Keep this book. You will need it and use it throughout your career.

About the American Hotel & Lodging Association (AH&LA)

Founded in 1910, AH&LA is the trade association representing the lodging industry in the United States. AH&LA is a federation of state lodging associations throughout the United States with 11,000 lodging properties worldwide as members. The association offers its members assistance with governmental affairs representation, communications, marketing, hospitality operations, training and education, technology issues, and more. For information, call 202-289-3100.

LODGING, the management magazine of AH&LA, is a "living textbook" for hospitality students that provides timely features, industry news, and vital lodging information.

About the American Hotel & Lodging Educational Institute (AHLEI)

An affiliate of AH&LA, the Educational Institute is the world's largest source of quality training and educational materials for the lodging industry. AHLEI develops textbooks and courses that are used in more than 1,200 colleges and universities worldwide, and also offers courses to individuals through its Distance Learning program. Hotels worldwide rely on AHLEI for training resources that focus on every aspect of lodging operations. Industry-tested videos, CD-ROMs, seminars, and skills guides prepare employees at every skill level. AHLEI also offers professional certification for the industry's top performers. For information about AHLEI's products and services, call 800-349-0299 or 407-999-8100.

About the American Hotel & Lodging Educational Foundation (AH&LEF)

An affiliate of AH&LA, the American Hotel & Lodging Educational Foundation provides financial support that enhances the stability, prosperity, and growth of the lodging industry through educational and research programs. AH&LEF has awarded millions of dollars in scholarship funds for students pursuing higher education in hospitality management. AH&LEF has also funded research projects on topics important to the industry, including occupational safety and health, turnover and diversity, and best practices in the U.S. lodging industry. For information, go to www.ahlef.org.

HOSPITALITY TODAY

An Introduction

Educational Institute Books

HOSPITALITY TODAY
An Introduction

Seventh Edition

Rocco M. Angelo, CHA
Andrew N. Vladimir, CHE

AMERICAN HOTEL & LODGING
EDUCATIONAL INSTITUTE

Disclaimer

This publication is designed to provide accurate and authoritative information in regard to the subject matter covered. It is sold with the understanding that the publisher is not engaged in rendering legal, accounting, or other professional service. If legal advice or other expert assistance is required, the services of a competent professional person should be sought.
   —From the Declaration of Principles jointly adopted by the American Bar Association and a Committee of Publishers and Associations

The authors, Rocco M. Angelo and Andrew N. Vladimir, are solely responsible for the contents of this publication. All views expressed herein are solely those of the authors and do not necessarily reflect the views of the American Hotel & Lodging Educational Institute (the Institute) or the American Hotel & Lodging Association (AH&LA).

Nothing contained in this publication shall constitute a standard, an endorsement, or a recommendation of the Institute or AH&LA. The Institute and AH&LA disclaim any liability with respect to the use of any information, procedure, or product, or reliance thereon by any member of the hospitality industry.

Editor: Jim Purvis

Cover photo: The Fairmont Chateau Lake Louise, Lake Louise, Alberta, Canada; courtesy of Fairmont Hotels & Resorts.

DEDICATION

To my dear friend and co-author
Andrew N. Vladimir
1932–2008

Contents

Preface

ANDY VLADIMIR AND I met in Puerto Rico in 1961 when I was the food and beverage director of the Loews Americana Hotel and his firm was contracted to create and execute the hotel's advertising and promotion. We had much in common and we became good friends. After I left Puerto Rico, we did not communicate until he arrived in my office at Florida International University almost twenty years later. We were both surprised, since neither one of us knew that we were associated with the same university. He was lecturing in the Business School but because of his experience in hospitality and tourism he felt he belonged in the Hospitality School. The dean and I agreed, and Andy was hired.

Many of you did not know that Andy had muscular dystrophy. Although I knew he had MD when he was hired, there were no visible signs of the terrible malady. As the MD asserted itself, Andy had to use a cane at first and later a motorized chair. Finally there came a point when driving each day to the university was no longer possible, and Andy retired from teaching. Eventually he lost his ability to move about except in his motorized chair or assisted by a caregiver, but he never lost his intellectual curiosity, his sense of humor, his drive to create, and his willingness to help others. Andy served on the board of Shake-A-Leg Miami, an organization that helps children and adults with physical, developmental, and economic challenges, and he had a leadership role in his church. Besides our textbook, he co-authored two books with Bob Dickinson, who was president of Carnival Corporation at the time. Andy also wrote a memoir and penned many articles about his experiences traveling as a disabled person. The progressive disease continued to take its toll but he never stopped planning for the future—a trip, an article, a project. Andy inspired me. The phrase "He always sees the glass as half full" is apt in describing his outlook on life. But, finally, the MD prevailed, and in December 2008 Andy passed away. We were co-authors, but friends first. I miss him.

During the time that I was working on this, the seventh edition of *Hospitality Today,* the United States and other parts of the world began to emerge from the largest economic downturn since the Great Depression more than seven decades earlier. From 2007 to early 2010, world travel declined, hotel occupancies and average rates fell, restaurant sales (especially for the high-priced restaurants) plunged, and private clubs lost membership. Business travel and conventions almost came to a standstill. Those consumers who continued to travel were trading down and focused on price. No segment of hospitality and tourism was immune from the economic disaster wrought by failures in the financial markets. The cruise lines fought for market by slashing prices, the casino hotels in Las Vegas offered room rates at unprecedented low rates, and hotels and restaurants across the country failed and shuttered their doors or surrendered the keys to the lender. There were hotels to be bought, but capital was unavailable. Unemployment in the United States reached double-digit levels. Hospitality enterprises fought to survive by cutting labor and other operating costs and lowering prices, or offering special incentives to lure customers back. By mid-2010 there were indications that the economy was improving, but many businesses remained cautious about hiring.

One thing was clear: organizational and staffing-level changes that were made out of necessity were here to stay. A number of hotel companies consolidated hotel administrative departmental positions into regional offices. Accounting, purchasing, human resources, and sales functions and staffs were centralized to handle clusters of hotels. Electronic advertising and promotions via e-mail and social media were on the rise at the expense of print advertising, requiring a new type of marketing expert on the staff. Despite the difficult times, many hotel companies pursued environmentally sound practices, creating corporate and hotel positions to manage their new "green" programs. The many hotel failures across the country spurred the growth of new small firms to asset-manage the distressed properties. Thus, while some positions within the hospitality industry were diminished or eliminated, others were created that offered new opportunities for hotel school graduates. The hospitality and tourism industries have been disrupted before by economic recessions, only to rebound to profitability. Students need not worry about the future if they are prepared to manage in a leaner and smarter environment.

Acknowledgments

An introductory text must cover many topics, requiring the author to research and write about a broad range of subjects. When Andy and I wrote the first edition twenty years ago, we worked on the book for more than a year. Once Andy asked me, "Will we *ever* finish this book?" I responded jokingly that we were writing the history of the world, Part One. Given all the subjects we were covering, it seemed that that was the case. For this edition, once I decided to revise the text on my own (with the exception of one chapter), I called on many industry friends and former students to critique what I wrote or to suggest revisions. This is my opportunity to thank all those who willingly came to my rescue. I will be eternally grateful for their generous assistance.

Former student and human resources expert Sabina Tonarelli-Frey deserves credit for being a contributing author of Chapter 13, "Managing Human Resources." As he has for past editions, Tom Hewitt, CEO of Interstate Hotels & Resorts, gave valuable commentary on management contracts for Chapter 15. Richard Brilliant, Vice President—Accounting & Audit for the Carnival Corporation, gave exceptionally good advice on the cruise line chapter and introduced me to Wayne Cimring, VP Cruise Operations Audit Services, and Richard Muth, VP Risk Advisory Services, who were both quite generous with their time. It was great to catch up over dinner with Brooke Patterson, Manager On Board Revenue, Celebrity Cruise Line, and get her thoughts on the cruise line chapter as well. Steve Bauman, VP Talent Acquisition and Selection, Marriott International Inc., clarified my list of Marriott brands. I wanted to make certain my information on Ritz-Carlton was correct, and Marco Selva, Regional Vice President—Florida at the Ritz-Carlton Hotel Company assured me I was on the right track. Duncan Dickson of the University of Central Florida's Rosen School of Hospitality Management is still an expert on Disney. The National Travel MONITOR is an invaluable marketing study, and Peter Yesawich of Ypartnership shared it with me, as he has done in the past. A number of aspects of technology were made clearer to me thanks to Jules Sieburgh, a technology consultant and long-time friend. Greg Bohan, Principal, Pinnacle Advisory Group, read my comments on feasibility studies and offered suggestions to make that segment better. Mark Woodworth, Executive Managing Director, PKF Consulting, and Robert Mandelbaum, Director of Research Information Services, PKF Hospitality Research, are always generous with the important data they generate. Michael Hudson, a former student and the current Owner/President of Site, Search & Select, read through the meetings chapter and gave me his thoughts. One of my FIU associates, Donald Rosellini, shared with me some of his great research and provided encouragement. In an example of taking advantage of one's family, I had my nephew, Vincent Angelo, Hotel Manager, Sheraton Nassau Beach Resort, Bahamas, critique my comments on Six Sigma. Thank you all for responding to my telephone calls, texting, and e-mails, and sharing your expertise with me and the many students who will benefit from this book.

Last but not least I must thank the team at the American Hotel & Lodging Educational Institute for their support and encouragement: Robert L. Steele III, President and Chief Operating Officer, and George Glazer, Senior Vice President. And what would I do without Jim Purvis? He is the best editor any writer could hope for and get. Jim edited five of the previous six editions of *Hospitality Today* and he has done it again with his usual high standards and good nature. Thank you, Jim, for your invaluable assistance and friendship.

Rocco M. Angelo
Key Biscayne, Florida

About the Authors

Rocco M. Angelo (left) is the Associate Dean of the School of Hospitality and Tourism Management at Florida International University, where he has held the Ellsworth M. Statler Professorship since 1993. He is also a Certified Hospitality Administrator (CHA). Prior to joining FIU, Mr. Angelo spent six years as manager of Laventhol & Horwath's Management Advisory Services division in New York City. He was responsible for supervising and conducting economic feasibility studies, operation and control analyses for hotels and restaurants, and tourism studies in the United States, Canada, and the Caribbean. He has managed a private club/hotel and has also worked in various management positions with ARAMARK and Loews Hotels. He was a consultant with Pannell Kerr Forster.

Mr. Angelo received B.S. degrees from Fordham University and the School of Hotel Administration at Cornell University, and an M.B.A. from the University of Miami. In 2009–2010 he was President of the Southeastern Federation of International CHRIE, the worldwide association of hospitality and tourism faculty. He has been honored at Florida International University with the Presidential Medallion for service and the FIU Alumni

Association's "Outstanding Faculty Award," which is presented to faculty members who have made a lasting impression on the lives of FIU alumni. He is a past president of the Cornell Hotel Society and in 2008 was recognized for service to that organization with the "Hotelee of the Year" award. He has taught courses at Cornell University, New York University, and the Centre International dé Glion in Switzerland.

Mr. Angelo has been an advisor to the Club Management Institute of the Club Managers Association of America, and is a member of the educational corporation of the Culinary Institute of America, the advisory board of Dade County's Academy for Tourism, and the Certification Commission of the American Hotel & Lodging Educational Institute. He has also served on the Scholarship and Grants Committee of the American Hotel & Lodging Foundation and was a trustee of the Caribbean Hospitality Training Institute. He is a past president of the Cornell Hotel Society International.

Mr. Angelo is the author of *A Practical Guide to Understanding Feasibility Studies.* He resides in Key Biscayne, Florida.

A ndrew N. Vladimir was an internationally recognized marketing consultant with a distinguished track record in the tourism industry. An Associate Professor Emeritus at the School of Hospitality and Tourism Management of Florida International University, Mr. Vladimir taught courses in service management, cruise line management, marketing communications, and promotion strategy.

Before joining FIU's faculty, Mr. Vladimir served as Director of Tourism for the Government of Bermuda, the only non-Bermudian ever to hold that post. Part of his responsibilities as Bermuda's chief tourism regulator was to oversee the government's marketing, advertising, and public relations programs.

Mr. Vladimir spent most of his career in the marketing and advertising business, with a special emphasis on hospitality, travel, and tourism. He held senior management positions with some of America's best advertising and public relations agencies, including Young & Rubicam, Norman Craig & Kummel, Kenyon & Eckhardt, and Ruder Finn. In addition, he headed his own advertising and public relations agencies in San Juan, Puerto Rico; Miami, Florida; and Seattle, Washington; and owned two travel agencies. In the course of his career Mr. Vladimir worked for such hospitality clients as McDonald's, Sonesta Hotels, Loews Hotels, Resorts International, Delta Airlines, Air France, and TravAlaska Tours. He was a featured speaker at three world congresses of the American Society of Travel Agents.

Mr. Vladimir is the author or co-author of *The Complete Twenty-First Century Travel, Tourism, and Hospitality Marketing Handbook* (Prentice-Hall, 2004), *Selling the Sea: An Inside Look at the Cruise Industry* (John Wiley & Sons, 1997), *The Complete Travel Marketing Handbook* (NTC Business Books, 1988), and *Fundamentals of Advertising* (Crain Books, 1984). He wrote hundreds of magazine and newspaper articles on travel and served as an expert witness in many trials involving the hospitality and cruise industries.

Mr. Vladimir held a B.A. degree from Yale University and an M.S. degree from FIU's School of Hospitality Management. He was also a graduate of Harvard Business School's Advanced Management Program and a Certified Hospitality Educator (CHE). He was a member of Delta Delta Phi, the hospitality honor society, and twice received Florida International University's teaching excellence award. He passed away in 2008.

Prologue:
A Brief History of Travel

S INCE THE WORD "TRAVEL" suggests pleasure and adventure to most people, it is not often remembered that "travel" is derived from the French word *travail*, which means "toil and labor." Prehistoric people moved about in search of food and shelter; their travels were by no means pleasant. Travel has been an arduous task for much of recorded history. In fact, only in modern times has travel become relatively comfortable.

Commerce was an important motivator of early travel. By 3000 B.C., caravan routes from Eastern Europe to North Africa and on to India and China were well established. Camels were favored pack animals—a healthy one could carry up to 600 pounds of cargo. By 1200 B.C., Phoenician merchant vessels were plying the Mediterranean, following sea routes stretching from Britain to Africa.

The Romans were the first to travel on land on a large scale. Their desire to expand the Roman Empire resulted in expeditions of discovery and conquest followed by massive road building. The first important Roman highway was the Via Appia, started in 312 B.C. By A.D. 200 the Romans had highways throughout their empire, from Hadrian's Wall in northern Britain to the Sahara Desert—highways that featured wheel-changing stations and rest houses every 15 to 30 miles.

People in ancient times traveled for pleasure as well. Hundreds of years before the birth of Christ, Greeks and barbarians (a "barbarian" was defined by the Greeks as anyone who was not Greek) traveled to the Olympic games. Health, too, provided an impetus for early travel. People believed that waters in certain locations possessed healing qualities, and they would go there to rest and recuperate. The Romans built spas as far away from Rome as Bath, England.

With the growth of organized religion, pilgrimages became common in many parts of the world. Muslims traveled to Mecca; Christians traveled to shrines all over Europe and beyond. A sense of the Christian pilgrimages in the Middle Ages is preserved in *The Canterbury Tales*, written in the fourteenth century by Geoffrey Chaucer. The book's narrator is a jovial innkeeper who hosts 29 pilgrims staying at the Tabard Inn in Southwark, England, and subsequently offers to accompany them on their journey to help make the trip an interesting one.

The first European traveler to popularize long-distance trips was Marco Polo. The desire for wealth sent this Venetian in 1275 to trade at the "Hall of the Barbarians" in Kublai Khan's empire. Polo returned from the Far East 20 years later to write a book about his adventures, titled *The Description of the World*, which later became known popularly as *Il milione—The Millions—*because of all the wealth he had allegedly acquired abroad. His adventures captured the imagination of courts all over Europe. Almost certainly, one reader of *Il milione,* who eventually set out to find some of the sights Polo catalogued, was Christopher Columbus.[1]

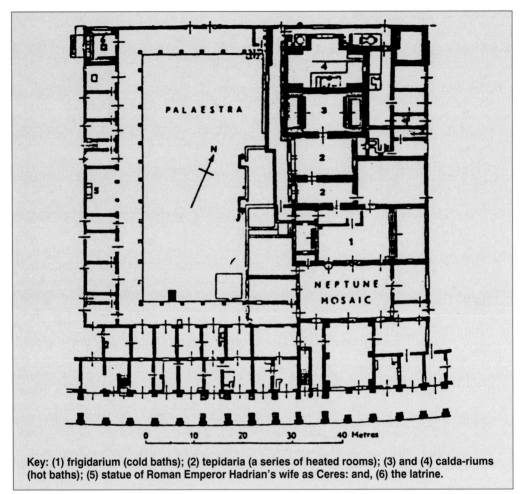

Key: (1) frigidarium (cold baths); (2) tepidaria (a series of heated rooms); (3) and (4) calda-riums (hot baths); (5) statue of Roman Emperor Hadrian's wife as Ceres: and, (6) the latrine.

A Roman spa. Source: Russell Meiggs, *Roman Ostia,* 2d ed. (Oxford: Clarendon Press, 1973).

In the capital city of Hangzhou, home of the "Great Kahn," one of the things that intrigued Marco Polo most was the vast abundance of food. Reay Tannahill, a food historian, points out that

> most countries had their cookshops, but none at this period were as advanced and varied as China's. As well as ordinary eating houses, there were fast-food restaurants, hotels, taverns, tea houses, noodle shops and wine shops, all with their own chef's specials—chilled fruits or honey fritters, steamed pork buns, won ton, barbecued meats, fish soups, and so on. Every morning between 1 A.M. and dawn the proprietors hurried off to one of the ten great specialist food markets of Hangzhou for the pork or silkworms or shrimp from which they made pies to serve with their drinks, or oysters, mussels, or bean curd that nourished the poorer classes.

> The fish market, according to Marco, was an extraordinary sight. Every day, "a vast quantity of fish is brought upstream from the ocean, a distance of twenty-five

miles. There is also abundance of lake fish, varying in kind according to season, which affords constant occupation for fishermen." So many fish were on sale at the market that "you would imagine they could never be disposed of. But in a few hours the whole lot has been cleared away."[2]

By the thirteenth century trade had emerged as the prime reason for travel. Improved navigation skills and the development of the magnetic compass took much of the uncertainty out of long, hard sea trips. Better world maps and two- and three-masted sailing ships helped open the oceans to further exploration in the fourteenth and fifteenth centuries.

During the Renaissance period (beginning in the fourteenth century in Italy and lasting in Europe into the seventeenth century), travel for cultural and artistic reasons became common. Soon it was popular for aristocrats, diplomats, scholars, and other young gentlemen and women to take an extended tour of the Continent, which came to be known as "The Grand Tour." Paris, Rome, Florence, Venice, Munich, Vienna, and other cities of central Europe were fashionable tour stops, and resorts and spas were developed to accommodate the tourists.

An enduring symbol of hospitality surfaced for the first time during this period. Early explorers who traveled to the West Indies were enchanted by pineapple fruit and brought it home to Europe to cultivate in their hothouses. By the seventeenth century it had become a very popular symbol in society and among royalty, and soon the motif appeared carved into their furniture, signifying bountifulness. When the colonists settled North America, they carried with them some of this furniture. Sea captains returning home from long trips would often place pineapples at the doors or on their gate posts to announce their arrival home and invite friends to stop in to celebrate. Today the pineapple remains a symbol of hospitality and welcome, and you can find it carved into the entrances of hotels, restaurants, and homes.

The Transportation Revolution

Modern technology became a major force in travel with the development of the steamship, locomotive, automobile, and airplane. These new forms of transportation put long-distance travel within the reach of more people than ever before by decreasing the amount of time and money necessary to take long trips.

Steamships

Travel to the New World for adventure and profit in the seventeenth and eighteenth centuries opened sea lanes and hastened the development of the great trans-Atlantic ocean liners that were to connect Europe and the Americas in the nineteenth century.

The first steamship to cross the Atlantic was the *Sirius* in 1838. In 1840 Samuel Cunard inaugurated regular passenger service across the Atlantic when he formed the British and North American Royal Mail Steam Packet Company, which later took its founder's name and became the Cunard Line. Sea voyages became the most romantic and luxurious form of travel, but only a few could afford them.

Exciting and luxurious as these early steamers may have seemed to landlubbers, the people who actually traveled on them were often uncomfortable during the trip. Harriet Beecher Stowe described a transatlantic voyage she took in 1854:

The R.M.S. *Titanic* on a trial run in 1912. It was the most luxurious ocean liner of its day.

> At night! the beauties of a night on shipboard!—down in your berth, with the sea hissing and fizzing, gurgling and booming, within an inch of your ear; and then the steward comes along at twelve o'clock and puts out the light, and there you are! Jonah in the whale was not darker or more dismal. There, in profound ignorance and blindness, you lie, and feel yourself rolled upwards, and downwards, and sidewise, and all ways, like a cork in a tub of water; much such a sensation as one might suppose it to be, were one headed up in a barrel and thrown into the sea.[3]

The most famous and tragic sea voyage of all was that of the *Titanic*. The 46,329-ton vessel offered a degree of luxury that was unheard of in the shipping world. One writer called the maiden voyage of the *Titanic* "the millionaires' special." The ship left port on April 12, 1912, and more than two thousand passengers and crew partied their way into the North Atlantic. Only 705 people survived the voyage. April 14, 1912—the night the *Titanic* struck an iceberg and sank—is one of the saddest days in the history of passenger shipping. A woman who survived the tragedy later wrote about that Sunday night in her diary:

> We dined the last night in the Ritz Restaurant. It was the last word in luxury. The tables were gay with pink roses and white daisies, the women in their beautiful shimmering gowns of satin and silk, the men immaculate and well groomed, the stringed orchestra playing music from Puccini and Tchaikovsky. The food was superb—caviar, lobster, quail from Egypt, plover's eggs, and hothouse grapes and fresh peaches. The night was cold and clear, the sea like glass. But in a few short hours every man in that room was dead except J. Bruce Ismay, Gordon Duff, and a Mr. Carter.[4]

Despite this disaster, transatlantic passenger service continued, and the great ocean liners such as the *Queen Mary,* S.S. *France,* and *United States* became known throughout the world as the flagships of their nations. Ocean liners were the principal form of luxury travel until the late 1950s, when commercial jets first entered transatlantic service. Soon the great ocean liners became relics of the romantic past. Today the *Queen Mary* is permanently docked and operated as a hotel in Long Beach, California; the S.S. *France* took on a new life as Norwegian Cruise Line's *Norway* until it was retired from service in 2006. Other older ships still ply the waves, operated by some of the smaller cruise lines.

Railroads

The first working locomotive was built in England in 1804. In 1830 the railroad age began with the opening of the Liverpool and Manchester Railway in England. One year later America's first public railway, the South Carolina Railroad, began service. It did not take long for entrepreneurs to sense the potential of the railroad to stimulate travel. In 1841 a Baptist preacher named Thomas Cook organized a rail tour from Leicester to Loughborough and back for 570 people to attend a temperance meeting, thus earning himself a place in history as the world's first recognized travel agent.

In the last half of the nineteenth century, railroads grew rapidly in Europe and elsewhere. The Union Pacific and the Central Pacific railroads joined their tracks at Promontory Point near Ogden, Utah, in 1869, making a transcontinental rail trip across America

In the nineteenth century, railroads put long-distance travel within the reach of ordinary Americans. (Courtesy of the State of Michigan Archives.)

Hotels were sometimes built well before the arrival of the railroad—or even before there was much of a town! (Courtesy of the State of Michigan Archives.)

possible for the first time. In 1891 construction started on the Trans-Siberian railroad, which would link Europe to Asia.

After rail travel became popular in Europe, the most desirable place to build a hotel in major European cities was next to the railroad station. In the United States, hotels and restaurants were built beside the railroad tracks as they crisscrossed the country. In many instances, hotels were built well *before* the arrival of the railroad or even before a town had sprung up. The idea was that a proper hotel would attract the railroads and, with them, settlers and commerce. Victorian novelist Anthony Trollope visited North America and makes this point in the book he wrote about his visit:

> In the States of America the first sign of an incipient settlement is a hotel five stories high with an office, a bar, a cloak-room, three gentlemen's parlours, a ladies' entrance and two hundred bedrooms....Whence are to come the sleepers in those two hundred bedrooms and who is to pay for the gaudy sofas and numerous lounging chairs of the ladies' parlours? In all other countries the expectation would extend itself simply to travellers; to travellers or to strangers sojourning in the land. But this is by no means the case as to these speculations in America. When the new hotel rises up in the wilderness, it is presumed that people will come there with the express object of inhabiting it. The hotel itself will create a population, as the railways do. With us railways run to the towns; but in the States the towns run to the railways. It is the same thing with the hotels.[5]

Resorts also had their beginnings with the growth of the railroad. The Catskill Mountains were a popular day trip by rail from New York City and eventually became the home of the "borscht circuit," a group of mountain resorts that featured many great entertainers in the 1930s, '40s, and '50s. Two of the most famous Catskill resorts were Grossinger's and the Concord. Soon railroad companies started developing resorts of their own. In Florida, Henry Flagler built The Breakers in Palm Beach and other hotels in Miami and Key West to accommodate passengers on his Flagler Line. In West Virginia, the Chesapeake & Ohio Railway company developed the Greenbrier Resort.

Trains significantly increased the amount of business travel. With that growth came a demand from business travelers for a uniform standard of hotel quality so that they could go from one city to another and enjoy similar services.

Automobiles

In the late nineteenth century, horses (for short distances) and trains (for long distances) were the two main modes of land travel in the United States and Europe. This began to change with the invention of bicycles. The bicycle was invented in Paris and first introduced to the European community at the 1867 Paris Exposition. Many people saw it as a faster, safer, more reliable, and less expensive means of transportation than the horse. Bicycles did not require feeding or care and they were not likely to throw off a rider in a fit of temperament. Bicycles did require, however, good, hard-surfaced roads—especially if you wanted to use them to cover long distances fast.

The automobile's potential as a convenient and inexpensive means of travel would not be fully realized until better roads were built. (Courtesy of the State of Michigan Archives.)

As bicycles grew in popularity, so did the demand for paved roads. It was these hard-surfaced roads that made the motor car a practical device for transportation. Not surprisingly, many of the first cars were made by bicycle manufacturers. Their dealers saw the car as an improved bicycle. Companies like Willys in America, Rover in England, Opel in Germany, and Peugeot in France were bicycle manufacturers that realized that many of their customers really wanted fast personal transportation, not bicycles, and that automobiles were the best way to satisfy that need.

As with the first bicycles, the first automobiles were built in France. The early Peugeot cars, built in 1889, were heavy tricycles powered by steam engines. Leon Serpollet, the inventor of the instantaneous steam generator, mounted one of his engines on a tricycle and drove it 295 miles from Paris to Lyon in 1890.[6] At the same time, steam-powered road vehicles of various designs were being built in the United States. In Lansing, Michigan, Ransom E. Olds built one of the earliest models in 1891, which he sold for $400 to a London patent medicine firm for use in its branch in Bombay, India.[7] Soon two American companies were producing steam cars in quantity—the Locomobile and the Stanley Steamer—that could be bought for as little as $600. Steam engines were inefficient, however. There was a brief period of interest in electric cars, but the limited storage capacity of their batteries severely restricted their use.

It was not until the gasoline engine (first invented in 1860 by Etienne Lenoir[8]) was perfected that the modern car became a reality. The first person to improve a gasoline engine to the point where it could be attached to a vehicle was Gottlieb Daimler, a German engineer. Daimler, along with his assistant William Maybach, built four experimental motor vehicles between 1885 and 1889. Their engine was the prototype of the modern automobile's power plant.[9] Unfortunately, Daimler crashed one of these vehicles into a wall, giving him another place in history as having the first automobile accident!

The French, who were already enthusiastic cyclists and had a network of good roads, first saw the potential of the gasoline-powered car. By 1901 about 130 automobile manufacturers are estimated to have been in business in the Seine Department of Paris alone, making the Paris metropolitan area the world center of automobile production.[10] At the same time, automobile production was beginning in the United States. Between 1900 and 1908, 485 companies entered the automobile production business in the U.S. Their customers were mostly wealthy professionals who used their vehicles for business travel.

It was Henry Ford who first realized that if an inexpensive car could be built, everyone would want one. In 1908 he introduced the Model T runabout—a 20 horsepower, 1,200 pound car—priced at $825. By 1916, using the assembly line to mass-produce cars, he was able to get the price down to $345. The Model T had none of the sleek lines or sophistication of the European cars being produced in Germany and France during the same period, but it was durable, easy to drive and repair, and its undercarriage was high enough off the road to clear the ruts made by the horse carts and wagons still traveling America's primitive roads. That was enough to make the Model T a huge success.

Cars completely changed the way people lived. It was no longer necessary to buy everything you needed in the town in which you lived. People could live farther away from work. Suburbs began to grow as people moved away from the crowded cities. Small, self-reliant agricultural communities lost many of their businesses and opened some new ones that were dependent on tourists. Touring and sight-seeing became increasingly popular as more Americans acquired cars. There were no places to stay, however. Hotels located in small towns had been built to accommodate traveling salesmen and

Many World War I pilots started independent, nonscheduled air transportation services after the war. Passenger comfort was not a consideration. (Courtesy of the State of Michigan Archives.)

did not have facilities to serve families with children. Until roadside eating and lodging establishments began to be built in the 1930s, early motorists brought tents with them and camped. It was not until after World War II that the highway hotel and restaurant chains we know today were conceived and built.

Today there are more than 237 million motor vehicles in operation in the United States, and Americans travel more than two trillion miles each year by motor vehicle. In fact, about 87 percent of daily trips take place in personal vehicles, and 91 percent of people commuting to work use personal vehicles.[11] Travel by car remains popular because it is affordable, flexible, and convenient.

Airplanes

The end of the First World War marked the beginning of commercial aviation on both sides of the Atlantic. The impetus, of course, was the experience gained in flying planes during the war and the number of trained pilots and mechanics available to exploit this new form of transportation. In 1919 the British launched their first trans-channel commercial flights linking the business capitals of London and Paris. Each flight took two and a half hours and the first planes used were converted bombers in which the pilot and the passenger sat in open cockpits.

In America the first commercial flights were inaugurated in 1918 as joint ventures of the U.S. Signal Corps and the U.S. Postal Service. These flights delivered mail only. However, many pilots who had learned to fly in the war bought surplus planes from the government and started independent nonscheduled service for passengers between various points. Soon, regular flights carried both mail and passengers between major cities.

The air age got a tremendous boost when a young stunt flyer named Charles Lindbergh, whose act of standing on the top wing of a looping plane thrilled crowds all over the country, decided to compete for a prize of $25,000 offered to the first person to fly solo across the Atlantic Ocean. At 7:55 A.M. on May 20, 1927, Lindbergh took off from Roosevelt Field on Long Island, New York, and landed at Le Bourget in Paris 33 hours and 39 minutes later. Lindbergh proved that the airplane was a practical means of traveling over long distances, and, as a result, investors who had been hesitant to put money into this new method of transportation lined up to back commercial aviation.

Also in 1927, a young World War I pilot, Juan Trippe, founded Pan American Airlines with a mail contract from the United States government to fly between Key West, Florida, and Havana, Cuba. The DC3, the first passenger aircraft that met the needs of the flying public, was introduced in 1936. In 1958 the first Boeing 707 went into service. It heralded the start of the jet age and provided a huge stimulus to both the tourist and business-traveler markets.

Almost from the beginning, commercial aviation has had a substantial impact on the hospitality industry. The airplane made affordable mass transportation over long distances possible. Resort areas such as the Caribbean and Hawaii, which had previously been accessible only by boat, could now be visited by a larger number of tourists. The airplane was a boon to the hospitality industry.

A Closer Look at the Hospitality Industry

Few people realize that there are at least three patron saints for those engaged in providing hospitality to others. The first of these is Saint Julian the Hospitaller. While many acknowledge that he may be mythical, he is listed in the *Oxford Dictionary of Saints* and has seven English churches dedicated to him.[12] In addition, he is depicted in stained glass windows in the cathedrals of Chartres and Rouen. He is the patron saint of innkeepers and travelers. His feast day, for those who wish to celebrate it, is January 29.

The legend goes that while Julian was away from home one day, a traveling couple knocked on the door of his house. His wife answered. She gave the tired travelers food and water and invited them to take a nap in her bed while she went to the market. While she was away, Julian (who was not yet a saint) came home to discover a man and woman asleep in his bedroom. Assuming it was his wife with another man, he killed them both on the spot. As he left the house he met his wife returning from the market. Because of this experience, he decided to spend the rest of his life being hospitable to strangers!

Although not as colorful, Saint Amand, a French monk who lived from 584 to 679, is recognized as the patron saint of innkeepers by the Roman Catholic Church, which holds his feast day on February 26.[13] Saint Amand began his work in Bourges, France, where he was a missionary. His work took him throughout Europe and he founded several monasteries in Belgium. Amand's monasteries were highly regarded as places where weary travelers could find comfortable lodging and good food, and he was supposed to have been a first-class manager.

The third saint, Saint Notburga, has a church dedicated to her in her hometown of Eben/Maurach, Austria. The church literature describes her as a "farm girl who dedicated her life to the welfare of servants," and she is considered the patron saint of food servers.

Saint Amand is a patron saint of innkeepers. (Courtesy of *Lodging Magazine*)

History of Lodging

No one knows exactly when the first inns opened; references to them go as far back as recorded history. But certainly the first inns were private homes that offered accommodations to travelers. By 500 B.C., ancient cities such as Corinth, Greece, had a substantial number of establishments that offered food and drink as well as beds to travelers.

The early Roman *hospitia* provided rooms and sometimes food, although whether they were provided hospitably is open to question. The *Cornell Quarterly,* quoting from *The Laws of Innkeepers,* says, "In ancient Rome, publicans and their houses were held in general contempt, just as they were in Greece. The Romans were a proud race who held that the business of conducting a tavern was a low form of occupation, and the running of such establishments was usually entrusted to slaves."

In the Middle Ages, inns built along the highways were of questionable reputation. There is an anonymous English verse written about an inn in Wales that depicts its lack of hospitality this way:

> If you ever go to Dolgelly,
> Don't stay at the Lion's Hotel;
> 'Cause there's nothing to put in your belly,
> And no one to answer the bell!

During this period, many landlords were predatory, and robberies of travelers were common.[14] Even today, the legend of the unscrupulous innkeeper is a part of our cultural heritage. In the popular musical *Les Misérables*, one of the most colorful and shady characters is the innkeeper Thénardier, who sings, "Charge 'em for the lice, extra for the mice!"[15]

By the middle of the seventeenth century the private inn was well established in England and on the Continent, and its reputation had improved. Samuel Johnson echoed a popular sentiment of the time: "There is nothing which has yet been contrived by man, by which so much happiness is produced as by a good tavern or inn."[16] Inns in those days were important social gathering places, and people congregated at the ones where political and literary figures stayed regularly. One collector of historical anecdotes tells of Thomas Telford, a British engineer who was considered something of a celebrity as well as delightful company: "In London, he stayed at the Ship Inn in Charing Cross, which was always crowded with his friends. A new landlord purchased the inn without knowing that Telford was about to move into a house of his own on Abingdon Street. When he found out he was utterly dismayed. 'Not leaving!' he exclaimed. 'I have just paid seven hundred and fifty pounds for you.'"[17] In France, large buildings that had rooms to let by the day, week, or longer were called *hotel garni*. The word "hotel" was first used in England in about 1760 by the Fifth Duke of Devonshire to name a lodging establishment in London.[18]

In 1794 the first hotel in the United States opened—the 70-room City Hotel on Broadway in New York City. Historian Daniel Boorstin notes that American hotels played a very different role than European hotels:

> Lacking a royal palace as the center of "Society," Americans created their counterpart in the community hotel. Hotels were usually the centers of lavish private entertainment (which, being held there, acquired a public significance) and of the most important public celebrations. The hotel lobby, like the outer rooms of a royal palace, became a loitering place, a headquarters of gossip, a vantage point for a glimpse of the great, the rich, and the powerful.[19]

One of the first hotels to clearly reflect this purpose in its architecture was the 170-room Tremont House, opened in Boston in 1829. Besides having a colonnaded marble portico, it featured formal public rooms with Ionic columns designed to give the hotel a palatial feeling. The Tremont was also the first hotel to have bellpersons, front desk employees, locks on guestroom doors, and free soap for guests. It is considered the first modern American hotel. Its designer, Isaiah Rogers, went on to build many other hotels and became one of the most influential hotel architects of the nineteenth century.

Hotels were often the first places where the public could experience new technology. The Tremont was one of the first large buildings in America to incorporate extensive plumbing facilities. The first public building to be heated by steam was the Eastern Exchange Hotel in Boston. Elevators were first introduced in hotels; New York's Fifth Avenue Hotel installed one in 1859. Less than three years after Thomas Edison announced in 1879 the commercial feasibility of his incandescent lamp, it was tried in hotels. The Hotel Everett on Park Row in New York City was the first hotel lit by electricity.[20]

Lodging Industry Pioneers. One of the first prominent hoteliers in the world started his career while still in his teens as an apprentice hotelkeeper in France. César Ritz (1847–1935)

Opening in Boston in 1855, the Parker House gave the world the near-perfect Parker House roll.

subsequently served as manager of the Grand National Hotel in Lucerne, Switzerland, and the Savoy in London, where he introduced live orchestras in the dining room, made evening dress compulsory, and restricted unescorted women.[21] Ritz went back to Paris to found his famous Ritz Hotel, a name that became synonymous with luxury and quality all over the world. Ritz was the first hotelier to give each guestroom a private bath, built-in closets, and telephones. No detail was too small for Ritz's personal attention. He invented the silk lamp shade so that the hotel's electric light bulbs would cast an apricot glow on ladies' faces instead of a harsh glare. On the opening day of the hotel, Ritz thought the dining room tables were two centimeters too high and had them cut down just hours before guests arrived.[22]

One of Ritz's close associates throughout his career was Georges Auguste Escoffier. Escoffier became famous in his own right, first as a chef and later for his innovative kitchen management techniques. Escoffier wrote a cookbook called *Le Guide Culinaire* (referred to by most today as *Escoffier*). Many premier hotels still serve dishes prepared from the book's recipes.

The oldest continuously operated hotel in America is the Parker House (now the Omni Parker House) on School Street in Boston. Founded in 1855 by a Massachusetts restaurateur, the Parker House was innovative in several ways. It was one of the first to deviate from the American Plan and embrace the more flexible European Plan (under the European Plan, guests paid separately for the cost of a room and whatever meals they ate). It was also the first hotel to offer meals whenever guests wanted them rather than at a fixed time, and it was the first building in Boston with a passenger elevator.[23] Undoubtedly its most famous innovation was the Parker House roll, a soft, sweet dinner roll "consumed with butter by the tons," according to James Beard.[24]

The need for a uniform hotel standard was first recognized by Ellsworth Statler. He started his hospitality career in 1878 as a bellhop in Wheeling, West Virginia. In 1908 Statler opened the first hotel bearing his name in Buffalo, New York. It featured telephones in every room, modern plumbing, ice water, full-size closets with lights, and other amenities. Soon he had other Statler hotels in Cleveland, Detroit, St. Louis, and Boston. Statler's genius was his ability to increase service and simplify operations on a chain-wide basis. He gave free morning newspapers to guests, provided radios at no extra charge, and even developed "The Statler Service Code," which all employees had to memorize and carry with them.

Another early hotel-chain pioneer was Conrad Hilton, born in 1887 in San Antonio, in the Territory of New Mexico. Young Conrad started his hotel career by renting rooms in his family's home to travelers. In 1919 he bought his first hotel, the Mobley, in Cisco, Texas. Hilton continued to buy hotels throughout his lifetime (he died in 1979), including the Waldorf=Astoria, which his company purchased control of in 1949, and the entire Statler chain, acquired in 1954.

The Sheraton chain—at one time the largest hotel chain in the world—was started in 1941 by Ernest Henderson, a Boston investor. The chain began when Henderson, along with associate Robert Lowell Moore, acquired several New England hotels in the mid-1930s. One of the hotels had an expensive electric sign on the roof bearing the name "Sheraton." Deciding it would be too costly to remove, the owners kept the sign and applied the name to all of their future hotels.[25] Henderson's primary interest was in new forms of financing and other methods for increasing equity.

The concept of standardized lodging accommodations built alongside U.S. highways was the brainchild of a former movie theater operator and land developer in Memphis, Tennessee, Kemmons Wilson. Wilson came home very unhappy from a family vacation because he thought he had been overcharged to stay in substandard motel rooms. In 1952 Wilson built his first Holiday Inn in Memphis. Its unique features included a restaurant—most motels did not have one—as well as two double beds in every room. Wilson did not believe in charging parents for lodging their children—he had three children of his own and paying extra for them when he stayed at a motel irked him. Another marketing innovation of Wilson's was a huge property sign (he had learned the value of distinctive signs from his years in the theater business). Wilson also recognized the value of retaining his guests. He instructed his managers to offer to make reservations by telephone for departing guests who wished to stay at another Holiday Inn down the road. Like Statler, Wilson offered free "extras" to his overnight guests—free TV, free ice, and a telephone in every room.

Walt Disney was one of the most remarkable entertainment and tourism pioneers of the twentieth century. Trained as a commercial artist, he used his creativity and imagination to establish and set the standard for vacation destinations that appeal to a family market. His vision for Disneyland came during trips to a California theme park with his daughters, where he got the idea to "create an entirely new kind of place—one that families could experience together, immersed in an atmosphere rich in detail and storytell-

The first Holiday Inn, Memphis, Tennessee. (Courtesy of InterContinental Hotels Group.)

ing."[26] Disneyland in California opened in 1955, followed by Walt Disney World Resort in 1971. In addition to creating theme parks and iconic animated characters, Disney was noted for being a film producer, director, and screen writer, and an innovative animator who won twenty-six Oscars and fifty-nine nominations for his work. At the time of his death at 65 in 1966, he had established an entertainment conglomerate that included theme parks, hotels, vacation clubs, cruise ships, and television and motion picture enterprises. Today the Disney entertainment empire includes eleven theme parks in five countries, thirty-eight hotels with 34,000 rooms, eight vacation clubs, and two cruise ships.

History of Food Service

About the same time that hotels were gaining a strong foothold on both sides of the Atlantic in the seventeenth century, restaurants were also achieving prominence. According to *Food in History*, professionally cooked food was not a new concept:

> It had been known in Mesopotamia in the time of Nebuchadnezzar, and the population of the Near East still, in medieval times, preferred not to cook at home but to buy forcemeat balls, roast mutton, fish fritters, pancakes, and almond paste sweets from the market. It may, indeed, have been from the Arab world, by way of Spain, that the custom of buying ready made food was reintroduced into Europe....[27]

An interest in preparing delicious food on a large scale was stimulated in Europe by Louis XIV of France. He made dining a state occasion. The first restaurant, as distinct from an inn, tavern, or food specialty house, was opened by Boulanger in Paris in 1765. The first London restaurants (which served mainly French food) were not established until about 1830.[28] While he was ambassador to France, Thomas Jefferson learned to appreciate French food and wines and used them in White House functions when he became president. In 1832 America's first continental-style restaurant opened—Delmonico's in New York City.

Food Service Pioneers. As well as encouraging the growth of hotels, the railroads were responsible for America's first restaurant chain. In 1875 a 40-year-old English immigrant, Fred Harvey, opened two small restaurants along the Kansas Pacific Railroad.[29] Soon he added more along the Atchison, Topeka, and Santa Fe route. Harvey was a stickler for fine food and quality. His menus featured such delicacies as fresh oysters, sea turtle, and charlotte of peaches with cognac sauce, served on fine linen in scrupulously clean dining rooms. Harvey was also famous for his food servers, who were known as "Harvey Girls." They were chosen to represent impeccable standards of cleanliness, mannerliness, and hospitality—qualities in short supply in the West of those days.

In 1925 Howard Johnson purchased a small drugstore in Wollaston, Massachusetts. He soon started selling a chocolate ice cream product he developed to supplement his

Ray Kroc opened his first McDonald's franchise in Des Plaines, Illinois, on April 15, 1955. Built on the original site, "Number One Store/Museum" is an almost exact replica of that first restaurant (a few concessions were made to accommodate museum visitors and staff). The "Speedee" road sign is the original. (Courtesy of McDonald's Corporation.)

drugstore's revenues. The ice cream did so well that Johnson added other flavors until he had developed the "28 Flavors" that became his trademark. Johnson was one of the first franchisors. By 1940 he had 100 roadside restaurants selling Howard Johnson's ice cream and other food.

Like Statler, Johnson was interested in standardization and quality control. The building, decor, and seating arrangements for each restaurant in the Howard Johnson's chain were standardized. Johnson also created a central commissary to make sure his restaurants' food products were consistent and of the proper quality. This commissary prepared frozen entrées for delivery to Howard Johnson's franchises all over the country. Johnson insisted that his franchisees buy everything from him and operate their restaurants exactly as he specified.

Finally, no discussion of food service pioneers would be complete without mentioning Ray Kroc, the man who founded McDonald's. Kroc was a milk shake–machine salesman who, at the age of 52, called on two brothers who had set up a hamburger stand in San Bernardino, California. They were not interested in expanding their concept, which featured large lighted golden arches, but Kroc was. Within 40 years of making a deal that allowed him to franchise the operation, Kroc had a chain of restaurants stretching first across the nation and then around the world. The success of McDonald's is due largely to its commitment to "QSC&V"—quality, service, cleanliness, and value—combined with a simple standardized concept utilizing many of the same ideas originally pioneered by Howard Johnson.

 Endnotes

1. *Encyclopedia Britannica*, 15th ed. (Chicago: Encyclopedia Britannica Inc., 1975), p. 757.

2. Reay Tannahill, *Food in History* (New York: Crown Publishers, 1988), p. 138.

3. Cited by Robert Wechsler in *All in the Same Boat: The Humorists' Guide to the Ocean Cruise* (Highland Park, N.J.: Catbird Press, 1988), p. 44.

4. Ellen Williamson, *When We Went First Class* (New York: Doubleday, 1977), p. 112.

5. Daniel J. Boorstin, *The Americans: The National Experience* (New York: Vintage Books, 1965), p. 141.

6. James J. Flink, *The Automobile Age* (Cambridge, Mass.: The MIT Press, 1992), p. 6.

7. Ibid.

8. Ibid., p. 10.

9. Ibid.

10. Ibid., p. 18.

11. These statistics were found in *Highway Statistics 2004*, U.S. Department of Transportation; and the Bureau of Transportation Statistics, www.bts.gov.

12. David Hughes Farmer, *Oxford Dictionary of Saints* (Oxford: Oxford University Press, 1987), pp. 243–244.

13. Mark Collins and Robert J. Collins, "In Noble Footsteps," *Lodging*, April 1995, p. 158.

14. "The Evolution of the Hospitality Industry," *Cornell Quarterly*, May 1985, p. 36.

15. *Les Misérables* by Alan Boubil and Claude-Michel Schonberg, based on the novel by Victor Hugo. Lyrics by Herbert Kretzmer. Copyright 1985 Exallshow Ltd.

16. Samuel Johnson, 21 March 1776, in *Boswell's Life of Johnson*, L. F. Powell's revision of G. Hill's edition, vol. 2, p. 452.

17. Clifton Fadiman, *The Little, Brown Book of Anecdotes* (Boston: Little, Brown, 1985), p. 536.

18. Donald A. Lundberg, *The Hotel and Restaurant Business*, 4th ed. (New York: Van Nostrand Reinhold, 1984), p. 21.

19. Boorstin, p. 135.

20. Ibid., p. 139.

21. Richard A. Wentzel, "Pioneers and Leaders of the Hospitality Industry," reprinted from *Hospitality Management* by Robert A. Brymer (Dubuque, Iowa: Kendall Hunt, 1991), p. 29.

22. "The Cowherd Who Made the Ritz Ritzy," *Lodging*, December 1993, p. 56. This article was adapted from a story by Mary Blume, published in the *International Herald Tribune*, 12 October 1993.

23. "Eating In, All-American Fare," *Lodging*, September 1994, p. 112.

24. Ibid.

25. Larry Littman, "Despite Its Rocky Start, Hotel Industry Continues to Flourish into the 1990s," *Travel Agent Magazine*, 26 February 1990, p. 62.

26. http://corporate.disney.go.com.

27. Tannahill, pp. 173–174.

28. Ibid., p. 327.

29. Information in this and the following paragraph is cited from John Mariani, "Working on the Railroad," reprinted in *Restaurant Hospitality*, January 1992, p. 71, from Mariani's *America Eats Out* (New York: Morrow, 1991).

Part 1
INTRODUCTION

1

Service Makes
the Difference

Outline

Competencies

1. Define "service" and summarize how service businesses differ from manufacturing businesses. (pp. 4–11)

2. Explain the importance of strategic planning, describe the strategic planning process, and summarize planning challenges in capacity-constrained businesses. (pp. 11–15)

3. Describe the basic components of a strategic service vision for service companies, summarize keys to delivering good service, and describe Disney's four basic service priorities. (pp. 15–23)

Page 1: The Fairmont Orchid, Kohala Coast, Hawaii; photo courtesy of Fairmont Hotels & Resorts.

I N MANY PARTS OF THE WORLD, hospitality has become a mature industry. That is to say, it has passed the stage of rapid growth and innovation. There are not many new inventions that affect the way we eat and sleep away from home. In the past, customers were easily able to tell the difference between one hotel or restaurant type or brand and another, because each was unique within its own market niche. Holiday Inns, Hyatt, McDonald's, and T.G.I. Friday's stood for something special and different. Within each chain the architecture, decor, amenities, and menus were similar. But there was a clear difference between chains. You could get hamburgers at McDonald's, but if you wanted chicken you headed to KFC. All Holiday Inns had swimming pools; Days Inn did not.

Many of these distinctions no longer hold true. As lodging and restaurant chains redefined themselves to appeal to broader markets, their uniqueness began to fade. Chicken is available not only at KFC, but at McDonald's, Burger King, and Wendy's. Dunkin' Donuts sells bagels, and if you want a bowl of chili you can find it at Wendy's as well as Chili's. Many Days Inn properties now have swimming pools, and the distinctions between hotel brands are blurring. Atriums used to be an exclusive feature of Hyatt, for example; now many hotels have them. They have even become common on cruise ships!

Because obvious physical and product differences have faded, consumers have looked for other ways to differentiate one brand from another. There are many possibilities to choose from. One difference is availability. Some lodging chains have many units in just about every major city; others have just a few. Another difference is price. A steak at Outback Steakhouse costs much less than one at Morton's.

However, the most compelling difference in the minds of many consumers is service. Why is this so? Much of the answer has to do with the busy lifestyles of today, which have shaped our priorities. The large number of two-income families and the growing number of single-parent families have made time a priority in the way we live our lives. Very few consumers today have the luxury of spending a lot of time shopping to find the best value, the highest quality, or the speediest service. The attitude today is that we demand these things, they are a given, and when we don't receive what we expect, we become dissatisfied.

There is another factor at work here. Many studies show that life has become much more stressful in the last 50 years. The "rat race" is no longer an elusive euphemism, but a reality. One way of escape is to purchase a service so that we don't have to do it ourselves. When we do this, we not only relieve some of the pressures of daily life, but we also expect to feel pampered, to feel more important. Someone else is cooking and serving dinner, making the beds, and providing the entertainment. Expectations are what service is all about, as we shall see throughout the chapter.

What Is Service?

Service is generally defined as "work done for others." But this definition falls far short of the real meaning of the word. If a customer sits down in a restaurant, orders a sirloin steak, medium rare, and then after waiting 30 minutes receives a baked chicken breast, we can hardly characterize this as "service." Yet it fits the definition of "work done for others"!

For a better understanding of what service can mean, let's look at a real service experience from one of the most highly praised hotels in the world. According to many travel

The atrium of the Loews Santa Monica Beach Hotel welcomes guests with its distinctive decor.
(Courtesy of Loews Hotels.)

writers and frequent-traveler surveys, one of the best hotels in the world is the Mandarin Oriental in Bangkok. Famous writers such as James Michener and Noel Coward have written books while staying there. The Oriental's service is considered to be unparalleled anywhere. How does it achieve this?

Guests who pre-register at the Oriental are asked what flight they will be arriving on and whether they would like limousine service to the hotel. (Traffic in Bangkok is horrendous, taxis are hard to come by, and the hotel's limo costs the same as a taxi.) As soon as guests pass through customs at the Bangkok airport, they are greeted by an assistant manager from the hotel. He takes their baggage checks, calls for a Mercedes limousine, and, while they are waiting for the car and the luggage, takes down all of their registration and credit card information. When they leave the airport, the assistant manager radios ahead with the guests' names and car number. When they pull up to the hotel entrance, the doorman greets them by name and another assistant manager escorts them immediately to their room. Depending on the level of accommodations, the Mandarin service does not stop there. Every room contains pre-printed personalized stationery. Guests staying in suites are immediately greeted by a butler who offers to unpack for them and press any wrinkled garments. Bowls of fresh fruit in every room are replenished several times a day. All employees greet guests by name. To ensure that the hotel can provide this kind of service, there is a staff-to-guest ratio of 3 to 1—an almost impossible level to achieve economically in most countries. Moreover, the hotel runs one of the best hospitality schools in the country. Top graduates are offered a job at the Oriental; others easily find positions at other hotels and restaurants.

Every step of the way, the Mandarin Oriental exceeds its guests' expectations of what it will be like to stay there. First-time guests do not expect to be greeted at the airport by an assistant manager, pre-registered while their luggage is being retrieved, greeted by name when they arrive, escorted to their room not by a bellperson but by another assistant manager, find personalized stationery, and so on. It is this ability to exceed expectations that has earned the hotel its outstanding international reputation.

Restaurant and hotel guests have certain expectations. Consider the elements that constitute what we would call "good service" at a fine restaurant. The first impression of what kind of service the restaurant offers occurs when guests call for a reservation. How gracious is the person on the other end of the line? Do they sound genuinely interested in taking the reservation, or do they act as if the call were an unwanted interruption? The next impression may be the valet parking. Are cars taken quickly? Are guests welcomed or simply handed valet parking tickets? When they walk through the door, who greets them and how? Is the dining room host well-groomed, polite, and concerned with the guests' needs (for immediate seating or a no-smoking table, for example)? When seated, how soon before their presence is acknowledged by a server (often simple eye contact is enough) and water and bread are placed on the table? How soon is the order taken? Is the food served on time? Do guests receive what they ordered, correctly prepared? Does the server remember who ordered what? These are just some of the standards that are used when guests form opinions about the restaurant. If all of the parts of this process are performed better than expected—that is, *if reality exceeds expectations*—then guests rate the service received as better than average, or high. If reality matches expectations—the guests get what they expected, no more and no less—then service is satisfactory. But if reality is less than what is expected, the service is considered poor.

One further note: Price may play an important part in how service is evaluated, because it influences customers' expectations. When customers buy a hamburger at a fast-food restaurant, what they expect is very different from when they buy a hamburger in the dining room of a fine hotel. In the latter case, they expect more because they are paying more.

It is important to remember that, in all cases, it is the person who is receiving the service (the customer), not the person who is delivering the service, whose expectations count. Too often managers assume that if they think they are providing good service, that must be so. It is difficult for some managers to recognize that their perceptions may differ considerably from their customers'.

With this background, we are now in a position to formulate a more precise definition of service, or, to be more exact, *good* service. One approach is to look at service as a *performance* directed at satisfying the needs of customers. This is a good analogy and one that is used quite often in books on service management. Those who like this approach compare what customers experience in a hotel or restaurant to what they experience in a theater. In a theater, the audience sees only what happens on stage—the front of the house. Many things happen behind the scenes—the back of the house. The use of these very terms by hotels comes directly from the theater. Hotel employees can be compared to actors on a stage. Indeed, at Disney resort hotels and theme parks all employees are "members of the cast" and are "on stage" as soon as they walk into the sight of any of the guests. Through this use of performance terminology, Disney reminds its employees that they are to "act" at all times the way guests expect them to act, not the way they may feel like acting!

In conclusion, we choose to define good service as *meeting customers' needs in the way that they want and expect them to be met.* Superior service, obviously, means exceeding customer expectations.

Challenges in Managing and Marketing Service Businesses

Traditionally, the management and marketing of service businesses (including hospitality businesses) have been described and studied in the same way as businesses that manufacture products. The view has been that management is management and marketing is marketing; once you understand the basic principles, it doesn't matter much whether you're marketing a bowl of soup in a restaurant or a can of soup in a supermarket.

We no longer believe this. There are in fact a number of very important differences that affect the way service enterprises have to be managed and marketed. Hotels and restaurants—which deal in such **intangible products** as comfort, security, and positive experiences—have very different management and marketing challenges than do businesses that create tangible products such as automobiles or boxes of cereal. Christopher H. Lovelock has identified differences between the two.[1] For hospitality businesses:

- The nature of the product is different.
- Customers are more involved in the production process.
- People are part of the product.
- It's harder to maintain quality control standards.
- The services provided can't be inventoried.

- The time factor is more important.
- Distribution channels are different.

Let's take a closer look at each of these differences and consider their implications.

The Nature of the Product

Manufactured goods are tangible products. We can pick them up, carry them around, or in some other way physically handle them. A service, on the other hand, as noted earlier, is a performance or process. Marketing a hotel or restaurant service, which of course involves the use of physical objects and goods such as beds and food, is quite a different thing from marketing the goods themselves. For example, when guests choose a hotel, they take into account such factors as the convenience of the location, amenities (spas, business centers, etc.), and the kind of service they expect. When they make a reservation, the hotel reserves a certain category of guestroom based on price, size, or location, but seldom reserves the exact room itself (except in the case of a room especially equipped for disabled guests)—the exact room is not assigned until check-in. When guests arrive they use the physical facilities and eat the food, but that's not all they are buying. They are also purchasing the performance of services by people who work in the hotel—room service, concierge service, valet service—all of which are intangible. The hotel must manage the production of these services as well as of the physical products, and must persuade potential guests to buy some things (services) that the hotel cannot show them a picture of, or even in some cases adequately describe.

The Customer's Role in Production

Customers have no involvement in the production of manufactured goods. Soup is produced and packaged at the factory and purchased by a consumer at a supermarket or convenience store. The people who make the soup never see the ones who eat it, and the ones who eat it don't go to the factory when they want a serving. The two activities, production and consumption, are completely separate. This is not true in a service-based business.

A restaurant or a hotel is, in a very real sense, a factory. A factory where service is produced for customers who come inside, see the workers who are putting together the service, and may even participate with them in producing it—for example, when guests assemble their own salads at a salad bar and thus become part of the food production and service process. Some kinds of services require more employee-customer interaction than others. But in any case, because it is part of the service (product), the interaction between employees and customers must be managed—a task that a manager of manufactured goods never has to face.

People Are Part of the Product

In a service business like a hotel or restaurant, customers not only come in contact with employees but with other customers as well. That makes the other customers a part of the product (which we define as a performance), and often defines the quality of the service. Have you ever been to a movie or play where the people around you wouldn't keep quiet and spoiled some of your enjoyment? What about a restaurant where you went for a quiet, romantic evening and there was a party of 12 loud people at the next table celebrating someone's birthday? Business travelers who pay $300 or more per night for a room in a

People are part of the product offered at hotels and restaurants. As a result, their service attitude plays a large part in delivering such "service products" as friendliness and positive experiences.
(Courtesy of Gaylord Opryland Resort and Convention Center Nashville, Nashville, Tennessee.)

city hotel can get very annoyed when their check-in is delayed by a busload of tourists who have just arrived, or when a group of conventioneers insists on being served breakfast before anyone else so they can be finished in time for their first meeting. Similarly, when you are dressed up to attend an elegant reception, the dress of the other guests adds to your own enjoyment.

In short, all of the people with whom a guest comes in contact, both other guests and employees, are an integral part of the service product. They often are the main difference in the quality of the experience one hotel provides over another.

Maintaining Quality Control

When a factory produces a product, the product can be inspected for quality before it goes out the door. As long as proper quality control procedures and inspections are in place, defective products are not delivered. But services, like other live performances, take place in real time. That means that mistakes are bound to occur. Professor Christopher Lovelock cites a former package-goods marketer who became a Holiday Inn executive and observed:

> We can't control the quality of our product as well as a Procter & Gamble control
> engineer on a production line can. … When you buy a box of Ivory, you can reaso
> ably be 99 and 44/100ths percent sure that this stuff will work to g

clean. When you buy a Holiday Inn room, you're sure at some lesser percentage that we'll work to give you a good night's sleep without any hassle, or people banging on the walls, and all the bad things that can happen in a hotel.[2]

No Inventories

Manufacturers can inventory their products in warehouses until they are needed. But because services are live performances, they cannot be made in advance or stored for future use. That means that there are times when the supply can't be produced on time because the demand is too great. Guests must be turned away from hotels that are completely occupied, or restaurant guests may wait an hour or more for a table. For this reason, service marketing often focuses on controlling demand.

The Importance of Time

Because most hospitality services are delivered (performed) in the "factory," customers have to be present to receive them (except when they order take-out food from a restaurant, and even then delivery—which is a service—is involved, and time is a crucial factor). When customers are present, they expect the service to be performed "on time," which in their minds means "when I want it." In a restaurant, guests not only expect that their orders will be taken promptly, but that the food will arrive in a reasonable amount of time. Time, then, often plays a more important role in producing services than in producing goods. Customers must wait for a service to be performed, perhaps just briefly, perhaps for a long time; they don't have to wait for a manufactured good—it is already sitting on

...art of the overall hospitality experience. (Courtesy of Gaylord ... Nashville, Tennessee.)

the shelf. Since customers must wait for a service, hospitality enterprises must devise strategies to keep them from feeling during the wait that they are being ignored or are not important.

Different Distribution Channels

Companies that manufacture goods move their products from the factory by trucks, trains, or airplanes to wholesalers, distributors, or retailers, who then resell them to the ultimate consumer. This is not the case with service companies, where customers come right into the factory or contact it directly. For instance, hotel customers may use phones or walk up to the front desk to make reservations. In either case, service businesses must train their employees to handle the marketing function of dealing with customers. Employees who manufacture goods do not for the most part require those skills. Even when intermediaries are involved (such as travel agents), transferring a service to a customer requires more "people skills" than transferring, from factory to warehouse to retail store, a physical product to a customer.

Achieving Superior Service in a Less-Than-Perfect World

The most important operational competency of top-level service managers is the ability to plan for the future. While day-to-day operations can be performed by others, someone must be thinking about next year and beyond. This is the job of top managers—to develop the strategy for survival that any business needs to succeed. It is also the key to providing superior service, which must begin at the very top of the organizational ladder.

Strategic Planning

Broad, long-range business planning is called strategic planning. Companies must formulate general business objectives for themselves, otherwise there is bound to be confusion about where they are going and how they intend to get there. These general business objectives are most commonly called a company's mission or values, and are expressed as a missio statement or a statement of core values. Here is the complete statement of core val Darden Restaurants, the largest full-service dining company in the world:

As an organization, we value:

- *Integrity and fairness.* It all starts with integrity. We trust in the fairness of each other to always do the right thing, to be forthright with ourselves and others, to demonstrate cou blame and to follow through on all our commitme

- *Respect and caring.* We reach out with respect interest in the well being of others. We kn power of understanding and the imm

- *Diversity.* Even though we have a our individual differences. W perspectives, attitudes, an ness. Our power of di

- *Always learning — always teaching.* We learn from others as they learn from us. We learn. We teach. We grow.
- *Being "of service."* Being of service is our pleasure. We treat people as special and appreciated by giving of ourselves, doing more than expected, anticipating needs, and making a difference.
- *Teamwork.* Teamwork works. By trusting one another, we bring together the best in all of us and go beyond the boundaries of ordinary success.
- *Excellence.* We have a passion to set and to pursue, with innovation, courage and humility, ever higher standards.
- Our Core Values communicate the behaviors and attitudes we cherish as we strive to deliver on Darden's Core Purpose. That's what motivates us to be the best.[3]

Note the order of the list. There is a belief that excellent service and teamwork are achievable when there is "integrity and fairness," "respect and caring," and a "common vision," but embracing and celebrating individual differences. You will learn to recognize the importance of all of these concepts.

The Strategic Planning Process. Once a mission has been clearly established and articulated, there is a series of steps a company must take to make that mission a guiding force.

Perform a SWOT analysis. SWOT stands for *strengths, weaknesses, opportunities,* and *threats.* To do a SWOT analysis, a company examines the internal and external environment in which it is operating. What are the strengths and weaknesses of its operation? What opportunities exist for growth? What ˈts exist, either from competitors or changing trends? The ultimate goal of th… to determine how well the company is serving current markets.

Formulate …lude adding more units, appealing to new market … ˈe, or developing new products. Marriott … additional types of Marriott hotels—for …ˈelers who like to stay in limited-service …d-stay market), and Fairfield Inns (to …ness travelers).

…ˈen developed, they must be imple- …ˈgies for attracting dieters is to add …ˈan be made in a uniform manner …rs for the salads' ingredients and

… fundamental issues must be

…employees. Continuing with …t explain to employees why …en if this strategy involves … organization.

…ˈucture must be changed …concentrate on improv- …ˈ of weekly paperwork …mers.

- *Corporate culture.* To implement a strategy, you need employees who buy into the corporate culture or way of doing business. They must share the same values and work ethic. Disney spends two days of employee orientation in telling new employees the history of the company. Walt Disney's life story is retold at length. Early Mickey Mouse cartoons are shown. New hires are taught the Disney language — words and concepts unique to the Disney organization. This helps promote a family or "tribal" feeling.

Monitor and evaluate results. After implementing strategies, managers must monitor them to make sure they are working. Some examples: Marriott and Hyatt read guests' online surveys carefully; Domino's Pizza surveys customers by phone.

Tim Firnstahl is the founder of SGE, Inc., a restaurant management company in Seattle. Firnstahl set an objective of making sure that guest satisfaction in all of his restaurants would be guaranteed. Then he developed a plan to reach that objective. He came up with a company slogan: *"Your Enjoyment Guaranteed. Always."* He reduced this to an acronym — YEGA — that all employees could easily remember. After a series of meetings in which Firnstahl explained what he had in mind, all of his 600 employees signed a contract pledging that they would follow through on the YEGA promise. "We created a YEGA logo and put it everywhere," says Firnstahl, "on report forms, on training manuals, on wall signs. We started *YEGA NEWS* and distributed YEGA pins, shirts, name tags, even underwear. We announced that failure to enforce YEGA would be grounds for dismissal." The final step was empowering employees to make the YEGA objective workable. With this in mind, Firnstahl instituted the idea that employees can and should do anything to keep the customer happy. "In the event of an error or delay, any employee right down to the busboy could provide complimentary wine or dessert, or pick up an entire tab if necessary."[4]

Planning Challenges in Capacity-Constrained Businesses

One important difference between service organizations and manufacturing firms, as pointed out previously, is the inability of service firms to inventory finished products. In the manufacturing of goods, peaks and valleys of supply and demand are managed, in part, by finishing and storing goods in advance of when they will be needed. Thus it is seldom, if ever, necessary to produce anything instantly to satisfy demand.

Since service firms cannot manufacture and store services, their financial success depends on how efficiently they match their productive capacity — their staff, equipment, and resources such as operating inventories — to consumer demand at any given moment. This is very difficult. When demand is low, production capacity will be wasted because there will be an oversupply of workers to serve the customers; when demand is higher than production capacity, there will be more guests than the workers or the building can serve and business will be lost. In other words, hotels and restaurants are **capacity-constrained businesses** and therefore must constantly manage both supply (production capacity) and demand.

Managing Supply. Let's first look at strategies for managing supply. In the case of hotels and restaurants, the ability to supply the products manufactured in the service "factory" is fixed. A hotel has a fixed number of beds; a restaurant has a fixed number of seats. These cannot be altered to increase capacity whenever demand is greater than capacity — that is, when there are more guests than there are hotel beds or restaurant seats. That means that a good part of the time hotels and restaurants must follow a **level-capacity strategy** in which the same amount of capacity is offered no matter how high the demand.

However, some hospitality firms can follow a **chased-demand strategy,** in which capacity can be varied to suit the demand level—in a limited way. For example, there is a measure of flexibility in some parts of a hotel, such as the space set aside for meetings and conventions. Another common tactic in hospitality firms is to have a certain number of part-time employees who work only when the demand is high. Sometimes firms such as caterers can rent extra equipment and thus increase their capacity as needed. Finally, companies can cross-train employees so that they can be shifted temporarily to other jobs as needed. In the long run, of course, a hotel or restaurant can increase its capacity by enlarging its current property or building a new, larger one.

Managing Demand. Because hotel and restaurant capacity is limited, it is important to put most of the strategic planning emphasis on managing demand. One of the goals of managers in a service business is to shift demand from periods when it cannot be accommodated (because the operation is already filled to capacity) to periods when it can be. One way to do this is to encourage business during slow periods. Some restaurants offer early-bird specials to increase demand early in the day, and lounges have happy hours to increase demand early in the evening.

While supply cannot be inventoried, sometimes demand can. This happens when managers or employees encourage customers to stand in line or sit in the restaurant's lounge until a table in the dining room becomes available. Taking reservations is another example of inventorying demand.

Many cruise lines attempt to manage demand by changing their ports of call seasonally over the course of a year. (Courtesy of Holland America Line.)

The most common method used to influence demand in the hotel industry is price. Using pricing strategies to control demand is risky unless the strategies are thoroughly understood. Hotels are faced with pricing decisions every day, such as whether to accept meeting and convention reservations at low group rates, or hold on to those guestrooms for later sale at higher rates to individual business travelers. One tool managers use to make such decisions is revenue management, a system that guides management in selling "the right product to the right customer at the right time for the right price."[5]

Sometimes the product itself can be varied to help balance supply and demand. Restaurants routinely change their menus and level of service between lunch and dinner. Cruise ships reposition themselves to call on ports in the Caribbean in the winter and Alaska in the summer. Sometimes different services can be offered at the same time to accommodate the demand levels of different groups, as with first-class, business-class, and economy-class airline seats—all on the same plane—or concierge floors in hotels.

Finally, communication strategies can play a large part in balancing demand levels. A carefully thought-out advertising schedule can enable resorts to influence demand by appealing to new market segments with special rates during the off-season; similarly, they can keep demand levels high during the regular season by targeting those guest groups willing to pay full rates.

One of the hard realities that prompts these tactics is that hotels and restaurants have a high level of fixed expenses because of their physical plant. These fixed expenses cannot be lowered, so strategies and tactics must be found to utilize a hotel or restaurant to its fullest possible extent. Even a marginal increase in business can produce a significant increase in profit once the break-even point is reached.

The Strategic Service Vision

James Heskett, professor emeritus of business administration at Harvard Business School, notes that all successful service companies share what he calls a "strategic service vision"—a blueprint for service managers. The components of this blueprint are: (1) targeting a market segment, and (2) focusing on a service strategy.[6] Let's discuss these elements in more detail, drawing from examples and ideas from the work of Heskett and others.

Targeting a Market Segment

There is no such thing as a product or service that appeals to everyone. Some people want hotels that have a good restaurant because they enjoy dining while they are traveling. Others don't care that much about food but value a hotel with a fitness club and spa where they can relax and exercise. Some travelers want a comfortable guestroom with a desk where they can work; others plan to spend little time in their room. Similarly, a restaurant can't appeal to everyone. People have different tastes in food and different ideas of what constitutes a pleasant experience when dining out. They differ in how much they are willing to pay for a meal.

Since hotels and restaurants cannot hope to appeal to everyone, they single out groups or market segments and attempt to provide products and services that, in the eyes of these consumers, are superior to those of competing hotels and restaurants. For example, the primary market for McDonald's has always been families with young children. Wendy's targets adults who want a hamburger cooked to order—historically, it has made little effort to attract children. At the high end of the hamburger-restaurant scale is Fuddruckers,

The furnishings, decor, layout, and design of a hospitality product are all affected by the needs and desires of the targeted market segment. Some target markets want little more than a comfortable room with few amenities, while others are looking for a vacation experience. (The Radisson Aruba; photo courtesy of Carlson Hospitality Worldwide.)

which serves larger and more expensive hamburgers and beer in an atmosphere designed to appeal to adults.

Focusing on a Service Strategy

The various service concepts that hospitality businesses adopt are not simply amorphous marketing ideas. A hotel or restaurant, including its services, is carefully designed to appeal to a limited segment of the market, *and the way service is delivered is tailored to match the expectations of the segment that it targets.*

Research has shown that most people believe buying an intangible service like a vacation or even a meal in a restaurant is more risky than buying a manufactured product. With a manufactured product, buyers have a better idea of what they're getting for their money, while with intangible products there may be some surprises. It is that element of uncertainty that poses the biggest challenge to service businesses. That is why it is so important for managers and employees to provide consistent services that meet an operation's standards.

Service Standards. Successful hospitality companies focus a good deal of management attention on establishing quality standards for services, communicating these standards to employees through training programs, and measuring performance. For example, one service standard that is frequently established and easy to measure is waiting time. Burger King and McDonald's have strict standards for how long customers are expected to wait for their food once it has been ordered. Many airlines and hotels with busy telephone reservation systems have set time limits for how long customers can be kept on hold before their call is handled. Restaurants often manage expectations by telling guests they will have to wait longer for a table than is actually the case. When they are given their table earlier than expected, guests conclude that they have been given special attention—thus their feeling of receiving good service is reinforced.

The way service is delivered must be tailored to match the expectations of the target market. Leaving flower petals on the sheets during turndown service, as is done at the Trump International Sonesta Beach Resort, would be a strangely out-of-place service at a budget hotel. (Courtesy of Sonesta International Hotel Corporation.)

Another quality control technique restaurants use is to set standards for how quickly a food server should approach a customer after he or she sits down at a table. At some operations the standard is for a server to go to the table immediately and say, "I'll be with you in a minute." Another restaurant may require bread and butter to be served at the same time, to further acknowledge the diners' presence.

Providing consistent services is extremely complex where customer contact is involved, especially when some of the lowest-paid employees make the most contacts. A former Marriott executive described one strategy he used to deal with the problem:

> The *Marriott Bellman* booklet is designed to convince our uniformed doormen that they represent an all-important first and last impression for many of our guests, that they must stand with dignity and good posture, and that they must not lean against the wall or put up their feet when sitting. . . . Bellmen are often looked at subconsciously by guests as being "Mr. Marriott himself" because many times a guest will speak to and deal with a bellman more often during a visit than with any other employee of the hotel.… They are coached to smile often and to do all they can to make the guest feel welcome and special.[7]

Marriott is known for setting exact standards—including service standards—for all of its jobs, and for communicating them clearly in writing as well as in training sessions.

The company continually measures how well standards are being met with frequent inspections, and it encourages its employees—through profit sharing, stock options, and other bonus programs—to provide good service.

Job Restructuring. An effective service strategy must also provide a means of achieving levels of productivity that will satisfy the business's economic goals as well as customer expectations. One way managers do this in service companies is by job restructuring—changing the nature of the work or the way it is done. For example, at Benihana restaurants, the chef prepares the food at a hibachi in front of guests, combining the jobs of food server and chef. Professor Heskett observes, "Given the nature of a service concept that combines quality food and entertainment at reasonable prices, as well as the exotic format of a Japanese restaurant, customers of Benihana readily accept a highly economic combination of jobs that is carried out in their full view."[8]

Payroll Control. Along with controlling the quality of service goes controlling payroll and other costs involved in providing that service. Any hotel or restaurant could schedule more than enough employees to give good service all the time, but that would not be profitable. Every operation must provide good, if not superior, service within its own economic constraints. Companies that do the best job of controlling service quality also excel at controlling labor and other costs, since clearly they are closely connected. Payroll control can be achieved by employee training and careful scheduling, a combination that almost always produces higher productivity and better service.

Remember Seattle restaurateur Tim Firnstahl and YEGA? Part of why Firnstahl designed YEGA was to help him identify systems that were not working and control costs that were out of line. Every time an employee gave a guest a free meal because of bad service, this was reported and considered by Firnstahl to be a "system failure cost." Whenever a meal was given away, Firnstahl asked, "Why is the system failing?" not "Why is the employee failing?" Asking the question proved to be highly productive.

"Our search for the culprit in a string of complaints about slow food service in one restaurant led first to the kitchen and then to one cook. But pushing the search one step further revealed several unrealistically complex dishes that no one could have prepared swiftly."[9] A service strategy helped identify a production problem.

Delivering on the Service Promise

Many theories and ideas about service have been mentioned so far in this chapter. The bottom line, however, is doing it—delivering on the promise that a company makes to its owners, employees, and customers. It is easy enough to write a mission statement that says, "We intend to be a premier and progressive lodging company," or, "Our goal is to deliver the best service of any restaurant chain in our class"—but how do you do it? What makes it really happen?

There are hundreds of suggestions that have been made on how to deliver exceptional service. Any good-size bookstore has at least a half-dozen books full of practical, tested ideas that work. The Harvard Business School has published hundreds of case histories that detail how and why companies succeed and fail. There are many fine training companies that offer seminars on every aspect of service. With all this information available, it is surprising that there is still so much poor service in the hospitality industry.

Keys to Delivering Good Service

Everyone understands that customers want superior service and that better service leads to better profits. Understanding it is one thing; doing it is another. This chapter does not offer a simple recipe for success or a prescription that can turn a one-star restaurant or hotel into a three- or four-star one—it's not that easy. But there are a number of things that any organization that cares about good service can do. Here are five of them:

1. *Don't forget who you are.* A classic story about forgetting who you are concerns People's Express, which in the early 1980s was the darling of the airline business. People's Express started as an airline that promised really low fares to leisure travelers who were willing to accept limited service in return. The airline's schedules weren't the most convenient, passengers had to buy a ticket on board instead of getting one ahead of time, at the airport people carried their own luggage to the plane, and if they wanted a meal during the flight they paid for it. People's Express employees didn't have a simple job description—they did whatever needed doing. Pilots, for example, also helped out on the ground, which allowed People's Express to save on labor costs. With this simple strategy, in five short years the company's value grew to almost $1 billion.

   As People's Express grew, it acquired more customers and planes. It decided to go after business travelers, and the company added a first-class section. Soon the company's sheer size meant that it had to change the way it did things. With a small customer base it was acceptable not to take reservations, but when thousands started showing up at the airport, the airline needed some means of forecasting who wanted to go where and when. That meant an expensive computerized reservation system and reservation agents who knew how to use it—just like the big airlines had. It was okay to ask pilots to help out on the ground when the company only had a few planes, but when it had more than 100, it needed the pilots in the air. All of this affected the company's ability to keep its costs down. Even worse, now it was competing with the major airlines for business. It forgot that it had succeeded by being a budget airline that targeted leisure travelers. Five years after the first plane left the ground, People's Express was sold and grounded forever.

   Companies that succeed create a service strategy for each market segment and stick to it. They make certain that everyone who works for them understands what they are selling and who they want to sell it to. They don't confuse or anger consumers by offering something they don't deliver.

2. *Encourage every employee to act like a manager.* Managers understand the need for repeat business; employees may not. Service-oriented companies motivate, train, and empower their employees to act like the company they work for is their own business. That means really caring when anyone has a problem, whether it's another employee or a guest. It also means making sure that they can solve problems they run into, which in turn requires that they be given the authority to make the necessary decisions. Authors William H. Davidow and Bro Uttal talk about Embassy Suites in their book *Total Customer Service: The Ultimate Weapon*. Embassy Suites, a division of Hilton Hotels Corporation, uses an upside-down organization chart to dramatize the idea that the front-line employees, the ones who deal with guests, are the most important people in the organization. It's not easy to find hotel managers who will accept the idea that when it comes to pleasing guests, the front desk employees may be more important than they are. Embassy Suites does that

by hiring managers who have the right attitude and then training them to help the people who work for them.[10]

3. *Handle moments of truth correctly.* Many of the duties performed by front desk agents or food servers are repetitive and sometimes performed in a depersonalized manner. As a result, guests may feel that they are being treated as mere numbers. To combat this guest perception, some companies have identified what they call **moments of truth.** The concept was popularized by Jan Carlzon, the CEO of Scandinavian Airlines System (SAS) in the early 1980s and is still viable today. Carlzon understood that there was a huge difference in the way SAS defined service levels and the way its customers defined them. "Each of our 10 million customers came in contact with approximately five SAS employees, and this contact lasted an average of 15 seconds each time. Thus SAS is 'created' in the minds of our customers 50 million times a year, 15 seconds at a time. These 50 million 'moments of truth' are the moments that ultimately determine whether SAS will succeed or fail as a company. They are the moments when we must prove to our customers that SAS is their best alternative," Carlzon explained.[11]

Service-oriented businesses concentrate their efforts on making sure that moments of truth are handled correctly. For hotels, an important moment of truth

Guests may experience more "moments of truth" with a door attendant than with any other employee. (Photo courtesy of Ernie Pick.)

occurs when guests check in or out and come face-to-face with a hotel employee. Although there are certain check-in/check-out routines that must be followed, guests should be given individual attention so they feel their needs are being addressed in a personal way. One way to do this is to make certain that front desk employees are trained to look up from their computer screens to give guests a warm welcome (by name, if possible), and continue to smile and make eye contact as they perform their duties for guests. Such seemingly small gestures go a long way toward establishing an overall atmosphere of attentive and pleasing guest service.

4. *Hire good people and keep them happy.* Turnover is the worst enemy superior service has. New people don't know what is expected of them and may have inadequate training or the wrong training. They are often unprepared to give good service. Superior companies make every effort to recruit, hire, and hold onto people who have the right personalities. (Many companies today hire for attitude rather than skill. Skills that are learned on the job are often more easily upgraded than attitudes that employees bring with them.) Service-minded companies regard their employees as being as important as their customers. That means training their employees well, motivating them, and rewarding them. This strategy is inevitably more cost-efficient and more successful than constantly finding and training new employees.

5. *Respond in a timely manner.* Most guests don't like to wait. Waiting, for them, is a hallmark of poor service. At limited-service establishments even five minutes may seem too long. At family restaurants, most guests expect their food to be on the table in 30 minutes or less. No one likes to be put on hold when making a reservation for an airline ticket, a hotel room, or a rental car. Long check-in and check-out lines spell disaster. None of these is a necessary evil. Excellent companies are constantly monitoring the waiting time of their guests and looking for ways to decrease it, or at least make it less stressful.

Every organization and every situation is unique. Managers need to develop their own lists of key service criteria and ways to implement them. It's the difference between winning and losing the battle for satisfied customers.

Service, Disney-Style

A careful look at the way the Walt Disney Company delivers service at its theme parks and resorts provides some insight into how superior service is delivered consistently. It starts with Disney's four basic service priorities: *safety, courtesy, show,* and *efficiency.* The order of these service priorities is important—first safety, next courtesy, then show and, lastly, efficiency. Disney personnel must think in that order.

Safety is of course a key element, especially in the theme parks, where the potential for accidents is ever-present. If an elderly person with a walker wants to go on the Haunted House ride in the Magic Kingdom, "cast members" (as all employees are called) are empowered to stop the ride while the guest is helped onto the walkway. At the same time, a recorded announcement is played for those on the ride: "Ladies and gentlemen, the ghosts and goblins have taken over for a minute." This is just one example of how cast members are trained to handle potential safety problems.

Courtesy is generated by Disney's attitude toward its employees and reinforced by specific training techniques in handling guests. A popular Disney saying is, "Our front line is our bottom line." Disney also believes that guests are always guests, whether they are right or wrong. That means that they are allowed to be wrong with dignity, never

At Walt Disney theme parks, service is a "performance" that focuses on interacting with guests and satisfying their needs. (Courtesy of Walt Disney World, Orlando, Florida.)

reprimanded or put on the defensive. If a guest has locked him- or herself out of a car, staff members react in a positive manner even though they know that what has happened is not their fault. They attempt to soften the situation by trying to make the guest feel okay. Body language also is considered a part of courtesy. Cast members are taught to use the "Disney point" when giving directions; the "Disney point" involves the entire palm or two fingers—never a single finger, which is considered rude! Another dimension of courtesy is the way the Disney cast interacts with guests. In the morning, when people are full of energy and ready to start off on a day of adventure, the staff too is upbeat and chatty. But at night, when people are tired and returning to their rooms or going home, unnecessary conversation is kept to a minimum.

The other two service priorities, *show* (entertainment) and *efficiency* are obvious throughout the Disney operation. As "cast members," all employees have a role in the show at Disney. Part of show integrity is to ensure that a cast member in a Frontierland costume does not appear in Tomorrowland, and that a server in Liberty Tree Tavern talks as if it were 1776. Video monitors, character appearances, and live performances are show elements that entertain guests during long waits for attractions. Parades, shows, and fireworks are used to draw crowds to specific areas of the park. Disney World in Florida efficiently solved a recurring and embarrassing problem for guests: remembering where they left their cars in a parking lot that is larger than California's entire Disneyland complex. When guests cannot find their cars, attendants simply ask them what time they arrived. With that information, it is easy to tell where to look for a car, because specific rows are filled at specific times!

Disney executives estimate that every cast member has 60 moments of truth every day. Clearly, Disney defines quality service as exceeding guest expectations during every one of those encounters. The Disney company helps its cast members exceed guest expectations by paying attention to the smallest details. This meticulous approach pays off, bringing customers back for repeat visits and making Walt Disney World the world's largest single tourist attraction.

Summary

Because many obvious physical and product differences among hospitality companies have faded, consumers have looked for other ways to differentiate one hotel and restaurant brand from another. The most compelling difference in the minds of many consumers is service. Good service is defined as meeting customer needs in the way that they want and expect them to be met. Superior service results from exceeding guest expectations.

Hospitality operations, which often deal in intangible services, have very different management and marketing challenges than do companies that deal exclusively in tangible products. For hospitality businesses, the nature of the product is different, customers are more involved in the production process, people are part of the product, it's harder to maintain quality control standards, the services they offer can't be inventoried, the time factor is more important, and distribution channels are different.

Broad, long-range business planning is called strategic planning. Companies must formulate general business objectives for themselves, otherwise there will be confusion about where they are going and how they intend to get there. These general business objectives are most commonly called a company's mission and are expressed as a mission statement. Once a mission has been clearly established and articulated, there is a series of steps a company must take: perform a SWOT analysis, formulate strategies, implement strategies, and monitor and evaluate results.

Hotels and restaurants are capacity-constrained businesses and must constantly manage supply and demand. Supply can be managed to a limited extent but, for hospitality businesses, it is more productive to focus on managing demand. Demand can be shifted, inventoried, and controlled by varying prices, changing service levels, or using communications strategies (such as advertising) to affect demand.

Successful service companies share a "strategic service vision"—a blueprint for service managers. The components of this blueprint are: (1) targeting a market segment, and (2) focusing on a service strategy. In addition, successful hospitality companies focus a good deal of management attention on establishing quality standards for services, communicating them to employees through training programs, and measuring performance. Job restructuring is another effective strategy.

There are many ways companies have found to make certain they deliver on their promise of quality service. Every organization and situation is different. The Walt Disney Company provides one example of how a hospitality company can consistently deliver superior service.

 # Endnotes

1. Christopher H. Lovelock, *Services Marketing,* 2d ed. (Englewood Cliffs, N.J.: Prentice-Hall, 1991), p. 7. The authors gratefully acknowledge the concepts formulated by Dr. Lovelock, upon which much of the following discussion is based.

2. Ibid., p. 9.

3. www.darden.com.

4. Timothy W. Firnstahl, "My Employees Are My Service Guarantee," *Harvard Business Review,* July–August 1989, p. 29.

5. Kathleen Cullen and Caryl Helsel, "Defining Revenue Management," HSMAI Foundation Special Report, 2006.

6. James L. Heskett, *Managing in the Service Economy* (Boston: Harvard Business School Press, 1986), pp. 5–25.

7. Ibid., pp. 96–97.

8. Ibid., p. 93.

9. Firnstahl, p. 30.

10. William H. Davidow and Bro Uttal, *Total Customer Service: The Ultimate Weapon* (New York: Harper Perennial, 1989), p. 115.

11. Jan Carlzon, *Moments of Truth* (Cambridge, Mass.: Ballinger, 1987), pp. 21–29.

Key Terms

capacity-constrained businesses—Businesses that produce "products" or services that cannot be inventoried or stored for future use. Success depends on their ability to efficiently match productive capacity to consumer demand at any given moment.

chased-demand strategy—A management strategy in which capacity can, to a limited extent, be varied to suit the level of demand.

intangible products—The primary products of hospitality-oriented organizations. Intangible products such as comfort, enjoyment, and pleasant experiences relate to guests' emotional well-being and expectations. They present very different management and marketing challenges than do tangible products such as automobiles or boxes of cereal.

level-capacity strategy—A management strategy in which the same amount of capacity is offered, no matter how high the consumer demand.

moments of truth—Critical moments when customers and staff members interact, offering opportunities for the staff to make a favorable impression, correct mistakes, and win repeat customers.

service—Meeting customers' needs in the way that they want and expect them to be met.

SWOT—An acronym for strengths, weaknesses, opportunities, and threats. A SWOT analysis helps companies assess how well they are serving their current markets, an important step in the strategic planning process.

Review Questions

1. How is "good service" defined? What constitutes superior service?

2. What are some challenges service businesses face when managing and marketing their products and services?

3. What are some of the intangible products that hotels and restaurants provide?

4. How does strategic planning help hospitality businesses provide good service? What is the strategic planning process?

5. How do capacity-constrained businesses such as hotels and restaurants manage supply and demand?

6. What are the components of a strategic service vision, and how do they help businesses deliver good service?

7. What are five things organizations can do that will help them deliver good service?

8. What are Disney's four basic service priorities?

Internet Sites

For more information, visit the following Internet sites. Remember that Internet addresses can change without notice. If the site is no longer there, you can use a search engine to look for additional sites.

Hotel Companies/Resorts

Days Inn
www.daysinn.com

Hilton Hotels
www.hilton.com

Holiday Inns
www.holiday-inn.com

Hyatt Hotels and Resorts
www.hyatt.com

Mandarin Oriental Hotel Group
www.mandarin-oriental.com

Marriott International
www.marriott.com

South Seas Plantation
www.captivavip.com/south-seas.htm

Walt Disney Corporation
www.disney.com

Restaurant Companies

Burger King
www.burgerking.com

Chili's Grill & Bar
www.chilis.com

Darden Restaurants
www.darden.com

Domino's Pizza
www.dominos.com

KFC
www.kfc.com

McDonald's
www.mcdonalds.com

Olive Garden
www.olivegarden.com

Outback Steakhouse
www.outbacksteakhouse.com

Pizza Hut
www.pizzahut.com

T.G.I. Friday's
www.tgifridays.com

Taco Bell
www.tacobell.com

Wendy's
www.wendys.

2

The Travel and Tourism Industry

Outline

Competencies

1. List recent world changes that affect the travel and tourism industry, describe in general terms the size of the industry, and explain the importance of the interrelationships within the industry. (pp. 30–35)

2. Summarize reasons people travel and describe types of travel research. (pp. 35–40)

3. Explain the social impact travel and tourism can have on a destination, discuss sustainable tourism development and ecotourism, and describe a plan for sound tourism development. (pp. 40–43)

Opposite page: An alpine ski resort—Crans-Montana, Switzerland.

T HE HOSPITALITY INDUSTRY is only one of several industries that together make up the travel and tourism industry. In this chapter, we will look at the scope and economic impact of travel and tourism, then examine how businesses within the industry are interrelated. We'll conclude the chapter with a discussion of why people travel, travel and tourism's effect on society, sustainable development, and ecotourism.

The Changing World

The world has been on an evolutionary path since the beginning of time. But never was the phenomenon of change as dramatic as in the twentieth century—more specifically, the period following World War II. The pace of change after 1945 was unprecedented, and there are no signs of it slowing down here in the twenty-first century.

More than any other factor, technology is responsible for transforming the way we live. Technological advancement drove much of the world from an agrarian to an industrial society and, beginning in the 1950s, into an information society. Technology has provided us with the means to travel faster and cheaper, manufacture goods more efficiently, and communicate with one another across the globe almost instantaneously. The Internet, e-mail, cell phones, voice messages, teleconferencing, and fax machines enable us to exchange information as fast as thoughts are conceived. Satellites and fiber-optic cables link North America, Europe, and the Far East, carrying voice and electronic communications faster and clearer every day. Even more significantly, new information-transfer technologies can carry a much greater volume of information and calls.

The world's population is growing. There are more than 8 billion people on the planet today; by 2050, it's estimated there will be 9.1 billion.[1] The world's population is not only growing; it is also aging (see Exhibit 1). In many parts of the world, declining birth rates will produce a population with a larger percentage of older people. As we age, we tend to accumulate wealth. Therefore, we can expect that more people will be able to travel and dine out in the years ahead.

Exhibit 1 Median Age by Major World Area			
Median Age (Years)			
	1950	**2005**	**2050**
World	24.0	28.1	38.4
More developed regions	29.0	38.8	45.6
Less developed regions	21.6	25.7	37.2
Africa	19.2	19.2	28.5
Asia	22.3	27.7	40.2
Europe	29.7	39.2	46.6
Latin America and the Caribbean	20.0	26.4	41.7
Northern America	29.8	36.4	42.1
Oceania	28.0	32.3	39.1

Source: United Nations Population Division, *World Population Prospects: The 2008 Revision.*

Drawing by Ed Fisher;©1988, The New Yorker Magazine, Inc.

There are many other trends affecting travel. In a number of countries the amount of leisure time is increasing. The United States offers fewer legal holidays to its workers than most other developed countries. While the average American gets 10 legal holidays a year (as does the average Japanese and Canadian), Germans receive 18 days annually, and citizens of Sweden and Denmark receive 30 days.

Many households have two income-earners. This means that there are more discretionary funds for travel and a greater need to take a vacation as a relief from stress. But two workers in one family also means shorter vacations. People today tend to take several short vacations during the year rather than one long one.

Seasonality has become less important in travel. Part of this is due to the increased tendency to take vacations when we can, not when we would like to. Also, more and more attractions tend to be "climate controlled." In Japan, for instance, there is an indoor ski resort that is 25 stories high and the length of six U.S. football fields. It holds up to 3,000 skiers, and its temperature is a constant 28°F (–2.2°C).

As a result of an increased awareness of the problems caused by pollution and over-development, sustainable tourism is being embraced by governments, the travel industry, and travelers. People all over the world are eager to visit the rain forests of the Amazon, the glaciers of Alaska, and the barrier reefs of Australia. The increasing affluence of younger travelers has fueled the relatively new adventure-travel business. There is an increasing interest in going to faraway or highly inaccessible places like central New Guinea or the North Pole. Tours and cruises now offer those options, among others.

In short, we are seeing significant economic, social, and political changes throughout the world. Some bode well for tourism; others, such as the increase in terrorism, do not.

The Nature of the Travel and Tourism Industry

When the United States Senate created the National Tourism Policy Act of 1981 to encourage the growth of tourism, it used the following definition of the **travel and tourism industry:**

> An interrelated amalgamation of those businesses and agencies which totally or in part provide the means of transport, goods, services, and other facilities for travel outside of the home community for any purpose not related to day-to-day activity.

Another definition that is somewhat similar but a bit clearer, and therefore the one we will adopt, is provided by Douglas Fretchling, professor of tourism studies at George Washington University. Fretchling defines the travel and tourism industry as "a collection of organizations and establishments that derive all or a significant portion of their income from providing goods and services purchased on a trip to the traveler." Exhibit 2 lists businesses that make up the travel and tourism industry. The businesses under the headings "Accommodation" and "Food and Beverage," along with institutional (generally nonprofit) food service operations, constitute the hospitality industry. As you can see, the hospitality industry is only part of the travel and tourism industry.

One way to define the size of the travel and tourism industry is to add up the amount of money spent on goods and services by travelers. Unfortunately, it's impossible to do this accurately. While just about everyone would agree that airlines and resorts receive almost all of their business from travelers, what about gift shops and gas stations? These businesses on the whole have no way of knowing what percentage of their customers are travelers and what percentage are local residents. Depending on their location, there may be a wide variation in the amount of business they get from each source. Although there is no way of knowing how much of their revenues are from travelers, for statistical purposes the total receipts of these types of businesses are included in projections of the size and scope of the travel and tourism industry.

Statisticians and economists measure the size of the travel and tourism industry by adding together the receipts of the businesses that compose it, but these figures do not tell the whole story. For example, one could argue that the amount of money a hotel takes in is not a true measure of its economic impact on the surrounding community. The real impact is also measured by the salaries the hotel pays to its employees, which they in turn spend on housing, clothes, and food for their families; by the taxes the hotel pays to local, state, and federal governments; by the amount of profits generated by local companies who sell goods and services to the hotel; and by the number of jobs the hotel creates that may keep people off the welfare rolls.

The World Travel & Tourism Council gives these examples of the impact of tourism on other industries:

- When American Airlines did an impact study of employment in the Miami–Dade County community, the company found that it generated 10 percent of the jobs in that area. Of these, 10 percent were directly in aviation and another 10 percent were

Exhibit 2   The Travel and Tourism Industry

Accommodation	Travel Agencies	Luggage
Hotels/Resorts	Tour Companies	Construction/Real Estate
Motels		
Hostels	Hotel/Restaurant Suppliers	Distillers/Brewers/Bottles
Caravans	Taxi Services	Auto/Aircraft Manufacturers
Camping		
	Cameras and Film	Motor Fuel Producers
Transportation	Maps, Travel Books	Clothing Manufacturers
Airlines		
Cruise Ships	Shopping Malls	Communication Networks
Rail		
Car Rental	Service Stations	Education/Training Institutes
Bus Coaches	Sporting Events	Recreation/Sporting Equipment
Attractions	Banking Services	Food Producers
Man Made		
Natural	Reservation Systems	Advertising Media
Food and Beverage	Auto Clubs	Cartographers/Printers
Restaurants	Entertainment/Arts Venues	Souvenirs
Fast Food		
Wine Merchants	Museums/Historical Sites	

Source: *Travel and Tourism—Jobs for the Millennium,* World Travel & Tourism Council.

in companies benefiting from spending by aviation employees. The other 80 percent were jobs in hotels, restaurants, department stores, and other local businesses relying on spending by American Airline passengers.

- It is estimated that at least 20 percent of the sales in London shops comes from foreign visitors.
- Surveys suggest that 50 percent of all photographs are taken by travelers.[2]

Industry analysts have a name for these indirect or hidden benefits—the **multiplier effect.** The multiplier effect is measured by adding up all the expenditures of travelers in a given geographic area and multiplying that figure by a factor (known as the multiplier) to arrive at the amount of additional income that is generated by these expenditures. While the multiplier effect is highly variable among cities and countries around the world, many industry analysts use a figure of 1.6 as a reasonable multiplier on a general basis.

Although it is difficult to accurately assess the size of the tourism industry, some figures are available that are truly astounding. According to the United Nations World Tourism Organization (UNWTO), in 2008 there were 922 million tourist arrivals

| Exhibit 3   Most Tourist Arrivals ||
Country	Arrivals (in millions)
France	79.3
United States	58.0
Spain	57.3
China	53.0
Italy	42.7
United Kingdom	30.2
Ukraine	25.4
Turkey	25.0
Germany	24.9
Mexico	22.6

Source: UNWTO World Tourism Barometer, World Tourism Organization, June 2009.

worldwide. Spending on international tourism reached $944 billion. France, the United States, and Spain had the most tourist arrivals, with China and Italy getting more than 40 million each (see Exhibit 3). Although travel and tourism suffered a downturn in the second half of 2008 due to the global economic decline, it is expected to resume its growth pattern. The World Travel & Tourism Council estimates that travel and tourism employment will grow from almost 220 million in 2009 to nearly 276 million in 2019, while the contribution of the sector to the Gross Domestic Product (GDP) is expected to rise from 9.1 percent to 9.4 percent during the same period.[3]

Interrelationships within the Travel and Tourism Industry

An important and unique feature of the travel and tourism industry is the interrelationship of the various parts of the whole. A trip may consist of an airplane flight, a car rental, a stay at a hotel, several restaurant meals, and some gift purchases. Each of these elements must work well in order for travelers to have a pleasant total experience.

For example, suppose the Smiths decide to fly from their home in Minneapolis to vacation at Walt Disney World in Orlando, Florida. The sum total of their experiences determines the quality of their vacation and the likelihood of their becoming repeat guests at Disney World. For instance, the Smiths might have a pleasant flight to Florida, but then their rented car could overheat, leaving them stranded for several hours and cutting short the day they were going to spend at EPCOT. Or their hotel could be undergoing refurbishing so that the pool and the restaurant are closed during their stay and the usually attractive lobby decor is covered with drop cloths and scaffolding. Even worse—suppose they arrive at the Magic Kingdom at a particularly busy time and find that the park has closed its parking lot and is not admitting any more visitors that day. Any of these incidents could spoil their entire vacation.

Travel-industry businesses have a symbiotic relationship, a mutual dependency. For any one of them to be entirely successful in pleasing the Smiths, all of them must do a good job. If the hotel stay was uncomfortable, the Smiths might enjoy Disney World but still feel on the whole that they had a less-than-perfect vacation. If the hotel did its job but Disney's park was overcrowded, the net sum of their experience could also be negative. Either way, in the long run, all of the travel businesses in the area will suffer if the Smiths do not return to Disney World and/or tell their friends in Minneapolis that a trip to Disney World is a disappointing experience.

Some destinations are so aware of this interrelationship that they go to extreme lengths to control all elements of the travel product. Bermuda, for instance, which is only 21 square miles in size, monitors the standards of all of Bermuda's hotels, restaurants, and attractions because it believes that if a visitor has a bad hotel room or a bad meal, he or she will go home feeling critical of the whole island. Since more than 40 percent of Bermuda's travel business is repeat, it cannot afford to disappoint its visitors.

Owners and operators of hospitality enterprises often underestimate the importance of the travel and tourism industry's interrelationships when considering how their enterprises are going to attract consumers. Such vacation spots as Hawaii depend on airlines to deliver almost all of their visitors. If airline fares are too high, tourism business suffers, no matter how strong or how effective marketing efforts are. Atlantic City is a highly successful destination for motorcoach tours from New York City, but that is entirely a function of the gaming industry that has grown in Atlantic City in the last two decades. Now the casinos depend on the buses, and the buses depend on the casinos. Neither could succeed without the other.

Why People Travel

Over the centuries, travel has developed for business, health, social, and cultural reasons. But at the most basic level, it can be said that the main reason people travel is to gather information. We want to know how our favorite aunt is doing in Nashville, so we take a trip to visit her. Businesspeople travel to see what is going on in their home office in Chicago or to find out what customers in Madrid think of their products. Some of us travel to France to see how the French vintners grow grapes and produce wine. Others go to Moscow and Beijing to learn more about Russian and Chinese culture.

Travel is an important part of our lives. It helps us understand ourselves and others. It is both an effect and a cause of rapid societal change. Technology has played a huge part in all of this. Commercial jet aircraft have brought foreign places closer, communications satellites bring news events from around the world into our living rooms, and the Internet connects us to people and places throughout the world via our personal computers. These technologies have stimulated interest in traveling abroad.

The three most important factors that determine the amount people spend for travel are employment, disposable income, and household wealth. The more money people who want to travel have, the more likely they are to travel, the more frequently they are likely to travel, and the farther they are likely to travel. Business travel is less susceptible to economic downturns than leisure travel, although not immune. For example, during the "Great Recession" of 2008/2009 business travel plummeted due to companies tightening their travel budgets. Research has shown that international travel patterns are very sensitive to shifts in exchange rates. The buying power of a traveler's own currency affects destination choices and the timing of trips.

It is important to note that not everyone is disposed to travel. Some people by their nature are stay-at-homes. Others get motion sickness, or don't like to fly, or simply won't travel no matter what their economic circumstances. Psychologist Frank Farley has studied the behavior of travelers versus nontravelers. "People who hesitate to travel may do so because of deep-seated fears," says Farley. "Travelers, though, seem stable enough to expose themselves to uncertainty and adventure. They worry less, feel less inhibited and submissive, and are more self-confident than stay-at-homes."[4] Farley found other differences between people who like to travel and those who would rather stay at home:

> Most passionate travelers are risk-takers in many areas of life. They're drawn not only to unknown lands but also to taking chances with their investment portfolios. However, their risk-taking is rational; it's based on a deep sense that they control their destiny. They enjoy life, love to play, and gravitate towards crowds and parties.[5]

The various reasons for why people travel can be placed into five broad categories:

1. *Recreation.* Recreation includes leisure and activities related to sports, entertainment, and rest. Beach vacations, ski vacations, and adventure travel such as whitewater rafting all fall into this category. Destinations such as the Caribbean, Disney World, and national parks benefit largely from recreational travel.

2. *Culture.* People travel for cultural reasons as well—a desire to learn about things and places that interest them. These interests can be historical, ethnic, educational, or they can relate to the arts or religion. Famous battlegrounds such as the beaches of Normandy, France, or the rolling hills of Gettysburg, Pennsylvania; cathedrals such as St. Peter's in Vatican City; California's Napa Valley; Kenya's national parks; and the Great Wall of China all have educational, religious, historical, or ethnic significance. Destinations often capitalize on these attributes to stage special events and festivals. The Salzburg Music Festival and the Mardi Gras in Rio de Janeiro and New Orleans are examples of cultural events that are marketed very heavily. Many destination areas and businesses within those areas have their own websites on which they list events, attractions, and other "things to do" for travelers (see Exhibit 4).

3. *Business.* Business travel is a significant portion of all travel. This category includes individual business travelers as well as travelers attending meetings and conventions. The trend now is to combine business and recreational travel—thus business meetings and conventions are held at resort hotels, at theme parks, and on cruise ships, and spouses and even children often come along.

4. *Visiting Friends and Relatives (VFR).* Research has shown that much travel involves visiting friends and relatives. This is difficult to measure, however, and has little economic impact compared to recreational, cultural, or business travel.

5. *Health.* Many persons travel to visit diagnostic centers and receive treatment at clinics, hospitals, or spas such as the Mayo Clinic in Rochester, Minnesota, or the Canyon Ranch in Tucson, Arizona. This type of travel, too, has relatively little economic impact.

Exhibit 4   Sample Tourist-Friendly Website

The neworleans.com website contains a wealth of information for travelers who want to make the most of their time in the area. (Courtesy of neworleans.com.)

Psychographic Research

Another kind of research that is helpful in understanding travelers and changing travel patterns is psychographic. **Psychographic research** attempts to classify people's behavior not in terms of their age or education or gender, but rather their lifestyles and values. Sometimes this information is more useful than **demographic information** in deciding what kind of amenities to offer in a resort or how to advertise a particular destination. For instance, the government of Bermuda conducted psychographic research in the United States to determine who would be most interested in going to Bermuda on vacation. In a sample of persons who were potential vacationers, three groups emerged:

- The **price and sights group.** These people were interested in seeing the most things for the least amount of money. They wanted tours that covered ten countries in nine days at a bargain price. For them, the best cruises were the cheapest ones that visited the most ports, and a good hotel was one that offered budget-priced accommodations within walking distance of everything they might want to see.

- The **sun and surf group.** These people sought a vacation where they could lie on a beach and get a golden tan. Value was important, but even more important was finding a destination where there was good weather, guaranteed sunshine, and a beautiful beach where they could soak up the sun and swim in clear waters.

Many people enjoy vacations with lots of recreational activities.

Vacationers in the sun and surf group seek a beautiful beach where they can soak up the sun and swim in clear waters.

- The **quality group.** The quality of the vacation experience was of paramount importance to this group. Members of this group felt they had worked hard for a vacation and now it was their turn to relax and be taken care of. This group valued destinations and accommodations that were first-class or deluxe. Service was very important—they wanted and expected lots of pampering and were willing to pay a fair price for it. They also wanted gourmet dining and sophisticated entertainment.

Yankelovich, Inc., is a marketing research firm that specializes in psychographic research. For many years it has studied how social, political, and economic changes affect the behavior of U.S. consumers. As it has in past years, Yankelovich teamed with Ypartnership, LLC (a marketing, advertising, and public relations agency), to track such trends as the types of vacations people are planning, their hotel and airline preferences, and attitudes toward modes of purchasing. Every year, results are tabulated and provided to subscribers through a service called the MONITOR™.

MONITOR research reveals that the economic downturn of 2008/2009 affected consumer attitudes. Travelers are making decisions with caution. There is a shift from extravagance and accumulation to a sense of responsibility; consumers are rejecting the "notion of obnoxious excess," wanting enriching experiences rather than repeating the past. An understanding of this new viewpoint can lead hospitality marketers and managers to new strategies and tactics in attracting new guests and bringing back old ones.[6]

Today's consumers are savvy technologically. They know how and where to find the help they need to make sound purchasing decisions. Everyone is wired, and new technologies and tools have erased old limits. Travelers shop for the best airline fares and hotel rates on travel service websites such as Expedia and Travelocity. More than 50 percent of U.S. consumers use the Internet when planning their trips. Those who fly to a vacation destination are more likely to use the Internet exclusively when planning a holiday.

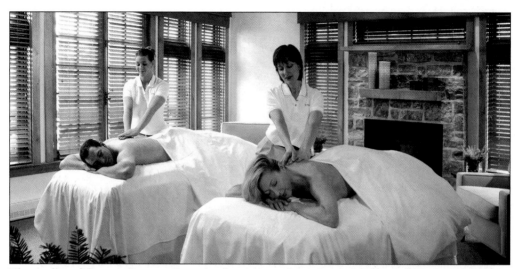

The quality of the vacation experience is of paramount importance for the quality group. Members of this group feel they have worked hard for a vacation and now it's their turn to relax and be taken care of. They want lots of pampering and are willing to pay a fair price for it. (Fairmont Le Château Montebello, Montebello, Quebec, Canada; courtesy of Fairmont Hotels & Resorts.)

However, only 20 percent who use the Internet go to blogs for information (although that percentage reflects an increase in blog usage). Among social media websites, YouTube.com is used most frequently, followed by Facebook.com and MySpace.com. Business travelers are more likely to use technology in planning a trip; 70 percent use the Internet solely for information, while 60 percent book their trip with a travel service, airline, or hotel website.

Leisure travelers took fewer trips in 2009 that required overnight accommodations, yet the primary reason for travel continued to be visiting friends or relatives. Most travelers stay in a hotel (75 percent) that they choose based on perceived value for the price, and they travel with another adult and without children. They seek beautiful scenery (70 percent), but their next preference is visiting places never visited before.

The bottom line of these major trends in lifestyle and buyer behavior is that the old ways of appealing to consumers don't work anymore. Everyone expects reliability, comfort, convenience, performance, and more. Marketers are learning to offer new points of difference in designs, emotions, and experiences. Every transaction must offer intangible rewards. There is no room for an average product anymore. People don't want to sleep in an average hotel or eat average food. Everything has to be special in one way or another. The new consumer mindset is that there is no reason to stick with the old when you are good at picking new options.

The Social Impact of Travel

Hotels, restaurants, and attractions can shape and change life in a community. For example, Huatulco, Mexico, was a town that hardly rated a dot on the map until Club Med decided to build there. Walt Disney World has changed the character of Orlando and Florida forever.

Travelers to any destination bring money and jobs, but they can also bring problems. Whenever you have increased travel to an area, you must provide additional public services such as police, fire fighters, water treatment plants, and solid waste disposal facilities. This may increase the cost of living for residents. Crime may increase. New airports bring with them pollution and noise; new hotels and shopping strips change the character of the local landscape. Residents may have limited or no access to beaches and other property that previously had been public.

For these and other reasons, many people feel that their communities have been negatively affected by travelers, and therefore they are not in favor of development that encourages more tourism. Some areas are ambivalent about the benefits of the travel and tourism industry and have not gone out of their way to attract tourists or develop facilities for them. Other communities, like Monroe County, Florida (where Key West is located), feel that they may have let development get out of hand and are now trying to put a cap on it.

In developing and Third World countries there are other problems. One is the enormous economic gap that exists between the travelers who stay in luxurious resorts and the employees who witness for the first time new lifestyles and behaviors that can change their own expectations and values. Local residents often try to emulate the dress styles and consumption patterns of visitors. An area's culture and traditional values can be eroded. Racial tensions are not uncommon as a result of these conditions. The seasonality of tourism poses another major problem. When the season is over, often there is a large number of dislocated, jobless workers who have no place to go and few other opportunities to earn a comparable living.

Today's hospitality managers are paying more attention to the social costs of travel and tourism. Modern planning methods make more use of impact studies that consider the social and environmental changes that can be brought about by increased travel to an area. Many countries have mounted impressive marketing campaigns in the off season to attract visitors and keep employment levels high. Countries like Turkey have developed arts and crafts industries so that workers can make products for tourists during the off season.

Pierre L. van den Berghe, a sociology professor at the University of Washington in Seattle, has studied the cultural impact of tourism in depth. He believes that, on the whole, the impact of tourism is positive:

> In complex and unpredictable ways, tourism changes not only the behavior of hosts—their presentation of self—but their very definition of self. Far from destroying local cultures, tourism more commonly transforms and revives them. Of all forms of outside contact and modernization that affect isolated local cultures, tourism is probably the least destructive, precisely because it imparts a marketable value to cultural diversity. If the quest for authenticity sometimes initially seems to undermine and corrupt local culture, it can revive and reinvigorate traditions that were languishing under the assault of other modernizing forces such as industrialization, urbanization, Christianization, or Western-style schooling.... Locals often have the vitality to recapture their own heritage, the creativity to invent a new, redefined authenticity, and the resilience to resist the encroachments of the global village. To paraphrase Mark Twain, news of the death of Third and Fourth World cultures is greatly exaggerated. And, where cultures die, tourism is seldom to blame.[7]

Sustainable Tourism Development

One answer to solving some of the problems that tourism brings with it is **sustainable tourism development,** a middle road between unbridled tourism development and public intervention to control tourism expansion. The World Tourism Organization states that "sustainability principles refer to the environment, economic, and socio-cultural aspects of tourism development, and a suitable balance must be established between these three dimensions to guarantee its long-term sustainability."[8] Tourism that has a low impact on a locale's environment and culture and conserves the ecosystem, while generating income and employment, is considered sustainable tourism. Controlling the number of visitors to parks to minimize damage to the flora and fauna, and limiting vehicular traffic at cultural sites to reduce air pollution and overcrowding are examples of responsible measures to limit damage to the environment. There is a growing realization that if tourism is to prosper at any location, there must be a balance between the needs of the visitors, the tourism industry, the community visited, and the environment. A sustainable tourism development program protects and enhances a locale's natural resources, conserves the local culture, contributes to cultural understanding, and benefits the economy of the community and its residents.

Ecotourism

An example of responsible tourism is **ecotourism.** Ecotourism is described as "responsible travel to natural areas that conserves the environment and improves the well-being of

Many of today's resorts try to blend in with the surrounding landscape. This is the 215-room Boulders Resort and Golden Door Spa in Carefree, Arizona; the rooms are in various one-story buildings (called "adobe casitas" and "pueblo villas") scattered among the boulders of the scenic desert foothills. (Courtesy of The Boulders Resort and Golden Door Spa—A Wyndham Luxury Resort in Carefree, Arizona.)

local people."[9] The rain forest in Costa Rica, the animal preserves in Kenya, and the Galapagos Islands are examples of sites that attract travelers who are ecologically and socially conscious. Since many of these sites are fragile and protected, visitation is on a small scale and is therefore low-impact. Just visiting an ecologically sensitive location is not ecotourism, unless there is a benefit such as building environmental awareness or providing funds for conservation.

There are a number of private operators of travel and tourism businesses who do business in fragile habitats and are sensitive not only to the habitats but to their inhabitants as well. Some operators take pains to develop resorts that blend in with their cultural and physical surroundings. Others hire and train local guides and support scientific environmental research. Those operators involved in ecotourism are careful that their operations will have minimal impact on the environment or the culture. These kinds of steps are the hallmark of real ecotourism.

Initially, travel to ecologically sensitive sites required forsaking comforts. Not anymore. One example of the many luxury resorts near ecologically sensitive areas is the Arenas Del Mar Hotel in Costa Rica. Located not far from a national park, the hotel uses solar power to heat water, advanced wastewater treatment, and nontoxic biodegradable cleaning products, among other environmentally protective measures. Room rates as high as $550 per night are charged during the peak season.[10]

The bottom line is that travel and tourism is an industry that has its benefits and its costs. Societies and governments must recognize both sides of the coin and plan for the proper balance for their own situation.

Planning for Tourism Development

One logical planning sequence for responsible tourism development consists of five steps:

1. *Define the scope of the project.* What is going to be built? Can it be done in a manner that is socially, environmentally, and economically sound?

2. *Analyze the market.* What need will this project fulfill? Will the existing infrastructure support it? What about seasonality? What is the demand potential? Who is the competition? Is there an available labor force?

3. *Create a master plan.* How is the land going to be used? What goes where? Is there a need for new roads, airports, or marine facilities?

4. *Determine who is going to develop it.* Some projects are built by governments, others by private developers. In the most successful projects, both are involved. Take Cancun, Mexico, where the development of the area as a resort destination was the result of a government initiative coupled with the desire of international hotel operators to expand into Mexico.

5. *Establish a timetable.* Is this a long-term plan or a short-term one? Is everything going to be done simultaneously or in incremental stages?

Summary

Technology has provided us with the means to travel faster and cheaper, produce more food with fewer farmers, manufacture goods more efficiently, and communicate with each other around the globe almost instantaneously. The world's population is changing. There are more of us than ever before and the population continues to grow—and grow older. Significant economic, social, and political changes occurred throughout the world in the latter part of the twentieth century, and the pace of change shows no sign of slowing down in the twenty-first.

There are many trends that affect travel. These include increased leisure time, greater discretionary funds for travel, less seasonality in travel, growing ecotourism, and adventure travel. Many of today's trends bode well for tourism; others, such as the increase in terrorism, do not.

Travel and tourism is now the world's largest industry. We cannot measure its size in receipts alone; adding expenditures like salaries and food purchases gives a truer measure. Moreover, the multiplier effect must be added to get the complete picture.

There are many components to the travel and tourism industry, including airlines, hotels, restaurants, and attractions. They are all interrelated, and the success or failure of one component can affect all of them.

Many of today's consumers want to be in charge of the decision-making process while buying hotel rooms and meals and making travel arrangements. They do their own research, using the Internet and other resources, then decide for themselves what they want to see and do, rather than take guided tours. They budget, but don't economize; they are willing to spend money on travel and other goods and services so long as they get value. They are motivated by three critical value constricts: self-invention, personal authenticity, and "advantage intangibles."

There is cause for concern about the cultural impact of tourism. Some believe that the effects of tourism can be detrimental. Others maintain that tourism can stimulate economic growth and preserve rather than destroy native cultures.

 # Endnotes

1. United Nations Population Division, 2009.

2. These examples are excerpted from "Travel and Tourism—Jobs for the Millennium," published by the World Travel & Tourism Council, January 1997. Many of the examples and figures in this chapter are based on material supplied by this organization, for which the authors are grateful.

3. *Travel & Tourism Economic Impact,* World Travel & Tourism Council, March 2009.

4. Daniel Goleman, "Head Trips," *American Health,* April 1988, p. 58.

5. Ibid.

6. The information in the following paragraphs is from the Ypartnership/Yankelovich, Inc., 2009 National Leisure Travel MONITOR™ and is used with their permission.

7. Pierre L. van den Berghe, "Cultural Impact of Tourism," VNR's *Encyclopedia of Hospitality and Tourism* (New York: Van Nostrand Reinhold, 1993), p. 627.

8. www.world-tourism.org/frameset/frame_sustainable.html.

9. www.ecotourism.org.

10. www.areanasdelmar.com.

 Key Terms

ecotourism—Responsible travel to natural areas that conserves the environment and improves the well-being of local people.

demographic information—Statistical information (such as age and income) about a population, used especially to identify markets.

multiplier effect—The hidden or indirect benefits of travel and tourism to a community, measured by adding up all the expenditures of travelers in the community and then multiplying that figure by a factor (known as the multiplier) to arrive at the amount of income that stays in the community and is generated by these expenditures.

price and sights group—The group of travelers interested in doing the most things for the least amount of money while on vacation.

psychographic research—Research that attempts to classify people's behavior in terms of their lifestyles and values.

quality group—The group of travelers for whom the quality of their vacation is of paramount importance. They want, and are willing to pay for, first-class accommodations and service.

sun and surf group—The group of travelers seeking a vacation spot where there is good weather, guaranteed sunshine, and a beautiful beach.

sustainable tourism development—Tourism that has a low impact on a locale's environment and culture and conserves the ecosystem, while generating income and employment.

travel and tourism industry—A collection of organizations and establishments that derives all or a significant portion of its income from providing goods and services to travelers.

Review Questions

1. How has technology transformed the way we live? What are some other economic and social trends that are affecting travel and tourism?

2. What are the components of the travel and tourism industry? How can the size of the travel and tourism industry be defined?

3. What is the multiplier effect?

4. How are the components of the travel and tourism industry interrelated?

5. Why do people travel?

6. What is psychographic research and how does it help the travel and tourism industry?

7. What are some of the ways that the travel and tourism industry can affect local communities?

Internet Sites

For more information, visit the following Internet sites. Remember that Internet addresses can change without notice. If the site is no longer there, you can use a search engine to look for additional sites.

Associations

Pacific Asia Travel Association
www.pata.org

Travel Industry Association of America
www.tia.org

Travel & Tourism Research Association
www.ttra.com

Organizations, Resources

Caribbean Tourism Organisation
www.doitcaribbean.com

World Travel & Tourism Council
www.wttc.org

Ecotourism Society
www.ecotourism.org

Yankelovich
www.yankelovich.com

World Tourism Organization
www.world-tourism.org

3
Exploring Hospitality Careers

Competencies

1. Describe in general terms the makeup and size of the lodging and food service industries, identify advantages and disadvantages of a career in hospitality, and list the personal characteristics that correspond to each of the three personal skills areas: data, people, and things. (pp. 50–56)

2. Summarize career options in the lodging industry, list the advantages of working in a chain hotel and an independent hotel, and describe typical management positions in lodging operations. (pp. 56–62)

3. Briefly describe segments of the food service industry and the career opportunities available within them, and outline career options in the club and cruise line industries. (pp. 62–66)

4. Describe career ladders in the hospitality industry, summarize the purpose and contents of a résumé, and explain how to prepare for a job interview, sell yourself during the interview, and effectively follow up after the interview. (pp. 66–71)

Opposite page: Fairmont Bab Al Bahr, Abu Dhabi, United Arab Emirates; courtesy of Fairmont Hotels & Resorts.

THIS CHAPTER FOCUSES on your career in the hospitality industry. The chapter opens with a short discussion of the industry's size. Next we look at the reasons people go into the hospitality field, and how to go about selecting a segment of the industry that interests you. Each segment, from hotels to institutional food service, is described. Finally, there are some ideas and suggestions for getting a job in the industry.

Hospitality Today

What *is* the **hospitality industry?** This is not an easy question, and books on the subject offer many different answers. Some view the hospitality industry as comprising four sectors: lodging, food, entertainment, and travel. However, usually the hospitality industry is viewed as encompassing mainly lodging and food service businesses. If we define the industry this way we can include such facilities as school dormitories, nursing homes, and other institutions (see Exhibit 1).

The U.S. hospitality industry has grown tremendously in recent decades. Some of the reasons for this growth are a generally higher standard of living among Americans, increased longevity as a result of medical advances, the growth in education, and the greater opportunities available in a rapidly developing society. Services and goods that in the past were only available to the privileged few can now be enjoyed by a much larger percentage of the population. For example, in the past ten years, the number of people who have flown on an airplane or taken a cruise has increased dramatically.

We can get an idea of the hospitality industry's size by examining some of the statistics for the lodging and food service industries.

Lodging

The World Tourism Organization estimates that there are more than 19 million hotel rooms in the world. More than 4.5 million of those are in the United States. The number of rooms continues to increase, as new hotels, resorts, and other lodging facilities open every year.

Exhibit 1 The Hospitality Industry		
Lodging Operations	**Food Service Operations**	**Other Operations**
All-suite hotels	Commercial cafeterias	Airlines
Casino hotels	Education food service	Campgrounds
Conference centers	Employee food service	City clubs
Full-service hotels	Full-service restaurants	Country clubs
Limited-service hotels	Health-care	Cruise ships
Resorts	Lodging food service	National parks
Retirement communities	Quick-service restaurants	
	Recreational food service	
	Social caterers	

The U.S. lodging industry employs about 1.8 million people, both part time and full time. Hotel managers and assistant managers account for 200,000 jobs. Self-employed managers—primarily owners of small hotels and motels—hold a significant number of those jobs. Clearly, you don't have to work for someone else to succeed in the lodging business!

Continued expansion of the lodging industry is inevitable. No one knows precisely how many new hotels and other lodging properties will be built in the next decade, or where most of them will be located. All that can be said with certainty is that career opportunities in lodging will continue to grow.

Food Service

According to the National Restaurant Association (NRA), food service industry sales are about 4 percent of the U.S. gross domestic product. For every dollar spent on food, 48 cents are spent in a food service operation. An estimated 13 million people, 9 percent of the U.S. work force, are employed in the industry.[1]

The *Restaurant Industry Operations Report*, published annually by the NRA, highlights some interesting facts about the food service business:

* The restaurant industry is expected to add 1.8 million jobs over the next decade, with employment reaching 14.8 million by 2019.

From line cook to award-winning chef, there are plenty of career opportunities in the hospitality industry if cooking is your passion.

- Most eating-and-drinking places are small businesses. More than nine out of ten have fewer than fifty employees.

- More than seventy billion meals and snacks are eaten in restaurants and school and work cafeterias each year.[2]

Most hospitality students tend to view the food service business in terms of full-service and "quick-service" (fast-food) restaurants. As can be seen from Exhibit 1, other food service operations deserve serious consideration as well. For example, contract food companies operate cafeterias, dining rooms, snack bars, and catering facilities in office buildings, factories, universities, sports arenas, and retirement homes. Three of the largest companies in these fields are Sodexo, ARAMARK, and Compass Group. Social caterers such as Glorious Foods in New York City offer opportunities for interesting careers. They cater 3,000 events a year, such as the opening night of the New York City Ballet and the Metropolitan Opera. Many hospitals now have the equivalent of a hotel food and beverage manager in charge of their food service. Gourmet meals and wine are available to patients in some hospitals. Hospitals run employee cafeterias, special dining rooms for doctors, and coffee shops for visitors. To maximize kitchen use, some hospitals also market off-premises catering as well.

Careers in the Hospitality Industry

Why do people go into the hospitality industry? If you were to ask people who have spent their careers in this business what they like most about it, you would get a wide variety of answers. Some of the most popular are:

- *The industry offers more career options than most.* No matter what kind of work you enjoy, and wherever your aptitudes lie, there is a segment of the industry that can use your talents (take another look at Exhibit 1!).

- *The work is varied.* Because hotels and restaurants are complete production, distribution, and service units, managers are involved in a broad array of activities.

- *There are many opportunities to be creative.* Hotel and restaurant managers might design new products to meet the needs of their guests; produce training programs for employees; or implement challenging advertising, sales promotion, and marketing plans.

- *This is a "people" business.* Managers and supervisors spend their workdays satisfying guests, motivating employees, and negotiating with vendors and others.

- *Hospitality jobs are not nine-to-five jobs.* Hours are highly flexible in many positions. (Some see this as a disadvantage, however.)

- *There are opportunities for long-term career growth.* If you are ambitious and energetic, you can start with an entry-level job and move up. The industry is full of stories of people who started as bellpersons or cooks and rose to high management positions or opened their own successful businesses.

- *There are perks associated with many hospitality jobs.* If you become the general manager of a resort, you can dine at its restaurants with your family and friends, and use its recreational facilities. Airline and cruise employees get free or reduced-fare travel.

If you are ambitious and energetic, you can start with an entry-level hospitality job and move up quickly. The industry is full of stories of people who started out as bellpersons, bartenders, or cooks and rose to high management positions or opened their own successful businesses.

Despite these advantages, there are some aspects of the business that many people don't like:

- *Long hours.* In most hospitality businesses the hours are long. The 40-hour work-week is not the norm, and 50- to 60-hour workweeks are not unusual.

- *Nontraditional schedules.* Hospitality managers do not work a Monday-through-Friday schedule. In the hospitality field you will probably often find yourself working when your friends are relaxing. As one manager told his employees, "If you can't come to work Saturday or Sunday, don't bother to come in on Monday."

- *Pressure.* There are busy periods when managers and employees are under intense pressure to perform.

- *Low beginning salaries.* Entry-level jobs for management trainees tend to be low-paying compared to some other industries.

Selecting an Industry Segment

As we have pointed out, one of the attributes that prompts many people to enter the hospitality industry is its diversity. It is difficult to imagine another industry in which there are as many different kinds of work. Before a hotel, restaurant, or club is built, for example, a feasibility study is made by a management consulting firm. Research-oriented hospitality graduates often join consulting firms for the opportunity to combine their interest in

Work schedules are highly flexible in many hospitality positions.

collecting and analyzing data with their interest in hotels and restaurants. Others work for hotel owners and investors as asset managers, the guardians of the owner's investment.

Management positions abound in the hospitality industry. Although hotels and restaurants may represent the largest sectors, they are by no means the only ones. Hospitality managers are needed in clubs, hospitals, nursing homes, universities and schools, cafeterias, prisons, corporate dining rooms, snack bars, management companies, airlines, cruise ships, and many other organizations. Within these organizations you can go into marketing and sales, rooms management, housekeeping, cooking, engineering, dining-room management, menu planning, security, accounting, food technology, forecasting and planning, computer technology (management information systems), recreation, entertainment, guest relations, and so on. Moreover, you have a wide choice of places to live—you can choose between warm climates and cold; cities, suburbs, and even rural areas; any region of the country or the world. There simply is no other industry that offers more diverse career opportunities.

Skills Inventory. One of the best ways to select a career niche you will be happy with is to start by listing your own skills. What are the tasks you do best? Most skills fall into one of three areas: skills dealing with data, skills dealing with people, or skills dealing with things. You will probably find that the majority of your skills will fall into one or two of these areas.

People whose skills fall into the data group are often good in subjects such as math and science, and enjoy working with computers. They tend to like such activities as analyzing information, comparing figures, working with graphs, and solving abstract problems. Such individuals might enjoy doing feasibility studies for a hospitality management consulting firm. They might also be happy in the corporate planning departments of large hotel and restaurant chains, where data is analyzed and demand is forecast. Most auditors and accountants fall into the data-skills group.

If you like to deal with people, you probably enjoy helping them and taking care of their needs. You can take and give advice and instructions. You may also enjoy supervising and motivating other people, and may find that they respond to your leadership. Individuals with people skills are often good at negotiating and selling—they like to bargain and are not afraid to make decisions. In the hospitality industry, general managers and marketing and sales managers of hotels often fall into this category. So do independent restaurant owners, catering managers, and club managers.

The third group of skills are those dealing with things. If you excel in this area, you may be good at building or fixing things. You like to work with your hands and use tools and gadgets. You enjoy setting things up—when there is a party in your house you like to put up the decorations, for example. If your skills lie here you may be attracted to food production jobs. Chefs, bakers, and cooks all like working with things. So do the engineers who manage the hotel's physical plant.

Positions Available in Travel-Related Businesses

Tourist Bureau Manager	Tour Wholesaler
Travel Journalist/Writer	Reservation Agent
Promotion/Public Relations Specialist	Interpretive Specialist (Museums, Destination Information, Crafts, Art, etc.)
Marketing Representative	Curriculum Specialist
Group Sales Representative	Business Travel Specialist
Tour Operator	Financial Analyst
Travel Agency Manager	Teacher/Instructor
Recreation Specialist	Transfer Officer
Tour Escort	Market Researcher
Retail Store Manager	Group Sales Manager
Incentive Travel Specialist	Association Manager
Consultant	Tour Broker
Translator	Public Relations Officer
Planner	Tour Operator
Sales Manager	Receptionist
Policy Analyst	Tour Leader
Campground Manager	Meeting/Conference Planner
Research/Statistical Specialist	Guide
Marina Manager	Ski Instructor
Economist	Advertising Agency Account Executive
In-Transit Attendant	Convention Center/Fair Manager
Resident Camp Director	Sales Representative
Motor Coach Operator	Guest House/Hostel Manager
Concession Operator	Entertainer
Auto/Recreation Vehicle Rental Agency Manager	Program Specialist
Destination Development Specialist	Recreation Facility/Park Manager
Information Officer	Promoter
Travel Agent	
Travel Counselor/Sales Manager	

Source: *A Guide to College Programs in Hospitality, Tourism, & Culinary Arts,* Ninth Edition (Richmond, Va.: International CHRIE, 2006).

There are plenty of opportunities in the hospitality industry for individuals with people skills.
(Courtesy of Starwood Hotels & Resorts Worldwide, Inc.)

Most of us have skills in more than one area. It is important to identify your skills and rank them according to how much you enjoy using them. This will help you find a career niche that suits you.

Career Options

The type of business you choose for your first hospitality job puts you into a definite career slot. While skills and experience are usually transferable within a particular industry segment (such as resort hotels), generally you cannot easily jump from one kind of industry segment to another. For example, it's unlikely you would progress from managing a Taco Bell to managing food service in a hospital, or from managing a Motel 6 to managing a Ritz-Carlton. However, you might go from being a hotel manager for Hyatt to being a hotel manager of a large cruise ship such as the *Grand Princess*. It's important to note that owners and operators of motels and fast-food restaurants often have incomes that are as high as, or higher than, those of managers at some deluxe hotels. With this in mind, let's take a look at the career options open to you.

Lodging

There are many types of lodging properties to choose from. There are luxury hotels such as the Mandarin in San Francisco and the Four Seasons in New York. There are full-service hotels operated by such companies as Hilton, Marriott, Starwood, and Hyatt. Resorts are another type of hotel. Some resorts, like the Boca Raton Hotel and Beach Club in Florida and the Arizona Biltmore, are geared to convention groups. Others, such as the Williamsburg Inn in Virginia and the Trapp Family Lodge in Vermont, cater to individuals and small meetings. Finally, there are casino hotels like the Wynn in Las Vegas and Borgata in Atlantic City. These specialized operations are organized and managed differently from other hotels.

People who choose the lodging industry as a career often do so because they enjoy traveling and living in different places. Hotel management personnel are in great demand,

If you like to work with your hands, use tools, and set things up, you might enjoy working in a food production position such as hotel chef. (The Sonesta Beach Resort Key Biscayne; photo courtesy of Sonesta International Hotel Corporation.)

and since most large hotels belong to chains, managers are often offered opportunities to move into new positions in different geographic locations. Some people enjoy working in large metropolitan areas and in the course of their careers may live in New York, Chicago, and San Francisco. Others like warm weather resorts and may start in Miami, then move to a better position in Puerto Rico, then on to Hawaii, and so forth. Managers who like to ski or climb mountains often opt for hotels in the Rocky Mountains, the Cascades, or the Berkshires of New England. Some people enjoy quiet suburban life and move their families to communities where there are independent inns or conference centers. At an independent hotel you are not as likely to be uprooted from your home and community by a transfer.

Would you rather be part of a large chain or work for an independent operation? There are many opportunities in both areas. The arguments for working for a large chain include:

- *Better training.* Companies such as Ritz-Carlton and Hyatt have very sophisticated operating systems. Being trained in these systems provides valuable additional education and experience.

- *More opportunities for advancement.* Hotel managers of chain properties who wish to advance might be offered opportunities for promotions within the division in which they work or, if none are available there, in different divisions. Hotel managers who work for very large hospitality organizations might apply for positions in the time-share or food service divisions of their companies. Since large chains have many units, there are simply more places to climb the ladder of success.

- *Better benefits.* You are more likely to get superior life and health insurance benefits, more generous vacation and sick time, use of a company car, moving expenses, stock purchase options, and so forth from a large chain.

A career with an independent operation also offers some advantages, however:

- *More chances to be creative.* You will have a chance to set standards and initiate changes instead of just adhering to company programs and rules.

- *More control.* You are more likely to be in control of your own destiny. In large chains, decisions that involve your salary, advancement, and place of residence are often made by persons in corporate headquarters thousands of miles away. In an independent operation, however, you deal on a regular basis with the people who will be deciding your fate. And, as mentioned earlier, with an independent property you are not likely to be transferred.

- *Better learning environments for entrepreneurs.* Independent operations offer better learning environments for entrepreneurs, because all of the financial and operating decisions are made on-site. That means you will have a better opportunity to understand how and why things are done the way they are. If you intend to buy your own lodging operation some day, you will learn more at an independent than at a chain operation where data is forwarded to headquarters for analysis.

Management Positions within Lodging Operations. Whether the lodging property is part of a chain or an independent operation, as a hospitality student you have a wide variety of management positions open to you. Many people enjoy aiming for the top administrative job of general manager, but others prefer to specialize in such areas as:

- Catering
- Engineering

- Food and beverage

- Finance and accounting

- Human resources

- Marketing and sales

- Rooms management

- Management information systems (MIS)

Let's take a look at management positions in these areas.

The **general manager** is the chief operating officer of a hotel. He or she is responsible for attracting guests and making sure they are safe and well-served while visiting. The general manager supervises hotel staff and administers policies established by the owners or chain operators. Chains such as Holiday Inn and Marriott have very specific service, operating, and decorating standards. The general manager must see that all departments adhere to those standards.

Most general managers hold frequent meetings with their department heads. If a convention is about to arrive, for example, the general manager will want to make sure that the staff is aware of all the details necessary to make the conventioneers' stays pleasant—details regarding limousine service, check-in procedures, banquets, meeting rooms, audiovisual facilities, entertainment, and so on.

The general manager's main responsibility is the financial performance of the business. The compensation a general manager receives is often tied to the profitability of the business he or she manages. Hiring and firing when necessary is also part of a general manager's job. The general manager can be involved in union negotiations as well.

Good general managers are skilled at getting along with people. They are able to forge positive relationships with employees, guests, and members of the community at large. They believe in teamwork and know how to get things done through other people. Effective general managers are also technically proficient. They do not subscribe to "seat of the pants" managing; instead, they study problems and carefully formulate short- and long-term solutions.

Catering managers promote and sell the hotel's banquet facilities. They plan, organize, and manage the hotel's banquets, which can range from formal dinners to picnic buffets. Knowledge of food costs, preparation techniques, and pricing is essential. Good catering managers are also aware of protocol, social customs, and etiquette. Creativity and imagination are useful qualities as well.

Chief engineers are responsible for the hotel's physical operation and maintenance. This includes the electrical, heating, ventilating, air conditioning, refrigeration, and plumbing systems. Chief engineers must have extensive backgrounds in mechanical and electrical equipment and may need numerous licenses.

Food and beverage managers direct the production and service of food and beverages. They are responsible for training the dining room and kitchen staffs and ensuring quality control. Food and beverage managers at large properties work with their head chefs to plan menus and with their beverage managers to select wines and brands of liquor. At small properties the food and beverage manager has sole responsibility for these tasks. Menu pricing and cost control are also the province of the food and beverage manager.

Food and beverage managers must have a keen interest in food and wines and an up-to-date knowledge of food trends and guests' tastes. Because food and beverage service is offered from 15 to 24 hours a day, managers in this field must be prepared to work long

Large chains such as Hyatt frequently offer training programs, placement assistance, good benefits, and numerous opportunities for advancement. (From the Hyatt website at www.hyatt.com.)

shifts and endure periods of pressure—dealing with unexpectedly large dinner crowds, serving a banquet, and so on.

The **controller** is in charge of the accounting department and all of its functions, such as the management of credit, payroll, guest accounts, and all cashiering activities. The controller also prepares budgets and daily, weekly, and monthly reports showing revenues, expenses, and other statistics that managers require. Controllers are detail-oriented people and favor an analytical approach to business problems.

Human resources managers are responsible for recruiting and training the majority of the hotel's employees. They are also in charge of employee relations, which includes counseling employees, developing and administering programs to maintain and improve employee morale, monitoring the work environment, and so on. An important part of the human resources manager's job is to oversee compliance with equal employment opportunity and affirmative action laws and policies. People who choose human resources as a career usually have a good deal of empathy and are excellent negotiators.

The marketing and sales function at a hotel consists of several different activities. Sometimes a large hotel will have two managers overseeing marketing and sales. In that case, the **marketing manager** develops and implements a marketing plan and budget. The marketing plan lays out how the hotel intends to attract business. It includes sections on meeting and convention sales, local sales, advertising, and promotion plans. The marketing manager is also in charge of corporate accounts and may work with an advertising and public relations agency. The **sales manager** conducts sales programs and makes sales calls on prospects for group and individual business. He or she usually reports to the marketing manager. People who work in marketing and sales tend to be service-oriented and possess good communication skills.

Resident managers are often the executives in charge of a hotel's rooms division. Their areas of responsibility include the front office, reservations, and housekeeping, as well as sources of revenue other than the food and beverage department, such as gift shops and recreational facilities. In small hotels, resident managers are also in charge of security. They report directly to the general manager and share responsibility for compliance with budgets and forecasts. Resident managers are good leaders and have many of the same qualities that general managers have.

Management information systems (MIS) managers are the computer experts in a hotel. They are in charge of the computers used for reservations, room assignments, telephones, guestroom status reports, accounting functions, and labor and productivity reports. They often know how to write simple computer programs and easy-to-follow instructions for using computers. They have good problem-solving aptitudes and oral and written communication skills.

People who work in marketing and sales tend to be service-oriented and possess good communication skills.

The salaries for the hotel management positions just described vary according to the area of the country, the size of the property, and the work experience of the individual. However, Exhibit 2 gives a good indication of average management salaries in various positions. Chapter Appendix A lists hotel management positions, titles, and advancement opportunities.

Food Service

There is also a wide variety of job opportunities and geographic locations to choose from within the food service industry. Those who are interested in commercial food service often choose between independent and chain restaurants.

Independent Restaurants. At the top of the restaurant spectrum are luxury restaurants, which are for the most part owned and operated by independent entrepreneurs. Within the trade, these restaurants are sometimes called "white tablecloth" restaurants. Most of their patrons are on expense accounts. Le Cirque and the Four Seasons in Manhattan are perennial favorites in this class.

Guests at luxury restaurants usually receive superior service. Some luxury restaurants, for example, feature French service, in which meals are served from a cart or *guéridon* by formally dressed personnel. Tables are waited on by servers, a *chef de rang*, and an apprentice called a *commis de rang*. In the back of the house there is a classic kitchen in the tradition of **Escoffier,** with an executive chef and a brigade of cooks organized into departments, each headed by a *chef de partie*.

Contrary to popular belief, luxury restaurants are not necessarily high-profit ventures. Often, their rent and labor costs are high, and there is intense competition for a limited number of guests. These restaurants are usually open for both lunch and dinner (some only

Exhibit 2	Compensation: Lodging Properties					
Position— Median Salaries	Nationwide	<150 rooms	150–350 rooms	350–550 rooms	550–800 rooms	>800 rooms
Dir. of Human Resources	$59,717.79	$50,923.20	$53,073.75	$66,342.19	$78,464.00	$82,202.98
Dir. of Mgmt. Info. Systems	$54,636.35	N/A	$53,045.00	$53,225.90	$59,879.81	$60,972.78
Dir. of Revenue Management	$65,637.72	N/A	N/A	$56,992.00	$72,406.00	N/A
Dir. of Sales	$68,269.98	N/A	N/A	$78,550.98	$89,413.16	$99,495.45
Dir. of Sales & Marketing	$70,344.30	$50,020.35	$64,767.95	$86,320.00	$106,527.88	$120,052.92
Director of Catering	$58,595.52	N/A	$49,288.24	$63,028.49	$64,875.00	$91,090.36
Director of Food & Beverage	$70,119.20	$54,991.66	$61,902.98	$78,283.78	$87,418.16	$97,095.35
Director of Rooms	$63,688.50	$51,864.78	$59,685.43	$64,675.96	$68,871.10	$73,607.80
Executive Housekeeper	$39,493.50	$28,032.16	$40,314.20	$49,565.25	$58,682.06	$65,563.62
Front Office Manager	$38,478.47	$28,700.47	$39,392.81	$45,020.35	$46,439.53	$58,073.75
General Manager	$85,616.75	$55,112.82	$102,625.37	$129,368.80	$150,002.10	$165,970.07
Resident Manager	$81,384.42	N/A	$79,610.62	$91,552.22	$100,997.68	$103,076.19
Restaurant Manager	$37,151.62	$33,171.09	$37,131.50	$39,392.81	$45,010.18	$42,436.00
Sales Manager	$40,272.82	$34,929.07	$39,558.84	$43,519.45	$46,439.53	$48,888.31

*N/A = Not available.

Source: www.hvs-executivesearch.com. Visit this Internet site and click on "Products," then "Free Compensation Reports" for the most up-to-date numbers.

offer dinner), but the work starts early in the morning, when much of the food is purchased fresh and delivered for cooking that day, and runs until midnight or even later.

Many hospitality students aspire to run and eventually own a luxury restaurant. The top restaurants are very sophisticated operations and have a substantial volume of business—some sell as much as $30 million in food and beverages annually. Most do considerably less: $5 million to $6 million is a more typical figure for this kind of establishment. The best way to the top is to work in a luxury restaurant and learn the ropes. Many of these restaurants are owned by an individual. They are usually sold to an employee or other entrepreneurs who can get financing when the owner retires. Banks and other lending institutions look to see what experience the prospective owner has before approving loans, so a good track record in management positions at similar restaurants is your best ticket for getting the financing you need to buy your "dream" restaurant.

Chain Restaurants. Chain restaurants recruit the majority of their managers from hospitality schools. Entry-level jobs for graduates with hospitality degrees are often on the assistant-manager level, with progression to manager, then district manager responsible for a group of restaurants, and then regional manager.

Restaurant chains are the fastest growing part of the restaurant business today. Many of these chains are made up of fast-food restaurants or, as they prefer to be called, "quick-service" restaurants. Menus rarely change in these restaurants. Their strategy calls for delivering a large number of meals at fairly low prices. The free-standing buildings they occupy are usually specially built food-production factories filled with specially designed equipment. Minimum-wage employees turn out a standardized product. Successful quick-service chains depend on a large number of units so that they can engage in regional and national marketing and advertising programs. Expansion is usually accomplished through franchising, although some of the largest quick-service chains own as many as 30 percent of their units. Small quick-service chains such as Subway average as little as $375,000 annually per unit, but large chains like McDonald's average more than $1.5 million per unit.

Many hospitality students bypass quick-service management opportunities. This is often a mistake. Many of these jobs pay well and offer security and excellent benefit packages. For example, Burger King multi-unit managers can earn between $55,000 and $100,000 a year, plus benefits and bonuses. In addition, if you dream of owning your own franchise, the franchise company may help you if you've worked hard and well in one of their units. Domino's Pizza recruits many of its franchisees from its store managers and helps them arrange financing. Burger King and McDonald's have leasing programs that allow successful managers to lease units and pay the rent out of sales until they can afford to buy their unit.

Dinner houses, also known as casual restaurants, are another type of chain restaurant. Such well-known companies as Applebee's, Chili's, Outback Steakhouse, and Olive Garden lead the pack. These companies are popular career choices for hospitality graduates because they offer many opportunities for advancement.

Social Caterers. Social catering is another part of the food service industry that many hospitality graduates become interested in. Catering is another business that is most often started by independent entrepreneurs, as it requires very little start-up capital—facilities can be rented as needed, equipment can usually be leased on a short-term basis from restaurant supply houses, and food servers can be hired as needed. In some cases, caterers provide only food; in others, they are responsible for tables, chairs, utensils, tents, servers, and decorations.

Contract Food Companies. Contract food companies are generally hired by organizations whose major business purpose is not food service, but they provide it for some reason. The biggest users of contract food services are large manufacturing and industrial concerns in which workers have a short lunch period. Contractors such as ARAMARK and Sodexo operate cafeterias and executive dining rooms for these companies. The service is often subsidized by the contracting company, which may supply the space and utilities and, in some cases, underwrite some or all of the food costs. Schools and colleges, hospitals, sports arenas, airlines, cruise ships, and even prisons use contract food companies. In the case of airlines, meals are cooked and prepackaged in central commissaries and then delivered to the airplanes for preparation and service as needed.

Contract food management is somewhat unusual because the manager must please two sets of employers—the manager's home office and the client that has contracted for the service. Many contract food programs, such as those at schools and hospitals, have strong nutritional requirements as well. Others, such as airline programs, require a knowledge of advanced food technology.

Careers in contract food service are attractive to many hospitality majors. Contract food managers work more regular hours and are under less pressure than restaurant managers. Why? Because many of the users of contract food service, such as office building tenants, work a regular 40-hour week, Monday through Friday, which allows the contract food managers to work more normal hours. Also, contract food managers are able to predict with more certainty how many people they are going to feed, what they will feed them, and when the meals will be served.

Because of the large volume of meals involved, contract food managers must be highly skilled in professional management techniques and cost control. For this reason, contract food companies usually hire people with experience within their industry and recruit from hospitality schools.

Institutional Food Service. Although contract food companies can supply food for schools and hospitals, the majority of these institutions handle their own food service programs. Most public schools belong to the National School Lunch Program established by the federal government in 1946. The purpose of this program is twofold: (1) to create a market for agricultural products produced by America's farmers, and (2) to serve a nutritious lunch to schoolchildren at a low cost. Public elementary schools tend to offer only those menu items that qualify for government support, but many high schools add items such as hamburgers, French fries, and even diet sodas. High school food managers work hard to come up with creative and innovative menu plans to keep students in school cafeterias. Even the look of school cafeterias has changed as managers have developed new methods of merchandising food.

Colleges and universities have also experienced changes in their food service programs. Because more students live off-campus now, there is a trend toward flexible meal plans in which students have a choice of how many meals they wish to purchase from the institution. To compete successfully, many universities have opened special table-service restaurants in addition to their traditional cafeterias. Another move has been to offer a more varied cafeteria menu featuring salad bars and popular items such as croissant sandwiches, bagels, lox and cream cheese, and even Belgian waffles for breakfast. Some universities have brought quick-service outlets such as Pizza Hut and Taco Bell on campus.

Hospital programs are usually administered by a trained dietitian or a professional food service manager working with one. Menus are generally simple and nourishing. In the past, most hospitals had a central kitchen where all foods were prepared and then sent in insulated carts or trays to the patients' rooms. Some hospitals have decentralized their food service. With a decentralized system, the hospital purchases frozen and portion-packed entrées and salads and keeps them in small pantries in various parts of the hospital. The meals are then plated and heated in microwave ovens as needed. Another trend has been the attempt to turn hospital food service from a cost center into a revenue center. Some hospitals sell take-home food to doctors and employees and even do outside catering.

As you can see, institutions are beginning to compete with commercial food service operations for consumers. This means that there are more opportunities than ever before for hospitality students to enter what is clearly a growing field.

Management Positions within Food Service. A restaurant is usually a small business, with average sales of $535,000 annually.[3] That means that most of the management opportunities in this field, even with large chains, lie in operations or "hands-on" management, as opposed to corporate staff jobs behind a desk. The duties of a food service manager are similar across the spectrum of food service operations, from an independent restaurant to a cruise ship to a retirement home.

The Chili's Grill & Bar restaurant chain staffs its units with a general manager and three restaurant managers. The general manager is responsible for overall operations, while each restaurant manager has specific functional duties—managing the dining room, handling beverage service, or supervising the kitchen staff. This simple management structure and division of duties is similar for many other commercial food service operations. Other typical food service management positions include chef, maître d', and banquet manager. Exhibit 3 lists median salaries of general managers, assistant general managers, and other food service managers and executives. Appendix B at the end of the chapter lists food service management positions, titles, and advancement opportunities.

Clubs

Clubs are another career option open to you. Clubs are very different from other types of hospitality businesses because the "guests"—the club members—are also the owners in many cases. There are country clubs, city clubs, luncheon clubs, yacht and sailing clubs,

Exhibit 3	Compensation: Restaurant Properties
Position–Median Salaries	**Nationwide**
Chief Operating Officer/President	$291,747.50
Director Human Resources	$97,696.34
Director Training	$84,686.34
Senior VP Operations	$173,891.06
Area Manager	$77,567.50
Unit General Manager	$51,358.17
Unit Assistant General Manager	$37,507.59
VP Development	$156,001.78

Source: www.hvs-executivesearch.com. Visit this Internet site and click on "Products," then "Free Compensation Reports" for the most up-to-date numbers.

military clubs, tennis clubs, even polo clubs—all with clubhouses and other facilities that must be managed. Some, like the Yale Club in New York City, offer complete hotel services. Large clubs have many of the same positions found in hotels and restaurants: a general manager, a food and beverage director, a catering director (weddings and parties are an important part of club operations), and a controller.

Today there are more than 14,000 recreational and social clubs in the United States that lease or own their facilities and have them run by professional managers. Most clubs are nonprofit organizations owned by, and run for the benefit of, the members. Some clubs are built by developers as part of housing developments and are proprietary, for-profit enterprises.

Many hospitality managers enjoy working in clubs. First of all, unlike chain food service and hotel operations, there is a chance to exercise one's own imagination and creativity in such matters as menu selection, party planning, and sporting events. Secondly, you interact with the owners (members) in a more direct way. Moreover, clubs with sports facilities often host celebrity tournaments that bring with them media coverage. This can make the job even more stimulating. Since the nature of clubs often requires specialized training and knowledge (in such areas as golf, tennis, and marina operations), club managers often come up through the ranks.

Cruise Lines

There are opportunities both on shore and at sea within the cruise industry. Shoreside positions include marketing, accounting, provisioning, itinerary planning, and hotel operations. At sea, there are the same kinds of jobs any fine resort has. Salaries are competitive. Persons who are attracted by travel may enjoy operations jobs at sea but should be prepared to spend a minimum of nine out of every twelve months away from home. Living conditions don't allow for much privacy either, but many like the feeling of extended family that often occurs among staff members on a ship.

Looking for a Job

Many hospitality students have a preconceived idea of the job they want in the industry. They may have had an enjoyable part-time or summer job in a restaurant or hotel, for example. Or their parents, a family friend, or someone else they admire may have been in the business and advised them to take a particular position. In the view of career counselors, however, it's better to keep an open mind. If you don't explore other career possibilities, you might overlook opportunities that could be more appealing in the long run. A sound understanding of your goals and lifestyle, and a thorough knowledge of the companies that might be interested in what you offer, is an important foundation for your career search.

Every job you take should move you closer to your final goal. If you look at jobs as stepping-stones on a **career path** or **career ladder** (see Exhibit 4), there are several questions you should answer before you decide whether a job is right for you:

- What can I learn from this job that will contribute to my career goals?

- What are the long-term opportunities for growth in this company?

- What is this company's reputation among the people I know? Is it a good place to work? Does it deliver on its promises to employees?

Exhibit 4   Sample Career Path—Steak 'n Shake

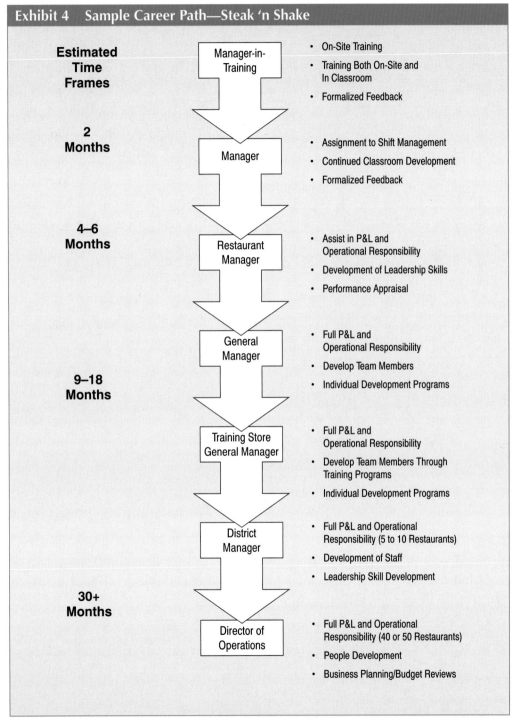

Estimated Time Frames

| | Manager-in-Training | • On-Site Training
• Training Both On-Site and In Classroom
• Formalized Feedback |

2 Months

| | Manager | • Assignment to Shift Management
• Continued Classroom Development
• Formalized Feedback |

4–6 Months

| | Restaurant Manager | • Assist in P&L and Operational Responsibility
• Development of Leadership Skills
• Performance Appraisal |

| | General Manager | • Full P&L and Operational Responsibility
• Develop Team Members
• Individual Development Programs |

9–18 Months

| | Training Store General Manager | • Full P&L and Operational Responsibility
• Develop Team Members Through Training Programs
• Individual Development Programs |

| | District Manager | • Full P&L and Operational Responsibility (5 to 10 Restaurants)
• Development of Staff
• Leadership Skill Development |

30+ Months

| | Director of Operations | • Full P&L and Operational Responsibility (40 or 50 Restaurants)
• People Development
• Business Planning/Budget Reviews |

This career path shows the sequence of jobs a manager trainee may take in the Steak 'n Shake Company as he or she moves up the corporate ladder. (Courtesy of Steak 'n Shake Company.)

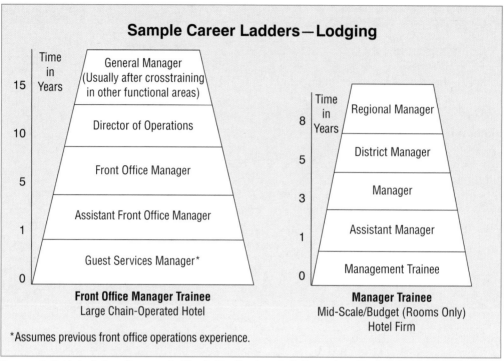

Sample Career Ladders—Lodging

Time in Years

15 — General Manager (Usually after crosstraining in other functional areas)

10 — Director of Operations

5 — Front Office Manager

1 — Assistant Front Office Manager

0 — Guest Services Manager*

Front Office Manager Trainee
Large Chain-Operated Hotel

Time in Years

8 — Regional Manager

5 — District Manager

3 — Manager

1 — Assistant Manager

0 — Management Trainee

Manager Trainee
Mid-Scale/Budget (Rooms Only)
Hotel Firm

*Assumes previous front office operations experience.

Source: *A Guide to College Programs in Hospitality, Tourism, & Culinary Arts,* Ninth Edition (Richmond, Va.: International CHRIE, 2006), p. 19.

- How good is the training program? Will the company really make an effort to educate me?

- What is the starting salary? What about other benefits? Do they add up to a competitive package?

- How do I feel about the location? Will I be living in a place where I can be happy? What about proximity to friends and relatives?

Your First Moves

While you are still in school, you probably will want to gain some job experience in the hospitality industry. To do that, you will need some basic knowledge of how to prepare a résumé and handle a job interview. The following sections contain information that may be useful to you.

Your Résumé. Whether you mail in a reply to a newspaper ad or apply for a job in person, a basic tool you will need is a well-prepared, typed or printed (not handwritten), and attractive résumé. What follows is a brief introduction to the art and science of writing a good résumé. There are many excellent books in bookstores and libraries on creating résumés; our best advice is to find one and read it!

Purpose of a résumé. Many job seekers do not understand the purpose of a résumé. Put yourself in the shoes of an interviewer. You have just placed an ad in your local newspaper seeking a front desk agent for your hotel. It is not unlikely that you will receive 100 résumés or more for this job. Obviously you can't interview 100 people in person. Their résumés, and the cover letters that usually accompany them, serve as screening guides. They are tools that the interviewer uses to decide whom to see. The purpose of your résumé, therefore, is to make certain that you will be one of the handful of people who will actually be interviewed. Your résumé will not get you a job—no one is hired on the basis of a résumé alone.

A résumé is an *advertisement for yourself*. Its purpose is to convince the person doing the hiring that he or she should not fill the job without talking to you first. Résumés have other purposes as well. They introduce you to your prospective employer and provide a brief summary of your educational and employment background. However, their main purpose is to pre-sell you to the company, to persuade the interviewer before the interview starts that you may be the best person for the job.

Contents of a résumé. Once you understand the purpose of a résumé, the information that goes into one and in what order becomes clearer. Start with the length. Your résumé should not run more than one page. Interviewers don't have time to read more than that, and they don't need to read more in order to decide whether they want to interview you. Remember, your résumé will end up in a file with many others. The interviewer will skim through the file to find the most likely candidates. What should be at the top of the page, after your name, address, and phone number? Whatever you can say that is most likely to make the interviewer want to read more about you.

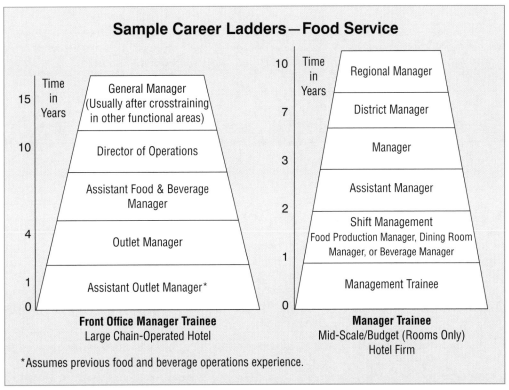

Source: *A Guide to College Programs in Hospitality, Tourism, & Culinary Arts,* Ninth Edition (Richmond, Va.: International CHRIE, 2006), p. 20.

Many of the best résumés start with a section called "Summary of Qualifications." Continuing with our example, suppose you are applying for the front desk position and you have worked at another hotel as a front desk agent. What you would want to put in this section is, "One year of experience as a front desk agent at a major hotel." In most cases, however, you will not have had previous experience. That does not mean you are not qualified for the job. Maybe you worked at a quick-service restaurant while you were in high school, in which case you could say, "Experienced at greeting and serving customers." It may well be that you've never held a job before. Your qualifications then might be something like the following: "A personable, enthusiastic worker, quick learner, good team player." This is the section that you use to market or sell yourself, to show that you have the skills, experience, and basic credentials for the job. If you have received any awards or recognition ("Named 'Employee of the Month'"), this is the place to mention it, to separate you from the crowd.

The next section of a résumé is often a direct presentation of your skills and experience. Here you will be more specific: "One year's experience as a front desk agent at the 100-room Hampton Inn. Duties included taking reservations, checking in and checking out guests, and handling complaints."

What if you've never held a front desk position before? You want to show that the jobs you have held or the work you've done has contributed to your ability to do the job in question. If you said that you were a "personable, enthusiastic worker," you might note that you were a shift leader at McDonald's last summer, or even "Head of the prom committee at Northside High."

List your education at the bottom of your résumé. Why not put your education at the top? Because most interviewers are not looking for a specific educational background, they are looking for someone who can do the job. If they think you can do it, then they'll read your entire résumé carefully and call you in. If they don't, they won't care about your schooling.

Should you list your hobbies? Only if they relate to the job you're trying for. If you're applying for a job as a cook and your hobby is collecting or writing recipes, that would be relevant. But if what you do in your spare time is collect stamps or play the saxophone, leave it out. It not only won't help, it might even hurt (the interviewer might hate the saxophone!).

Other personal information also has no place on a résumé. Your height, weight, age, race, or marital status should not be part of your résumé unless it bears directly on the job qualifications. While some books suggest enclosing a picture, we don't recommend it. Your physical appearance has nothing to do with your ability to do the job, and might unconsciously prejudice the interviewer not to see you. We also don't recommend putting references on résumés. Usually you will be asked for references at the interview if they are wanted—why waste valuable space? Nor should you state a desired salary. Once the company decides it wants you and you decide you want the job, then you can discuss salary.

Finally, avoid gimmicks or being "creative" with your résumé. You want to present yourself as a professional, responsible, and reliable individual. Unusual résumés do not promote that image. (See Chapter Appendix C for a sample résumé.)

Preparing for the Interview. You should know as much as possible about your prospective employer before you walk in the door. You want to be informed, because that will make it easier for you to hold a conversation and you will sound more enthusiastic. If you're applying to a hotel or restaurant chain, there's a lot of information in the library from trade periodicals, on the Internet, and in Dun & Bradstreet reports.

Dressing for the Interview. The way you are dressed makes a big difference in the way you are perceived. If you are applying for a management position, you should consider how you would dress if you were working at the firm, and then dress slightly better. Research shows that reactions to clothing styles, colors, and combinations are fairly predictable. Remember, you want to project a professional, responsible image. The interview is not the time to make a bold or unusual fashion statement.

How to Be Interviewed. An interview is your opportunity to sell yourself, or rather to sell your prospective employer on offering you a job. Once you get the offer you can decide whether to take it, but the name of the game is to convince the interviewer to want to hire you.

Going into an interview with this attitude has several implications. First, it gives you a sense of confidence. You are not going to sit back and wait to see what the interviewer asks, because he or she might not ask about the things that make you a superior candidate. You are going to control, to the extent you can, what is talked about. This is not as hard as it sounds. One good way to start off and gain control of the interview is to ask questions. If you have done your homework about the company, some questions will naturally occur to you. Asking questions shows that you are a person who is very interested in working for the company. The answers to your questions may give you clues that will help you sell the interviewer on hiring you.

The more you know about the company (and the interviewer) before you start answering questions, the better job you can do of answering them. Generally, industry recruiters look for people who not only possess specific skills, but also understand the dynamics of our changing business. They want good communicators and leaders who can motivate others, show them what needs to be done, and teach them how to do it. Industry recruiters look for well-rounded individuals who understand financial issues, legislative issues, ethical issues, and, above all, human resources issues.

Often, interviewers have a checklist of topics they want to cover in the interview. Don't be put off; you can still ask your questions in between their questions. Always answer their questions directly and honestly. If you don't know the answer to something, say so. The best thing you can do is sound positive. You want to be remembered after you leave the room as someone who is enthusiastic, confident, energetic, and dependable. Shape every answer to reinforce those images.

Under no circumstances should you say anything bad about a former employer. To do so suggests that you might be disloyal or dishonest.

Finally, encourage the interviewer to make you an offer. Like any good salesperson, ask for the order! Once you have a job offer, you can weigh it along with other possibilities.

After you leave you should always write a follow-up thank-you letter. Thank the interviewer for the time he or she spent with you and for considering you for the position. If you were impressed with the company, say so! Tell the interviewer that you're certain you can make a contribution and you hope you'll be hearing from him or her soon.

If you are offered a job, respond within the time requested. You might have additional questions, so contact the person making the offer to clarify details. If you need more time to make your decision, ask for it. When you have decided, be prompt in letting your prospective employer know. If you call to turn down the offer, follow up with a letter in which you thank the person for his or her interest in you. Remember, you may meet this recruiter again during your career under different circumstances.

Summary

The hospitality industry's growth in recent decades has been due in part to the average individual's higher standard of living, higher level of education, and longer life span. The greater opportunities available in rapidly developing societies have also contributed to industry expansion.

The hospitality industry offers many career options. The work is varied and there are numerous opportunities for advancement. Some people, however, don't like the occasional pressures and long hours that go along with many hospitality jobs. Management positions in a hotel include general manager, catering manager, chief engineer, food and beverage manager, controller, human resources manager, marketing and sales manager, resident manager, and management information systems manager. Management positions in a restaurant include general manager, restaurant manager, chef, maître d' hotel, and banquet manager.

It's important to select the segment of the industry that will best suit you. To do this you must know whether you work best with data, people, or things. Once you have considered your strengths and weaknesses, you are in a position to evaluate areas of specialization. Your choices include hotels, restaurants, clubs, catering operations, contract food companies, institutional food service, and more.

Three important job-seeking skills are preparing a good résumé, dressing correctly for an interview, and conducting yourself appropriately during an interview. The purpose of your résumé is to gain an interview. It is an advertisement for you; use it to emphasize your special skills and experience. Research the company you will interview for, dress conservatively for your interview, and "sell yourself."

Endnotes

1. *2008 Restaurant Industry Operations Report* (Washington, D.C.: National Restaurant Association, 2009).

2. *2009 Restaurant Industry Operations Report* (Washington, D.C.: National Restaurant Association, 2010).

3. *2005 Restaurant Industry Operations Report* (Washington, D.C.: National Restaurant Association, 2004).

Key Terms

career path/career ladder—A series of positions an individual may take on the way to his or her ultimate career goal. Some companies lay out sample career paths or ladders for their employees.

catering manager—A hotel manager responsible for arranging and planning food and beverage functions for (1) conventions and smaller hotel groups, and (2) local banquets booked by the sales department.

chief engineer—Responsible for a hotel's physical operation and maintenance.

controller—Manages the accounting department and all of its functions, including management of credit, payroll, guest accounts, and cashiering activities.

Escoffier, Georges Auguste—A French chef (1847–1935) who is considered the father of modern cookery. His two main contributions were (1) the simplification of classical cuisine and the classical menu, and (2) the reorganization of the kitchen.

food and beverage manager—Directs the production and service of food and beverages.

general manager—The chief operating officer of a hotel or restaurant.

hospitality industry—Lodging and food service businesses that provide short-term or transitional lodging and/or food.

human resources manager—In charge of employee relations within an organization.

management information systems (MIS) manager—Manages a hotel's computerized management information systems. May write simple computer programs and instruction manuals for employees.

marketing manager—Develops and implements a marketing plan and budget.

resident manager—In charge of the rooms division in a mid-size to large hotel. Sometimes resident managers are also in charge of security.

sales manager—Conducts sales programs and makes sales calls on prospects for group and individual business. Reports to the marketing manager.

Review Questions

1. What is the hospitality industry?
2. What are some of the advantages and disadvantages of a career in hospitality?
3. How can a skills inventory help you decide on a career path?
4. What are some career options in the hotel industry?
5. What are the advantages of working for a large hotel chain? for an independent hotel?
6. What are some career options in the food service industry?
7. Should a hospitality student bypass quick-service management opportunities? Why or why not?
8. What are some of the questions you should ask yourself before you decide that a job is right for you?
9. What should appear on a résumé? What should not appear?
10. How should you prepare for, and conduct yourself during, a job interview?

Internet Sites

For more information, visit the following Internet sites. Remember that Internet addresses can change without notice. If the site is no longer there, you can use a search engine to look for additional sites.

Associations

Asian American Hotel Owners Association
www.aahoa.com

American Hotel & Lodging Association
www.ahla.com

American Hotel & Lodging Educational Institute
www.ahlei.org

Club Managers Association of America
www.cmaa.org

Hospitality Financial & Technology Professionals
www.hftp.org

National Restaurant Association
www.restaurant.org

Casinos

Bally's
www.harrahs.com/brands/ballys/hotel-casinos/ballys-brand.shtml

Caesars
www.harrahs.com/brands/caesars/hotel-casinos/caesars-brand.shtml

Circus Circus
www.circuscircus.com

Harrah's Casino
www.harrahs.com

Luxor Casino
www.luxor.com

MGM Grand
www.mgmgrand.com

The Mirage
www.mirage.com

Trump's Taj Mahal
www.trumptaj.com

Wynn Las Vegas Resort
www.wynnlasvegas.com

Hotel Companies/Resorts

Hilton Hotels
www.hilton.com

Hyatt Hotels
www.hyatt.com

Mandarin Oriental Hotel Group
www.mandarin-oriental.com

Marriott International
www.marriott.com

Ritz-Carlton Hotels
www.ritzcarlton.com

Starwood Hotels
www.starwoodhotels.com

Trapp Family Lodge
www.trappfamily.com

Westin Hotels
www.westin.com

Organizations, Consultants, Resources

Hcareers
www.hcareers.com

Hospitalitycareernet.com
www.hospitalitycareernet.com

Hospitality Net
www.hospitalitynet.org

World Tourism Organization
www.world-tourism.org

Restaurant Companies

Burger King
www.burgerking.com

Canteen
www.canteen.com

Chili's Grill & Bar
www.chilis.com

Domino's Pizza
www.dominos.com

McDonald's
www.mcdonalds.com

Pizza Hut
www.pizzahut.com

Taco Bell
www.tacobell.com

Tavern on the Green
www.tavernonthegreen.com

Chapter Appendix A

Key Hotel Management Positions

Title	Department	Description	Advancement Opportunity
Food and Beverage Controller	Accounting	Controls food and beverage costs through menu planning and pricing/purchasing decisions, storage, issuing. Works closely with management and provides advice through consultation and reporting.	Assistant Controller
Assistant Controller	Accounting	Functions as office manager with responsibility for preparation of financial statements.	Controller
Controller	Accounting	Acts as financial advisor to management in achieving profit objectives through detailed planning, controlling costs, and effectively managing assets and liabilities of the hotel.	Area/Regional Controller
Director of Operations	Administration	Usually the number two manager in a hotel, responsible for the management of the all operating departments, such as food and beverage, housekeeping, etc.	General Manager
General Manager	Administration	Supervises all activities within the hotel. Responsible for the coordination of all departments.	Regional and Corporate Positions
Director of Engineering	Engineering	Responsible for the maintenance of the physical and mechanical plant.	Regional Team
Steward	Food and Beverage	Purchases and supervises the receipt and storage of food/beverage for the hotel.	Restaurant Manager
Director of Food and Beverage	Food and Beverage	Oversees entire food and beverage department.	General Manager
Catering Manager	Food and Beverage	Sells banquets and supervises banquet services.	Director of Food and Beverage

Title	Department	Description	Advancement Opportunity
Convention Services	Food and Beverage	Acts as liaison between meeting planners and the hotel. Responsible for execution of major functions.	Catering, Manager/Director of Food and Beverage
Front Office Manager	Front Office	Acts as a liaison between the guest and the hotel for reservation, registration, and information.	Cross-training in other divisions—Director of Operations
Reservations Manager	Front Office or Marketing	Oversees reservations functions, plans for reservations and yield management.	Front Office, Manager/Director of Marketing
Housekeeping Manager	Housekeeping	Supervises the work of room attendants and housepersons in assigned areas.	Director of Housekeeping
Director of Housekeeping	Housekeeping	Supervises all housekeeping personnel. In charge of all renovation and purchases of housekeeping supplies.	Cross-training in other divisions—Director of Operations
Director of Marketing	Marketing	Oversees all marketing and sales functions, develops marketing and sales plans.	Cross-training in other divisions—Director of Operations
Director of Sales	Sales	Sells convention facilities for meetings, banquets, and receptions. Sells rooms to volume purchasers, such as corporate travel directors of large companies.	Director of Marketing

Source: *A Guide to College Programs in Hospitality, Tourism, & Culinary Arts,* Ninth Edition (Richmond, Va.: International CHRIE, 2006).

Chapter Appendix B

Key Food Service Management Positions

Title	Department	Description	Advancement Opportunity
Beverage Manager	Beverages	Orders for and stocks bar, maintains inventories of liquor and glassware, supervises bartending personnel.	Food Production Manager
Dining Room Manager	Dining Room	Supervises all dining room staff and activities, including staff training, scheduling, time records, and assigning work stations.	Assistant Manager
Pantry Supervisor	Pantry	Supervises salad, sandwich, and beverage assistants. May also supervise cleaning crews and requisition cleaning supplies.	Food Production Manager
Cook or Sous Chef	Kitchen	Prepares and portions out all food served. In large restaurants often responsible for specific items such as soups, sauces, or meats.	Executive Chef
Pastry Chef or Baker	Kitchen	Bakes cakes, cookies, pies, and desserts, as well as bread, rolls, and quick breads.	Executive Chef
Executive Chef	Kitchen	Responsible for all quantity and quality food preparation, supervision of sous chefs and cooks, and menu-recipe development.	Assistant Manager
Food Production Manager	Kitchen	Responsible for all food preparation and supervision of kitchen support staff and baker, upholding sanitation standards and cost control.	Assistant Manager

Title	Department	Description	Advancement Opportunity
Purchasing Agent	Management	Orders, receives, inspects, and stores all goods shipped by suppliers. Oversees distribution to different food preparation departments. Often assists executive chef or assistant manager.	Assistant Manager
Assistant Manager	Management	Performs specified supervisory duties under the manager's direction.	Food Service Manager
Food Service Manager	Management	Responsible for profitability, efficiency, quality, and courtesy of the entire food service operation.	Multiunit Regional Manager
Personnel Director	Management	Responsible for hiring and training of food service personnel, administration of employee relations, benefits, safety, and communications.	Regional Personnel Manager
Merchandising Supervisor (Local)	Management	Plans and carries out advertising and promotional programs to increase sales. May also handle public relations activities.	Regional Merchandising Manager

Source: *A Guide to College Programs in Hospitality, Tourism, & Culinary Arts,* Ninth Edition (Richmond, Va.: International CHRIE, 2006).

Chapter Appendix C
Sample Résumé

Chris Jones
911 Maple Avenue
Miami, Florida 33000
(305) 555-1234
Jones@abc.com

Summary of Qualifications:

Experienced at supervising and training front desk and dining room staff, and implementing quality procedures.

Experience

January 20XX to Present

Front Desk Supervisor, The Royal Plaza Hotel, New York, NY. Supervised front desk operations for the 300-room luxury hotel, trained shift staff, and implemented quality policies.

September 20XX to December 20XX

Assistant Manager, Global Restaurant, Miami, FL. Responsible for dining room service staff, food and beverage inventory control, and opening and closing for a 150-seat casual restaurant.

April 20XX to August 20XX

Front Desk Clerk, The Limited-Service Hotel, Miami, FL. Trained and worked at the front desk of this 130-room limited-service hotel, responsible for guest check-in and check-out and answering guest inquiries.

Education

USA University, School of Hospitality Management, Bachelor of Science Degree, December 20XX

Activities

The College Hotel Club: President

Sales & Marketing Association: Treasurer

The Community Charity

Computer Skills

Microsoft Word, Excel, PowerPoint, Web CT

Languages

Fluent in Spanish and French

References

On request

Part 2
Hospitality
Organizations

4

Understanding the Restaurant Industry

Outline

Competencies

1. Describe in general terms the size of the restaurant industry, list restaurant industry segments, and describe eating and drinking places. (pp. 84–90)

2. Describe food service outlets in lodging operations; the transportation, recreation and sports, business and industry, educational, health care, and retail food service markets; corrections and military food service; and contract food management companies. (pp. 90–95)

3. Summarize some of the pitfalls of starting a new restaurant, cite reasons restaurants may fail, and outline some of the issues involved in starting a new restaurant, such as developing a concept, selecting a site, having a feasibility study done, and thinking "green." (pp. 95–105)

Opposite page: An outdoor cafe near Strasbourg, France.
Page 81: Fairmont Singapore, Singapore; courtesy of Fairmont Hotels & Resorts.

THIS CHAPTER DESCRIBES the diversity and complexity of the various segments of the restaurant industry. We will take a look at eating and drinking establishments; hotel food and beverage operations; food service for airlines, trains, and cruise lines; the recreational, business and industry, educational, health care, retail, corrections, and military markets; and contract food management companies. Since owning their own restaurant someday is the dream of many who enter the restaurant industry, there is a section on how to start a new restaurant. The chapter concludes with a topic of growing importance: the "greening" of restaurants.

Today's Restaurant Industry

The restaurant industry runs the gamut from gourmet restaurants to hot dog stands. The National Restaurant Association (NRA) estimated 2009 food service sales at $566 billion, and the industry employed 13 million people in 945,000 establishments. The overall impact of the industry on the U.S. economy exceeds $1.5 trillion. Restaurant industry sales equal four percent of the U.S. gross domestic product. The percentage of the food dollar spent away from home is 48 percent. On a typical day in the United States, 130 million individuals are patrons of food service establishments.[1]

The restaurant industry is truly an equal opportunity employer. It employs more minority managers than any other industry: 57 percent are women, 14 percent are African-American, and 16 percent are Hispanic. Someone entering the food service field might work for a small, independent operator who runs a **fine-dining restaurant,** pizza parlor, or ice cream stand. Working at an independent operation is good training for future entrepreneurs. Another career track might begin in the management training program of a large corporation like Darden, which operates the full-service restaurants Red Lobster, Olive Garden, Longhorn Steakhouse, Seasons 52, the Capital Grille, and Bahama Breeze. There are many opportunities in the quick-service field with McDonald's, KFC, Wendy's, and other companies. The Walt Disney Corporation runs a huge number of diverse food operations and actively recruits hospitality graduates to manage its theme park restaurants and snack bars. Airline meals are supplied by in-flight catering operators such as Gate Gourmet International. Many big banks, insurance companies, and advertising agencies have executive dining rooms run by professional food service managers. Contract food companies such as ARAMARK, Sodexo, the Compass Group, and others place managers in executive or employee dining facilities; in schools, colleges, and universities; and at tourist attractions such as the Getty Center and J. Paul Getty Museum in Los Angeles. As you can see, there are many career choices in the restaurant industry.

Restaurant Industry Segments

The restaurant industry includes many different types of facilities and markets. For reporting and other purposes, the industry can be divided into the following segments:

- Eating and drinking places
- Lodging
- Transportation

- Recreation and sports

- Business and industry

- Educational

- Health care

- Retail

- Corrections food service

- Military food service

- Contractors

Eating and Drinking Places. Eating and drinking places constitute the largest segment of the restaurant industry, accounting for almost 70 percent of total industry sales. This segment includes full-service restaurants, quick-service restaurants, commercial cafeterias, social caterers, ice cream and frozen custard stands, and bars and taverns. Over 88 percent of this segment's sales are made by full-service and quick-service restaurants, which offer the most opportunities for hospitality students. For this reason, most of this section deals with these industry segments.

Full-service restaurants. There is a wide variety of **full-service restaurants.** According to one generally accepted definition, full-service restaurants are restaurants that:

- Feature a dozen or more main-course items on the menu, and

- Cook to order

Full-service restaurants are generally categorized in terms of price, menu, or atmosphere. There are other ways to categorize them, of course. They can be casual or formal, for example. These categories are not mutually exclusive. Many full-service restaurants—as well as other restaurant operations—can fit into more than one category.

Price. When the focus is on price, restaurants can be categorized as luxury, high-priced, mid-priced, or low-priced establishments. An example of a luxury restaurant is Per Se in New York City, where dinner for two—appetizer, entrée, dessert, coffee, and accompanying bottle of wine—would cost over $200 per person. Luxury restaurants are generally small and independently operated. They feature well-trained, creative chefs and employ skilled dining room servers headed by a maître d'hotel and a cadre of captains. Some luxury restaurants offer table-side cooking. To provide the necessary—and expected—high level of service, luxury restaurants employ more kitchen and dining room employees per guest than do other types of restaurants.

Some luxury restaurants are tourist attractions famous the world over, such as the Eiffel Tower Restaurant in Paris. Others, such as Masa's in San Francisco, cater to "regulars"—members of the jet set, movie stars, corporate executives, and others who lead the lifestyle of the rich and famous. Typically, such establishments are owned or co-owned by a chef who supervises the cooking in the kitchen. While fine-dining restaurants have historically featured French cuisine, this is no longer the case. Today's top restaurants often feature regional specialties and **fusion cuisine,** which blends ingredients and flavors from all over the globe. The industry is led today by innovative young chefs, many of whom have been trained in the United States at places like the Culinary Institute of America in Hyde Park, New York, and Johnson & Wales University, headquartered in Providence, Rhode Island.

High-priced restaurants are also usually independently owned and operated, but most have larger seating capacities than luxury restaurants. Menus are extensive, and service can range from formal at New York's Le Cirque to casual at Joe's Stone Crab in Miami Beach. Every year, *Restaurants & Institutions* ranks the top 100 independent full-service restaurants in America in order of total sales. The Top 20 list appears in Exhibit 1.

Menu. Restaurants such as steak houses and seafood restaurants are full-service restaurants defined in terms of menu. For example, Outback Steakhouse specializes in beef, while Red Lobster features shrimp, crab, and lobster on its menu. **Ethnic restaurants** feature a specific cuisine as their distinctive theme. Romano's Macaroni Grill features Italian food, for example. Other ethnic restaurants serve Chinese, Greek, Japanese, Polynesian, Scandinavian, Korean, or Indian food, to name a few.

Atmosphere. Some restaurants are known primarily for their atmosphere—that is, for their unique architecture, decor, and/or setting. Show business and sports motifs—currently very fashionable in the industry—provide themes for a growing number of popular restaurants. The Hard Rock Café chain, which started in London and now has restaurants in major cities around the world, features rock-and-roll music memorabilia from Elvis Presley and the Beatles to contemporary rock stars. Old-fashioned stainless-steel-and-Formica diners have plenty of atmosphere and continue to be a popular part of the nostalgia niche-market segment.

Other categories. Full-service restaurants can be categorized in other ways besides price, menu, or atmosphere. For example, there are **casual restaurants.** Casual restaurants are distinguishable by their combination of decor, informal atmosphere, and eclectic menus that draw from ethnic and traditional offerings. Almost all casual restaurants are chain-affiliated. Olive Garden, T.G.I. Friday's, and Ruby Tuesday are all casual restaurants, one of the largest segments within the full-service category (see Exhibit 2). Applebee's and Chili's are two of the largest chains in this segment. Part of Applebee's success is the attention the chain devotes to the location of each restaurant. Although there is uniformity in the chain's concept, 40 percent of Applebee's menu items are tailored to regional food preferences.

Family restaurants—another mainstay in the full-service restaurant category—cater to families, with an emphasis on satisfying the needs of children (see Exhibit 3). Family restaurants serve breakfast, lunch, and dinner, offering traditional menu items. Their pricing falls between casual dinner houses and quick-service restaurants. A major source of revenue for some family restaurants (such as Cracker Barrel) is an on-site gift shop.

Quick-service restaurants. The distinguishing features of **quick-service restaurants** are that they offer a narrow selection of food, provide limited service, and focus on speed of preparation and delivery. Quick-service restaurants focus on convenience. Burger King, KFC, and Taco Bell fall into this category. Because convenience is such an important element of a quick-service restaurant's appeal, many stay open from early morning until very late at night.

Exhibit 4 lists the top 25 restaurant chains. Note that the vast majority are quick-service restaurants. The largest group of quick-service restaurants by far specializes in hamburgers, and the leader of the pack is McDonald's, with more than 31,000 units serving nearly 50 million customers each day in more than 118 countries. The largest McDonald's in the world is in Orlando, Florida; it seats more than 400 people on two levels. The busiest, on Pushkin Square in Moscow, serves 40,000 customers per day.

McDonald's is a leader in innovative marketing approaches. For example, for the 2008 Olympics in Beijing, McDonald's created Asian-inspired versions of its food in its restaurants around the world—a Beijing Burger with chop suey and breaded sticks of

Exhibit 1   Top 20 Independent Full-Service Restaurants

Rank	Restaurant	2008 F&B Sales	Meals Served/ Year
1	Tao Las Vegas Restaurant & Night Club Las Vegas	$68,406,696	785,000
2	Tavern on the Green New York City	34,221,691	476,899
3	Joe's Stone Crab Miami Beach	28,827,328	320,000
4	Smith & Wollensky New York City (Third Avenue)	28,595,000	387,000
5	Tao Asian Bistro New York City	24,433,601	385,000
6	Old Ebbitt Grill Washington, D.C.	23,330,827	800,000
7	Buddakan New York City	21,602,008	237,898
8	Gibsons Bar Steakhouse Chicago	20,753,314	335,899
9	Joe's Seafood, Prime Steak & Stone Crab Chicago	20,500,000	410,000
10	Joe's Seafood, Prime Steak & Stone Crab Las Vegas	20,300,000	400,000
11	Fulton's Crab House Lake Buena Vista, Florida	20,140,933	421,519
12	Mix Las Vegas	19,500,000	190,000
13	SW Steakhouse Las Vegas	19,500,000	170,000
14	Sparks Steak House New York City	19,400,000	270,000
15	Bob Chinn's Crab House Wheeling, Illinois	19,242,677	652,991
16	Prime One Twelve Miami Beach	18,900,000	155,000
17	Rumjungle Las Vegas	17,900,000	300,000
18	Prime Steakhouse Las Vegas	17,877,624	129,548
19	Devito South Beach Miami Beach	17,800,000	140,000
20	'21" Club New York City	17,324,066	138,790

Source: Adapted from "Top 100 Independent Restaurants of 2008," *Restaurants & Institutions* website, September 18, 2009. You can visit the *Restaurants & Institutions* website—www.rimag.com—to search for the latest industry statistics.

Exhibit 2   Top 15 Casual Restaurant Chains, Ranked by U.S. Systemwide Sales

Rank	Chain	U.S. Systemwide Sales (in millions)
1	Applebee's Neighborhood Grill & Bar	$4,486.5
2	Chili's Grill & Bar	3,961.0
3	Olive Garden	3,250.0
4	Red Lobster	2,537.0
5	Outback Steakhouse	2,478.0
6	T.G.I. Friday's	1,935.0
7	Ruby Tuesday	1,553.0
8	The Cheesecake Factory	1,395.0
9	Buffalo Wild Wings Grill & Bar	1,229.4
10	Red Robin Gourmet Burgers & Spirits	1,175.6
11	Texas Roadhouse	1,155.0
12	P.F. Chang's China Bistro	919.7
13	Hooters	916.0
14	Longhorn Steakhouse	880.0
15	California Pizza Kitchen	681.3

Source: Adapted from "Top 100," *Nation's Restaurant News,* June 29, 2009, p. 60. You can visit the *Nation's Restaurant News* website—www.nrn.com—to search for the latest industry statistics.

Exhibit 3   Top 8 Family-Dining Restaurant Chains, Ranked by U.S. Systemwide Sales

Rank	Chain	U.S. Systemwide Sales (in millions)
1	International House of Pancakes/IHOP	$2,419.0
2	Denny's	2,318.0
3	Cracker Barrel Old Country Store	1,872.2
4	Bob Evans Restaurants	1,000.0
5	Waffle House	973.0
6	Perkins Restaurant and Bakery	780.0
7	Steak 'n Shake	696.0
8	Friendly's Ice Cream	642.1

Source: Adapted from "Top 100," *Nation's Restaurant News,* June 29, 2009, p. 80. You can visit the *Nation's Restaurant News* website—www.nrn.com—to search for the latest industry statistics.

rice in Latin America, a 310-calorie chicken Olympic sandwich in Denmark (created with the help of dietitians from the Danish Olympic team), and so on. The packaging for these new creations featured competing athletes. Some McDonald's units offer computers with limited Internet access and computer game kiosks for kids. In Boca Raton, Florida, the customers of one McDonald's can eat amid a small motorcycle museum that displays motorcycle paraphernalia and a Harley-Davidson. In Hong Kong, there is a McDonald's at the racetrack; a McDonald's in Rovaniemi, Finland, has a drive-through unit designed for snowmobiles.

The type or number of menu items alone does not determine who is successful in the quick-service category. A commitment to good service and providing nutritional menu choices has taken center stage. McDonald's guarantees hot food; fast, friendly service; and double-check drive-thru accuracy. A survey of operators, customers, and chefs conducted by the National Restaurant Association found that customers have become more health-conscious and concerned about sustainability or how and where their food was produced. Seventy-six percent of the adults who were queried said they were trying to

Exhibit 4   Top 25 Restaurant Chains, Ranked by U.S. Systemwide Sales

Rank	Chain	Concept	Parent Company	Sales (in millions)
1	McDonald's	Sandwich	McDonald's Corp.	$29,987.5
2	Subway	Sandwich	Doctor's Associates Inc.	9,637.5
3	Burger King	Sandwich	Burger King Holdings Inc.	9,264.0
4	Wendy's	Sandwich	Wendy's/Arby's Group Inc.	8,009.0
5	Starbucks Coffee	Coffee	Starbucks Corp.	7,755.0
6	Aramark Food & Support Services	Contract	Aramark Holdings Corp.	6,740.0
7	Taco Bell	Sandwich	Yum! Brands Inc.	6,700.0
8	Pizza Hut	Pizza	Yum! Brands Inc.	5,500.0
9	KFC	Chicken	Yum! Brands Inc.	5,200.0
10	Dunkin' Donuts	Coffee-Snack	Dunkin' Brands Inc.	4,955.0
11	Applebee's Neighborhood Grill & Bar	Casual	DineEquity Inc.	4,486.5
12	Chili's Grill & Bar	Casual	Brinker International Inc.	3,961.0
13	Sonic Drive-In	Sandwich	Sonic Corp.	3,811.1
14	Arby's	Sandwich	Wendy's/Arby's Group Inc.	3,254.0
15	Olive Garden	Casual	Darden Restaurants Inc.	3,250.0
16	Domino's Pizza	Pizza	Domino's Pizza Inc.	3,057.4
17	Jack in the Box	Sandwich	Jack in the Box Inc.	3,048.3
18	Chick-fil-A	Chicken	Chick-fil-A Inc.	2,962.3
19	Dairy Queen	Sandwich	Berkshire Hathaway Inc.	2,600.0
20	Red Lobster	Casual	Darden Restaurants Inc.	2,537.0
21	Outback Steakhouse	Casual	Bain Capital LLC	2,478.0
22	Panera Bread	Bakery-Cafe	Panera Bread Co.	2,447.0
23	International House of Pancakes/IHOP	Family	DineEquity Inc.	2,419.0
24	Denny's	Family	Denny's Corp.	2,318.0
25	Papa John's Pizza	Pizza	Papa John's International Inc.	2,041.6

Source: Adapted from "Top 100," *Nation's Restaurant News,* June 29, 2009, p. 36. You can visit the *Nation's Restaurant News* website—www.nrn.com—to search for the latest industry statistics.

First Pizza Delivery in Outer Space

In 2001, the quick-service restaurant chain Pizza Hut made history when "the world's first space-consumable pizza" was safely delivered to the International Space Station. Cosmonaut Yuri Usachov, the station's commander, had the honor of eating the first piece, after heating the pizza in the space station's oven. It had a crispy crust, pizza sauce, and cheese, but was also a little different from the typical Pizza Hut product: it was seasoned with extra spices (especially salt, since taste buds become a little dulled in space) and was topped with salami rather than pepperoni (the chain's most popular topping), because pepperoni did not pass the rigorous 60-day testing process the pizza had to undergo before being approved for space. The delivery and consumption of the salami pizza was the culmination of nearly a year of collaboration between Pizza Hut and Russian food scientists.

As one spokesperson for Pizza Hut put it, "As a leader in the pizza delivery business, we're determined to give customers what they want, when they want it and where they want it, even if they are in space. Wherever there is life, there will be Pizza Hut pizza."

eat healthier. Accordingly, chefs placed nutrition and health high on their list of considerations in menu planning, and chefs and operators ranked "healthy kids' meals" as one of the "hottest trends."[2]

Hospitality-school graduates tend to look at careers in quick-service restaurants last, preferring to work for major fine-dining restaurants. But quick-service companies offer graduates a chance to assume positions of great responsibility quickly, and the pay is very good, due to their liberal bonus and incentive plans.

Lodging. Food service outlets in lodging operations range from gourmet restaurants to coffee shops and even quick-service outlets. Lodging food service sales are tremendous: Marriott Hotels and Resorts alone had food sales of $1.258 billion. Food sales for the top seven hotel chains totaled $5.856 billion.[3]

In recent years, hotels and motels have marketed their food service outlets more aggressively. According to Jean-Georges Vongerichten, an outstanding chef who operates hotel and free-standing restaurants in the United States, Europe, and Asia, "the expectations for a hotel restaurant are far superior to what they were ten years ago. This is true for both the United States and Europe."[4] Hotel food service can be a powerful marketing tool. The presence of the renowned Joël Robuchon in the New York Four Seasons Hotel suggests that the hotel itself is also a world-class facility.

Transportation. Travelers eat at highway stops; on airplanes, ships, and trains; at airport terminals and train stations; and at other facilities in the transportation market — a market that enjoys about $3.8 billion in sales each year.[5]

Cruise lines put a great deal of emphasis on their food service. Industry surveys cite the food served shipboard as one of the top reasons for taking a cruise and selecting a specific line. Royal Caribbean International's 142,000-ton *Voyager of the Seas* carries 3,114 passengers and a crew of 1,181; fully 30 percent of the crew works in the kitchen. Royal Caribbean has won numerous international awards for its food. Some of the other cruise lines contract their food and beverage service out to Apollo Ship Chandlers, an award-winning company cited for its outstanding food service by *Onboard Services Magazine, Condé Nast Traveler,* and *Porthole Cruise Magazine.*

Food service outlets in lodging operations range from gourmet restaurants to coffee shops and even quick-service outlets. This deli is one of four food and beverage outlets in the Renaissance Nashville, a convention hotel. (Courtesy of the Renaissance Nashville Hotel, Nashville, Tennessee.)

Food service in airports and train terminals is often provided by restaurants—frequently limited-menu restaurants—and contract food companies such as ARAMARK that bid for the opportunity to sell food in the terminals. Most airlines buy their in-flight meals from Gate Gourmet International and LSG Sky Chefs. Airport food service is changing as well. Airlines are now serving fewer in-flight meals. Increased security means that people get to airports earlier and stay longer, which gives them more time to eat and shop, including buying meals to take on board their planes.

Recreation and Sports. The recreation and sports market includes food service facilities located at sports arenas, stadiums, race tracks, movie theaters, bowling alleys, amusement parks, municipal convention centers, and other attractions. All together, this is a $27.3 billion market.[6] In many cases, recreational-market food service facilities are concessions run by contract food companies such as Centerplate and Sports Services, a division of Delaware North Companies.

The food served at recreational facilities varies greatly. For example, theme parks such as Walt Disney World sell everything from lollipops in kiosks to lobster tails in gourmet restaurants. Soldiers Field in Chicago, home of the Chicago Bears, has 200 food and beverage outlets scattered throughout the stadium. The stadium has 130 suites where food and drink is served, in addition to a dining room that is open on game days. At Busch Stadium in St. Louis, fans can watch chefs prepare fresh food in the facility's open-design kitchen. The concessionaire at both stadiums is SportsService.

Business and Industry. The business and industry market consists of non-food service businesses that offer on-site food service to their employees. Most businesses that provide employee meals use contract food companies such as Sodexo, ARAMARK, and the Compass Group. At the Bristol-Meyers Squibb facilities in New Jersey and Connecticut, Sodexo Corporate Services provides food service and other conveniences for 12,000 employees. There are a total of eight full-service employee dining rooms, two table-service restaurants, three bakery cafes, seven satellite cafes, four employee stores, two hair salons, and an e-store providing Internet service. In addition to substantial food items such as pizzas and roast beef sandwiches, employees have other options. Programs such as "Your Health Your Way" offer menu selections for various diets (low-fat, low-calorie, low-carbohydrate), while "World's Fare" provides choices from an international menu.

Contract food companies face increasing competition in the business and industry market from quick-service and limited-menu restaurants and are responding by entering into agreements with some of these companies to operate franchises.

Educational. The educational market includes schools that operate their own restaurants and schools that contract with food service companies to manage their food service. This more than $30.3 billion annual market is made up of food service in colleges, universities, and primary and secondary schools. One of the biggest changes in college food service programs has been the gradual shift from mandated meal plans to à la carte operations. Due in part to this shift, many college food service operators have become revenue producers instead of revenue consumers for their colleges.

Another change in college food service is the growing use of brands. Today's students grew up eating at branded restaurants and they expect to see these familiar brands at school. Brands such as Starbucks, Wendy's, and Subway, among others, are found on campuses across the country. At New York University, Chick-fil-A and Quiznos replaced other operations in response to student food preference surveys.

More than 29 million primary and secondary school students eat lunch at school each day. One company, Chartwells School Dining Services (a division of the Compass Group), manages the food service at 88 public schools in Oklahoma City. The challenge for Chartwells and other contract companies is to provide nutritional meals that are similar to the quick-service food that appeals to students.

Some school districts and universities still believe they can outdo contract food companies. For example, the Hillsborough County Public School system in Florida operates its own food service. Notre Dame's food service, once managed by a contract company, is now being run by the university for its more than 10,000 students.

Health Care. The health care market consists of three principal segments: hospitals and other medical centers, nursing homes, and retirement communities (including congregate food sites—community-sponsored meal centers for senior citizens).

Many experts believe that there is enormous potential for food service management companies in the health care market. This can be attributed to a combination of factors—rapidly changing lifestyles, an aging population, skyrocketing medical costs, restricted federal funds, and a lack of family support systems. Sodexo, ARAMARK, and Morrisons have over 2,000 health care accounts in North America and the United Kingdom. Each of these companies provides everything from bedside meals for patients to food service in staff and visitor dining rooms and cafeterias, some of which feature mall-style food courts with such well-known brands as Burger King, Wendy's, Starbucks, and Subway.

The health care food service market continues to grow. This facility is part of the University of Nebraska Medical Center. (Courtesy of Sodexo.)

Many health care facilities run their own food service departments, some of which can be quite extensive. One example is the Florida Hospital Medical Center, which serves as a community hospital for Orlando and as a major tertiary referral hospital for central Florida and much of the southeast United States, the Caribbean, and Latin America. It has a Nutritional Services Department that boasts impressive food service statistics. It serves seven hospitals, provides meals for 1,785 beds, serves 1.8 million meals each year, and grosses almost $12 million in retail food sales. Many hospitals operate vending machines, visitor coffee shops, employee cafeterias, special dining facilities for doctors, day-care food programs for employees' children, regular patient food programs, and special patient food programs that can include gourmet meals (with accompanying wines) served in patient rooms.

Retail. Two trends in food service worth noting are the tendency of Americans to eat food prepared outside the home, as evidenced by the steady growth in restaurant food sales, and the growth in the take-out and delivery segment of the market. It is clear that Americans are cooking less; it is also clear that there is a growing inclination to buy food prepared outside the home and bring it home to consume it. This last development is in line with marketing trends in other areas such as home electronics and furniture, where research has shown that, at an increasing rate, people use their homes as recreational and entertainment centers.

A good part of retail business take-out sales comes at the expense of traditional restaurants and quick-service outlets. This is due, among other reasons, to increased marketing by convenience stores and supermarkets of their prepared take-out foods.

Supermarkets are increasing the size and scope of their take-out-food operations. Some industry observers expect the average supermarket to increase in size from its present 30,000–50,000 square feet to 200,000 square feet (2,790–4,650 square meters to 18,600 square meters). Much of that space will be devoted to pre-cooked take-out dishes and sit-down food service areas. Many supermarkets already offer take-out salad bars in addition to their traditional deli sections. Using ovens in their bakeries, many of today's supermarkets are preparing a complete line of food products for their small in-store restaurants and cafeterias. Supermarket research shows that supermarket produce is perceived to be fresher than that sold in most restaurants. Some supermarkets are taking advantage of this perception by selling a wide range of freshly prepared salad and vegetable dishes. Some have hired chefs to work in open kitchens so that customers can actually see that dishes are prepared with fresh—not frozen—ingredients.

Another supermarket food service trend is the growth of food courts. Supermarket chains are installing food courts (similar to those found in shopping malls) in hopes of winning back some of the food dollars they have lost to restaurants.

Corrections Food Service. Correctional institutions—state and federal prisons and local jails—constitute another segment of the food service industry. Correctional institutions often have a hard time attracting and retaining food service staff because they cannot offer much professional career growth. However, the unique challenge they do offer can be attractive to some people. A prison must offer a **cyclical menu** that is not overly repetitive and has the flexibility to meet special religious and medical dietary needs, while still offering a bit of creativity in both preparation and presentation. Theft is another problem encountered by prison food service systems, so stringent controls must be used. Food costs are a further constraint on operations. Correctional institutions often have limited budgets for food service; economies of scale can thus make a substantial difference in the type and variety of food that can be offered to inmates.

Because they enjoy economies of scale, contract food companies are now successfully competing in this area. For example, ARAMARK, through its Correctional Services group, operates the food service at more than 500 correctional facilities in North America. Also, the company provides other support services such as laundry management and commissary services. ARAMARK's unique culinary training program, Inmate to Workmate, deals with preparing inmates for their transition to the community by offering skill training and classroom instruction in food production.

Military Food Service. Military food service is a very specialized area. Nevertheless, it deserves mention because of its diversity in terms of geography, type of facility, and size. Jobs in military food service range from space shuttle food preparation, to aircraft carrier or nuclear submarine mess operations, to Army, Navy, Air Force, Marine, and Coast Guard officers' club management at bases all over the world. Both civilian and military personnel are employed by many of these facilities.

Contractors. Contract food management companies are the major operators of noncommercial food service. The largest are Compass Group, ARAMARK, and Sodexo (see Exhibit 5). Contract food management companies are hired to operate restaurants and other

Exhibit 5	Top Contract Food Management Companies	
Rank	**Chain**	**Gross Revenue (in millions)**
1	Compass Group Americas Division	$9,000
2	ARAMARK Corp.	8,925
3	Sodexo, Inc.	7,700
4	Delaware North Companies	2,200
5	Centerplate	793
6	Guest Services, Inc.	334
7	AVI Food Systems	320
8	Guckenheimer Enterprises, Inc.	300
9	Thompson Hospitality Services	270

Source: Adapted from Mike Buzalka, "FM Top 50 Management Companies," www.food-management.com, September 2009. You can visit www.food-management.com to search for the latest industry statistics.

food service outlets in convention centers, sports arenas, tourist attractions, colleges and schools, office buildings, manufacturing plants, and health care facilities. Contractors are hired by businesses and other clients that want to provide food service to patrons and/or employees, yet do not want to get involved in an activity (preparing and serving food) that is outside their expertise. Unlike free-standing, single-concept restaurants, many contract locations have multiple restaurant concepts. For example, at a corporate headquarters, the food service might consist of an upscale cafeteria, a quick-service outlet, a tableservice restaurant, and banquet facilities.

Contract food management companies offer numerous careers in restaurant management. Many contractors recruit on college campuses.

In addition to food service, some contract food management companies provide housekeeping, grounds maintenance, laundry, and other services for their clients. This diversification has enhanced management opportunities in the field. For example, a college food service manager may be offered a higher salary to accept the added responsibility of managing the housekeeping department in the building in which the food service outlet is located.

Starting a New Restaurant

Many students dream of owning their own restaurant someday. To be sure, huge fortunes have been made in the restaurant business. The entire Marriott empire grew from a single Hot Shoppe Restaurant opened in 1927 in Washington, D.C., by J. Willard Marriott, a 27-year-old sheep herder from Salt Lake City, Utah. America's largest grossing independent restaurant, the Tavern on the Green in Manhattan, was the creation of Warner LeRoy, whose father, Mervyn LeRoy, produced the movie *The Wizard of Oz*. Warner LeRoy made his fortune by understanding the meaning of showmanship in the restaurant business—his employees often referred to him as a "food impresario." Norman Brinker, creator of many casual dining restaurants, started out as a busperson and went on to create Chili's and other successful restaurant chains.

The restaurant business is one of the easiest businesses to enter. Novices see few barriers — comparatively little capital and virtually no experience are needed. Used commercial ovens, stoves, and other fixtures are readily available. Almost any location will do — they think — and no special skills or technology are required. Most of the labor can be obtained at minimum wage. Anyone can cook, right?

Staying in business is the real challenge. Being a good cook, a popular host, and a creative promoter are not enough when it comes to running a successful restaurant. Because the business is far more complicated than it appears, those who study the industry at colleges or universities have a much better chance of succeeding. Without business knowledge, prospects can be bleak. Professors at Cornell and Michigan State studied restaurant failures and found that 57 percent of surveyed restaurants failed within three years; 70 percent closed their doors after ten years.[7] Actual figures may be even higher, since many restaurants simply close their doors when they have exhausted their capital and become unrecorded failures.

Why Do Restaurants Fail?

There are several reasons why so many restaurants fail every year:

- *Lack of business knowledge.* The first and most important reason restaurants fail is due to an operator's simple lack of business knowledge. Successful restaurant operators have a working knowledge of marketing, accounting, finance, law, engineering, and human resources. Knowing and loving food is not enough to operate a thriving food service operation. Tim and Nina Zagat, the creators of the ZAGAT guides and surveys that rate restaurants in a number of cities, observed in the *Wall Street Journal* that "a good restaurateur must exhibit unerring real estate instinct, a grasp of financial controls, a flair for interior design, and a sense of popular trends. He needs to be adept at hospitality, publicity, and procurement."[8]

- *Lack of technical knowledge.* The second reason for failure is an operator's lack of technical knowledge. Attorneys, accountants, movie stars, and sports figures have all tried the restaurant business. In general, those who have succeeded either invested capital or simply lent their names to the enterprise in return for a share of the profits; they left the planning and operating to professional restaurateurs. Successful restaurant operators must understand site selection, menu planning, recipe development, purchasing, production techniques, and sophisticated service procedures that make it possible to deliver a consistent and reliable experience that meets guest expectations.

- *Lack of sufficient working capital.* A third reason for restaurant failure is a lack of sufficient working capital. In the restaurant business, where word-of- mouth recommendations are so important, it takes time to develop a solid guest base. New restaurants usually lose money for a while. Many new operators badly underestimate the amount of capital they will need (to pay for food, labor, and fixed operating expenses) until they reach the break-even point, which can be six months to a year down the road — or never.

Industry Innovators

Thomas Keller
Chef, Restaurant Owner

Every once in a while a new chef bursts on the scene who captures the imagination of the entire restaurant industry worldwide. Thomas Keller is one of those people. His restaurant, The French Laundry, has been named the best restaurant in the world by *Restaurant Magazine. Bon Appetit, Esquire, Gourmet,* and *Zagat* have all named it the best restaurant in America. *Time* has picked him as America's best chef. Located in Yountville, California, in the Napa Valley, The French Laundry has five stars from the *Mobil Travel Guide.* Another restaurant of Keller's, Per Se (in the Time Warner Center in New York City), has three Michelin stars—the only restaurant in all of Manhattan with that ranking.

Keller was born at Camp Pendleton, Oceanside, California, in 1955, the son of a Marine drill instructor. Eventually the family settled in Palm Beach, Florida, where Keller spent his teenage years.

In an interview at Powell's bookstore in San Francisco, Keller talked about his education as a chef: "I have no formal culinary training. My mother ran a restaurant and said, 'Do you want to be a chef?' I said yes. She said, 'Here you go, you're the chef. Now learn how to cook.'"

In his cookbook, *The French Laundry Cookbook,* Keller explains his philosophy. "When you acknowledge, as you must, that there is no such thing as perfect food, only the idea of it, then the real purpose of striving toward perfection becomes clear: to make people happy. That's what cooking is all about. But to give pleasure, you have to take pleasure yourself. For me it's in the satisfaction of cooking every day—culling salmon, or portioning foie gras—the mechanical jobs I do daily, year after year. This is the great challenge: to maintain passion for the everyday routine and the endlessly repeated act, to derive deep satisfaction from the mundane."

Keller clearly is a perfectionist. He tells his readers, "Cooking is not about convenience and it's not about shortcuts. The recipes in this book are all about wanting to take time to do something priceless. Our hunger for the twenty-minute gourmet meal, for one-pot ease, and pre-washed, precut ingredients has severed our lifeline to the satisfactions of cooking. Take your time. Take a long time."

So what does Keller do at the French Laundry that is so innovative? To begin with, his cooking is characterized by small portions served slowly over a long period of time. Some diners finish their meals in two and a half hours, others take four. Keller offers a nine- (or more!) course meal served in very small portions. Typical dishes include Pearls and Oyster (glistening caviar and oysters on a bed of creamy tapioca), Warm Fruitwood-Smoked Salmon with Potato Gnocchi and Balsamic Glaze, or Braised Stuffed Pig's Head. Tongue-in-cheek recipe names like "Macaroni and Cheese" (a.k.a. Butter-Poached Maine Lobster with Creamy Lobster Broth and Mascarpone-Enriched Orzo) and "Banana Split" (actually, Poached Banana Ice Cream with White Chocolate-Banana Crepes and Chocolate Sauce) belie the complexity of the dishes.

(continued)

Industry Innovators *(continued)*

"Where do I want you to be after you've eaten something? I want you to be thinking, 'God, I wish I had a little more of that.' Your memory of that taste is excellent. Also, it's more healthy—in the Japanese way—to extend the meal for a longer period of time. It helps your body digest the food, instead of packing your body with so much food that you're uncomfortable for hours afterward. This way you're able to taste better and you know when you've had enough."

Another thing Keller wants you to be thinking is that the $210 bill per person (including service) is worth every penny. The fact that the restaurant is typically booked three or four months in advance is all the proof that is needed that it is.

Source: Adapted from Thomas Keller, *The French Laundry Cookbook* (New York: Atrium Books, 1999).

Building a Successful Restaurant

Let's assume that you have enough business knowledge, technical knowledge, and capital to start a restaurant and keep it going until you reach the break-even point. What's the first step? How do you decide what kind of restaurant it should be and where it should be located?

Many would-be restaurateurs approach this issue by first deciding what kind of restaurant they would like to have and then picking a location they're comfortable with. You might want to operate an Italian restaurant in the neighborhood where you live, for example. You may then decide to negotiate a lease in a nearby shopping center where some space is available, come up with a name, and hire a contractor to "build out"—do the interior construction needed to add finishing touches to the restaurant, such as Roman columns, trellises from which grapes can be hung, or other details suggesting an Italian setting.

While this approach might succeed, modern management theory suggests that this is putting the proverbial cart before the horse. In the above scenario, you decided on the restaurant's concept and location without any regard for who your guests are likely to be or who your competitors are. The big chain restaurants and franchisors have a different approach. Their focus is more on marketing—they have already decided who their customers are going to be (families with children, for example) and their task now becomes one of finding and serving them. Fred Turner, former president of McDonald's, was quoted as saying, "We lead the industry because we follow the customers."[9] Part of what makes McDonald's successful is that its product and service concepts are developed in response to customer and potential customer input. For example, McDonald's started serving breakfast not to keep stores open longer—although that was a consideration—but because it recognized customer demand for earlier hours and breakfast items.

The Concept. Before selecting a concept for your restaurant, you should first ask yourself:

* Who are the people I hope to attract? Are they families, businesspeople, tourists, or other guest groups?

* What guest needs am I trying to satisfy? Do these people want fast-food or fine dining?

Before selecting a concept for your restaurant, you should first ask yourself questions such as "Who are the people I hope to attract? What guest needs am I trying to satisfy?" (The Radisson Aruba; photo courtesy of Carlson Hospitality Worldwide.)

- Where do these people live and work? Are they located near my proposed location?

- When do they buy? Do they eat out at lunch and dinner, or only at dinner? What are their peak days and hours for dining out?

- How do they buy? Do they dine in, take out, or want delivery?

- How much competition is there now and is there likely to be in the near future?

- What are the current competitors' menus, prices, and hours of operation?

Only after you have addressed all of these questions are you ready to develop a concept. The concept consists not only of the products and services your proposed restaurant will offer, but also the manner in which you will present them. The restaurant's name, atmosphere, location, and menu prices are all elements of the concept. In other words, the concept is the physical embodiment of the answers to the questions you have just asked. It is your idea of a restaurant that will attract the customers you have targeted.

How do you arrive at a concept? A new restaurant's concept can come from an existing concept—as when a restaurant chain expands—or from individuals who create fresh concepts, usually after considering the questions posed above. In either case, the foundation of the concept is the menu. Will it be ethnic, regional American, eclectic, traditional, or limited? One way to address this question is to study market trends in terms of the popularity of various menu items. Much of this information is available in trade media research (e.g., magazines such as *Restaurants & Institutions* and *Nation's Restaurant News)* as well as from trade associations like the National Restaurant Association.

Once you've decided on the menu, you can put many other aspects of the concept into place—decor, number of seats, type of service, hours of operation, pricing structure, and, finally, the investment required.

You may modify the final investment figure several times in the course of creating your restaurant. To begin with, market research is likely to influence some of the elements of the concept; remember that the focus must be on the potential guests' needs and preferences. Resource limitations may pose another constraint. Most restaurateurs do not have unlimited funds. Even large restaurant chains are concerned with how long it will take a new restaurant to break even and make a profit. This means that the amount of capital available for investment may be established early on, and that amount, in turn, may affect many elements of the concept (some elements may have to be scaled back if investment capital is lacking, for example).

Site Selection. Another important decision you must make about your proposed restaurant is its location. A restaurant site can be an undeveloped lot where a new building must be constructed, or a lot with an existing restaurant (or a building that can be converted). Of course, there is no such thing as a universally ideal restaurant site. Some restaurants should be in areas where there is a substantial amount of foot traffic; others should be near a busy highway intersection. Many fast-food or quick-service restaurants consider their primary, secondary, and tertiary markets to be within a one-, two-, and three-mile radius, respectively. On the other hand, table-service restaurants regard these markets to be within a one-, three-, and five-mile radius. Still others rely on neighborhoods with certain predetermined characteristics, such as a minimum number of households within a certain radius or a minimum average household income. In any case, a restaurant's site has a tremendous influence on its success.

Expanding restaurant chains like Chili's Grill & Bar and Olive Garden provide examples of how site selection works. Most chains start by selecting cities or metropolitan areas with a certain-size population that has an average disposable income within a certain range. For instance, one chain's criterion might be "to locate our new restaurants in cities of more than 250,000 people, where the average annual household income is $30,000 or more." If you want to open a Denny's franchise, they require a minimum of 40,000 permanent population and a median household income of $32,000–$50,000 within their trade area. Often, rather than thinking in terms of cities or metropolitan areas, sites are selected in specific **areas of dominant influence (ADI).** ADIs describe areas covered by major television station signals, as measured by Arbitron, a national TV rating service. By selecting a site in this manner, a chain knows in advance that it will be able to advertise economically using television.

Restaurant sites often fall into one of four areas:

- *Central-city business and shopping districts.* These are near office buildings, down-town department stores, or major commercial hotels.

- *Shopping centers.* Modern shopping centers provide a central focus in suburban communities. City government offices, churches, recreational facilities such as movie theaters and fitness centers, and restaurants usually are in or near shopping centers.

- *Planned communities.* Planned communities can be large suburban developments or urban renewal projects.

- *Highway intersections.*

Usually, large restaurant chains carefully analyze market data in new locations, to match potential guest profiles with chain standards. Outback Steakhouse used to focus on establishing sites in residential neighborhoods, where it thought its dinner-only concept would find the most patrons. While it hasn't abandoned those areas, Outback has discovered other successful sites for its restaurants. These include expressway interchanges, shopping malls, and hotel districts that are some distance from suburban communities. With prime real estate becoming harder to find, Outback is also building restaurants in secondary locations and expanding its sign program.[10]

A good site possesses certain specific characteristics. First, the site must be easily visible. If the proposed site is situated off a highway, it should be near a clearly marked or well-known exit. It should also be possible to put up a sign that can be seen far enough in advance from either direction so that a driver can slow down and exit safely. If the restaurant is in a major shopping complex, the site should not be off in a corner where no one will see it. It should be visible from the parking lot, where shoppers entering the mall or movie theater are bound to notice it.

Second, a good site is easily accessible. Some otherwise favorable sites are rejected because they are hard to find or are on side streets or one-way streets that are inconvenient for customers. Moreover, the restaurant must be accessible to the market it intends to serve. Depending on the type of restaurant, "accessible" can range from a few minutes' walk to a one-hour drive. Restaurants that serve upscale markets or have unique themes may have a large geographic range, while limited-menu or quick-service restaurants tend to serve markets no more than five square miles (13 square kilometers) in size.

The third consideration is parking. There must be sufficient spaces on-site for peak periods, unless valet parking off-site is provided to accommodate busy times.

The fourth consideration is availability. Can the property be rented or purchased? When? Are there any zoning restrictions?

A fifth factor to consider is affordability. An undeveloped lot may require extensive and costly site preparation. Are power and other utilities readily available or must they be brought in? What are the terms of the purchase? If you are buying a building on the lot, is the seller willing to help with the financing? Are the taxes reasonable? Can the building be leased? Will the landlord pay for remodeling costs and other improvements, or must you? Since under-capitalization is a major cause of restaurant failure, you must be careful not to commit yourself to higher rent or remodeling costs than you can afford. You should be conservative when deciding what you can afford, because business may not go as well as you expect.

The feasibility study. After finding a possible site, restaurateurs usually have a **feasibility study** done. These studies are similar to the feasibility studies that are done for new hotels. The major difference is that the demand for hotel rooms is usually generated by travelers or others coming from outside a hotel's immediate area, while the demand for restaurants is mostly local. Therefore, local market characteristics are more important for restaurants. Feasibility studies help a restaurateur decide if a particular location is right and if a restaurant has a good chance of success.

In addition to data on local population characteristics, a good deal more information is available from many sources. The National Restaurant Association (www.restaurant. org) publishes a number of studies that provide data for feasibility analysts, such as:

- Restaurant Spending Report

- Tableservice and Quickservice Restaurant Trends

- Restaurant Industry Forecast

- Restaurant Performance Index

- Restaurant Trendmapper

- Employment by State

The Bureau of Labor Statistics publishes an annual Consumer Expenditure Survey based on consumer interviews and purchase diaries. This survey is available from the Government Printing Office in Washington, D.C. Using the Consumer Expenditure Survey and data collected from specific zip codes and other sources, several other research services can report exactly how often and which meals people in those zip codes eat out, what they like to eat, and how much they spend. A computer database called PRIZM, available through the Claritas Corporation, provides demographic and lifestyle information for the entire United States by zip code.

As you can see, feasibility study writers can draw from many sources to produce qualitative and quantitative analyses of proposed restaurant operations. A feasibility study can identify possible guest markets for a proposed restaurant, evaluate the proposed site, and analyze the financial prospects of the restaurant.

The financial analysis portion of the study also contains a capital investment budget. The purpose of a capital investment budget is to make certain that enough capital will be available for the following items:

- Land and construction costs (or extended lease costs on an existing building)

- Equipment

- Furniture and fixtures

- Working capital

- Pre-opening expenses for inventory

- Pre-opening staff salaries and training expenses

- Pre-opening advertising and promotion

Finally, the study should contain a proposed operating budget for the restaurant's first three years. Without this information, it's impossible to tell when the proposed restaurant will make money. The budget lets investors and managers know how much cash will be required to meet initial expenses until the restaurant makes a profit. The budget may reveal that the restaurant, as conceived, will never make money, and therefore adjustments must be made.

"Greening" the Restaurant

In 1971, Alice Waters opened Chez Panisse in Berkley, California, serving organically grown food in season from the local area. She became an activist for what is known now as the sustainable food movement, and many consider Chez Panisse the beginning of the "green" movement in the hospitality industry. In recent years this socially responsible movement has caught on with the public and with business owners who recognize the fragility of the world's finite resources and the need for conservation and the promotion of health. Besides, many green initiatives are just plain good business sense, such as curbing energy consumption; lower energy consumption means reduced operating costs. Restaurants are major consumers of resources. Each year the average restaurant uses 800,000 gallons of water, 500,000 kilowatt hours of electricity, and generates 100,000 pounds of garbage.[11]

A National Restaurant Association consumer survey revealed that "sixty percent of adults say they are more likely to visit a restaurant that offers food that was grown in an organic or environmentally friendly way."[12] Approximately 41 million consumers follow the principles of Lifestyles of Health and Sustainability (LOHAS).[13] In the United States, the market for goods and services that are sustainable and environmentally sound is more than $200 billion. Reducing consumption and serving healthy sustainable food is environmentally responsible and good business practice.

"Greening" a restaurant is not an easy task, and what constitutes a green restaurant is evolving. However, the Green Restaurant Association has established a certification program for both existing and new restaurants. Seven categories are evaluated, with points assigned for each category. An existing restaurant can achieve a total of 100 to 470 points to be certified; four stars are awarded to restaurants achieving the maximum number of points, two stars for 100 points. The program does allow for improvement. For example, if a dishwasher is replaced with a more environmentally efficient one that uses less water and energy, additional points would be granted and the certification upgraded.

Using fresh fruits and vegetables organically grown in the local area is a hallmark of many "green" restaurants.

Seven Principles of Sustainable Food

According to London-based Sustain, the alliance for better food and farming, people and businesses adopting a sustainable approach to food should:

1. Use local, seasonally available ingredients as standard, to minimize energy used in food production, transport, and storage.
2. Specify food from farming systems that minimize harm to the environment, such as certified organic produce.
3. Limit foods of animal origin (meat, dairy products, and eggs) served, as livestock farming is one of the most significant contributors to climate change, and promote meals rich in fruit, vegetables, whole grains, and nuts. Ensure that meat, dairy products, and eggs are produced to high environmental and animal welfare standards.
4. Exclude fish species identified as most "at risk" by the Marine Conservation Society, and choose fish only from sustainable sources—such as those accredited by the Marine Stewardship Council.
5. Choose Fair Trade Federation–certified products for foods and drinks imported from poorer countries, to ensure a fair deal for disadvantaged producers.
6. Avoid bottled water and instead serve plain or filtered tap water in reusable jugs or bottles, to minimize transport and packaging waste.
7. Promote health and well-being by cooking with generous portions of vegetables, fruit, and starchy staples like whole grains; cutting down on salt, fats, and oils; and cutting out artificial additives.

Source: www.sustainweb.org/sustainablefood.

Here are the seven point categories for green restaurant certification:

1. Water Efficiency
2. Waste Reduction and Recycling
3. Sustainable Furnishings and Building Materials
4. Sustainable Food
5. Energy
6. Disposables
7. Chemical and Pollution Reduction[14]

The Microsoft headquarters in Redmond, Washington, was the first corporate dining facility to receive the Green Restaurant Association's Certified Green Restaurant status. Since it was an existing facility serving 24,000 meals daily, construction and equipment changes were necessary. Its "green" initiatives include a composting and recycling program, the elimination of all Styrofoam containers, and conversion of grease and oil from the kitchens into biodiesel fuel.

The National Restaurant Association's Conserve program to educate restaurant owners and operators and encourage them to be more environmentally responsible is delivered through its conserve.restaurant.org website. In addition to tips on recycling, water and energy conservation, and "green" construction, the site has a "virtual restaurant" that you can tour for hints on how to make specific restaurant areas "greener."

What this all adds up to is that if you are considering starting a new restaurant, you must also take today's "green revolution" into consideration.

Summary

Food service is a huge industry. Career opportunities abound throughout the various industry segments, which include eating and drinking places; lodging operations; transportation, recreational, business and industry, educational, health care, and retail markets; corrections and military food service; and contract food management companies. Eating and drinking places constitute the largest segment of the restaurant industry. This segment includes full-service restaurants, quick-service restaurants, commercial cafeterias, social caterers, ice cream and frozen custard stands, and bars and taverns.

Over 88 percent of sales from the eating-and-drinking-places segment are from full-service and quick-service restaurants. Consequently, these restaurants offer the most opportunities for hospitality students. Full-service restaurants are generally categorized in terms of price, menu, or atmosphere. The distinguishing features of quick-service restaurants are that they offer a narrow selection of food, provide limited service, and focus on speed of preparation and delivery.

Compared to other industries, the restaurant industry offers unmatched opportunities for entrepreneurship. Restaurant entrepreneurs have followed various paths to success. Some have created entire restaurant chains; others have nourished a single restaurant to perfection. However, success is far from guaranteed: approximately 70 percent of new restaurants that open in a given year will be out of business within ten. Restaurants often fail because their operators lack business and technical knowledge, or because there is insufficient working capital.

Successful restaurateurs start by focusing on the needs and preferences of their potential guests. Then they develop a restaurant concept. Next, they select a site. During the site-selection process, a feasibility study is done to analyze the local market. Such studies typically include a financial analysis and capital investment budget.

Today's restaurant operators and patrons are showing increasing interest in environmental issues. The non-profit Green Restaurant Association has established a seven-category certification program for "green" restaurants. Through its Conserve program, the National Restaurant Association provides guidelines for recycling, water and energy conservation, and green construction standards. If you are considering starting a new restaurant, you must take the "green revolution" into consideration.

Endnotes

1. Unless otherwise noted, the statistics quoted in this and the following paragraph are from the 2009 National Restaurant Association's website at www.restaurant.org. Please visit this site for the latest statistics.

2. *2009 Restaurant Industry Forecast,* National Restaurant Association, pp. 16–18.

3. *Nation's Restaurant News,* June 29, 2009, p. 68.

4. Mary Scoviak-Lerner, "Great Hotel Restaurants," *Hotels,* August 2000.

5. *2009 Restaurant Industry Forecast* (Washington, D.C.: National Restaurant Association, 2009).

6. Ibid.

7. *Nation's Restaurant News,* November 10, 2003, p. 25.

8. *Wall Street Journal,* November–December, 2000.

9. Ron Zemke and Dick Schaaf, *The Service Edge* (New York: New American Library, 1989), p. 297.

10. Deborah Silver, "Site Seeing," *Restaurants & Institutions,* January 15, 2000.

11. www.usatoday.com (5/19/2008).

12. National Restaurant Association, Consumer Survey, 2008.

13. www.lohas.com.

14. www.dinegreen/restaurants/standards.asp, the Green Restaurant Association. See this website for more details concerning the point system.

 Key Terms

areas of dominant influence (ADI)—A term used in the television industry to describe areas covered by the signals of major television stations as measured by Arbitron, a national TV rating service.

casual restaurant—A restaurant distinguishable by a combination of decor, informal atmosphere, and eclectic menu that draws from ethnic and traditional offerings.

cyclical menu—A menu that changes every day for a certain number of days, then repeats the cycle. A few cycle menus change regularly but without any set pattern. Also known as a cycle menu.

ethnic restaurant—A restaurant featuring a particular cuisine, such as Chinese, Italian, or Mexican.

family restaurant—A restaurant that caters to families—with an emphasis on satisfying the needs of children—that serves breakfast, lunch, and dinner, offering traditional menu items.

feasibility study—A study commissioned by developers and prepared by consultants that seeks to determine the potential success of a proposed business on a proposed site.

fine-dining restaurant—A restaurant that features luxury dining and an exciting menu (not necessarily French or haute cuisine, however), and employs well-trained, creative chefs and skilled food servers. Fine-dining restaurants are generally small and independently operated, with more employees per guest than other types of restaurants.

full-service restaurant—A restaurant that (1) has more than a dozen or so main-course items on the menu, and (2) cooks to order.

fusion cuisine—A style of cooking in which chefs take ingredients or techniques from more than one cuisine and create new dishes with the results.

quick-service restaurant—A restaurant that focuses on convenience, offers a narrow selection of food, and provides limited service and speedy preparation.

Review Questions

1. What segments constitute the restaurant industry?

2. What characterizes a full-service restaurant? a quick-service restaurant?

3. What are some characteristics of the transportation, recreational, business and industry, educational, health care, and retail food service markets?

4. What are some of the challenges that are unique to corrections food service?

5. What are three common reasons for restaurant failure?

6. What are some strategies for building a successful restaurant?

7. What four general urban areas make good sites for restaurants?

8. What are some desirable characteristics any restaurant site should have?

9. What are some components of a feasibility study for a new restaurant?

Internet Sites

For more information, visit the following Internet sites. Remember that Internet addresses can change without notice. If the site is no longer there, you can use a search engine to look for additional sites.

Associations

American Hotel & Lodging Association
www.ahla.com

National Restaurant Association
www.restaurant.org

Publications and Other Resources

Claritas Corporation
www.claritas.com

LSG Sky Chefs
www.lsg-skychefs.com

Culinary Institute of America
www.ciachef.edu/

Nation's Restaurant News
www.nrn.com

Gate Gourmet International
www.gategourmet.ch

Restaurants & Institutions
www.rimag.com

Johnson & Wales University
www.jwu.edu

Zagat
www.zagat.com

Restaurants and Other Food Service Companies

ApolloShipChandlers, Inc.
www.apolloships.com

ARAMARK Corporation
www.aramark.com

Applebee's Neighborhood Grill & Bar
www.applebees.com

Canyon Ranch Health Resorts
www.canyonranch.com

Centerplate
www.centerplate.com

Chili's Grill & Bar
www.chilis.com

Compass Group
www.compass-group.com

Cracker Barrel Old Country Store
www.crackerbarrel.com

Delaware North Companies
www.delawarenorth.com

Domino's Pizza, Inc.
www.dominos.com

Ed Debevic's Restaurants
www.eddebevics.com

KFC Corporation
www.kfc.com

McDonald's
www.mcdonalds.com

Metromedia Restaurant Group
www.metromediarestaurants.com

Olive Garden
www.olivegarden.com

Outback Steakhouse
www.outbacksteakhouse.com

Pizza Hut
www.pizzahut.com

Rainforest Café
www.rainforestcafe.com

Red Lobster Restaurants
www.redlobster.com

Romano's Macaroni Grill
www.macaronigrill.com

Sodexo
www.Sodexousa.com

Spaghetti Warehouse
www.meatballs.com

Steak and Ale
www.steakale.com

Taco Bell
www.tacobell.com

T.G.I. Friday's
www.tgifridays.com

Wendy's
www.wendys.com

5
Restaurant Organization and Management

<table>
<tr>
<td>

Outline

Organizing for Success
   Guests
   Ambience
   Menu
Restaurant Controls
   Financial Controls
   Operational Controls
Summary

</td>
<td>

Competencies

1. Describe the importance of guest information and restaurant ambience to a restaurant's success, and summarize rules for creating menus. (pp. 112–119)

2. Give examples of guest menu preferences in different parts of the United States and the rest of the world, describe menu categories, and summarize the importance of menu design and menu pricing. (pp. 119–125)

3. Summarize the impact of computers and the Internet on restaurant controls; identify methods of financial and operational control; list the control points of the food cost control cycle; and describe the menu planning, forecasting, purchasing, receiving, storing, and issuing control points of the cycle. (pp. 125–135)

4. Describe the producing, serving, and customer payment control points of the food cost control cycle, outline methods of food cost analysis, and explain how managers can control labor and beverage costs. (pp. 135–141)

</td>
</tr>
</table>

Opposite page: The Sonesta Beach Resort Taba; photo courtesy of Sonesta International Hotel Corporation.

I N THIS CHAPTER WE WILL FOCUS first on organizing a restaurant for success. We will discuss the importance of guests, ambience, and menus. Then we will describe financial and operational controls for restaurants, including accounting systems, budgeting, menu planning, forecasting, purchasing, receiving and storing, issuing, producing, serving, customer payment, food cost analysis procedures, and computerized point-of-sale systems. We will briefly consider labor costs, then conclude the chapter with a discussion of beverage control.

Organizing for Success

Restaurant managers must have a broad base of skills to run a restaurant successfully. These include marketing skills (to bring guests in) and quality control and service skills (to satisfy guests so they will want to return). Of course, having guests does not guarantee a profit; restaurants have gone bankrupt even when running at capacity every night. Often, the difference between successful and unsuccessful food service operations is that the successful ones are organized. Managers of well-organized restaurants are able to budget and control expenses so that they maximize profits. Even the success of managers of nonprofit or subsidized operations, such as school food programs, is measured in financial terms—by their ability to control expenses and operate within their budget limitations.

All types of food service operations have the same mission—to prepare and serve food while staying within financial guidelines. Because their mission is the same, they all operate under similar principles of management and control.

Three elements crucial to the success of any restaurant are its guests, ambience, and menu.

Guests

Everything starts with the guest or customer. Finding and holding on to this elusive creature is the most important factor in the success of any business. Once you understand where guests will come from and what needs they will have, you can determine the feasibility and optimal location of any new food service operation. But a thorough knowledge of guests tells us a good deal more than simply where to put the restaurant. Guests' wants and needs guide new restaurateurs in formulating menus, determining ambience, setting the level and style of service, and creating advertising and marketing plans.

The marketing research that goes into a feasibility study for a new restaurant is only the beginning. Guest research must be updated continually, because we live in a dynamic society where markets change quickly. Continual research makes it possible not only to measure current guest preferences but to discover trends—how those preferences are changing and how fast.

Restaurants with long, successful track records and loyal guests have sometimes lost their guests' allegiance virtually overnight. According to management consultants Albrecht and Zemke, guest loyalty "must be based on a continuously satisfying level of service."[1]

The key word is "continuously." It is not hard to find examples of restaurants that lost touch with their guests and either failed or fell under the control of new companies with new concepts. For example, Sambo's, a limited-menu chain popular for many years, derived its name and decor from the children's story "Little Black Sambo." The civil rights movement focused attention on the racial aspects of Sambo's concept, and the chain died a painful death. The Royal Castle hamburger chain started during the Depression, offering 24-hour service and five-cent hamburgers. Over the years, the units became too small, old-fashioned, and limited in their menu choices. Soon the land on which the 175 restaurants rested was worth more than the company, and the company was liquidated. Then there was the Victoria Station restaurant chain. It had an attractive concept—restaurants in the form of a cluster of railroad cars that served extraordinarily good roast beef and generous drinks at reasonable prices. But beef consumption began to decrease and the restaurant's concept became less popular. The owners tried many new concepts, one after the other, leaving customers guessing about what they might find on their next visit. Eventually, most customers went elsewhere.

Guest attitudes and desires change constantly. At the moment, casual-dining restaurants are popular segments of commercial restaurants. This segment is loosely defined as restaurants where patrons can dine for about $15, and includes such popular chains as Applebee's, Chili's, Olive Garden, and The Cheesecake Factory. In response to consumer attitudes, The Cheesecake Factory has introduced an entirely trans-fat-free menu and is offering "weight management salads" throughout the day. On the other hand, Red Lobster, a Darden restaurant, has continued its successful "Endless Shrimp" promotion that offers all the shrimp you can eat.

Dining out, it seems, has become more routine than occasional, and, for many, the tried-and-true Big Mac or Whopper with fries doesn't cut it anymore. Many people see dining out as an affordable indulgence.[2] The National Restaurant Association reports that 45 percent of adults say restaurants are an essential part of their lifestyle. There are 945,000 restaurant locations in the United States, and that number is growing.[3]

Smoking in restaurants is a good example of how consumer preferences have changed over the years. Twenty years ago, every restaurant offered ash trays on every table. By the end of the 1980s, surveys showed that more than three-quarters of guests wanted separate smoking and no-smoking restaurants. Several states have banned all smoking in all restaurants. McDonald's has implemented 100 percent no-smoking policies in all of its company-owned units in the United States and has urged its franchisees to do the same.

Nutrition awareness has dramatically changed the way guests view menus. Freshness has become an important attribute for menu items, partly because it denotes a more nutritious and therefore healthier product. Restaurant analysts have seen a continuing escalation in the demand for fresh-baked breads and pastries. There has also been an increase in the popularity of fruit and vegetable menu offerings.

However, whether a trend appears to be taking hold or an old one losing ground is not a reason in itself to make dramatic changes in methods of operation. Few trends are universal. Different regions of the country and different countries have their own values; what is true in California may be less true or not true at all in Vermont. Therefore, restaurateurs should use national surveys and studies only as guides. Whether they apply to your city and your restaurant can only be determined by asking your guests.

Ambience

In successful food service operations, all types of elements play a role. The decor, lighting, furnishings, tableware, menu, service methods and personalities of the servers, and even the guests all combine to create a feeling about or an identity for a restaurant—that is, they create the restaurant's atmosphere or mood, its **ambience.** Ambience often leads guests to choose one restaurant over another. For some patrons, a restaurant's ambience may be as important as the food, or even more important.

The menu is an important element in setting the overall ambience of a restaurant. The artwork on Carrabba's menu cover, a fine-dining scene in the Italian countryside, reflects Carrabba's goal of serving authentic Italian food and giving guests an upscale version of the casual-dining experience.

Freshness is an important attribute for menu items. Here Executive Chef John Cordeaux tends to his herb garden on the roof of The Fairmont Royal York in Toronto, Canada. (Courtesy of Fairmont Hotels & Resorts.)

A restaurant's ambience can even enhance how its food tastes to guests. One reason restaurateurs like to locate seafood restaurants next to the water is that there is a suggestion that the fish they serve are fresh. The restaurants in the Fuddruckers hamburger chain feature a glass-enclosed refrigerated room where fresh sides of beef hang; customers can view the beef while they stand in line for their hamburgers. This reinforces Fuddruckers' claim that its hamburgers are fresh and made on the premises, and may help convince customers that Fuddruckers' hamburgers taste better than those made from frozen hamburger patties.

A legendary industry story about designing a restaurant's ambience to satisfy the clientele comes from the early days of McDonald's. Founder Ray Kroc decided to concentrate on reaching families with young children. Why? Research showed that this was a large and growing market segment. The research also showed that the children often cast the deciding vote on which restaurant a family visited. With that in mind, Kroc and his associates designed a restaurant that not only served food children would like, but served it in a setting that small children would feel comfortable in. Kroc ordered cameras mounted on three-foot-high tripods to photograph a prototype McDonald's restaurant. Looking at the restaurant through the eyes of a child made the necessity for some changes immediately evident. Counters, for example, were lowered so a child could order without having to strain or stand on tiptoe. Seats and tables were also lowered. The interior was accented with bright yellow and red—the same colors used on many toys at the time.

REISINGER
Zagreb
CROATIA

Cartoonists & Writers Syndicate

"One more mackerel and two more calamari."

Source: Cartoon by Resinger, appearing in Zagreb, Croatia; Cartoonists & Writers Syndicate, New York, New York.

Benihana is another restaurant chain that owes much of its success to ambience. Japanese immigrant Rocky Aoki, the chain's founder, was a stickler for authentic detail. Not only did he train his chefs at a special school in Tokyo before bringing them to the United States, he imported wooden beams from Japan at great expense to create the atmosphere of an authentic Japanese inn. Many of Aoki's advisors told him that this was an unnecessary expense, since the same look could be produced with American materials, but Aoki refused to compromise.

Restaurant designers today talk about "fusing the decor with the region." Colonial-style furnishings and fabrics are often used in New England inns. Nautical themes are popular for restaurants located in seaports, and Southwest native decor predominates in cities like Santa Fe, New Mexico.

The ambience of a restaurant's building can dictate the restaurant's concept. For example, some restaurants are housed in landmark buildings (the Space Needle in Seattle, Washington, to name one) or historic railroad stations. In Europe, castles, country houses, and châteaus are favored locales for restaurants because of their distinctive character.

The decor, furnishings, lighting, tableware, menu, and other factors all combine to create a restaurant's ambience. As you can see, these two restaurants have a very different ambience. (Bottom photo from Fairmont Chicago, Millenium Park, is courtesy of Fairmont Hotels & Resorts.)

Menu

A restaurant's menu is usually the most important element of its success. For that reason, we will discuss menus in some detail. A menu is much more than a list of items for sale. The menu helps define and explain what the restaurant is all about. It should represent what its guests expect and want. There is also a more subtle dimension. The menu should state what the restaurant does best. Unfortunately, what a restaurant does best sometimes changes. This is often the case with independent restaurants that are showcases for famous chefs. Cooking is a creative process; dishes conceived by one chef are not always as deftly executed by assistants and successors. This is one of the main reasons the menus of gourmet independent restaurants should and do change—so that the restaurants they represent can put their best foot forward.

Basic Rules. There are some basic rules that good restaurateurs follow when creating menus:

- *Give guests what they want.* Offer your guests what they are looking for at your restaurant. If your restaurant emphasizes convenience and speed of service, then be certain that menu items that take a long time to prepare are not on the menu. If Italian specialties are what you promise, you must offer more than just spaghetti and lasagna.

- *Use standard recipes.* **Standard recipes** are formulas for producing a food or beverage item that specify ingredients, the required quantity of each ingredient, preparation procedures, portion size and portioning equipment, garnish, and any other information necessary to prepare the item (see Exhibit 1). Standard recipes are an essential part of quality control. Guests who come to your restaurant for the Dover sole *à la meunière* expect it to look and taste the same every time they come back for it.

- *Match the menu to the staff's abilities.* Make certain that all of the items on the menu can be correctly prepared and served by your staff. Servers' abilities are especially important when the menu includes items that are prepared tableside.

- *Take equipment into account.* Consider the limitations of your kitchen equipment. Menu items that call for grilling should not be broiled; grilled items do not taste the same as broiled items. Dishes that should have authentic wood-smoke flavors require a hickory or mesquite grill.

- *Provide variety and balance.* Present a variety of items, colors, and textures in your menu. Much of any restaurant's business is repeat, especially at lunchtime. Daily or weekly specials can ensure that there are varying choices for guests. Strive for balance, so that foods complement each other or contrast nicely. Cream soups should not be followed by main courses with cream sauces. Some items should be heavy, others light. Since poultry and meat are white or brown, liven up their presentation with colorful vegetables.

- *Pay attention to the season.* Food costs are higher and quality is lower when you use fresh fruit or vegetables that are out of season. Menu items calling for fresh ingredients that are not readily available should perhaps be dropped from the menu until the ingredients are in season again.

- *Keep nutrition in mind.* Probably a certain number of your guests are committed to eating nutritious meals. Many of today's consumers try to eat a balanced diet. They may also be interested in reducing their intake of salt, fat, or sugar. Don't make that difficult to do in your restaurant.

- *Use food wisely.* Strive for a menu that will produce profits. Carefully plan how to use perishable items and make full use of leftovers. Throwing away food is like throwing away money. Smart chefs use meat and vegetable scraps (left over from

Exhibit 1   Sample Standard Recipe

Fish Fillet Amandine

Yield: _____ Size: _____		Yield: 60 Size: 6 oz	IX. MAIN DISHES—FISH 2 Baking Temperature: 450ºF Baking Time: 14-15 min
Amount	**Ingredients**	**Amount**	**Procedure**
_____	Fish, fillets, fresh or frozen 6 oz portion	22 ½ lb	1. Defrost fillets if frozen fish is used. 2. Arrange defrosted or fresh filets in single layers on greased sheet pans.
_____	Almonds, toasted, chopped or slivered	1 lb	3. To toast almonds: 　a. Spread on sheet pans. 　b. Place in 350ºF oven until lightly toasted. 　　*Approximate time:* 15 min
_____ _____ _____ _____ _____ _____	Margarine or butter, softened Lemon juice Lemon peel, grated Salt Pepper, white Weight: Margarine-almond mixture	2 lb 8 oz ½ cup 2¾ oz 4 tbsp 1 tbsp 4 lb	4. Add almonds, lemon juice, lemon peel, salt, and pepper to softened margarine or butter. 5. Mix thoroughly. 6. Spread margarine mixture on fillets as uniformly as possible. 7. Bake at 450ºF for approx. 15 min or until fish flakes when tested with fork. 8. Sprinkle lightly with chopped parsley or sprigs of parsley when served.

preparing other menu items) for stews and soups. Day-old bread can be used for stuffings and croutons. Good menu planners automatically think of daily specials that chefs can prepare using leftovers from the previous day's production.

Menu Preferences. Successful restaurant chains know that menu preferences vary significantly by region. In the United States, people in New England have significantly different tastes than do people in the South or West. Germans from Berlin prefer different dishes than their Bavarian cousins in Munich. Northern Chinese food is much spicier than that of southern China. Darden Restaurants (which, as mentioned earlier, operates the Red Lobster and Olive Garden chains) is careful to make sure that, although the restaurants in each of its chains look alike and have many of the same basic items, regional preferences are taken into account. Olive Garden, for example, has many different menus for its more than 650 restaurants. By offering seasonal and "test" menu items and conducting tens of thousands of customer interviews nationwide, Olive Garden was able to put together a data bank to help in designing new menus. This research showed executives that customers in coastal areas preferred more seafood dishes on the menus, while those in the Midwest preferred

SCOTT
London
ENGLAND

Cartoonists & Writers Syndicate

"If my French is correct, it says 'turkey leftovers'!"

Source: Cartoon by Scott, appearing in London, England; Cartoonists & Writers Syndicate, New York, New York.

more meat options. Before entering a new market, Olive Garden executives sample food at potential competitor restaurants to measure local spice preferences.

Global food chains keep their signature items on all menus the world over, but they also add items that appeal to local tastes. McDonald's serves fried yucca sticks in Venezuela and an egg, rice, beans, and chorizo platter for breakfast in Mexico. In the Middle East, regional menu items include a folded tortilla sandwich filled with spiced beef. Pizza Hut, a division of Yum! Brands Inc., in China serves French restaurant–style escargot in garlic oil and ostrich-topped pizza. Pizza Huts in Hong Kong offer many more pasta dishes than their counterparts in the United States, since the Chinese have never been large consumers of cheese.[4]

Menu Categories. There are two menu categories based on how the menu is scheduled: fixed menus and cyclical menus. Menus can be further categorized as breakfast, lunch, dinner, or specialty menus.

Fixed menus. A **fixed menu,** also known as a static menu, is typically used for several months or longer before it is changed. Daily specials may be offered, but a set list of items forms the basic menu.

Quick-service operations are examples of restaurants with fixed menus. They can get away with offering the same menu items every day because the items they serve—typically hamburgers, chicken, pizza, or Mexican foods—appeal to a broad market. Many chain-operated full-service restaurants also feature fixed menus.

One of the principal advantages of a fixed menu is its simplicity. Purchasing, staffing, and inventory control are straightforward and uncomplicated. Even the equipment requirements are minimal and less complex. But there are disadvantages. A fixed menu provides no variety and few options for coping with increased costs other than raising menu prices. One solution to the lack of variety is to expand the fixed menu from time

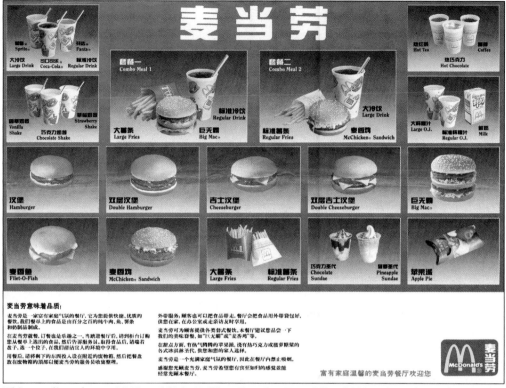

This tray liner from a McDonald's in Beijing, People's Republic of China, introduces the Chinese to McDonald's products by illustrating the menu items. (Courtesy of McDonald's Corporation.)

to time by adding new menu items on a temporary or permanent basis. Burger King's Bundles of Burgers and McDonald's Shamrock Shakes are both examples of temporary items. Both chains added salads and desserts on a permanent basis to provide more variety and achieve a higher average check per customer.

Some restaurants, such as independent family restaurants, offer daily specials to put a little variety in their fixed menus. The specials are usually printed on a separate sheet and inserted into the regular menu. Adding daily specials to an otherwise fixed menu helps keep regular customers who occasionally want to try something different.

Cyclical menus. A **cyclical menu** is a menu that changes every day for a certain number of days before the cycle is repeated. Desktop publishing makes changing printed cyclical menus easy and inexpensive.

Institutional food service operations and commercial operations that are likely to serve guests for an extended period of time use cyclical menus. A cruise ship where guests typically stay for a week needs a seven-day cyclical menu so that different menus can be offered each day. Menus can be numbered and may run from #1 to #7 before starting with #1 again. Cruise lines that offer longer cruises or whose clientele often take back-to-back cruises may use a much longer cycle menu; Seabourn Cruise Line has a 14-day cycle menu. Hospitals, where patients might be confined for prolonged periods, sometimes use long cycles. Nursing homes may use a very long cycle menu.

This menu from Outback Steakhouse helps position the restaurant as an exotic and fun place to eat ("no rules") where the food is "just right."

Specialty menus. **Specialty menus** differ from typical breakfast, lunch, and dinner menus. They are usually designed for holidays and other special events or for specific guest groups. Most restaurants offer a specialty menu featuring turkey and ham at Thanksgiving and Christmas, for example. Catered events such as birthdays, weddings, bar and bas mitzvahs, and other social occasions may call for specialty menus. In some

Industry Innovators

Drew Nieporent
Owner
Myriad Restaurant Group

When Drew Nieporent opened Montrachet in 1985 in Manhattan's TriBeCa neighborhood, he was described by Alex Witchel in the *New York Times* as a pioneer of "the style of casual but elegant dining that celebrates high quality and shuns pretension." He was just 30 years old at the time, but he understood food, service, and quality, and how to style it for the changing dining scene. Placing his first restaurant in TriBeCa was an inspired move.

TriBeCa, the triangle below Canal Street in lower Manhattan, was a residential area in the early nineteenth century that became commercial as the populace moved north. However, by the mid-1960s most of the businesses had moved, leaving the stores and lofts to artists seeking affordable rents. Drew was introduced to TriBeCa while training for the New York Marathon and racing through its streets. His dream to create and own restaurants was about to begin. He found a location, hired his first chef, David Bouley, and plunged ahead. Within seven weeks of opening Montrachet, the restaurant received three stars from the *New York Times* critic. Drew's entrepreneurial career was underway and TriBeCa was launched as a trendy restaurant area.

One of Montrachet's early customers was the actor Robert De Niro, who proposed that Drew open another restaurant in the area. Tribeca Grill was opened in 1990, and more of Drew's creations were to follow—thirty-three restaurants in twenty-five years, some of which are Centrico, Corton, and Nobu restaurants in New York and London. Corton opened in 2008 in the former location of Montrachet and, like its predecessor, received two Michelin stars in its inaugural year. Drew also opened a wine shop in mid-Manhattan, the award-winning Crush Wine & Spirits.

In 1992 Drew formed his company, the Myriad Restaurant Group. Why the name "Myriad"? According to Drew, myriad's meaning of "endless" and "countless" represents the journey he is on that started with his small, ninety-seat restaurant, Montrachet, and has now grown to a $100 million business that continues to evolve. He does not consider Myriad a restaurant chain, but a group of various brands. Myriad is a consulting firm as well, with projects across the United States and in Moscow.

How did Drew's career begin? He wanted to own restaurants from the time he was ten years old, and he set out to prepare himself. First there was a formal education at Cornell University's School of Hotel Administration. While a student there, he spent the summers working on world-class cruise ships, the *Vistafjord* and the *Sagafjord*. After graduating from Cornell, he worked for the great creative restaurateur Warner LeRoy at two of the most unique restaurants in New York, Maxwell's Plum and Tavern On The Green. That experience was followed by positions at three of New York's acclaimed French restaurants, Le Périgord, La Grenouille, and Le Regence at the Plaza Athénée Hotel. Drew's well-rounded background of theory and practice was ready to be unleashed. He opened Montrachet, and the rest, as they say, is history.

At the time of the tragic terrorist attacks on the World Trade Center, all of Drew's restaurants were near Ground Zero. Only emergency traffic was allowed in the TriBeCa area after the terrorist attack, so the restaurants were closed for more than two weeks.

Industry Innovators *(continued)*

However, Drew continued to pay his staff and, with them, helped feed the rescue workers. He believes you are defined by the acts you perform for those less fortunate, and he proves the point by giving time to many charities. For his humanitarian efforts, he and the Myriad Restaurant Group have received numerous awards.

Drew has mentored many young men and women who aspire to be the next generation of restaurant trendsetters. Here is his advice to students seeking careers in the restaurant industry: "Nothing replaces professional experience. Find the right opportunities that will allow you to build a proper foundation to launch a career. That could be working at a three-star restaurant or even a McDonald's. They both provide you with a unique education. My advice is to pursue the restaurant business if it excites you the way it excites me. There are easier ways to earn a living, and the obstacles can be daunting, but, if you have that dream—go for it!"

cases, specialty banquet menus may be created. There are many other kinds of specialty menus used by restaurants, such as children's, early-bird, beverage, senior citizens', dessert, and take-out.

Specialty menus are marketing tools—extra incentives to bring patrons in. Their only limit is the menu planner's imagination.

Menu Design. Like a brochure for a hotel, a menu is a sales tool and motivational device. A menu's design can affect what guests order and how much they spend. The paper, colors, artwork, and copy all can influence guest decisions and help establish a restaurant's ambience and image; therefore, the look and language of the menu should be closely tied to the restaurant's concept.

When guests sit down at a restaurant table, there is no question about whether they are going to buy something; the question is how much they are going to spend. Blackboards, tent cards, well-trained food servers, and—most important—a well-designed menu can all influence that decision and, ultimately, affect the restaurant's bottom line.

Menu Prices. The goal in establishing menu prices is to bring in sufficient revenue to cover operating costs and overhead, and to provide a reasonable return on investment. In other words, price is related to costs and investment. Clearly, a restaurant with a low investment and low operating costs should be able to charge less than one with high costs and a larger investment. Quick-service restaurants use computer-designed, standardized facilities and specialized equipment to prepare their menu items. The result is a relatively low investment cost plus low operating costs, since the menu and the equipment are designed for use by unskilled labor and with a limited menu in mind. Other operating costs are also kept to a minimum because nothing is added to the system that is not absolutely necessary for the smooth functioning of the unit. Therefore, prices in quick-service restaurants can be kept low.

On the other hand, restaurants such as Charlie Trotter's in Chicago are designed to offer extraordinary dining. These restaurants have lavish appointments, are located on valuable real estate, and provide luxury service with a menu requiring highly skilled chefs, cooks, dining room captains, and servers. Luxury restaurants charge high prices to cover their high food and operating costs and high overhead. They can do this because their guests are willing to pay for a fine-dining experience.

"We use the cheapest ingredients and pass the savings on to you."

Drawing by Weber; ©1998, The New Yorker Magazine, Inc.

There are a number of mathematical models and other methods that are used to set menu prices. Most of them involve a markup over food and labor costs. Whatever method is used, you should ask some basic questions after pricing menu items:

- Are these prices appropriate for my type of operation? Cafeterias usually charge less than tableservice restaurants for the same items, for example.

- Will my guests feel that I am offering a good price/value relationship? In other words, will they feel they're getting a good deal for their money?

- Are my prices competitive? What do similar restaurants in this same locale charge?

- Do these prices deliver a fair profit? Profit, of course, depends on many factors, but, generally, people who invest in restaurants expect their original investment to be paid back in three to five years.

Remember that, for most menu items, the lowest price you can charge a customer is governed by the need for the restaurant to make a profit, but the highest price you can charge is governed by the customer's perception of the item's quality and value.

Restaurant Controls

Control is one of management's fundamental responsibilities. Effective control is a result of establishing standards based on the needs of guests and the goals of the business. This principle holds true for all types of food service operations. Whether the establishment

Exhibit 2   On-Line Restaurant Reservations

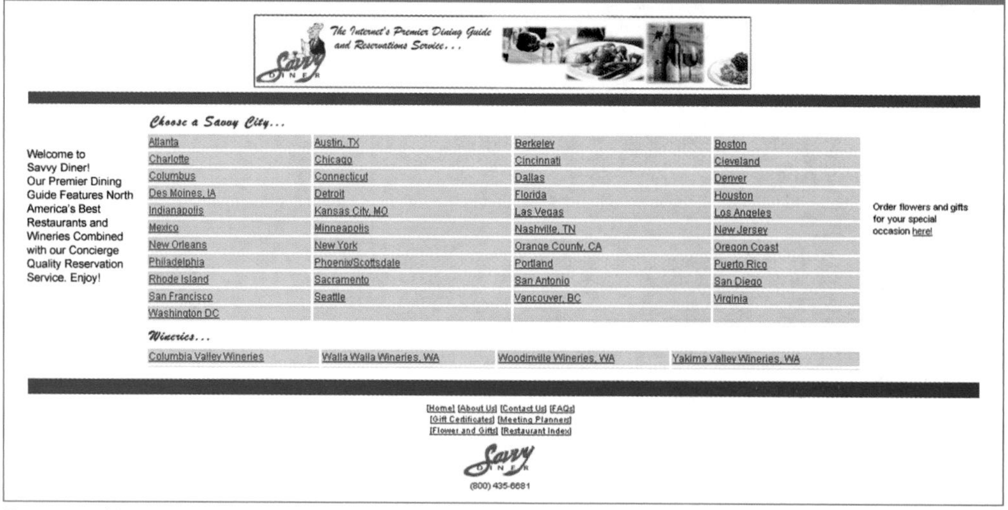

Courtesy of Savvy Diner.

is a fine-dining restaurant, a quick-service outlet, or even an institutional food service operation, managers must establish standards for financial performance, operations, and quality control. Without standards, there can be no real management, only organized confusion.

Clearly, running a successful food service operation requires attention to details. Each day, managers must keep track of reservations, the number of people in the restaurant, what guests are ordering, and how much they're spending. They also need to be aware of the restaurant's inventory, operating costs, and profit picture. The answer to keeping track of all these things lies with information technology. Computers, computer networks, and the Internet have revolutionized the restaurant industry.

Look at what is happening on the Internet right now. Restaurant operators are collecting reservations from all over the world using their own websites and other Internet reservation systems, such as SavvyDiner.com. This system lists restaurants in more than 30 major cities, displays their addresses and their menus, shows a photo of each establishment, and takes and confirms reservations (see Exhibit 2).

Purchasing can also be done on the Internet. For example, some restaurant operators develop and post their shopping lists online for preferred vendor prices. Foodgalaxy.com is an example of a site that operates this way.

Computer-based food and beverage systems have revolutionized restaurants by increasing the efficiency of front- and back-of-the-house operations. With a point-of-sale (POS) system, servers need not roam far from their dining room stations and can still get their food and beverage orders to the kitchen or the bar by using a touch-screen terminal in the dining room or a wireless handheld device that transmits the order to either a printer or a video display. These terminals and handheld devices also allow servers to print and settle guest checks, whether guests pay by cash, payment card, or—in the case of hotel restaurant customers—wish to post the charges to their guest folio.

For high-volume table-service restaurants, a table management system can be invaluable in improving service by reducing the guest's wait, allowing staff to utilize tables as soon as they are free, and balancing work load. The system, which can be part of a reservation and wait-list management system, is managed through touch-screen monitors that graphically display the table layout at the host's station as well as stations throughout the restaurant. As a table becomes available, the server indicates its availability by touching the table icon, causing the corresponding icon on the host's screen to be identified.

Back-of-the-house computer operations include labor and scheduling management programs and an inventory/purchasing (I/P) system. Menu items sold are transmitted to the I/P system, where they are broken down into their major ingredients and those ingredients deducted from inventory. Management reports—covering such topics as sales analysis, server sales, menu mix, complimentary meals/beverages, and labor costs—can be generated at any interval during the meal period or at the close of business.

In the following sections we will take a look at the financial and operational controls—many enhanced by the use of computers—that restaurant managers use in order to meet guest expectations and achieve their operations' financial goals.

Financial Controls

Financial controls are tools managers use to measure the worth of a restaurant and its level of sales, costs, and profitability. They include such documents as balance sheets, statements of income, and statements of cash flow. Managers use an accounting system to gather the financial information that makes control possible.

Accounting Systems. An accounting system that provides usable and sufficient information for management decisions is the basis for sound financial control. One such accounting system is the *Uniform System of Accounts for Restaurants.* This system is similar to the *Uniform System of Accounts for the Lodging Industry* in that it establishes categories of revenues and expenses, as well as formats for financial statements. The *Uniform System of Accounts for Restaurants* provides a common language for the restaurant industry, so operators can compare the performance of their restaurant with other restaurants in the same chain, with similar establishments in different chains, or with industry performance as a whole.

The following sections discuss two important components of the *Uniform System of Accounts for Restaurants:* the balance sheet and the statement of income.

The balance sheet. A restaurant's balance sheet shows the restaurant's financial condition on a given day. It is similar in many ways to a hotel's balance sheet (in fact, to any business's balance sheet), but there are differences. For example, although many restaurants accept credit cards as well as cash, they are, in fact, cash businesses, since the credit card companies rapidly redeem the charges. Therefore, unlike many other kinds of businesses, restaurants do not have high levels of accounts receivable on their balance sheets—that is, money due them from customers.

The statement of income. A statement of income shows the results of operations—the sales, expenses, and net income of a business—for a stated period of time. Whereas a hotel has a number of services for sale, a restaurant basically sells only food and, in some cases, alcoholic beverages. (There are exceptions, of course, such as theme restaurants, which may also sell T-shirts, caps, and other souvenirs; and restaurants with gift shops.) Hence, the statement of income generally is uncomplicated and relatively easy to understand.

Exhibit 3 shows an income statement for the fictional St. Julian Restaurant. Note the division of sales into "food" and "beverage" sales. (Food sales include sales of nonalcoholic beverages; beverage sales are sales of alcoholic beverages.) The cost of sales is also divided into "food" and "beverage" categories, representing the cost of the food and

Exhibit 3 Sample Statement of Income

St. Julian Restaurant
Income Statement
Month Ending January 31, 20XX

Sales	Amount ($)	Percent*
Food	$ 577,823	77.9%
Beverages	163,927	22.1
Total Food and Beverage Sales	741,750	100.0
Cost of Sales		
Food	235,174	40.7
Beverages	45,736	27.9
Total Cost of Sales	280,910	37.9
Gross Profit		
Food	342,649	59.3
Beverages	118,191	72.1
Total Gross Profit	460,840	62.1
Other Income	8,250	1.1
Total Income	469,090	63.2
Operating Expenses		
Salaries and Wages	196,563	26.5
Employee Benefits	35,604	4.8
Direct Operating Expenses	51,923	7.0
Music and Entertainment	6,676	.9
Marketing	17,802	2.4
Utility Services	18,544	2.5
Administrative and General	40,055	5.4
Repairs and Maintenance	12,610	1.7
Total Operating Expenses	379,777	51.2
Income Before Occupancy Costs, Interest, Depreciation and Income Taxes	89,313	12.0
Occupancy Costs	29,670	4.0
Income Before Interest, Depreciation and Income Taxes	59,643	8.0

*All ratios are to total sales except cost of sales and gross profit, which are ratios to their respective sales.

beverages sold to guests. "Other income" includes income derived from service charges, cover and minimum charges, banquet room rentals, and gift shop sales. Although this other income can be profitable, usually it is not very significant in food service operations. "Operating expenses" relate to the entire operation, with "salaries and wages" the largest single controllable expense.

"Occupancy costs" relate to the fixed costs of the restaurant, such as rent, real estate taxes, and insurance on the building and its contents. The levels of these expenses do not vary with sales, as operating expenses do—with the exception of rent on the land or building(s), which may contain a percentage clause related to sales. (For example, the rent may be $20,000 a year plus 2 percent of gross sales.)

Operational Controls

Budgeting. Budgeting—the forecasting of revenues, expenses, and profits—is another tool managers must use to track a restaurant's performance and make necessary adjustments. The headquarters of many chain restaurants collects the sales figures from each restaurant in the chain on a daily basis, using computer hookups. This process is called "polling." Managers at headquarters then compare actual sales with forecasted sales and take appropriate action. If sales are down, management can increase advertising, lower prices, add promotional items to the menu, or take other steps. Without standards and budgeting procedures, restaurant managers can and sometimes do allow difficult situations to develop past the point where anything can be done about them and financial disaster becomes almost a certainty.

Many management experts feel that budgeting for the first year of operation for any food service enterprise is as much an art as a science. The reason, of course, is that the venture is new—there are no sales history records on which to base forecasts. That means that estimates of the number of guests to expect and the expenses that are likely to be incurred ought to be made by persons with restaurant experience or with at least a solid understanding of what goals are reasonable in terms of revenues and costs. Once the business has been running for a year or more and has a track record, the forecaster's work becomes easier.

Since food is the primary tangible item for sale in a restaurant, the procedures related to menu planning, the acquisition of food products, and the processing of food through storage, production, and service are important elements of a restaurant's control system. Equally important is control over labor costs. The cost of food sold plus payroll costs and employee benefits (such as paid vacation, sick leave, employee meals, and bonuses) constitute the largest costs of operation. Together they are known as **prime costs**, representing approximately 60 percent of sales. While all expenses must be controlled, prime costs are management's major concern.

In the following sections we will discuss strategies for controlling food, labor, and beverage costs.

Controlling Food Costs. **Food cost** is defined as the cost of food used in the production of a menu item. To control food costs, most restaurants use a system of control points that are linked in a cycle similar to the one shown in Exhibit 4. A problem anywhere in the food cost control cycle can weaken the operation's control over food costs. Let's take a closer look at each of the cycle's control points.

Menu planning. Once a restaurant is in operation, ongoing market research is needed to update the existing menu or develop a new one. Such research includes periodic analyses of menu items sold. Computerized point-of-sale systems make this analysis easier. Sales of

Exhibit 4   Food Cost Control Cycle

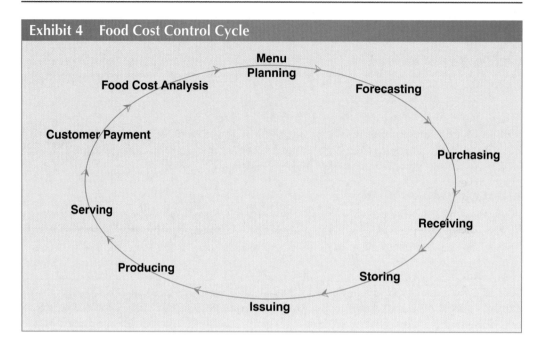

menu items can be tracked by meal period or, if necessary, by the hour. This information can help menu planners develop a menu guests will like. (The choice of menu items is not unlimited, however; menu planners must keep in mind their operation's concept, equipment, staff, and budget.) With such research in hand, the planner can remove menu items that are not selling and replace them with items that may prove more popular.

To achieve an optimal mix of popular and profitable menu items, restaurant managers perform a menu analysis. The following discussion is not intended to give you a detailed understanding of menu analysis; its purpose is to introduce you to the subject and acquaint you with some of the methods used in the industry.

There are a number of ways to analyze a menu. The earliest was proposed by Jack Miller, who used a "cost percentage" scheme that suggested that the best menu items ("winners") were those that achieved the lowest food cost percentage and the highest popularity.[5] A second method, proposed by Michael Kasavana and Donald Smith of the Boston Consulting Group, placed all menu items into a chart consisting of four sections labeled **stars, plowhorses, puzzles,** and **dogs.** Under this system, the best items (stars) were those that produced the highest **contribution margin** (the menu item's selling price minus the cost of the food that went into preparing the item) and the largest sales volume. A third method was suggested by David Pavesic. Pavesic said that the best items, the **primes,** were those with a low food cost and a high contribution margin, which he weighted by sales volume.[6] All of these methods rely on averages to separate the winners from the losers.

David Hayes and Lynn Huffman suggested a fourth method that created an individual profit and loss (P&L) statement for each menu item. Their system calculates the P&L for each item by allocating all variable and fixed costs incurred in the restaurant among the items on the menu. Variable costs are those that change when business volume changes (for example, costs for food servers or table linens). A fixed cost is an item, such as insurance, which does not vary according to volume. The best menu items, according to Hayes and Huffman, are those that contribute the greatest profit.

Finally, Mohamed E. Bayou, assistant professor of accounting at the University of Michigan, and Lee B. Bennett, an experienced restaurant-chain controller, have proposed a method (see Exhibit 5) that begins by analyzing the profitability of the restaurant as a whole, and then the profitability of each of its meal segments (breakfast, lunch, dinner, and catering). Once this is done, a margin for each menu category, such as appetizers, entrées, and desserts, is calculated, and from there a margin for each item within the category is established. On the surface, this procedure sounds complicated, but when Bayou and Bennett surveyed the managers of 103 tableservice restaurants in southeastern Michigan, they found that 55 percent used an approach that was similar to their "segment-contribution analysis" method.[7]

Professor Stephen Miller suggested that "the proliferation of personal computers and low-cost, easy-to-use software means virtually any organization can quickly and easily perform menu analyses anytime at little or no additional expense."[8] Miller called his system "The Simplified Menu-Cost Spreadsheet." Under Miller's system, a spreadsheet listing all ingredients and their costs is first set up, then the cost of menu items and side dishes is calculated along with selling price and **gross profit.** A portion of Miller's spreadsheet is reproduced in Exhibit 6.

Forecasting. Once the menu is created and a restaurant has been open long enough for a sales pattern to be established, management should forecast total expected business by meal period and menu item in order to determine purchasing needs and plan production. Accurate forecasting keeps food costs down because food is not purchased to be left sitting in a storeroom, perhaps to spoil before it is needed.

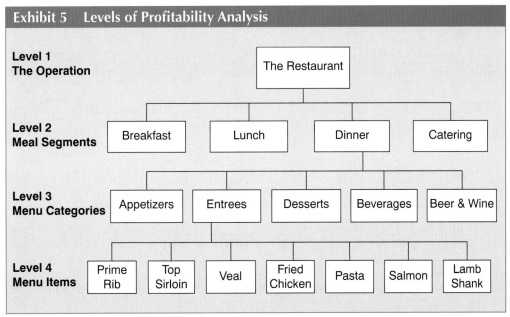

Exhibit 5   Levels of Profitability Analysis

Source: Mohamed E. Bayou and Lee B. Bennett, "Profitability Analysis for Table-Service Restaurants," *Cornell Quarterly,* April 1992, p. 53.

Exhibit 6	Sample Menu-Cost Spreadsheet					
E	F	G	H	I	J	K
Menu Item	Cost Per Entrée	Cost of Side Dishes	Total Cost	Selling Price	Food-Cost %	Gross Profit
Beef Kebob	$2.82	$1.25	$4.07	$8.75	46.51%	$4.68
Chicken Kiev	$2.07	$1.25	$3.32	$8.50	39.06%	$5.18
Chopped Beef Stk	$0.93	$1.25	$2.18	$7.95	27.42%	$5.77
Delmonico Stk	$5.46	$1.25	$6.71	$9.95	67.44%	$3.24
Filet Mignon	$4.43	$1.25	$5.68	$15.95	34.61%	$10.27
Fried Shrimp	$3.62	$1.25	$4.87	$9.95	48.94%	$5.08
Lamb Chops	$3.15	$1.25	$4.40	$12.95	33.98%	$8.55
Liver & Bacon	$1.49	$1.25	$2.74	$7.50	36.53%	$4.76
London Broil	$1.80	$1.25	$3.05	$8.95	34.08%	$5.90
Perch	$1.84	$1.25	$3.09	$8.95	34.53%	$5.86
Pork Chops	$1.49	$1.25	$2.74	$8.50	32.24%	$5.76
Prime Rib	$6.50	$1.25	$7.75	$14.95	51.84%	$7.20
Scallops	$4.22	$1.25	$5.47	$11.95	45.77%	$6.48
Scrod	$2.11	$1.25	$3.36	$8.95	37.54%	$5.59
Seafood Kebob	$3.27	$1.25	$4.52	$9.95	45.43%	$5.43
Seafood Platter	$3.99	$1.25	$5.24	$15.50	33.81%	$10.26
Sole/Crabmeat	$4.20	$1.25	$5.45	$10.95	49.77%	$5.50
Strip Steak	$4.99	$1.25	$6.24	$14.95	41.74%	$8.71
Swordfish	$4.94	$1.25	$6.19	$12.95	47.80%	$6.76
Turkey	$1.59	$1.25	$2.84	$8.25	34.42%	$5.41
Whitefish	$2.73	$1.25	$3.98	$12.95	30.73%	$8.97

Source: Stephen G. Miller, "The Simplified Menu-Cost Spreadsheet," *Cornell Quarterly,* June 1992, p. 87.

Purchasing. In any food service operation, the goal in purchasing is to keep food costs at a planned, budgeted level by obtaining the right product for the best price. To accomplish this, **purchase specifications** must be developed for all food items used in the restaurant, so that bids based on those specifications can be obtained from suppliers. A purchase specification is a detailed description of a food item for ordering purposes (see Exhibit 7). The description might include size by weight ("3 lb. chicken") or by volume ("#2 can"); grade ("Rib of Beef—USDA Prime" or "Peaches—Fancy"); and packaging ("Iceberg Lettuce—24 count" or "Eggs—30 dozen").

Exhibit 7   Sample Purchase Specification Format

(name of food and beverage operation)

1. Product name:

2. Product used for:

> Clearly indicate product use (such as olive garnish for beverage, hamburger patty or grill-fry for sandwich, etc.).

3. Product general description:

> Provide general quality information about desired product. For example, "Iceberg lettuce; heads to be green and firm without spoilage, excessive dirt or damage. No more than 10 outer leaves. Packed 24 heads per case."

4. Detailed description:

> Purchaser should state other factors that help to clearly identify desired product. Examples of specific factors, which vary by product being described, may include:
>
> | | | |
> |---|---|---|
> | • Geographic origin | • Grade | • Density |
> | • Variety | • Product size | • Specific gravity |
> | • Type | • Portion size | • Container size |
> | • Style | • Brand name | • Edible yield, trim |

5. Product test procedures:

> Test procedures can occur at the time the product is received and/or after product is prepared/used. For example, products that should be at a refrigerated temperature upon delivery can be tested with a thermometer. Portion-cut meat patties can be randomly weighed. Lettuce packed 24 heads per case can be counted.

6. Special instructions and requirements:

> Any additional information needed to clearly indicate quality expectations can be included here. Examples include bidding procedures, if applicable, labeling and/or packaging requirements, and special delivery and service requirements.

According to Lendal H. Kotschevar, author of *Management by Menu* and other food service industry texts, most food specifications should include the following:

- Name of the item
- Grade of the item, brand, or other quality information
- Packaging method, package size, and special requirements
- Basis for price—by the pound, case, piece, or dozen
- Miscellaneous factors required to get the right item, such as the number of days beef should be aged, the region in which the item is produced, and the requirement that all items be inspected for wholesomeness[9]

Purchase specifications enable the restaurant's purchaser to communicate to suppliers an exact description of what is needed to meet the restaurant's standards. Veteran operators are able to establish these specifications based on need and personal experience. Beginners and others who would like assistance can turn to sources such as the United States Department of Agriculture at www.usda.gov.

Once you have developed purchase specifications, the next task is to determine how much of each item to purchase. As explained earlier, the best way to accomplish this is to forecast the number of guests you expect and identify the menu items they are most likely to order. Delivery schedules also play a part in determining how much to order. Delivery schedules depend in part on the restaurant's location in relation to its suppliers—the greater the distance, the costlier the deliveries. Many restaurants order large quantities of the items they can stock up on (such as nonperishable items) so fewer deliveries are needed. Restaurants typically like to receive fresh fish and produce daily; meats twice weekly; canned and frozen items weekly or biweekly; and nonperishable items, such as napkins or sugar packets, quarterly or even semi-annually. The level of inventory already on hand is another obvious factor in determining how much to order. Computers make it easier to track inventory levels closely and make rate-of-consumption information on individual items readily available. Once this is done, supplies can be ordered directly on the Internet.

Receiving. Acceptable receiving procedures mandate that the employees receiving the food items clearly understand the food specifications adopted by the restaurant. Receiving clerks help keep food costs down by verifying that:

- The items delivered are those ordered and correspond to the quantity on the supplier's invoice

- The quoted price and the invoice price are the same

- The quality and size of the items delivered match the restaurant's specifications

In addition, receiving clerks handle the initial processing of invoices and deliver the food to the kitchen or to storage areas. Some operators favor a **"blind receiving"** system. With this system, suppliers give the receiving clerk a list of items being delivered but not the quantities or weights. This forces the clerk to count or weigh the incoming products and record his or her findings on the invoice. Later these figures are compared with (1) the supplier's invoice received by the accounting office, and (2) the restaurant's purchase order.

Receiving clerks must check large shipments on a random basis for quality and count. Items that do not meet the restaurant's standards are generally returned and a credit is recorded on the invoice. Those items that are acceptable are placed in storage, ready to be used as needed.

Controlling the receiving process is an important part of keeping food costs down, because receiving is an area in which dishonest employees or suppliers can take advantage of employers. For example, suppliers may deliver a lower-grade product than ordered, with the hope that it will pass unnoticed, or use extra packing material to increase the weight of goods delivered.

Storing. Food storage facilities consist of dry storerooms, refrigerators, and freezers. Ideally, food storage areas should:

- Have adequate capacity

- Be close to receiving and food preparation areas

- Have suitable temperature and humidity levels

- Be secure from unauthorized personnel

- Be protected from vermin and insects

In addition, careful consideration should be given to storage shelves and the arrangement of items within the storage facility. Obviously, the items used most frequently should be stored near the entrance. Sometimes goods are stored on shelves by groups ("vegetables" might be one group, for example) and then alphabetically within those groups (asparagus, broccoli, cauliflower, corn, and so on).

A standard inventory system of **first-in, first-out (FIFO)** is almost always adopted. With this system, older products (those received first) are stored in front so that they will be used first; newer shipments are stored behind them for use later. Proper storage reduces spoilage and waste.

Issuing. Formal procedures for transferring food from storage to production or service areas are an essential part of any control system. The purpose of such procedures is to keep track of inventory usage and make sure only authorized employees take food from storage.

In some instances, a small amount of food goes directly from the receiving area to the kitchen or dining room, bypassing the issuing system used to requisition food from storage areas. This is known as a **direct purchase.** Most direct purchases consist of items that will be used that day, such as fresh-baked goods and fresh fish. Food service operations can calculate their daily food costs by adding together direct purchases and storeroom issues.

The bulk of the inventory received in each shipment goes to various storage areas. Items from storage are issued using a requisition system. A **requisition form** identifies the person who ordered the items and the type, amount, and price of each item. Sometimes the area the items are going to—for example, the pantry or kitchen range area—is identified. Although many operations manually calculate the cost of requisitioned food, the trend is to use computerized systems to calculate this cost. Some operators track food by categories such as meat, fish, fresh produce, or staples. This enhances control by showing how the restaurant uses specific food categories and, within each category, specific food items.

Modern food service operations with relatively uncomplicated menus have been the first to adopt computerized issuing. For computerized issuing to work, standard recipes must be used. When food is requisitioned for a specific menu item, the computer determines the quantity to be issued based on the standard recipe. Computerized issuing systems work best in hospitals, schools, and other institutional food service operations that prepare large numbers of the same types of meals. Few hotels have adopted the system, due to their many different restaurant concepts and menus. But as new software becomes available, this technology is expected to spread.

Producing. Standard recipes are essential in controlling food costs. With a standard recipe, managers can calculate exactly how much it should cost to produce each menu item. As a result, managers have something to compare actual costs with, and can take into consideration the cost of producing menu items when setting menu prices. Standard recipes are also important in controlling labor costs, since employees using such recipes require less training and supervision.

Standard recipes play a major role in customer satisfaction. By using standard recipes, operators are able to provide consistency in quality and quantity no matter who is in the kitchen. Standard recipes enable restaurants to ensure that every time a repeat customer orders a particular item, the same product and portion will be served.

Serving. If service is not friendly and efficient, all other efforts in the control cycle are in vain, because most guests will stop going to a restaurant where they receive poor service. Well-trained food servers who know the menu and have good people-skills can help overcome production problems. However, if servers are not attentive to the needs of guests, the best efforts of the chef and others in the kitchen will not be enough to produce a satisfactory experience. It is a mistake to assume that operations that do not offer table service need not be concerned with their level of service. Even the food servers in a cafeteria serving line help set the mood for guests.

Customer payment. Obviously, a restaurant can't recoup its food costs if customer payments are not collected. There is no one universal payment system—systems vary from operation to operation. Here are some of the ways payment can be settled:

- The guest pays a cashier who tabulates the food order (as in a cafeteria).

- The guest pays an order-taker/cashier who rings up the order on a cash register before the food is delivered (as in quick-service operations).

- The server writes the order and prices on a check, or the order is machine-printed and priced on a check. The check is then settled in one of the following ways: (1) the guest pays the cashier; (2) the guest pays the server, who pays the cashier; or (3) the guest pays the server, who maintains a bank.

The goal of any cash control system is to ensure that what comes out of the kitchen is in fact served, recorded as a sale, and paid for. In those establishments where the server takes the order, the server writes the order on a check. The original is kept for presentation to the guest for payment at the end of the meal, and will eventually be placed in the cash register. A duplicate is carried to the kitchen so that production personnel know what to

Servers have a tremendous impact on the guests' experience—and the bottom line.
(Courtesy of Darden Restaurants.)

Computerized point-of-sale systems help servers place orders and record sales; such systems are an important element of a restaurant's operational controls. (Courtesy of MICROS Systems, Inc.)

prepare. As mentioned earlier, computerized point-of-sale systems can help servers perform this process faster and with less legwork. Servers input the order into a handheld or stationary point-of-sale terminal in the dining room. The order is electronically transmitted to the kitchen, where it is shown on a kitchen video display monitor or printed by a small work-station printer. Whether checks are recorded manually or by computer, control records (that is, the machine data, the check, and the duplicate check) are created that can be reconciled at the end of the meal.

   Food cost analysis. A common statistic used throughout the food service industry is the **food cost percentage.** This number represents the cost of food sold to guests in a given period (the month of June, for example), divided by food sales for the same period.

   To reach the **cost of food sold,** one must deduct meals that are consumed but not sold, such as complimentary meals. The cost of food sold is based on beginning inventories, closing inventories, and food purchases for the period between the two inventories, minus complimentary meals. The following figures illustrate how this works:

Beginning Inventory	$20,000
Add Food Purchases	+ 15,000
Total	$35,000
Deduct Closing Inventory	− 4,000
Cost of Food Consumed	$31,000
Deduct Employee Meals ($1,500)	
and Complimentary Meals ($500)	− 2,000
COST OF FOOD SOLD	$29,000

Assume food sales for this period (the month of June, for example) were $100,000. To compute the food cost percentage, the formula is:

$$\frac{\$29{,}000 \text{ (cost of food sold)}}{\$100{,}000 \text{ (food sales)}} \quad = \quad .29 \times 100 = 29\%$$

In this example, 29 percent reflects the actual cost of food sold (expressed as a percentage of food sales) during June. This percentage has little value unless it can be compared to a goal or an acceptable food cost percentage range established by management.

How do managers come up with a food cost goal or an acceptable range within which food costs should fall? They often use a standard cost system based on standard recipes. Since each standard recipe is an exact formula for making X number of menu items, the exact or standard cost of preparing a menu item can be computed. Continuing with our example, the restaurant manager can total the standard costs for all the menu items sold during June, divide this figure by the total menu item sales for June, multiply by 100, and come up with the **standard food cost percentage,** which would match the actual food cost percentage for June if everything worked exactly as it should have. Assuming the manager assessed standard food costs in June at $27,000, the standard food cost percentage would be calculated as follows:

$$\frac{\$27{,}000 \text{ (standard food costs)}}{\$100{,}000 \text{ (food sales)}} \quad = \quad .27 \times 100 = 27\%$$

In this case, the standard food cost percentage for June is 27 percent. The actual food cost percentage for June was 29 percent—2 percentage points higher than the standard. Since a standard food cost represents the ideal cost that management can expect if everything goes exactly as planned, the actual food cost percentage is almost always higher than the standard food cost percentage. Management at each restaurant must determine an acceptable limit for actual food costs. For example, one operation may set a limit of 2 percentage points over standard food costs. This means that if the standard food cost percentage for a period of time is 22 percent, an actual food cost percentage of 24 percent or below for that time period is acceptable.

Each individual menu item has a standard food cost percentage and, of course, some menu items have a higher food cost percentage than others. However, it is unwise to decide to keep an item on the menu or add a new one by looking at the item's food cost percentage alone. The following comparison between two menu items shows why:

	8 oz. Filet Mignon	Smoked Salmon
Menu Price	$24.00	$14.00
Standard Food Cost %	52%	25%
Gross Profit	$11.52	$10.50

The smoked salmon has a lower food cost percentage, which is desirable, but the filet mignon provides a higher gross profit. Obviously, it's preferable to sell the filet mignon, despite the higher costs associated with it, because its gross profit gives the operation $1.02 more ($11.52 – $10.50) to cover other costs and add to profits.

Controlling Labor Costs. The cost of payroll and employee benefits averages about 30 percent of sales for most full-service restaurants. This is a high figure when you consider that restaurants have more entry-level and minimum-wage employees than most other businesses. Food service is highly labor-intensive, and quality service on any level demands that employees be well-trained, efficient, and productive. Quick-service restaurants and cafeterias have lower payroll costs primarily because of their methods of service and, in the case of quick-service restaurants, their limited menu and production-line system of food preparation.

Commercial food service establishments have a unique problem in controlling payroll. The amount of money an operation must allocate to payroll depends on two factors: (1) the rates of pay for employees, and (2) the time required to do a given job—that is, productivity. While payroll costs escalate every year, productivity does not. Indeed, many full-service restaurants prepare and serve food today with the same type of equipment and in the same way as did restaurateurs many years ago. (Even quick-service restaurants with new technology will always need a base staff.) As a result, the industry, for the most part, has responded to higher payroll costs by raising menu prices rather than increasing employee productivity, adhering to the conventional wisdom that you cannot raise productivity when you are dealing with low-paid, inexperienced personnel.

You also can't raise productivity if there aren't enough customers in the restaurant. Even the hardest-working employees can't be productive if there is no one to serve, and even the best managers can only trim payroll costs to a certain point, because a minimum number of employees must be on hand when a restaurant opens, even when business is projected to be terrible. Therefore, keeping payroll costs in line depends in part on having a concept and menu that appeal to the target market and having a marketing program strong enough to keep guest demand high.

Controlling Beverage Costs. In recent years, the dangers of excessive alcohol use have gained greater recognition in the United States and elsewhere. Nevertheless, wine, malt beverages (beer, ale, stout), and distilled spirits—the major categories of alcoholic beverages—are still an important part of restaurant revenue. Alcoholic beverages account for 10 to 15 percent of sales in casual-dining chains and 20 to 30 percent in upscale restaurants. These sales are highly profitable because of the high markup on beverages. In fine restaurants, a markup of 100 percent for a bottle of wine is not unusual. Most drinks are easy to pour or mix, and the labor and beverage costs combined represent a small part of the sales price.

For restaurant managers, purchasing alcoholic beverages is relatively uncomplicated compared to purchasing food. Purchase specifications are limited to brand (Dewars White Label scotch, Budweiser beer, Robert Mondavi wine); size (liters, quarts, fifths, kegs); and, in the case of wine, vintages. Competitive bidding is usually not necessary. Some states, known as monopoly or control states, set beverage prices and allow beverage purchases to be made only from state-owned stores. Most states, however, are license states. In these, operators can buy from private wholesalers licensed by the state. Even in these states, state laws are typically designed to limit price wars, and prices do not vary a great deal among wholesalers. Most license states publish a monthly master list of wholesalers in the state, the beverages they carry, and the prices they charge.

Receiving is also straightforward. For example, weighing or checking for wholesomeness is not necessary. The receiving clerk simply verifies that what was ordered—brand, size, amount, and vintage—is what was delivered and billed on the invoice.

With beverages, secure storage is of prime importance. Access to beverage storage areas should be limited to authorized personnel. All items should be grouped by brand. Wine bottles should be stored on their side or bottom-up to keep the cork moist. Temperature control during storage is crucial. For example, the ideal storage temperature for red wines is 65°F (18.3°C) and for white wines 45°F to 50°F (7.2°C to 10°C).

**"And what is your preference in wine --
single or double figures?"**

Source: Cartoon by Levin, appearing in the United States, Cartoonists & Writers Syndicate, New York, New York

Issuing is generally done by requisition. If a restaurant has more than one bar, separate requisitions are written by personnel at each bar. Some operations stamp their liquor bottles with their name or logo to prevent unscrupulous bartenders from bringing in their own bottles, pouring drinks from them, and pocketing the money.

In most operations, a perpetual inventory of beverage items is maintained either manually or by computer. A **perpetual inventory** is a record that shows what should be on hand in the storeroom at any one time. It is compiled from daily invoices and requisitions by adding each day's purchases and subtracting each day's issues. Of course, inventory levels should be checked by a physical count on a regular basis, usually monthly. The perpetual inventory system is particularly helpful for purchasing managers, since it tracks inventory usage on a daily, weekly, and monthly basis.

Control over individual drink sales may take one or more forms. Many operators have employed automated systems with electronic or mechanical devices attached to each bottle that record every drink poured. The advantages are obvious. The manager or owner can easily determine how many drinks have been sold and thus what the receipts should be. The system reduces loss from spillage and overpouring and prevents a bartender from underpouring or offering complimentary drinks to friends. The disadvantage of an automated system is that it impedes those bartenders who make pouring drinks a theatrical presentation.

Managers can control the amount of beverages on hand at a bar by establishing a "par." A **bar's par** is the amount of each type of beverage that managers want to be available behind the bar. It is based largely on expected consumption. Levels are set high enough so that the bar will not run out of an item during a bartender's shift, but not so high that theft is encouraged. At the end of each shift, empty bottles are replaced so that the bar's beverage stock is at par for the next shift.

Beverage control is crucial to running any establishment that sells beverages to customers. Product consistency and the threat of theft are the primary areas of concern. Only through proper controls can these concerns be addressed and customer satisfaction and profitability be ensured.

Summary

Food service operations that are organized for success focus on their guests. Since guest preferences and tastes constantly change, a restaurant's management team should keep track of local and national trends and conduct ongoing research of its own customers to make sure that the restaurant's concept and menu reflect current preferences.

A restaurant's ambience is also important to its success. Decor, lighting, furnishings, and other features should all be a natural extension of a restaurant's concept.

A third important element of a successful restaurant is its menu. A good menu offers customers what they want, is based on standard recipes that can be prepared and served by the restaurant's staff, takes into account equipment limitations, and lists a variety of items. Menus can be categorized as either fixed or cyclical. Menus can be further categorized as breakfast, lunch, dinner, or specialty menus. It should be remembered that the menu is primarily a sales tool that should be constructed and presented with marketing in mind.

Pricing menu items correctly is also a key element of organizing for success. Menu prices are related to costs and investment. Basic considerations when setting menu prices include the type of operation, the customers' perception of the price/value relationship, the competition, and the desired level of profit.

Sound financial management is achieved through efficient budgeting, using a system such as the *Uniform System of Accounts for Restaurants*. Components of this system include a balance sheet and a statement of income. A successful operation keeps its costs within budgeted levels. Prime costs are the most important costs for management to control. Prime costs consist of the cost of food and the cost of payroll and related employee benefits.

There are many control points in the food cost control cycle that help restaurant managers keep food costs down. The first is menu planning. A correctly planned menu has few, if any, unpopular menu items. This helps control food costs by reducing or eliminating the need to purchase food for unpopular menu items; such food may spoil and have to be thrown away before it is used. Accurate forecasting also helps to reduce food costs because unnecessary food is not ordered. A restaurant's purchaser can minimize food costs by obtaining the right products for the best price. Purchase specifications play an important role in this. If suppliers have a restaurant's purchase specifications in hand as they're formulating a bid, their bids are more likely to be truly comparable, since they are all basing their bids on the same criteria. Today, some restaurants are using the Internet to purchase items online.

Receiving procedures can also affect food cost. What is received must be verified and compared with what was ordered.

Storing and issuing also require attention if food cost is to be adequately controlled. Storage facilities must protect the operation's inventory from deterioration and theft. Issuing procedures allow managers to keep track of inventory and calculate a daily food cost figure. Daily food cost is calculated by adding together direct purchases and storeroom issues.

Standard recipes that yield standard portions reduce food waste. Standard recipes also reduce food and labor costs. The cost of preparing menu items can only be calculated accurately when standard recipes are used.

Service and cash control concerns include the manner in which customer payments are handled. This varies by type of establishment, but the goal of all cash control systems is to ensure that what comes out of the kitchen is in fact served, recorded, and paid for. Getting instant reporting from computerized point-of-sale (POS) systems can make a substantial difference to restaurant operators. Computers connect the dining room to the kitchen, generate customer checks, sales reports, and inventory lists.

Food cost calculation is essential for the operation of a successful and profitable establishment. A restaurant's overall food cost percentage for a given period is calculated by dividing the cost of food sold during the period by total food sales during the same period. Each menu item has its own food cost percentage and contribution margin. Although, as a rule, a low food cost percentage is desirable for a menu item because a high contribution margin results, some items with high food cost percentages also have high contribution margins. Therefore, operators should keep contribution margins as well as food cost percentages in mind when making decisions about whether to drop or add menu items.

Payroll expenses, including employee benefits, represent about 30 percent of sales in the food service industry, but payroll costs vary considerably by type of establishment.

Alcoholic beverages account for approximately 29 percent of sales in medium-priced full-service restaurants—sales that have a high profit margin. Purchasing beverages is fairly uncomplicated, since purchase specifications are largely limited to brands and sizes, and competitive bidding is not necessary. Receiving is also straightforward. Issuing is usually tracked by a perpetual inventory system that shows what ought to be on hand in the beverage storeroom. These records should be checked by taking a physical inventory on a regular basis, usually monthly. Finally, a bar par, based mostly on expected consumption, is established at each bar.

 # Endnotes

1. Karl Albrecht and Ron Zemke, *Service America* (Homewood, Ill.: Dow Jones-Irwin, 1985), p. 49.

2. Jennifer Ordonez, "Casual Dining Chains Feast on Increase In Customers," *Wall Street Journal*, July 11, 2000.

3. www.restaurant.org.

4. *Nation's Restaurant News*, April 11, 2005, and *Nation's Restaurant News*, August 15, 2005.

5. Mohamed E. Bayou and Lee B. Bennett, "Profitability Analysis for Table-Service Restaurants," *Cornell Quarterly*, April 1992, p. 50.

6. Ibid.

7. Ibid., p. 55.

8. Stephen G. Miller, "The Simplified Menu-Cost Spreadsheet," *Cornell Quarterly*, June 1992, p. 85.

9. Lendal H. Kotschevar, *Management by Menu*, 2d ed. (Chicago: National Institute for the Foodservice Industry/William C. Brown, 1987), p. 261.

Key Terms

ambience—The decor, lighting, furnishings, and other factors that create a feeling about or an identity for a restaurant.

bar par—The amount of each type of beverage established for behind-the-bar storage, based on expected consumption.

blind receiving—A receiving system in which the supplier gives the receiving clerk a list of items being delivered but not the quantities or weights, thereby forcing the clerk to count or weigh the incoming products and record the results. These results are later compared with the supplier's invoice.

contribution margin—A food or beverage item's selling price minus the cost of the ingredients used to prepare the item.

cost of food sold—The cost of the food that is sold to a guest.

cyclical menu—A menu that changes every day for a certain number of days, then repeats the cycle. A few cyclical menus change regularly, but without any set pattern. Also known as a cycle menu.

direct purchase—Food sent directly from the receiving area to the kitchen or dining room rather than to a storage area.

dogs—Unpopular menu items with a low contribution margin.

first-in, first-out (FIFO)—An inventory method for rotating and issuing stored food that requires items that have been in storage the longest to be used first.

fixed menu—A menu with a set list of items that is used for several months or longer before it is changed. Also known as a static menu.

food cost—The cost of food used in the production of a menu item.

food cost percentage—A ratio comparing the cost of food sold to food sales, calculated by dividing the cost of food sold during a given period by food sales during the same period.

gross profit—Price minus the cost of food.

perpetual inventory system—A system for tracking inventory by keeping a running balance of inventory quantities—that is, recording all additions to and subtractions from stock.

plowhorses—Popular menu items with a low contribution margin.

prime costs—The cost of food sold plus payroll costs (including employee benefits). These are a restaurant's highest costs.

primes—Menu items with a low food cost and a high contribution margin.

purchase specifications—A detailed description—for ordering purposes—of the quality, size, weight, and other characteristics desired for a particular item.

puzzles—Unpopular menu items with a high contribution margin.

requisition form—A written order used by employees that identifies the type, amount, and value of items needed from storage.

specialty menu—A menu that differs from the typical breakfast, lunch, or dinner menu. Specialty menus are usually designed for holidays and other special events or for specific guest groups. Examples include children's, beverage, dessert, and banquet menus.

standard food cost percentage—The ideal food cost percentage that managers should expect when a menu item is prepared according to its standard recipe. It is calculated by dividing the standard food cost of the menu item by its sale price and multiplying by 100.

standard recipe—A formula for producing a food or beverage item specifying ingredients, the required quantity of each ingredient, preparation procedures, portion size and portioning equipment, garnish, and any other information necessary to prepare the item.

stars—Popular menu items with high contribution margins.

Review Questions

1. What are the most important success factors for a restaurant?

2. Why is keeping up with customer preferences so important?

3. How does ambience contribute to a restaurant's success?

4. What are some basic rules to keep in mind when creating menus?

5. How do fixed menus differ from cyclical menus?

6. What is a balance sheet? a statement of income?

7. What control points make up the food cost control cycle?

8. A purchase specification should include what kinds of information?

9. What is the food cost percentage and how is it calculated?

10. In what ways does beverage cost control differ from food cost control? In what ways is it similar?

Internet Sites

For more information, visit the following Internet sites. Remember that Internet addresses can change without notice. If the site is no longer there, you can use a search engine to look for additional sites.

Point-of-Sale (POS) Systems

Javelin POS
www.racoindustries.com/jviper2.htm

MICROS Systems, Inc.
www.micros.com

Resources

Foodgalaxy.com
www.foodgalaxy.com

Savvy Diner
www.savvydiner.com

Restaurant Companies

Applebee's Neighborhood Grill & Bar
www.applebees.com

Benihana
www.benihana.com

Burger King
www.burgerking.com

Chili's Grill & Bar
www.chilis.com

Darden Restaurants
www.darden.com

Fuddruckers
www.fuddruckers.com

KFC
www.kfc.com

McDonald's
www.mcdonalds.com

Olive Garden
www.olivegarden.com

Pizza Hut
www.pizzahut.com

Red Lobster
www.redlobster.com

Ruby Tuesday
www.ruby-tuesday.com

6

Understanding the World of Hotels

Outline

Competencies

1. Briefly describe the dynamic hotel industry, and summarize information about important hotel guest segments. (pp. 148–156)

2. Describe center-city, resort, suburban, highway, and airport hotels, including their services and facilities, and summarize their historical development. (pp. 156–164)

3. Explain various ways hotels can be owned and operated, distinguish chain hotels from independent hotels, and explain how hotels can be categorized by price. (pp. 164–173)

4. Describe the following hotel categories: all-suite hotels, conference centers, timeshare properties, condominium hotels, and seniors housing. (pp. 173–180)

5. Outline the following steps in developing and planning new hotels: site selection, the feasibility study, and financing. (pp. 180–187)

Opposite page: The Ritz-Carlton, Key Biscayne; photo courtesy of Ernie Pick.

THIS CHAPTER EXAMINES the dynamic hotel industry. We will discuss types of hotel guests and the various types of hotels they patronize. You will learn about hotel branding concepts and some of the differences between chain and independent hotels. Major industry players will be identified so you can become familiar with the business philosophies of the most successful hotel companies. The growing trend to make hotels "greener" will be discussed. Finally, there is a section on developing and planning new hotels. Included in this section is information on the use and structure of feasibility studies.

Hotels: A Dynamic Industry

The hotel industry is undergoing many changes. The demand for hotels is affected as the economic fortunes of countries, regions, and cities rise and fall. Each year, companies and hotels change ownership and new companies and brands enter the marketplace. Brand names that are popular today may not be around in the next decade. For example, Renaissance Hotels of Hong Kong acquired Stouffer Hotels (formerly a U.S.-based company) from the Nestlé Corporation of Switzerland and converted all of the Stouffer hotels into Renaissance hotels, which were then acquired by Marriott International. The Stouffer hotel name no longer exists.

As you can see, the hotel industry is a global industry. InterContinental Hotels, headquartered in London, operates hotels in 100 countries and territories; the French company Accor has hotels in 90 countries; U.S.-based Marriott International has hotels in 66 countries; and Hilton has hotels in 79 countries.

Industry Trends

In the 1960s, the development of new locations fueled the expansion of the U.S. hotel industry. Prior to that time, hotels were built primarily in city centers and resort areas. As commerce and industry spread from urban centers to rural, suburban, and airport locations, hotel companies like Hilton, Sheraton, and Marriott recognized opportunities to develop their brands in these new locations.

In the 1970s, intense competition among established and emerging hotel chains created a need for chains to better differentiate their product. Some did this with architecture and decor—for example, the atrium lobby became Hyatt's signature for its Regency brand. Hotel companies adopted distinctive motifs—Ritz-Carlton's decor was traditional, Hyatt's was contemporary.

Pampering the hotel guest was the strategy of the 1980s. Room and bathroom amenities—specialty soaps, sewing kits, mouthwash, shampoo, and a variety of other personal-care items—could be found in most hotels, whatever the rate category. Of course, the higher-rate hotels provided the most elaborate amenity packages. Some first-class and luxury hotels set aside one or more guest floors as "club" areas. For a higher rate, club guests could enjoy a number of special services, including an exclusive club desk for check-in and check-out, and complimentary breakfasts, afternoon teas, evening cocktails, and before-bed snacks served in the club's private lounge. Exercise rooms—even complete spa facilities—were added to many hotels to satisfy travelers' growing interest in physical fitness. Hotels with predominantly business-traveler markets added

Some hotels set aside one or more guest floors as "club" areas. For a higher rate, club guests can enjoy a number of special services, including an exclusive club desk for check-in and check-out, and complimentary breakfasts, afternoon teas, evening cocktails, and before-bed snacks served in the club's private lounge. (The Sheraton Gateway Hotel, Toronto; photo courtesy of Starwood Hotels & Resorts Worldwide, Inc.)

business centers to provide secretarial and translating services as well as computer and fax capabilities.

In the early 1990s, the concept of quality service as a differentiating factor came to the fore. Hotel companies implemented quality-assurance programs and referred to the quality of their service in their advertising. For the first time, a hotel company—The Ritz-Carlton—won the prestigious Malcolm Baldrige National Quality Award.

As the 1990s progressed, the industry emphasized innovation and new business strategies. Segmentation was one of the most important strategies implemented by many hotel chains to increase their market share. Actually, the concept was not new. Hilton and Sheraton each had established hotel and inn divisions 40 years before; the hotels were in cities, the inns in suburbs, at airports, and off highways. But in the 1990s, segmentation was based not on location, but on market. Between 1992 and 1996 there were 25 new brand announcements. Some of these brands were divisions of established chains, such as Marriott International's TownePlace Suites.

At the end of the twentieth century and the beginning of the twenty-first, mergers, acquisitions, and joint ventures changed lodging's competitive environment both here and abroad. The following are just some of the notable transactions that occurred within the hotel industry:

- The Blackstone Group, a private investment and advisory firm, purchased Wyndham International and its real estate holdings for $3.24 billion, and then spun 14 of Wyndham's top resorts and seven of its own properties into a new LXR Luxury Resorts division.

- Hilton Hotels Corporation acquired the lodging assets of Hilton Group plc (Hilton International), combining both companies for the first time since the founder, Conrad Hilton, sold the international division more than 40 years ago. Hilton Hotels is now the fourth largest hotel chain in the world, with more than 2,800 hotels in 93 countries.

- The Blackstone Group, in the biggest hotel deal in history, acquired Hilton Hotels for $26 billion. By the end of 2007, Blackstone controlled fifteen brands with 560,000 rooms worldwide.

- Microsoft Chairman Bill Gates and Prince Al-Waleed bin Talal of Saudi Arabia acquired 95 percent of Four Seasons Hotels and Resorts for $3.8 billion.

Acquisitions were not the only vehicle for growth. Hotel companies also expanded through partnerships and alliances. For example, Carlson Hospitality Worldwide, owners of Radisson Hotels, partnered with Four Seasons Hotels and Resorts of Canada. The agreement gave Carlson rights to the Four Seasons name and to the development of new hotels, while Four Seasons continues to manage existing and new properties.

Going Green

Going "green"—that is, conducting business in a way that shows concern for the environment—is a big trend today within the hotel industry. Individual hotels and even the headquarters buildings of hotel chains are now being built with environmental concerns in mind. For example, Hilton moved its headquarters during the summer of 2009 from Beverly Hills, California, to a new building in Virginia that is LEED Gold certified. ("LEED" stands for Leadership in Energy and Environmental Design.) Marriott is going for LEED certification in the "Commercial Interiors" category in a company building that pre-dates the LEED program.

The LEED certification program was introduced in 2000 by the U.S. Green Building Council (USGBC), a non-profit organization. The program contains benchmarks for the design, construction, and operation of green buildings that focus on five categories (with prerequisites and points for each):

- Sustainable site development

- Water savings

- Energy efficiency

- Materials selection

- Indoor environmental quality[1]

The outcome of the LEED assessment determines which of four levels a hotel or other building will achieve: certified, silver, gold, or platinum. There is a rating system for new buildings—"LEED for New Construction and Major Renovations"—and for existing buildings—"LEED for Existing Buildings: Operations and Maintenance." The goal of the program is to encourage a move toward sustainable practices. As of mid-2009 there were thirteen new hotels and three existing properties in the United States that were certified,

Bardessono, a 62-room boutique luxury inn and spa in Yountville, California, is one of only two hotels in the world to have received LEED Platinum certification from the U.S. Green Building Council. To help it achieve this certification, Bardessono uses solar and geothermal energy, sophisticated energy management systems, sustainable building materials, and organic landscape management practices. (Courtesy of Sam Dyess and WATG.)

with more than 500 registered to go through the certification process. One of the first hotels to receive LEED certification was the Orchard Garden Hotel in San Francisco. Since the Orchard Garden received its certification, the cost of going green has been decreasing. Stefan Mühle, the hotel's general manager, says that some "green" building materials are becoming mainstream and less expensive.[2] A challenge for hoteliers who are seeking LEED certification is that the program was designed for office buildings, not hotels. A hotel-specific certification is being created.

Green certification is an official announcement to the public that a hotel is environmentally efficient, but certification isn't necessary to create an eco-sensitive hotel operation. The American Hotel & Lodging Association has published a list of eleven minimum guidelines that can be adopted to begin the process of becoming environmentally friendly:

1. Each hotel should form an environmental committee that is responsible for developing a green plan for energy, water, and solid waste use.

2. Manage your hotel's environmental performance by monitoring the electric, gas, water, and waste usage information on a monthly and annual basis.

3. Replace incandescent lamps with compact fluorescent lamps wherever possible.

4. Install digital thermostats in guestrooms and throughout the hotel.

5. Implement a towel and/or linen reuse program.

6. Install 2.5 gallons per minute (or less) showerheads in all guestroom baths and any employee shower areas.

7. Install 1.6-gallon toilets in all guestrooms.

8. Implement a recycling program to the full extent available in your municipality, and document your efforts.

9. Implement a recycling program for hazardous materials found in fluorescent bulbs, batteries, and lighting ballasts through licensed service providers.

10. Purchase Energy Star–labeled appliances and equipment.

11. All office products should have 20 percent or more post-consumer recycled content.[3]

Almost all of the major hotel chains have initiated green policies. For example, Wyndham Worldwide, as part of its WyndhamGreen program, has adopted sustainable staff uniforms and green cleaning products. As Marriott hotels use up their inventory of supplies, those supplies are being replaced with greener products. In Europe, Scandic Hotels has replaced bottled water in restaurants and meetings with filtered water from taps. It appears that the "green revolution" is here to stay, and these and many other hotel companies are responding.

Hotel Guests

Hotels are in the business of attracting guests. The most important guest segments that constitute the market for the hotel industry are:

- Corporate individuals
- Corporate groups
- Convention and association groups
- Leisure travelers
- Long-term stay/relocation guests
- Airline-related guests
- Government and military travelers
- Regional getaway guests[4]

We'll take a look at each of these guest segments in the following sections.

Corporate Individuals. Corporate individuals are hotel guests who are traveling for business purposes and are not part of any group. They usually stay one or two nights. The top six factors that determine the hotels they select are:

1. Location

2. Previous experience with the hotel

3. Price/value

4. Room rate

5. Previous experience with the hotel chain

6. Recommendation of friend or associate[5]

Less than 15 percent of business travelers use a travel agent when making hotel reservations, while 61 percent use the Internet (up from 22 percent in 2000). Business travelers' use of the Internet to make hotel reservations is steadily increasing. Their preferences are a hotel chain's website first, and an online travel agent such as Expedia and Travelocity next.[6]

Business travelers want clean, functioning rooms and friendly, efficient service. On-site services that they desire are: complimentary breakfast included in the guestroom rate, a casual three-meal restaurant, complimentary airport shuttle service, and express check-in and check-out. Business travelers have very definite ideas about what hotels should make available to help them get their work done on the road. Free high-speed Internet access in the guestroom is their highest priority, followed by wireless Internet access in public areas and business services such as copying and faxing. Only about one quarter of business travelers desire concierge floors and even fewer want spa services.[7]

Business travelers care about recognition and special treatment. Frequent-stay programs such as Marriott Rewards, Hilton HHonors®, and Starwood Preferred Guest have

A business traveler typically desires a room with a desk to work on, a comfortable chair, a desk phone, good lighting, and, increasingly, an Internet connection. (Courtesy of Wyndham.)

Corporate groups tend to prefer hotels with intimate meeting rooms and private dining facilities.
(The Fairmont Waterfront, Vancouver; photo courtesy of Fairmont Hotels & Resorts.)

proven particularly effective with part of this market segment. Individual corporate travelers are often members of airline frequent-flyer programs, and they may choose to patronize hotels (and rental car companies) tied in with such programs.

Corporate Groups. **Corporate groups** travel purely for business purposes but, unlike individual corporate travelers, they are usually attending a small conference or meeting at their hotel or at another facility in the area, and their rooms are booked in blocks by their company or a travel agency. These travelers usually stay from two to four days. While top managers are typically assigned single rooms, middle- and lower-level managers often share rooms.

   Corporate groups favor hotels that offer intimate meeting rooms and private dining facilities. Several conference centers with these features have been constructed in suburban locations conveniently located near major cities and airports. The idea is to do away with big-city distractions and give participants a chance to interact not only during meetings but between them as well.

Convention and Association Groups. Generally, what distinguishes **convention and association groups** from other corporate groups is their size. The number of people in a convention or association group can run well into the thousands. For example, the annual meeting of the American Association of Orthodontists typically attracts about 20,000 delegates, and every year the National Restaurant Show in Chicago attracts approximately 90,000 visitors. Modest-size hotels with limited function space often compete for this group business in slow periods by offering extremely competitive rates. Convention delegates usually share rooms and stay three to four days. Large convention groups choose their venues several years in advance, so a hotel's selling efforts are often prolonged and may involve cooperation from airlines and local convention and visitors bureaus.

Leisure Travelers. **Leisure travelers** often travel with their families on sight-seeing trips, or on trips to visit friends or relatives (VFR travel). Except at resorts, they typically spend only one night at the same hotel, and a room may be occupied by a couple as well as one or more children. Because they typically travel during peak season, leisure travelers usually pay high rates, unless they are members of such organizations as the American Automobile Association or the American Association of Retired Persons, which have been able to negotiate discounts with many hotels.

Long-Term Stay/Relocation Guests. **Long-term stay/relocation guests** are primarily individuals or families relocating to an area and requiring lodging until permanent housing can be found. Often they are corporate, government, or military personnel. Their needs include limited cooking facilities and more living space than is available in a typical hotel room. All-suite and extended-stay hotels such as Embassy Suites and Residence Inns by Marriott are examples of products designed specifically for the needs of long-term guests. A Residence Inn unit is about twice the size of an average hotel room and typically contains a living area, a bedroom, extra closet space, and a small kitchen.

Leisure travelers often travel as a family during peak seasons. (Sheraton Safari Hotel Lake Buena Vista, Orlando, Florida; photo courtesy of Starwood Hotels & Resorts Worldwide, Inc.)

Airline-Related Guests. Airlines negotiate rates with hotels for airplane crew members, and for passengers who need emergency accommodations because they are stranded by some unforeseen event such as a winter storm. Rooms for **airline-related guests** are usually booked in blocks at rock-bottom prices.

Government and Military Travelers. **Government and military travelers** are reimbursed on fixed per diem allowances, which means they only receive a certain amount for lodging expenses no matter what they have to pay for a room. Therefore, as a general rule these guests stay only in places that have negotiated acceptable rates with their organizations or offer very low rates.

Regional Getaway Guests. **Regional getaway guests** are important to hotels that normally cater to commercial and convention groups on weekdays. Such hotels promote special weekend packages designed to entice nearby residents to leave the kids at home, check into a hotel for Friday and Saturday nights, and enjoy a night or two "on the town." Family packages are also available. Rates are discounted substantially and often include some meals and entertainment.

Guest Mix. **"Guest mix"** refers to the variety or mixture of guests who stay at a hotel. A hotel's guest mix might consist of 60 percent individual business travelers, 20 percent conventioneers, and 20 percent leisure travelers, for example. Guest mix is carefully managed in successful hotels.

With few exceptions, hotels—no matter where they are located or what their price structure is—strive to capture multiple market segments. A hotel's guest mix depends on its location, size, facilities, and operating philosophy. To fill up rooms not booked by convention groups, hotels geared to convention sales seek individual business travelers and vacationers willing to pay nondiscounted rates. At any one time, a hotel such as the 2,000-room New York Hilton in Manhattan will lodge several groups, some individual business travelers, families on vacation, airline crews, and government employees. By diversifying their guest base, hotels hope to minimize the effect of seasonality, economic recessions, and changing market dynamics.

There are dangers inherent in this strategy, however. Sometimes different kinds of guests do not mix well together. For example, business executives paying top rates for their rooms may be annoyed to find a noisy tour group blocking their way to the coffee shop in the morning. Some luxury hotels control their mix very carefully, only allowing groups on weekends and, even then, setting up special facilities for group registration and dining so the groups will not interfere with regular guests.

Hotel Categories

It's important to understand the ways in which hotels are categorized. Hotels can be categorized by location, ownership, price, and other factors (such as service, guestroom format, or clientele).

Location

Many hospitality publications and consulting firms categorize hotels by location. Some of the most generally recognized hotel-location categories are:

- Center-city
- Resort

How the U.S. Government Categorizes Lodging Properties

The U.S. government, along with Canada and Mexico, has its own way of categorizing hotels and other lodging properties. The basis of government classification is the North America Industry Classification System (NAICS). Industries in the "accommodations" sub sector, 721, provide lodging or short-term accommodation for travelers, vacationers, and others. The sub-sector is organized into three industry groups: (1) Traveler Accommodation, (2) Recreational Accommodation, and (3) Rooming and Boarding Houses.

- Suburban
- Highway
- Airport

Center-City. After the Great Depression of the 1930s, there was a considerable amount of rebuilding and construction in the United States as part of President Franklin Roosevelt's New Deal. One result of that program was that by 1941, when America entered World War II, most cities had at least one downtown hotel built to create jobs and stimulate the economy. Major cities like New York, Chicago, and Los Angeles had many downtown hotels, some of them internationally famous. These hotels were usually built near railroad stations, for at that time railroad stations were located at or near the center of a city's business district. This followed the pattern that had been established in other major cities of the world as early as the late nineteenth century. London's famous Savoy Hotel, built in 1889, and Frankfurt's Parkhotel are early examples of this trend. In New York City, the Commodore (the Grand Hyatt Hotel now occupies the site) was built right over Grand Central Station. In St. Louis, the Head House (now the Hyatt Regency) was part of Union Station. Other popular downtown locations for hotels were near centers of government such as city halls and courts, and in financial districts such as merchandise marts or stock exchanges. Up until the 1940s, virtually all of the nation's important business took place near these downtown areas.

After World War II the face of the world began to change. In the United States, automobiles and airplanes replaced trains as the favored means of transportation. Automobiles and good road systems made suburbs possible. Soon the suburbs began attracting office parks, shopping centers, airports, and other businesses. Downtown areas in many parts of the country began to decline. This was not the case in Europe, where trains remained a popular means of transportation. As a consequence, the downtown centers of major European capitals continued to flourish.

But most Americans were not ready to let their downtown metropolitan areas die. In the mid-1960s a trend began (which is still continuing today) to restore and rebuild downtown areas. This included building new hotels and refurbishing many of the old ones. In 1969 the Parker House in Boston was totally renovated and is now operated by Omni Hotels. In Seattle, the Four Seasons hotel company purchased the historic Olympic Hotel from Westin. (It is now a Fairmont Hotel.) In 1986, Washington D.C.'s Willard Hotel—the hotel of choice for foreign dignitaries, several presidents-elect, and other notables in the nineteenth century—was reopened as an InterContinental hotel after $113 million was invested in its restoration. The 3,000-room Conrad Hilton Hotel in Chicago, built in 1927, was closed in 1984 and reopened in 1988 as the Chicago Hilton and

Towers after a $180 million renovation. The Roosevelt Hotel in New York City near Grand Central Station, named for President Theodore Roosevelt and first opened in 1924, was refurbished in 1997.

The majority of downtown or **center-city hotels** today are properties built within the last 40 years. Along with these hotels, skyscrapers such as the John Hancock Building in Chicago and the Columbia Center in Seattle have sprung up. These buildings kept corporate headquarters in town and attracted new businesses as well. As you would expect, the hotels that surround them attract mostly business travelers. Most guests who stay in center-city hotels are corporate individuals or convention guests. In general, center-city hotels achieve the highest average room rate of all the nonresort hotel categories. These hotels cost more to develop and operate than hotels in other categories because of the high cost of real estate, construction, and urban wages.

Most of today's center-city hotels are full-service facilities operated or managed by hotel chains. In addition to rooms, center-city hotels may have a coffee shop as well as other restaurants, at least one bar or cocktail lounge, room service, laundry and valet services, a business center, a newsstand and gift shop, and a health club.

Because of the unpredictable arrival and departure times of the business clientele who patronize these properties, extended room service hours are considered essential. The room service menu for the Oriental Hotel in Bangkok states that if guests do not see anything on the menu that they like, the kitchen will be pleased to prepare a requested dish for them at any hour!

Many older center-city hotels have no parking facilities on the premises and must offer valet services to park guest automobiles off-site. Consequently, parking fees can be high. Some of these hotels contract at special rates with nearby independent garages, thus lowering their costs somewhat.

Resort. **Resort hotels** are generally found in destinations that are desirable vacation spots because of their climate, scenery, recreational attractions, or historic interest. Mountains and seashores are favorite locales. It is not unusual for resorts to have elaborately landscaped grounds with hiking trails and gardens as well as extensive sports facilities such as golf courses and tennis courts.

The Romans were the first to build hotels for recreational purposes, usually near hot springs. Famous spas dating back to the Roman Empire still exist, though in modern form, in Baden-Baden, Germany; Bath, England; and other countries. In the United States, early resorts were linked to the transportation system—the highways, rivers, and railroads. Reputedly, the first American resort advertisement appeared in 1789 for Gray's Ferry, Pennsylvania. Guests were offered fishing tackle and free weekly concerts. Transportation to and from nearby cities was provided by "a handsome State Waggon mounted on steel springs, with two good horses."[8]

Early American resorts were also built around hot or mineral springs. The Greenbrier in White Sulphur Springs, West Virginia; the nearby Homestead in Hot Springs, Virginia (which owns 15,000 acres of Allegheny mountain forests); and the many facilities in Saratoga Springs, New York—all survive today as popular vacation destinations.

Major growth in U.S. resorts came in the nineteenth century. The Mountain View House in Whitefield, New Hampshire, opened in 1865. The Hotel del Coronado near San Diego opened its doors in 1888. That was the same year Henry Flagler opened the Ponce de Leon in St. Augustine, Florida, followed by the Royal Poinciana in Palm Beach in 1893 and the Royal Palm Hotel in Miami in 1896. Another great resort, the Grand Hotel

The Grand Hotel on Mackinac Island, Michigan. It first opened its doors in 1887 and has 385 guestrooms, "no two decorated the same." Mark Twain lectured there in 1895 (admission was $1). Two movies have been filmed at the hotel, *This Time for Keeps,* starring Jimmy Durante and Esther Williams, and *Somewhere in Time,* starring Christopher Reeve, Jane Seymour, and Christopher Plummer. In 1989 the U.S. Department of the Interior designated the Grand Hotel a National Historic Landmark.

on Mackinac Island in northern Michigan, opened in 1887 and has preserved its original turn-of-the-century atmosphere to this day—helped greatly by the island's ban on all automobiles.

The first American resorts were summer retreats only. In the winter, fashionable people stayed in the cities to work and attend the opera, theater, and other cultural events; they went to the mountains and seashore in the hot summer months to escape the heat of the city. California resorts were the first to solicit winter vacation business, followed by Florida hoteliers who recognized the potential profit in offering those in northern cities a way to get out of the cold.

European resorts also were first built as summer retreats, only later becoming popular in the winter as well. The Palace, a famous Swiss resort in St. Moritz, was founded in 1856 by Johannes Badrutt. His clientele came only in the summer, until one year Badrutt made a bet with some of his wealthy British guests. He told them that if they would visit him in the winter, he would charge them nothing if they did not agree that wintering in St. Moritz was more pleasant and not as cold as staying home in London. They came, and Badrutt won his bet. Today the Palace dominates St. Moritz and remains one of Europe's most luxurious resorts, attracting royalty and celebrities from all over the globe.

A resort's guest base may vary greatly according to the season. For example, in Palm Springs, California, the winter months are the peak season. That is when movie stars and

Resort hotels are generally found in destinations that are desirable vacation spots because of their climate, scenery, recreational attractions, or historic interest. This is the Sheraton Moorea Lagoon Resort & Spa, located on Moorea, one of the islands of Tahiti. The resort features 54 over-the-water bungalows, each with a viewing panel in the floor that allows guests to watch the region's brightly colored fish swim beneath their feet. (Courtesy of Starwood Hotels & Resorts Worldwide, Inc.)

other celebrities are in town and rates are at their highest. In the summer, when temperatures often approach 100 degrees in the shade, the same resorts offer bargain prices to tour operators, conventioneers, and individual guests who could never afford to come during the cooler months.

Early resorts did not have extensive entertainment or recreational facilities. The principal activities consisted of dining, walking, climbing, horseback riding, swimming, and lawn games. These resorts all featured large verandas with comfortable chairs for sitting, reading, and enjoying the scenery. Dinner was served early, and many guests retired to their rooms by 10 P.M. On weekends there might be a dinner dance. Contemporary resorts offer much more to their guests. In Las Vegas resorts, for example, there are nightly shows featuring star entertainment, all-night casinos, discos, elaborate health spas, two or even three golf courses, tennis courts, boating, arts and crafts classes, and children's programs. Fine dining is an important part of all resort operations. Guests expect it and are not willing to pay high room prices unless the resort has a superior restaurant.

Successful resorts achieve higher occupancy and higher sales per room than other categories of hotels. However, resorts are the most expensive hotels to operate. They average a higher number of employees per room, and thus their payrolls are much higher than for other kinds of hotels.

A resort's decor is influenced by its locale. This resort is in sunny Acapulco, Mexico.
(Photo courtesy of Ernie Pick.)

Business travelers make up nearly half of the resort lodging market for large resort hotels that have conference and convention facilities. In smaller resorts the guest mix may be skewed toward leisure visitors, but groups and meetings nevertheless remain important target markets. Because of the significance of the revenue from business guests, many resorts added or increased amenities that are important to this market segment, such as full-service business centers.

Suburban. With the rebirth of American cities in the two decades after World War II, the U.S. economy expanded rapidly, and construction of major office buildings in downtown areas reached a new peak of activity. Landowners soon realized that new buildings commanded a much higher rent than older ones, and real estate prices in many downtown areas doubled and tripled.

Many corporations that did not want to pay the higher downtown rents moved to the suburbs. Land there was available at a more reasonable price and, with improved highway systems, proliferating suburban housing developments, and gigantic new suburban shopping centers, it made sense to relocate. IBM, for example, moved its world headquarters from Manhattan to Armonk, New York. Many of the other large business tenants in Manhattan moved to Connecticut, New Jersey, and upstate New York.

Inevitably, a strong demand arose for building new hotels near these suburban businesses. Land developers recognized this need and found meeting it particularly attractive. Unlike suburban townhouses and rental apartments, a hotel seemed to be a more profitable investment. After all, when you rented out a new apartment you were tied into a lease at a set price for a year or more. Inflation could easily erode your profits because you couldn't raise the rent whenever you wanted to cover increased costs. A hotel was different; you were not locked into fixed rates at all. If your costs went up, you could raise rates in less than 24 hours. While many land developers didn't know the first thing about running a hotel, a solution was readily available. Large hotel chains were selling franchises, and management companies were available to completely take over the new hotels from those developers who were not really interested in hotelkeeping.

In addition to the new businesses, there were other reasons for locating hotels in the suburbs. Newer and larger hotels offering parking space and other amenities could be built much more economically in suburban locations than downtown. Moreover, the growth of motels (which were on their way to being called motor hotels), combined with the need for suburban accommodations, further eroded the desirability of building hotels downtown.

Today it is difficult to distinguish between a **suburban hotel** and any other kind of hotel. It is the location that makes the difference. Nevertheless, there are some characteristics that suburban hotels have in common:

- As a group, they tend to be somewhat smaller than downtown hotels. Many suburban properties have 250 to 500 rooms and limited banquet facilities.

- They are primarily chain affiliated; just about every major chain operates suburban properties.

- Their major source of revenue is from business-meeting and convention attendees and from individual business travelers.

- They often have the same kinds of facilities that center-city hotels offer. Because they depend heavily on local patronage, restaurants in suburban hotels frequently offer superior dining experiences. Hotel services such as laundry, valet, and room service are on a par with center-city standards.

- Many of these properties have sports and health facilities as well as swimming pools.

- Suburban hotels are often cornerstones of their communities. They frequently host weddings and bar/bas mitzvahs as well as weekly meetings of such major service clubs as Rotary and Kiwanis.

Highway. As soon as America began to develop its highway system in the 1920s and 1930s, small **tourist courts** began to spring up along major roads such as the Boston Post Road (U.S. Highway 1) from Maine to Florida. At first these tourist courts were a row of simple cabins with direct access to the outside. Many of them did not even have private baths. These early motels averaged 20 cabins or rooms and were usually owned by a couple who lived on the premises and did all the work. No effort was made to provide food or other services. Because rooms were sometimes rented for just a few hours with no questions asked, early highway motels in some communities developed an unsavory reputation.

It was not until after World War II, when the pent-up demand for automobiles and travel was finally released, that the highway motel business really grew. With the new interstate highways came a need for families and businesspeople to have a safe and comfortable place to stay en route to their destination. One of the first to recognize this need was Kemmons Wilson, whose Holiday Inn chain was launched in 1952 in Memphis, Tennessee. One of Wilson's major innovations was to put a restaurant in his motel so that travelers could eat a meal without leaving the property. This upgraded the status of these properties considerably, making them more like hotels. Soon the evolution from tourist court to motel to motor hotel was complete. Today's **highway hotels** offer the same facilities found in downtown and suburban hotels, but with a distinct identity of their own.

Most highway hotels feature a large sign that can be seen from the highway and an entrance where travelers can leave their automobiles while they check in. Parking space is plentiful and the atmosphere is informal. Beyond that, the distinction blurs—a highway hotel can be just like any other hotel except that it is on the highway.

Most highway hotels are franchised. The nature of highway hotels—often located away from urban centers—presents management and quality control problems that can best be solved by independent entrepreneurs operating a franchise.

Highway hotels have a lower number of employees per room than suburban or center-city hotels. This is because highway hotels generally provide fewer services. Guests spend less time at this kind of hotel than in other kinds of hotels; consequently, total sales per room are generally lower. Like most other types of hotels, highway properties depend mainly on commercial traffic.

Airport. It did not take long for hotel chains to identify another growing need for hotel space in the United States—guestrooms near airports. The majority of **airport hotels** today are affiliated with chains. Even though airport hotels tend to have difficulty attracting weekend guests because most airline travel occurs on weekdays, airport hotels enjoy some of the highest occupancy rates in the lodging industry. In fact, demand can be too high at times. A problem that airport hotels face is the need to respond to a high demand almost immediately. A severe snowstorm or an airline strike can fill up an airport hotel instantly and put a severe strain on the rooms division and food service facilities.

Airport hotels such as the Fairmont Vancouver Airport address the need for guestrooms near airports. Such hotels have occupancy rates among the highest in the lodging industry. (Courtesy of Fairmont Hotels & Resorts.)

Airport hotels in the United States and Europe have begun changing from facilities designed just for overnight guests to hotels that can accommodate the needs of business travelers who may plan to stay more than one night and might require meeting space. Why are they changing? Because fewer guests are airline passengers. Busy industrial parks have sprung up in areas surrounding major airports. Hotels near the airports serving London, Brussels, and Frankfurt draw much of their business from executives visiting nearby firms, and many of these executives arrive by auto.

Ownership

Hotels can also be categorized by ownership. There are six different ways hotels can be owned and operated. Hotels can be:

- Independently owned and operated.
- Independently owned but leased to an operator.
- Owned by a single entity or group that has hired a hotel management company to operate the property.
- Owned and operated by a chain.
- Owned by an independent investor or group and operated by a chain.
- Owned by an individual or group and operated as a franchise of a chain. The franchise holder may be an individual or a management company.

An **independent hotel** is not connected with any established hotel company and is owned by an individual or group of investors. A **management company** contracts with hotel owners to operate their hotels. The management company may or may not have any of its own funds invested. It is usually paid by a combination of fees plus a share of revenues and profits. A **hotel chain** is a group of affiliated hotels.

A **franchise** is the authorization granted by a hotel chain to an individual hotel to use the chain's trademark, operating systems, and reservation system in return for a percentage of the hotel's revenues plus certain other fees, such as advertising fees. A **franchisor** is the party granting the franchise; Holiday Inn Worldwide is an example of a franchisor. A **franchisee** is the party granted the franchise. A franchisee can be a hotel management company—Interstate Hotels, for example—or an individual who has applied and been granted a license to do business under the franchisor's name.

There are also **referral systems.** Referral systems tend to be made up of independent properties or small chains that have grouped together for common marketing purposes. Best Western is the largest of these. Its properties have no common designs or standard amenities, but a room at a Best Western can be reserved anywhere in the United States through a central reservations number.

Chain Hotels. Hotel chains account for a large percentage of the world's hotel room inventory. The largest of these chains, InterContinental Hotels Group in England, owns seven brands, including InterContinental, Holiday Inn, and Crowne Plaza (see Exhibit 1), and is represented in most countries of the world. Wyndham Worldwide, the second largest chain, is a franchise system that owns such brands as Wyndham Hotels & Resorts, Travelodge, and Ramada. All of its more than 7,000 hotels are franchises.

In the past, the world's most deluxe hotels were independent. There was a perception that a chain could not possibly achieve the level of service of an independent hotel owned and operated by hoteliers who were there every day. This is no longer true.

Exhibit 1 Top 25 Hotel Chains

Rank 2008	Company/ Headquarters	Rooms 2008	Hotels 2008
1	IHG (InterContinental Hotels Group) Windsor, Berkshire, England	619,851	4,186
2	Wyndham Hotel Group Parsippany, N.J. USA	592,880	7,043
3	Marriott International Washington, D.C. USA	560,681	3,178
4	Hilton Hotels Corp. Beverly Hills, Calif. USA	545,725	3,265
5	Accor Paris, France	478,975	3,982
6	Choice Hotels International Silver Spring, Md. USA	472,526	5,827
7	Best Western International Phoenix, Ariz. USA	305,000	4,000
8	Starwood Hotels & Resorts Worldwide White Plains, N.Y. USA	284,800	942
9	Carlson Hotels Worldwide Minneapolis, Minn. USA	151,077	1,013
10	Global Hyatt Corp. Chicago, Ill. USA	114,332	375
11	Westmont Hospitality Group Houston, Texas USA	106,097	689
12	TUI AG/TUI Hotels & Resorts Hannover, Germany	83,728	297
13	Jin Jiang International Hotels Shanghai, China	80,164	465
14	Golden Tulip Hospitality Group Amersfoort, Netherlands	76,779	788
15	The Rezidor Hotel Group Brussels, Belgium	76,740	361
16	Extended Stay Hotels Spartanburg, S.C. USA	76,384	686
17	Sol Meliá SA Palma de Mallorca, Spain	76,335	304
18	LQ Management LLC Irving, Texas USA	75,832	721
19	Group du Louvre Torcy, France	61,077	856
20	Vantage Hospitality Group Westlake Village, Calif. USA	60,354	845

(continued)

Exhibit 1	*(continued)*		
Rank 2008	**Company/ Headquarters**	**Rooms 2008**	**Hotels 2008**
21	Home Inns Shanghai, China	55,578	471
22	MGM Mirage Las Vegas, Nev. USA	49,919	17
23	NH Hoteles SA Madrid, Spain	49,677	341
24	Barceló Hotels & Resorts Palma de Mallorca, Spain	47,000	186
25	Interstate Hotels & Resorts Arlington, Va. USA	46,448	226

Source: Adapted from "*Hotels'* Corporate 300 Ranking," *Hotels*, July 2009. You can visit *Hotels'* website—www. hotelsmag.com—to search for the latest industry statistics.

Most travel writers consider the Oriental Hotel in Bangkok to be the world's single best hotel. The Oriental is part of the Mandarin chain, with 22 hotels. The Ritz-Carlton Hotel Company, a division of Marriott International, manages a chain of hotels in the United States and abroad. It was awarded—twice!—the Malcolm Baldrige National Quality Award (in 1992 and 1999), which was created by the U.S. Congress to recognize quality achievements. It is the only hotel company ever to win this prestigious award. Four Seasons Hotels and Resorts of Toronto, Ontario, Canada, operates first-class hotels all over the world, including London's famous Inn on the Park.

It should be noted that the figures in Exhibit 1 can be somewhat misleading without a more complete understanding of these organizations. For example, the "Hotels" column does not indicate how many of the properties are company-owned, franchised, under management contract, or simply independent hotels that have banded together solely to advertise and set up a common reservation system. The largest chains on the list are primarily franchisors or management companies, or both. For example, all of the hotels under the Wyndham and Choice brands are franchised. InterContinental, Marriott, and Hilton hotels have both franchised and managed hotels in their portfolios. Companies such as Marriott develop a hotel and sell it once it has achieved a stable income stream, but retain the management. Best Western International does not own, franchise, or manage any of its properties. The only affiliation among Best Western hotels is that all of them are part of a common reservation and marketing system.

Independent Hotels. Most hotels that are classified as independent are independently owned and managed but are allied with a referral or marketing association. Three such associations are Preferred Hotels & Resorts Worldwide, The Leading Hotels of the World, and Relais & Chateaux. The Cloister at Sea Island, Georgia, and the Peabody Orlando in Florida are Preferred hotels. The famous Le Bristol Hotel in Paris and the Setai Hotel in Miami Beach are members of The Leading Hotels of the World. Relais & Chateaux properties include Lake Placid Lodge in upstate New York, and Las Mañanitas in Cuernavaca, Mexico.

The Broadmoor is an independent resort that is allied with Preferred Hotels & Resorts Worldwide. The Broadmoor has earned the Mobil Five-Star and the AAA Five-Diamond ratings every year since the awards were established. (Courtesy of The Broadmoor, Colorado Springs, Colorado.)

It is sometimes difficult to differentiate hotels that are independent from those that are actually managed or owned by chains. For example, the Pierre Hotel in New York City, which many consider to be a fine independent hotel, is actually owned and managed by the Taj Hotels chain.

Price

Another way of categorizing—or **segmenting**—hotels is by the prices they charge. Hotel chains create several different brands or hotel names that offer different benefits and charge different prices. This is a favored strategy for marketing manufactured consumer products. For example, General Motors manufactures economy automobiles (Chevrolets, Saturns), mid-price automobiles (Pontiacs, Buicks) and luxury cars (Cadillacs). The idea is that different segments of the consumer market are attracted to different brands at different price levels, and if you want to sell a car to everyone you must have different kinds of cars with different prices. When Henry Ford started his automobile business, his intention was to offer only one kind of car—a basic black Model T that he could sell for the lowest-possible price of $500. It was not until General Motors demonstrated that it could sell more cars by having a range of brands at different price levels that Ford decided to change his strategy of offering only one product at a rock-bottom price.

Similarly, in the lodging industry the major hotel chains started by offering one kind of brand only. Initially these were mid-price products introduced by Sheraton, Hilton, and Marriott in the 1940s and '50s. They were priced to appeal to the largest segment of the traveling public—mid-level business executives. Top executives in those days wouldn't dream of staying at a chain hotel—they stayed at independent properties or properties that may have been part of a group but were perceived to be unique or independent, such as the St. Regis Hotel in New York City.

As the market for mid-price hotels became saturated, some of the leading hotel chains developed new concepts to appeal to a growing economy-minded market. Also, there was increasing demand from families and businesspeople for more spacious, reasonably priced hotel accommodations. The industry responded by developing several full-service and limited-service brands at different prices.

Today, most hotel chains have properties in one or more full-service or limited-service segments. For example, through development and acquisition, Marriott International has chosen to enter every price category in an effort to maximize its market share. Marriott adheres to the philosophy that, if it is no longer possible to appeal to everyone with one kind of hotel, it will build/acquire as many kinds of hotels as necessary to ensure that as many people as possible who stay in hotels will stay at a Marriott property (see Exhibit 2). On the other hand, Four Seasons identifies its expertise not in the management of hotels in general, but in the management of luxury hotels. To maintain this specialized identity, Four Seasons manages only first-class hotels that appeal to its current guest base.

Three broad categories of hotels distinguished by price are (1) limited service—economy and budget, (2) mid-price—full-service and limited-service, and (3) first-class/luxury. We will take a brief look at each of these categories in the following sections.

Limited Service: Economy and Budget. There are many **limited-service hotels** in the marketplace today (see Exhibit 3). The first hotel chain to go after a low-price consumer market was Holiday Inn. Holiday Inns were not budget properties, however. Their construction costs were relatively high because they included restaurants and other amenities and services, and their aim was to provide a better product than previously available on the highway.

Exhibit 2	How Marriott Segments the Market		
	Hotels & Resorts	**Extended-Stay**	**Vacation Ownership**
Luxury	Ritz-Carlton Hotels J.W. Marriott Hotels & Resorts Edition		The Ritz-Carlton Club Grand Residences by Marriott
Full Service	Marriott Hotels & Resorts Renaissance Hotels & Resorts	Marriott Executive Apartments	Marriott Vacation Club
Upper Moderate	Courtyard SpringHill Suites	Residence Inn Execustay	Horizons
Moderate	Fairfield Inn & Suites	TownePlace Suites	

Marriott has decided to follow a segmentation strategy and offer different products at different prices for different markets.

Exhibit 3	Top 25 Limited-Service Hotel Chains			

2009 Rank	Chain	Franchise, Ownership, Membership	Guest-rooms	Properties
1	Holiday Inn Express	Franchise, own	169,227	1,889
2	Hampton Inn/Inn & Suites	Franchise, own	158,434	1,607
3	Days Inn	Franchise	152,557	1,878
4	Super 8	Franchise	130,056	2,098
5	Comfort Inn	Franchise	113,782	1,455
6	Courtyard by Marriott	NA	102,523	731
7	Motel 6	Franchise, own	92,873	917
8	Quality	Franchise	83,648	888
9	La Quinta Inns & Suites	Franchise, own	74,287	708
10	Hilton Garden Inn	Franchise, own	57,482	419
11	Americas Best Value Inn	Own, membership	52,585	809
12	Econo Lodge	Franchise	51,490	824
13	Fairfield Inn by Marriott	Franchise	49,651	556
14	Howard Johnson	Franchise	45,084	471
15	Comfort Suites	Franchise	40,890	526
16	Extended Stay America	Own	40,426	365
17	Country Inns & Suites by Carlson	Franchise, own	37,068	464
18	Travelodge	Franchise	36,203	482
19	Homewood Suites by Hilton	Franchise, own	27,913	253
20	Sleep Inn	Franchise	26,478	359
21	Springhill Suites by Marriott	Franchise	23,181	199
22	Clarion	Franchise	23,031	173
23	Microtel Inns & Suites	Franchise	21,431	301
24	Candlewood Suites	Franchise, own	20,024	196
25	Rodeway Inn	Franchise	19,904	336

Source: Adapted from "Hotel & Motel Management's 2009 Limited-Service Hotel-Chain Survey," *Hotel & Motel Management,* February 2009. You can visit *Hotel & Motel Management's* website—www.hotelmotel.com—to search for the latest industry statistics.

It was not until the 1960s that the first budget motels were introduced—Motel 6 in California, Days Inn in Georgia, and La Quinta in Texas. Sam Barshop, founder of La Quinta, explained his idea this way: "We have a very simple concept. What we're doing is selling beds. Not operating restaurants, not running conventions—just selling beds." By eliminating the restaurants and the lobby and meeting space that Holiday Inns offered, La Quinta and other budget properties were able to offer Holiday Inn–type rooms at 25 percent less. Some chains, like Motel 6, sold rooms for as low as $6. They were able to

Wyndham Hotel Group's Days Inn brand is one of the largest limited-service hotel chains. (The Days Inn Montreal Downtown, Montreal; photo courtesy of Wyndham Hotel Group.)

offer such low prices by using modular and prefabricated construction materials and choosing less-than-ideal locations where land costs were lower. These chains offered hardly any amenities at all. In the early days, some had a coin slot in their guestroom television sets for pay-as-you-view TV!

The early budget motel segment has evolved into two price levels, **economy hotels** (the lowest-rate hotels) and **budget hotels** (limited-service hotels with slightly higher rates than economy hotels). Both of these hotel segments have a low per-room construction cost. Because they provide limited services and facilities, labor and other operating costs are well below those for full-service hotels. However, pricing varies by market area and is affected by inflation. Generally, rates are offered at 20 to 50 percent below prevailing mid-market rates. Of course, hotel rates are constantly changing. Holiday Inn, once at the low end of the price scale, is now considered a mid-price hotel. However, Holiday Inn developed a concept, called Holiday Inn Express, to compete at the low end of the market. Choice Hotels International, the fifth largest hotel company worldwide, developed Comfort Inn and Comfort Inn Suites as part of its low-price strategy.

Mid-Price: Full-Service and Limited-Service. In the 1960s, Sheraton, Hilton, Ramada, Quality Inns, and Holiday Inn used the term "inn" to designate their mid-price products. At that time the mid-price hotel segment was the fastest-growing segment of the industry. Fueled by a growing economy and the development of automobile and commercial air traffic, a strong need existed for mid-price lodging facilities with restaurants and some other amenities (such as lounges and meeting space) previously found only in higher-price establishments. Today, however, the term "inn" no longer identifies a specific price category. For example, Hampton Inns and Days Inns are both economy products.

Mid-price hotels are attractive to many consumers who want to trade up from the economy/budget segment. When the rate difference between first-class and mid-price hotels is not significant, travelers are drawn to the higher-class hotels, but when rates are significantly different, mid-price hotels become more attractive. The challenge for mid-price hotels is to maintain a guest-pleasing, clearly drawn middle position between increasingly upscale hotels in the economy/budget segment and first-class hotels with low (for the segment) room rates.

Sheraton introduced Four Points Hotels, a mid-price concept that is, in some cases, a re-branding of Sheraton Inns. Although the facilities have not necessarily changed, the name has changed because the term "inn" was considered to represent a limited facility. Holiday Inn Select and Hilton Garden Inns are other brands that compete in the mid-price segment.

First-Class/Luxury. At the top of the price scale there is a range of **first-class/luxury hotels,** from the full-service hotels of Hyatt, Hilton, and Marriott to the luxury properties of Four Seasons, Ritz-Carlton, and InterContinental. Before these chains offered successful luxury hotels, "luxury chain hotel" was considered a contradiction in terms. By definition, a luxury hotel used to be an independent property in which the owner/manager was present to greet guests and see that their every need was satisfied. A perfect example of this kind of property was the Ritz Hotel in Paris on the Place Vendôme. Its founder, the legendary César Ritz, set unusually high standards for facilities and services. But Ritz also recognized the marketing advantages that could accrue from having more than one Ritz Hotel and so, with his partner Georges Auguste Escoffier, he acquired an equity interest in the Carlton Hotel in London and then formed the Ritz-Carlton chain. Other luxury chains followed. One highly successful example is the Canada-based Four Seasons hotel

The St. Regis in Aspen, Colorado, is a luxury mountain resort. (Courtesy of Starwood Hotels & Resorts Worldwide, Inc.)

Industry Innovators

J. W. Marriott, Jr.
Chairman of the Board and Chief Executive Officer
Marriott International Inc.

J. W. "Bill" Marriott did not start the Marriott empire—he inherited it from his father, who opened his first Hot Shoppe restaurant in 1927 in Washington, D.C. In one sense, the company that Bill Marriott runs today is very much the same as it was in 1985, the year his father died and Bill was named chairman of the board. The same core values and corporate culture that the senior Marriott instilled continue, but Bill Marriott has transformed the company. The company that once concentrated its efforts on a few brands of hotels and restaurants is now the world's leading lodging and contract services conglomerate. Marriott split his operations into Marriott International (in charge of Marriott's various lodging chains) and Host Marriott Corporation (in charge of lodging real estate investment opportunities).

Marriott International operates and franchises a broad portfolio of lodging brands, which include full-service Marriott Hotels & Resorts; Renaissance Hotels; The Ritz-Carlton Hotels & Resorts; and Marriott Conference Centers. Residence Inn, TownePlace Suites, Marriott Executive Apartments, and ExecuStay are Marriott's extended-stay and corporate accommodations. The company also has three limited-service lodging brands—Courtyard, Fairfield Inn, and SpringHill Suites—and three vacation-ownership resort brands.

Host Marriott Corporation is one of the largest real estate companies in the world; its assets exceeded $8 billion in 2000. The company's portfolio consists of 122 full-service hotels with almost 58,000 rooms. HMSHost operates food, beverage, and retail concessions in airports, along tollroads, and in shopping and entertainment centers. Sodexo is a provider of outsourced food service and facilities management to U.S. and Canadian businesses, healthcare facilities, colleges and universities, and primary and secondary schools.

A devout Mormon, Bill Marriott has always been known for his ethics, solid values, and integrity. He believes that if he takes good care of his employees, they'll take good care of his guests. He spends about one-quarter of his time on the road, practicing what he calls "management by walking around." For Bill Marriott, this means talking with employees on the job, eating with them in company cafeterias, having photos taken with them—and paying attention to details. It is not unusual, on these visits, for Bill to suggest changes in the restaurant food, to order new pillows for guestrooms, or to pick up trash. Perhaps this is Marriott's most unique characteristic as a CEO. Raised in the business, he understands the importance of guest satisfaction to his huge empire, and that is where he concentrates his efforts. "I'll come up with some of our ideas but, really, I'm not so much a deal-cutter as an operations man," he says.[9] Marriott offers these rules for success:

- Continually challenge your team to do better.

- Celebrate your people's success—not your own.

(continued)

Industry Innovators *(continued)*

- Do it now. Err on the side of taking action.
- It's more important to hire people with the right qualities than people with specific experience.
- Eliminate the cause of a mistake—don't just clear it up.[10]

---

company. The company's strategy is to operate only mid-size hotels of exceptional quality and have the finest hotel or resort in each destination where it locates.

Other Hotel Categories

Other hotel categories include all-suite hotels, conference centers, timeshare properties, condominium hotels, and seniors housing. We'll take a look at each of these categories in the following sections.

All-Suite Hotels. There are a number of all-suite hotel chains in the industry today, including Embassy Suites and Residence Inn by Marriott. Although all-suite chains can be viewed as a different kind of hotel chain, they also provide a way for traditional hotel chains to expand their product.

Suites often appeal to business executives, who may wish to hold private gatherings in their room outside of a bedroom setting. (Courtesy of the Renaissance Nashville Hotel, Nashville, Tennessee.)

When **all-suite hotels** were first introduced, the concept was simple—two connected hotel rooms for approximately the price of one, at a price much lower than that for a traditional hotel suite. One room was furnished as a typical hotel guestroom with a bed, the other with a fold-out sofa (or a table and chairs) in place of the bed. The first all-suite hotel was built in 1961—the Lexington Apartments and Motor Inn in Grand Prairie, Texas. It took 11 years for one of the major chains to embrace the idea; Guest Quarters Suite Hotels opened its first property in Atlanta in 1972. Residence Inns developed an all-suite concept in the early 1980s and had more than 100 hotels when it was acquired by the Marriott Corporation in 1987.

All-suite hotels were originally positioned to attract extended-stay travelers, but they proved popular with other kinds of travelers as well. An all-suite hotel gave guests more private space, but the trade-off was that much of the hotel's public space—the lobby, meeting rooms, health club, and (most importantly) restaurant and kitchen—was eliminated.

All-suites continue to develop and be embellished; today there are all-suite hotels that are upscale, mid-price, extended-stay, and resort. Some of these hotels still embrace the original concept, but others have added back the lobbies, restaurants, health clubs, and more.

All-suite hotels appeal to several kinds of travelers. Business travelers are still the primary target and account for two-thirds of the guests. Executives find all-suites attractive because they can hold private meetings in their room outside of a bedroom setting. Families also like all-suites. The children can sleep in their own alcove on bunk beds or on the convertible sofa in the living room, leaving the parents with the master bedroom. And the ranges and microwave ovens that are part of many all-suite guestrooms are great for preparing meals or popping popcorn while watching the news or the movie of the week.

Conference Centers. Although all hotels with meeting facilities compete for conferences, there are specialized hotels called **conference centers** that almost exclusively book conferences, executive meetings, and training seminars. While they provide most of the facilities found at conventional hotels, conference centers are built to provide living and conference facilities without any of the outside distractions that might detract from meetings held in ordinary hotels.

According to the International Association of Conference Centers, for a facility to be classified as a conference center, a minimum of 60 percent of its total sales must come from conferences and, of the facility's total meeting space, 60 percent must be devoted exclusively to meetings.[11]

Conference centers almost always have more audiovisual equipment on-site than is available at other hotels. Theaters, videotaping facilities, closed-circuit television, secretarial services, and translation facilities are common amenities. Conference centers are usually accessible to major market areas but are in less busy locations. They range in size from 20 guestrooms (The Council House in Racine, Wisconsin) to 1,042 guestrooms (the Q Center in St. Charles, Illinois). Revenues from conference centers are as much as 15 percent higher than those from full-service hotels.

As with other kinds of hotels and resorts, conference centers can be classified according to usage. There are four general classifications:

- *Executive conference centers*, which cater to high-level meetings and seminars.

- *Corporate-owned conference centers*, used primarily for in-house training.

Many hotel companies are rethinking their public spaces and taking innovative approaches.
(Courtesy of Fairmont Hotels & Resorts.)

- *Resort conference centers,* which provide extensive recreation and social facilities in addition to conference facilities.

- *College and university conference centers,* which tend to be used mostly by academic groups. These facilities range from dormitory accommodations to modern hotels.

Such hotel chains as Hilton and Marriott include conference centers among their hotel brands. Conference centers operated by American Express, IBM, and the Chase Manhattan Bank are used expressly for private conferences. Private and public universities such as Columbia, Duke, Babson, and the Universities of Virginia and Pennsylvania have entered the conference-center business with great success, attracting overseas visitors and weekend meetings.

One company that specializes in conference-center management is Benchmark of Woodlands, Texas. Benchmark manages more than 22 corporate, executive, and resort conference centers in 14 states, Japan, and Panama. Another company that specializes in this segment is Dolce Hotels and Resorts, which operates 22 conference hotels and resorts in the United States, Canada, and Europe.

Timeshare Properties. During the 1960s and 1970s, when inflation was a serious problem in many countries, time-sharing—which first started in the French Alps in the 1960s—seemed like an idea whose time had come. Many people enjoyed taking their vacation every year at the same time and at the same place. Many Californians, for example, went to Hawaii every winter for a week or two, rented a hotel room at the same property, played the same golf course, and had a group of friends who would go at the same time. The more affluent Californians bought condominiums, but for most people it didn't make sense to buy a $40,000 to $100,000 condominium that they might use for only a few weeks a year.

The **timeshare condominium** concept seemed the perfect answer. Instead of selling people entire condominiums, developers reasoned, why not sell them only one-twelfth of one, which would give them the use of it for 30 days—or even one-fiftieth of one, which would allow buyers to use the condo for one week every year? (Typically, timeshare properties set aside two weeks each year for maintenance, so a year, for sales purposes, consisted of 50 weeks.) Buyers could pick their own month or week and actually own the condo for that period of time. If they couldn't go on their designated week, they could trade with other owners. By buying a block of time in a timeshare condominium they would not only be assured of getting the accommodations they wanted when they wanted them, but over the years their rate would stay the same even if hotel-room rates doubled or tripled. Moreover, if they got bored with going to the same place every year, they could join an exchange company such as Interval International or RCI and trade the use of their timeshare unit for another timeshare unit somewhere else in the world. For example, Interval International has 2,000 affiliated resorts in 75 countries, and 1.8 million timeshare owners as members. Disney, Marriott, Starwood, and Four Seasons timeshare divisions are some of the brands that are clients of the exchange company.

The timeshare concept arrived in the United States in the 1970s. Problems with the first timeshare developments occurred when too many unscrupulous developers tried to unload bankrupt or aging hotels and condominiums by luring purchasers with high-pressure sales tactics. In a number of cases, management of such facilities was left to unsuspecting buyers who lacked the technical expertise needed to operate a timeshare property. Consequently, many properties were poorly maintained and a number went bankrupt. The federal government and most of the states enacted consumer protection laws and policies, including a grace period for buyers to reconsider their decision to purchase a timeshare. It was not until the 1980s, when respected companies such as Disney entered the arena, that timesharing became a serious contender for the vacation market. Other well-regarded companies soon followed: Hilton, Marriott, Hyatt, and Four Seasons.

Hotel companies are entering the timeshare business for a number of reasons. First, of course, is the potential for profit. The average vacation-ownership package includes a two-bedroom unit and costs about $16,000 for one week. If a unit is sold out for the year (as just mentioned, timeshare properties usually set aside two weeks each year for maintenance, so a sell-out would mean that the unit was sold for 50 weeks), the total revenue on that unit is $800,000. After deducting approximately 50 percent for sales and marketing costs, about $400,000 remains to cover general and administrative costs and profit.

The timeshare business has other advantages for hotel companies, especially in mixed-use projects—a project comprising timeshare units and a resort hotel, for example. With this type of mixed-use project, operating expenses such as housekeeping can be shared between the resort and the timeshare units, and timeshare residents can increase the resort's food and beverage revenue.

From a management standpoint, there are significant differences between managing traditional hotels and timeshare facilities. Timeshare properties—where there is deeded interest—are considered harder to manage because owners are always present and concerned about their investments. Managers must deal with numerous owners, all of whom have their own ideas about improvements. Selling must be handled more aggressively and sales costs are considerably higher for timeshare properties than for traditional hotels. After all, when a deeded interest is involved, you are selling a piece of property, not simply an overnight stay. Salespersons with strong closing techniques are required for the initial sell-out period.

Initially, the majority of timeshare units sold were deeded one-week intervals. While that type is still popular, many timeshare resorts and companies now offer more flexible systems, such as vacation clubs that feature point systems. They do not include a deeded interest but are structured more like a membership. These point systems enable buyers to purchase a minimum number of points, rather than time or property; buyers "spend" these points like currency to select their timeshare location, preferred time of year, number of nights, and type of unit. Buyers can use their points all at once, or spread them throughout the year for shorter vacations. Timeshare units may be sold on a floating-week basis as well. This method allows the owner to select a period in which the week purchased will be used. For example, a family may want the option of choosing their one week during the summer season when school is closed. The average timeshare owner is forty-eight years old, is college educated, makes more than $92,000 per year, and owns his or her primary residence (see Exhibit 4).[12]

Timesharing is big business. There are more than 5,000 timeshare resorts worldwide, with over six million unit owners. The United States currently dominates the industry, with more than 1,600 timeshare resorts. Florida and California have the highest number. The leading timeshare companies (in terms of units) are Wyndham, Marriott, Vacation Resorts International (VRI), and Westgate.

Condominium Hotels. Somewhat similar to timeshare properties are properties known as condominium hotels. (In a timeshare hotel, the owner has a deed for 1/52 of a unit and can use the unit for one week a year; a condominium room or apartment is wholly owned by the purchaser.) Also called condo hotels or even condotels, condominium hotels first surfaced in the 1960s and weathered some difficult early years as a result of dishonest

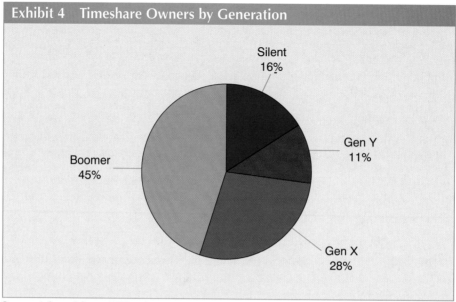

Exhibit 4   Timeshare Owners by Generation

Source: Adapted from *AIFVacation Timeshare Owners Report, 2009 Edition,* prepared by Penn, Schoen & Berland Associates.

practices by some developers. A condo hotel is one in which investors take title to specific hotel rooms. Investors stay in their rooms whenever they wish, and inform management of the times during the year when they will not be using their rooms. When an investor does not occupy his or her hotel room, it is placed in the pool of hotel rooms available for renting to vacationers and other travelers. Investors expect to receive a gain from the increase in value of the condominium hotel over time, as well as ongoing income from the rental of their rooms.

After years of little growth in the condominium hotel segment, the concept has become popular in resort areas such as South Florida, Hawaii, and Las Vegas, and even in some cities such as New York and San Francisco. The difficulty in obtaining financing for full-service and resort hotel projects has made mixed-use properties that include a transient hotel and a condominium hotel component attractive to developers. By selling hotel rooms or apartments as condominium units, the developer can transfer much of the development costs to the purchasers of the condominiums.

There are three types of mixed-use condominium hotels:

- One type has a number of condominium units in the hotel that are sold to people who use them as a primary residence. These residences are not placed in a rental pool. The Ritz-Carlton in Boston is an example of this type of development.

- Another type of mixed-use condominium hotel has condominium units located in a separate wing of the hotel, such as the Ritz-Carlton Hotel in Key Biscayne, Florida. These units are vacation homes, not primary residences, and are rented to transient guests by the hotel when the owners are away.

- There is a type of mixed-use condominium hotel in which each room is sold as a condominium to one or more investors. In this case, the owners are interested in a return on their investment, rather than an additional residence. An example of this type of condominium hotel is The Westin Grand Hotel in Vancouver, Canada.[13]

In all types of condominium hotels, the permanent residents and the transient guests receive the customary hotel services, such as housekeeping and room service.

Seniors Housing. "**Seniors housing**" is hard to define, because each state uses unique terms and regulatory controls for this portion of the lodging industry. What follows is a generally accepted classification of the various types of seniors housing:

- *Independent-living units.* Independent-living units are apartments, condominiums, or co-ops for seniors who function independently (that is, who have no serious health problems requiring assistance of some kind).

- *Congregate communities.* Congregate communities are made up of rental units with tie-ins to services such as meals, housekeeping, transportation, and social activities.

- *Assisted-living facilities.* Assisted-living facilities are apartments with private bathrooms and kitchenettes for seniors who need assistance with the activities of daily living (bathing, dressing, or eating), but who do not require continuous skilled-nursing care.

- *Continuing-care retirement communities (CCRCs).* Continuing-care retirement communities provide a full range of long-care services, such as home care and independent-living, assisted-living, and skilled-nursing care.

Adding to the confusion about seniors housing is the fact that several of these categories can exist in the same facility. For example, a single seniors-housing development might offer independent, congregate, and assisted-living units to meet the various needs of its clientele.

Seniors housing has gotten the attention of hotel corporations and major real estate developers with hotel interests. The reason for this growing interest is the "graying of America," which so many marketing people have commented on and written about. In the past, many elderly Americans moved in with their children; retired to states like Florida, Arizona, or California; or entered nursing homes. However, today's senior citizens are a different breed. For example, the very term "senior" is rejected by some older citizens. They think of themselves as active, mature people with distinct needs. They are, on the whole, more educated and affluent than their parents. And many of them prefer the new varieties of seniors housing to other options.

There is no doubt that these new "life-care" centers (as they are sometimes called to distinguish them from "health-care" facilities like nursing homes) are targeted at the affluent, because prices are typically high. Residents can buy apartments or rent them; they typically get small studios or one- or two-bedroom apartments with small kitchens where they can prepare their own meals, although usually at least two meals a day are included in the rent or maintenance plans. Often there are scheduled activities every day, including trips to shopping malls and grocery stores, movies, and fitness centers. Market studies show that seniors housing appeals mostly to women (approximately 75 percent of residents), especially widows. Married couples account for most of the other residents.

Marriott was one of the first hotel companies to enter this market when it established its Senior Living Services division in 1984. The division has since been sold to Sunrise Senior Living in McLean, Virginia, which is now the largest provider of seniors housing in the United States. The Hyatt Corporation started Classic Residence by Hyatt to develop and manage high-end independent, assisted-living, and skilled-nursing facilities.

Developing and Planning New Hotels

Before a new hotel is built, (1) a site is selected, (2) a feasibility study is conducted to determine the potential success of the planned hotel, and (3) financing is arranged.

Site Selection

Choosing the site for a hotel is usually first in a series of critical decisions affecting the eventual success of the hotel. The site must be accessible to the market it hopes to attract. If the location is downtown, for example, it should be convenient to the central business district, the financial district, the entertainment district, or a major convention hall. It also should be accessible by public transportation. If it is a highway location, whether the highway is a major route and will continue to be one should be established. Many of the old "ma and pa" tourist courts and motels were put out of business when new freeways and turnpikes bypassed their locations. On the other hand, the site criteria for resort hotels might be quite different. Many resorts are deliberately developed off main routes and might not be easily accessible. One example of a hotel in a somewhat isolated location is the Caneel Bay resort on St. John, U.S. Virgin Islands. In order to reach the hotel you must fly to St. Thomas and take a taxi service to the ferry to be transported to St. John.

Site selection is a critical aspect of hotel planning and development. (The St. Regis Princeville Resort; photo courtesy of Mark Silverstein and WATG.)

Site selection must take local zoning laws and ordinances into consideration, because zoning may significantly limit the construction options available. (Courtesy of The Luxor, Las Vegas, Nevada.)

The site must be adaptable to the type and size of the proposed hotel. A 400-room commercial hotel with meeting space can't be built on a site where zoning laws prohibit a building of that size. Zoning ordinances could also limit the type and size of ancillary facilities that would make the property more attractive and marketable, such as restaurants and lounges. Parking requirements are another consideration. Many cities have ordinances that dictate the number of parking spaces that must be available to employees and guests. That requirement must be satisfied before a hotel can be constructed.

The Feasibility Study

After the site is selected, a market study and financial analysis to determine the potential return on investment, called a **feasibility study,** is conducted. This study can help investors decide whether the hotel project they are considering is economically viable. Among other things, a feasibility study determines the size and scope of the potential guest market for the new hotel. It would be unwise to construct a hotel without first making sure that a market for it exists and learning about the market's size and characteristics. The kinds of questions the study should address include: What kind of hotel is most likely to succeed in this location? What types of guests is it likely to attract? How much will these guests be willing to pay? What occupancy rate can be expected? How many competitors are there and where are they located? Are there any other hotels planned for the area, and, if so, at what stage of development are they in the planning process?

A feasibility study helps prospective owners in a number of ways. They can use the study to help them obtain financing and negotiate contracts for a franchise, lease, or management contract. A feasibility study can guide planners and architects of the facility. A study also helps the new hotel's management team formulate operating and marketing plans and prepare the initial capital and operating budget.

Feasibility studies are typically conducted at the request of lenders, investors, franchisors, or management companies. Usually the person or persons conducting the study are independent consultants, although it is not uncommon for developers, management companies, or institutional investors to conduct their own study as well.

The person or consulting firm commissioned to conduct a feasibility study should have expertise and prior experience in the areas of hotel marketing, operations, and finance. There are a number of domestic and international companies that are considered experts in these disciplines, including HVS International and PricewaterhouseCoopers. Personnel in these firms are often graduates of hospitality management schools.

Most feasibility studies are performed to determine the suitability of a location for a hotel-chain property. Hotel chains already have brand-name recognition, tested hotel concepts, and established markets. Consumers have definite expectations of these hotels. Therefore, an important purpose of a feasibility study is to find out whether the proposed site and hotel can meet these consumer expectations.

The Report. The final product of a feasibility study is a written report that typically includes the following sections.

Market area characteristics. This section contains a review of demographic and relevant economic data for the area surrounding the site. The purpose is not to provide an in-depth economic evaluation, but to obtain a sampling of those factors that support or reject the need for the proposed hotel. For example, a profile of the commercial and industrial sectors of the area can indicate the degree of economic stability and strength of the market. Population statistics, along with growth trends and income levels, are valuable for determining the potential demand for hotel restaurants and catering facilities. Employment statistics are helpful as well. Not only are they another indicator of economic strength, but they also may be useful in forecasting potential employment problems or opportunities in operating the hotel. Highway traffic counts, air arrivals and departures, and tourism statistics often are analyzed in relation to their potential impact on the proposed project.

Site and area evaluation. The father of the modern American hotel, Ellsworth Statler, was reputed to have said that there were three reasons for a hotel's success: location, location, and location. That maxim may be as true today as it ever was. As pointed out earlier, convenience and accessibility are key components to a new hotel's success. There may be a real demand, but if the proposed hotel is not easily accessible to the source of that demand, it cannot succeed. Moreover, ideally the proposed hotel should be *more* accessible than existing or proposed competing hotels.

Accessibility is a relative concept, of course, which varies according to the kind of facility proposed. Club Med has built one of the largest hospitality organizations of its kind by going into areas that are by definition inaccessible—except to its own guests. To make sure that guests can get to its hotels, Club Med often charters aircraft and buses, and it has even developed airports in partnership with governments (as was necessary

Accessibility is a relative concept that varies according to the type of facility proposed. This Club Med village in Martinique fits Club Med's definition of accessible. (Courtesy of Club Med.)

in Mexico). Resort hotels may not need to be accessible by automobile as long as they are convenient by air, train, bus, or even ferry (ferries serve Nantucket Island in Massachusetts, for example). On the other hand, highways are the lifelines of motels.

Finally, the reputation of the area may well be an important factor in determining the feasibility of the proposed hotel. Travelers avoid areas with high crime rates, blatant poverty, or political unrest. Unless there is an overriding reason for building a hotel in these areas, they are best avoided.

Competition analysis. A good feasibility study carefully describes all of the competition and proposed future competition in the area in order to reveal the size and nature of the market as it currently exists. Facilities, services, and price levels of competitors are noted. This section of the report is a good place to look for opportunities that may have been overlooked or simply not taken advantage of by competitors. There may not be a fine-dining restaurant in the area, for example, or there may be a need for a health club—both of which a hotel could include in its concept.

Demand analysis. The feasibility study must answer a number of questions about potential guests. Who are they and where are they going to come from? How many are there? Is this number likely to grow or decline in the future? Which hotels are they going to now? How are we going to take these guests away from those hotels? (It should be noted that other than the existing demand for hotels within a competitive set, additional demand can be induced by a new hotel that is unlike any of the competition.) A detailed approach to demand analysis is a vital part of any sound marketing plan.

If demand is expected to be generated from local industry and commercial activity, then surveys of potential guests in the area are one of the best ways to confirm that demand. On the other hand, if the potential market is anticipated to come from incoming travelers such as conventioneers and sightseers, measured by current occupied room

Because Club Med seeks to appeal to guests who want a unique vacation experience in a beautiful natural setting, Club Med properties (such as this one on Bora Bora) are usually built in remote areas. (Courtesy of Club Med.)

nights and a projection of future room demand by market segment. Then the market survey should be extended to cover those groups. The market as a whole must be quantified, measured by current occupied room nights and a projection of future room demand by market segment. Then the potential for the proposed property to gain a fair share of that market must be appraised.

Proposed facilities and services. After analyzing market area characteristics, evaluating the site, reviewing the competition, and preparing a demand analysis, the next step in a feasibility study is the proposal of facilities and services. At this stage the analysts conducting the study are expected to recommend the size and type of facilities the proposed hotel should have, as well as the services that should be provided. Their goal is to establish a market difference that gives the hotel a competitive advantage. Recommendations may cover architectural and design considerations as well as overall concept and ambience.

Financial estimates. The last section of the study contains estimates of revenues and expenses, based on (1) the proposed hotel's type and the services it will offer, and (2) the size of the projected guest demand.

Feasibility studies vary at this point. Some will present estimates of operating results only, while others, at the request of those commissioning the study, provide additional information, such as (1) the fixed charges that can be anticipated—for example, property taxes, the cost of insurance on buildings and contents, and interest on borrowed capital and depreciation; and (2) an analysis of the expected return on investment (ROI). A study that includes ROI is a true feasibility study. (However, in order to calculate the return on investment, an estimate of construction and development costs must be obtained, usually from other experts.) Most studies end at the point of forecasting income before fixed charges—that is, they estimate only operating revenues and expenses. Those studies are known as market studies with estimates of operating revenues and expenses.

Financing

Investors who are asked to participate in the financing of a new hotel look carefully at several components:

- *The land on which the hotel will be built.* How large is the site? What condition is it in? What is its appraised value? What is its market value? What has comparable land sold for in the last year?

- *The building.* What construction costs are involved? How long will it take to construct the hotel?

- *Furniture, fixtures, and equipment (FF&E).* What is needed to decorate rooms and public areas? What types of equipment are necessary? How much will FF&E cost?

In addition to these **hard costs,** there are some **soft costs** that should be factored into any financing package:

- *Architectural fees.* These include site elevations, final blueprints from which contractors will work, and models.

- *Pre-opening expenses.* Certain members of the management team will be on board months before opening day. New managers and employees must be trained. Security guards will be needed to protect the property. An advertising campaign should begin several months before opening day. Working capital will also be needed until the hotel is open and generating its own.

- *Financing costs.* Financing costs include interest on loans, and brokerage fees paid to lenders.

There are two general types of hotel financing—permanent financing loans and construction financing loans.

Permanent financing loans are long-term mortgage loans—traditionally no longer than 25 years. Long-term mortgage loans are obtained from institutions such as insurance companies, pension funds, and banks. These lending institutions provide the financing and charge interest at what the going rate is when the loan is made. In addition, they sometimes take an equity position in the property—that is, they become part-owners of the hotel. Historically, these institutions have put up as much as 65 to 75 percent of the cost of the entire project. The developer, either alone or with partners, provides the remainder, as lenders do not wish to loan money to projects if the developer is unwilling or unable to risk any of his or her own funds.

A **construction financing loan** is obtained from a bank or a group of banks. It is a short-term loan to be used while the hotel is being built, with repayment to be made in three years or less. In most cases the construction financing loan is approved only after

Hotel Industry Financial Rewards/Benefits

Type of Reward/Benefit	Explanation
Favorable Tax Treatment	Personal property within a hotel can be depreciated over a short period of time. As such, hotels generate tax shelter benefits via associated depreciation and amortization write-offs.
Potential for Significant Profits	As soon as the income from a hotel reaches the breakeven point, profits tend to increase rapidly. A large portion of hotel expenses are fixed and do not vary significantly with occupancy, therefore profits increase with occupancy.
Potential for Value Appreciation	The financial returns from a hotel investment are derived from the annual cash flow after debt service (equity dividend), mortgage amortization, and the potential value appreciation realized when a property is sold. Mortgage amortization also creates equity.
Inflation Hedge	Hotel rates can be adjusted daily, within the limits of market conditions.
Part of a Global Industry	Travel and tourism is the world's largest employer and industry, with strong growth prospects over the next ten years.
Intangibles	Trophy-asset and investment-grade hotel properties can strengthen an investor's portfolio, prestige, and standing in the financial community.

Financial Risk in the Hotel Industry

Type of Risk	Explanation
Cyclicity and Operating Leverage	Small movements in occupancy and ADR have had profound impacts on net operating income. A hotel's significant operating leverage heightens its sensitivity to economic cycles and necessitates underwriting to a higher debt service coverage ratio than for other property types. Because of the higher operating leverage inherent to the lodging sector, investors can naturally expect higher return potential compared to other types of real estate investments. However, the downside risk in the hotel industry is greater if economic or company-specific issues produce insufficient cash flow to cover the high fixed-cost structure of this asset class.

(continued)

Financial Risk in the Hotel Industry (continued)	
Type of Risk	**Explanation**
Interest Rate Risk	The unexpected change in interest rates is a risk. Changes in interest rates impact hotel investments because they are highly leveraged. This means that increased interest rates lower returns, or can make a proposed project not feasible. Additionally, required investor returns tend to move with interest rates. With interest rates rising, the value of the future is discounted. Higher interest rates make it harder to earn those profits. The rise in interest rates will also cause P/E multiples to decline.
Supply-Side Risk	A spike in hotel construction gives pause to investors and triggers scrutiny. The critical issue is whether supply is growing faster than demand. Many hotel markets are currently suffering from supply growth that is running ahead of demand. Part of the reason is that the capital suppliers are hotel companies, not traditional real estate financing sources.

Source: Adapted from *PKF Consulting.*

permanent financing, known as **"take-out,"** has already been granted, since once the hotel opens and the permanent financing is in place, part of the permanent financing will be used to pay off the construction financing loan.

Summary

The hotel industry is dynamic. Each year companies and hotels change ownership, and new companies and brands enter the marketplace. The hotel industry is also global. Mergers, acquisitions, and joint ventures have changed the competitive environment both in the United States and abroad.

There is growing sensitivity to the environment among hotel owners and customers, resulting in more eco-sensitive hotels. Some hotels are opting for LEED (Leadership in Energy and Environmental Design) certification, while others are adopting programs to make themselves more environmentally friendly. Almost all of the major hotel chains throughout the world have initiated "green" policies.

Hotel guests can be classified by market segment. The major market segments are corporate individuals, corporate groups, convention and association groups, leisure travelers, long-term stay/relocation guests, airline-related guests, government and military travelers, and regional getaway guests. "Guest mix" refers to the variety or mixture of guests who stay at a hotel.

Hotels can be categorized by location: center-city, resort, suburban, highway, and airport are common categories.

Center-city hotels are typically full-service hotels located near their city's government or financial district. Most guests who stay in center-city hotels are in the "corporate individual" or "convention guest" categories.

Resorts are built in destinations that are desirable because of climate, scenery, recreational facilities, or historic interest. Many resorts are patronized for health reasons. While early resorts were usually open only in the summer, today most resorts are open year-round. Most resort business comes from leisure travelers, but resort-use by businesses for meetings and incentive programs can be a significant source of revenue. Most resorts are still independent operations. They are expensive to build and operate.

Suburban hotels followed corporations and factories that relocated from downtown to the suburbs because of land costs. Suburban hotels tend to be somewhat smaller than downtown properties and are primarily chain-affiliated. Individual business travelers represent their single largest market, although their food and beverage operations are often patronized by the local community.

Highway hotels have evolved from early tourist courts. Large signs, easy access, and ample parking facilities are distinguishing characteristics. Many are franchised. Business travelers are their main source of revenue.

Airport hotels are for the most part affiliated with chains and enjoy some of the highest occupancy rates in the lodging industry. Their biggest operating problem is the need to respond to high demand instantly when weather or other conditions delay flight arrivals and departures.

Hotels can also be categorized by ownership. A majority of hotels are owned, leased, managed, or franchised by a chain. Nevertheless, many independent hotels have overcome the chains' advantage of economies of scale with other business strategies that allow them to compete effectively. Business philosophies vary from chain to chain. Some hotel chains prefer to own, others to franchise, and others to manage. Many have a mix of the three. In addition, there are some successful management companies that operate and manage chain properties.

Hotels can also be categorized by price. The most important classifications are: (1) limited service—economy and budget, (2) mid-price—full-service and limited-service, and (3) first-class/luxury.

A significant development in the hotel industry has been the growth of segmentation strategies. In order to capture more guest markets, companies like Marriott International now offer a complete line of properties that range from economy to luxury.

Other types of hotels include all-suite hotels, conference centers, timeshare properties, condominium hotels, and seniors housing.

Feasibility studies are conducted when new hotels are developed and planned. They help prospective owners obtain financing and help managers prepare operating and marketing plans. Location is a key consideration in all new hotel projects.

Hotel financing covers hard costs, such as the land; building(s); and furniture, fixtures, and equipment; as well as soft costs, such as architectural fees, pre-opening expenses, and financing costs. Financing for new hotels is usually provided in two types of loans—long-term permanent financing loans (mortgage loans) and short-term construction financing loans.

Endnotes

1. U.S. Green Building Council, www.usgbc.org.

2. "In the LEED," *Lodging,* February 2009, p. 34.

3. www.ahla.com/green.

4. Albert J. Gomes, *Hospitality in Transition* (Houston, Texas.: Pannell Kerr Forster, 1985), pp. 32–34. Although the hotel industry has been through many changes since Gomes' book was published, the industry's guest markets can still be categorized as described in the following sections.

5. The Ypartnership/Yankelovich, Inc., 2009 National Business Travel MONITOR.

6. Ibid.

7. Ibid.

8. Donald E. Lundberg, *The Hotel and Restaurant Business,* 5th ed. (New York: Van Nostrand Reinhold, 1989), p. 185.

9. Anthony Falola, "The Bill Marriott Way," *The Washington Post,* 19 August 1996, p. 12.

10. Ibid., p. 13.

11. "Conference Centers," *The Convention Liaison Council Manual,* 6th ed. (Washington, D.C.: Convention Liaison Council, 1994), p. 17.

12. *AIF Vacation Timeshare Owners Report,* Penn, Schoen & Berland Associates (www.arda.org).

13. Steve Rushmore, "What Is a Condo-Hotel? *Hotels,* November 2004.

Key Terms

airline-related guests—Airplane crew members; airline passengers needing emergency accommodations are also included in this guest category.

airport hotels—Full-service hotels built near airports.

all-suite hotel—A hotel that features units made up of two connected hotel rooms that sell for approximately the price of one, at lower prices than traditional hotel suites. One room is furnished as a typical hotel guestroom with a bed, the other with a fold-out sofa and/or table and chairs.

budget hotels—A type of limited-service hotel. Budget hotels have low construction and operating costs, allowing them to charge between $45 and $60 per night.

center-city hotels—Full-service hotels located in downtown areas.

conference centers—Specialized hotels, usually accessible to major market areas but in less busy locations, that almost exclusively book conferences, executive meetings, and training seminars. Some conference centers provide extensive leisure facilities.

construction financing loan—A short-term loan to be used while a hotel is being built, with repayment to be made in three years or less.

convention and association groups—Groups of businesspeople attending a convention or association meeting. The number of people attending can run into the thousands.

corporate groups—Small groups of people traveling for business purposes, usually to attend conferences or meetings.

corporate individuals—Individuals traveling for business purposes.

economy hotels—A type of limited-service hotel. Economy hotels have the lowest construction and operating costs, allowing them to charge 25 percent less than budget hotels.

feasibility study—A study commissioned by developers and prepared by consultants to determine the potential success of a proposed hotel on a proposed site.

first-class/luxury hotels—Hotels with high room rates and exceptional service and amenities.

franchise—Refers to (1) the authorization given by one company to another to sell its unique product and service, or (2) the name of the business format or product that is being franchised.

franchisee—The individual or company granted a franchise.

franchisor—The franchise company that owns the trademark, products, and/or business format that is being franchised.

government and military travelers—Travelers in government or the military on a fixed per diem allowance who typically are reimbursed for hotel and other travel expenses.

guest mix—The variety or mixture of guests who stay at a hotel or patronize a restaurant.

hard costs—The land; building; and furniture, fixtures, and equipment (FF&E) costs that are basic to hotel and restaurant development.

highway hotels—Hotels built next to a highway. These hotels typically feature large property signs, an entrance where travelers can leave their cars as they check in, and a swimming pool. Parking space is plentiful and the atmosphere is informal.

hotel chain—A group of affiliated hotels.

independent hotel—A hotel owned by an individual or group of investors not connected with any hotel company.

leisure travelers—Vacationing travelers—often entire families—who typically spend only one night at a hotel unless the hotel is their destination.

limited-service hotels—Hotels that do not offer the full range of services customarily associated with hotels. For example, they do not have restaurants or bars. Types of limited-service hotels include budget and economy hotels.

long-term stay/relocation guests—Individuals or families relocating to an area who require lodging until permanent housing is found.

management company—A company that manages hotels for owners, typically in return for a combination of fees and a share of revenues. A management company may or may not have any of its own funds invested in a hotel that it manages.

mid-price hotels—Hotels that offer facilities and services similar to those at first-class/luxury hotels, but at average rates. They have restaurants and bars, and many have meeting space. Average prices vary by market.

permanent financing loan—A long-term mortgage loan for a hotel, usually up to 25 years. Long-term mortgage loans are obtained from institutions such as insurance companies, pension funds, and banks.

referral systems—Independent hotels or small hotel chains that do not share common operating systems, decor, purchasing systems, etc., but are linked by (1) a common reservation system, and (2) a common marketing strategy. The reservation system and marketing campaigns are funded by the hotels in the referral system.

regional getaway guests—Guests who check into a hotel close to home—with or without children—in order to enjoy a weekend away from daily responsibilities.

resort hotels—Usually located in desirable vacation spots, resort hotels offer fine dining, exceptional service, and many amenities.

segmenting—A method of categorizing hotels by the prices they charge.

seniors housing—Long-term living facilities for senior citizens.

soft costs—Development costs other than land; building; and furniture, fixtures, and equipment (FF&E) costs for a hotel or restaurant project. Soft costs include architectural fees, pre-opening expenses (for advertising and employee training, for example), and financing costs.

suburban hotels—Hotels located in suburban areas. Suburban hotels typically belong to a major hotel chain and have 250 to 500 rooms as well as restaurants, bars, and other amenities found at most downtown hotels.

take-out—The permanent financing secured for a new hotel.

timeshare condominiums—Condominiums for which an owner can purchase a portion of time at the condominium—typically one month to one week—for one-twelfth or one-fiftieth of the condominium's price, and share the condominium with other owners. Owners have the right to stay at the condominium during their assigned time or to trade their slot with another owner.

tourist courts—The forerunners of motels, built along highways in the 1920s and 1930s. Typical tourist courts consisted of a simple row of small cabins that often had no private baths.

Review Questions

1. How has the hotel industry changed in recent decades?

2. How can hotel guests be categorized?

3. What are some of the differences between a center-city hotel and a resort hotel?

4. What are some characteristics of suburban hotels? highway hotels? airport hotels?

5. What are some of the various ways hotels can be owned and operated?

6. How can hotels be categorized by price?

7. What are some characteristics of all-suite hotels? conference centers? timeshare properties?

8. Seniors housing can consist of what types of units/facilities?

9. What is a feasibility study and what does it cover?

10. In terms of new hotel projects, what are hard costs? soft costs?

Internet Sites

For more information, visit the following Internet sites. Remember that Internet addresses can change without notice. If the site is no longer there, you can use a search engine to look for additional sites.

Hotel Companies/Resorts

Accor
www.accor.com

Bellagio
www.bellagiolasvegas.com

The Bristol Hotel
www.hotel-bristol.com

Choice Hotels International
www.hotelchoice.com

Club Med
www.clubmed.com

Days Inn
www.daysinn.com

Dolce
www.dolce.com

Doubletree Hotels
www.doubletreehotels.com

Embassy Suites
www.embassy-suites.com

Four Seasons Hotels and Resorts
www.fourseasons.com

The Golden Nugget
www.goldennugget.com

The Greenbrier Resort
www.greenbrier.com

The Hotel Hershey
www.hersheypa.com/
accommodations/hotel/index.html

Hilton Worldwide
www.hilton.com

Holiday Inn Worldwide
www.holiday-inn.com

Howard Johnson
www.hojo.com

Hyatt Hotels & Resorts
www.hyatt.com

InterContinental Hotels & Resorts
www.intercontinental.com

Interstate Hotels
www.interstatehotels.com

Lake Placid Lodge
lakeplacidlodge.com/intro.htm

La Quinta Hotels
www.laquinta.com

Las Mañanitas
www.lasmananitas.com.mx

The Leading Hotels of the World
www.lhw.com

Mandarin Oriental Hotel Group
www.mandarin-oriental.com

Marriott International
www.marriott.com

The Mirage
www.mirage.com

Motel 6
www.motel6.com

The Oriental, Bangkok
www.mandarin-oriental.com/bangkok

Preferred Hotels & Resorts Worldwide
www.preferredhotels.com

Ramada
www.ramada.com

Relais & Chateaux
www.relaischateaux.com/Accueil

The Ritz-Carlton Hotel Company
www.ritzcarlton.com

The Roosevelt Hotel
www.theroosevelthotel.com

Sheraton Hotels
www.sheraton.com

Starwood Hotels & Resorts Worldwide
www.starwood.com

Super 8 Motels
www.super8.com

Taj Hotels
www.tajhotels.com

TownePlace Suites
www.towneplace.com

Treasure Island at The Mirage
www.treasureislandlasvegas.com

Westin Hotels & Resorts
www.westin.com

Willard InterContinental Washington
www.washington.interconti.com

Wingate Inns
www.wingateinns.com/ctg/cgi-bin/
Wingate

Organizations, Consultants, Resources

Accenture
www.accenture.com

American Society of Association
  Executives
www.asaenet.org

Host Hotels & Resorts
www.hosthotels.com

HVS International
www.hvsinternational.com

International Association of Conference
  Centers
www.iacconline.com

PricewaterhouseCoopers
www.pwc.com

Smith Travel Research
www.str-online.com

Travelocity
www.travelocity.com

Publications

Hotel & Motel Management
www.hmmonline.com

Lodging
www.lodgingmagazine.com

Meetings & Conventions
www.meetings-conventions.com

Timeshare Companies

Interval International
www.intervalworld.com

Resort Condominiums International
www.rci.com/index

Vacation Resorts International
www.vrivacations.com

Seniors Housing

American Seniors Housing Association
www.seniorshousing.org

Classic Residence by Hyatt
www.hyattclassic.com

Senior Housing Net
www.seniorhousing.net

Sunrise
www.sunrise-al.com

7

Hotel Organization and Management

Outline

Competencies

Opposite page: The Sheraton Hong Kong Hotel & Towers; photo courtesy of Starwood Hotels & Resorts Worldwide, Inc.

I N ORDER TO GAIN A PERSPECTIVE on how hotels are organized, a few hotel characteristics should be noted at the outset:

- All hotels are in the business of renting rooms.
- Hotels vary in size from under 100 rooms to over 5,000.
- Hotels vary in type. They can be center-city hotels, resorts, highway properties, conference centers, and so on.
- Hotels vary in the nature and extent of their facilities. Some hotels offer only rooms, while others have coffee shops, gourmet restaurants, swimming pools, golf courses, and other facilities.
- Hotels vary in the level of service they offer. For example, some offer 24-hour room service, others offer room service from 7 A.M. to 10 P.M. only, and some do not offer room service at all.

Clearly, hotels are not all alike. No matter what category a hotel falls into, however, it must be organized in order to: (1) coordinate the many specialized tasks and activities necessary to attract and serve guests, and (2) produce a reasonable profit consistent with the amount of money and time invested in the enterprise. Organizing is one of the principal jobs of management.

How Is a Hotel Organized?

In order to attract and serve guests and make a reasonable profit, hotels are organized into functional areas or divisions[1] based on the services the hotel provides. For instance, all hotels have a rooms division to manage guestrooms. If the hotel operates a restaurant or lounge, it is likely to have a food and beverage division as well. Within each division there are specialized functions. The rooms division handles reservations, check-in and check-out activities, housekeeping tasks, uniformed service (bellstaff) activities, and telecommunications service. At a small hotel, these functions are performed by personnel who report to and take their instructions from the general manager. At a large hotel, rooms personnel report to a rooms division manager. The tasks each employee is responsible for also vary with the size of the hotel. For example, in a small hotel, one person behind the front desk may act as receptionist, cashier, and hotel operator. In a large hotel, different individuals handle these jobs.

Revenue Centers versus Cost Centers

The divisions in a hotel can be categorized as revenue centers or cost centers. **Revenue centers** generate income for the hotel through the sale of services or products to guests. **Cost centers,** also known as support centers, do not generate revenue directly. Instead, they support the proper functioning of revenue centers.

Probably the easiest way to understand revenue and cost centers is to take a look at hotel organization charts. Exhibit 1 shows a typical organization chart for a small hotel. As you can see, this hotel has four divisions: front office, housekeeping, food and beverage, and building maintenance. The general manager supervises four people, each of whom has the responsibility and the authority to take care of one of the four principal areas in

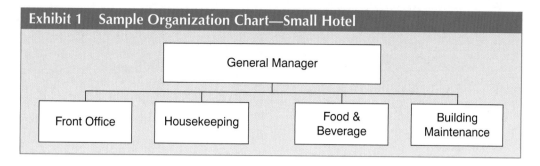

Exhibit 1   Sample Organization Chart—Small Hotel

this hotel. These individuals may or may not supervise other employees, depending on the size of the property. For example, at a very small property, building maintenance may be handled by just one person.

Let's examine a much larger hotel that has a more complex organization (see Exhibit 2). The divisions and departments shown in Exhibit 2 can be categorized like this:

Revenue Centers	Cost Centers
Rooms	Marketing
Food and Beverage	Engineering
Telecommunications	Accounting
Concessions, Rentals, Commissions	Human Resources
Fitness and Recreation Facilities	Security

In order to make hotels more efficient and profitable, there is a trend to combine some departments and eliminate certain middle-management positions. At some hotels, the rooms operation and food and beverage operation have been combined into one division, for example. Those areas responsible for generating revenue, such as sales, guestroom reservations, and catering, might be combined into a revenue division. Finally, there might be an administrative division that includes human resources and accounting.

In some hotel chains, regional management clusters have been formed. Under this system, a single manager—i.e., general manager, controller, or human resources director—is in charge of more than one hotel in the region.

At other hotels a different kind of reorganization is taking place. Based on management concepts that put the customer first, front-line employees are being given more authority to solve guest problems and make other decisions—by themselves or in teams. Authority is pushed down to the lowest level in the organization. For some hotels, the sample organization charts shown in this chapter may be more representative of the functions that occur in a hotel rather than the individuals who do the job.

Now let's take a closer look at each revenue and cost center.

Revenue Centers

The two main hotel revenue centers are the rooms division and the food and beverage division. Other revenue centers include the telecommunications department; concessions, rentals, and commissions; and fitness and recreational facilities.

Exhibit 2   Sample Organization Chart—Large Hotel

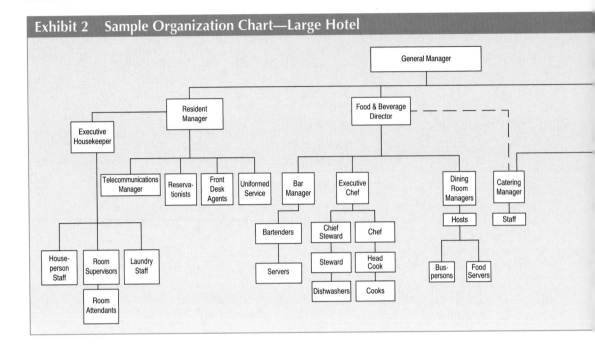

Rooms Division

In most hotels, the **rooms division** is the major division and the central reason for the business entity. (Casino hotels are an exception to this rule, since their rooms are occupied by guests whose primary reason for being at the hotel is to gamble.) Most of any hotel's square footage is devoted to guestrooms and areas that support the operation of those rooms. Therefore, the major segment of the building investment and, in most cases, the land cost is related to the rooms division.

For all hotels except casino hotels, guestroom rentals are the single largest source of revenue (see Exhibit 3). Rooms not only occupy the most space in a hotel and produce the most revenue, they generate the most profit. In a study of U.S. hotels published by PKF Hospitality Research, rooms division income (defined as room revenues or sales less room operating expenses) amounted to 74 percent of rooms revenue. In other words, for every dollar spent on guestrooms, 74 cents were available for general overhead after deducting the direct rooms division expenses.[2]

Organization of the Rooms Division. No matter what the size or category of hotel, rooms divisions are organized and function in a similar manner. Large hotels have more departments and personnel within the division, but this does not change the basic tasks that must be performed.

In a small hotel, the general manager or owner directly oversees the rooms division because of its paramount importance. In a mid-size to large hotel (300 rooms or more), there is likely to be a rooms manager or an executive assistant manager in charge of rooms. In either case, the rooms division is usually organized like the sample division shown in Exhibit 4. As you can see, the rooms division has four departments or functions:

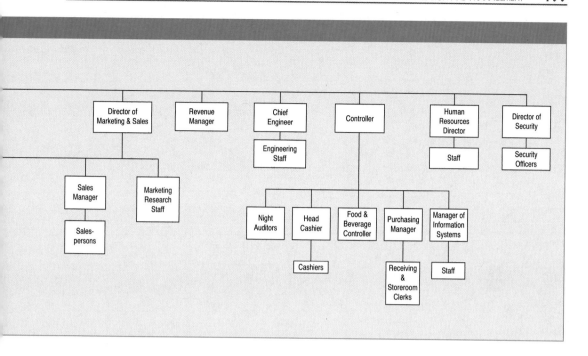

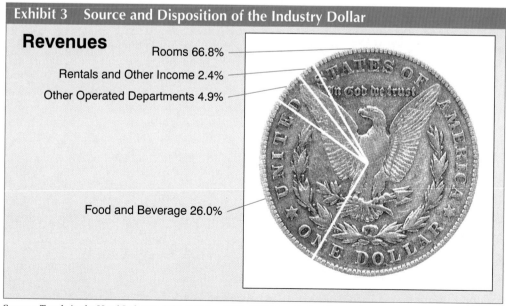

Source: *Trends in the Hotel Industry,* USA Edition 2009, PFK Hospitality Research.

Exhibit 4   Sample Organization Chart—Rooms Division

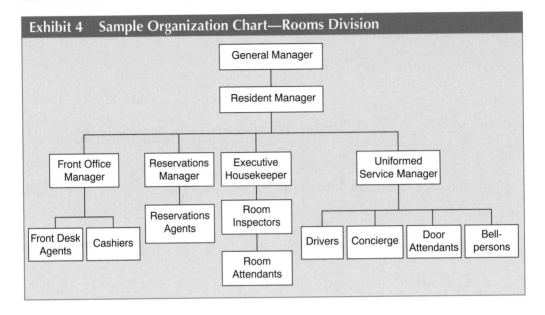

- Front office
- Reservations
- Housekeeping
- Uniformed service

Front office. The **front office** is the command post for processing reservations, registering guests, settling guest accounts (cashiering), and checking out guests. Front desk agents[3] also handle the distribution of guestroom keys and mail, messages, or other information for guests.

The most visible part of the front office area is of course the front desk. The front desk can be a counter or, in some luxury hotels, an actual desk where a guest can sit down and register. Traditionally, the front desk was placed so that the person behind it had a view of both the front door and the elevator. This was so front desk agents could discourage unwelcome individuals from entering and keep non-paying guests from departing. Because of modern credit and security procedures, such front desk placement is no longer necessary.

The duties of front desk agents include:

- Greeting guests
- Registering guests
- Establishing a method of payment for the guestroom—credit card, cash, or direct billing
- Assigning guestrooms that are unoccupied and have been cleaned
- Assigning guestroom keys to guests
- Informing guests about their room location and special hotel facilities, and answering questions about the property and the surrounding community

Most of any hotel's square footage is devoted to guestrooms and areas that support the operation of those rooms. For all hotels except casino hotels, guestroom rentals are the single largest source of revenue. (Courtesy of The Palazzo Las Vegas.)

- Calling a bellperson to assist guests with their luggage, if such service is normally provided

In small and mid-size hotels the front desk agent is also the cashier. Although the front desk station and cashier's station are usually separated in large hotels, employees are often cross-trained to handle both jobs. One important duty of a cashier (or a front desk agent performing cashier duties) is to post charges to guest accounts. This means that the cashier must make sure that all of the expenses a guest incurs, such as restaurant bills and telephone calls that were charged to the guestroom, are added to the bill before it is presented. This task is not necessary in hotels that have a computerized **property management system (PMS)** that interfaces with a point-of-sale (POS) system and automatically posts charges to guest accounts. Once the posting has been accomplished (either manually or electronically), guests can settle their account when they check out. Checking out guests requires tact and diplomacy. Guests often have questions about their charges and, in some cases, may not even be aware that they incurred a charge when using a particular service (such as making telephone calls).

Computerized property management systems have simplified check-in. For example, in one high-end hotel chain, guests with reservations are greeted personally at the door by an employee, who then escorts the guests to a special rack. In the rack is a packet for each pre-registered guest. The packet contains a room key and a registration card already filled out. The employee checks with each guest to see if the information is correct. If it is, the employee offers to escort the guests to their guestrooms or simply gives directions. Another hotel chain has a similar program, in which guests go directly to a special station, have an imprint of their credit card taken, and are given an arrival packet that includes a room key. At other hotel chains, guests can even check in by phone before they arrive at the hotel. In still others, check-in is done when guests arrive at nearby airports.

Self-service kiosks in hotel lobbies provide an even more simplified check-in system. From the kiosk, guests can check in simply by inserting their credit cards into the machine to retrieve reservation information. The kiosk will then dispense a room key, completing the guest check-in process. Upon checking out, guests can use the kiosk's terminal to pay their bills and print a receipt. Check-out information is then transmitted to the property management system. Guests can also fill out satisfaction surveys at this time.

Many hotels allow guests to review their bills on the television screens in their guestrooms and then send a signal through the channel selector to acknowledge that their accounts are in order and authorize payment. The bills are then charged to the guests' credit cards. Copies of the guests' hotel bills can be mailed directly to their homes or offices, or picked up in the lobby when the guests depart. In guestrooms with fax machines, bills can be faxed to guests in their guestrooms on check-out day.

Another common front office procedure to facilitate checkout is to slip copies of final bills under the doors of guestrooms during the night, while guests are sleeping. This system saves time because guests don't need to request their bills, and it allows guests time to study their bills before checkout. If guests have no questions, they can simply phone the front desk and tell the cashier that they agree with the charges as posted. Any charges incurred between the time a bill is okayed and the time checkout actually occurs are added to the guest's final account. The total amount of guest charges will appear on the guest's personal or corporate credit card statement.

This system presumes that the guest has used a credit card and that an imprint of that card was taken at registration. Usually, approval of the card and the guestroom charges is obtained from the credit card company at check-in, not checkout. If a credit card is not used, then the cashier must handle payment by cash or check according to the hotel's policies.

Another important duty performed at the front desk is the **night audit.** The night audit is a review of the guest accounts, also known as accounts receivable, for a single day. The purpose of a night audit is to reconcile the charges or postings to each guest account with the income of each department. For example, the total of room service charges for a day must equal the total of all the room service charges to the guest accounts. Night audits are usually done between 11 P.M. and 6 A.M., when there are few other distracting duties and the hotel's sales outlets are closed. In a small hotel, the night audit is performed by the front desk agent on duty. In a larger property, an auditor from the accounting division usually is assigned this task.

The typical metal guestroom keys and locks have been replaced in most hotels by electronic locking systems that operate with plastic **card keys**—and sometimes with a guest's own credit card. An electronic connection between guestroom door locks and a console at the front desk makes it possible to code a card key with each check-in, matching the card-key's code with a code programmed into the console for the guest's room. When the guest inserts the card key into a slot in the guestroom doorknob assembly, the door is unlocked. The door will stay locked if someone tries to use a card key with a code that does not match the electronic code for the lock. These card keys usually do not have the name of the hotel or the room number on them, so if they are lost they are of no use to whoever finds them. Some card-key systems connect guestroom locks to a central computer so that the hotel has a record of everyone who has entered the room (each housekeeping and maintenance employee's key registers its owner's code), along with the time of entry.

In addition to all of their other duties, front desk employees, in most cases, represent the first and last (and often the only) contact the guest has with hotel personnel. The front desk agents' ability to make guests feel welcome and special has a tremendous impact on the quality of a guest's experience. It's essential, therefore, that the front desk staff be well-trained and that morale be kept high so that interactions with guests and among staff members are always positive.

In order to improve guest relations, more and more hotels are encouraging front office and other employees to take the initiative in resolving disputes themselves rather than referring them to a supervisor. For example, the Ritz-Carlton hotel chain permits all employees to deduct up to $2,000 from a guest's bill if the guest has a legitimate complaint.

Reservations. Another part of the rooms division is the **reservations department** or office. A reservations department should be staffed by skilled telemarketing personnel who are able to accept reservations over the phone, answer questions about the hotel and its facilities, and quote guestroom rates and available dates. Since some callers are shopping around, reservationists should be trained to sell the property as well as simply accept reservations. Reservationists also process reservations that arrive through a central computer reservation system (CRS) or through third parties such as travel agents and hotel representatives, who typically contact hotels by telephone or use the Internet. Most hotels have their own websites where guests can make reservations directly.

When travel agents and hotel representatives call in a reservation, their calls must be handled with skill and efficiency if they are to be served properly. They require immediate and correct information on current room status. These travel professionals are compensated by commissions that the hotel sends to them after guest stays are completed. Naturally, a major concern of theirs is that the hotel will keep accurate records so that they will be paid promptly.

The largest percentage of advance reservations comes into hotels through direct inquiry, either by telephone or the hotel brand website. The remainder are received through the following sources:

- The Internet (e.g., Expedia, Orbitz, Travelocity—known as online travel agents or OTAs)
- Travel agents
- Hotel representatives
- Tour operators
- Independent reservation systems
- Airlines, cruise lines, and other transportation companies

Many hotels use **revenue management** techniques in the pricing and selling of rooms. For many years, airlines have used sophisticated revenue management pricing systems. These are automated marketing programs that allow the airlines to control the inventory and pricing of airplane seats by forecasting the demand for seats on a given flight or route and then adjusting prices to maximize revenue. Revenue management for hotels means using information, historical and current, to enhance a hotel's ability to carry out a number

More and more companies are allowing guests to tour their properties, find answers to common questions, plan their vacations, and make reservations on the Internet. (Courtesy of Walt Disney World, Orlando, Florida.)

of common business practices, and thereby increase both its revenues and its customer service capabilities. These practices include:

- Setting the most effective pricing structure for guestrooms

- Limiting the number of reservations accepted for any given night, room type, or length of stay, based on the expected profitability of a reservation

- Reviewing reservation activity to determine whether any inventory control actions should be taken (for example, lowering rates)

- Negotiating volume discounts with wholesalers and groups

- Providing customers with the right product (the right guestroom type, rate, etc.)

- Obtaining more revenue from current and potential business

- Enabling reservations agents to be effective sales agents rather than merely order takers

Eric Orkin, an industry consultant, says:

> Performance benchmarks in the hotel industry are commonly keyed to room-night or dollar volume. Volume criteria like these make perfect sense when selling a product with a sustained value, but the value of a hotel room varies from day to day and over time. For example, a room on a Saturday during New England fall foliage season is a lot more valuable than the same room on a "mud season" night in the spring. Less obvious, the value of that fall foliage night was high until two days before the date, when bad weather caused a major tour to cancel. Because the hotel was now faced with the prospect of empty rooms, the value of the hotel's rooms dropped.[4]

Revenue management requires the use of complex computer programs to (1) forecast the number of reservations a hotel can expect on a given day (as well as cancellations and no-shows), (2) track the availability of guestrooms, and (3) compute the maximum rates that those rooms can be sold for, based on availability, demand, and other factors which fluctuate.

As revenue management systems become more sophisticated, their scope is expanding. For example, today many hotel companies use revenue management systems to manage their meeting space as well as their guestroom space. By tracking demand for meeting space, the goal of "total hotel revenue management" is to maximize the revenue stream of both room inventories (guestrooms and meeting rooms).

Some hoteliers feel that revenue management systems sometimes encourage discounting. Others see revenue management as incompatible with good customer service, because room rates that frequently change can confuse guests. But, properly used, there is no doubt that revenue management can be an effective reservations tool.

Housekeeping. The **housekeeping department** is another department of the rooms division. Housekeeping is responsible for cleaning the hotel's guestrooms and public areas. In most hotels, this department has the largest staff. In a large hotel, the housekeeping department might consist of an executive housekeeper, an assistant housekeeper, room inspectors, room attendants, a houseperson crew (which cleans the public areas and handles the logistics of moving housekeeping supplies throughout the hotel), a linen room supervisor and attendants, laundry employees, and personnel in charge of employee uniforms (see Exhibit 5). Hotels with laundry and valet equipment may use it only for hotel linens and uniforms and send guest clothing to an outside service where it can be handled with specialized equipment.

An executive housekeeper has an enormous amount of responsibility—not only for cleaning and maintenance, but also for training staff and controlling large inventories of linens, supplies, and equipment.[5] Room inspectors supervise room attendants. Room attendants are responsible for cleaning guestrooms according to specified procedures and

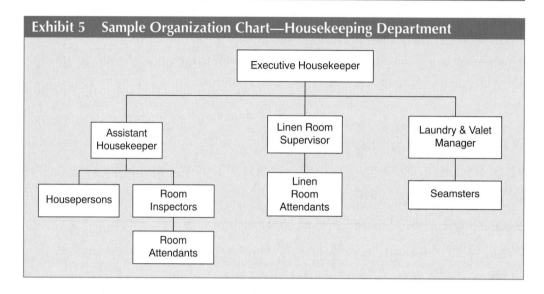

Exhibit 5   Sample Organization Chart—Housekeeping Department

for maintaining a predetermined level of supplies in the linen closets located on each hotel floor. They are usually assigned a quota of rooms to clean in a given number of hours. Fifteen guestrooms per shift is average, although this figure may vary considerably because of such conditions as geographic location, union contracts, the size of the property, and the wage scale. In most hotels, room attendants are paid relatively low wages.

When guests check out, it is the room attendants' responsibility to clean the guestrooms so that they are available again for rental. This includes such duties as:

- Removing soiled linen and towels and replacing them with fresh ones
- Checking the bed and blankets for damage
- Making the beds
- Emptying trash
- Checking the guestroom for broken appliances, damaged shades or blinds, and leaky faucets
- Checking closets and drawers for items forgotten by guests
- Cleaning the guestroom and bathroom
- Replacing bathroom towels and amenities

Some hotels contract with outside cleaning services to clean the hotel's lobbies, restaurants, restrooms, and windows. With the exception of windows, much of this cleaning must be done late at night, and hotels often find it difficult to find supervisors and employees willing to work at those hours. Contract cleaning firms, many of whom handle office buildings and airline terminals as well, are geared to efficiently handle these cleaning tasks during unusual work hours.

Uniformed service. The **uniformed service department** is sometimes referred to as the guest service department. Employees in this department include bellpersons (so called because originally they were summoned by a bell), a concierge, and transportation or valet-parking employees. Some large hotels have door attendants who move luggage from cars or taxicabs into the hotel.

Room attendants are responsible for cleaning guestrooms according to procedures specified by the hotel. (The Westin Calgary, Calgary, Canada; photo courtesy of Starwood Hotels & Resorts Worldwide, Inc.)

Bellpersons move guest luggage to and from guestrooms. They also escort guests to their rooms, inspect guestrooms while rooming the guest, and explain the features of the room and the hotel to guests. Bellpersons should possess a detailed knowledge of the hotel, including the hours of operation of the hotel's restaurants, lounges, and other facilities. They should also know the local community.

Some hotels have adopted the European system of concierge service. The concierge performs many of the functions that a host might perform for guests in his or her home. The goal is to give guests personal and attentive service. The concierge is the main source of information about the hotel. He or she is not only familiar with the hotel's facilities and services but also has a thorough knowledge of the local area. A good concierge knows what's going on in town. He or she can recommend a romantic candlelit bistro within walking distance or the best steak house in the city. The concierge can make reservations and get theater tickets—or suggest someone who can. He or she can also recommend secretarial services and copying centers, order limousines, and perform many other services that give guests the feeling that they are important and well cared for.

Transportation services include valet parking, either in the hotel's own garage or a nearby facility. If other transportation services are provided, such as airport shuttle service, these are normally handled by the same department. In most large hotels, garages and limousines are handled by outside contractors.

Measuring the Performance of the Rooms Division. The three most commonly used room department statistics for measuring department performance are the **average daily rate (ADR), occupancy percentage,** and **revenue per available room (RevPAR).** These statistics can be calculated daily or for any other time period.

The average daily rate is simply the amount of rooms revenue divided by the number of rooms occupied for the same period of time. Here is an example of how this is calculated for a single day and a three-day period:

Day	Rooms Revenue	÷	Rooms Occupied	=	Average Daily Rate (ADR)
Monday	$23,800		170		$140.00
Tuesday	$30,000		185		$162.16
Wednesday	$29,000		178		$162.92
Three-Day Figures	**$82,800**		533		$155.03

In this example, $155.03 indicates the average amount of revenue for each of the 533 occupied rooms for the three-day period. Most hotels have a number of rate classes targeted at different market segments. There may be different rates for government employees, corporate travelers, and senior citizens, among others. The rates also vary according to room size, location, furnishings, and service. For example, a large corner guestroom on a high floor overlooking a park is more expensive than a smaller room on a lower floor that faces an alley. The price the room is finally sold for will depend on who it is sold to, the location, the day of the week, and possibly the season of the year. Management's goal is to sell the most expensive rooms first. However, guests usually request the lowest-priced rooms. Therefore, the average daily rate is an indicator of the sales ability of those taking reservations, as well as the demand for the various types of guestrooms.

An equally important marketing statistic is the occupancy percentage. It is computed by dividing the number of rooms occupied by the number of rooms available for sale for the same period and multiplying by 100. The number of rooms available for sale may be different from the number of rooms in the hotel. This discrepancy occurs when rooms are being used to house managers and other personnel on a permanent basis, or when rooms are being remodeled. Like the average rate, the occupancy percentage can be calculated for any period of time:

Day	Rooms Occupied	÷	Rooms Available	× 100 =	Occupancy Percentage
Monday	170		200		85.0%
Tuesday	185		200		92.5%
Wednesday	178		200		89.0%
Three-Day Figures	**533**		600		88.8%

Revenue per available room (RevPAR) is a third common statistic operators use in evaluating the performance of the rooms department. It is computed by dividing room revenue by the number of available rooms for the same period. Alternatively, it can be determined by multiplying the occupancy percentage by the average daily rate for the same period:

Day	Occupancy Percentage	×	Average Daily Rate	=	RevPAR
Monday	85.0%		$140.00		$119.00
Tuesday	92.5%		$162.16		$150.00 (rounded)
Wednesday	89.0%		$162.92		$145.00 (rounded)
Three-Day Figures	88.8%		$155.03		$138.00 (rounded)

These three statistics are used by managers to assess how the hotel is doing in relation to the budget and forecast of performance. Using these same forecasts, the marketing department can see which weeks and months ahead need extra sales efforts. It should be noted that these figures cannot be used by themselves to measure a hotel's financial performance. A hotel might have a 99 percent occupancy percentage and still be failing if the average daily rate or revenue per available room is not high enough to cover all costs and provide a reasonable return on investment.

Food and Beverage Division

Although in most hotels the rooms division generates the greatest amount of revenue, this is not always the case. In a few hotels (most often resorts and convention properties with extensive banquet sales), the **food and beverage division** may produce as much or more revenue as the rooms division. This is because guests in resorts tend to stay on the premises and may be less price-sensitive because they are on vacation. In convention hotels, the added food sales come from the multitude of restaurants, banquet rooms, and bars typically found in a convention property.

Whether the food and beverage operation is large or small, most hotel managers have found that their food and beverage facilities are of paramount importance to the reputation and profitability of the hotel. There is no doubt that in many cases the quality of a hotel's food and beverages powerfully affects a guest's opinion of the hotel and influences his or her willingness to return. In fact, some hotels are as famous for their restaurants as for their guestrooms. For example, the Four Seasons Hotel in New York City has the L'Atelier de Joël Robuchon, operated by the celebrated French chef.

Successful hotel operators no longer consider dining facilities merely a convenience for guests. A hotel's food and beverage outlet(s) must attract members of the local community, convince hotel guests to dine on the premises, and return a fair profit. The **capture rate**—that is, the percentage of guests who eat meals at the hotel—is measured regularly by many hotels.

Except for limited-service hotels and motels (which achieve that status in large part by staying out of the restaurant business), virtually all lodging facilities offer some level of food and beverage service. Large hotels usually have a wide array of facilities, while small properties may have just one dining room that serves breakfast, lunch, and dinner. Exhibit 6 lists the types of food and beverage outlets that may be found in a hotel.[6]

Selecting Food and Beverage Outlets. There are several criteria managers use to decide what type of food and beverage service should be offered in any given hotel. Managers

Exhibit 6 Types of Hotel Food and Beverage Outlets	
Food Service	**Beverage Service**
Dining Room	Cocktail Lounge
Specialty Restaurant	Public Bar (for guests)
Coffee Shop (mid-price restaurant)	Service Bar (for servers)
Supper Club	Banquets
Snack Bar	Discotheques
Take-Out	Mini-Bars (in guestrooms)
Cafeteria	
Room Service	
Banquets	
Employee Food Service	

should think about these carefully, both in the initial planning stages of a new hotel and as a hotel matures and the market it appeals to changes.

The first criterion is the type of hotel. Does this property primarily serve transient businesspeople or conventioneers? Is the property a resort? Business clientele are more interested in private dining, while convention hotels need ballrooms for large gatherings. Resorts often do well with specialty restaurants.

Next is the class of hotel. Five-star hotels need five-star restaurants. Moderate-price hotels could not sustain this kind of restaurant quality, nor would their guests expect it.

Competition is another consideration. What kinds of restaurants are already available in the area? If you are surrounded by Italian restaurants, putting one in your hotel would probably not be a good idea. It might be wiser to try something completely different.

Product availability also counts. A fresh-fish restaurant might have a difficult time making it unless it limited itself to the kind of fish that is readily available. The cost of flying in fresh Maine lobster and Dover sole could easily price it out of the market.

Availability of labor is another important consideration. A menu that requires a lot of employees—for example, one that features tableside cooking with dishes like Steak Diane and desserts such as crêpes Suzette—might not be practical in a tight labor market.

Finally, there is the question of demand. Certain kinds of food are more popular in some areas of the country than others. Mexican restaurants are more in demand in the Southwest than the Northeast, for example. Is the type of restaurant in the hotel one that the hotel's guests will want to patronize?

Organization of the Food and Beverage Division. The food and beverage division of a major hotel can be complex, offering a variety of different kinds of restaurants and bars, each with its own unique decor, menu, and style of service. Such a division requires well-trained employees and highly skilled and versatile managers in the kitchen, bar, and service areas.

We can examine an organization chart of a typical food and beverage operation in a mid-size hotel to get an idea of how a food and beverage division works (see Exhibit 7). As can be seen from the exhibit, the person in charge of the food and beverage division reports to the general manager and is known as the food and beverage manager. (Some

Exhibit 7 Sample Organization Chart—F&B Division in a Mid-Size Hotel

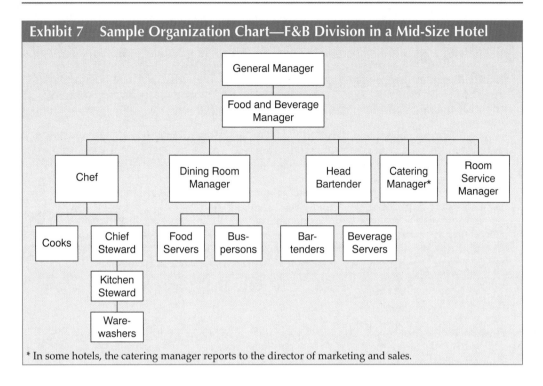

* In some hotels, the catering manager reports to the director of marketing and sales.

hotels assign this function to an executive assistant manager.) Since this job entails responsibility for a major business entity of the hotel that is staffed by persons with specialized technical skills, the food and beverage manager should have a thorough knowledge of general business and management practices. He or she should also be well-versed in the technical aspects of food and beverage preparation and service.

Reporting to the food and beverage manager is the chef, sometimes called the executive chef or head chef, who is in charge of the kitchen staff. An important member of the chef's team is the chief steward, who directs the kitchen steward and warewashers and makes sure all dining rooms, bars, and banquet rooms have sufficient inventories of clean china, glassware, and silverware.

The dining room manager must see that guest service goes smoothly, that there is a sufficient number of food servers and buspersons on duty, and that all dining room employees are well-trained and are meeting the property's service standards. The job may also include training new employees.

In mid-size hotels with a lounge, a head bartender oversees the lounge's operation. He or she supervises bartenders and beverage servers. The catering manager and room service manager are in charge of food and beverage areas that will be discussed briefly in the following sections.

Catering. The food and beverage divisions of some hotels contain catering departments. (It should be noted that some hotels with catering operations choose to place catering in their marketing and sales department rather than the food and beverage division.) A **catering department's** importance is twofold. Not only is it an image-maker for the hotel, but it also can be the most profitable segment of the food and beverage division. Catering arranges and plans food and beverage functions for (1) conventions and smaller

Meal Plans

There are several meal plans that hotel food and beverage divisions offer. They include the Full American Plan, the Modified American Plan, the Continental Plan, and the European Plan.

The Full American Plan and the Modified American Plan are usually seen in resort hotels. Under the Full American Plan, the room rate quoted includes all major meals—breakfast, lunch, and dinner. In effect, guests are offered a package price that includes their room and all three meals for as long as they stay. This has great appeal to guests who are concerned with the total cost of their resort vacation and like to budget for it ahead of time. The Modified American Plan provides two meals only—usually breakfast and dinner.

The Continental Plan includes a continental breakfast with the room rate. This plan is also called a Breakfast Plan, and in Bermuda it's known as the Bermuda Plan. With the European Plan, no meals are included in the room rate.

Isolated resorts with few or no restaurants in the surrounding area and no centers of population nearby are more likely to offer an American Plan. These types of resorts were especially popular in the early 1900s, when travelers stayed at resorts for two weeks or more. Most guests today don't want to be locked into a meal plan—they prefer the freedom to try other restaurants in the area. As a result, offering a meal plan is not a growing hotel service, since demand for it, on the whole, is decreasing. Hotel managers can be sympathized with for wishing this were not so. From the hotels' standpoint, there is much better control over purchasing, preparing, and staffing when the number of meals that will be served is known in advance. Moreover, both American plans guarantee food revenue and, to a great degree, beverage revenue as well, since guests often order cocktails before dinner, wine with dinner, or after-dinner drinks.

hotel groups, and (2) local banquets booked by the sales department. Catering sales, in some instances, represent as much as 50 percent of a hotel's total food and beverage sales.

Catering is a highly competitive business in most market areas. To succeed, a catering department must have employees with a broad range of abilities and knowledge. Good catering departments excel in sales, menu planning, food and beverage service (including wines), food production, product knowledge, cost control, artistic talent, and a sense of theater. All of this requires sound technical knowledge as well as skillful use of the hotel's facilities and equipment.

The catering manager generally reports to the food and beverage manager. There are exceptions to this rule, however. In some hotels, the catering manager reports to the director of sales or directly to the hotel's general manager; in such instances, the catering manager's main responsibility is to sell catered events to clients rather than actually manage the events. When hotels are organized in this manner, a banquet manager in charge of the catering area's food production usually reports to the food and beverage manager. Such a division of labor separates the catering area's selling function from the production and service function. To help cut costs, some hotels combine the positions of food and beverage manager and catering manager.

Room service. Most hotels with a food and beverage division provide some type of food service to guests in their rooms. **Room service**—or "private dining," as the highly marketing-oriented Walt Disney Corporation refers to it—is one of the most difficult areas of hotel food service to manage and has the greatest potential for losing money.

There are two main difficulties with room service. First, food and beverages are served at great distances from production areas. In resorts where there are cottages for

A hotel's catering department can account for as much as 50 percent of a hotel's total food and beverage sales. This outdoor banquet is set up on the hotel's grounds. (The Westin La Paloma, Tucson, Arizona; photo courtesy of Starwood Hotels & Resorts Worldwide, Inc.)

guests, electric carts are often used to transport food. Because of frequent stops along the way, there is a real likelihood of hot items arriving cold and cold items becoming tepid. Second—and, again, because of distance—the productivity of food servers is low; in the same amount of time, restaurant servers can take care of many more guests than room service personnel can. The revenue generated, therefore, is often not sufficient to cover costs. These problems are exacerbated by the fact that the greatest demand for room service is at breakfast, and the most popular type of morning meal is the continental breakfast (juice or fruit, roll with butter and jam, and a beverage). This meal has a low check average.

To deal with room service costs, many hotels charge higher prices for room service food, as well as an additional charge per order (or per person) for the service. The cost problem can be further alleviated by limiting (1) the number of items on the room service menu, and (2) the hours of service. This does not solve the problem of potentially inferior food quality, however, nor meet the desire on the part of some guests to have a wide variety of food available on the room service menu.

When it comes to room service at luxury resorts, presentation is often as important as the food itself. (Courtesy of The Broadmoor, Colorado Springs, Colorado.)

To retain food quality, the food must be delivered to the room as quickly as possible and at the appropriate temperature. This requires proper equipment and a highly efficient room service organization. Many hotels use a doorknob menu that invites guests to order their breakfast the night before, indicating on the menu the items they want and the time they would like to be served. Guests then place the menus on the outside doorknobs of their rooms, for collection during the night. This allows the hotel to do a better job, because the hotel can plan the number of breakfasts to be served in each time period and organize delivery to the rooms.

Because of the problems associated with delivering a satisfactory room service experience, some hotels have been cutting back on room service, curtailing the number of hours it is available or doing away with it altogether. On the other hand, some first-class and luxury hotels view room service as an opportunity. Hoteliers at these properties see it as part of the overall guest experience. To help guarantee its success, they have redesigned their menus to focus on foods that travel well, while still providing a variety of selections. For example, Ritz-Carlton includes pizza, hamburgers, and salads; The Four Seasons serves home-style dishes such as chicken pot pie and meat loaf.

Support and control services. Support and control services related to the food and beverage division include the **purchasing department** and the accounting division. Large hotels have a purchasing manager who is responsible for buying all of the products used in the hotel, including food and beverage items. Usually, orders are given to the purchasing department by the chef, by the bar manager (or head bartender), or by the food and beverage manager. The purchasing department then seeks competitive bids from suppliers, giving them precise specifications for each of the food and beverage items being ordered.

The control aspect of food and beverage is generally under the supervision of the hotel's controller. Reporting to the controller are:

- Receiving clerks, who verify the number and quality of food and beverage items received

- Storeroom clerks, who are responsible for properly storing and issuing items from the food and beverage storeroom

- Cashiers in restaurants, coffee shops, and other food and beverage outlets, who handle the settlement of guest checks

Some properties also have a food and beverage controller who reports to the hotel's controller. This individual is the food and beverage expert in the controller's office and is responsible for ensuring that optimum financial efficiency is attained in the food and beverage division. A food and beverage controller's duties include:

- Tracking food and beverage costs

- Monitoring ordering and receiving procedures, including adherence to purchase specifications

- Costing and pricing menu items

- Conducting monthly storeroom inventories

- Keeping management informed of costs and, when necessary, recommending actions to lower costs

- Creating monthly and daily reports on food and beverage costs

In some hotels, the food and beverage controller reports to the food and beverage manager. From a control standpoint, this arrangement is not desirable, because the food and beverage controller, in effect, is the watchdog over the food and beverage division, with his or her reports serving as an evaluation of the division. However, the food and beverage controller is sometimes positioned that way because the job is often an early step in the career path toward food and beverage manager.

Problems in Food and Beverage Operations. Although the food and beverage divisions of many hotels show a substantial profit in all of their food and beverage operations, not all food and beverage divisions are profitable. Some lose money in all areas, while others lose money in their food operations but make a profit with their beverage operations. Sometimes losses are attributed to bad management alone, but there are a number of other common reasons for losses in food and beverage operations:

- *Long hours of operation.* Hotel restaurants must maintain an adequate level of service even during slow periods in order to satisfy the needs of hotel guests. But the low volume of business during slow times is not always sufficient to cover the cost of operation. Tightly managed employee scheduling can help alleviate this problem.

- *Low check averages.* Low-priced breakfasts and inexpensive snacks served at odd hours are frequently cited as reasons for unprofitability. Clever marketing of more profitable items can help overcome this problem.

- *Too many facilities.* Trying to satisfy a wide variety of hotel guests by having several different types of food and beverage facilities tends to be inefficient from a cost standpoint. However, proper planning, central kitchens, and coordinated menus (so that different recipes use many of the same ingredients) can help solve this problem.

- *High turnover.* Because of the increasing complexity of hotel food and beverage divisions, there is a greater need for highly paid personnel. This labor cost cannot be avoided. What can be avoided is a high turnover rate among this group, which increases recruiting and training costs. Good human resources management can make a real difference here.

- *Costly entertainment.* Some hotels with several restaurants and bars hire entertainers to entice guests into a night out. Although entertainment is a specialized business, prices charged by entertainers are negotiable. Hotels that use experienced booking agents often have lower entertainment costs and get better entertainers.

- *Insufficient marketing.* In the past, few hotels marketed their food and beverage outlets; some are still guilty of that omission today. But one of the most significant changes in most hotels in recent years is that they are aggressively marketing their restaurants and lounges. Now many hotels compete successfully with free-standing restaurants by employing some of the same techniques that these independents have used so effectively: exciting themes and decor, interesting and dramatic menus, and quality entertainment.

Other Revenue Centers

Telecommunications Department. Hotel managers know that good telecommunications service adds to a guest's positive impression of the hotel, while poor service causes frustration and a negative impression. This can result in lost repeat business.

The use of modern telecommunications equipment has lessened the guest's dependence on the hotel's telephone operators. Many hotel telecommunications services can be accessed directly by dialing a given extension. For example, guests can retrieve their own phone messages, if they are taken (or recorded) correctly, by dialing a digital code. Wake-up calls can be automated, although clock radios in guestrooms often eliminate the need for these calls completely. Local and long-distance calls do not require the assistance of the hotel's operator. As a result, the **telecommunications department** in a modern hotel not only provides better service than ever before but has a greater potential for profit. There is no doubt that good phone service is appreciated, and guests may be willing to pay extra for it. One example is offering in-room Internet service.

Many first-class hotels offer guests a voice-mail service that allows them to send and receive recorded messages. Beeper service and cellular phones are also offered, so that guests can contact business clients quickly, whether the guests are in the hotel or out at a meeting. AT&T has an over-the-phone translation service. A non-English-speaking guest simply calls a front desk agent, who can contact an AT&T operator to act as a translator for the guest and the front desk agent.

Of course, many guests today own cell phones, which has had a substantial impact on guest use of hotel telephone services; other guests use calling cards when traveling. As a result, telephone revenues are declining in many hotels.

Concessions, Rentals, and Commissions. If there is enough guest demand, a hotel has the potential to sell more than rooms, food, and beverages. Gift shops, newsstands, flower shops, laundry and dry cleaning services, beauty salons, jewelry stores, secretarial services, and even office space are just a few of the types of services that can be made available within the hotel and accessible through the lobby or a separate street entrance. Hotel management has the choice of either operating these services themselves or bringing in others to do it for them.

A **concession** is a facility that might well be operated by the hotel directly, such as a beauty salon or fitness club, but instead is turned over to an independent operator who is responsible for the concession's equipment, personnel, and marketing. The hotel's income from concessions is determined in several ways. It can be a flat fee, a minimum fee plus a percentage of the gross receipts over a specific amount, or simply a percentage of total gross sales.

Rentals are common in many properties. With a rental, the hotel simply rents space to an enterprise such as an office or a store. The rent charged is typically spelled out in a lease, which is usually long term, with options to renew and annual rent adjustments specified.

Commissions are fees paid to the hotel by suppliers that are located outside the hotel but provide services for hotel guests. Some examples are car rental agencies, photographers, and dry-cleaning services. They pay a commission to the hotel based on a percentage of their gross sales to guests.

One important aspect of these kinds of arrangements is that unless the company or individual providing the service within the hotel is recognized in its own right (such as the Canyon Ranch Spa in the Venetian Hotel in Las Vegas), as far as most guests are concerned, their relationship is not with the vendor but with the hotel. Therefore, the quality and service standards of vendors must conform to the rest of the hotel's operation, or they can negatively affect the guest's perception of the hotel itself. For example, if a gift shop sells tasteless novelties, guests are likely to conclude that the hotel itself has those same tastes and standards. An agreement with a vendor should explicitly spell out standards of cleanliness,

If there is enough demand, a hotel has the potential to sell more than rooms, food, and beverages to guests. This is a gift shop in The Fairmont Pierre Marques, Acapulco, Mexico. (Courtesy of Fairmont Hotels & Resorts.)

personnel dress codes, and other "image" issues, as well as more practical matters such as hours of operation.

Fitness and Recreational Facilities. Today's businessperson may well travel with a pair of running shoes and feel that a daily run or workout of some kind is important. Hotels that have recognized this and provided workout facilities and indoor swimming pools have been able to capitalize on this new demand and increase their guest base. Other hotels have not kept up with the times and have lost guests who insist on some provision for exercising while they are away from home.

Often guests are not charged for the use of basic exercise facilities, although there may be a fee for extras like massages, rental bicycles, or the use of a luxury spa. Some hotels have recognized the potential to sell access to their health club to office workers and residents near the hotel and have sold health club memberships, thus turning what started out as a cost center into a revenue producer.

Another growing trend in travel is to combine business with pleasure. It is not uncommon to see businesspeople traveling with their spouses and children. As a result, some properties have installed video game rooms, which have turned out to be exceedingly popular. Such rooms can gross more than $500 per week, with approximately half of that ending up on the bottom line as profit for the hotel.

Many hotels and resorts now provide fitness centers for their guests. This is a fitness center in The Fairmont Acapulco Princess, Acapulco, Mexico. (Courtesy of Fairmont Hotels & Resorts.)

A major source of recreation revenue comes from pay TV in guestrooms. There are many systems for delivering television programming to hotel guestrooms and lounges. In addition to regular broadcast channels, there are cable channels such as HBO, Showtime, ESPN, and MTV. First-run movies are also available on a pay-per-view basis. This is one service that a deluxe or even middle-market hotel can hardly afford not to offer. Many guests expect to be able to watch movies in their room—often with pizza or popcorn delivered by room service.

Cost Centers

As mentioned earlier, cost or support centers are hotel divisions that do not directly generate revenues. These divisions include:

- Marketing and sales
- Engineering
- Accounting

- Human resources
- Security

Marketing and Sales Division

The mission of a hotel's **marketing and sales division** is to (1) identify prospective guests for the hotel, (2) shape the products and services of the hotel as much as possible to meet the needs of those prospects, and (3) persuade prospects to become guests. This task begins before the first brick is laid.

One way to understand marketing is to look at what it is not. Marketing is not selling. It has been said that the difference between marketing and selling is that selling is getting rid of what you have, while marketing is having what people want. If you have what people want and you tell them about it, sales will come easily—assuming that not too many others have it at the same place for the same price at the same time! If you don't have what people want and you are forced to get rid of what you have, you may have to discount it or promote it heavily, and even then it might not sell.

Marketing a hotel is not an activity confined to the marketing and sales division; every employee is involved in providing what guests want. It is part of the job of the marketing and sales division to understand the needs and wants of the hotel's guests and advise management of them, so that managers can train employees in how to meet those needs and wants.

The marketing and sales division is charged with the responsibility of keeping the rooms in the hotel occupied at the right price and with the right mix of guests. It accomplishes this through many activities, including:

- Contacting groups and individuals
- Advertising in print and on radio, television, and the Internet
- Creating direct mail and public relations campaigns
- Participating in trade shows
- Visiting travel agents
- Arranging **familiarization tours** (free or reduced-rate travel packages designed to acquaint travel agents and others with the hotel and stimulate sales)
- Participating in community activities that raise the community's awareness of the hotel

On average, hotels spend approximately five percent of sales on such efforts. This figure is misleading, however, and should be considered cautiously. For example, marketing a new hotel is much more expensive than marketing an established one. The marketing expenses involved in opening a new hotel, such as parties for community leaders and familiarization tours for travel agents, are often capitalized and charged off over a period of time. The cost of reservation systems is often charged to the rooms division, although it could be argued that such a system is a marketing tool and ought to be treated as a marketing expense.

In most large hotels, the marketing and sales division is headed by a director of marketing and sales (see Exhibit 8). Reporting to the director is a sales manager, an advertising and public relations director, and a convention sales manager. Each of these individuals

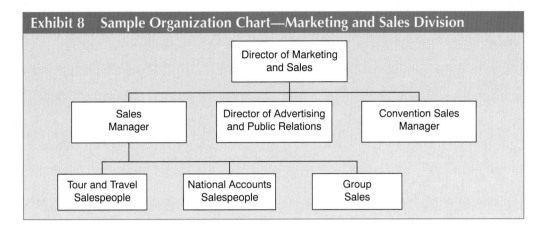

Exhibit 8 Sample Organization Chart—Marketing and Sales Division

heads a department that is responsible for a distinct and separate activity within the overall marketing mission.

The sales department is responsible for prospecting for business and making sales calls on individuals and companies. The advertising and public relations department attempts to attract guests through advertising and create a positive image of the hotel. Commonly used public relations techniques are news releases about the hotel and its employees or guests, and involvement by managers and employees in community service. The convention sales manager specializes in finding and booking group and convention business.

In many ways, the marketing and sales function of a hotel can be considered the very essence of the operation. A frequently quoted remark by management consultant Peter Drucker puts it this way: "There is only one valid definition of business purpose: to create a customer."[7]

Engineering Division

Taking care of the hotel's physical plant and controlling energy costs are the responsibilities of the **engineering division.**[8] The physical upkeep of the building, furniture, fixtures, and equipment is essential to:

- Slow a hotel's physical deterioration
- Preserve the original hotel image established by management
- Keep revenue-producing areas operational
- Keep the property comfortable for guests and employees
- Preserve the safety of the property for guests and employees
- Create savings by keeping repairs and equipment replacements to a minimum

The engineering division is also responsible for heating and air-conditioning systems and the systems that distribute electricity, steam, and water throughout the property.

In order to accomplish the many tasks of the engineering division, several types of technicians may be employed: electricians, plumbers, carpenters, painters, refrigeration and air-conditioning engineers, and others. The division is headed by a chief engineer.

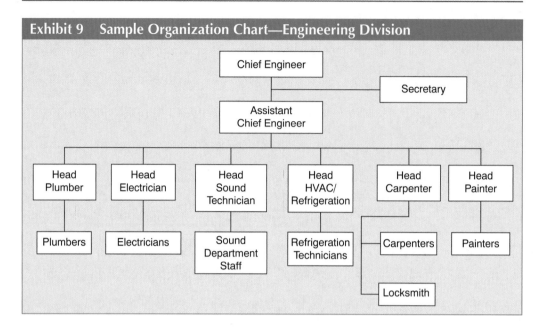

Exhibit 9   Sample Organization Chart—Engineering Division

In small hotels, one all-purpose engineer may perform all engineering functions or subcontract work as needed. In a large hotel, the chief engineer may be called a plant manager. When the size of the hotel warrants, there is also a secretary or administrative assistant to deal with the logistics of handling repair requests and scheduling service. Exhibit 9 shows a sample organization chart for the engineering division of a 700-room convention/resort hotel.

The maintenance and repair work performed by the engineering staff is one of two kinds: preventive or as needed. Preventive maintenance is a planned program of ongoing servicing of the building and equipment in order to maintain operations and prolong the life of the facility. Outside contractors may be hired for some jobs either on an as-needed basis or through a service contract. An important aspect of maintenance work is that in all areas there should be documentation to track labor and material costs. A master checklist groups the preventive maintenance work to be done on a daily, weekly, and monthly schedule. Detailed equipment checklists outlining tasks to be performed and how long it should take to perform them assist managers in scheduling employees.

In addition to preventive maintenance, the engineering staff performs routine repairs. Repair logs should be used to keep track of the start and finish of each repair assignment. Major projects that require the purchase of building materials may also be undertaken by the engineering division. Management usually determines whether extensive repairs or replacement of equipment not covered by service contracts is to be done by the hotel's own staff or given to an outside contractor.

In a study of full-service U.S. hotels, PKF Hospitality Research reports that its sample spent 4.8 percent of total sales on maintenance. Utility cost was 4.1 percent.[9]

Accounting Division

A hotel's **accounting division** is responsible for keeping track of the many business transactions that occur in the hotel. The accounting division does more than simply keep

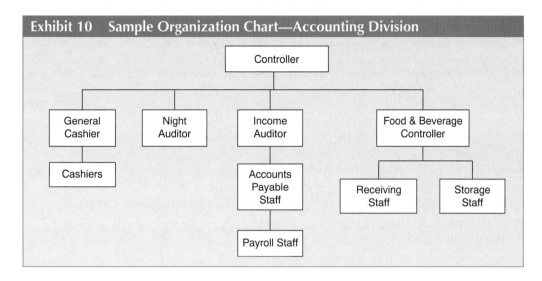

Exhibit 10   Sample Organization Chart—Accounting Division

the books—financial management is perhaps a more appropriate description of what the accounting division does. A sample organization chart of an accounting division is shown in Exhibit 10.

The responsibilities of the accounting division include:

- Forecasting and budgeting

- Managing what the hotel owns and what money is due from guests

- Controlling cash

- Controlling costs in all areas of the hotel—revenue centers as well as cost centers and payroll

- Purchasing, receiving, storing, and issuing operating and capital inventory such as food and beverages, housekeeping supplies, and furniture

- Keeping records, preparing financial statements and daily operating reports, and interpreting these statements and reports for management

In order to accomplish these diverse functions, the head of accounting—the controller—relies on a staff of auditors, cashiers, and other accounting employees. Not all of the controller's staff works in the hotel's accounting office; accounting functions are performed throughout the hotel. For example, credit staff, front office cashiers, and night auditors work in the front desk area. Cashiers work in the restaurant and bar. The food and beverage controller is sometimes located in the receiving area, and others responsible for control functions, such as receiving clerks, are close to the hotel's service entrances.

The accounting division bridges and interacts with all of a hotel's revenue and cost divisions. In many cases, the controller reports directly to the corporate controller of the parent company (if the hotel is part of a chain or some other corporation). He or she is responsible for all of the control functions within the hotel and, in that capacity, also reports to the hotel's general manager.

Human Resources Division

Good managers see themselves as developers of people and as guardians of their company's most important asset—its employees. Thus, the old-fashioned personnel division has gone the way of the dinosaur. In the old days the personnel manager of a company was little more than a clerk. His or her job was to accept applications, check references, and keep records of who was hired, fired, and promoted.

Today's **human resources division** does much more. Modern human resources managers are concerned with the whole equation of people and productivity—as well as salaries, wages, and benefits. Their job description includes recruiting, hiring, orienting, training, evaluating, motivating, rewarding, disciplining, developing, promoting, and communicating with all the employees of the hotel.

Security Division

The security of guests, employees, personal property, and the hotel itself is an overriding concern for today's hotel managers. In the past, most security precautions concentrated on the prevention of theft from guests and the hotel. However, today such violent crimes as murder and rape have become a problem for some hotels. Many hotels now worry about terrorism threats. Hotel owners and operators are concerned about their ethical and legal responsibility to protect guests and their property. Not giving security the attention it deserves can be costly. Courts have awarded plaintiffs thousands (in some cases, millions) of dollars as a result of judgments against hotels for not exercising reasonable care in protecting guests.[10]

A hotel security program should be preventive. While ultimate responsibility for security remains with the general manager, most hotels have one or more security officers on staff who are professionally trained in crime prevention and detection.

Traditionally, security has been the responsibility of the front office. The trend today is to give security the status of an independent division or department reporting directly to the general manager or resident manager. In large hotels, the head of the **security division** may be called the chief of security. This person usually has an extensive background in law enforcement.

Those involved in security should have specialized training in civil and criminal law. They must work closely with local police and fire departments to ensure that all regulations pertaining to hotels are enforced. Applicants for security positions should be trained in self-defense.

A comprehensive security program includes all of the following elements:

- *Security officers.* Security officers make regular rounds of the hotel premises, including guest floors, corridors, public and private function rooms, parking areas, and offices. Their duties involve observing suspicious behavior and taking appropriate action, investigating incidents, and cooperating with local law enforcement officials.

- *Equipment.* Security equipment includes two-way radios; closed-circuit television (CCT) and motion sensors to monitor entrances, elevators, and corridors; smoke detectors and fire-alarm systems; fire-fighting equipment, including extinguishers, hoses, and fire axes; and adequate interior and exterior lighting.

- *Master keys.* Security officers should be able to gain access to guestrooms, storerooms, and offices at all times.

- *Safety procedures.* A well-designed security program includes evacuation plans in case of fire, bomb threats, terrorism, or some other emergency. All employees should be familiar with these plans. Employee training and procedure manuals should include sections on safety.

- *Identification procedures.* Every employee should be issued an identification card that includes his or her photo. Name tags for employees who are likely to have contact with guests not only project a friendly image for the property but are also useful for security reasons.

Compliance with the ADA

As a result of the Americans with Disabilities Act (ADA), all of the divisions of a U.S. hotel must modify existing facilities to some extent and incorporate design features into new construction that make hotel facilities accessible to disabled persons.[11] Disabled persons, as defined by the ADA, include persons in wheelchairs, other persons with mobility impairments who may suffer from neuromuscular conditions such as multiple sclerosis and muscular dystrophy, and persons with sensory impairments such as blindness and deafness. The ADA covers employees as well as guests.

All hotels are expected to have at least four percent of their parking spaces designated as "handicapped" (the figure drops to two percent if the parking lot has more than 100 spaces). Parking spaces for persons with disabilities must be wide enough for wheelchairs to be unloaded from a van or other vehicle; wheelchair users must be able to easily enter the hotel by means of accessible ramps and doors. Entrances to hotels must have accessible pick-up and drop-off points without curbs or any other obstructions for a person using a wheelchair or crutches.

Many areas within hotels are affected by the ADA. One section of the registration desk should be low enough for a person in a wheelchair to comfortably see over it. Ramps should be equipped with handrails; stairs require handrails and beveled risers. Restrooms must have accessible stalls that are wide enough for a disabled person to receive assistance from another individual if needed, or to allow a blind person to enter with a guide dog. Meeting rooms must be equipped with special listening systems for persons who are hearing impaired. If platforms are used in meeting rooms, they must have accessible ramps. Restaurants must have "accessible paths" at least 36 inches (91.4 centimeters) wide between tables or counters and bars. Merchandise racks in hotel retail shops must be spaced far enough apart for persons in wheelchairs to move around and between them.

Guestrooms must be fitted with equipment that can be manipulated by persons with severe arthritis, an amputation, or poor control of their hands. Visual fire alarms are required in guestrooms designated for hearing-impaired guests. Numbers on guestroom doors must be tactile so they can be read by touch.

Many of these changes involve new construction or modifications of existing facilities that are "readily achievable." In time, hopefully, all public facilities in the United States, including hotels, restaurants, museums, theaters, shops, and even parks, will have made the changes necessary to be fully accessible to disabled persons. Other countries, notably the United Kingdom and Germany, are making great strides in this area as well.

Control Systems

An important part of managing is to measure performance levels and take corrective action if they do not meet the goals of the enterprise. In order to maintain control over all aspects of an organization, managers and owners must first establish goals against which results can be measured. For example, an organization may establish a payroll goal of 30 percent of revenues—that is, the operating plan is to spend 30 percent or less of sales on salaries and other payroll expenses. The plan may also provide that a variance of 2 percent is acceptable, but that anything above that is not. If payroll expenses exceed 32 percent, management must take action.

The ideal control system allows managers to quickly recognize and correct deviations from the operating budget (or some other management standard) before they become major problems. One way hotel managers accomplish this is to have accurate forecasting systems. To continue with our payroll example: By being able to forecast with a high degree of accuracy what sales are likely to be in a given period, managers can adjust staffing levels accordingly to meet the payroll goal. For instance, if the dining room manager knows from sales history records that on Monday evenings in February the dining room is likely to serve only 100 meals, then the number of food servers and cooks that will be required is no longer a matter of guesswork but can be carefully planned. Of course, current hotel occupancy and other circumstances must also be taken into account.

In too many cases, corrections are made long after the problem starts. The longer the period between the variation from property goals and the correction, the weaker the control system and the greater the potential for lost revenue and increased costs.

Training plays a key role in control systems. A certain number of errors by front desk personnel and food servers is inevitable—no human system is perfect. But careful training can minimize errors and bring performance levels up to standard.

Many of management's goals can be quantified. The more specific the goal and the easier it is to quantify, the more likely it is that the goal will be met. Guestroom occupancy levels, guest counts in restaurants, and revenue and expense targets are examples of quantifiable goals. Not all goals are easy to measure. For example, an operating plan might have a goal of increasing guest satisfaction or employee morale. However, even there it is possible to be more specific and measure the results accordingly.

Two of the most important types of controls for hotel managers are financial controls and quality controls.

Financial Controls

Among the most useful **financial control** tools are financial statements. Investors use them to monitor profitability; lenders view them as measures of financial stability; managers base their planning on them and monitor the success of their planning with them.

In order to understand a hotel financial statement, it is necessary to be familiar with the hotel industry's financial terminology and to understand the manner in which revenues and expenses are grouped by hotel division.

Uniform System of Accounts. In March 1926 the American Hotel & Lodging Association (at that time it was called the American Hotel Association of the United States and Canada) adopted a manual called the *Uniform System of Accounts for Hotels.* The system was formulated by a committee of accountants and hoteliers in New York City. The ninth edition bore a new title to better encompass all segments of the industry: *The Uniform System of Accounts for the Lodging Industry.*

The *Uniform System of Accounts for the Lodging Industry* classifies the different types of hotel revenues and expenses, and groups them in the statement of income by division or department. The **statement of income** is one of management's major control tools. It shows the total sales by product or service category (rooms, food, beverage, and so on) for a stated period of time, the expenses incurred in generating those sales, and the profit earned or the loss incurred as a result of those activities (see Exhibit 11).

There are three types of hotel expenses: divisional expenses, overhead expenses, and fixed charges or capital costs. Divisional expenses include a wide range of items, such as rooms division payroll expenses, restaurant laundry, and telephone supplies like message pads and pencils. Overhead expenses are costs such as marketing and energy—costs that relate to the entire hotel and not to one specific division. Fixed charges or capital costs are

Exhibit 11   Sample Hotel Statement of Income

XYZ Hotel
Statement of Income
For the year ended December 31, 20XX

Net Revenue		
Rooms	$ 1,897,500	69.2%
Food	548,410	20.0
Beverage	112,424	4.1
Telecommunications	49,357	1.8
Other Operated Departments	93,230	3.4
Rentals and Other Income	41,131	1.5
Total Departmental Revenue	2,742,052	100.0%
Costs and Expenses		
Rooms	493,569	18.0
Food	408,728	16.0
Beverage	54,841	2.0
Telecommunications	27,421	1.0
Other Operated Departments	54,841	2.0
Administrative and General	227,590	8.3
Franchise Fees	85,004	3.1
Marketing	152,354	5.0
Property Operation and Maintenance	152,333	5.0
Utility Costs	112,424	4.1
Management Fees	76,777	2.8
Rent, Property Taxes, and Insurance	142,587	5.2
Interest Expense	329,046	12.0
Depreciation and Amortization	249,527	9.1
Total Costs and Expenses	2,567,042	93.6
Income Before Income Taxes	175,010	6.4

expenses related to the investment, such as insurance on the building and contents, and interest on the mortgage loan.

The uniform system also classifies **assets** (something of value that is owned) and **liabilities** (what is owed to creditors). Examples of assets might be the hotel building itself, furniture and equipment, and courtesy vans to transport guests to and from airports. Liabilities include items such as the mortgage loan and food purchases for which payment is due. All of these items are grouped together in the financial statement known as the **balance sheet** (see Exhibit 12). A balance sheet reports the financial position of a business by presenting its assets, liabilities, and owner's or shareholders' equity on a given date.

Quality Controls

It is a relatively simple task to standardize the quality and cost of a manufactured product. This is because products, whether they be toasters or skis, are produced in a factory under strictly controlled conditions. Some assembly lines are computerized, and many use robots to perform some functions. Moreover, quality control inspectors not only monitor all operations but can inspect each finished item before it leaves the plant and a consumer purchases it.

Service businesses such as hotels operate under an entirely different set of circumstances. The "product" that a hotel produces—the experience of staying there—is manufactured in the hotel "factory" right in front of the consumer. For example, a guest enters a hotel, goes into the lounge, sits down at a table, and orders a strawberry daiquiri. The product in this case is not simply the daiquiri—it also includes the lounge, the server, and the bartender who mixes the drink. It is this total experience that the guest pays for. If the guest had just wanted a strawberry daiquiri, he or she could have made one at home or bought a bottled one at the corner liquor store.

Because of the nature of a service business, it is extremely difficult to standardize or even control the service that guests receive. There are too many variables that can interfere with the process—including the guests, who, for example, may be rude and provoke employees to be rude in return.

Opportunities for guest dissatisfaction abound. Take our guest who ordered the strawberry daiquiri. Possibly the guest had to wait for a table because none was available or the host was out of the room temporarily. Maybe the seating was prompt, but the guest had to wait longer than expected for the order because the ice machine or the drink mixer was broken. Perhaps the bartender was preoccupied with a personal problem instead of concentrating on fixing a perfect strawberry daiquiri. Even if everything else goes well, it can all be spoiled if the guest has to wait too long for the check or if there is a mistake on it. All of these possibilities exist whenever a guest enters the lounge. Any of them can affect the quality of the experience (the product) and thus the guest's perception of the lounge and the hotel. This one transaction is a single example of the many kinds of things that can go wrong in a hotel that is open 24 hours a day, seven days a week, where guests interact regularly with, and receive service from, front desk agents, food servers, room attendants, bellpersons, concierges, valets, maintenance people, and gift shop employees.

Why is guest satisfaction so important? Because dissatisfied guests may not come back, and may tell their friends about their unpleasant experiences, which jeopardizes the profit objectives of the organization.

One of the best ways to keep guests satisfied is through product and service consistency. Therefore, product and service is of primary importance. Consistency can only be achieved through **quality controls** such as:

Exhibit 12   Sample Hotel Balance Sheet

ABC Hotel
Balance Sheet
December 31, 20XX

ASSETS

Current Assets

Cash	$ 58,500	1.9 %
Short-Term Investments	25,000	.8
Accounts Receivable (net)	40,196	1.2
Inventories	11,000	.3
Prepaid Expenses	13,192	.4
Total Current Assets	147,888	4.6

Property and Equipment

Land	850,000	26.2
Building	2,500,000	77.0
Furniture and Equipment	475,000	14.6
Total	3,825,000	117.8
Less Accumulated Depreciation	775,000	23.9
Total	3,050,000	93.9
Leasehold Improvements	9,000	.3
China, Glassware, and Silver (net)	36,524	1.1
Total Property and Equipment	3,095,524	95.3

Other Noncurrent Assets

Security Deposits	1,000	–
Deferred Charges	3,000	.1
Total Other Assets	4,000	.1
Total Assets	**$3,247,412**	**100.0 %**

LIABILITIES AND STOCKHOLDERS' EQUITY

Current Liabilities

Accounts Payable	$ 13,861	.4 %
Federal and State Income Taxes Payable	16,545	.5
Accrued Payroll	11,617	.4
Other Accrued Items	7,963	.2
Unearned Revenue	3,764	.1
Current Portion of Long-Term Debt	70,000	2.2
Total Current Liabilities	123,750	3.8

Long-Term Debt

Mortgage Payable, less current portion	2,055,000	63.3
Total Liabilities	**2,178,750**	**67.1**

STOCKHOLDERS' EQUITY

Common Stock, par value $1, authorized		
and issued 50,000 shares	50,000	1.5
Additional Paid-In Capital	700,000	21.6
Retained Earnings	318,662	9.8
Total Stockholders' Equity	1,068,662	32.9
Total Liabilities and Stockholders'		
Equity	**$3,247,412**	**100.0 %**

- Setting standards that answer the needs and expectations of guests
- Selecting employees who are capable of achieving those standards and who are motivated to do so
- Conducting continual training and certification programs for all employees at every level
- Involving employees in structuring job descriptions, setting performance standards, and solving work problems
- Having a feedback system so that all managers and employees know they are achieving what they have set out to do—satisfy the guest
- Rewarding managers and employees for achieving quality goals

Quality programs at hotels go by various names: "quality assurance" (QA) and "total quality management" (TQM) are two examples. Hilton Hotels has the Balanced Scorecard quality program that evaluates financial, operational, and employee performance (as well as customer perceptions) against predetermined objectives and performance measurements. In other words, is the hotel achieving what it wants to achieve from the standpoint of profitability, customer and employee satisfaction, and innovation? Starwood uses Six Sigma, a system to improve the quality of the operation by identifying and reducing defects and improving efficiency. Although their names vary, the goal of all such programs is to provide quality service to guests.

Setting Standards. Quality is an overriding concern in the hotel industry, but what does "quality" mean? There is no universal industry agreement on what quality is, nor should there be. Quality has to do with guest expectations versus reality. When guests check into a $40-a-night budget hotel, they expect a certain standard of service and no more. If they get what they expect (or a little more), they have enjoyed a quality experience from their point of view. If they get less than what they expected or thought they were paying for, then they will think they received poor-quality service. The formula is the same for a hotel room that costs $250 a night. A guest who pays that amount has certain expectations. His or her perception of quality depends to a large degree on whether those expectations are met or exceeded.

Most hotels strive for quality for their type of product and target market. Quality, then, means that the guest experience—in terms of the cleanliness of the rooms, the taste and presentation of the food, and the physical condition of the hotel—is consistent with what the management has promised and is trying to deliver.

The Ritz-Carlton Hotel Company is known for setting very high standards. According to the management of the Ritz-Carlton chain, "Customer satisfaction is a deeply held belief at the Ritz-Carlton and begins with an absolute understanding of the needs and expectations of our customer." The chain achieves this understanding by forming focus groups of Ritz-Carlton current and prospective guests and by recording guest preferences that are detected and reported by all employees. This information is used to set guest-service standards.

To achieve quality standards, hotel managers—with the help of individual employees and "quality teams" formed from hotel personnel—must create procedures for hotel staff to follow. For example, when a room attendant has finished cleaning a guestroom, the position of the furniture, the number of towels and other guest amenities, and—most important—the overall cleanliness of the room must be exactly the same every day for every room. How many towels to leave in the bathroom or what constitutes "clean" should not be left to the discretion of the person doing the cleaning. Procedures must be established for each task to be performed. At the same time, a standard of what is acceptable and what is not must be spelled out for each procedure. It is not reasonable to set standards without specifically detailing the procedures that must be followed in order to achieve those standards.

The following example of a food service procedure and standard concerns the task of greeting guests at a table:

> *Procedure:* After table is seated, greet the guest(s): "Good morning. May I offer you some coffee?" Be pleasant, unhurried. Pour coffee with cup on table, and to right of guest. If tea is served, the tea pot is served on a butter plate with a doily, lemon on top of tea pot.
>
> *Standard:* Make the guest feel comfortable. Strike a positive note in your "beginning" with the guest.

Selecting Employees. Ritz-Carlton emphasizes the importance of employee selection in its quality management program. Ritz-Carlton's managers have devised a highly sophisticated predictive instrument, using superior employees as benchmarks, that allows them to determine whether the candidates for a specific position are capable of living up to the chain's service standards.

Training Employees. It is not enough for a hotel to establish standards and procedures and select employees to carry them out. Employees must be shown how to perform the procedures. Employees who have never cleaned a guestroom or waited on a table can't be expected to know what to do simply because they've been given a manual.

To succeed, training must be ongoing and have the full commitment of management. At Ritz-Carlton, all hotels have a director of human resources on staff who is assisted by the hotel's quality leader, who acts as an advisor. Each work area has a departmental trainer who is charged with the training and certification of new employees in that area.

Involving Employees. All successful quality programs use a participative style of management. Judy Z. King, owner and president of Quality Management Services, lists basic beliefs in employee involvement in problem-solving:

1. The person doing the job knows how the job can be done better.

2. Problem-solving and decision-making should be done at the lowest capable level in the organization.

3. People are the greatest untapped resource in the organization.

4. People will meet expectations if they have been enabled to do so and, with encouragement, will exceed them.[12]

Ritz-Carlton employees are expected and empowered to solve problems. On the Ritz-Carlton "Service Values" card that every employee carries, it says, "I own and immediately resolve guest problems." Employees are encouraged to break out of their regular routine and solve guest problems immediately and ensure that they do not recur. Teams of workers from different divisions are often put together to resolve conflicts between internal operation problems and external guest expectations.

Evaluating Quality Programs. Management must verify the consistency of product and service quality in order to evaluate the success of its quality efforts. Ritz-Carlton, for example, depends heavily on real-time reports, called "guest incident action forms," that are generated daily by employees. These reports are analyzed and quickly acted on so that incidents of guest dissatisfaction will not be repeated.

One of the simplest ways to evaluate the quality of an operation is called "management by walking around." Successful hotel managers have found that taking periodic tours of the hotel and staying alert to what is going on around them is one of the best ways of ensuring that the quality program is working. There is a saying in the United States Navy that also applies to the hotel business: "You get what you inspect, not what you expect."

Guest satisfaction surveys are another important evaluation tool. Most chains use an electronic survey e-mailed to hotel guests within twenty-four hours of departure. Guests are asked to evaluate the reservations process and the service they received at the hotel by selecting a degree of agreement with a statement about the facilities and the service. Almost all surveys ask if the guest would stay at the hotel again and the likelihood of recommending the hotel to others. Experience has shown that open-ended questions that ask guests to write a description of their experiences do not work as well as simple rating scales, where guests can indicate their level of satisfaction with various components of the hotel's service and facilities. There should be room on the survey, however, for guests to add comments if they choose and identify employees whom they wish to single out either positively or negatively.

Another evaluation method involves hiring outside inspectors, usually referred to as "mystery shoppers." These inspectors, who are not known to hotel employees, make reservations, stay in a guestroom, eat in the dining room, check out, and then prepare elaborate reports on the level of service they received. Some hotels announce inspections in advance and the inspectors are known. While employees often favor this system, the level of management confidence in the results of such inspections tends to be much lower.

Rewarding for Achievement. Today, hotel management executive compensation almost always includes both a salary and a bonus. The bonus can be quite substantial and is a result of hotel owners' desire to motivate their executives to a higher level of performance. Very often bonuses are tied to achieving or surpassing specific goals in the areas of financial performance or guest satisfaction.

Employee recognition programs are also common. These may involve posting photographs of the "employee of the month" in a special frame in the lobby, giving gift certificates or other monetary rewards to high-achieving employees, or setting aside special parking spaces for employees in recognition of their superior job performance.

Hotel Technology

Technology plays a vital roll in managing a hotel and providing service to hotel guests.[13] Technology applications have been designed for almost every aspect of hotel operations and control. However, there is no one system that manages all the functions even within individual departments. For example, the rooms department may have one system for guest check-in and check-out, another for voice mail, another for the electronic door locks, and yet another for in-room entertainment. These systems act as one because they are designed to integrate, or interface, with each other.

What follows is a list of some of the most common technology applications that a hotel might have.

Property Management System. A property management system (PMS) performs most functions that affect a guest's stay at the hotel. This system shows room availability, handles guest check-in and check-out, maintains a current record of all guest charges, and accepts payment (cash or payment card) when the guest checks out. Other functions of the system include describing the physical characteristics of guestrooms, such as the view, whether there is a balcony, the type of bed, etc., so that the front desk agent has sufficient data to assign a room that will best satisfy the guest.

A number of hotels have kiosks in their lobbies where guests can check in and check out. With the swipe of a payment card or the input of a reservation number, guests can identify themselves; the kiosk has the capability to then assign a room and dispense a key. The guest can check out at the kiosk or use the television remote control and follow the commands on the television screen, and so check out before he or she leaves the guestroom. With such a property management system, guests can use the television to view their hotel bills at any time. An interface between the PMS and the kiosk or television is necessary to perform the functions described.

Room reservations may come to a hotel through a central reservations system (CRS), via the Internet, or through a global distribution system (GDS). In all of these cases, an interface with the hotel's PMS is necessary to provide rates and availability to these outlets, to get the reservation to the property, and to have it available on the PMS when the guest arrives at the hotel.

Another important interface with the PMS is the hotel's revenue management system, which sets the rates in the PMS that are then available to the CRS, Internet outlets, and the GDSs.

Point-of-Sale System. The point-of-sale (POS) system in a hotel's food and beverage outlets must interface with the hotel's PMS in order to verify a hotel guest's name and room number when the guest wants to make a purchase. Once verified, the guest's restaurant or bar charge is accepted and transferred to the guest folio.

Sales and Catering System. Hotels with function rooms that have a considerable number of meetings and catered events would find a sales and catering system helpful. Through an interface with the PMS, the sales staff has access to guestroom availability when negotiating dates with prospective group clients. The system also has the description and availability of all meeting rooms. This facet is especially important in large convention hotels that have a sizeable sales staff that is selling to different types of clients. Menus for all types of occasions are a feature that allows clients to see what type of food the hotel considers its specialty. An important aspect of a sales and catering system is its ability to prepare contracts for customer signature and prepare banquet event orders for distribution to departments in the hotel involved in putting on the customer's event.

Inventory/Purchasing System. An inventory/purchasing (I/P) system for hotels is similar to I/P systems for restaurants. An I/P system tracks inventories of food and beverages by increasing quantities when items are purchased and decreasing them when they are requisitioned out of storage. The system stores recipe costs and vendor lists, generates reorder reports based on par levels of food or beverage items, and prepares purchase orders.

Accounting System. A hotel's accounting system maintains records of all a hotel's financial transactions. It is referred to generally as a "back office" system, since it performs out of sight of guests. The system deals with the hotel's general ledger, accounts payable, accounts receivable, and payroll (when payroll is not outsourced to a service company). The general ledger is a record of balance sheet and income statement accounts, and accounts payable is what the hotel owes to its creditors.

Telecommunications System. Today many hotel guests use their mobile telephones to communicate with family, friends, and business associates. However, guestroom telephones are still necessary for wake-up calls and other communications between hotel and guests, and for safety and security reasons. A hotel's call accounting system (CAS) is the software that manages calls made from guestrooms, sending cost information to the hotel's PMS/guest folios. When least-cost routing was adopted by hotels, the CAS searched for the least-expensive carrier to use for the destination of a telephone call. The cost of calls was reduced further with the adoption of Voice over Internet Protocol technology that transmits a call over the Internet rather than a regular telephone line. An important aspect of a hotel's telephone service for guests is voice mail, a system that allows messages to be left for guests during their stay at the hotel.

Electronic Door Lock System. Today it is rare to find a hotel with metal keys for its guestrooms, although there are some small hotels and inns that still use metal keys to help create the ambience of less hectic days. Most hotels use an electronic locking system with plastic key cards that are programmed to open a door during a defined guest stay. In some hotels, the guestroom key card is programmed not only to open the guestroom door, but also to allow hotel entry late at night, or to allow guests access to special facilities such as the hotel's swimming pool, exercise room, or business center.

Energy Management System. The basic guestroom energy control still found in many hotels is the guest-operated thermostat. More current equipment includes occupancy sensors that adjust guestroom temperature based on guest occupancy. The system is activated by the PMS, which sends a message to the guestroom HVAC equipment when a guest checks in or departs.

Internet Access. Most travelers today expect wired or wireless Internet access, and most hotels provide this service. Because of security issues and concerns about the pirating of sensitive business information, some companies prefer that their traveling executives use wired connections.

Television System. Guests need not be restricted to the television stations' programming. Video-on-demand or pay-per-view options allow guests to select from a wider menu of programs or movies any hour of the day or night and have their selections charged to their guest account. Some guestroom television systems provide music and video-game options as well as television and movie programming. As mentioned earlier, in many hotels guests can also use the television to review their accounts and check out.

Minibars. The mechanical or stand-alone minibar still found in most hotels requires an attendant to check usage and restock. More current minibars are connected with a PMS interface. Each time an item is removed, it is charged to the guest account. While this system is more expensive, it can reduce labor costs, since an attendant is not required to visit all the rooms but only those that have inventory depleted (this also means one less guest disturbance).

Summary

To efficiently run their hotels, hotel managers organize them into various functional areas and then delegate responsibility and authority. The functional areas are divided into revenue and cost (or support) centers. Divisions such as rooms and food and beverage are revenue centers; others, like engineering and accounting, are cost centers. The number of such centers (or divisions) depends on the size of the hotel.

In most hotels, the rooms division is the largest and generates the most revenue and profit. It generally consists of four departments: front office, reservations, housekeeping, and uniformed service. Front office duties include checking guests in and out, posting charges to their accounts, and collecting payments. In small hotels, front desk agents may also accept reservations, relay messages to guests, and handle the telephone switchboard.

A hotel's reservations department should be staffed by skilled telemarketing personnel who are able to accept reservations over the phone, answer questions about the hotel and its facilities, and quote guestroom rates and available dates. Since some callers are shopping around, reservationists should be trained to sell the property as well as simply accept reservations.

The housekeeping department is responsible for cleaning guestrooms and public areas. Often it has the most employees. Besides cleaning, the housekeeping department also takes care of laundry and valet services.

Uniformed service employees deal with guest luggage and transportation, and provide concierge services.

The food and beverage division is of paramount importance to a hotel's profitability and reputation. There may be many different types of food and beverage outlets in a hotel. Factors that influence the level of food and beverage service that a hotel offers include the type of hotel, the class of hotel, the competition, product availability, availability of labor, and guest demand. The food and beverage manager typically has restaurant managers, beverage managers, and a catering director reporting to him or her. Support and control personnel for the food and beverage division include purchasing managers, receiving clerks, storeroom clerks, cashiers, and a food and beverage controller.

The overall profitability of food and beverage operations depends on several factors, including hours of operation, guest check averages, the number and kind of facilities, employee turnover, entertainment costs, and marketing.

A well-managed telecommunications department can also contribute to a hotel's profits. Modern systems have made a big difference in the way hotel telecommunications departments function and have helped increase guest satisfaction with service.

Concessions, rentals, and commissions are other sources of hotel revenue. However, managers should make sure that the standards of concessionaires are compatible with the hotel's.

Guests' changing lifestyles have made hotel health spas, cable movies, and video game rooms popular with guests and therefore important services for many hotels to offer.

The marketing, engineering, accounting, human resources, and security divisions of a hotel are considered cost or support centers. The marketing division is charged with identifying prospective guests, communicating their needs and wants to hotel management, and persuading prospective guests to stay at the hotel. To accomplish these tasks, the marketing division usually has a director of marketing and sales, a sales manager, a director of advertising and public relations, a convention sales manager, salespeople, and support staff.

The engineering division takes care of the hotel's physical plant and utility systems. The division is headed by a chief engineer, assisted by his or her own staff and outside contractors. Most preventive maintenance duties and repairs are performed by hotel staff.

The accounting division is charged with the hotel's financial management. Accounting is headed by a controller who oversees the general cashier, the night auditor, the income auditor, and the food and beverage controller.

The human resources division is responsible for recruiting, hiring, orienting, training, evaluating, motivating, rewarding, disciplining, developing, promoting, and communicating with hotel employees.

Security of hotel employees and guests is of overriding importance. Hotel security programs are preventive and should be under the direction of a person with law enforcement experience.

As a result of the Americans with Disabilities Act (ADA), all of the divisions of a U.S. hotel must modify existing facilities to some extent and incorporate design features into new construction that make hotel facilities accessible to disabled persons. Disabled persons, as defined by the act, include persons in wheelchairs, other persons with mobility impairments who may suffer from neuromuscular conditions such as multiple sclerosis and muscular dystrophy, and persons with sensory impairments such as blindness and deafness. The ADA covers employees as well as guests.

Hotel managers have two major kinds of controls: financial controls and quality controls. Important financial controls are the hotel's financial statements. These statements are based on those found in the *Uniform System of Accounts for the Lodging Industry*. In this accounting system, hotel expenses are classified as divisional, overhead, and fixed. Assets and liabilities are also classified.

Quality controls are essential in order to ensure that standards established by management are adhered to. Hotel managers must establish standards appropriate for their type of hotel, create procedures, and select employees carefully if quality guest service is to be achieved. All quality programs require employee involvement. Employees are encouraged to solve problems that interfere with good guest service. To be optimally effective, quality programs should be evaluated to make sure they are truly working, and both managers and employees should be rewarded for achieving quality goals.

Technology plays a vital roll in managing a hotel and providing service to hotel guests. Computer applications have been designed for almost every aspect of hotel operations. Two of the most widely used are the property management system (PMS), which performs most functions that affect a guest's stay at the hotel, and an accounting system that records and analyzes the hotel's financial transactions.

Endnotes

1. The use of the terms *division* and *department* is not standardized in the industry. Some properties call their main functional areas (rooms, food and beverage, etc.) departments; the smaller functional areas within departments (room service, for example) may be called sub-departments. Large properties often call their main functional areas divisions, and units within divisions, departments. Neither option is better than the other. For consistency, however, throughout this chapter we will call the main functional areas "divisions" and the smaller areas "departments."

2. *Trends in the Hotel Industry, USA Edition, 2009,* PKF Hospitality Research.

3. The titles for front desk employees vary within the industry. Hotels may refer to their front desk employees as front desk agents, front desk clerks, guest service representatives, front

office agents, or something similar. However, for the sake of consistency we will refer to front desk employees as front desk agents throughout the chapter.

4. Eric B. Orkin, Yield Management Conference, March 26–27, 1992, Dallas, Texas.

5. The housekeeping department, from an executive housekeeper's perspective, is the subject of Margaret M. Kappa, Aleta Nitschke, and Patricia B. Schappert, *Managing Housekeeping Operations*, 2d ed. (Lansing, Mich.: Educational Institute of the American Hotel & Lodging Association, 1997).

6. For students desiring a good introductory text to food and beverage operations, see Jack D. Ninemeier, *Management of Food and Beverage Operations*, 4th ed. (Lansing, Mich.: Educational Institute of the American Hotel & Lodging Association, 2005).

7. Peter E. Drucker, *Management: Tasks, Responsibilities, Practices* (New York: Harper & Row, 1974), p. 61.

8. For more information on the responsibilities of a hotel's engineering division, see David M. Stipanuk, *Hospitality Facilities Management and Design*, Third Edition (Lansing, Mich.: Educational Institute of the American Hotel & Lodging Association, 2006).

9. *Trends in the Hotel Industry, USA Edition, 2009*, PKF Hospitality Research.

10. Legal ramifications of hotel security are covered in Jack P. Jefferies and Banks Brown, *Understanding Hospitality Law*, 4th ed. (Lansing, Mich.: Educational Institute of the American Hotel & Lodging Association, 2001). The security responsibilities of hotel managers and hotel security programs are the subjects of Raymond C. Ellis, Jr., and David M. Stipanuk, *Security and Loss Prevention Management*, 2d ed. (Lansing, Mich.: Educational Institute of the American Hotel & Lodging Association, 1999).

11. Much of the following information appeared in John P. S. Salmen, "The ADA and You," *Lodging*, November 1991, pp. 97–107.

12. Judy Z. King, Sixth Annual AH&LA National Conference for Quality, San Francisco, July 7–9, 1993.

13. For this section on hotel technology, the authors relied on *An Introduction to Hotel Systems*, Second Edition (Lansing, Mich.: American Hotel & Lodging Educational Institute, 2006), and information provided by technology consultant Jules Sieburgh.

Key Terms

accounting division—The hotel division responsible for keeping track of the many business transactions that occur in the hotel and managing the hotel's finances.

assets—Resources available for use by a business, i.e., anything owned by the business that has monetary value.

average daily rate (ADR)—A key rooms department operating ratio: rooms revenue divided by number of rooms sold. Also called average room rate.

balance sheet—A financial statement that provides information on the financial position of a hotel by showing its assets, liabilities, and equity on a given date.

capture rate—The percentage of hotel guests who eat meals at the hotel.

card keys—Plastic cards, resembling credit cards, that are used in place of metal guestroom keys. Card keys require electronic locks.

catering department—A department within the food and beverage division of a hotel that is responsible for arranging and planning food and beverage functions for (1) conventions and smaller hotel groups, and (2) local banquets booked by the sales department.

commissions—Retailers located off the hotel site (such as gift shops, car rental agencies, and photographers) that pay a commission to the hotel based on a percentage of their gross sales to guests.

concessions—Facilities that might well be operated by the hotel directly, such as a beauty salon or fitness club, but are turned over to independent operators. The hotel in turn receives a flat fee, a minimum fee plus a percentage of the gross receipts over a specific amount, or a percentage of total gross sales.

cost centers—Divisions or departments within a hotel that do not directly generate income; they provide support for the hotel's revenue centers. Also known as support centers.

engineering division—The hotel division responsible for taking care of the hotel's physical plant and controlling energy costs.

familiarization (fam) tours—Free or reduced-rate travel programs designed by hotel personnel to acquaint travel agents and others with the hotel and stimulate sales.

financial controls—Financial statements, operating ratios, and other financial statistics that hotel managers can use to keep track of operations and make sure financial goals are being attained.

food and beverage division—The hotel division responsible for preparing and serving food and beverages within the hotel. Also includes catering and room service.

front office—A hotel's command post for processing reservations, registering guests, settling guest accounts, and checking guests in and out.

housekeeping department—A department of the rooms division responsible for cleaning the hotel's guestrooms and public areas.

human resources division—The hotel division responsible for recruiting, hiring, orienting, training, evaluating, motivating, rewarding, disciplining, developing, promoting, and communicating with hotel employees.

liabilities—Obligations of a business—largely indebtedness related to the expenses incurred in the process of generating income.

marketing division—The hotel division responsible for identifying prospective guests for the hotel, conforming the products and services of the hotel as much as possible to meet the needs of those prospects, and persuading prospects to become guests.

night audit—An accounting task usually performed between 11:00 P.M. and 6:00 A.M. after all of a hotel's sales outlets are closed. A night audit (a) verifies that guest charges have been accurately posted to guests' accounts, and (b) compares the totals of all accounts with sales reports of operating departments.

occupancy percentage—A ratio indicating hotel management's success in selling its main "product"—guestrooms. It is calculated by dividing the number of rooms occupied by the number of rooms available for a given period.

property management system (PMS)—A computerized system that helps hotel managers and other personnel carry out a number of front-of-the-house and back-of-the-house functions. A PMS can support a variety of applications software that helps managers in their data-gathering and reporting responsibilities.

purchasing department—The hotel department responsible for buying, receiving, storing, and issuing all the products used in the hotel.

quality controls—Standards of operation, quality assurance programs, and other controls that seek to establish and maintain hotel products and services at quality levels established by management.

rentals—Enterprises such as offices or stores that pay rent to a hotel.

reservations department—A department within a hotel's rooms division staffed by skilled telemarketing personnel who take reservations over the phone, answer questions about facilities, quote prices and available dates, and sell to callers who are shopping around.

revenue centers—Divisions or departments within a hotel that directly generate income through the sale of products or services to guests.

revenue management—A hotel pricing system adapted from the airlines that uses a hotel's computer reservation system to track advance bookings and then lower or raise guestroom prices accordingly—on a day-to-day basis—to yield the maximum revenue. Before selling a room in advance, the hotel forecasts the probability of being able to sell the room to other market segments that are willing to pay higher rates.

revenue per available room (RevPAR)—A statistic used by hotel managers to evaluate the performance of the rooms department. It is computed by dividing room revenue by the number of available rooms for the same period. It also can be determined by multiplying the occupancy percentage by the average daily rate for the same period.

rooms division—The largest, and usually most profitable, division in a hotel. It typically consists of four departments: front office, reservations, housekeeping, and uniformed service.

room service—The department within a food and beverage division that is responsible for delivering food and beverages to guests in their guestrooms. May also be responsible for preparing the food and beverages.

security division—The hotel division responsible for the protection of guests and their property, employees and their property, and the hotel itself.

statement of income—A financial statement of the results of operations that presents the sales, expenses, and net income of a business for a stated period of time.

telecommunications department—The hotel department responsible for providing telephone, Internet, and other communications services to hotel guests.

uniformed service department—A hotel department within the rooms division that deals with guests' luggage and transportation and provides concierge services. Also referred to as the guest service department.

Review Questions

1. What is the difference between a hotel revenue center and cost center?

2. Which division provides the largest source of revenue for most hotels?

3. What are some of the duties of a front desk agent?

4. How is a typical housekeeping department organized?

5. Why do some food and beverage divisions lose money?

6. What are the marketing division's challenges and responsibilities? the engineering division's? the accounting division's?

7. How do the new human resources divisions differ from the old personnel divisions?

8. What are the elements of a good hotel security program?

9. What are two of the most important types of controls for hotel managers and how are they used?

Internet Sites

For more information, visit the following Internet sites. Remember that Internet addresses can change without notice. If the site is no longer there, you can use a search engine to look for additional sites.

Hotel Companies/Resorts

Club Med
www.clubmed.com

Four Seasons Hotels
www.fourseasons.com

Grand Casinos
www.grandcasinos.com

Hilton Hotels
www.hilton.com

Holiday Inn
www.holiday-inn.com

Mandarin Oriental Hotel Group
www.mandarin-oriental.com/
mohg-hotels/mohg/

Marriott International
www.marriott.com

Opryland Hotel
www.gaylordhotels.com/
gaylordopryland

Paris Las Vegas
www.parislasvegas.com

Ritz-Carlton Hotels
www.ritzcarlton.com

St. Michaels Harbour Inn
www.harbourinn.com

Swissôtel
www.swissotel.com

Walt Disney Corporation
www.disney.com

Westin Hotels
www.westin.com

Organizations, Consultants, Resources

Americans with Disabilities Act
www.jan.wvu.edu/links/adalinks.htm

AT&T
www.att.com

PKF Consulting
www.pkfc.com

Publications

Lodging
www.lodgingmagazine.com

8
Club Management

Outline

Background on Clubs
Types of Clubs
    City Clubs
    Country Clubs
    Other Clubs
Club Ownership
    Equity Clubs
    Corporate or Developer Clubs
Club Organization
    The Club Manager
Club Operations
    Revenue
    Expenses
    Control
Summary

Competencies

1. Summarize background information about clubs; list and describe types of city clubs; and describe country, yacht, fraternal, and military clubs. (pp. 244–252)

2. Compare equity clubs with corporate or developer clubs; outline club organization and the duties of, personal attributes of, and advancement opportunities for a club manager; list and describe typical revenue sources for clubs; and give examples of club expenses and controls. (pp. 252–263)

Opposite page: Photo courtesy of the Boca Raton Resort & Club.

I N THIS CHAPTER we will discuss the organization and management of private clubs. The chapter explains the different kinds of clubs and their membership composition. It also describes how clubs are owned, organized, and managed. We then examine the unique aspects of clubs, including their sources of revenue, and profile several prominent clubs and their memberships.

Background on Clubs

Private clubs are gathering places for club members only. They bring together people of like interests. Those interests could be recreational, social, fraternal, or professional.

Private clubs are not an invention of modern society. Wealthy citizens of ancient Greece and Rome formed clubs. Clubs have been an integral part of the social fabric of upper-class English society for centuries. As the English colonized the world, they established clubs. English social clubs and the golf club of St. Andrews in Scotland are the forerunners of city clubs and country clubs in the United States. Some U.S. city clubs, such as the Somerset Club in Boston, the San Francisco Commercial Club, and the Wilmington Club in Delaware, date back to the mid-nineteenth century. Perhaps the oldest country club—founded in 1882—is located in Brookline, Massachusetts.

In many parts of the world the club you belong to is an indication of your position in society. Comedian Groucho Marx sent a telegram to the Friar's Club in Manhattan, to which he belonged: "Please accept my resignation. I don't want to belong to any club that will accept me as a member." Marx was commenting on the fact that many people join clubs to enhance their own social status. While some clubs continue to be vestiges of the class system, by and large the exclusionary aspect of private clubs in the United States has changed due to equal rights legislation and society's increased social consciousness.

Today there are about 14,000 private clubs in the United States, providing diverse opportunities in management. Private club management is closely related to hotel and food service management. Often the manager of a club is called the chief operating officer (COO). Many of a club manager's responsibilities in the areas of guest relations, human resource management, marketing, control, and maintenance are similar to those of a hotel manager's. Most clubs have dining facilities. In fact, some have multiple dining rooms and lounges as well as extensive private meeting rooms for catered events. In addition to these facilities, many city clubs have gymnasiums, racquetball courts, and guestrooms for overnight guests. Country clubs may have dining rooms, meeting rooms, one or more golf courses, a tennis club, a beach club, and even a skeet- and trap-shooting club. Such country clubs are like resort hotels, except that they are not open to the public.

Clubs managed by the same company, as well as independent city and country clubs, have various types of reciprocal agreements so that their members can use the facilities of similar clubs when traveling. For example, the members of the historic Georgetown Club in Washington, D.C., may dine at the Los Angeles Athletic Club, stay overnight at the Fort Orange Club in Albany, New York, or London's Oxford and Cambridge Club, and play golf at the Dataw Island Club in South Carolina. Typically, members secure an introductory guest card or letter of introduction to the club they wish to visit before leaving on their trip, although simply presenting their current membership card to their own club will often get them into an affiliated club.

Many clubs provide attractive and distinctive dining facilities for their members. (Courtesy of New York Athletic Club, New York, New York.)

There are some similarities in the organization of clubs and hotels. A basic difference between clubs and hotels is that the club's "guest" is a dues-paying member with a financial and emotional attachment to the club, whereas hotels are open to the public and the relationship between the guest and the hotel is less personal.

Types of Clubs

There are two basic types of private clubs: city clubs and country clubs. There are also some private clubs that do not easily fit into either of these classifications, which we will discuss under a third classification called "other private clubs."

City Clubs

City clubs vary in size, type, facilities, and membership. Some city clubs own their own real estate; others lease space in office buildings or hotels. What they have in common is that food service is generally offered and a manager is hired to oversee the entire operation. The basic types of city clubs are:

- Athletic
- Dining
- Professional
- Social
- University

Athletic. Athletic clubs are as varied as the club industry itself. The New York Athletic Club, founded in 1868, occupies an entire building in midtown Manhattan, with extensive health and sports facilities, 200 guestrooms, a dining room with a sweeping view of Central Park, a Tap Room and Cocktail Lounge, and extensive meeting and banquet rooms. (Travers Island, the club's 30-acre "summer home" on Long Island Sound, has a clubhouse, an Olympic-size saltwater pool, and facilities for tennis, rowing, and yachting.) The Dayton Racquet Club in Dayton, Ohio, is a more modest facility located on the top floor of a 29-story office building. Squash is the main athletic activity, but fitness equipment and an aerobic studio are available. The club also has dining facilities.

Dining. The number of dining clubs located in office buildings proliferated in the 1960s. Building owners offered them mainly to induce companies to lease office space. Many dining clubs are only open for lunch—these clubs are usually referred to as luncheon clubs. In some instances, facilities that are used exclusively as private luncheon clubs during the day are open to the public for dinner in the evening. Some dining clubs located in downtown office buildings remain open for cocktails after work, and a few even serve dinner and cater private functions, but most shut down quite early unless they have some lodging facilities.

Professional. Professional clubs are dining and social clubs for people in the same profession. Clubs of this nature include the Press Club in Washington, D.C., for journalists, the Lawyers' Club in New York City for attorneys, and the Friars Club (also in New York City) for actors and other theater people.

One famous professional club located on Gramercy Park in New York City is the National Arts Club, founded in 1898 by Charles de Kay, at that time the literary and art critic for the *New York Times*. De Kay's aim was to unite all the arts—painting, sculpture, music, and literature—and provide a place for serious art patrons to mingle with the men and women whose works they admired and collected.[1] Mark Twain was one of the early members of this club, as was the American painter George Bellows.

Social. Members of a social club may have no affiliation except that they enjoy being in each other's company. These clubs were modeled originally after men's social clubs in London such as Boodle's, St. James, and White's, where persons from similar backgrounds could meet with each other at the end of the day for cocktails and general companionship or entertainment unrelated to business. Indeed, in some social clubs it was considered bad manners to talk about business.

The New York Athletic Club, founded in 1868, is a world-famous city club. (Courtesy of New York Athletic Club, New York, New York.)

The oldest social club in America is said to be the Fish House in Philadelphia, founded in 1832. To ensure that the Fish House would always be socially oriented rather than business oriented, it was formed as a men's cooking club, with each member taking turns preparing meals for the membership.[2] Social clubs in Manhattan include the Union League Club, founded in 1863; the Knickerbocker Club, started by author Washington Irving for gentlemen with New York roots; and the Links Club, which was originally established "to promote and conserve throughout the United States the best interests and true spirit of the game of golf." Links Club members include business leaders and politicians from all over the country. In New Orleans there's the Louisiana Club, and on the West Coast the most famous social club is San Francisco's Bohemian Club, founded in 1872. This club, which occupies a handsome red-brick Georgian clubhouse on the side of Nob Hill,

Travers Island, the New York Athletic Club's 30-acre "summer home" on Long Island Sound, features a clubhouse and an Olympic-size saltwater swimming pool. It also has facilities for tennis, rowing, and yachting. (Courtesy of New York Athletic Club, New York, New York.)

has a 750-seat theater where members perform amateur theatricals. The club also owns a 280-acre estate in the Sierra Nevada, where members gather every summer for a two-week "encampment," during which there are poetry readings, musical productions, and concerts presented by the club's own 70-piece orchestra.[3]

In recent years social clubs have been founded for other purposes besides leisure, recreation, and camaraderie. One such club is the Commerce Club in Atlanta, Georgia, whose stated purpose is "to provide, for the political, business, and civic leadership of metropolitan Atlanta, club facilities and programs designed to stimulate and maintain vigorous and healthy communication and discourse on issues of common interest affecting metropolitan Atlanta, in an environment offering comfortable surroundings, modern meeting facilities, and the finest food and service."

University. University clubs are private clubs for university graduates or individuals otherwise affiliated with a university (university employees, for example). Some clubs of this nature are quite open. For instance, the University Club in Seattle is not affiliated with any university, and to be eligible to join you only have to be a university graduate. Other university clubs are for graduates of specific schools and exist in cities where there may be a large concentration of alumni who either live there or visit often. In New York City, for example, Harvard, Princeton, Yale, Cornell, and the University of Pennsylvania have their own clubs with restaurants, health clubs, guestrooms, and regular activities such as lectures and concerts. The Harvard, Yale, and Princeton clubs are owned by their members, but the Cornell and University of Pennsylvania clubs are university-owned. The largest of these clubs is the Yale Club. Guestrooms, dining facilities, meeting and banquet rooms, an indoor swimming pool, and a gymnasium are provided for Yale (and Dartmouth) alumni. The club stands on the exact spot where one of Yale's most celebrated sons, Nathan Hale, uttered the famous phrase, "I regret that I have but one life to give for my country," before being hanged by the British during the Revolutionary War for spying.

Country Clubs

The largest type of private club is the country club. **Country clubs** are primarily recreational and social facilities for individuals and families who live nearby. These clubs often have separate children's facilities and do a large catering business, since it is common for members to hold bar and bat mitzvahs, weddings, and other social events at them. Dining, golf, and social status are the most important reasons for joining a country club.

Since country clubs need a great deal of land (one 18-hole golf course typically requires a minimum of 110 acres), they are usually located in suburban or rural areas. Exceptions sometimes occur when a nearby city develops to the extent that the urban sprawl comes up to or surrounds the club. The Hillcrest Country Club in Los Angeles is a case in point. When it opened in 1920, the locale was suburban Los Angeles. Now it is surrounded by Beverly Hills and Century City. Other once-suburban country clubs include the Chevy Chase Country Club in metropolitan Washington, D.C., and the Everglades Country Club on fashionable Worth Avenue in Palm Beach, Florida.

In some cases, new country clubs are financed by prospective members, who are asked to invest in the club by buying shares of stock. A new club can cost $50 million to build. It is not unusual for members who wish to join to be asked to buy as much as $150,000 worth of stock, as well as pay membership dues of at least $1,000 a month.

In addition to a clubhouse with one or more dining rooms and function rooms, most country clubs have at least one golf course and one swimming pool. In the 1970s, the popularity of tennis grew so much that tennis courts became almost a mandatory part of a country club's recreational facilities. In a study conducted by the Club Managers Association of America (CMAA), 80 percent of the country clubs reporting had outdoor tennis courts and 10 percent had indoor courts. Other facilities mentioned in the study were steam rooms, fitness and exercise rooms, paddle tennis, and racquetball.

There are a number of country clubs known for their beautiful facilities and exclusivity. One such is the Owentsia Club in Lake Forest, Illinois, its name derived from the Iroquois word meaning "a meeting place in the country for sporting braves and squaws." The golf course of the Mid-Ocean Club in Bermuda (founded in 1921) was played by Sir Winston Churchill, presidents Dwight Eisenhower and George H. W. Bush, and baseball legend Babe Ruth; the *World Atlas of Golf* calls its par-4 fifth hole "one of the world's unforgettable holes."[4] Other clubs are famous for their outstanding golf courses and the tournaments

The private pool at Spa Palazzo, part of the Boca Raton Resort & Club. The pool and other spa facilities, such as treatment rooms, saunas, steam rooms, whirlpools, and soaking tubs, are open to guests as well as club members. (Courtesy of the Boca Raton Resort & Club.)

held there. Examples include the Pebble Beach Country Club in Pebble Beach, California, and the Royal St. George's Golf Club in Sandwich, England.

Other Clubs

There are other types of private clubs that engage professional managers to operate their facilities and manage their social and recreational programs.

Yacht. Yacht clubs are located near large bodies of water. Their main purpose is to provide marinas and other boating facilities for boat owners. While many of these clubs have tennis courts, swimming pools, and elaborate clubhouses with dining rooms and lounges, others provide only the bare necessities of dock space, fuel, and boating supplies. One famous yacht club is the Grosse Pointe Yacht Club in Grosse Pointe Shores, Michigan, founded in 1923 by a group that included automaker Edsel Ford. The club's facilities include an enormous ballroom, a domed main dining room overlooking the harbor, and slips for 300 boats.

Fraternal. The Elks and the Veterans of Foreign Wars are examples of fraternal clubs. Fraternal organizations sometimes own or rent entire buildings or floors within a building. Some offer food and beverage service, overnight accommodations, and rooms for meetings and recreation. Fraternal clubs also require professional managers.

Military. The armed services operate officers clubs and noncommissioned officers clubs. Most have clubhouses with dining and function facilities. Some have lodging facilities, recreational facilities, and social programs similar to civilian private clubs and resorts. One such facility is the Hale Koa Hotel at the Armed Forces Recreation Center in Fort DeRussy, Hawaii, which is on one of the nicest parts of Waikiki Beach. In Europe, the armed forces

The main purpose of yacht clubs is to provide marinas and other boating facilities for boat owners.

operate hotels and recreation centers in Garmisch, Berchtesgaden, and Chiemsee—all in Bavaria. In recent years the Department of Defense has hired civilians to manage military clubs instead of using military personnel.

Club Ownership

Private clubs are usually owned in one of two ways. A club can be owned by some of its members; such clubs are called equity clubs. Those members who fund the purchase or development of an equity club are known as founder-members. Or a club can be owned by a company that sells memberships in the club. These for-profit clubs are known as corporate or developer clubs, or—less frequently—as proprietary clubs.

Equity Clubs

Equity clubs are generally nonprofit, since they are typically formed not for money-making purposes but simply for the enjoyment of their members. Members are either (1) founder-members, or (2) other members who pay a one-time initiation fee and annual dues. If an equity club has an excess of revenues over expenses, the profits are not given back to the founder-members but are invested in improving the club's facilities and services. Because equity clubs are not formed to make a profit, the nonprofit statute of the tax law exempts the club from federal and state income taxes, although clubs may be required to pay taxes on unrelated income (such as nonmember functions) as well as federal and state payroll taxes.

Nontransfer of profits to members is only one part of what gives an equity club its nonprofit status. To receive a tax exemption, an equity club must be formed solely for pleasure and recreation, and must not discriminate on the basis of sex, race, or religion against anyone who wishes to become a member. Discrimination is often practiced on other grounds, however. Sometimes clubs charge high initiation fees or require members to buy expensive bonds or membership shares. And it is perfectly within the rights of a club to turn down applicants because they are not qualified by reason of accomplishment, professional occupation, or—as in the case of the Bohemian Club—artistic talent.

Corporate or Developer Clubs

As mentioned earlier, **corporate clubs** or developer clubs operate for profit and are owned by individuals or corporations. Persons who wish to become members purchase a membership, not a share in the club. Members may or may not be involved in running the club. Sometimes developers sell or turn over the club to its members when all memberships are sold. The cost of the clubhouse is paid for by initiation fees or real estate sales.

Corporate or developer clubs proliferated with the real estate boom in office buildings, condominiums, and single-housing developments. Just as having a dining club in office buildings helped developers rent office space, a country club at the center of a condominium or housing development was a good marketing tactic that not only helped to sell or lease properties but raised their prices by offering an added value to buyers.

The major company in the business of club management is ClubCorp. This Dallas-based company owns or operates more than 170 country clubs, city clubs, sports clubs, and resorts nationwide. It was in 1984, with the purchase of the Pinehurst Resort and Country Club, that ClubCorp broadened its business by going into resort hotel management. This was not surprising, in view of the similarities between country clubs and resorts. Later, it

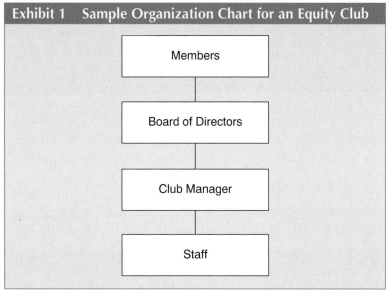

Exhibit 1   Sample Organization Chart for an Equity Club

Members

Board of Directors

Club Manager

Staff

In an equity club, the members own the club and elect a board of directors (who are also members of the club) to oversee the budget and set club policies. The club manager reports to the board or a member of the board.

added daily-fee golf courses to its management portfolio. In 2006, ClubCorp was acquired by KSL Capital Partners, a leading private equity firm.

Some corporate or developer clubs are built exclusively for the use of employees of particular companies and are owned and operated by those companies. The DuPont Country Club in Wilmington, Delaware, is one of those clubs. Only employees of the DuPont company, members of their immediate families, and retired employees may join this club. The 6,000-member club is one of the largest private clubs in the world. Its facilities include 19 outdoor clay tennis courts and six hard courts, a lawn-bowling green, three 18-hole golf courses, and a fitness center. There are two dining rooms, two ballrooms, and eight banquet rooms.

Club Organization

How a club is organized depends to a large extent on whether the club is nonprofit or for-profit. In a nonprofit equity club, the members elect a board of directors (sometimes called a board of governors) to oversee the budget and set policy affecting membership and club use. The board is the governing body, and the club manager reports to the board and implements its policies and decisions (see Exhibit 1). In a for-profit corporate or developer club, the club manager reports to and receives instructions as to club policies, procedures, and standards from the club's owners (see Exhibit 2). A corporate or developer club may have a board of directors made up of club members, if the owners wish to give the members some sense of authority, but generally this board merely advises the owners and does not make policy.

Exhibit 2   Sample Organization Chart for a Corporate or Developer Club

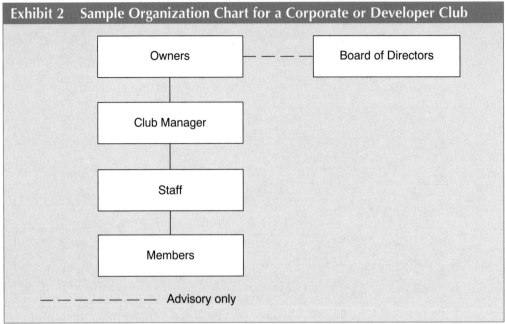

In a corporate or developer club, the club is owned by a corporation or developer, not the club's members. Members may or may not be involved in running the club. For example, the club's owners may form a board of directors, made up of club members, to advise them on club matters. The club manager reports to the corporation or developer, not the club's members.

The number of members on an equity club's board usually ranges from 12 to 25, although sometimes it is even higher. Board officers typically include a chairperson (usually last year's president), president, vice president, and treasurer.

Committees are extremely important to club morale and operation because they allow more members to participate in club leadership. In addition to special committees that are appointed for specific social or sporting events, clubs generally have five standing committees: a house committee, a membership committee, a finance and budget committee, an entertainment committee, and an athletic committee.[5]

The Club Manager

Club managers were not considered to be necessary until the early 1920s. Up to that time, most private clubs were managed by their members, through the club's standing committees and board of governors. Generally, the clubhouse was run by a steward, and the sports facilities were overseen by a sports professional. Today, club management is a profession requiring special training and expertise.

The duties of a **club manager** can vary considerably, depending on the kind of club he or she works for and the way it is organized. Some clubs have a general manager in the club manager position; others have a clubhouse manager. The difference is that a general manager has responsibility for all the employees of the club, while a clubhouse manager may only be responsible for employees working in the clubhouse. For example, a country

City Club Organization

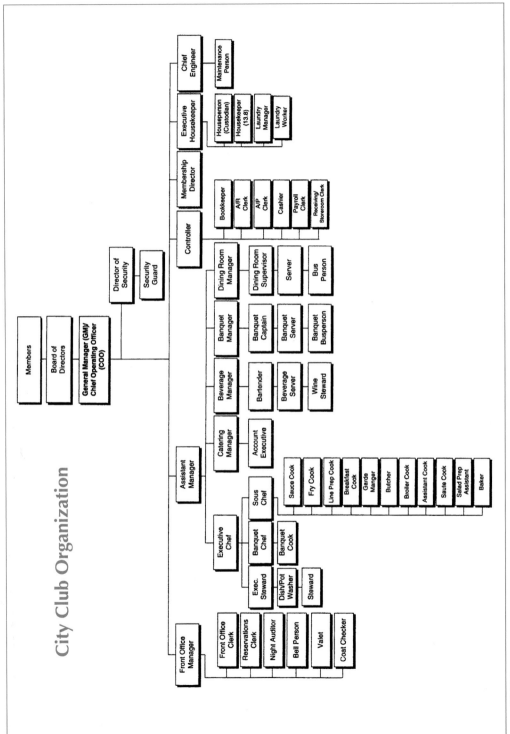

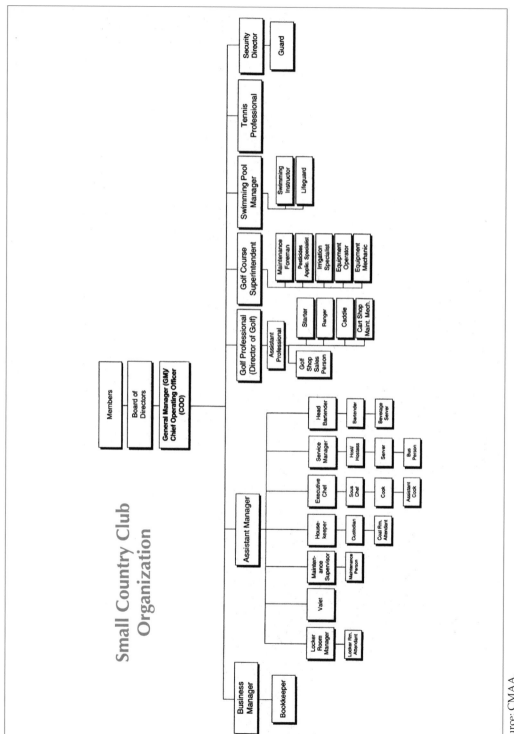

Small Country Club Organization

Source: CMAA.

club may have a clubhouse manager in charge of clubhouse operations and personnel, while the club's sports facilities are operated by athletic professionals. A list of the areas of competency needed by club general managers is shown in Exhibit 3. In corporate or developer clubs the trend is to have one general manager in charge of everything, because members are too busy to take an interest in all of the details involved in running a club.

According to CMAA, club managers who excel have certain personal qualities and abilities in common:

1. Effectiveness in interpersonal relations

2. Dedication—commitment to the welfare of the club

3. Integrity

4. A strong sense of organization and an ability to administer

5. Creativity and vision

6. Intelligence

7. Professionalism

8. An ability to communicate well

9. Strong leadership capabilities

10. Industry experience[6]

In one respect, a club manager's job is more complex than that of a hotel or restaurant manager's. The jobs are similar to the extent that all of these managers must manage physical facilities, employees, and services in order to meet economic objectives. In addition, each must hire, train, fire, and set standards of service. Where the jobs differ—and what makes a club manager's job more complex—is that club managers must share planning and budgeting responsibilities with an on-site board of directors, and club members have a more direct say in whether a manager keeps his or her job than hotel or restaurant guests do. In an equity club, a club manager must find a way to keep two groups relatively happy: (1) a board whose members may have diverse points of view because they were elected by different factions within the club's membership that do not agree, and (2) a variety of members with differing wants and needs. To do this, a club manager must be a master politician.

Advancement in the club management field may require more mobility than in the hotel field. According to surveys done by CMAA, fewer than 20 percent of all CMAA-member club managers were employed as an assistant manager or department head at the same club they now manage.[7] An assistant manager or department head who wishes to advance usually must move to a different club. Club managers who wish to advance to a larger and more prestigious club obviously have to change jobs, which usually requires moving. But many club managers develop such a satisfying relationship with club members and officers that they never consider moving on.

Club Operations

Clubs are similar to other hospitality businesses in that they generate revenue and incur expenses. Differences between clubs and other hospitality businesses can be found in the clubs' sources of revenue.

Exhibit 3   Club Management Competency Areas for the GM/COO

I.   Private Club Management
History of private clubs
Types of private clubs
Membership types
Bylaws
Policy formulation

Board relations
Chief Operating Officer concept
Committees
Career development
Club job descriptions

II.   Food and Beverage
Sanitation
Menu Development
Nutrition
Pricing concepts
Food and beverage trends
Ordering/receiving/inventory

Quality service
Creativity in theme functions
Design and equipment
Food and beverage personnel
Wine list development

III.   Accounting and Finance in the Private Club
Accounting and finance principles
Uniform system of accounts
Financial analysis
Budgeting
Cash flow forecasting
Compensation and benefit administration

Financing capital projects
Audits
Internal Revenue Service
Computers
Business office organization
Long-range financial planning

IV.   Human and Professional Resources
Employee relations
Management styles
Organizational development
Balancing job and family responsibilities

Time management
Stress management
Labor issues
Leadership vs. management

V.   Building and Facilities Management
Preventive maintenance
Insurance and risk management
Clubhouse remodeling and renovation
Contractors
Energy and water resource management

Housekeeping
Security
Laundry
Lodging operations

VI.   External and Governmental Influences
Legislative influences
Regulatory agencies
Economic theory
Labor law

Privacy
Club law
Liquor liability
Internal Revenue Service

VII.   Management
Communication skills
Professional image and dress

Effective negotiation
Member contact skills

VIII.   Marketing
Marketing through in-house publications
Working with the media

Marketing strategies in a private club environment

IX.   Sports and Recreation
Golf operations management
Golf course management
Tennis operations
Swimming pool management

Yacht facilities management
Fitness center management
Other recreational activities

Source: CMAA.

Exhibit 4   Sources of Club Revenue

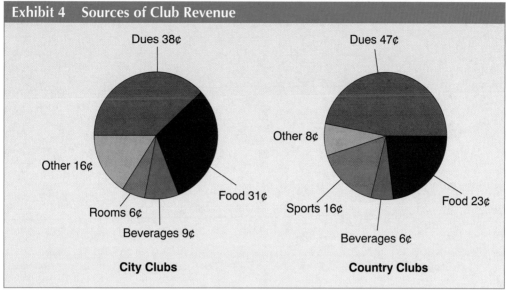

City Clubs: Dues 38¢, Other 16¢, Rooms 6¢, Beverages 9¢, Food 31¢

Country Clubs: Dues 47¢, Other 8¢, Sports 16¢, Beverages 6¢, Food 23¢

City Clubs   **Country Clubs**

Source: *Clubs in Town & Country,* North America Edition, 2009 (Fairfax, Va.: PKF North America Network, 2009), pp. 9, 19.

Revenue

Since a club is a private enterprise used primarily by members, the bulk of its revenue is derived from its members (see Exhibit 4). Typical sources of club revenue are:

- Membership dues
- Initiation fees
- Assessments
- Sports activities fees
- Food and beverage sales
- Other sources of revenue (such as rooms revenue)

Membership dues, initiation fees, assessments, and sports activities fees help set clubs apart from hotels and restaurants, since hotels and restaurants do not earn revenue from these sources.

Membership Dues. Membership dues are the cost to a member for the exclusivity of the club. Unlike an operation open to the public, a private club has a limited number of patrons and hence a limited source of revenue. Membership dues subsidize all of the club's operating costs and fixed charges. Dues vary based on the type of club (city or country), the number of members, and the extent of the club's facilities and services. Because country clubs are generally more expensive to operate than city clubs, they usually have higher dues. According to a study by PKF North America Network, in 2009 the income per member derived from dues alone averaged $6,032 for country clubs, compared to only $2,752 for city clubs.[8]

It is common for a club to have several different membership dues based on different types of membership. This makes it possible for more persons to join and thus increases the membership base, which decreases costs for each member.

A good example of how a city club offers different types of memberships is the Cornell Club of New York. The Cornell Club occupies a 15-floor building with guestrooms, dining rooms, a lounge, a health club, and private meeting rooms. Here are the different types of memberships (each with a different dues structure) that are available:

- Resident—a member who resides or works within New York City

- Suburban—a member who resides within 50 miles of New York City but not within the city itself and does not work in New York City

- Nonresident—a member who resides more than 50 miles from New York City

Each of these memberships has six different levels of dues, based on the number of years the member has been out of college. It is presumed, of course, that the members who have been graduates for the greatest number of years can afford the highest dues.

In addition to these memberships, the Cornell Club offers special memberships for persons who are not Cornell graduates but are associated with the university (such as full-time faculty and staff). These special memberships are also categorized as resident, suburban, or nonresident. There is even a Cornell couple membership and a spouse membership.

Country clubs usually have a larger number of membership categories than city clubs. Some people are just interested in a social membership at a country club—they wish to eat there and socialize with friends at the swimming pool but are not interested in playing golf or tennis. Other members want to make full use of the club's recreational facilities and purchase a regular or active membership. Some clubs offer single or family memberships. A few country clubs have a nonresident category. Many have a lifetime membership option for those willing to make a large one-time payment for lifetime privileges.

An example of a club that offers its members a wide variety of memberships is the Grosse Pointe Yacht Club. This club offers a choice of an active membership or a social membership. An active member can vote and enjoys all privileges (dining, tennis, pool, bowling, paddle tennis, and boating). A social membership excludes voting and boating. Within each of the two categories there are three levels of dues defined by age, beginning with members aged 21–25. There is even a special membership for clergy.

Initiation Fees. Most clubs charge new members an **initiation fee,** which in most cases is nonrefundable. Clubs vary in how they handle initiation fees. Some consider them contributions to capital and show them as additions to founder-members' equity (for equity clubs) or owners' equity (for corporate or developer clubs). Others add them to reserve funds for specific capital improvement projects such as refurbishing the clubhouse. Initiation fees typically range from $500 to $10,000, although a few clubs charge $100,000 or more.

Assessments. One-time or periodic **assessments** are sometimes imposed on members instead of increasing dues. Some assessments cover operational shortfalls. Others are used to raise capital for improvements to the club. Assessments are unpopular with members, since they are unanticipated expenses. Therefore, instead of assessments, many clubs prefer to impose minimum spending requirements, usually on food and beverages. If a member does not spend a specified amount on food and beverages either on a monthly, quarterly, or annual basis, a bill is sent for the difference.

Fees for golf and other sports activities account for a significant portion of country club revenues.

Sports Activities Fees. City clubs do not record revenue from sports activities because they typically do not charge members extra for using the club's recreational facilities. On the other hand, **sports activities fees** (including golf) account for 16 percent of total country club revenues.[9] In country clubs where golf and tennis are significant activities, a golf professional and a tennis professional are responsible for programs in these sports. Fees are charged for playing tennis or golf and, in the case of golf, rental fees are charged for golf carts.

A golf course is an expensive facility, each year costing more than $114,699 per hole to maintain.[10] As Exhibit 5 shows, revenue derived directly from golf operations covers only about half of golf costs. Membership dues or profits from other departments are necessary to make up the difference.

Sometimes other recreational facilities exist, such as a swimming pool, a health spa, and volleyball or squash courts. Members at most country clubs pay fees to use these facilities, with the exception of the swimming pools; swimming is usually free. If a club offers a lot of sports options, an athletic director might well be added to the staff to supervise all of the club's recreational facilities and programs.

Clubs with athletic facilities have committees for specific sports. Country clubs with a golf course have a **golf committee** that reports to the club's board and advises it on golf course policies such as appropriate course use and the course's hours of operation. The

Exhibit 5 Golf Course Expenses	
Average Cost per Hole	**All Country Clubs in the Study**
Payroll	$ 56,715
Payroll Taxes and Employee Benefits	12,737
Course Supplies and Contracts	14,580
Repairs and Maintenance	5,975
Other Costs	24,692
Total Golf Department	$114,699
Less: Golf Revenue	53,030
Net Golf Expenses	$ 61,669

Source: *Clubs in Town & Country,* North America Edition, 2009 (Fairfax, Va.: PKF North America Network, 2009), p. 11.

committee works with the club's management in planning tournaments and preparing the golf course budget.

Food and Beverage Sales. After dues income, sales of food and beverages are the major source of revenue in both city clubs and country clubs. Like hotels and resorts, clubs often have more than one dining facility. City clubs with a single dining room tend to keep it formal and add a more informal tap room or grill. Country clubs usually operate snack bars at the pool or golf course, an informal dining room for lunch, and a formal dining room.

A club's dining facilities must compete with restaurants in the surrounding area in terms of food quality and value. The Lake Merced Golf Club near San Francisco conducts wine tastings and frequently puts on special dinners prepared by renowned European chefs to draw members away from competing restaurants. Club chefs are often promoted heavily and in some instances have become celebrities. Former executive chef Thomas Catherill of the Cherokee Town and Country Club in Atlanta is a gold medalist from the Culinary Olympics in Frankfurt, Germany. In Dallas, the Club at San Simeon lured a sizable share of banquet business away from prominent hotels by offering the locally renowned cuisine of their club chef.

In general, club members hold their club to higher standards of food quality and service than public restaurants. For this reason, in many cases food service becomes the main focus of the club, requiring the greatest part of the club manager's efforts.

Other Sources of Revenue. In addition to membership dues, initiation fees, assessments, sports activities fees, and food and beverage sales, there are other sources of revenue for clubs. Most clubs charge **visitors' fees** for nonmembers who are guests of members and use rooms, buy food and beverages, or use recreational facilities. Often there are service charges on food and beverage sales, which may be distributed to employees or, as in most cases, used to offset the club's labor costs. City clubs with overnight accommodations generate revenue from guestroom sales and may offer laundry and valet services for a fee. Country clubs have pro shops, operated by the club or by a concessionaire, that sell sports equipment, apparel, and (in some cases) a broad range of gift items.

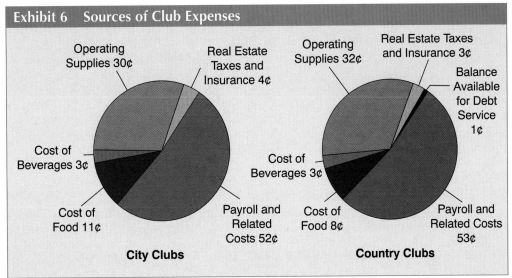

Exhibit 6   Sources of Club Expenses

Operating Supplies 30¢

Real Estate Taxes and Insurance 4¢

Cost of Beverages 3¢

Cost of Food 11¢

Payroll and Related Costs 52¢

City Clubs

Operating Supplies 32¢

Real Estate Taxes and Insurance 3¢

Balance Available for Debt Service 1¢

Cost of Beverages 3¢

Cost of Food 8¢

Payroll and Related Costs 53¢

Country Clubs

Source: *Clubs in Town & Country,* North America Edition, 2009 (Fairfax, Va.: PKF North America Network, 2009), pp. 9, 19.

Expenses

Payroll and related costs are the single largest expense in operating a club, representing 52 percent of club expenses in city clubs and 53 percent in country clubs (see Exhibit 6). The largest segment of payroll expenditure is in the food and beverage operation. The second largest expense for both country clubs and city clubs is "operating supplies," at 30 percent and 32 percent, respectively.

Control

Like hotels and restaurants, clubs have a uniform accounting system; the *Uniform System of Financial Reporting for Clubs* is in its sixth revised edition.[11] In addition to a classification of accounts, the system provides for a reporting method that separates revenues and expenses into departments. This allows a club's managers, board of directors, members, and—if it is a corporate or developer club—owners to easily review operating results by department.

Summary

Private clubs date back to ancient Greece and Rome, but the true forerunners of American private clubs (which now number more than 14,000) are the social and golf clubs of England and Scotland. While there are many similarities to managing clubs and hotels, there are some differences as well.

There are two basic types of clubs—city clubs and country clubs. City clubs can be categorized as athletic, dining, professional, social, or university.

Athletic clubs are often quite large, sometimes occupying entire downtown buildings, and may include lodging and dining facilities as well as gymnasiums, swimming pools, and courts for squash, handball, and racquetball.

Dining clubs are generally found in office buildings. Many of these clubs are open only for lunch.

A professional club is a dining or social club for people in a particular profession. There are clubs for lawyers, actors, artists, journalists, and other professionals.

Social clubs were originally modeled after men's social clubs in England. Although most social clubs do not discriminate on the basis of sex, race, or religion, some try to limit their membership to persons of the same social and economic background.

University clubs are private clubs for university graduates. Some university clubs have dining and meeting rooms, guestrooms, and extensive libraries and recreational facilities.

The largest type of private club is the country club. Country clubs are primarily recreational and social facilities for individuals and families who live nearby. Since country clubs need a great deal of land for their golf course(s) and other facilities, they are usually located in suburban or rural areas.

Other kinds of clubs include yacht clubs, fraternal clubs, and military clubs.

Most private clubs are equity clubs or corporate (or developer) clubs. Equity clubs are owned by a group of founder-members and are generally nonprofit, since they are formed not for money-making purposes but only for the enjoyment of their members. Corporate or developer clubs are for-profit clubs owned by individuals or companies that sell memberships in the clubs.

A club's organization depends on whether it is an equity or a corporate or developer club. The club manager is the hired professional responsible for guiding all of the elements of a club's operation.

The bulk of club revenues is derived from club members. These revenues fall into the following classifications: membership dues, initiation fees, assessments, sports activities fees, food and beverage sales, and other sources of revenue.

Membership dues are the cost to a member for the exclusivity of the club. It is common for city and country clubs to have several different types of memberships. A city club might have different membership dues for resident, suburban, and nonresident members, reflecting the location of the member's residence in relation to the location of the club. Country clubs tend to use a different type of dues structure, based on use of recreational facilities, a member's age, and other factors. In addition to dues, clubs generally charge initiation fees and, in some cases, special assessments.

Next to dues, food and beverage sales are the major source of club revenue. Other sources of revenue include guestroom sales (for city clubs), visitors' fees, and service charges on food and beverage sales. A club's payroll and related costs are its largest expense.

Like hotels and restaurants, clubs have their own uniform system of financial reporting that helps club managers control and manage operations.

Endnotes

1. Carole Klein, *Gramercy Park: An American Bloomsbury* (Boston: Houghton Mifflin, 1987), p. 159.

2. Stephen Birmingham, *America's Secret Aristocracy* (New York: Berkley Books, 1990), p. 209.

3. Ibid., p. 213.

4. Bermuda Department of Tourism.

5. Ted E. White and Larry C. Gerstner, *Club Operations and Management,* 2d ed. (New York: Van Nostrand Reinhold, 1991).

6. Club Managers Association of America, *Club Management Operations,* 4th ed. (Dubuque, Iowa: Kendall-Hunt, 1989), p. 27.

7. Ibid., p. 32.

8. *Clubs in Town & Country,* North America Edition, 2009 (Fairfax, Virginia: PKF North America Network, 2009), pp. 4, 13.

9. Ibid., p. 6.

10. Ibid., p. 11.

11. The *Uniform System of Financial Reporting for Clubs,* Sixth Revised Edition, was published in 2003 by the Educational Institute of the American Hotel & Lodging Association (2113 N. High Street, Lansing, Michigan, 48906), in cooperation with the Club Managers Association of America (which owns the copyright) and Hospitality Financial and Technology Professionals (HFTP), the international society for financial and technology professionals in the hospitality industry.

Key Terms

assessment—A one-time or periodic charge imposed on private club members to cover operational shortfalls or raise capital for improvements to the club.

city club—An urban recreational and social facility that can be categorized as athletic, dining, professional, social, or university.

club manager—The hired professional responsible for guiding all of the elements of a private club's operation. Often referred to as the club's general manager or chief operating officer (COO).

corporate club—A for-profit private club owned by an individual or a company that sells memberships in the club. Also called a developer or proprietary club.

country club—A private recreational and social facility for individuals and families who live in the surrounding area.

equity club—A nonprofit private club whose members buy shares in the club and, after expenses have been paid, invest any revenues left over into improving the club's facilities and services.

golf committee—A private country club committee composed of club members who establish golf course policy, review golf course budgets and operations, and oversee the care of the golf course(s).

initiation fee—A typically nonrefundable charge that new members must pay to join a private club.

membership dues—The cost to a private club member for the exclusivity provided by the club's limited membership. Membership dues subsidize all of the club's operating costs and fixed charges.

sports activities fees—Fees that country clubs charge members and visitors for using the club's recreational facilities.

visitors' fees—Charges to nonmembers of a private club who are guests of members and use rooms, buy food or beverages, or use recreational facilities.

Review Questions

1. What is a basic difference between clubs and hotels?
2. What are the similarities and differences among the various types of city clubs?
3. What are the similarities and differences between city clubs and country clubs?
4. What are two basic ways private clubs can be owned?
5. What are some criteria an equity club must meet to maintain its nonprofit status?
6. How is an equity club organized? How is a corporate or developer club organized?
7. What are some opportunities and problems associated with a career in club management?
8. What are typical sources of club revenue?
9. What are some common types of club memberships?
10. What are typical sources of club expenses?

Internet Sites

For more information, visit the following Internet sites. Remember that Internet addresses can change without notice. If the site is no longer there, you can use a search engine to look for additional sites.

Associations

American Hotel & Lodging Educational Institute
www.ahlei.org

Club Managers Association of America
www.cmaa.org

International Health, Racquet & Sportsclub Association
www.ihrsa.org

National Club Association
www.natlclub.org

National Restaurant Association
www.restaurant.org

Organizations/Resources

ClubCorp
www.clubcorp.com

Club Services, Inc.
www.clubservices.com

The Virtual Clubhouse
www.club-mgmt.com

9

An Introduction to the Meetings Industry

Competencies

1. List and describe types of meetings typically held in lodging facilities, explain the role of civic and government organizations in the meetings industry, and describe where most meetings are held. (pp. 270–276)

2. Outline the meeting planning process and summarize career opportunities in the meetings industry. (pp. 276–287)

Opposite page: The Fairmont Battery Wharf, Boston, Massachusetts; photo courtesy of Fairmont Hotels & Resorts.

ANY DISCUSSION OF THE MEETINGS INDUSTRY should begin with a definition of what we mean by a meeting. For the purposes of this chapter, we define a **meeting** as a planned event in which a group of people gather together to accomplish something. The gathering can take place in a hotel, on a cruise ship, in a convention center, or at airports or colleges. It can also take place at several locations simultaneously through teleconferencing.

A meeting can consist of a few people in a conference room or 100,000 delegates at a major convention center utilizing a dozen or more hotels in a large city. In some cases, especially when a convention is involved, a meeting may include a trade show. For example, the International Hotel and Restaurant Exposition, held annually in New York City, consists of a general industry association meeting, at which industry issues and trends are discussed; committee meetings; educational programs; and a trade show. At the trade show, vendors of products and services such as furniture, property management systems, and design services demonstrate and explain what they have to offer. There are also numerous receptions, meals, and other social events held all over the city in conjunction with the exposition.

In order to stage such complicated events, many specialized services, facilities, and technologies are used. For example, transporting a huge body of people to a single location at the same time involves the use of airlines, motorcoaches, limousines, and rental cars. Meeting planners must arrange for this transportation. They must also book hotels to house and feed the delegates, and reserve convention centers to hold the meetings and trade shows. Vendors must contract with exhibit designers to build booths where the vendors will show their products. Meeting planners may contract with audiovisual and satellite services to record and film the guest speakers or produce and broadcast the presentations.

Types of Meetings

The **meetings industry** is also referred to as the meetings, incentive travel, conventions, and exhibitions industry (MICE). Types of meetings within the industry are association meetings, corporate meetings, and trade shows/expositions.

Association Meetings

Many people belong to an association of some kind. Associations range from trade groups, such as the American Medical Association (AMA), to social groups, such as the American Association of Retired Persons (AARP). Labor unions, like the Teamsters or the American Federation of Labor–Congress of Industrial Organizations (AFL-CIO), are also associations. Service associations include the Junior Chamber of Commerce (Jaycees) and the Rotarians.

Some associations are large enough to employ a full-time meetings and travel department. Exhibit 1 shows a sample organization chart for such a department.

Virtually all associations hold at least one annual meeting when the entire association gets together to elect officers, set budgets, and plan activities. Association members take this opportunity to learn about the issues that may affect their future, such as government regulation. In between these annual meetings, members network with each other and hold local chapter meetings.

Exhibit 1   Sample Organization Chart for a Large Association's Meetings and Travel Department

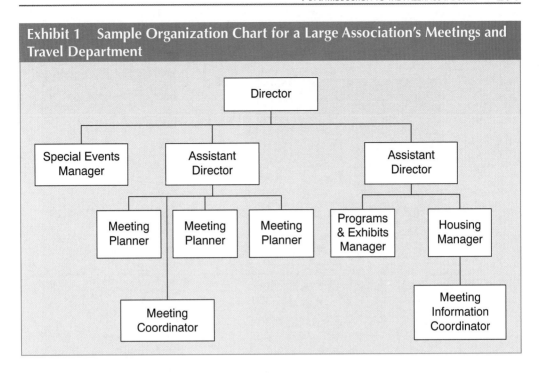

Some associations meet frequently. Besides annual national or international conventions, some associations hold regional meetings, board meetings, and educational seminars. These meetings typically range in length from one day to one week. For example, in a typical year the American Bar Association might hold an annual meeting (attended by 12,000 delegates), a mid-year meeting (attended by 3,200 delegates), and 350 local meetings throughout the year.

An important characteristic of association meetings is their timing cycle. National or international meetings or conventions are usually held annually. Often the site is selected two to five years before the event, especially when large numbers of persons are involved. (Smaller meetings are scheduled as needed, with a typical lead time of five to eight months.) These large conventions usually last from three to five days. From a large association's point of view, the number of cities that can accommodate 50,000 delegates or more is limited. Sites must be selected years in advance to be sure that hotel rooms and airline seats are available. The goal of hotels and convention centers is to maximize the use of their facilities, and this long lead time allows them to plan sales and marketing efforts.

The need for adequate exhibit space is another important characteristic of association meetings. More than 40 percent of all conventions feature exhibitions that require at least 20,000 square feet (1,860 square meters) of exhibit space.

Attendance at association meetings is voluntary, so association meeting planners must pay special attention to site selection and social programs.

Corporate Meetings

According to the Professional Convention Management Association, the types of corporate meetings held off company premises include:

Unique French Ambiance

2,916 Rooms and 300 Suites

130,000 Sq. Ft. of Meeting Space

8 Distinctive French Restaurants

Give Your Next Convention a French Twist.

They've never experienced a convention like this. Non? That's because until now, there's never been a place like this. The romance and excitement of Paris mixed with casino action fantastique and a full complement of business and convention resources. Not to mention, the musical spectaculaire Notre Dame de Paris, suave European service and beautiful view of the Strip from our 50-story Eiffel Tower. So don't gamble on your next convention, book Paris Las Vegas. They'll love "vous" for it. For reservations, call 1-800-722-5597 or visit www.paris-lv.com.

Attendance at association meetings is voluntary, so association meeting planners must pay special attention to site selection. This ad asks meeting planners to consider all of the advantages of booking a convention at the Paris Las Vegas. (Courtesy of Paris Las Vegas, Las Vegas, Nevada.)

- *Management meetings.* Management meetings include everything from financial reviews to strategic planning sessions. Management meetings make up the largest category in the corporate meetings market. Average attendance: 45.

- *Training seminars.* Training seminars rank second in number of meetings held. They provide training for employees at all levels.

- *Sales meetings (both national and regional).* Sales meetings are essential for teaching sales techniques, introducing new products, building morale, and motivating sales personnel. National sales meetings average 3.6 days with 104 attendees. Regional sales meetings average 42 attendees and last an average of 2.5 days.

- *New product introductions.* New products are showcased to employees at new product introductions. These meetings are also used to motivate dealers or distributors who are not employees (for example, introducing new car models to dealers). New product introductions last 2 days on average; average attendance is 60 people.

- *Professional and technical meetings.* Professional and technical meetings are used to provide information or teach new techniques to employees who work in technical and professional fields. Accountants need to learn about new tax laws and rulings every year, for example.

- *Incentive trips.* Often a combination of meetings and recreation, incentive trips are rewards to customers, retailers, distributors, or employees. Spouses are often invited to attend.

Training seminars are often held in hotels.

- Louisiana Old State Capitol

This magazine ad, placed by the Baton Rouge Area Convention & Visitors Bureau, is aimed at meeting planners and asks them to consider Baton Rouge as a meetings destination because "business and pleasure have never mixed so well."

- *Stockholders meetings.* Stockholders meetings are annual events usually lasting a day, with an average attendance of 95 owners of company stock.

- *Other corporate meetings.* Other corporate meetings include press conferences, public forums, and any other meetings a corporation might sponsor.

Corporate meetings require much less lead time than association meetings, since for the most part they are smaller and don't last as long. Because corporate meetings are often mandatory, corporate meeting planners do not need to take as much care to promote the meeting or plan special social programs as do association meeting planners.

Trade Shows/Expositions

Trade shows, also known as **expositions,** usually take place at convention centers, at exhibit halls, or in exhibit space in hotels. Sometimes public arenas are used. Trade shows are sponsored by trade associations, private companies who are in the business of organizing trade shows, or by governments. Trade shows can be part of a convention or association meeting. When they are, they can represent a significant amount of revenue for the sponsoring association.

Most trade shows can be placed within one of four categories:

- Industrial shows
- Wholesale and retail trade shows
- Professional or scientific exhibitions
- Public or consumer shows

Industrial shows are events used by manufacturers of equipment and products to exhibit their products to other manufacturers. At an industrial show, buyers are typically purchasing materials and inventory that they will remanufacture into a processed product or resell either as-is or in some adapted form.

Wholesale and retail trade shows are collections of exhibits that are specific to one or more closely allied or associated trades. In most instances the buyers represent businesses that are shopping for services and products to use in the conduct of their business. The World Travel Mart, held annually in London, is an example of a wholesale and retail trade show. At this show, several hundred hotels, airlines, cruise lines, tour operators, and tourism boards from major countries staff booths and attempt to persuade travel agents to recommend their offerings. One of the largest wholesale and retail trade shows in the United States is held every May in Chicago by the National Restaurant Association. This show attracts almost 2,000 exhibitors and is attended by more than 90,000 delegates from all over the world.

Professional or scientific exhibitions are usually associated with meetings of professional groups, educators, scientists, and other people who could be considered end users.

Public or consumer shows are the only wholesale and retail trade shows open to the public. Many newspapers and other media sponsor travel shows for their advertisers. At these shows, the public can browse among exhibits prepared by destinations, hotels, tour operators, and cruise lines; view videos; and listen to presentations about various vacation options. Other popular consumer shows include antique shows, art shows, and other shows that appeal to collectors.

The Role of Civic and Government Organizations

Almost every city has a **convention and visitors bureau (CVB)** or a chamber of commerce. These are nonprofit organizations whose job it is to market their destinations. States and counties often have their own tourism departments. Virtually every country in the world has a Department or Ministry of Tourism that often includes a division whose function is to attract meetings and conventions. These entities field salespeople to call on meeting planners. They also run advertisements in meeting publications suggesting that their locations are ideal for a meeting or convention. They help groups find meeting sites and accommodations, and organize activities for delegates. They will frequently offer personnel to assist with greeting and registering delegates as well.

Where Meetings Are Held

Almost any kind of facility can be used to hold a meeting. Meetings have been held in amusement parks, football stadiums, and castles. All modern cruise ships have conference centers and meeting rooms. Such business accounts for between one and fifteen percent of cruise line business, depending on the line. Meetings have even been held on luxury trains such as the Orient Express. However, most meetings are held in hotels or motels.

Almost all of the business of conference centers, which are specifically designed to house small meetings, comes from the meetings market segment. Conference centers range in size from 32 guestrooms to 400. Some are owned by corporations, which use them primarily for their own purposes and occasionally rent them out to other corporations and, in some cases, even open them to the public on weekends. Corporations that own their own conference centers include American Express, Xerox, IBM, and Chase Manhattan Bank. Many universities have also built conference centers. For example, Columbia University has Arden House on its Harriman, New York, campus.

Virtual Meetings

Teleconferencing has been around for many years but has never caught on as an alternative to live meetings. But as the technology continues to improve and companies become more cost-conscious, "virtual meetings" are becoming more popular. Starwood Hotels & Resorts and Marriott International are two companies in the forefront of providing telepresence suites in some of their meeting rooms. "Telepresence" is a system that attempts to simulate a face-to-face experience by using half a conference table facing high-definition screens. Projected onto the screens are life-size images of meeting participants who are at similar locations at a distant site. The set-up of the room, including the color of the wall at the distant site in another Starwood or Marriott hotel, is similar, giving the impression that everyone is in the same room.[1]

The Meeting Planning Process

The meeting planning process comprises three parts: planning the meeting itself, choosing a location, and choosing a facility.

The website for InterContinental Hotels Group provides helpful information to meeting planners—both professional and "occasional." (Courtesy of InterContinental Hotels Group.)

Planning the Meeting Itself

To do a good job, a meeting planner must know the objective(s) of the meeting. This will give him or her a better idea of how much time to schedule for the meeting, what time of year to schedule it, and what type of format or agenda is best. The following sections will cover each of these meeting planning components: objectives, scheduling, and format.

Objectives. One of the first questions a meeting planner must deal with is the objective(s) of the meeting. There are three general meeting objectives: business, educational, or social (or any combination of the three). The appropriateness of a meeting site depends on the meeting's objectives. For example, a two-day meeting of quick-service franchisees from all over the United States might best be held in a centrally located large hotel in (or connected to) a major airport, so that attendees can get to the meeting site and return home quickly and economically. On the other hand, a sales meeting meant to motivate salespeople to

MEETING AND BANQUET FACILITIES

LOBBY LEVEL

ROOM	DIMENSION	CEILING HT.	SQ. FT.	BANQUET	RECEPT.	THEATRE	SCHOOL
Combined Pompeii & Imperial Rooms	68 x 150	18'/15'	10,200	850	1,100	1,100	650
Pompeii	68 x 85	18'	5,780	450	600	600	350
Combined Imperial A & B	68 x 65	15'	4,420	400	500	500	325
Imperial A	68 x 33	15'	2,200	200	250	250	165
Imperial B	68 x 33	15'	2,200	200	250	250	165
Mona Lisa	70 x 73	16'	5,100	300	350	350	225
Cotillion	85 x 71	20'	6,000	350	500	400	250
Rotunda	29 x 29 (Round)	12'	660	35	50	50	35
Porch	61 x 50	—	3,050	350	425	425	280
Ocean Lounge	56 x 30	—	1,680	125	200	200	75
Regency Court (Pre-function area)	—	—	2,500	—	200	—	—

MEZZANINE LEVEL

ROOM	DIMENSION	CEILING HT.	SQ. FT.	BANQUET	RECEPT.	THEATRE	SCHOOL
Paladium	44 x 37	13'	1,630	100	150	150	100
Board Room	17 x 15	10'	260	25	30	30	20
Sales Board Room	32 x 15	10'	480	30	45	45	25

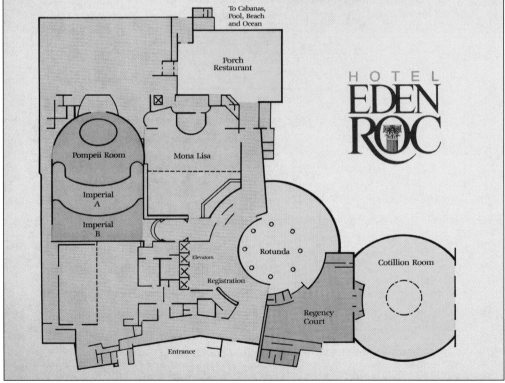

Charts like this one help meeting planners determine whether a given hotel has the right meeting room(s) for their meetings. "Banquet," "Recept.," "Theatre," and "School" refer to seating styles or plans; the numbers below these columns show how many chairs will comfortably fit into each meeting room listed on the left. Note that the number of chairs that can be accommodated in each room changes dramatically, depending on the seating plan. (Courtesy of Eden Roc Hotel and Marina, Miami Beach, Florida.)

exceed their quotas in the year ahead and reward them for their past year's performance is frequently held at a resort in a warm climate (Hawaii and Florida are popular destinations). Cruise ships are also popular for such meetings.

Scheduling. The next issue to address is the amount of time needed to achieve the meeting's objectives. The dates of the meeting are also important. A toy show must occur early enough in the year for retailers to place their orders in time for Christmas. Boat shows are typically held in the spring, just before the boating season begins. Television executives gather every January to show off new programs to advertisers and stations so that the fall season programming can be finalized. Meeting planners should be careful to pick a time that does not conflict with another meeting that might require the presence of or attract the same delegates. Planners should also avoid religious and national holidays.

Format. Once the length of the meeting and the dates have been established, it is time to make decisions about the meeting's format. The format is the overall schedule of events—what is going to happen during the meeting and in what order? When will the meeting start and finish? What will be the times and lengths of meals? coffee breaks? social events? How many general sessions, round-table discussions, and workshops will there be? If there is a trade show, when will it open and close? How many exhibitors will be involved and how much time will they need to accomplish their objectives? If there are tours, when will they occur and how long will they take?

Choosing a Location

Some meeting locations are predetermined. Many corporations hold their meetings at their own headquarters, for example. Other organizations change the meeting site from year to year to ease the travel costs for delegates from different geographic areas. Location is also affected by the nature of the organization. One would not expect a religious group to meet in Las Vegas or Atlantic City, where many of the leisure activities available are not compatible with the group's values. The transportation logistics involved are also a consideration. How accessible is the meeting site to airports? In Europe, where trains are used extensively for inter-city travel, accessibility to the train station can be a major consideration.

Choosing a Facility

Once the location has been chosen, a facility must be selected. Will it be a resort, a center-city hotel, a conference center, or a cruise ship? A facility's size and cost are two of the major considerations here.

In terms of size, a facility must have enough guestrooms, meeting rooms, and exhibit space. Factors to consider when choosing a facility include the following:

- Are the guestroom accommodations adequate? Are there a sufficient number of suites for VIPs and hospitality functions? What about the availability of smoking and no-smoking rooms?

- Are there computer connections in the guestrooms? Is wireless connectivity available in the lobby and other public areas?

- Can the meeting rooms be set up in a variety of styles? Theater, schoolroom, and hollow square are some of the basic styles (see Exhibit 2).

Exhibit 2   Sample Meeting Room Setups

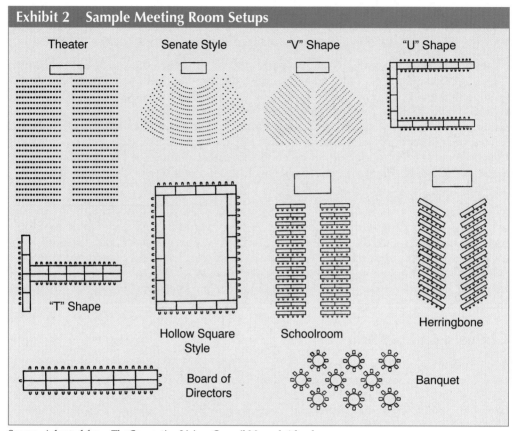

Source: Adapted from *The Convention Liaison Council Manual,* 4th ed.

- What types of amenities and recreational facilities are offered? This can be very important for meetings where relaxation is an objective. Some groups insist on resorts with golf courses, tennis courts, and spas; others want hotels located in or near scenic attractions.

- Are the meeting rooms adequately soundproofed? Meetings and activities in adjoining rooms should not intrude on each other.

- Does the resort, hotel, or cruise ship offer adequate audiovisual facilities? Is there a good sound system, especially for large rooms? What about the lighting? State-of-the-art lighting facilities include track lighting and theatrical lighting equipment. What kind of projection equipment is available? A group can rent much of this equipment from suppliers other than the hotel, but the hotel's meeting rooms must have enough outlets and electrical power to accommodate it.

- How far are the meeting rooms from the guestrooms? Can the meeting rooms be reached without climbing stairs? Are there a sufficient number of conveniently located elevators or escalators? These access issues have taken on added importance since the passage of the Americans with Disabilities Act.

This meeting room features a board of directors setup. (Courtesy of Fairmont Hotels & Resorts.)

Of course, an association or corporation's budget is an important determining factor in where the meeting will be held. Some industry groups can afford to meet at upscale hotels; others have more modest budgets. The price of many items is a matter of negotiation between the hotel and the meeting's sponsor. Questions for negotiation include whether there will be a charge for meeting room space, what the functions will cost, whether the hotel is willing to pay for a function (such as a manager's reception), what the guestrooms will cost, and how many guestrooms will be provided on a complimentary basis.

Here is a list of the top ten criteria deemed important by meeting planners in selecting a meeting site:

- Price of hotel rooms
- Available meeting space
- Willingness to negotiate
- Service standards
- Price of meeting space
- On-site meeting services
- Available hotel rooms
- Attrition rates
- On-site amenities
- Complimentary services[2]

Meetings Industry Careers

Persons who plan, organize, and coordinate meetings, conventions, and trade shows may have various job titles. Only in the largest associations are such people engaged full time in meeting planning and have titles such as "meeting planner," "meeting coordinator," or "exhibits manager" (see Exhibit 1). Many **meeting planners** have job titles that relate to other activities they perform, such as sales, marketing, or administration. For example, the marketing manager of a company may also be its convention manager or meeting planner. For the purposes of this discussion, however, we will refer to all those who plan and organize meetings, conventions, and trade shows as meeting planners.

This is an example of a herringbone meeting room setup in the British Columbia Ballroom at The Fairmont Hotel Vancouver in Vancouver. (Courtesy of Fairmont Hotels & Resorts.)

This is an example of a schoolroom setup. (Courtesy of Fairmont Hotels & Resorts.)

As mentioned earlier, persons who are actively engaged in meeting planning can be found in associations, corporations, governments, and travel agencies. There are also association management companies that include meeting planning among the management services they provide to clients. Independent meeting planners not associated with a company are another type of meeting planner. While these independent professionals are known as "meeting planners" in North America, in other parts of the world they are called professional conference or congress organizers (PCOs). Associations for meeting planners include Meeting Professionals International, the International Society of Meeting Planners, the Professional Convention Management Association, the American Society of Association Executives, and the Society of Government Meeting Professionals.

There are a number of tasks that meeting planners routinely perform and must be skilled at. The Convention Industry Council in McLean, Virginia, which certifies meeting planners and awards the designation of Certified Meeting Professional (CMP), lists 25 tasks meeting planners should be able to perform. Among the most important of these are:

- Establishing meeting objectives
- Selecting meeting sites and facilities
- Negotiating with facilities
- Budgeting
- Handling reservations, housing, and food and beverage issues efficiently
- Choosing from transportation options (air and ground)

A "U" shape setup. (Courtesy of Fairmont Hotels & Resorts.)

- Planning programs
- Planning meeting room setups
- Managing exhibits
- Selecting guest speakers
- Booking entertainment

In order to perform these tasks successfully, meeting planners must be superb negotiators and diplomats. The organizations they work for and the persons who attend the meetings expect them to choose the best sites and arrange for the best accommodations and transportation at the lowest prices. They want their food and beverage service and their social events to be superior—and they expect all of this to happen without any mishaps or delays. Meeting planning is a difficult job, requiring a high degree of specialized knowledge.

During the actual meeting, the planner is usually busy and under a great deal of pressure to keep things moving smoothly and resolve problems that come up. Meeting planners often arrive at a site a day or two in advance, to ensure that all of the elements they have negotiated and contracted for are in place. Are the hotels prepared to receive the delegates? Is transportation in place? Are the meeting rooms arranged as they should be? Have the arrangements for guest speakers been confirmed? Are there any problems with setting up the trade show? Cellular telephones and short-wave radio communications are often required to keep the planner in touch with the hotel staff in different parts of the hotel (and in touch with various hotels within the city, in the case of a large convention).

Even when things are going well, unanticipated events can threaten a convention's success. Speakers can fail to show up, hurricanes and snow storms can disrupt transportation arrangements, and fires, strikes, or demonstrations can occur. Good meeting planners devise contingency plans to handle all of these situations.

After a meeting is over, the meeting planner must still deal with a number of crucial tasks. Equipment and exhibit booths must be packed and shipped. Invoices from hotels, restaurants, and other facilities must be checked and settled. Equally important, the meeting must be evaluated from the point of view of the attendees, the sponsor, and the exhibitors. This information provides feedback for future meeting planning.

Travel and Tourism Careers Associated with Meeting Planning

Up to this point, we have discussed the meeting planners that the hospitality industry serves—the part-time or full-time meeting planners in associations, corporations, or other groups. Now let's look at some of the careers within the travel and tourism industry that may involve you in the meetings market.

Event Planner. Special event planning has become a popular career track in a number of hospitality schools, due to the growing demand for professional management. Individuals; companies; and charitable, social, and trade organizations rely on trained and experienced people to create and execute their events. The diversity of events that a professional event planner might be called upon to create and execute is one aspect of the career that is especially appealing for many. Although some independent event planners specialize in certain kinds of events (weddings, for example), others accept the challenge of any type of event—personal, cultural, leisure, or organizational. Weddings and anniversaries are personal events, while an art fair is an example of a cultural event. Leisure events include concerts and organized recreational activities. Events produced for businesses or charitable groups are classified as organizational. All types of events, no matter the category, require organizational skills and technical knowledge on the part of the event planner.

Companies that have many events throughout the year might have their own in-house event planners, or they might call upon an event planning company or independent event planner. Hospitality school graduates have numerous opportunities for careers in event planning. They can join an organization's event department or a company specializing in producing special events, or become an independent planner.

Event planners coordinate every aspect of the event. In some cases they may select the city or the hotel, or some other venue (such as a park, convention center, or historical building). Bryant Park in New York City is the venue for Fashion Week when the world's famous couturiers show their fashions. The Baltimore Aquarium and the Smithsonian Institution in Washington, D.C., rent certain areas to event and meeting planners for dinners and receptions. The center of downtown Aspen is used for the three-day Wine & Food Classic event.

Since event planners must deal with other contractors such as caterers, audiovisual companies, decorators, florists, and transportation companies, they must have knowledge of those functions. Creativity is an important trait for an event planner. Many clients expect the planner to recommend a unique location or create a one-of-a-kind event.

Hotel Careers Associated with Meeting Planning. Many hotel careers touch the meetings industry or involve meeting planning. The hotel's sales manager is usually instrumental in bringing meetings business to the property. Some hotel salespeople specialize in meetings business. These salespeople usually spend many years cultivating relationships with professional meeting planners and learning about their businesses or activities. They often know as much or more about professional meeting planning than their clients. Many of them have built a "following," and when they move to a new property they sometimes bring their clients with them.

In small hotels, the person who sells a meeting or convention to a group is responsible for coordinating the meeting as well. At large hotels that do a lot of convention business, once the sale is made, the job of working with the group is turned over to a **convention services manager (CSM)**, a relatively new position in the hotel business. The convention services manager sees to it that everything the hotel promised the group, whether in the contract or orally, is delivered. In some hotels this job is quite important, and the CSM reports directly to the hotel's general manager and has a department staffed by several persons.

Another key hotel staff member involved in meeting and convention planning is the catering manager. The catering manager is the person in charge of banquets and other food and beverage operations that are not connected with room service or the hotel's restaurants and lounges. In addition to preparing some of the food for large conventions, many catering departments do their own marketing, and solicit and handle the arrangements for small meetings such as weddings, monthly meetings of a business or civic club, and dinners honoring elected officials.

Careers in Convention and Visitors Bureaus. Since the CVB for a destination is the entity responsible for marketing that destination to meeting planners, it follows that the job of the CVB's chief executive is a marketing one. In many instances the CVB handles tourism development and visitor information services as well. CVBs usually have a sales department that works closely with the area's hotels and exhibition facilities to bring business to the destination. Associations often will contact a CVB and ask for the names of hotels in the area that meet certain criteria for their meetings. For example, an association meeting planner might ask for a list of downtown hotels with 100 rooms available from March 5–8 that also have 10,000 feet of exhibit space. The CVB will usually tell all of their members about this inquiry so that those who are interested can contact the meeting planner directly. CVBs almost never book hotel rooms for meeting planners, but in some cities they serve as the marketing and sales arm for the city's convention center. CVBs also place advertising on behalf of their destinations, produce brochures and films, research potential markets, and provide maps and other materials to visitors who request them.

Careers in Tourism Departments. As mentioned earlier, many states, countries, and other political and geographic entities have their own department or ministry of tourism.

Some tourism departments are well-funded and spend significant amounts on advertising and promoting their destinations. Tourism departments maintain overseas offices with salespersons who call on travel agencies and tour operators to persuade them to promote their destination. In some destinations, the Department of Tourism stages or helps fund events such as festivals, golf or tennis tournaments, sailing regattas, and even dog shows. Typically these departments employ nationals of their country to attend trade shows and create and coordinate events designed to entice travelers to visit their countries. Career opportunities consist of positions in sales and administration.

Careers as Exhibitors or Exhibit Designers. There is an entire category of professionals who do nothing but design, promote, and manage exhibits and trade shows. **Exhibitors** and **exhibit designers** have their own association, the Trade Show Exhibitors Association. They even have their own annual trade show, where they learn about the newest ideas and designs in exhibit building. The firms in which these professionals work may hire exhibit halls, rent space to exhibitors, and promote shows directly to the trade or to the public. Sometimes when a trade show is connected to a convention, the convention organizers will contract out the promotion and management of the show to an exhibitor rather than handle it themselves.

Designing and building exhibits, shipping them, and erecting them on-site is another large industry. Some of this work is done by full-service exhibit houses, some by custom designers. There are also a number of advertising agencies that are skilled in helping their clients design and build trade exhibits. Finally, there are manufacturers of "off-the-shelf" exhibits that come in modular form and can be customized to fit any exhibit situation. All of these firms have career opportunities for specialists who sell, design, and produce exhibits.

Summary

A meeting is any group of people who gather together for a specific purpose. A meeting can consist of a few people in a conference room. In contrast, a convention might have 100,000 delegates at a major convention center using a dozen or more hotels in a large city. Many specialized services, facilities, and technologies may be used.

Meetings are held by associations, corporations, and governments. There are also trade shows or expositions that may be a part of or independent from a meeting or convention.

Four kinds of trade shows are industrial shows, wholesale and retail trade shows, professional or scientific exhibitions, and public or consumer shows.

Convention and visitors bureaus are nonprofit organizations that market the destinations in which they are located. Governments may play a similar role.

Almost any kind of facility can be used to hold a meeting. Meetings have been held at amusement parks, football stadiums, and castles. However, most meetings are held in hotels and motels. Conference centers, universities, and cruise ships also serve as popular meeting venues. Virtual meetings are becoming more popular because of new teleconferencing technology.

One of the first questions a meeting planner needs to address is the objective (or objectives) of the meeting. Some meeting locations will obviously be more appropriate than others, once objectives have been set. The next question that must be addressed is the amount of time needed to achieve the stated objectives. The dates of the meeting are also important. Once the length of the meeting and the dates have been established, it is time to make some decisions about the format—the meeting's overall schedule of events. What is going to happen during the meeting and in what order?

Some meeting locations are predetermined. Many corporations hold their meetings at their own headquarters, for example. Other organizations move their meetings around to ease the travel costs for delegates from different geographic areas. Once the location has been established, a facility must be chosen. Size and cost are two of the major considerations here. Other considerations include guestrooms, meeting rooms, amenities and recreational facilities, soundproofing, audiovisual systems, adequate access, and budget.

Meeting planners may hold a variety of job titles within an organization. Few do it full time. Persons who are actively engaged in meeting planning can be found in associations, corporations, governments, and travel agencies. There are also association management companies and independent meeting planners.

Meeting planners are involved in everything from establishing meeting objectives and selecting sites to budgeting, selecting guest speakers, and booking entertainment. The best meeting planners are superb negotiators and diplomats. During the actual meeting, the planner is usually very busy and under a great deal of pressure to keep things moving smoothly and resolve problems that come up. After a meeting is over, there are still a number of crucial tasks left for the meeting planner. Evaluation for future planning purposes is one of the most important of these.

Special event planning has become a popular career track in many hospitality schools. One can work as an event planner for a company that has many events throughout the year, join an event-planning company, or become an independent contractor. Creativity is an important trait for an event planner.

Many of the travel and tourism industry careers associated with serving the meetings market are found in hotels. Hotel sales managers and their staffs, convention service managers, and catering managers all play key roles.

Convention and visitors bureaus employ marketing staffs to handle tourism development and sell their destinations to meeting planners. Tourism departments, which are usually branches of governments, do the same but often on a global scale.

Finally, there is an entire category of professionals who do nothing but design, promote, and manage exhibits and trade shows. Some exhibit design work is done by full-service exhibit houses, some by custom designers. There are also a number of advertising agencies that are skilled in helping their clients design and build exhibits. There are manufacturers who produce "off-the-shelf" exhibits that come in modular form and can be customized to fit any exhibit situation. All of these firms have career opportunities for people who want to sell, design, and produce exhibits.

Endnotes

1. "Business Today," *New York Times*, November 10, 2009.
2. Convention South, PKF Hospitality Research, September 2009.

Key Terms

convention and visitors bureau (CVB)—A nonprofit service organization that promotes a destination and sometimes provides services for meetings and conventions.

convention services manager (CSM)—A member of a hotel or resort's staff who is responsible for all aspects of a convention.

exhibit designer—Someone who designs a display booth or area to show products or services to prospective buyers.

exhibitor—The company or organization sponsoring an exhibit booth.

meeting—A planned event in which a group of people gather together to accomplish something.

meeting planner—Someone who plans meetings for an association, a corporation, or some other group.

meetings industry—An industry that comprises meetings (small meetings, conventions, trade shows, etc.), meeting planners, meeting sponsors (associations, corporations, etc.), and meeting suppliers (facilities as well as firms that supply services for meetings—audiovisual firms, exhibit design companies, and so on). Also referred to as the conventions, expositions, meetings, and incentive travel industry (CEMI).

trade show—An exhibit of products and services that is usually closed to the public. Also called an exposition.

Review Questions

1. What types of meetings do associations typically hold?
2. Why is it important for large associations to select meeting sites years in advance?
3. What types of meetings do corporations typically hold?
4. How is planning an association meeting different from planning a corporate meeting?
5. What are the various types of trade shows?
6. What roles do civic and government organizations play in the meetings industry?
7. Where are association and corporate meetings typically held?
8. What are some factors a meeting planner must consider when choosing a facility?
9. What are some of the tasks meeting planners should be able to perform?
10. What are some of the travel and tourism careers associated with the meetings industry?

Internet Sites

For more information, visit the following Internet sites. Remember that Internet addresses can change without notice. If the site is no longer there, you can use a search engine to look for additional sites.

Associations

American Society of Association Executives
www.asaenet.org

Association of Destination Management Executives
www.adme.org

Connected International Meeting Professionals Association
www.cimpa.org

Convention Industry Council
www.conventionindustry.org

Destination Marketing Association International (DMAI)
www.iacvb.org

Hospitality Sales & Marketing Association International
www.hsmai.org

International Association for Exposition Management
www.iaem.org

International Society of Meeting Planners
www.iami.org/ismp.html

Professional Convention Management
Association
www.pcma.org

Society of Government Meeting
Professionals
www.sgmp.org

Publications

Meetings & Conventions
www.meetings-conventions.com

Resources

Convention Industry Council
www.conventionindustry.org
www.conventionindustry.org/glossary

Trade Show Exhibitors Association
www.tsea.org

10

Floating Resorts: The Cruise Line Business

Outline

Competencies

1. Summarize the beginnings of the cruise industry, describe the birth of modern cruising, and describe the cruise industry of today. (pp. 294–303)

2. Explain how a cruise ship is organized and managed. (pp. 303–320)

Opposite page: A cruise ship off the coast of Santorini, Greece.

IN NOVEMBER 2009 the largest and most expensive cruise ship ever built sailed into Port Everglades in Fort Lauderdale, Florida, arriving from the place where it was built (Turku, Finland). The *Oasis of the Seas*, a Royal Caribbean International ship, is big by any measurement. Costing $1.4 billion, it has 2,160 cabins that can accommodate 5,400 passengers who can sleep, dine, and be entertained on sixteen decks and seven themed "neighborhoods" located throughout the vessel. This magnificent ship symbolizes just how far the modern cruise line industry has come in the last few decades.

The cruise industry has experienced impressive growth since 1970, when it is estimated that just 500,000 people took a cruise each year. By 2008 more than 13 million people took a vacation on a cruise ship somewhere in the world every year. Growth in demand required expanded fleets. More than one hundred new cruise ships have been launched since 2000,[1] the *Oasis of the Seas* being one of them. This dramatic growth bodes well for hospitality program graduates who want to consider a career in the cruise industry. The passenger services aboard these ships are managed by hotel managers (many of whom come from fine hotels and hospitality schools), who supervise food and beverage managers, executive chefs, maître d's, and chief housekeepers, among others. A majority of these managers are recruited from North America and Europe and are offered salaries competitive with land-based resorts. Even on land there are many hospitality-related positions now available in the cruise industry. Carnival Cruise Lines, the world's largest cruise company, employs more than 37,000 people in hotel and food service operations, sales and marketing, entertainment and casino management, itinerary planning, finance, human resources, information systems, marine operations, and new construction.

Yet cruise lines are still in their infancy. Only 20 percent of U.S. adults have ever taken a cruise. It is, however, the fastest growing of all segments in the hospitality industry, and it appears to generate the highest rates of customer satisfaction. Almost 94 percent of all passengers express satisfaction with their cruise, and 54 percent are "extremely satisfied."[2]

In this chapter we will explore (1) the evolution of the cruise industry from steamship transportation to floating vacation resorts, (2) cruise line management, and (3) career opportunities for those who are interested in this exciting and dynamic industry.

Early Cruises

If you define a cruise as going to a number of ports for the purpose of sight-seeing, and then ending up back where you started, then perhaps the first person to take a cruise and write about it was the noted English novelist William Makepeace Thackeray. In 1844 the Peninsula and Oriental Steam Navigation Company, popularly known as the P&O, invited Thackeray to travel on board its ships to Greece, the Holy Land, and Egypt. His book *Notes of a Journey from Cornhill to Grand Cairo* told of the trip. Thackeray reported getting seasick; complained about the prices, bugs, and lack of pretty women in Athens; and objected to the beggars he encountered while climbing the pyramids in Egypt. Even so, he said he had a good time and recommended that others consider taking the journey.

The first American-origin cruise was probably the 1867 voyage of the paddle-wheel steamer *Quaker City*, with a similar itinerary as Thackeray's cruise except that it started from New York. Among the passengers was the American humorist Mark Twain,

Royal Caribbean's *Navigator of the Seas* outside Miami. Royal Caribbean is considered a popular-priced, mass-market cruise line. (Courtesy of Royal Caribbean International.)

who chronicled his adventures in *The Innocents Abroad.* Twain, too, became a cruising enthusiast. He described how every evening after dinner, guests would promenade the deck, sing hymns, say prayers, listen to organ music in the grand saloon, read, and write in their journals. Sometimes dances were held on the upper deck, accompanied by music that Twain did not particularly enjoy. "However," he wrote, "the dancing was infinitely worse than the music." When the ship rode to starboard, "the whole platoon of dancers came charging down to starboard with it, and brought up in mass at the rail; and when it rolled down to port, they went floundering down to port with the same unanimity of sentiment. The Virginia reel, as performed on board the *Quaker City,* had more genuine reel about it than any reel I ever saw before."[3]

Transportation and Immigration

From the time of the *Quaker City* up to the late 1950s, far more people crossed the Atlantic from necessity rather than for pleasure. This was the period of immigration, and travel conditions for most passengers crossing the Atlantic were miserable. Even for those traveling first class, the trip was often uncomfortable, because voyages were long and there were no ports to stop at. Shipbuilders tried their best to make people forget that they were at sea. The English architect Arthur Davis, who designed some of the great Cunard liners, put it this way:

> The people who use these ships are not pirates, they do not dance hornpipes; they are mostly seasick American ladies, and the one thing they want to forget when they are on the vessel is that they are on a ship at all. If we could get ships to look inside like ships, and get people to enjoy the sea, it would be a very good thing; but all we can do as things are is to give them gigantic floating hotels.[4]

The other objective, of course, was to make the ships go as fast as possible so that the voyages would last only a few days instead of two weeks. On the whole this strategy worked, and passengers began to regard steamships as both luxurious and unsinkable.

This complacency was shattered when, on her maiden voyage, one of the most luxurious ships afloat, the White Star liner *Titanic,* sank in the North Atlantic in the early morning hours of April 15, 1912, after striking an iceberg. This 46,329-ton liner (less than one-third the size of today's largest ships) carried 2,228 passengers and crew. In two hours and forty minutes, 1,523 perished. They were mostly second- and third-class passengers, trapped because *Titanic's* 20 lifeboats could only carry about half of those on board. At first, because most passengers were convinced that the ship would not sink, they did not rush to fill the boats. Confusion and unpreparedness compounded the problem; 40 percent of the available lifeboat seats stayed empty as the boats were lowered. Boat number one was launched with only five passengers and seven crew. It had a capacity of 40!

The sinking of *Titanic* was one of the saddest nights in maritime history. Stories of courage and cowardice survive to this day. For example, Isidor Straus, co-owner of Macy's Department Store, and his wife, Ida, were returning home from a vacation on the French Riviera. Mrs. Straus refused to board a lifeboat without her husband. "I will not be separated from my husband," she said. "As we have lived, so shall we die. Together." Historians tend to blame Captain Edward Smith (who went down with his ship) and White Star's Managing Director Bruce Ismay (who was on board but managed to escape), because allegedly they were eager to run on schedule and arrive at the announced time, when the press would be waiting. Even though they were advised there were icebergs in the area (another ship, the *Californian,* just 20 miles away, had stopped for the night because of the same warnings), the ship did not slow down.

After the *Titanic* disaster, ships crossing the North Atlantic were moved to a more southerly route, more lifeboats were added, 24-hour wireless watches at sea were required, and other safety measures were implemented.

New Passengers and New Directions

By the 1920s, the transatlantic passenger business was booming again—until the United States curtailed its open-door immigration policy. Since the passenger lines earned most of their revenue from this source, a new kind of passenger had to be found. Fortunately, World War I had created an interest in Europe among Americans. Immigrants' accommodations were turned into "tourist class" cabins, and soon they were filled with teachers, students, and sightseers who wanted to see London, Paris, and Rome, or visit some of the famous European battlegrounds they had read about. There was another incentive as well. Prohibition had dried up America in 1920. Those who enjoyed a martini or scotch and soda could get as many as they wanted on an ocean voyage!

Spending a week at sea soon became the fashionable thing to do. The press ran frequent articles about the lavish and expensive first-class lifestyles displayed on board, where people dined, danced, and partied all night with exciting, interesting, and often rich companions. Going to Europe on a transatlantic liner was the best of all travel experiences.

In 1929, the Great Depression began. Many people could no longer afford to go to Europe for their vacations. As a result, steamship lines started to offer cheaper alternatives. These included short, inexpensive vacation/party cruises to Nova Scotia, Nassau, and Bermuda. The ships used for these cruises had been designed for transatlantic traffic and were not really suited for cruising, especially in warm waters. They were not air-conditioned, and their lack of outdoor deck space and swimming pools did not give the feeling of a resort at all. As the cruising market grew, however, new and more luxurious ships were deployed, and with them came more expensive and longer itineraries. Ships became lighter colored, more open, and more resort-like. Posters showed passengers dressed in leisure clothes around an outdoor pool instead of dressed in business suits strolling around an enclosed deck.

Up to World War II, the major steamship lines were owned by European interests. When the war started, almost all of their vessels were converted into troop ships or stayed in port. This situation continued until 1945, when the rebuilding of Europe once again spurred a growing demand for ocean liners. For the first time the United States recognized that it might need its own troop ships and subsidized the building and operation of new vessels. The *United States,* launched in 1951, was designed to be the fastest ship of its size afloat. On her very first transatlantic crossing she set a new world record of 3 days, 10 hours, and 40 minutes, beating *Queen Mary's* record by a full 10 hours.

The post-war boom marked the last days of the great steamship liners. Besides the *United States* and *Queen Mary,* there were the *Queen Elizabeth,* the French Line's *France,* Holland America's *Rotterdam,* and a host of sleek Italian liners built for warm-water cruising in the Mediterranean. These ships crossed the Atlantic, cruised to exotic ports, and circled the globe.

The cruise world started to come apart in 1958. That was the year that Pan American World Airways offered its first nonstop, transatlantic crossing on a Boeing 707 jet. Ocean-going passenger ships were effectively out of business as a means of transportation. Some ships were moth-balled, such as the *United States.* Others were scrapped. The *Queen Mary* became a landlocked hotel in Long Beach, California. The *France* was converted to a cruise ship, and it continued to sail as the *Norway* until 2006, when it was retired from service and scrapped.

The Birth of Modern Cruising

There were no modern cruise lines until the early 1960s, when Miami entrepreneur Leslie Frazer chartered two ships, the *Bilu* and *Nili,* and marketed them exclusively for cruises.

In 1966, Ted Arison, a young Israeli from Tel Aviv who had started and lost two air cargo businesses, joined with Norwegian Knut Kloster to bring the *Sunward,* the first new vessel built especially for cruising, into the market. They formed a cruise line called Norwegian Caribbean Line (now called Norwegian Cruise Line) to market the vessel. By 1971 the NCL fleet had added three more ships, the *Starward, Skyward,* and *Southward.* NCL helped transform South Florida's cruise industry from a regionally marketed collection of old transatlantic liners to a nationally marketed business featuring brand-new vessels designed specifically for Caribbean cruising.

At the same time, a former Miami Beach hotelier named Ed Stephan had dreams of starting his own cruise line. After producing some designs and plans, he traveled to Norway and enlisted the help of prominent shipping executives. Thus another industry giant, Royal Caribbean Cruise Lines (now Royal Caribbean International), was born. RCCL quickly launched a modern fleet based on Stephan's innovative designs of ships with a sleek, yacht-like profile and an observation lounge located in the ship's funnel, high above the superstructure, which was inspired by Seattle's Space Needle. By 1972 the RCCL fleet consisted of the *Song of Norway, Nordic Prince,* and *Sun Viking.*

By the early seventies, the U.S. cruise business was no longer limited to Florida. A Seattle businessman, Stanley McDonald, founded Princess Cruise Lines on the West Coast, offering cruises to the Mexican Riviera. It was an instant hit, and by 1972 Princess had four vessels. At the same time a former bush pilot, Chuck West, was building a seasonal cruise business along Alaska's Inside Passage. West's cruise line was part of his overall tour operation, which he called Westours.

In 1977 Princess scored a coup that would forever change the image of cruising. Most people had no idea what taking a cruise was like. A television production company, Aaron Spelling Productions, decided to use a luxury cruise ship as the location for a major TV series. Princess made two of their vessels, the *Island Princess* and the *Pacific Princess*, available for the filming. The series was called *The Love Boat,* and in nine years of production it featured stories of people who fell in love, solved personal problems, or just had a great adventure while on a cruise. There is little doubt that the program popularized the idea that a cruise was a vacation that wasn't just for the rich and famous.

Carnival Is Born

Partnerships do not always work out well, and in 1971 the most successful of them all, between Ted Arison and Knut Kloster, broke up. Arison decided to leave Norwegian Cruise Line and start his own business. With the help of a friend, Meshulam Riklis, Arison bought a laid-up ocean liner, the *Empress of Canada*, renamed it the *Mardi Gras*, and founded Carnival Cruise Lines.

A Carnival cruise ship. Carnival is the largest cruise line in the industry.

Princess Cruise Lines made this ship, the *Island Princess,* available to Aaron Spelling Productions for the television series *The Love Boat,* which ran from 1977–1986. *The Love Boat* forever changed the image of cruising. (Courtesy of Princess Cruises.)

What is now the world's largest cruise line did not have a very auspicious beginning. When the *Mardi Gras* entered service on March 7, 1972, she ran aground at the tip of Miami Beach shortly after leaving the dock. She sat there for a full 24 hours while tourists along the shoreline gazed at her in amazement before she was refloated. It did not help that Carnival's only ship was an old one competing in a sea of new vessels. Carnival's vice president of sales and marketing at that time, Bob Dickinson, mulled over the problem of how to get more people to take a Carnival cruise. He concluded that people were not really looking for a specific ship or port when they went on a cruise vacation; what they really wanted was to have fun. Dickinson's solution was to provide more activities and entertainment onboard ship than Carnival's competitors and call his ship "The Fun Ship." This was a total reversal of cruise marketing. Up to that time, cruise promotion had been destination-driven. Dickinson decided to make the ship itself the destination. Because it was an old ship, the company was forced to offer very low prices, which attracted a younger crowd. Until then, cruises had been viewed as suitable only for wealthy older people. This was a whole new market. The younger age and informality of the passengers added to the "fun" on the ship, and Carnival was able to deliver on its promise. By 1975 the line was profitable and started adding more ships to the Carnival fleet. Dickinson's strategy, which changed consumers' perception of cruising from a rather stodgy pastime for the rich to a fun and affordable vacation for the masses, was probably the defining event in the development of the modern cruise industry.

The Cruise Industry Today

Cruise lines are divided into four market segments by the Cruise Lines International Association. The largest category by far is the contemporary/value segment, which is dominated by the popular-priced, mass-market lines. These lines tend to get a lot of their business from first-time cruisers. Carnival, Norwegian, and Royal Caribbean are all part

Industry Innovators

Richard D. Fain
Chairman and CEO
Royal Caribbean International

It's not difficult to understand why just about everyone in the cruise industry considers Richard Fain to be a world-class innovator. All you have to do is look at Royal Caribbean' s *Oasis of the Seas*, launched in October 2009. She is the world's largest cruise ship at 225,282 gross registered tons, and, at 1,184 feet, is longer than any aircraft carrier in the U.S. fleet. It is so tall (240 feet high) that it has a retractable funnel/smokestack in order for it to get under the Verrazano-Narrows Bridge in New York City harbor.

Step into this goliath of a vessel and you encounter things you never expect to find on a cruise ship. Start by gazing at a zip line that stretches diagonally nine decks above an open-air atrium. Stroll along Central Park, one of seven themed neighborhoods, and enjoy the thousands of tropical plants—the first park at sea. Play on the nine-hole miniature golf course or jog on the almost half mile jogging track. There is much on this ship that is new and innovative to cruising, including 28 multilevel urban-style loft suites boasting floor to ceiling windows, an aquatic amphitheater that serves as a pool by day and a dazzling oceanfront theater by night, and a handcrafted carousel.

While these types of imaginative features may be unusual for an ordinary cruise ship, they are not for a Royal Caribbean ship, not since Richard Fain first became involved with the company full time in 1988. Fain, a graduate of the University of California-Berkley and the Wharton Business School, developed a passion for the cruise industry. He had been working for International Utilities, a holding company whose portfolio included a Norwegian shipping company, Gotaas-Larsen. Gotaas-Larsen, in turn, owned part of a cruise line in Miami called Royal Caribbean. Eventually, Fain rose in the company from being a junior executive, fresh out of college, to a managing director of Gotaas-Larsen and then the president of Royal Caribbean.

Fain's first big challenge was to build a bigger cruise line, one way or another. Royal Caribbean's biggest competitor at the time was Carnival, which had grown by building a fleet of new ships. Fain and his team envisaged a new paradigm, which they would introduce with a new ship, the *Sovereign of the Seas*. The largest ship afloat at that time was 47,262 tons. "There had been this old folk war of what cruising was all about – a romantic image of sorts. The image was small ships, highly personalized service, a relatively passive experience, and quite regimented. You went to dinner in the main dining room, went to the show, and then you went to bed. What we thought people wanted was more choices, more things to see and do; a more active vacation." That was all very well, but there was no way to put more things to do on a conventional cruise ship of the time. You needed a much bigger ship—a mega ship. "We also thought that if we had a large enough ship, it would appeal to more different groups of people, allowing us to serve all of them on the same vessel. There was a synergistic effect."

When the *Sovereign of the Seas* was introduced at 73,192 tons, the reaction from the cruise industry and the cruising public was electric. Cruise critic Ethel Blum was awe-struck: "In the five-story open lobby, brass-trimmed glass elevators glide up and down,

(continued)

Industry Innovators *(continued)*

their gleaming reflections glancing off marble walls. People walking past pause to lean against a brass railing to look far below at a white baby grand piano where a man in a red jacket is playing light classics beside three fountain pools. Almost every major city in America has one of these grand hotels with majestic staircases and ethereal space. The only difference is, this one is scheduled to sail off into the sunset at 5:30."

Industry competitors thought Fain had gone off the deep end, because the costs to operate these mega ships were so high. "Our costs were higher," says Fain," but our view was that the economy of scale of the larger ships meant you could give a passenger more, and so it was more valuable to him or her. At the same time, the larger ship gave us an economy of scale which meant it was less costly to produce, so that our vision was that we could make a ship larger and even more attractive, and that was contrary to the accepted vision of the day."

The 70,000-ton ship soon became the new standard for the industry. In 1991, Carnival introduced the Fantasy class ship (70,367 tons), and by 1998 had built eight of them. Royal Caribbean was already thinking far ahead of the curve, and in 1999 introduced the Voyager class – 142,000 tons each. The 160,000-ton *Freedom of the Seas* is an extended version of that, but it did not stay the largest ship in the world for long. Until someone builds something bigger, Royal Caribbean will have the record for the world's largest cruise ship—the *Oasis of the Seas* (and its sister ship, *Allure of the Seas*)—a record it will probably hold for quite a few years.

Fathering the mega ship is hardly Fain's only claim to fame. In search of a premium brand of cruise ship, something more luxurious than the Royal Caribbean brand could offer, the company purchased Celebrity Cruise Lines in the late 1980s. Seeking to give the line a marketing position that could not be preempted easily, they hired perhaps the world's most famous French chef of the time, Michel Roux, to design special menus and recipes for the ships. Celebrity today is one of the world's best luxury cruise lines, as voted by readers of some of the top travel magazines. Since Royal Caribbean bought it, Celebrity has grown from 3,000 berths to 15,000.

Both Royal Caribbean and Celebrity are known for their strong advocacy of "doing the right thing." They have gone overboard to see that nothing on their ships goes overboard, literally, with what they call their "Save the Seas" program. Beyond that, they have created the "Ocean Fund," which has already distributed over $8 million to more than 40 conservation organizations. In the area of handicapped accessibility, Royal Caribbean has advertised itself as the most accessible cruise line for persons with disabilities, and has gone far beyond ADA standards. For example, all ships have pool lifts so persons in wheelchairs can take a swim. "It's the right thing to do," says Fain, "and with 54 million persons with some kind of disability in the United States today, and the baby boomers growing older themselves, it's good business."

Fain's senior executives describe him as a sociable man with a good sense of humor, but one who is relentless in his search for perfection. He constantly questions everything the company is doing, to see how and if it can be done better, and is impatient with executives who haven't got a good answer for that question.

of this segment. The premium cruise lines charge more and carry fewer passengers per **ton** of space. (In the shipping business, the tonnage of a ship usually refers to the ship's volume, not weight.) Celebrity, Holland America, and Princess are in this category. The luxury segment is the top of the line. Seabourn, Crystal, Cunard, and Silversea are all examples of luxury cruise lines. The final segment is called "specialty" lines. These vessels

The Promenade Deck on one of Royal Caribbean's mega ships, the *Freedom of the Seas.* **This ship has a passenger capacity of 3,634, and among its onboard attractions are an ice-skating rink, nine-hole miniature golf course, surf park, and this spacious promenade featuring shops and restaurants.** (Courtesy of Royal Caribbean International)

specialize in niche destinations and include Sea Dream Yacht Club, Windstar, and various riverboat cruises.

There are three giant players in the industry: the largest is Carnival, with twelve brands; next is Royal Caribbean, which also operates Celebrity Cruises and Azamara Club

Cruises, and owns Pullmantur (based in Spain) and CDF Croisieres de France; the third largest is Genting Hong Kong, owner of Star Cruises (the largest cruise line in Asia) and Norwegian Cruise Line (NCL).

The average cruise passenger is 51, has a household income of $64,000, and pays $200 a day for an all-inclusive vacation that includes a cabin, four to five meals a day, and entertainment.[5]

Cruise Ship Organization

As we have said, cruise ships today are floating vacation resorts. In some ways they are very similar to a hotel as far as organization. While each cruise line has its own unique organization for its ships, in general all cruise ships follow a similar organizational pattern. Exhibit 1 shows a cruise ship organization chart of the Vista-class ships from the Holland America Line. At the top is the captain, who has four persons directly reporting to him: the chief officer, the chief engineer, the hotel manager, and the environmental officer.

Because this chapter concentrates on the hospitality aspects of a cruise, after discussing the captain's position we will focus on the hotel manager and those who report to him.

The Captain

Although a cruise ship can be compared to a hotel, it is in fact a vessel at sea and is therefore first and foremost operating under maritime laws. It is under the command of the **captain**, who is responsible for the ship's operation and the safety of all aboard. It is the captain's job to see that all company policies and rules are followed, as well as national and international laws. The captain has legal authority to enforce these laws, an authority granted by the country in which the ship is registered.

Vessels also must comply with the laws of the ports they sail from and to. For example, personnel from the U.S. Coast Guard and the U.S. Centers for Disease Control and Prevention regularly inspect all ships sailing to and from U.S. ports for compliance with U.S. safety and sanitation laws.

As just mentioned, directly reporting to the captain are the **chief officer** (called the staff captain on some lines), who is second in command and also the captain's deputy; the chief engineer, who is in charge of the ship's physical plant; the hotel manager; and the environmental officer, who is responsible for compliance with international and local environmental regulations. These persons (and some members of their staffs) are officers and wear uniforms with appropriate stripes indicating their rank and department. To some extent a cruise ship is a paramilitary organization. Rank, regulations, and discipline are taken very seriously. All officers have duties they must perform, otherwise they are subject to discipline. Unlike hotel or restaurant employees on land, a cruise ship's officers and crew members cannot walk off the job or refuse to obey commands.

The Hotel Manager

Among the senior officers reporting to the captain, the **hotel manager** has the largest staff (see Exhibit 2). The hotel manager and the people working for him or her are directly responsible for creating the vacation experience that the cruise line offers. Today many cruise-ship hotel managers are recruited from land-based resorts. For example, both

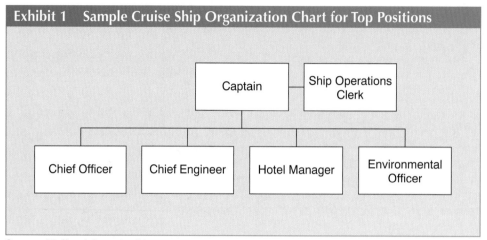

Exhibit 1   Sample Cruise Ship Organization Chart for Top Positions

Source: Holland America Line.

Carnival and Royal Caribbean recruit at schools of hospitality management for entry-level positions in their hotel divisions.

This job has some similarities but also many differences to a general manager's job in a land-based hotel. One major difference is that there is no sales or marketing staff to supervise; another is that passengers do not have to check in (that is, arrange for their length of stay and pay for their accommodations) onboard the ship: these functions are performed on shore. Besides being ultimately responsible for food and beverage services and housekeeping services, the hotel manager may be responsible for medical care, entertainment, and shore excursions. In addition, there are casino operations, the beauty salon, the health spa, gift shops, photography services, and more to oversee. On some cruise lines many of these services are concessions. For instance, cruise-ship beauty salon and health spa services typically are provided by Steiner-Transocean, a London-based company. The large lines run their own food and beverage operations, but some of the smaller ones use outside caterers, known as ship's chandlers, to provide both the food and the personnel. In these cases, the hotel manager is responsible only for housekeeping duties and planning social activities for passengers.

Just as the scope of their duties varies from cruise line to cruise line, some hotel managers are given more autonomy than others. There are vessels where virtually every decision is made on shore in advance or is relayed to the hotel manager via e-mail or satellite telephone when the ship is at sea.

Hotel managers on cruise ships typically spend four months at sea, followed by two months off. Many have families who join them occasionally on short cruises. Salaries are competitive with land-based jobs. Indeed, considering that for much of the year their housing, medical care, and food are supplied free of charge, hotel managers on cruise ships often fare better economically than their land-based counterparts.

Other Officers

Under the hotel manager on most cruise ships are a purser, food and beverage manager, chief housekeeper, cruise director, and human resources manager. We will take a look at

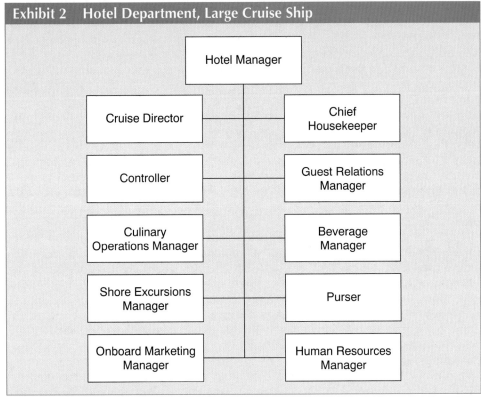

Exhibit 2 Hotel Department, Large Cruise Ship

Source: Holland America Line.

these positions in the following sections. (It should be mentioned that large cruise ships—Holland America's Vista class, for example—have others reporting to the hotel manager, such as a controller, shore excursions manager, onboard marketing manager, and guest relations manager. The onboard marketing manager is responsible for all of the ship's concessions, including the casino. You will note in Exhibit 2 that instead of a single food and beverage manager, this position's responsibilities have been divided into two positions, a culinary operations manager and a beverage manager. In such a circumstance, all kitchen and dining room staff report to the culinary operations manager.)

The Purser. One of the most important departments in the hotel division is the purser's office. The **purser** is the ship's banker, information officer, human resources director (except on larger ships), and complaint handler. The purser is also second in command of the hotel division and is in charge of the division whenever the hotel manager is off the ship. The purser's office runs the ship's front office, including the management of guest accounts or folios, and clears the ship at foreign ports. In some ways it is similar to the front office department of a hotel.

On some ships the purser is responsible for revenue accounting, while on others it is an accounting function managed by a controller. The purser (and the controller, if the ship is large enough to justify such a position) reports to the hotel manager. Whether a purser or a controller performs the function, the system of revenue control is the same. All sales at outlets onboard the ship, such as dining rooms, bars, and shops, are captured on a point-of-sale system (POS) that interfaces with the ship's property management system (PMS) and are recorded on the guests' folios.

Most cruise ships use a credit system to handle guest accounts. Checks and/or cash are not accepted for transactions onboard. After passengers board they are asked to come to the purser's office and register their credit card (if they have not already done so before boarding the ship). All charges incurred on board are then billed to that card. If they don't have a credit card, they are asked for a cash deposit. When the deposit is used up, credit is cut off until another cash deposit is made. Ships do not accept checks because there is no feasible method for clearing them while at sea or in a foreign port. Technology makes it possible for the ships to issue an all-purpose, magnetic-coded card to each passenger that serves as his or her identification, door key, and charge card. On some cruise lines, these cards also show the bearer's cabin number, dining time, and table assignment, and even serve as a security device to track who has gone ashore and returned.

The purser holds most of the money on the ship and acts as a central bank for the ship's cash needs at the front desk and for payroll and the casino. Passengers can convert their traveler's checks in the purser's office to get cash for duty-free shopping or for playing games of chance in the ship's casino. The purser provides currency exchange and makes change. The amount of cash a large ship carries can be substantial; more than $500,000 is not unusual.

The purser's staff also handles passenger problems like lost luggage, broken plumbing, and cabin upgrades (when they are available). The job is considered attractive. Living conditions are good, and pursers are allowed to mingle with passengers in specified public areas when they are off duty.

Flags of Convenience

The laws under which a cruise ship operates depend on where it is registered. The choice of country depends on many factors, including the financing of the vessel, the cost of operation, and/or the route the vessel sails. The flag-of-convenience tradition dates back to the early days of naval warfare, when merchant ships—to avoid being attacked—carried the flag of a neutral nation, thus protecting their passengers and cargo from the ravages of war.

Staffing considerations play an important part in the decision about which country's flag a cruise ship will sail under. Many countries, including the United States, Norway, and Britain, have strict regulations concerning unionized labor that tend to create a high labor cost for cruise lines. Countries such as Panama, Liberia, Bermuda, and the Bahamas do not have such laws and thus many cruise ships are registered there.

Unions are not the only issue. Some countries require that a large proportion of the crew serving on a cruise ship flying their flag must be citizens; for example, the United States requires that all cruise ships registered as U.S. ships must employ only officers licensed in the United States, and three-quarters of the unlicensed crew must be U.S. citizens. Cruise lines do not like to operate with these types of labor restrictions, because they wish to recruit from various countries to find the best people for the job. The British, Italians, Greeks, Dutch, and Norwegians are all known for their nautical skills and rigorous training, for example; similarly, French, German, and Austrian food service personnel are in high demand. Major cruise lines recruit from all of these groups, and therefore their ships have a truly international flavor that would be impossible to achieve if they flew the flags of countries with restrictive labor laws.

The Food and Beverage Manager. Research shows that one of the most important components of every cruise, from the passengers' point of view, is the food. It is the thing people are most likely to remember and talk about. Over the years, cruises have built a reputation for serving very good food and a lot of it. It goes back to the early days of steamship travel, when César Ritz designed a Ritz-Carlton restaurant for the Hamburg-Amerika line. While food is included in the price of every cruise, beverages are not (except on the most luxurious of ships), and they are the largest single source of onboard revenue for all of the major lines. These two factors make the job of the **food and beverage manager** the linchpin of every successful cruise. In addition to feeding the passengers, the food and beverage department is also responsible for feeding the ship's crew members—a challenging task because they are onboard for months at a time, represent many different cultures and nationalities with different tastes, have nowhere else to go, and must be satisfied if they are to satisfy guests.

Reporting to the food and beverage manager typically are the assistant food and beverage manager, executive chef, maître d' (dining room manager), bar manager, and provision master or storekeeper (see Exhibit 3).

Food and beverage managers who come from a hotel background describe their job as being very different on a cruise ship. Dedrick Van Regemorter, a 15-year Marriott veteran and now a hotel manager with Holland America, makes these observations:

> There is a tremendous difference between food and beverage services in a hotel and onboard a ship. The ship is a very closed environment. You live with the people you work with, so it's extremely important to develop good interpersonal skills. Also, the number of stripes you carry on your shoulders is very important. It makes a big difference in the amount of attention you get from others.
>
> My responsibilities are also different. While I do all of the ordering as far as items and quantity, I don't get involved with the financial details. In a hotel, I had to control wages, overtime, and other costs, as well as generate income. I do have a consumption budget, but I don't worry about food costs. I don't even know what it costs to feed a passenger.
>
> Serving tables on a cruise ship is very different from a hotel as well. The group being served stays the same for a whole week. This enables the waiter to develop a relationship with the guests and learn their preferences. After the first night, experienced servers remember whether guests like coffee, tea, or espresso, regular or decaffeinated, with or without sugar and cream. In a hotel, waiters have other concerns, such as handling cash and the number of people they have to serve at one time.
>
> Another difference is the way we do our cooking. The majority of our galley crew are trained cooks. The levels and positions are different. We still use the traditional French culinary setup. We use a lot more labor, which in part accounts for the high quality of our food. We do everything from scratch. We bake our own bread daily. We make our stock from bones. We buy a whole hindquarter and cut it down. Nothing goes to waste. We don't have leftovers. We have a limited storage capacity and no trucks come by to take away what we don't use. We know exactly how many people are coming and what they will order. That's because even though we have a lot of choices, we serve the same menu on every cruise.
>
> Our passengers expect quite a bit when it comes to food. They don't expect the same things they would have at home or even in an ordinary restaurant. I like to compare the food we serve daily to what you might order when you go to that extraordinary restaurant for a special occasion. That's why lunch is four or five courses, and dinner six or seven. If you feel like eating lobster or rack of lamb, price is no consideration because you've already paid for it.

Exhibit 3   Food and Beverage Department, Large Cruise Ship

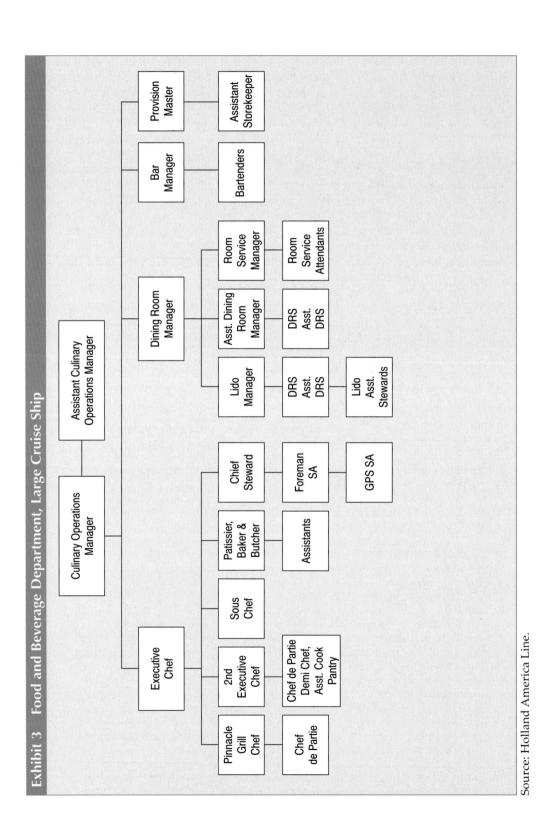

On land it's not possible to give 800 people a quality dining experience in an hour and forty minutes. But I have 107 people in our galley and they don't have to worry about what people are going to order or when to prepare it. All they have to worry about is taking orders from 108 waiters and cooking them individually. Having a ship that's consistently full removes a lot of uncertainty and allows us to produce really fine food and serve it in style.[6]

Several points that Van Regemorter makes are important to note. Safety, sanitation, and health are the most important considerations on any ship. That means that the **galley**, the shipboard equivalent of a kitchen, must be a highly disciplined operation. Everything must be done according to regulation; there can be no exception. There are many instances where one small error has caused hundreds to get sick. As Van Regemorter points out, one of the ways this discipline is achieved, which is very different from in a hotel or restaurant on land, is that everyone is taking orders from a person who has not just economic power over them but legal power. Not obeying orders from an officer on a ship is a form of mutiny. In reality, everyone strives very hard to get along, because it is not practical to quit in the middle of the ocean thousands of miles away from home! Food and beverage managers need even better people skills—including tact and diplomacy—than land-based F&B managers, because they must work long hours with their employees every single day for months at a time.

Another important difference that should be noted, which was also alluded to by Van Regemorter, is that the food and beverage department on a ship has less direct involvement with food costs than a land-based resort. The cruise industry calculates its costs very carefully, but this is done by managers in cruise-line offices on shore. Computer perpetual inventory systems provide a very detailed analysis of the food and beverage items consumed aboard ship, together with a daily food cost expressed in dollars per passenger day. Management expects the ship's food staff to be only generally aware of these daily costs but to respond to them, if necessary, so that both guest satisfaction and corporate financial targets are maintained.

The luxury cruise lines spend $25–$30 per day per passenger on raw food costs, premium lines spend $12–$18, and mass market lines spend $8–$11. That includes breakfast, lunch, dinner, midmorning snacks, afternoon tea or ice cream, a late buffet, and 24-hour room service. One of the reasons for these low prices is the enormous economies of scale that are possible. For example, each week Carnival Cruise Lines uses 34,000 pounds of tenderloin, 71,200 pounds of chicken, over 500,000 eggs, and 53,540 bottles of wine. This kind of consumption and the resulting cost savings through bulk purchasing are only possible because Carnival, like all the major lines, standardizes menus on its ships whenever possible. To facilitate this, cruise lines typically build several ships of the same size and class, which allows them to have similar galleys and passenger counts. Predictable demographics and ship itineraries make accurate forecasting possible. Royal Caribbean knows that when its ships put escargot on the French evening menu, which occurs on the fifth night out, 22 percent of the 1,800 passengers on each ship will most likely order it. Standardization is everything.

Serving is another very different matter on a cruise ship. The problem is time. Except for the smaller luxury ships, none of today's cruise vessels has enough main dining room seats to handle more than half of its passengers at the same time. While two dinner **sittings** was the former standard (and still is on some ships), today's lifestyles demand a more flexible approach to dinner. For example, Carnival offers four sittings in its main dining room; Norwegian Cruise Line lets passengers dine anytime during an extended

Multiple dining rooms—featuring different menus—help cruise ships deliver a high-quality dining experience for every passenger. (Courtesy of Norwegian Cruise Line and Royal Caribbean International.)

Holidays happen on cruise ships, too, and the cruise lines' food and beverage departments plan for them. This Thanksgiving menu is from Royal Caribbean International. (Courtesy of Royal Caribbean International.)

time period between 5:30 P.M. and 10 P.M. Almost all cruise lines are including daytime dining options.

On the dinner menu of every cruise line there is always a choice of four or five appetizers, a couple of soups and different salads, four or five entrées, and several desserts. (It is, in fact, this abundant choice that helps create the feeling of fine dining as opposed to banquet service.) Many people order wine as well. Because the dining experience is such an important part of a cruise vacation, passengers must not feel that they are being rushed or are receiving banquet-style service. On the contrary, most cruise passengers expect their server to know them by name, be aware of their preferences, discuss each menu item with them, and exchange a menu item for another if it doesn't meet their expectations. Since the server's compensation comes almost entirely from tips, it is important that he or she meet or exceed passenger expectations. The average food server's base salary is less than

This is a view of the Grand Pacific Main Restaurant on the Norwegian Cruise Line ship *Pride of Hawaii;* it is just one of more than a dozen food and beverage outlets on the ship. The restaurant's artwork was inspired by the menu covers from the old Matson Line, whose passenger ships sailed from San Francisco to Honolulu in the early part of the twentieth century. (Photo courtesy of Ernie Pick.)

The "lido deck" is the deck on which the ship's main swimming pool is located. A large outdoor swimming pool is a prominent feature of many of today's cruise ships. (Courtesy of Norwegian Cruise Line.)

$100 monthly plus room, board, and medical services. But their tips (on the major lines, passengers tip an average of $3 to $4 per person, per day, in the dining room and the same to cabin stewards) make it possible to bring home compensation of $24,000 a year—tax-free in most cases and with virtually no expenses!

The cruise lines use many strategies to turn the tables in their dining rooms without making passengers feel rushed. For instance, typically there are two live shows each evening in the ship's main auditorium. There are more live shows in the alternate auditorium (and sometimes a midnight performance as well). Passengers who want a good seat for a show—or a movie—leave the dining room promptly after dinner. Movie theaters showing first-run productions are a staple of some ships. Holland America's movie theaters on its newest ships (the *Amsterdam,* for example) are especially luxurious, and match most theaters you're likely to find on land.

To respond to the demand of passengers who do not want to eat at specified times, many ships offer food and beverage outlets in addition to their main dining rooms. For example, Crystal Cruises offers two or more alternative dining venues on its ships. The ships of some other cruise companies have opened up their lido deck dining-area for informal dining at night, in addition to its normal operating times during the day. (The **lido deck** is the deck on which the ship's main swimming pool is located.) Some ships have 24-hour pizzerias. The dining concept embraced by most major lines is that passengers should be able to eat when they want, where they want, and with whom they want rather than at fixed times and fixed tables.

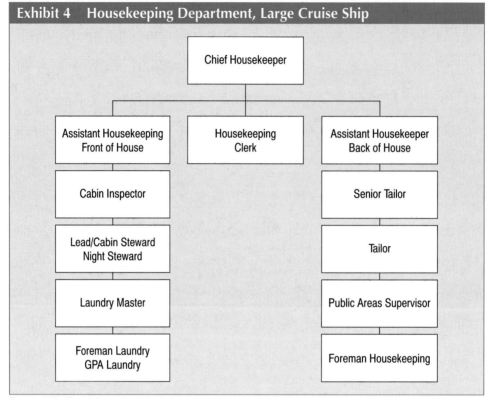

Exhibit 4   Housekeeping Department, Large Cruise Ship

Source: Holland America Line.

Just as the passengers need to be fed at all hours, so do the officers and crew. Dining facilities are usually open for them many hours of the day, with cooks on duty.

Finally, students should understand that as important as the food is to the passengers, beverages are even more important to the cruise lines. Beverages are the single largest source of onboard revenue on major mass-market cruise lines. As a rule, ships generate more bottom-line profit selling drinks than they do in their casinos or shops. For this reason, drinks are served in almost every part of the ship at any time when a particular area is likely to be in use. Moreover, drinks often must be served promptly because passengers are on some kind of schedule, wanting cocktails before dinner or a drink before a show starts, for example. This level of service requires a substantial commitment of well-trained personnel who can mix and serve a large number of drinks fairly rapidly. This staff must be well supervised.

The Chief Housekeeper. The **chief housekeeper** (also called the chief steward) runs a department that is very similar to the housekeeping department of any hotel (see Exhibit 4). The chief housekeeper's staff is responsible for the cleaning and general maintenance of all cabins and interior areas on the ship. The staff controls a large inventory of bed and bath linens, soaps and other bathroom amenities for passengers, and cleaning supplies and chemicals. (A perpetual inventory is used to track most of these operating supplies.) The department staff is also responsible for passenger laundry and dry cleaning, as well as cleaning all cabin linens, table linens, towels, and the crew's uniforms. The housekeeping department's cabin stewards are also responsible for cabin food service, and for loading and unloading luggage and delivering it to passengers' cabins.

The most important difference between housekeeping on shore versus at sea is that in hotels guests rarely interact on a regular basis with the persons who clean their rooms; on ships they always do. Cabins on a ship are regularly serviced twice a day—generally while passengers are having breakfast and again while they are at dinner. In addition, cabin stewards are on duty a good part of the morning and evening (70 hours a week is normal for this position), and assist passengers with other matters such as lifeboat drills, wheelchairs, pressing passengers' clothes for the captain's party for those passengers who request it, etc. Like the ship's food servers, cabin stewards depend largely on tips for their overall compensation, so they learn their guests' names and generally find as many ways as they can to be helpful. Good cabin stewards can be crucial to a guest's total cruise experience.

The busiest day for the housekeeping department is **turnaround day.** This is the day a ship finishes a cruise and starts another one. A typical 70,000-ton vessel may have 600 or more cabins, with an average of two persons in each cabin. Each cabin may have two to three pieces of luggage. That's 2,400–3,600 pieces of luggage to be unloaded and loaded in a single day! Moreover, departing passengers are usually off the ship between 9 and 10 A.M. and by noon new passengers begin to arrive. The ship often sails by 5 P.M. That means that all of the ship's cabins must be completely cleaned, linens changed, and all major lounges and other public spaces vacuumed and polished—all in three or four hours.

The Cruise Director. The **cruise director** and his or her staff are among the most visible crew members on board, from the passengers' point of view (see Exhibit 5). Members of this department are the entertainers, musicians, and children's counselors, and they direct all of the passenger-entertainment activities.

An important part of the cruise staff's job is to sell and coordinate the shore excursions. **Shore excursions** are a significant part of onboard revenue for any cruise line. In Alaska, passengers can go white-water rafting, walk on or fly over glaciers, and attend salmon bakes. In the Caribbean there are snorkeling expeditions, beaches, tours of old sugar plantations, visits to Mayan ruins, rain forests and volcanoes, opportunities to play golf, visit nightclubs, go shopping, and more. In the Mediterranean there are tours to the Acropolis in Athens, gondola rides in Venice, and visits to Pompeii in Naples. Typically these tours are contracted from local tour operators. They are sold in advance on the ship so that when it arrives in port a sufficient number of tour buses and guides are available for each activity. It is important that tours run as scheduled, since ships spend a limited amount of time in port. This can be a logistical problem when you are handling five or six different tours for more than a thousand passengers.

Before a ship arrives in port, a member of the cruise staff usually gives a destination-and-shopping talk in one of the ship's auditoriums to interested passengers. All of the large cruise lines recommend certain onshore shops whose merchandise they know to be fairly priced and reliable. These shops pay a promotional fee to the cruise line, in return for which their location and merchandise are promoted by the line. Often the cruise line guarantees that if there is any problem with a purchase and the shop will not make an adjustment, the line itself will.

Another important duty of the cruise staff is to prepare the daily activity calendar. The ship publishes a daily schedule for all passengers; it is distributed in their cabins the night before. If the ship is going to be in port, the schedule shows its arrival and departure times, tour departure times, when the ship's meals will be served and where, what activities

Exhibit 5   Cruise Director's Staff, Large Cruise Ship

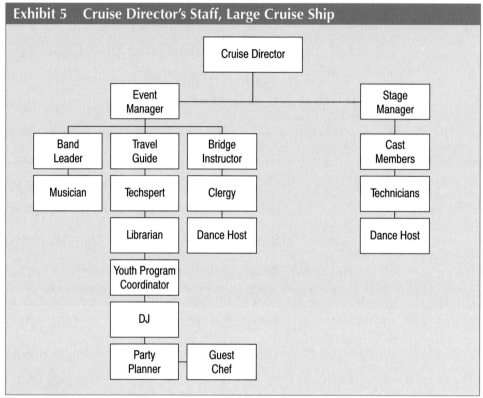

Source: Holland America Line.

there will be for those who are staying on the ship, library hours, the times that movies will be shown onboard, and other news of interest to passengers. When the ship has a day at sea, the cruise staff usually is very busy running a myriad of activities. There are aerobic classes; bingo games; tennis tournaments; dance lessons; carved-ice and cooking demonstrations; talks on such topics as personal finances, popular health issues, or the history and politics of the region the ship is sailing in; art auctions; bridge lessons; and more. All of these activities must be scheduled, promoted, and run by the cruise department.

Finally, the cruise director is responsible for monitoring the quality of the live shows and other entertainment that are offered nightly to passengers. The revues and other acts are cast, rehearsed, and produced by people outside the cruise department; in most instances they are the work of independent producers and agents. Carnival Cruise Lines is an exception; it produces and stages all of its own entertainment. Royal Caribbean produces some of its own entertainment and subcontracts the rest. In some cases the cruise director or a member of the cruise staff acts as the master of ceremonies. The cruise director is also responsible for providing feedback to the home office concerning audience reaction. Obviously the demographics of the passengers, which vary by season and itinerary, affect the suitability of the entertainment.

The Human Resources Manager. The human resources function of recruiting and hiring staff is done by land-based, not shipboard, human resources personnel. Background checks, medical exams, and visa requests must be done before a crew member is hired and

(Courtesy of Cunard Line.)

In January 2004 the *Queen Mary 2* sailed on her 14-day maiden voyage from Southhampton, England, to Fort Lauderdale, Florida. The flagship of the Cunard fleet, she was the most expensive cruise ship ever built at that time. She has 14 decks, 5 pools, 10 restaurants, a casino, a Canyon Ranch SpaClub, and a full-scale planetarium, among other features. She boasts the largest ballroom, library, and wine collection at sea. There is a kennel on the ship, for passengers who want to bring their pets along; avid golfers can play a virtual round of golf onboard. Renowned artists from around the world were commissioned to produce more than 300 original works of art (valued at more than $5 million) for the ship.

It's interesting to compare the *Queen Mary 2* with another British liner, the *Titanic*, which was the biggest and most expensive ocean liner of her day:

	Titanic	*Queen Mary 2*
Length:	882 feet	1,132 feet
Width:	92.5 feet	135 feet
Height:	175 feet	236 feet
Decks:	8	14
Gross tons:	46,328	151,400
Horsepower:	55,000	157,000
Top speed:	24 knots	30 knots
Approx. Cost:	$400 million*	$800 million

*In today's dollars; $7.5 million in 1912 dollars

Elegant dining options are a feature of many cruise ships. This is the main dining room of the *Freedom of the Seas*. (Courtesy of Royal Caribbean International.)

placed with a ship. Land-based human resources staff must arrange for getting the newly hired crew members to their ship assignments, which could be thousands of miles from the ship line's home base. Once the crew is aboard, the ship's human resources manager is responsible for ongoing training and crew welfare. Recreation and educational programs are necessary to occupy crew members during their free time. Members of the crew are allowed to charge purchases they make onboard ship and, accordingly, folios must be established for them. This is another responsibility of the ship's human resources department.

The Physician. In the hotel business, when guests get sick, a doctor is called in; if guests need further medical attention, they are rushed to a hospital. Since this is not possible on a ship at sea, all cruise ships carry a **physician** and at least one nurse.

The nature of the business makes this a critical position on any ship. Despite the fact that the age of the average cruise passenger is getting younger, cruise ships get a good number of older and disabled passengers. *Freedom of the Seas* has 32 cabins for the disabled, *Carnival Destiny* has 25 cabins, and Holland America's *Rotterdam VI* has 23. All modern cruise ships are completely accessible, which also makes them attractive for older passengers or those with arthritis or other mobility problems. Considering that cruise ships are not yet subject to the Americans with Disabilities Act because they sail under **flags of convenience,** they appear to be way ahead of the hotel industry in this matter. The reasons are simple: the disabled market is a large one (49 million Americans reported suffering from some kind of disability in 1997), targeting it is a sound marketing strategy, and it produces profits. Moreover, it's the right thing to do. Princess has created the "Love Boat Access Program," which includes a brochure highlighting the features for the disabled on each ship, many of which were suggested by passengers. These features include wheelchair gangways, Braille elevator buttons, phone amplifiers, and visual smoke detectors. Princess also developed tenders (launches that run between the ship and shore) that are designed to board wheelchairs, as well as gangway crawlers that carry persons in wheelchairs and others who find ascending steep stairways difficult. Most ships accommodate Seeing Eye dogs for the blind and other service animals.

To assist the physician, modern cruise ships are equipped with state-of-the-art medical centers. Physicians onboard ships have emergency-room training, and their equipment includes cardiac defibrillators, x-ray machines, operating tables, hospital beds, and enough prescription drugs to stock a small pharmacy! Consequently, the lead nurse is responsible for a perpetual inventory system to control the drugs. The object of onboard medical care is to treat minor injuries and stabilize major medical conditions until patients can be evacuated. Operators don't like to talk about it, but ships have morgues as well.

Princess's former fleet medical officer, Dr. Allister Smith, points out that, statistically speaking, only three percent of passengers may become critically ill and that his medical staff treats more crew members than passengers. Smith says practicing medicine at sea is not the same as onshore:

> Time, which is one of the main tools doctors use, is taken away from you at sea. If a patient has certain symptoms ashore, you can wait and see what happens. But with a passenger, if the ship is in port and the patient perhaps seriously ill, a decision must be made on the spot to put him ashore.

Environment, Health, Safety, and Security

All of the major cruise lines have policies and procedures to protect the environment and to ensure the health, safety, and security of passengers and crew. Carnival, for example, has a maritime policy and compliance group that deals with these issues, develops standards, and shares best practices with all of their brands. International, national, and local regulations set many of the standards to protect the environment in matters related to the discharge of black water (sewage) and gray water (shower and sink water), disposal of garbage, air emissions, and oily discharge.

Health maintenance is of course primarily a personal matter but cruise ships carrying thousands of passengers and crew must be concerned about spreading sickness. Today, hand-sanitizer dispensers are placed at the beginning of the buffet lines on most cruise ships, and reminders are posted throughout the ships advising crew and passengers to wash their hands often, especially after using the lavatory. In order to minimize slips and falls, warning notices are placed throughout the ships, calling attention to steps and wet decks. On all Carnival ships, U.S. standards are followed for food handling, storage, and preparation, and the maintenance of kitchen equipment. Fire prevention and the capability to repress any fire that might occur is a major concern of all cruise lines. Accordingly, smoking policies are strictly enforced and fire extinguishing equipment checked on a regular basis.

The cruise lines are responsible for passenger and crew security while they are onboard, but security issues may arise as well when passengers are at a port-of-call. Procedures are set to deal with any threats that may arise at a port or at sea. All Carnival brands, for example, have an emergency response system in place to deal with a variety of safety and security issues.

Summary

The cruise industry has experienced impressive growth since 1970, when it was estimated that just 500,000 people took a cruise each year; today that number has increased to more than 13 million. The passenger services aboard cruise ships are managed by hotel managers, pursers, food and beverage managers, chief housekeepers, cruise directors, and human resources managers, many of whom come from fine hotels and hospitality schools. Only 20 percent of Americans have ever taken a cruise.

If you define a cruise as going to a number of ports for the purpose of sight-seeing, and then ending up back where you started, then perhaps the first person to take a cruise and write about it was the noted English novelist William Makepeace Thackeray. In 1844 the Peninsula and Oriental Steam Navigation Company, popularly known as the P&O, invited Thackeray to travel on board its ships to Greece, the Holy Land, and Egypt. His book *Notes of a Journey from Cornhill to Grand Cairo* told of the trip. The first American-origin cruise was probably the 1867 voyage of the paddle-wheel steamer *Quaker City,* with a similar itinerary as Thackeray's cruise, except that it started from New York. Among the passengers was the American humorist Mark Twain, who chronicled his adventures in *The Innocents Abroad.*

From the time of the *Quaker City* up to the late 1950s, far more people crossed the Atlantic from necessity rather than for pleasure. This was the period of massive immigration to the United States, and travel conditions for most passengers crossing the Atlantic were miserable. Even for those traveling first class, the trip was often uncomfortable, because voyages were long and there were no ports to stop at.

Up to World War II, the major steamship lines were owned by European interests. When the war started, almost all of the vessels were converted into troop ships or stayed in port. This situation continued until 1945, when the rebuilding of Europe once again spurred a growing demand for ocean liners. For the first time, the United States recognized that it might need its own troop ships, and subsidized the building and operation of new vessels. The *United States,* launched in 1951, was designed to be the fastest ship of its size afloat.

The post-war boom marked the last days of the great steamship liners. Besides the *United States* and *Queen Mary,* there were the *Queen Elizabeth,* the French Line's *France,* Holland America's *Rotterdam,* and a host of sleek Italian liners built for warm-water cruising in the Mediterranean.

The cruise world started to come apart in 1958. That was the year Pan American World Airways offered its first nonstop, transatlantic crossing on a Boeing 707 jet. Ocean-going passenger ships were effectively out of business as a means of transportation.

Modern cruising was born in the 1960s and 1970s with the formation of Norwegian Caribbean Line, Royal Caribbean Cruise Lines, Princess Cruise Lines, and Carnival Cruise Lines. Carnival's strategy of focusing on the cruise ships themselves as the center of the cruise vacation experience changed consumers' perception of cruising from a stodgy pastime for the rich to a fun vacation for the masses. This marketing innovation was probably the defining event in the development of the modern cruise industry.

Cruise lines are divided into four market segments by the Cruise Lines International Association: contemporary/value, premium, luxury, and specialty lines. The average cruise passenger is 51 years old, has a household income of $64,000, and pays $200 a day for an all-inclusive vacation that includes a cabin, meals, and entertainment.

Today's cruise ships are floating vacation resorts, and in some ways they are very similar to hotels in how they are organized. At the top is the captain, who is responsible for the ship's operation and the safety of all those onboard. Four people typically report directly to the captain: the chief officer, the chief engineer, the hotel manager, and the environmental officer. The hotel manager is in charge of the ship's hotel division and oversees a purser, food and beverage manager, chief housekeeper, cruise director, human resources manager, physician, and sometimes the heads of other smaller departments and concessions. Besides being ultimately responsible for food and beverage services and cabin services, the hotel manager may also be responsible for entertainment and shore excursions.

The purser is the ship's banker, information officer, human resources director (on small cruise ships), and complaint handler. The purser is second in command of the hotel division.

The food and beverage manager oversees the assistant food and beverage manager, executive chef, maître d', bar manager, and provision master. Because of safety and sanitation requirements—as well as passenger expectations—food and beverage operations on cruise ships are highly disciplined operations. Beverages are the single largest source of onboard revenue on every major cruise ship.

The chief housekeeper is responsible for the cleaning and general maintenance of all cabins and interior areas of the ship. The housekeeping department also takes care of passenger laundry and dry cleaning, as well as cleaning all cabin linens, table linens, towels, and the crew's uniforms. The busiest day for the housekeeping department is turnaround day, when the ship finishes a cruise and starts another.

The cruise director's staff directs all guest activities and includes entertainers, musicians, and children's counselors. They also sell and coordinate shore excursions and prepare the daily activity calendar.

The human resources manager is responsible for the crew's welfare and ongoing training. This manager is responsible for the recreation and educational programs necessary to occupy crew members during their free time.

Modern cruise lines pay a great deal of attention to medical care. All ships carry at least one physician and a nurse. The physician typically has a state-of-the-art medical center onboard with which to treat patients. A determined devotion to accessibility makes cruise ships attractive vacations for disabled and older persons.

Endnotes

1. Cruise Line Industry Association, Source Book, 2009 Profile, www.cruising.org.

2. 2008 Cruise Market Profile Study, Cruise Lines International Association.

3. Much of the information cited in this chapter was originally researched and developed by Bob Dickinson and Andy Vladimir for *Selling the Sea: An Inside Look at the Cruise Industry* (New York: Wiley, 1997).

4. John Maxtone-Graham, *The Only Way to Cross* (New York: Macmillan, 1972), pp. 112–113.

5. Estimated figures compiled from various trade sources.

6. Dickinson and Vladimir, pp. 88–92.

Key Terms

captain—The person on a cruise ship who is responsible for its operation and the safety of all those onboard. The captain sees that all company policies and rules, as well as national and international laws, are followed.

chief housekeeper—The person on a cruise ship who is responsible for the cleaning and general maintenance of all cabins and interior areas on the ship. The chief housekeeper is also responsible for passenger laundry and dry cleaning, as well as cleaning cabin linen and table linen, towels, and the crew's uniforms. Also called the chief steward.

chief officer—The captain's second in command and deputy. Also called the staff captain on some cruise lines.

cruise director—Oversees a staff responsible for managing a ship's entertainers, children's counselors, and guest activities, including selling and coordinating shore excursions.

flag of convenience—The flag of the country where a cruise ship is registered and under whose laws it must operate.

food and beverage manager—The person on a cruise ship who is responsible for providing quality food and beverage service to passengers and crew members. Typically reports to the hotel manager.

galley—The shipboard equivalent of a kitchen.

hotel manager—The person on a cruise ship who runs the hotel division. Besides being ultimately responsible for food and beverage services and housekeeping services, the hotel manager may oversee medical care, entertainment, shore excursions, casino operations, the beauty salon, the health spa, gift shops, photography services, and more—in short, everything that helps create the vacation experience that the cruise line offers.

lido deck—The deck that contains a cruise ship's main swimming pool. It is usually a center for many onboard activities.

physician—The person on a cruise ship who is responsible for the medical care of passengers and crew members; he or she typically has a state-of-the-art medical facility in which to work and one or more nurses to assist in the care of patients.

purser—The second in command within the hotel department and a cruise ship's banker, information officer, human resources director, and complaint handler.

shore excursions—Specially arranged trips, tours, and activities that occur off the ship. They are a significant part of onboard revenue for any cruise line.

sitting—The time allotted for serving one complete meal to a group of diners.

ton—A unit for measuring the total cubic capacity of a cruise ship.

turnaround day—The day when a cruise ship finishes one cruise and starts another.

Review Questions

1. What were some of the early beginnings of the cruise industry?
2. What four major cruise lines were born in the mid-1960s to early 1970s?

3. What unique characteristics did Carnival introduce to the cruise industry?

4. What are some of the responsibilities of a cruise ship captain? a cruise ship's hotel manager?

5. What are the purser's responsibilities? the food and beverage manager's?

6. What important duties are overseen by the chief housekeeper? the cruise director? the physician?

7. How does the Seabourn case study illustrate the type of quality service cruise lines seek to provide to their guests?

 Internet Sites

For more information, visit the following Internet sites. Remember that Internet addresses can change without notice. If the site is no longer there, you can use a search engine to look for additional sites.

Cruise Lines

Carnival Cruise Lines
www.carnival.com

Crystal Cruises
www.crystalcruises.com

Cunard Cruise Lines
www.cunardline.com

Disney Cruise Lines
www.disneycruise.com

Holland America Line
www.hollandamerica.com

Norwegian Cruise Line
www.ncl.com

Princess Cruises & Tours
www.princesscruises.com

Royal Caribbean International
www.rccl.com

Seabourn Cruise Line
www.seabourn.com

Silversea Cruise Lines
www.asource.com/silversea

Windstar Cruise Lines
www.windstarcruises.com

Other Cruise Resources

Cruise Lines International Association
www.cruising.org

Cruise Magazine
www.cruisemagazine.net

Cruise Travel Magazine
www.cruisetravelmag.com

General Cruise Travel
www.travelpage.com/cruise.htm

Porthole Cruise Magazine
www.porthole.com

Titanic.com
www.titanic.com

11

Gaming and Casino Hotels

Outline

Competencies

1. Summarize the history of gaming around the world and in the United States, describe casino hotels, and explain differences between the organization and management of casino hotels and other types of hotels. (pp. 326–336)

2. Describe casino operations, including casino games, terminology, employees, customers, marketing, and controls and regulation. (pp. 336–346)

Opposite page: Part of the Las Vegas skyline at night; photo courtesy of Ernie Pick.

T HIS CHAPTER IS ABOUT GAMBLING, or *gaming*, which is what it has come to be called in the industry; the two words are interchangeable. For the most part we will focus on gaming within hotels, although free-standing casinos, riverboat gambling, offshore gaming junkets, and Internet gambling are proliferating. We will start with a brief history of gaming, then look at casino hotels—including the games that are played there, who plays them, and who conducts them. The chapter concludes with a discussion of how casinos within hotels are marketed, controlled, and regulated.

The Story of Gaming

No one knows when gambling first started. The first recorded accounts date back to early Chinese dynasties in 2300 B.C. Some of the earliest pieces of gaming evidence we have come from ancient Egypt; dice have been found by archeologists in pyramid excavations. As near as we can tell, gamblers back then faced the same problems that they do today. People who couldn't pay their gambling losses were punished and made to work off their debts! Ancient Greeks considered gambling immoral but it occurred anyway; historians tell us that Greek soldiers played dice before the offensive against Troy. Both the Old and New Testaments mention gambling. Indeed, Roman centurions gambled for Christ's robes at his crucifixion. While there were laws barring gambling during the early period of the Roman Empire, gambling was later embraced and became a popular diversion for Roman citizens. Romans enthusiastically bet on gladiators, the lions against the Christians, chariot races, and other sports held in venues like the Coliseum.

After the Crusades (circa A.D. 1100–1300), gambling spread throughout Europe. In fact, games that evolved into dice games, roulette, and blackjack had their roots in medieval times. Craps, for instance, began as a game called "hazard" that was played by English knights. By the seventeenth century, forms of roulette and blackjack were popular in Europe.

The elegant casinos of Baden-Baden, Germany, and Monaco in Monte Carlo were built in the mid-nineteenth century and became a favorite of European royalty and the aristocracy. Gambling was legalized in Great Britain in the 1960s to assist churches in collecting funds. Today, Austria, Egypt, Poland, Turkey, Russia, Macao, Australia, New Zealand, and the Philippines, among other countries, have popular gambling facilities. At least 22 jurisdictions in the Caribbean have casinos. In many countries, casinos are owned or controlled by the government.

Gaming in the United States

Following Columbus's discovery of the New World, Spanish and Portuguese sailors brought dice and cards with them on the first expeditions; in leisure moments, they raced their horses, wagering on the results. Indians shaped their own dice from fruit pits and joined in the games.

Early American colonists developed a taste for gambling as well. It was one way, for example, to raise needed funds to fight the Revolutionary War. They justified their popular lotteries by using the money raised to fund other worthy causes, such as municipal projects, colleges, and universities. Columbia, Dartmouth, Harvard, and Yale were all partially funded by lotteries. Card games, too, were widely played.

TOP 20 U.S. CASINO MARKETS BY ANNUAL REVENUE

Casino Market	2008 Annual GROSS Revenues*
1 Las Vegas Strip	$6.121 billion
2 Atlantic City, N.J.	$4.545 billion
3 Chicagoland, Ind./Ill.	$2.251 billion
4 Connecticut	$1.571 billion
5 Detroit	1.360 billion
6 Tunica/Lula, Miss.	$1.105 billion
7 St. Louis, Mo./Ill.	$1.031 billion
8 Biloxi, Miss.	$951.27 million
9 Shreveport, La.	$847.61 million
10 Boulder Strip, Nev.	$836.60 million
11 Reno/Sparks, Nev.	$779.38 million
12 Kansas City, Mo. (includes St. Joseph)	$756.22 million
13 Lawrenceburg/Rising Sun/Belterra, Ind.	$731.65 million
14 New Orleans, La.	$701.37 million
15 Lake Charles, La.	$651.23 million
16 Downtown Las Vegas, Nev.	$582.46 million
17 Laughlin, Nev.	$571.18 million
18 Black Hawk, Colo.	$508.69 million
19 Yonkers, N.Y.	$486.46 million
20 Council Bluffs, Iowa	$468.52 million

*Gross revenue is earnings before taxes, salaries, and expenses are paid — the equivalent of sales, not profit.

Source: The Innovation Group, May 2009.

By the early nineteenth century some places within the United States had established reputations as favorite gambling destinations. The most prominent of these was New Orleans, conveniently situated on the Mississippi River and a major port. By 1810 the city was said to have as many gambling halls as the four largest American cities put together. But gambling attracted criminals as well as average citizens. Riverboats were known to be home to cardsharps and professional gamblers, and there were many instances of travelers being cheated out of all their money.

Prior to 1861 and the start of the Civil War, there was a move to prohibit gambling in most states. In the latter part of the nineteenth century, lotteries were outlawed by the federal government. However, other forms of gambling continued to survive in a few places, including on riverboats plying the Ohio and Mississippi rivers, as well as in the states that were on those rivers.

Gaming in Nevada and New Jersey. By the early twentieth century, gambling had become illegal in most states. Even Nevada, which had allowed it since 1868, outlawed it in all forms in 1910. But, in 1931, during the Great Depression, Nevada's state legislature decided to revive gaming as a means to economic recovery. Almost all forms of gambling were again permitted.

The first Nevada casinos were mostly converted stores, but by 1935 clubs began to appear, first in Reno, and later in Las Vegas. In 1946 the Flamingo Hotel and Casino opened—the first elegant casino hotel that included entertainment. Opening night featured a bevy of Hollywood movie stars as performers and guests. They would return regularly, giving Las Vegas a reputation as a glamorous vacation spot. With the opening of The Mirage Hotel & Casino Resort in 1989, the era of the mega-destination resort began. The Mirage cost $630 million and was the most expensive casino hotel to be built anywhere in the world up to that time. Other mega-hotels would follow, and today Las Vegas is the home of nineteen of the twenty-five largest hotels in the world, each of them a casino hotel located on the Las Vegas Strip. The largest is the Las Vegas Sands Megacenter, with 7,128 rooms, 2.2 million square feet of meeting and exhibit space, 30 restaurants, and more than 60 retail shops.

Harrah's is the largest casino company in the world, with 39 casinos in the United States and casino interests on four continents. In addition to operating casino hotels in Las Vegas under the Harrah's name, the company runs Caesars Palace, Paris Las Vegas, Rio, and Bally's. The MGM Mirage Company has the largest number of casino hotels in Las Vegas, including four of the world's largest hotels: the MGM Grand, the Mandalay Bay, ARIA, and the Bellagio.

In 1976 legalized casino gambling was allowed in depressed Atlantic City, New Jersey, mainly for many of the same economic reasons that had appealed to Nevada. The first casino hotel was created by Resorts International (which had already developed Paradise Island in the Bahamas).

Today, gambling in one form or another is permitted almost everywhere in the United States. Hawaii and Utah are the only two states that prohibit all forms of gambling.

Riverboat and Offshore Gambling. By 1997 six states had legalized riverboat gambling, giving it a firm foothold. Laws concerning these gambling operations, however, vary considerably. For example, in Iowa the boats are required to leave the shore and take gamblers on cruises. In Illinois, cruises last for approximately two hours. In Mississippi the boats are not allowed to leave the dock at all and guests can gamble as long as they wish. Some major hospitality companies have taken an interest in riverboat gambling operations.

In coastal states such as Florida, Georgia, and Texas, offshore gambling is gaining in popularity. Large tour boats and even a few small, obsolete cruise ships offer gambling "cruises to nowhere." These boats sail three miles offshore before they open their casinos, and they usually stay out three or four hours.

Indian Gambling. With the passing of the Indian Gaming Regulatory Act (IGRA) in 1988, Congress made it legal for Native Americans to open casinos on their property in states where gambling was allowed. The purpose of the act was to promote tribal economic development, protect Indian gaming from organized crime, and establish an appropriate regulatory body. Today Connecticut, Minnesota, Florida, and many other states have major casino operations on reservations. In fact, the largest casino in the world—Foxwoods Resort Casino—is located on an Indian reservation in Ledyard, Connecticut; it is run by the Mashantucket Pequot Tribal Nation. Besides three hotels, there is a casino with more than 7,000 slot and video poker machines, 380 gaming tables, and a 3,800-seat bingo hall.

The major casino hotels in Las Vegas are not known for their understated architecture. This is a view of the Luxor Resort & Casino, completed in 1993 at a cost of $375 million. It has 4,408 guestrooms (including 447 suites) and more than 120,000 square feet of gaming area. (Courtesy of Luxor Resort & Casino, Las Vegas, Nevada.)

Casino Hotels

The best way to understand casino hotels is to think of them not as hotels with casinos attached, but rather as casinos with guestrooms, restaurants, shopping arcades, and even theme parks attached. A description of what casino hotels are like appeared in award-winning humorist Dave Barry's syndicated newspaper column:

> We stayed at Caesars Palace, a giant hotel-casino decorated to look exactly the way the Roman Empire would have looked if it had consisted mainly of slot machines. Caesars also features roughly four zillion flashing lights, huge toga-clad statues that move, cocktail waitresses designed by Frederick's of Rome, and a bar on a large indoor boat that is actually floating. ("Mom, I think maybe you've had enough, you might...." SPLASH. "MAN OVERBOARD!")
>
> In other words, by Vegas standards, Caesars is very understated. It's a traditional Amish farm settlement compared to the casino next door, the Mirage, which

has real dolphins, albino tigers, an indoor rain forest, and an outdoor volcano that erupts on schedule. (You're going to see more and more hotels installing volcanoes in response to demand from the business traveler.) Also, right behind the front desk is a giant aquarium containing sharks. So you definitely should not mess with the Mirage. ("Were you planning to pay for those hotel towels in your suitcase, Mr. Furbitt? Or would you prefer to *take a little swim?*")[1]

At New York–New York Hotel & Casino, guests can stroll through Central Park, ride the Manhattan Express roller coaster, shop along Park Avenue, and visit a huge replica of the Statue of Liberty. At the Venetian, guests can take a gondola ride on a re-creation of the Grand Canal.

The $1 billion MGM Grand is, for the moment, the world's third-largest hotel. Besides seven restaurants, 5,044 guestrooms (including 751 suites), 29 private villas, and a casino the size of four football fields (with 3,000 slot machines), the hotel boasts two wedding chapels for couples who want to get married during their stay.

The Palazzo, developed by the Las Vegas Sands company at a cost of $1.8 billion, is the largest building in terms of floor space in the Western Hemisphere. It opened in December 2007 as an extension of The Venetian Casino Resort and is the largest LEED-certified building in the United States.

The Mirage features an artificial volcano that "erupts" (with the help of 3,000 lights computerized to simulate flowing lava) every 15 minutes from dusk to midnight. (Courtesy of The Mirage, Las Vegas, Nevada.)

At New York–New York Hotel & Casino, guests can shop along Park Avenue, ride a roller coaster, and visit a 150-foot-tall replica of the Statue of Liberty. (Courtesy of New York–New York Hotel & Casino, Las Vegas, Nevada.)

In December 2008 Steve Wynn opened the Encore Hotel, a $2.3 billion casino resort with 2,034 guestrooms. It is connected to the Wynn by a shopping arcade and was originally conceived as an expansion of that hotel but developed its own identity as a resort. The hotel features five restaurants and seven bars, a 74,000-square-foot casino, a nightclub, and 27,000 square feet of retail space. One of the restaurants, a 152-seat steakhouse, is named Sinatra after the departed crooner Frank Sinatra and has on display Grammy and Oscar statuettes on loan from the Sinatra estate.

One of the most ambitious projects to be developed in Las Vegas is the MGM Mirage's City Center. Located on the Strip between the Monte Carlo and the Bellagio, it is a sixty-seven-acre hotel, residential, and entertainment complex that cost $8.5 billion. Three hotels with a total of 6,000 hotel rooms share the site with 2,400 condominiums. The Vdara, the Mandarin Oriental, and the ARIA hotels opened in December 2009. ARIA is the first hotel on the Las Vegas Strip to generate its own electricity.

Revenue

Before the advent of the mega-casino resorts, the casino was the major source of revenue at Las Vegas hotels. Gambling accounted for about 58 percent of total hotel revenue. The win percentage of the various gambling games breaks down as follows:

The Golden Nugget has undergone many renovations since its grand opening in 1946. It has 1,907 guestrooms and 45,000 square feet of casino space. (Photo courtesy of Ernie Pick.)

Baccarat	10.70%
Blackjack	11.58
Craps	13.72
Roulette	20.13
Slot Machines	6.16[2]

In 1989 the Mirage Hotel & Casino Resort set a new standard for casino hotel development by making the hotel itself an attraction through architecture, design, and entertainment. Meanwhile, at Caesars Palace, Wolfgang Puck opened his famous Spago restaurant and started a trend of upscale celebrity chef restaurants that was adopted by others, establishing Las Vegas as a culinary capital. Today, casino hotels have a more diversified revenue stream than in the past. As hotel developers made the rooms and suites more luxurious, higher room rates were charged. Shopping arcades are an integral part of every mega-resort, and shopping has become a major part of the vacation experience in Las Vegas. The Forum Shops of Caesars Palace was the first shopping arcade destination. In its more than 800,000 square feet of space, there are one hundred and sixty mostly upscale boutiques and specialty food shops. Brand names such as Burberry, Dior, Versace, and Gucci are located there. It is the highest-grossing mall in the United States. The Wynn Las Vegas has an art gallery with fifteen priceless paintings, including a Rembrandt, Picasso, and Vermeer. Las Vegas has become a center of dining, entertainment, and luxury shopping, resulting in a more varied economic base. While gambling still accounts for most of a casino hotel/resort's revenue at 40 percent, rooms now account for 26 percent of revenue, food 15 percent, beverage 5 percent, and "other" 14 percent.[3]

Exhibit 1   Sample Casino Hotel Organization Chart

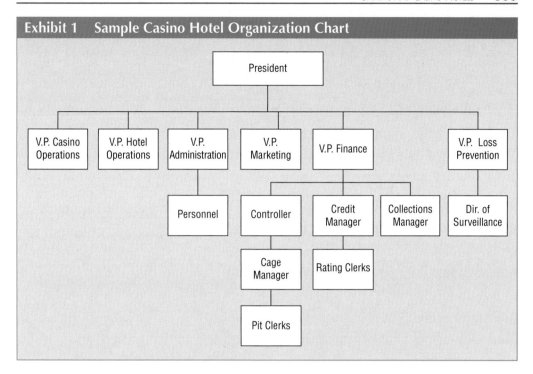

Organization and Management

The most striking difference between a casino hotel and other types of hotels is in the organization and management of the facility. The importance of this point cannot be overemphasized, because it changes completely the way casino hotels are operated compared to traditional hotels. In casino hotels, the hotel operation is subordinate to the gambling operation. The vice president of hotel operations is not in complete control of the hotel; he or she reports to a higher resident authority who usually holds the title of hotel president. There is also a vice president of casino operations who is as important as the hotel manager when it comes to making decisions about almost everything. That's not all. Other vice presidents also make a lot of decisions that, in a typical hotel or resort, are usually handled as part of hotel operations. In Exhibit 1, note that there are a total of six vice presidents reporting to the president. In addition to the vice presidents of hotel operations and casino operations, there's a vice president of administration (who handles human resources), a vice president of marketing, a vice president of finance, and a vice president of loss prevention (security). Why have these departments been separated from the hotel operation? Because decisions made in these departments affect not just hotel operations but casino operations as well.

For example, controls, credit, and the management of cash are not matters for either the hotel manager or the casino manager to determine independently, because decisions about them affect both the hotel operation and the casino operation. Therefore, there is a separate finance department. Marketing, too, is unique. Gamblers are one audience, resort and convention guests another. But they're all at the same property at the same time.

The bottom line is that the vice president of hotel operations in many large Las Vegas and Atlantic City casino hotels is not in charge of the entire hotel; rather, he or she is only

Exhibit 2   Sample Organization Chart for Hotel Operations within a Casino Hotel

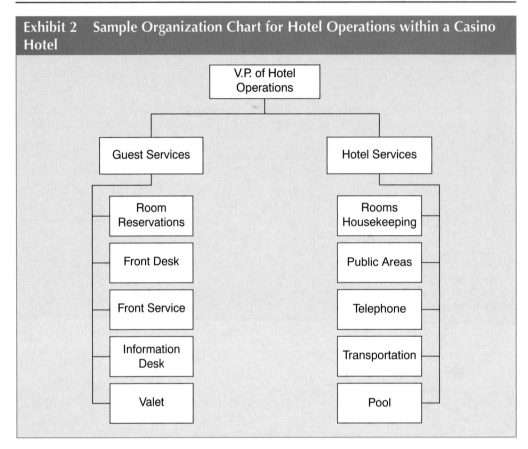

in charge of the rooms department and hotel services such as the spa, transportation, and pool (see Exhibit 2).

The Importance of Food and Beverages. While food and beverage operations are extremely important to any resort operation, in casino hotels they play an added role. They make gaming convenient by "fueling" the players. It isn't necessary to wander far or leave the premises in order to get any kind of dining experience—from a pastrami sandwich to a Châteaubriand.

In some casino hotels, the food and beverage department is operated as a separate division under its own vice president. At the Mirage, this division, which has 14 food outlets, is the largest of all in terms of number of employees. The MGM Grand has seven fine-dining restaurants—all of them imaginatively decorated—as well as a variety of other outlets, including a 24-hour café and a New York–style deli. The amount of food consumed daily at the hotel during a peak business period is mind-boggling: 10,000 eggs, 2,650 pounds (1,193 kilograms) of beef, 640 pounds (288 kilograms) of chicken, and 270 pounds (122 kilograms) of shrimp, for example. An in-house bakery, which produces 99 percent of MGM Grand's baked goods, prepares 9,000 rolls, 3,000 pastries, 200 cakes, and 150 pies each day. As many as 80,000 cocktails are poured on a busy day.[4]

One successful marketing tool for casino-hotel food and beverage departments has been the use of brand name restaurants. At the Bellagio there is Aqua, from San Francisco, and Circo, a sibling of Le Cirque in New York. At the Mandalay Bay Hotel there's a China Grill.

Service Demands. Service operations in casino hotels are unique as well. Both entertainment and food are important components of the gambling experience. They provide opportunities for winners to celebrate and losers to console themselves. Because of all the services they provide, casino hotels are even more labor-intensive than other kinds of hotels. Elaborate and extensive entertainment and multiple dining facilities with all-night service mean that the number of employees per hotel room may be three or four times higher than in conventional hotels and resorts.

Despite the complexity of operating casino hotels, they are tremendously attractive cash cows to knowledgeable operators who have experience in running them. Although not all casino hotels have been financially successful, those that are successful generate profits far in excess of other hotels.

One typical source of tension that may arise among casino managers, hotel managers, and food and beverage managers is how much money the casino division will be charged for complimentary rooms and food and beverages, given to guests to encourage them to come to the hotel and gamble. Another source of tension between the casino division and the rooms division involves guestroom inventory. Research has shown that most people take gambling trips—especially to Las Vegas and Atlantic City—on impulse, planning them no more than 48 hours in advance. This means that a casino hotel must keep a

The Paris Las Vegas, developed by Park Place Entertainment at a cost of $785 million, has 2,916 guestrooms, 13 restaurants, 100 gaming tables, more than 2,000 slot machines, and a 50-story replica of the Eiffel Tower. (Courtesy of Paris Las Vegas, Las Vegas, Nevada.)

certain number of guestrooms available at all times for this last-minute traffic. On the other hand, popular resort hotels with casinos tend to fill their guestrooms five or six weeks in advance, especially around holidays. Enough rooms must be held open so that the hotel is not forced to turn away gamblers—its most profitable source of revenue—due to lack of rooms. However, if too many rooms are held, the hotel is stuck with empty guestrooms that could have been sold. As you can see, casino hotel managers must perform a fine balancing act to plan correctly.

Casino Operations

Since the hotel operations within casino hotels are very similar to hotel operations within all types of hotels and resorts, in this chapter we will concentrate on what makes casino hotels unique: their casino operations. In the following sections we will describe casino games, then look at casino terminology, employees, customers, marketing, and controls and regulation.

Casino Games. There are basically two types of casino games: (1) those classified as table games, and (2) slot machines. The most common table games include baccarat, blackjack, craps, and roulette.

Table games. *Baccarat* was named after an Italian word meaning "zero." It went from Italy to France in the fifteenth century, where it was known as *Chemin de Fer.* The object of the game is to come as close as possible to the number 9, which is known as a "natural." (Scoring an 8 is the second-best hand and is also known as a natural.) It is played with eight complete decks of cards. The cards are shuffled by the croupier (dealer), cut, and placed in a special box referred to as the "shoe." The shoe is passed to a player who becomes the banker. The first and third cards dealt from the shoe constitute the player's hand; the second and fourth cards are the banker's hand. Face cards and 10 count as 0, aces count as 1, and all other cards count at face value. The hand with the highest point total closest to 9 wins.

Blackjack is played at a table that can seat up to eight players across from a dealer. Here the object is to get closer to 21 than the dealer. (All players play against the dealer, not against each other.) Players who go over 21 automatically lose. The shoe can contain between one and eight decks. The dealer gives each player two cards face up; the dealer gets one card face up and one card face down. Kings, queens, jacks, and 10s each count as 10. Aces count as 1 or 11, as the player or dealer wishes. All other cards count at their face value. Additional cards may be distributed to each player, if the player desires, and the dealer may or may not take additional cards, depending on the initial hand dealt. The game continues until all the players stand pat with their hands; each player's total is then compared with the dealer's total to see who won.

Craps is considered by many players to be the most exciting game in any casino. Because there are so many betting variations, craps can be a complicated game. It is played on a rectangular table covered with green felt. The table is marked with all of the possible bets that can be made. A pair of dice is thrown by one of the players designated as the "shooter." Other players bet with or against the shooter by putting their chips on sections of the table that are marked *pass* line, *don't pass* line, *come* field, etc.

In the most basic bet, players who bet on the pass line win if the shooter rolls a 7 or 11; they lose if the shooter rolls "craps," which is 2, 3, or 12. Of course there are many other ways to win and lose and the action moves very fast—which is why the game is often perceived as difficult.

Industry Innovators

Stephen A. Wynn
Chairman & CEO
Wynn Resorts, Limited

Although Steve Wynn is generally credited with igniting the spark that turned Las Vegas, Nevada, into the glittering wonder it has become today, he does not gamble. "If you want to make money in a casino, own one," he is widely quoted as saying. Wynn knows what he's talking about. His father was a compulsive gambler who ran bingo parlors. When he died leaving huge debts, Wynn and his wife took over the parlors and the debts. It took them years to pay off creditors while running the games themselves.

His father had always wanted to open a casino in Las Vegas, and in 1967 Wynn moved there with his family to fulfill his father's dream. He bought an interest in the Frontier Hotel and became the slot manager. Unknown to him, the hotel was owned by Detroit mobsters. When he found out, he sold his shares.

Wynn's next venture was a profitable real estate deal that made enough money to enable him to invest in a rundown casino, the Golden Nugget. By the time he was 31, he took control of the Golden Nugget and became the youngest casino owner in Nevada history. At that time, almost all casinos were dimly lit, smoke-filled rooms with questionable clientele. Wynn changed that by transforming the Golden Nugget into a sparkling, bright gaming hall that attracted legitimate high rollers.

Using his Las Vegas property as collateral, Wynn then opened the Golden Nugget in Atlantic City. In 1987, he sold his operations to the Bally Corporation and used the proceeds, along with money raised by issuing bonds, to build the Mirage Resort, which opened in 1989.

The Mirage was the first of a new kind of Las Vegas hotel—designed to be a family attraction. Guests enter through a lush, tropical atrium filled with palm trees and waterfalls. Behind the front desk is a gigantic coral-reef aquarium stocked with sharks and other large fish. The Mirage is also home to two unique animal habitats: a dolphin habitat and the Secret Garden, where six rare white lions and tigers live.

Next to the Mirage, Wynn opened Treasure Island in 1993. The hotel's theme is pirates, and every hour there is a realistic mock battle that includes the complete destruction and sinking of a replica of a British frigate.

In 1998, Wynn opened the Bellagio, a $1.6 billion property that he says is the "most romantic hotel in the world." This resort features an 8.5 acre man-made lake with shooting fountains choreographed to music.

In May of 2000, MGM Grand, Inc., acquired all of the Mirage Resort properties for $6.4 billion. That left Wynn without a hotel—but not for long. A few months later he acquired the 200-acre Desert Inn property in Las Vegas and developed there a new 60-story casino hotel which opened in April 2005. In September 2006 the Wynn Macau Hotel Casino opened and in December 2008 he opened the 2,034-room Encore next to the Wynn Las Vegas.

(continued)

Industry Innovators *(continued)*

Wynn is known for being politically active, especially for environmental causes. He personally led a measure to ban all personal watercraft (jet skis) from Lake Tahoe where he lives, arguing that they were polluting the lake. He has also taken the lead in fighting for laws to control erosion, traffic, and air pollution in Las Vegas. He is a member of the board of trustees of his alma mater, the University of Pennsylvania, and the George Bush Presidential Library. In the May 2006 issue of *Time,* Steve Wynn was honored in the "Builders and Titans" category of the publication, recognizing his extraordinary ability to influence the world of business.

Roulette is the simplest table game of them all. In American roulette the table consists of a revolving wheel in which there is a ball and slots numbered from 1 to 36; in addition, there are two symbols, 0 and 00 (in most other countries there is only one zero). On the table there is a diagramed area with each number and symbol marked. Players place their chips on a number or symbol and the dealer spins the roulette ball in the opposite direction of the spinning wheel. When the ball falls into a slot on the roulette wheel, the dealer places a marker on the winning number on the table layout and pays the winning bet(s), if any.

Manual dexterity is an important skill for dealers. This dealer is conducting a game of blackjack.

Roulette is the simplest of the casino table games.

Of the table games, blackjack is the most popular in the United States, followed by craps and roulette. People who gamble regularly know that a player has a good chance of winning in blackjack, where the house odds (depending on the player's skill level) can be less than two percent. With craps, the house advantage is only 1.4 percent. In American roulette the house advantage is 5.26 percent.

In European casinos, where roulette is the most popular game, gaming is generally considered more of an entertainment than a way of winning money. The odds are a little better for players of French roulette, however, because the wheel has only one 0. With French roulette, the house advantage is only 2.63 percent.

Slot machines. Much of the gaming in American casinos involves slot machines. Slots are by far the most profitable games from a casino's point of view—not only because the percentage of money the casino keeps is usually high, but because slots are the least labor-intensive of all games, requiring no dealers or other attendants, except for employees who maintain the machines, make change, and empty and refill the hoppers. There are also a high number of bets made every hour on a slot machine, and the more bets, the more the casino makes.

The amount of money slot machines pay out is controlled in every jurisdiction. For example, in Atlantic City, slot machines must pay back 83 percent, or 83 cents out of every dollar bet; the house keeps 17 cents. Nevada does not regulate the payback but the Gaming Control Board, as a policy, does not approve any game that pays back less than 75 percent. In order to attract business in competitive markets, casinos may pay back more, hoping to make their profit on the increased betting volume. Some casinos in Nevada have been known to pay back 99 percent in winnings.

Casino Terminology. Before we go any further, we should introduce some key terms used in casino management:

- *Markers.* **Markers** are printed or written forms that look like bank checks; they are used to extend credit to a player. They are IOUs that players can give to dealers to buy chips, instead of using cash. Markers have no cash value; they simply record the amount of credit that the casino is willing to extend to a player. Typically the casino agrees not to cash these markers for 30 or 45 days, giving the player time to deposit enough money in his or her bank account to cover them.

- *Cashier's cage.* The **cashier's cage,** generally referred to simply as "the cage," is where chips and cash are stored, where checks are cashed, where credit cards are accepted, and where markers are approved. It is the control center for the flow of chips to and from tables.

- *Pit.* A group of tables within a casino that defines a management section is called a **pit.** A pit can be made up of tables featuring the same game, or tables featuring a combination of games. For example, there may be four craps tables and four roulette tables in one pit, or simply eight craps tables. The manager of a pit is called the **pit boss.**

- *Fill and credit slips.* Each gaming table has an inventory of chips. At the end of each shift the inventory at each table is restored to the original amount. If the inventory is depleted, a **fill slip** is completed and additional chips are issued from the cage. If there is an excess of chips, a **credit slip** is completed and the extra chips are returned to the cage.

  In modern casinos these pieces of paper have been replaced by a computer network so that requests can be transmitted electronically from the pit. If there is no computer system, security guards are utilized to carry credit and fill slips back and forth to the cage.

- *Drop box.* Each gaming table is equipped with a box that locks in place beneath the table. Cash and markers received from players are deposited through a slot into the **drop box.** At the end of a shift, boxes are removed from the tables and brought to a count room. At specific times they are opened and the contents counted carefully under strict supervision. When the box is removed from a gaming table, the slot is automatically locked and can be reopened only by keys that are under the control of the casino's accounting team.

- *Table drop.* The **table drop** is the amount of money and markers in a gaming table's drop box that players have exchanged for chips at that table. It may or may not represent the amount placed on bets at that table, since players often carry chips from one table or game to another, or cash them in. The table drop, however, is a good measure of the gaming activity within a casino.

- *Slot drop.* Unlike the table drop, where all money and markers deposited are counted, the **slot drop** represents the amount of money put into a slot machine *less the amount paid out.* For example, if $100 is put into a slot machine and $90 is paid out, the slot drop is $10 or 10 percent.

- *Table win.* The **table win** is the amount bet at a table minus the amount that is paid back to the players. It is calculated as follows:

	Opening chip inventory
+	Fill slips
−	Credit slips
−	Closing chip inventory
TOTAL =	Total chips won or transferred from the table

Once the total chips won or transferred from the table are determined, a second calculation is required to arrive at the table win:

	Table drop
−	Total chips won or transferred from the table
TOTAL =	Table win

- *Hold percentage.* The **hold percentage** is a calculation to determine the percentage of chips purchased at a table by customers that is won back by the casino. It is calculated as follows:

$$\text{Win} \div \text{Drop} = \text{Hold}$$

For example, if the table win is $1,000 and the table drop is $4,000, then the hold is 25 percent. In other words, the casino won (kept) 25 percent of the chips purchased at that table.

Casino Employees. Casinos are staffed by **croupiers,** or dealers, whose job it is to conduct the table games, collect bets, and pay the winning bets of players, using chips. Casino managers expect dealers to be friendly and fast. Manual dexterity and math skills are also important. Like all casino employees, dealers are carefully screened for honesty. They are also under constant electronic and personal surveillance. Some U.S. dealers earn as much as $50,000 per year if they deal in high-action games; the average salary is $25,000 to $30,000. Dealers also may earn large sums in tips. Some players not only tip dealers generously, they place a bet for the dealer at the same time they place one for themselves (for good luck).

Floor people are casino employees who supervise dealers. They are trained to enforce good dealing procedures, resolve disputes, and watch for cheaters. Today's cheaters are often extremely sophisticated; some use computers and other electronic devices. A floor person will usually supervise two to four tables, and reports to a pit boss.

A pit boss manages a larger group of tables and pays special attention to tables with high action. A big part of a pit boss's job is to make sure that gamblers placing large bets are happy. Often pit bosses act as hosts for these gamblers.

The person in charge of the casino at any given time is the shift manager. Shift managers work six to eight hours at a time. Under the shift manager is the games manager, who is responsible for all of the table games.

All of these employees have high-pressure jobs because they are responsible for so much cash. In a large casino it is not unusual for betting activity to reach $1 million an hour. Many casinos win $1 million for their owners in an 18-hour day.

Exhibit 3 Compensation: Gaming Properties

Position	Minimum	50th Percentile	Maximum
General Manager	$ 180,081.41	$ 353,031.60	$ 827,502.00
Dir. Sales & Marketing	$ 94,953.33	$ 163,514.40	$ 281,138.50
Dir. Food & Beverage	$ 60,867.52	$ 110,864.05	$ 180,353.00
Dir. Human Resources	$ 77,660.11	$ 137,917.00	$ 275,104.13
Bonus			
General Manager	$ 0.00	$ 79,164.90	$ 325,307.59
Dir. Sales & Marketing	$ 0.00	$ 15,084.13	$ 86,060.21
Dir. Food & Beverage	$ 0.00	$ 4,215.00	$ 30,600.00
Dir. Human Resources	$ 0.00	$ 5,116.00	$ 27,539.27

Source: adapted from www.hvs.com/staticcontent/library.

Students who are interested in a career in gaming usually get specialized training and experience, which is available at gaming institutes. These are private schools that teach the skills needed to fill jobs such as croupier and casino manager. The majority of hospitality students, however, are drawn to a casino's hotel operations and food and beverage operations, which are extensive in the gaming industry. Career tracks in the rooms, food and beverage, and sales and marketing divisions—all leading to general management positions—are possible at casino hotels. Exhibit 3 shows average salaries for hospitality positions in gaming properties.

Casino Customers. Casinos often divide their customers into two broad groups: grind players and high-end players. Both are vital to the long-term health of a gaming establishment.

Grind players generally enter a casino with a budget. They have decided to play $25, $200, or some other relatively modest amount. When their budgeted amount is gone or when they have won enough to make them feel lucky, they happily leave. Gaming for them is a form of entertainment, and their losses are viewed as the price of that entertainment.

High-end players (often called "high rollers" or "high-stakes players") are a different breed of gambler. Gaming for them represents a chance to experience a meaningful risk, a big thrill, for which they are prepared to put down a large amount of money. It is difficult to estimate how much a high-end player will bet, because it depends on a casino's particular market. A player with $5,000 to spend during a weekend of gambling would typically be considered a high-roller. Some high-end players bet much more than that, however—sometimes as much as $500,000 on a single bet!

High-end players play regularly and expect to suffer big losses at times. They minimize their losses by negotiating with the casinos where they play regularly. Rebates, gifts, free guestrooms, and free food are four common ways casinos help ease the sting of losing. Often the value of these rebates and complimentary items can reach as high as 25 to 50 percent of what the player lost. Rebates are most common in baccarat, where typically the highest sums are wagered; rebates are negotiated in advance.

Casino managers have been known to present Rolex watches to high-end players and their spouses when they arrive at the hotel. These players may leave with a Lexus or BMW if their losses (the casino's winnings) are significant enough.

On the Las Vegas strip, the highest rollers of all are called "whales." One of these is Kerry Packer, an Australian media tycoon. During one July weekend at the Bellagio in Las Vegas, Packer reportedly lost $20 million, a loss so huge that it sent ripples through casino stocks on Wall Street and spurred heated debate back in Australia. "This is not someone else's money, this is mine and I'm entitled to spend it any way I choose," Packer said. "I understand that it's a lot of money and I understand how it comes as a shock to some. But the truth of the matter is that I like to have a bet now and then." Packer is also reputed to be one of the biggest winners in Las Vegas history; in 1995 he reportedly won more than $20 million at the MGM Grand. Packer likes baccarat and blackjack, and he plays hard and fast, betting up to $250,000 a hand and playing several hands at a time. He gambles for short stints, a few hours at a time, making him even more threatening to a casino's bottom line; if he gets ahead, he's out the door before the house can recover.[5]

Some high-end players have "personal representatives" who approach the casino's managers to negotiate terms before the players arrive. This representative asks questions like the following:

- What kind of action are you expecting? (How much money do you expect my client to play?)

- How many hours a day do you expect my client to play?

- What percent of my client's gambling losses will you cover through complimentary items?

- How long will you hold my client's markers?

- Will you give my client a discount if he or she pays off the markers immediately?

- Will you offer a suite and food and beverages for some of my client's friends and relatives who don't gamble but would like to stay at your hotel?

A personal representative usually receives a commission of ten percent of the money the casino wins from the client.

Casino Marketing. There are three separate markets that casinos generally target. The *high-end,* as we have discussed, is made up of those people who are willing to gamble $5,000 or more on every visit to a casino. Since they are, for the most part, experienced gamblers who play regularly and make credit arrangements in advance, they are well known to casino operators. This kind of gambler is recruited through agents and friends. Marketing to them consists mainly of offering rebates; complimentary lodging, food, and entertainment; and often gifts as well.

The *middle-range* customer can be described as the person who spends between $3,000 and $5,000 per gambling trip. Many casinos call this segment their core market. The key to marketing to these customers is first to be able to identify and track them—a task that has become much easier because of computer technology. Modern casinos use an automated rating system that tracks frequency of play, amount of time played, the particular games played, and the size of the average bet to assign a theoretical value or a certain number of points to players. With this information a direct-mail campaign can be created offering

The Wynn Las Vegas Resort and Country Club covers 215 acres and cost $2.7 billion to construct, making it the largest privately funded construction project in the nation. At 60 stories, the resort is one of the tallest buildings in Las Vegas. It opened its doors on April 28th, 2005.

everything from junkets to room discounts and special events for those who qualify. What is offered is calculated very carefully, based on how much a player is expected to (or agrees to) play. Some casino hotels comp up to 40 percent on table games and 30 percent on slot machines of the total amount the player gambles, whether the player wins, loses, or breaks even. This sum is applied against the room and food and beverage charges that the player incurs at the hotel.

Casino junkets are sometimes advertised or organized by brokers. Junkets are partially or completely paid trips to a casino. Guests generally agree, in advance, to play a certain amount of money over a certain period of time—usually four hours a day. Casino personnel monitor the action carefully. These junkets often lure first-time visitors who may then be invited back based on their observed performance.

Once a casino has identified one of these valuable middle-range players, it may send him or her a regular newsletter, along with invitations to play in special tournaments, join the casino's VIP club, and attend parties or events organized around special holidays.

Low-end players are very important for the health of any casino. Because their game of choice is often slot machines, they help create a busy ambience and can be very profitable, since the house odds on slots are significantly better than with other games. Bus tours, which are particularly popular in Atlantic City because of its proximity to New York City and Philadelphia, are the major marketing tool for this market. These tours operate on regular schedules. Players on a tour are usually refunded the amount of the bus fare in the form of vouchers good for free meals, show tickets, and rolls of quarters or tokens for playing the slots.

Typically, low-end players on bus tours spend about six hours in town. To keep players in a particular casino—so they won't wander off to visit a competitor down the street—casinos may offer free cocktails and hold frequent drawings for automobiles and cash.

Future marketing trends. As gaming continues to grow, gamblers have become more sophisticated. Casinos that cater to the grind market have been forced to offer complimentary items to grind players who've learned that part of the game is to recover some of your losses. Many casinos in Las Vegas have formed slot clubs. These clubs cost nothing to join. Members are issued electronic cards, which they enter into slot machines before starting to play. The cards record the volume of play, and players are awarded points based on how much they bet. These points can be exchanged for food, beverages, guestrooms, or gifts.

Casino Controls and Regulation. Because of the high volume of cash and credit transactions that occurs in casinos, controls within them must be stringent. There are many opportunities for customer and employee dishonesty. Because a casino's gambling operations do not earn money by selling services or products such as overnight accommodations or food, there is no way of measuring what has been "sold." Nor is it practical to record every single gambling transaction. So how does a casino make certain it keeps all of the cash it earns?

There are three kinds of controls that casinos use:

- *Accounting controls* include sophisticated formulas to calculate expected profitability by the game, by the table, and by the shift. As we have mentioned, there are numerous credit and cash control procedures that are carefully followed as well.

- *Equipment controls* involve equipment such as electronic surveillance cameras, safes, lock boxes, etc.

- *Human controls* are found at every staff level, from pit bosses to security guards. There are on-site inspectors (electronic as well as human) monitoring every part of the casino and every transaction.

Casinos are carefully regulated by the governments that sanction them. This is necessary to ensure that the government collects its share of the proceeds, as well as to discourage organized criminal activities. Legislation usually dictates the casino's size, types of games permitted, investigation and licensing of employees, hours and days of operation, marketing activities, and type and size of public space.

While regulations differ from state to state, the Nevada model of gaming control is widely copied. Nevada has two bodies that deal with gaming and report directly to the governor: the Gaming Commission and the Gaming Control Board. The Gaming Commission is charged with enacting necessary gaming regulations, issuing licenses, and handling disciplinary matters; the Gaming Control Board investigates applicants, enforces regulations, and audits the books and control systems of casinos.

Summary

The first recorded account of gambling dates back to early China. Today, casinos exist in many countries. Usually they are owned or controlled by the government.

Gambling was accepted early on in regions of the United States, and riverboats became popular venues. But by the early twentieth century, gambling had become illegal in most of the country. In 1931 it was revived in Nevada, and in 1976 it became legal in New Jersey. Today, gambling exists in most states in one form or another—if not throughout the state, it can be found on Indian reservations, riverboats, and offshore.

The best way to understand casino hotels is to think of them not as hotels with casinos attached, but rather as casinos with guestrooms, restaurants, shopping arcades, and even theme parks attached. In casino hotels, the hotel operation is subordinate to the gambling operation. As a result, many activities that come under the hotel manager's jurisdiction in non-casino hotels, such as food and beverage service and marketing, are separated from the hotel manager's duties in casino hotels. This may cause some tension between the hotel manager and the casino manager of a casino hotel.

There are basically two types of casino games: table games and slot machines. The most common table games include baccarat, blackjack, craps, and roulette. Of the table games, blackjack is the most popular in the United States, followed by craps and roulette. Slots are the most profitable games because of the percentage of money the casino gets to keep and the low labor requirements.

Casino employees include croupiers (dealers), floor people, pit bosses, and shift managers. From an operational point of view, casinos often divide their customers into two broad groups: grind players and high-end players. While those are the two kinds of customers playing, from a marketing point of view there are three separate markets that casinos generally target with their promotional activities: high-end, middle-range, and low-end. Different strategies are used to attract each market.

There are three kinds of controls that casinos use: accounting controls, equipment controls, and human controls. Casinos are carefully overseen by the governments that sanction them. While regulations differ from state to state, the Nevada model of gaming control is widely copied.

Endnotes

1. Dave Barry, *Tropic Magazine, The Miami Herald,* 31 January 1993.

2. Center for Gaming Research, http://gaming.unlv.edu, *Nevada Gaming Research Report,* December 2008.

3. Deutsche Bank, Gaming & Lodging, November 12, 2009.

4. Deborah Silver, "Lion's Share," *Restaurants & Institutions,* May 1, 2000.

5. Rebecca Trounson, "Big Spender Not Sweating Fat Vegas Loss," *Miami Herald,* October 2, 2000.

Key Terms

cashier's cage—Generally referred to simply as "the cage," this is the area within a casino where chips and cash are stored, where checks are cashed, where credit cards are accepted, and where markers are approved. It is the control center for the flow of chips to and from gaming tables.

credit slips—Forms that state the amount of excess chips at each gaming table at the end of a shift. Extra chips are returned to the cage along with the credit slips.

croupier—An attendant or dealer at a gaming table who conducts the game, collects bets, and pays the winning bets of players, using chips.

drop box—A locked box beneath each gaming table into which the cash and markers received from players are deposited. At the end of a shift, boxes are removed from the tables and brought to a count room, where they are opened and the contents counted under strict supervision.

fill slips—Forms that state the amount of chips short at each gaming table at the end of a shift.

floor people—Casino employees who supervise dealers. They are trained to enforce good dealing procedures, resolve disputes, and watch for cheaters.

grind players—Gamblers who budget a modest amount for gaming and usually leave the casino when that amount is used up. They view gaming as entertainment, and their losses as the price of that entertainment.

high-end players—Gamblers who gamble regularly, are prepared to gamble a large amount of money, and expect to suffer big losses at times. Often called "high rollers" or "high-stakes players," high-end players may bet as much as $500,000 on a single bet.

hold percentage—A calculation to determine the percentage of chips purchased at a gaming table by customers that is won back by the casino. It is calculated as follows: Win ÷ Drop = Hold. For example, if the table win is $1,000 and the table drop is $4,000, then the hold is 25 percent—that is, the casino won (kept) 25 percent of the chips purchased at that table.

markers—Printed or written IOUs that extend credit to a player; players can use them, rather than cash, to buy chips from dealers. Typically the casino agrees not to cash markers for 30 or 45 days, giving players time to deposit enough money in their bank account to cover their markers.

pit—A group of gaming tables within a casino that defines a management section. A pit can be made up of tables featuring the same game, or tables featuring a combination of games. For example, there may be four craps tables and four roulette tables in one pit, or simply eight craps tables.

pit boss—The manager who oversees a group of gaming tables, called a pit, within a casino.

slot drop—The amount of money put into a slot machine, less the amount paid out. For example, if $100 is put into a slot machine and $90 is paid out, the slot drop is $10 or 10 percent.

table drop—The amount of money and markers in a gaming table's drop box that players have exchanged for chips at that table. The table drop is a good measure of gaming activity within a casino.

table win—The amount bet at a gaming table minus the amount that is paid back to the players.

Review Questions

1. What is the early history of gaming? How did gaming in the United States evolve?

2. How are casino hotels organized and managed differently from other types of hotels?

3. What are the two basic types of casino games?

4. What are some of the key terms used in casino management?

5. What are the job responsibilities of croupiers? floor people? pit bosses?

6. What two broad groups of casino customers are vital to the long-term health of a gaming establishment, and what are their characteristics?

7. What types of incentives do casinos give to high-end, middle-range, and low-end players?

8. How are casino operations controlled and regulated?

Internet Sites

For more information, visit the following Internet sites. Remember that Internet addresses can change without notice. If the site is no longer there, you can use a search engine to look for additional sites.

Casinos

Bellagio
www.bellagiolasvegas.com

Caesars Palace
www.caesarspalace.com

Casino Windsor
www.casinowindsor.com

Circus Circus Las Vegas Hotel Resort
  and Casino
www.circuscircus.com

Excalibur Hotel and Casino
www.excaliburlasvegas.com

Foxwoods Resort Casino
www.foxwoods.com

Golden Nugget Casino
www.goldennugget.com

Harrahs Casino
www.harrahs.com

Imperial Palace Hotel/Casino
www.imperialpalace.com

Island Casino
www.islandcasino.com

Las Vegas Hilton
www.lv-hilton.com

Luxor Hotel and Casino
www.luxor.com

MGM Grand
www.mgmgrand.com

The Mirage
www.mirage.com

Monte Carlo Resort & Casino
www.monte-carlo.com

New York–New York Hotel & Casino
www.nynyhotelcasino.com

The Orleans Hotel & Casino
www.orleanscasino.com

Trump Taj Mahal
www.trumptaj.com

Treasure Island
www.treasureislandlasvegas.com

Tropicana Casino & Resort
www.tropicanalasvegas.com

Trump Entertainment Resorts
www.trumpcasinos.com

The Venetian
www.venetian.com

Wynn Las Vegas
www.wynnlasvegas.com

Part 3
HOSPITALITY MANAGEMENT

12

Managing and Leading Hospitality Enterprises

Competencies

1. Describe the basic goals and tasks of managers, and trace the development of management theories, beginning with the first management theorist, Robert Owen, and continuing with the classical school and the behavioral school of management. (pp. 354–364)

2. Explain the quantitative, systems, contingency, quality focus, and customer focus schools of management. (pp. 364–370)

3. Discuss quality management and summarize four basic strategies of effective leaders. (pp. 370–375)

Opposite page: Wingate Inn, Atlanta-Buckhead Georgia; photo courtesy of Wyndham Hotel Group.
Page 351: Loews Miami Beach Hotel; photo courtesy of Ernie Pick.

THIS CHAPTER BEGINS by defining the task of managers. It traces the evolution of management theory and discusses seven schools of management thought—the classical, behavioral, quantitative, systems, contingency, quality focus, and customer focus schools. The chapter then turns to reengineering and its application to hotels before concluding with a discussion about the importance of leadership.

A Manager's Job

It is usually easy to single out the managers in a hotel, restaurant, or club. Managers have titles. They usually have nice offices. Often their jobs come with perks such as company cars, country club memberships, and expense accounts. But what exactly do managers do? This question cannot be answered precisely or easily. Managers in different businesses do different things, and the entire field of management is changing rapidly as the world moves from a manufacturing-based to a service-based economy.

Peter Drucker, probably America's greatest management theorist, says a manager has two broad goals. The first is "creation of a true whole that is larger than the sum of its parts, a productive entity that turns out more than the sum of the resources put into it."[1] Drucker compares a manager to a conductor of an orchestra who is able to pull together the music played by each musician into a beautiful symphony. Unlike conductors, who have a composer's score in front of them and only have to interpret it, managers must do more, says Drucker. They must write their own score, and in that sense managers are composers as well as conductors. On the other hand, the Four Seasons hotel company sees each of its managers as "a coach-player, someone deeply involved in the experience of both customers and employees alike," says Executive Vice President Nick Mutton.[2]

The second broad goal of a manager is to "harmonize in every decision and action the requirements of [the] immediate and long-range future." In other words, a manager must consider not only the needs of today but also the needs of next year and beyond. "He not only has to prepare for crossing distant bridges—he has to build them long before he gets there."[3]

These two goals separate managers from supervisors. Supervisors are generally concerned with implementing established policies. Although supervisors may act like orchestra conductors at times—that is, lead and direct their employees—it is not their job to compose the music as well; that has already been done by higher-level managers. Nor do supervisors worry about the long-range future; their job is to take care of what is going on today.

This is not to imply that a manager does not do supervisory work. Managers do other things besides manage, but they always focus their activities on creating and harmonizing—or should, if they want to be effective managers.

Management Tasks

According to Drucker, a manager has five basic tasks:

- Setting objectives
- Organizing
- Motivating and communicating

- Measuring performance
- Developing people[4]

Let's take a look at each of these in turn.

Setting Objectives. A manager sets objectives. Unlike a worker or supervisor, a manager must decide what goals and objectives his or her department or organization should strive to achieve. The manager then decides what work must be done to reach those objectives and, lastly, directs and communicates with his or her employees to get the work done.

The Ritz-Carlton Hotel Company has twice won the Malcolm Baldrige National Quality Award, an award established by the United States Congress to recognize U.S. companies that have achieved excellence through adherence to quality-improvement programs. Ritz-Carlton has a set of "Service Values" that embody the service objectives of its managers (see Exhibit 1). The "Service Values" card, a pocket-size card that all staff members must carry with them while at work, clearly states in the "Credo" the company's objective to create a certain kind of hotel:

> The Ritz-Carlton is a place where the genuine care and comfort of our guests is our highest mission.

> We pledge to provide the finest personal service and facilities for our guests who will always enjoy a warm, relaxed, yet refined ambience.

> The Ritz-Carlton experience enlivens the senses, instills well-being, and fulfills even the unexpressed wishes and needs of our guests.[5]

Organizing. A manager organizes. A manager must analyze the work that his or her department is responsible for, divide that work into various jobs, and assign the jobs to employees, some of whom might have to be trained. All the classic management texts emphasize that managers must know how to delegate. According to author Wess Roberts, even Attila the Hun, a brilliant fifth-century leader who forged a conglomeration of 70,000 barbarians into a well-disciplined army, understood this concept. Attila is credited with having these ideas:

- Chieftains should never delegate responsibilities necessitating their direct attention.
- Those actions that don't require a chieftain's direct handling are appropriately delegated to the one most able to fulfill the assignment.
- Realize that a chieftain cannot accomplish every responsibility of his office by himself. Should he prove otherwise, a leader should understand that he is, in fact, chieftain over little or nothing at all.[6]

Motivating and Communicating. A manager must turn a group of individuals into a team that works together. To do this, managers must have excellent "people skills." They must be good at listening to employees with problems and helping them work out solutions. They must make wise and fair decisions regarding compensation and promotions. They must instinctively understand how to encourage and reward superior performance.

At Lettuce Entertain You Enterprises (LEYE), the Chicago-based restaurant company that operates in five states with many different concepts, owner Richard Melman believes keeping people happy is one of the most important reasons for LEYE's success. LEYE's partners are granted an equity stake. All employees qualify for such benefits as divorce therapy, while getting married earns you a $50 bonus. New parents get a $100 check and a silver spoon from Tiffany's.[7]

Exhibit 1   Ritz-Carlton's Service Values

THREE STEPS OF SERVICE

1.
A warm and sincere greeting.
Use the guest's name.

2.
Anticipation and fulfillment
of each guest's needs.

3.
Fond farewell.
Give a warm good-bye
and use the guest's name.

MOTTO

"We are Ladies and Gentlemen serving Ladies and Gentlemen."

THE RITZ-CARLTON®
CREDO

The Ritz-Carlton is a
place where the genuine care
and comfort of our guests is
our highest mission.

We pledge to provide the finest
personal service and facilities
for our guests who will always
enjoy a warm, relaxed, yet
refined ambience.

The Ritz-Carlton experience
enlivens the senses, instills
well-being, and fulfills even
the unexpressed wishes
and needs of our guests.

THE RITZ-CARLTON®
SERVICE VALUES

I AM PROUD TO BE
RITZ-CARLTON

1. I build strong relationships
and create Ritz-Carlton guests
for life.

2. I am always responsive to the
expressed and unexpressed
wishes and needs of our
guests.

3. I am empowered to create
unique, memorable and personal experiences for our
guests.

4. I understand my role in
achieving the Key Success
Factors, embracing Commu-
nity Footprints and creating
The Ritz-Carlton Mystique.

5. I continuously seek opportunities to innovate and improve
The Ritz-Carlton experience.

6. I own and immediately resolve
guest problems.

7. I create a work environment of
teamwork and lateral service
so that the needs of our guests
and each other are met.

8. I have the opportunity to
continuously learn and grow.

9. I am involved in the planning
of the work that affects me.

10. I am proud of my professional
appearance, language and
behavior.

11. I protect the privacy and
security of our guests, my
fellow employees and the
company's confidential information and assets.

12. I am responsible for uncompromising levels of cleanliness
and creating a safe and acci-
dent-free environment.

This is a partial reproduction of a small eight-sided card all Ritz-Carlton staff members are expected to carry whenever they are working, to remind them of the importance of serving customers well.
(Courtesy of The Ritz-Carlton Hotel Company, Atlanta, Georgia.)

Managers must know how to communicate effectively, both orally and in writing.

Above all, managers should know how to communicate—both orally and in writing—with their superiors and peers as well as with the people who report to them. The need for communication skills is often not recognized by those who want to become managers. Because of the nature of their jobs, managers have to "sell" their ideas to others. Selling an idea requires abilities ranging from writing a convincing memo or report to standing in front of a group and making a well-organized presentation. Communication skills can be developed through training and practice.

Measuring Performance. Managers decide what factors are important to the success of their organizations and then establish standards against which to measure individual or group performance. Domino's Pizza measures performance weekly by calling back a number of consumers who ordered pizzas from them. Store managers at Taco Bell spend most of their time out front where they can hear customer comments about the quality of their operations.

Managers at Marriott, besides regularly taking a scientific sampling of guests and non-guests, pay a great deal of attention to what is known as the "GSI"—Guest Satisfaction Index. This index is compiled from a survey that guests voluntarily fill out. As J. W. "Bill" Marriott, Jr., chairman of Marriott Corporation, puts it: "Measurement of customer perception causes a lot of focus just where we want it, on the customer."[8]

To measure performance, managers must collect statistical, financial, and qualitative data on how an organization or a department is doing, and then analyze and interpret the data for subordinates, superiors, and colleagues.

The Xerox Corporation pioneered a measurement technique that has been adapted by service companies in many industries, including hotel and restaurant chains. Xerox calls it **"competitive benchmarking":**

> Competitive benchmarking is the continuous process of measuring our products, services, and practices against our toughest competitors or those companies recognized as leaders. Benchmarking is a structured approach for looking outside our organization by studying other organizations and adapting the best outside practices to complement our internal operations and creative new ideas. It is an ongoing management process that requires constant updating and the integration of competitive information, practices, and performance into decision-making and communication functions at all levels of our business.[9]

Companies like Ritz-Carlton, Marriott, McDonald's, and Taco Bell all use benchmarking as a regular measurement tool. This is one reason for managers to acquire a sound knowledge of marketing research techniques, statistical analysis, and communication skills.

Developing People. A manager develops people, including himself or herself. Continual learning enables people to move ahead. Along with outside seminars and educational programs, ongoing on-the-job training is one of the main tools managers use to develop their employees. At Starbucks, partners are given extensive training in product knowledge, guiding principles for success, personal empowerment, and the importance of creating positive customer experiences. In fact, unlike most Fortune 500 companies, Starbucks spends more on training than it does on advertising.[10]

Successful managers recognize that the people who work for them are their most important resource. They also know that setting an example is the surest and best way to develop people. It is by following a good leader that people learn how to become leaders themselves. "What a manager does can be analyzed systematically," Peter Drucker said. "What a manager has to be able to do has to be learned (though perhaps not always taught). But [there is] one quality [that] cannot be learned, one qualification that the manager cannot acquire but must bring with him. It is not genius; it is character."[11] J. Willard Marriott, founder of the hotel chain bearing his name, believed the same. In a letter to his son when Bill Jr. took over the reins of the company, Marriott senior wrote, "A leader should have character, be an example in all things. This is his greatest influence."[12]

The Evolution of Management Theories

Although discovering the best way to manage people and work has been a concern dating back thousands of years, it was not until the nineteenth century, after the Industrial Revolution in England and the industrialization of other countries had begun, that the subject of management was systematically studied and written about.

Probably the first modern management theorist was a Scottish cotton mill manager, Robert Owen (1771–1858). Owen thought that a manager's job was to institute reform. He believed that the way to motivate his workers and increase their productivity was to treat them better. He reduced the length of the standard working day to 10½ hours, refused to hire children under the age of 10, and created an incentive pay system based on daily evaluations of an employee's work.

After Owen, other industrialists and theorists contributed their views about management. Over the years, seven schools of thought on management have emerged:

- The classical school
- The behavioral school
- The quantitative school
- The systems school
- The contingency school
- The quality focus school
- The customer focus school

The Classical School

The founder of the **classical school** was Frederick W. Taylor (1856–1915), an American industrial engineer who managed the Midvale Steel Company in Philadelphia. Taylor revolutionized the manufacturing process by coming up with scientific principles of production. According to Taylor's theories of scientific management, there was one best way to do every job; if managers analyzed what needed to be done to perform a job, they could come up with that best or most efficient way of performing it. Taylor believed that workers should be trained to do their jobs using only the "best way" that had been devised by management, and paid according to how fast and how well they performed. He suggested using a "differential rate system of piece work," under which one of two rates would be paid for a job: "a high price per piece, in case the work is finished in the shortest possible time and in perfect condition, and a low price, if it takes a longer time to do a job, or if there are any imperfections in the work."[13] Taylor also advocated "discharging workers and lowering the wages of the more stubborn men who refused to make any improvement." In 1912, in testimony taken by a committee of the House of Representatives investigating the practicality of using the "Taylor System" in government, Taylor compared workers to horses and said that just as a trotting horse was a "first class" horse not suited for hauling coal, so there were "first class" men who were better suited for some jobs than other men and so should be given those jobs.[14]

While Taylor's methods were widely hailed, many thought his approach was too hard-nosed and criticized him for comparing people to horses and for failing to take into

Robert Owen (left) was born in Scotland in 1771 and is considered perhaps the first modern management theorist. Among other reforms, he reduced the length of the standard working day to 10 1/2 hours and refused to hire children under ten years old. Frederick Taylor (1856–1915) was an American industrial engineer who revolutionized the manufacturing process by formulating scientific principles of production.

account the needs of workers. Because they felt that pushing workers to produce more was in some cases irrational and might ultimately result in fewer jobs, both unions and workers were critical of Taylor's ideas. In a strike at the Watertown Arsenal, government workers refused to adhere to what they called Taylor's "Stopwatch System" on the grounds that "it is not a question of what a job is worth, but is based upon the quickest time that one can make."[15] Taylor defended his point of view by saying that if labor and management cooperated, his system would work.

A one-time associate of Taylor's, Henry Gantt (1861–1919), added to Taylor's thinking by devising a control system for production-scheduling so that managers could forecast how much work should be expected from each employee. His Gantt Chart, which identifies work progress and deadlines in a visual form, is still used today.

Frank Gilbreth (1868–1924) and his wife, Lillian Gilbreth (1878–1972), contributed much to the classical school of management. Frank was an efficiency expert; Lillian was an industrial psychologist. By doing a series of motion studies, Frank was able to reduce the number of motions needed to lay a brick from 18 to 5. If bricklayers were trained to lay bricks using Gilbreth's five-step system, their productivity would triple. Gilbreth's research was a logical continuation of Taylor's idea that a "best way" could be found for every job. Lillian concentrated her efforts on studying worker fatigue. She advocated standard work days, lunch periods, and regular breaks for all employees. The Gilbreths also developed what they called a **"three position plan of promotion,"** in which workers would do their own jobs while at the same time preparing themselves for promotion by learning the next higher job, and also training workers below them to take over their job when the promotion actually came. That way every worker would always be looking forward to, and preparing for, a better job.

While one group of classical management theorists was developing systems to increase worker efficiency and productivity, another group was concerned with organizational theory—that is, defining the duties and functions of managers. The leader in this area was Henri Fayol (1841–1925), a French engineer and the manager of a large coal mining enterprise. Fayol was interested in what managers contributed to a business and how businesses were organized. From his studies, Fayol came up with a number of management principles. Fayol believed that these principles could be applied to any situation. Much of what we consider to be general management theory today was first articulated by Fayol in his 14 principles of management (see Exhibit 2). In Fayol's view, the manager's primary role was to be a regulator and integrator, taking all of an organization's rules, structures, and traditions and making them work together.

In summary, theorists of the classical school were mostly concerned with productivity. According to these theorists, workers were rational people interested primarily in making money. The classical school of management emphasizes satisfying employees' economic needs (pay them better for doing more work) and physical needs (don't tire them out) but ignores their social needs for respect and recognition. While many of the ideas developed by Taylor and his followers are still used today, we recognize now that scientific management ignores the human desire for job satisfaction. In service businesses such as hotels and restaurants, this human factor can make the difference between providing a good product and a bad one.

The Behavioral School

In recent years, many managers have recognized that the classical approach to management has serious limitations, especially when applied to service industries. To begin with, the

Exhibit 2   Fayol's 14 Principles of Management

1. Division of work. In Fayol's words, specialization leads to "more and better work with the same effort." This concept eventually led to the modern assembly line. Fayol believed specialization applied to managers as well as workers.

2. Authority and responsibility. Fayol defined authority and responsibility as "the right to give orders and the power to exact obedience." Managers need both authority and responsibility to accomplish things.

3. Discipline. Discipline is a function of leadership. Poor leadership produces poor discipline. Managers should enter into fair agreements with employees, and then both sides must respect and adhere to all the rules. When the rules are violated, managers must, for the well-being of the business, apply certain sanctions.

4. Unity of command. "For any action whatsoever an employee should receive orders from one superior only," said Fayol.

5. Unity of direction. Those activities in an organization having the same objective should be under the direction of one person with a single plan. In other words, one person should be in charge of sales, another finance, and so forth.

6. Subordination of individual interest to general interest. The interests of a single employee or group of employees are less important than the interests of the whole organization.

7. Payment of personnel. Workers should be paid at a rate that is fair and affords satisfaction to both employers and employees. Fayol advocated (1) paying workers by either time or piece or by the job, (2) giving bonuses, and (3) providing for employee welfare through better working conditions. He did not favor profit sharing except for senior managers, on the grounds that it was impractical.

8. Centralization. "The issue of centralization or decentralization is a simple question of proportion; it is the matter of finding the optimum degree of centralization for the particular concern." Managers must centralize things enough so that they can maintain control, but they also must give workers some authority so that they can perform their jobs. This balance will vary in different organizations, so managers must be flexible and seek the best degree of centralization.

9. Scalar chain. This is "the chain of superiors in a firm ranging from the ultimate authority to the lowest ranks." Generally, Fayol felt it was a mistake to deviate from this without reason, but he also believed that there were times when this might be necessary.

10. Order. "There must be a place appointed for each thing and each thing must be in its appointed place." Similarly, "there must be an appointed place for every employee....As in the case of orderly material arrangement, charts or plans facilitate the establishment and control of human arrangements."

11. Equity. Managers must be impartial and at the same time understanding in dealing with their employees. Fayol advocated both kindliness and justice.

12. Stability of tenure of personnel. A high employee turnover rate is not good for any organization. Organizations should have policies and plans that help them retain workers.

13. Initiative. Employees must be encouraged to show initiative on the job. "Thinking out a plan and ensuring its success are two of the keenest satisfactions that an intelligent person can experience," said Fayol. While some mistakes might occur, allowing employee initiative injects zeal and energy into an enterprise.

14. Esprit de corps. "Union is strength." Promoting team spirit is a key factor in good management. "Dividing enemy forces to weaken them is clever, but dividing one's own team is a grave sin against the business." Fayol also advocated oral communications rather than written ones because written ones might be misunderstood.

Source: Adapted from Henri Fayol, *General and Industrial Management,* revised by Irwin Gray (New York: Institute of Electrical and Electronic Engineers Press, 1984), pp. 61–82.

relatively stable and predictable business environment enjoyed by the classical theorists is a thing of the past. In today's business world, chaos and ambiguity are the norm. This means that rigid systems and rules no longer work as well as they used to. Managers must be more flexible and adaptable. In service industries especially, regulations and formal procedures may interfere with an employee's ability to satisfy consumer expectations. In addition, employees today are better educated and want to make their own decisions as much as possible.

For these and other reasons there has been a movement toward a human relations or **behavioral school of management.** Behaviorists attempt to find ways of motivating workers besides using the rules, systems, and wages proposed by classical management thinkers.

One of the first behaviorists was Chester I. Barnard (1886–1961), president of the New Jersey Telephone Company. Barnard believed that only when the goals of employees as well as employers were being satisfied could an organization grow and prosper. People want to work within an organization, said Barnard, because they want to accomplish more than they can do alone. Therefore, if management can mesh the personal goals of its employees with the organization's overall goals, a company should be successful.

A landmark in the development of behavioral management theory occurred when George Elton Mayo (1880–1949), a Harvard Business School professor, evaluated some studies on human behavior in work settings performed at the Western Electric Company's plant in Hawthorne, Illinois. Conducted between 1924 and 1933, these **"Hawthorne studies"** revolutionized the way managers looked at human relations problems. The Western Electric company designed and conducted the experiments to assess the effects of lighting conditions on workers. In the first experiment (which spanned three years), two groups of workers were segregated from the rest and each group was placed in its own "test room." Each test room started out with the same amount of light, with both groups performing the same task. For one group the light level was gradually increased over a period of time and, as expected, the group's productivity increased. Next the light level was gradually lowered and, to the surprise of the researchers, productivity increased again. Moreover, in the other test room, where the light remained constant, productivity also increased! The company's puzzled researchers decided that there must be other factors at work besides the amount of light.

At that point the researchers started a second series of experiments, this time looking at other variables that might be affecting productivity. Five workers were placed in a separate test room and given varied rest periods, shorter work days, a shorter work week, and higher wages. The researchers acted as supervisors in this set of experiments and allowed the workers a say in deciding when and how long their rest periods would be. On the whole, performance improved, but there were unexpected variations.

In the midst of these experiments, Mayo and his associates became involved, and they began to suspect that the real agent of change was the human factor:

> The records of the test room showed a continual improvement in performance of the operators regardless of the [experimental] changes made during the study. It was also noticed that there was a marked improvement in their attitude toward their work and working environment. This simultaneous improvement in attitude and effectiveness indicated that there might be a definite relationship between them. In other words we could more logically attribute the increase in efficiency to a betterment of morale than to any of the...alterations made in the course of the experiment....Comment after comment from the girls indicates that

they have been relieved of the nervous tension under which they previously worked. They have ceased to regard the man in charge as a boss...[and] they have a feeling that their increased production is in some way related to the distinctly freer, happier, and more pleasant working environment.[16]

Subsequently, 21,126 workers of the plant were interviewed over a period of three years to check the findings of the test group. Mayo and his associates eventually determined that their findings were valid. The employees worked harder and more efficiently when they knew that management was interested in them and that they had the ear of a sympathetic supervisor. This was far more important in motivating them than was the level of lighting or even the amount of money they were paid. This finding—that there was a clear link between supervision, morale, and productivity—was subsequently labeled the **Hawthorne effect,** and Mayo's book, *The Human Problems of an Industrial Civilization,* became a bestseller in business circles.

The idea that managers should concentrate on employee motivation was developed further by Abraham Maslow (1908–1970).[17] Maslow's idea was that we all have a system of priorities in our needs. Maslow defined a hierarchy of needs and theorized that we try to satisfy our needs progressively—that is, we satisfy one group of needs first because they are the most basic (or strongest), then go on to the second group, and so forth.

Group I needs are physiological. These are our most powerful needs, and until they are satisfied we are not interested in anything else. They are our needs for water, food, and shelter.

Group II needs are the safety needs—our needs for protection and security. As soon as we are satisfied that we have a roof over our heads and something to eat, these needs emerge as primary.

Social or belonging and love needs are in Group III. Once we have food, shelter, and security, the next thing we hunger for is love, affection, and a feeling that we belong to a community or group. These needs are all part of a need to relate to others around us.

Group IV needs are esteem needs. All of us need to think well of ourselves and have others think well of us. We want to achieve some degree of independence, and be recognized and appreciated for our work.

Self-actualization needs make up Group V. These are needs for fulfillment—to express ourselves and reach our full potential. These needs are the highest of all and they emerge only after all other needs are met.

Another theory of how human beings are motivated was suggested by Douglas McGregor (1906–1964), a professor of psychology at Massachusetts Institute of Technology. McGregor said managers tend to believe one or the other of two basic sets of assumptions about human nature and behavior, and these assumptions governed a manager's behavior and management style.

McGregor labeled the first set of assumptions **Theory X,** and said they represented the "traditional view of direction and control." Theory X assumptions are:

- The average human being has an inherent dislike of work and will avoid it if possible.

- Because people dislike work, most people must be coerced, controlled, directed, and threatened with punishment to get them to put forth adequate effort toward the achievement of organizational objectives.

- The average employee prefers to be directed, wishes to avoid responsibility, has relatively little ambition, and wants security above all.[18]

McGregor thought that while most managers believed these assumptions, they were really nothing more than self-fulfilling prophecies. In fact, McGregor said, if more managers would change their assumptions to **Theory Y,** which is based on a whole different set of ideas, workers would behave entirely differently. The assumptions of Theory Y are:

- Working is as natural as playing or resting. The average human being does not inherently dislike work.

- External control and the threat of punishment are not the only means of encouraging employees to work toward organizational objectives. Employees will exercise self-direction and self-control in the service of objectives to which they are committed.

- Commitment to objectives is a function of the rewards associated with achieving those objectives. The most significant of such rewards—the satisfaction of ego and self-actualization needs—can be direct products of efforts directed toward organizational objectives.

In the final analysis, McGregor believed that managers who did not try to control their employees through formal structures, but instead tried to motivate them by encouraging and challenging them, would be the most successful.

The Quantitative School

While the behavioral school of thought founded by Barnard and Mayo influenced a great number of managers, there were still some unanswered questions. For one thing, not all companies that improved working conditions achieved the expected results. It turned out that in many instances the corporate culture, salary levels, or the way the company was organized played a more important part in determining motivation and productivity. In other words, the problem of how to motivate workers turned out to be much more complex than was realized by any of the early behavioral researchers.

A new approach that would integrate the management ideas of the classical and behavioral schools was needed. To many, the answer lay in a mathematical approach to management problems, using models created during World War II when scientists developed radar, missiles, and the atomic bomb. This approach depended on two cornerstones, *operations research (OR)* and *management information systems (MIS).* Managers trained in the **quantitative school** use complex mathematical decision–making models based on consumer research to determine the probability of success for a new restaurant location or to project the optimum number of guestrooms for a given hotel site. From this they are able to determine the cost of construction, the number of employees needed to operate the property, and the expected return on investment (ROI) for the owners. Management information systems give hotel and restaurant managers the information they need to make decisions. For example, reservation systems project occupancy rates and income for future periods of time so that hotel managers can modify their marketing activities accordingly. Property management systems report how income and expenses change on a daily basis. Revenue management systems guide managers in setting optimum rates.

A major problem with quantitative management is that it tends to direct a manager's attention to short-term goals such as achieving the lowest possible costs and the highest profits. Doing this often results in ignoring such critical factors as employee morale, employee turnover, and—most important—customer satisfaction. Moreover, important activities such as training and R&D (research and development) are often put on the back burner because they don't make an obvious contribution to the bottom line. In recent years

MBA programs at major universities have modified their curriculum to de-emphasize the role of quantitative methods in decision-making. While quantitative methods remain an important management tool, they should be regarded as just one weapon in a manager's arsenal of techniques.

The Systems School

According to the **systems school,** a company is a system composed of many interrelated departments, which in turn is part of a larger external environment (made up of such things as competing companies, the economy in general, and societal values) that influences its behavior. Managers cannot act independently—what they can or cannot accomplish depends on other managers inside their company and on outside environmental factors. For example, the decisions made by a hotel's food and beverage director as to what kind of food will be served and at what price will affect the types of groups that the sales department can attract to the hotel. Similarly, the number of rooms the sales department sells to groups affects the number of rooms that the rooms department has to sell to individual travelers. All of these decisions are affected by the external environment—how many other hotels are nearby, what their rates are, how strongly they are competing for each other's business, and consumer needs and wants.

Managers who favor the systems school view their organizations in terms of *internal systems* and *external systems.* Internal systems are not individuals or departments, but rather a means by which a service is delivered. For example, for a guest to check into a hotel, several departments are involved. The housekeeping department is responsible for seeing that the room is clean and ready on time. The front desk is responsible for checking in the guest and assigning a room. Someone from the uniformed service department escorts the guest to the room. This is a process involving many functions and several departments. The output is the guest settling down comfortably in his or her room.

External systems are those outside the hotel that the manager has no control over. These include economic conditions, government regulation, and actions by competitors. Suppliers, too, are part of external systems.

Internal and external systems are connected, and when they interact and cooperate with each other they can often produce *synergy,* which simply means that the sum of their actions may be greater than their parts. For example, hotels working together with each other and the local government may be able to reduce crime in an area and thus make it a safer and more attractive tourist destination.

Systems managers understand that they must view their organizations as a whole, not in parts. This is similar to the environmentalist view that we all live on Spaceship Earth and mutual cooperation is necessary for our survival. Managers who think this way not only look at the trees but see the forest. They understand that the quality of service their facility produces is the result of every input that is involved in the final output, which means every person's work has an impact on the final outcome. From this, as we will see, comes an important concept in the achievement and management of quality.

The Contingency School

The **contingency school,** sometimes referred to as the **situational management school,** recognizes that every situation is different and every manager is different. Contingency theorists suggest that there are few management principles that are as universal as Taylor, Fayol, and Mayo believed. Managers must be pragmatic and decide what is likely to achieve the needed results in any given situation. The solution may use classical, behavioral, or quantitative management ideas, depending on what the problem is and what resources are available to the manager to solve it. Managers must constantly adapt to changing circumstances, and the way to do this is to be flexible, keep an open mind, and change one's own behavior to fit the situation at hand.

Managers who are comfortable with the contingency theory are often especially adept in managing diverse work groups that contain people with different ethnic backgrounds. They can also do well working in foreign countries, where they are likely to be placed in situations where traditional management approaches don't work. These managers are often comfortable with change because they are willing to experiment and try new approaches.

One example of this kind of outlook can be found in U.S. managers who have tried to understand and borrow from Japanese management techniques. For example, Japanese managers and employees believe in the concepts of *kawaiso* and *kaizen. Kawaiso*, literally translated, means "pathetic" or "pitiable," but in management it refers to the obligation of a manager to take care of his or her employees, much as fathers or mothers are obligated to protect and care for their children. *Kaizen* refers to the Japanese belief that it is a worthy and important objective to continually search for a better way to do things and to thereby improve one's self. These two beliefs imply a reciprocal agreement between managers and workers. Managers are obliged to help and protect their employees, and employees are expected to help managers get the job done better by seeking better ways to do it and by improving their own skills.

The Quality Focus School

In the early 1980s, at the same time the contingency school was gaining popularity, U.S. managers began to focus their attention on quality management. It was a logical step, since the systems approach had highlighted the idea that service was a process, not a function, and that meant that the chain of events that constituted the process could be no stronger than its weakest link. Moreover, the success of Japanese management techniques, especially in the automobile industry, turned American eyes westward to more closely examine the reasons behind Japan's success.

What they found was that the Japanese had been enormously influenced by the work of two Americans, both in their 80s, whose ideas had received little attention in the United States. These two unsung quality management champions were W. Edwards Deming and Joseph Juran. A third American, Philip Crosby (who had started his own quality consulting business after working for ITT as vice president of quality), was also preaching the importance of quality and getting a considerable amount of attention. Each of these men had their own distinctive approach to quality management.[19]

Deming, an electrical engineer who first visited Japan in 1950, introduced the revolutionary concept that consumers were not only a part of any production line, they were the most important part. Furthermore, he told his audiences that the way to make a profit in business was to attract repeat customers who would tell others about your product or service. Deming summarized his views in a 14-point program that told managers what they needed to do if they expected to run quality operations:

> To begin, managers had to put aside their preoccupations with today to make sure there was a tomorrow. They had to orient themselves to continuous improvement of products and services to meet customers' needs and stay ahead of the competition. They had to innovate constantly and commit resources to

W. Edwards Deming, considered one of the founders of the quality focus school of management, was an electrical engineer whose ideas about quality helped bring about the Japanese economic resurgence of the 1980s and subsequently influenced American businesses.

support innovation and continuous quality improvement. They had to build quality in. They had to break down department and worker-supervisor barriers. They had to rid themselves of numerical targets and quotas and instead had to concentrate on improving processes, giving workers clear standards for acceptable work, as well as the tools needed to achieve it. Finally, they had to create a climate free of finger-pointing and fear, which blocks cooperative identification and solution of problems.[20]

Deming believed that, if managers did all of these things, not only would they achieve quality, but productivity would increase as well, because by building in quality you got the job done right the first time and thus had none of the costs associated with having to do it over or having to replace lost customers.

Joseph Juran, who first visited Japan in 1953 (just three years after Deming), told his audiences that the definition for quality was "fitness for use." In other words, said Juran, people said that a product or service had quality if they could be sure it would do what they expected it to do, the way they expected it to be done. The way quality was achieved was by utilizing a comprehensive approach that touched everything a company did—from designing its product or service, to developing the delivery system, to its relations with customers and even suppliers. Juran developed a cost-of-quality (COQ) accounting system. He identified four different kinds of quality costs:

- Internal failure costs (from defects identified before the product or service was delivered)
- External failure costs (from defects discovered after the product or service was delivered)
- Appraisal costs (for assessing the condition of the ingredients or materials used)
- Prevention costs (for keeping the defects from occurring in the first place)

In a restaurant, for example, an internal cost might be food that was improperly cooked in the kitchen and was replaced before it reached the guest. External costs might be the cost of replacing an order that was wrong, causing a server to bring french fries to a guest who ordered a baked potato. Appraisal costs could be the costs associated with inspecting food purchased from suppliers that did not meet specifications for quality, size, or amount. Examples of prevention costs are the costs of training and communicating with employees and suppliers so that defects in quality don't occur in the first place. Juran believed that it was not economically feasible to achieve zero defects because at some point the costs associated with doing so would become too high. He advocated an approach that would achieve optimal quality on a continuing basis.

Philip Crosby liked to argue that "quality is free." Crosby defined quality as "conformance to requirements" and believed that any product which consistently reproduced its design specifications was of high quality. Ultimately, the goal of quality improvement was zero defects, to be achieved through prevention, rather than after-the-fact inspection.[21] Crosby believed that, to achieve quality improvement, top management had to change its thinking. If managers expected imperfection, they would get it, for workers would understand that managers expected imperfection and tolerated it. But if managers set zero defects as their goal and communicated that standard to everyone who worked for them, then it would be possible to achieve perfection. To achieve perfection, companies had to focus on changing their corporate culture so that employees would become involved in and commit themselves to the idea of delivering the perfect product or service every time, no matter what it took. Unlike Juran, who focused on statistical and analytical tools for measuring the cost of quality, Crosby said if you focus on people instead of numbers you can achieve zero defects. Prevention costs will always be lower than the costs of correcting mistakes and losing customers, Crosby believed. Therefore, quality always costs less than controlling and correcting errors.

Ritz-Carlton officials have said that the ideas of Deming, Juran, and Crosby influenced them when setting up their own quality program.[22] Ritz-Carlton managers created a system for problem-solving that employees are expected to use:

1. Identifying and selecting the problem
2. Analyzing the problem
3. Generating potential solutions
4. Selecting and planning the solution
5. Implementing the solution
6. Evaluating the solution

Note the emphasis in this sequence on eliminating the problem. Ritz-Carlton strives for "100 percent compliance to customer requirements." Computerized guest profiles showing the preferences of repeat guests are kept on file. Managers receive daily quality production reports based on data from 720 work areas in each hotel. All workers are directed to continually identify defects throughout the hotel and are expected and empowered to solve guest problems as soon as they hear about them, doing "whatever it takes"—even if the problem involves a different department than the one they work for. No matter what their normal duties are, other employees must assist if aid is requested by a fellow worker who is responding to a guest complaint or wish.

Stories about the lengths the staff will go to satisfy guests abound. Nancy and Harvey Heffner of Manhattan were quoted in the *New York Times* as saying, "They can't do enough to please you." When the couple's son became sick in Naples, Florida, the hotel staff brought him hot tea with honey at all hours of the night. When Mr. Heffner had to fly home on business for a day and his return flight was delayed, a driver for the hotel waited in the lobby most of the night.[23]

Ritz-Carlton is just one of many companies that embraced the **quality focus school.** Two McKinsey & Company consultants, Thomas J. Peters and Robert H. Waterman, Jr., wrote *In Search of Excellence,* a study of 43 excellent, large companies. In summarizing their findings, Peters said, "In the private or public sector, in big business or small, we observe that there are only two ways to create and sustain superior performance over the long haul. First, take exceptional care of your customers...via superior service and superior quality. Secondly, constantly innovate. That's it. There are no alternatives in achieving long term superior performance, or sustaining strategic competitive advantage, as business strategists call it."[24]

Peters and Waterman turned the management spotlight onto customers and suggested that while all of the various management theories and systems had their place, managers must never forget that they are in business to satisfy customers, and all the systems in the world to motivate employees and organize them using scientific principles will not succeed unless the final outcome is a satisfied customer. Although quantitative management theorists generally recognized the importance of the external environment—including customers—Peters and Waterman said that customers should be the *most* important consideration when managers decide how to run their business. Peters, in fact, suggested that companies start drawing their organization charts upside down with customers at the top and presidents on the bottom![25] Under the Peters and Waterman model of excellent management, the principles of scientific management apply only so long as they help the company please the customer, and even wages should be tied to customer satisfaction. We have come a long way from Frederick Taylor, who believed in paying workers according to how well they met their manager's expectations, not their customers'.

The Customer Focus School

The **customer focus school** is just a logical extension of the quality management school and the work of Peters and Waterman. We now have a better understanding of the needs and wants of today's consumers and thus are better able to create services and products that address them. The marketing research firm Yankelovich, in its publication *National Leisure Travel MONITOR 2000,* outlines what it calls a revolution going on in the way companies market and operate hospitality products. "In order to be successful in this evolving environment, marketers of travel services must come to grips with the fact that market effectiveness in the 21st century will be driven by a new reality: a reborn realization that it is not about you; rather, it is about creating an environment for self invention for your customer. Prepare to witness the end of consumer dependence. You must regard the customer—yes, a single customer—as participating on a level playing field with you, the marketer. The new customer will not just choose between existing options. Instead, they will self-invent their own personalized solutions to meet their travel needs."[26] In the same study, 64 percent of consumers agreed with the statement, "Businesses care more about selling me products and services that already exist, rather than coming up with something that really fits my lifestyle." The bottom line is that the customer focus school of management thought calls on businesses to feel a new respect for interacting with customers.

Marcus Buckingham and Curt Coffman of the Gallup Organization have put together the results of two massive management studies conducted over a 25-year period in their book, *First, Break All the Rules: What the World's Greatest Managers Do Differently.*

Gallup surveyed over a million employees from a broad range of companies, industries, and countries. In the course of its surveys it looked at how great managers handled their customers. It discovered that great managers and their employees did everything in their power to build a growing number of loyal customers. They took prospects that had never tried their product or service and turned them into "advocates"—that is, customers who were exceedingly loyal. "They will not only withstand temptations to defect, they will actively sing your praises. These advocates are your largest unpaid sales force. These advocates, more than marketing, more than promotion, even more than price, are your fuel for sustained growth."[27] In other words, the focus of great managers should be on their customers.

Over the last 25 years, Gallup has also interviewed more than a billion customers. While customer needs vary by industry, there were four expectations that all customers had. These expectations are hierarchical—the lower-level expectations must be met before the customer is ready to pay attention to the higher ones.

The first of these is *accuracy*. Hotel customers, for example, expect the hotel to give them the room they reserved. Restaurant customers expect the waiter to bring them what they ordered.

The second is *availability*. Hotel customers expect their preferred hotel chain to have hotels in many cities, so they can stay in them when they travel. Restaurant customers expect their favorite restaurant to be nearby and to have adequate parking.

The third expectation is *partnership*. Customers want the businesses they patronize to listen to them, be responsive to them, and make them feel that they are on the same "team." That's why all airlines create loyalty clubs offering special treatment to frequent flyers.

The fourth and most advanced expectation is *advice*. Customers feel the closest bond to businesses that have helped them learn. The travel agents who succeed in today's environment have turned themselves into consultants. They don't try to "sell" anything. Instead, they take the time to discover their clients' needs and wants in terms of travel and then explain to them the various travel options that are available. Home Depot has been meeting this advice expectation for years. Its sales force is really a group of in-store experts who will teach customers everything from plant care to grouting.[28]

Quality Management

There are many differences between hospitality and manufacturing enterprises. Although restaurants produce a product, it is not a product that can be manufactured and stored for future sale in the same way as, say, an automobile. Hotels and restaurants are in the service business primarily and, as such, rely on their staff members to follow numerous procedures, react to customer needs, and deal with many uncertainties. The process of service does not begin until the customer initiates the transaction—for example, when a guest arrives at a restaurant or hotel, or makes a reservation before arriving. At that point the restaurant or hotel staff reacts to the guest's needs. Throughout the meal or the hotel stay there is a reliance on staff members to satisfy the customer's needs over and over again. Consequently there are many opportunities for failure.

Quality assurance or "QA" programs were established decades ago by most of the major hotel chains to deal with service failures or to anticipate problems. These systems consisted of understanding the problem (or the opportunity), analyzing it through data collection or incident reports, and finally establishing an improvement program. A hallmark of these systems was that they involved employees. Those who did the work were given responsibility for improving work processes and solving problems, and management was asked to create a work culture that empowered employees and allowed them to achieve their full potential. Later on, companies such as Starwood, Hilton, and Marriott adopted other quality improvement programs that dealt with work processes, work culture, and business opportunities.

Six Sigma

Although relatively new for hospitality companies, Six Sigma was developed in 1981 for Motorola, a manufacturing company. It is a strategy for businesses that allows companies to get work done faster and more efficiently. In other words, it is a process-improvement program that leads to more profitability by concentrating on reducing defects and cutting costs. Adopted in 2001 by Starwood, Westin, Sheraton, W, and St. Regis, among others, these companies credit the program with increasing their financial performance.

How does Six Sigma work? At Starwood, for example, there is a vice president in charge of the program. Reporting to the vice president but based mostly at individual hotels in the chain are Black Belts and Green Belts who have received training in Six Sigma methods and tools. Green Belts are full-time employees at a hotel who spend a portion of their time as Six Sigma coordinators. They are responsible for the details of the program. Black Belts are members of hotel executive committees who work on new quality projects and are a resource for the Green Belts. A regional or divisional full-time person has Master Black Belt status.[29]

The Six Sigma process seeks to identify customer needs, reduce costs, and/or increase profits. Projects to be worked on are revealed through guest comments or requests, or through staff observations of problems. Many initiatives also are derived from "Best Practices"—proven solutions adopted from other hotels. After a project is identified, information is gathered through compiling or researching statistics, observing the process that needs to be improved, conducting guest surveys, and so on. All of the facts are then analyzed. If it is a guest complaint or operational problem under review, the root cause is identified; if it is a new business opportunity, the details of the opportunity are outlined. Solutions are created and implemented, then a monitoring process is put into place.[30] Starwood used Six Sigma to identify the cause of increases in worker's compensation claims and develop safer work processes, to name just one quality project. When a study of frequent travelers found that 34 percent of them feel lonely while on the road, the Six Sigma process helped the hotel chain create a number of lobby activities, called "Unwind," that brought interested travelers to the lobby for social interaction. In 2006, Six Sigma programs were responsible for more than $100 million in profit for the company.[31]

Balanced Scorecard

Another quality management system used by hotel companies is the Balanced Scorecard. Adopted by Hilton and Marriott, the Balanced Scorecard evaluates a hotel's overall performance in relation to objectives and performance measures. In the early 1990s, Drs. Robert Kaplan (Harvard Business School) and David Norton presented in a book and various articles a system of performance measurement "that added strategic non-financial performance measures to traditional financial metrics to give managers and executives a more 'balanced' view of organizational performance."[32] This approach recognizes that the success of a business should not be evaluated on profit alone. If an enterprise is to survive and prosper long-term, other factors must be considered in evaluating success—for example, employee satisfaction and turnover, customer satisfaction, and market standing, to name a few. The Balanced Scorecard approaches evaluation from four viewpoints:

- The Learning and Growth Perspective relates to employee development, training, satisfaction, diversity, and turnover.

- The Business Process Perspective refers to business innovation, facilities and services that satisfy the customer, fulfilling the mission, and business strategy.

- The Customer Perspective is generally determined through guest satisfaction surveys e-mailed to guests immediately after departure.

- The Financial Perspective includes budgets, ratios, and other operating statistics.[33]

For many years, hotels and restaurants relied on financial data alone in evaluating their success, ignoring other factors that drive profitable, long-term growth. The Balanced Scorecard brings together both short-term and long-term goals.

The Importance of Leadership

Throughout this chapter we have referred to the persons who manage an organization as "managers." This is perhaps misleading. Warren Bennis—an industrial psychologist, an advisor to four American presidents, and a man who has been called the father of leadership theory—wrote a landmark book (together with Burt Nanus) called *LEADERS: The Strategies for Taking Charge.* Bennis and Nanus interviewed 60 successful CEOs, all presidents or chairs of boards, and 30 outstanding leaders from the public sector. Bennis concluded that these people succeeded not by being managers, but by being *leaders*. While Bennis acknowledged that both management and leadership were important, he said there was a profound difference between the two:

> To manage means to bring about, to accomplish, to have charge of, responsibility for, to conduct. Leading is influencing, guiding in direction, course, action, opinion. The distinction is crucial. *Managers are people who do things right and leaders are people who do the right thing.* The difference may be summarized as activities of vision and judgment—*effectiveness*—versus activities of mastering routines—*efficiency.*[34]

To make the distinction clear, Bennis quoted from an advertisement for United Technologies, headlined "Let's Get Rid of Management," that ran in the *Wall Street Journal.* Here is what the advertisement said:

> People don't want to be managed. They want to be led. Whoever heard of a world manager? World leader, yes. Educational leader. Political leader. Religious leader. Scout leader. Community leader. Labor leader. Business leader. They lead. They don't manage. The carrot always wins over the stick. Ask your horse. You can lead your horse to water, but you can't manage him to drink. If you want to manage somebody, manage yourself. Do that well and you'll be ready to stop managing. And start leading.[35]

After their research was complete, Bennis and Nanus concluded that all of the 90 leaders they interviewed employed four basic strategies:

- Strategy I: Attention through vision
- Strategy II: Meaning through communication
- Strategy III: Trust through positioning
- Strategy IV: Self-development

We'll discuss each of these strategies in the following sections.

Strategy I: Attention through Vision

Leaders create a focus for their organizations. Ray Kroc of McDonald's told Bennis, "Perhaps [the ability to lead] is a combination of your background, your instincts, and your dreams." Leaders have clear ideas of what they want their organizations to be like and they are good at instilling their ideas in their employees. Before the first load of concrete was poured, Walt Disney knew what Disneyland would look like, how people would feel after spending a day there, and how he would get them to feel that way. That was his vision. Kemmons Wilson dreamed of a network of roadside inns no more than 100 miles apart that would have special facilities for children. Leaders have a vision of what their organization will be like when everything is in place and working right.

Strategy II: Meaning through Communication

Bennis and Nanus point out that dreaming is not enough. Successful leaders are able to translate dreams into reality by getting others to share their dreams, commitment, and enthusiasm:

> How do you capture imaginations? How do you get people aligned behind the organization's overarching goals? How do you get an audience to recognize and accept an idea? Workers have to recognize and get behind something of established identity. The management of meaning, the mastery of communication, is inseparable from effective leadership.[36]

Effective leadership is accomplished partially through effective communication. Some leaders write inspiring memos. Others hold meetings complete with models, drawings, and charts to get their ideas across. Many use analogies, comparing what they want things to be like to something that everyone already understands. Bennis points out that such communication has little to do with facts—rather, it concentrates on direction. The idea is to get everyone in the organization to share the same ideas and dreams so that they will all hear the same music and play the same tune—based not on having a song book in front of them, but because they just know instinctively what the tune should sound like.

Strategy III: Trust through Positioning

Leaders not only have a vision and communicate that vision in a way that gets everyone behind it, they know how to steer a constant and steady course in the direction they have laid out. People who work for effective leaders trust their reliability. They know that their leaders are going to do what they have said they are going to do, whatever it takes. Ritz-Carlton's managers expect their employees to satisfy guests—whatever it takes—and every employee knows that they mean it. When Bennis and Nanus entered Ray Kroc's office, he showed them an elaborately framed statement that he said was his favorite inspirational message. The same message was in every other executive's office at McDonald's, in a place where no visitor could miss it. The statement, originally written by former U.S. President Calvin Coolidge, reads:

> Nothing in the world can take the place of persistence.
> Talent will not; nothing is more common than unsuccessful men with
>   great talent.
> Genius will not; unrewarded genius is almost a proverb.
> Education will not; the world is full of educated derelicts.
> Persistence and determination alone are omnipotent.

Effective leaders hold on to their principles, ideas, and visions and are not deterred by obstacles, no matter how insurmountable they seem. The people who work for them know this and trust them to carry out their vision. In this respect they are no different from the legendary generals in military history, whose soldiers knew that they would fight until they achieved victory and thus were willing to fight alongside them.

Strategy IV: Self-Development

Bennis believes that effective leaders are out on the front line leading the charge most of the time. "Our top executives spent roughly 90 percent of their time with others and virtually the same percentage of their time concerned with the messiness of people problems."[37] He calls this "the creative deployment of self." Leaders know what they are good at and they are constantly using their personal strengths to achieve their goals. At the same time, they understand their weaknesses and compensate for them. If they believe they can't compensate for their weaknesses (by surrounding themselves with a staff competent in the areas in which they do not excel, for example), they typically do not take the job. "It's the capacity to develop and improve their skills that distinguishes leaders from followers," Bennis says.[38] Leaders generally do this without being prodded. They have a strong feeling of self worth—who they are and what they can do—and they act based on that confidence in themselves and their own abilities.

At the same time, leaders value and respect others. They understand that you can't get others to follow you willingly unless it feels good to them. Leaders seldom criticize others. A former head coach of the Los Angeles Rams football team told Bennis and Nanus that he

> never criticizes his players until after they're convinced of his *unconditional* confidence. *After* that's achieved he might say (if he does spot something that can help a player), "Look, what you're doing is 99 percent terrific, but there is that 1 percent factor that could make a difference. Let's work on that."[39]

For decades the Wallenda family was the most famous international group of circus acrobats. They performed their daring tightrope and high-wire acts in every major circus all over the world. Their daring and skill were unmatched. Bennis and Nanus quote Karl Wallenda as saying, "Being on the tightrope is living, everything else is waiting."[40] Karl Wallenda died in front of an audience of thousands in San Juan, Puerto Rico, trying to walk a wire between two high buildings. The Wallendas were able to walk the tightrope because they didn't think about falling. They expected to win, not to lose.

James Burke, retired CEO of Johnson & Johnson and one of the most successful leaders of a global enterprise, likes to tell about the time as a young manager he made a terrible error that cost his company several million dollars. He was called by General Johnson, who he expected would fire him. Instead, Johnson praised him and told him that he admired managers who were willing to take risks and make mistakes. Even today at

Johnson & Johnson, managers who refuse to take risks and never make mistakes hardly ever get promoted.

Leaders are not afraid to make mistakes. They believe that making mistakes may be the best way to learn—not only about themselves but about their employees. This is where the key principle of **empowerment** comes from. Leaders empower their employees to solve problems. They expect that in doing so some will make mistakes. Some of these mistakes may even be costly. But employees who make mistakes learn from them and become better at doing their jobs. It makes their jobs more rewarding because they are given a chance to act like a leader—to climb on the tightrope and walk it and take responsibility for their own actions. Sure, there are risks, but there are also rewards. Companies that encourage their employees to take risks, to fail, and to be rewarded when they succeed develop a strong group of well-trained leaders who also know how to follow. In the best companies, all employees are encouraged to become leaders by taking customer problems into their own hands and solving them. They are empowered to solve them by being given the resources—whether it is money or the assistance of other people. This requires great trust on the part of their leaders—and a well-trained group of people as well, so they *can* be trusted—but, as Bennis points out, leaders who trust themselves understand instinctively that it is necessary to trust others.

Conclusion

In this chapter we have tried to illustrate that in the management of hospitality organizations there is no single model or style of managing that is appropriate in all circumstances or for all organizations. Managers have different personalities, and thus any two managers are likely to adopt different solutions to the same problem. There are no absolutely right or wrong ways of doing things. There are, however, certain management principles that are used in excellent companies and that seem to produce the best results. In order to apply these principles, managers must be able to do certain things, many of which cannot be taught in a classroom but must be learned by experience. Four management professors—Robert E. Quinn, Sue R. Faerman, Michael P. Thompson, and Michael R. McGrath—have put together eight managerial/leadership roles and their key competencies (see chapter appendix). Managers and aspiring managers would do well to keep these various management roles in mind and try to develop their skills in them as they pursue their careers.

Summary

A manager's job is similar to that of a conductor of an orchestra, in that he or she must take all of the individual parts of a company and harmonize them into a whole. The manager must also compose the music that the orchestra is going to play. Managers have five basic tasks to perform. They are: setting objectives, organizing, motivating and communicating, measuring performance, and developing people.

The classical school of management was founded by Frederick Taylor, who advocated scientific management. Taylor believed there was a best way to perform every job. Frank and Lillian Gilbreth looked for new ways to make people more efficient and studied worker fatigue. Henri Fayol developed 14 principles of management that included division of labor, unity of command, and centralization, among others. His work is the basis of the current systems approach used in industrial management today.

The behavioral school was founded by Chester Barnard, who believed in satisfying the needs of both employers and employees; and George Elton Mayo, who was a researcher involved in the Hawthorne studies. Mayo found that when managers paid positive attention to employees, employees worked harder and had better morale. Abraham Maslow identified a hierarchy of needs, starting with basic physiological needs and ranging up to self-actualization needs. Douglas McGregor developed Theory X and Theory Y, which represent opposing views about how people are motivated to work.

The quantitative school of management attempted to integrate the management ideas of the classical and behavioral schools. Managers using quantitative techniques apply mathematical decision-making models to management problems. A problem with the quantitative approach is that it tends to focus management attention on meeting short-term financial goals at the expense of employee morale, research and development, and other factors.

The systems school holds that all organizations are a system and therefore events or decisions that occur in one part affect every other part. Managers cannot act independently—what they can and cannot accomplish depends on other managers within the company and on outside environmental factors such as the state of the overall economy.

The contingency school proposes that every situation is different and every manager is different and thus there are no universal principles of management. Managers must be pragmatic and determine for each situation what actions are likely to achieve the results they want.

The quality focus school of management became popular in the 1980s, with the success of Japanese automobile companies. The Japanese were influenced by three Americans—W. Edwards Deming, Joseph Juran, and Philip Crosby—who were little known in the United States until their ideas helped Japanese companies achieve success. Deming emphasized that managers must look to the future, strive for continuous improvement in their products, and break down barriers between employees and managers. By building in quality, a company saved the costs associated with product recalls and lost customers.

Joseph Juran defined quality as "fitness for use." Consumers think they have a quality product if it performs what they expect it to perform, the way they expect it to perform. Juran believed that it was not possible to achieve zero defects, because at some point costs would become too high.

Philip Crosby argued that quality is "free," because the costs associated with preventing defects would always be lower than the costs of correcting mistakes and losing customers. He believed that if managers expected imperfection, that is what they would get; therefore they should expect perfection. They could achieve perfection by increasing employee involvement in improving work processes and gaining their commitment to make perfect products.

According to the customer focus school, a manager should concentrate on building loyal customers who are advocates. The customer focus school believes that businesses today must realize that what the customer wants to buy is more important than what businesses want to sell. The customers of the twenty-first century will not simply choose between existing options, if none of them suit their needs. Instead, they will endeavor to create personalized solutions to meet their needs.

Quality assurance or "QA" programs were established decades ago by most of the major hotel chains to deal with service failures or to anticipate problems. A hallmark of these programs was that the people involved in the work were given responsibility for improving work processes and solving problems. One QA program used within the hospitality industry is known as Six Sigma. The Six Sigma process seeks to identify customer needs, reduce costs, and/or increase profits; projects to be worked on are revealed through guest comments or requests, or through staff observations of problems. Another QA program used by hotels is Balanced Scorecard. The Balanced Scorecard takes into account non-financial factors such as employee satisfaction and turnover, customer satisfaction, and market standing as well as financial success when measuring a hotel's performance. The Balanced Scorecard recognizes that if a business is to prosper long-term, it must measure more than just profits.

Managers above all should be leaders. Successful managers know what they want their businesses to accomplish, clearly communicate that vision to their employees, are good at overcoming obstacles, and are out front leading the charge most of the time. They aren't afraid to make mistakes, and strive to improve themselves and their skills. Leaders also empower their employees to solve problems and become leaders themselves.

There are eight managerial/leadership roles that a manager must play. These are director, producer, coordinator, monitor, mentor, facilitator, innovator, and broker. To increase their chances for success, managers and aspiring managers should develop their skills in each of these roles.

Endnotes

1. Peter F. Drucker, *Management: Tasks, Responsibilities, Practices* (New York: Harper & Row, 1974), p. 398.

2. Interview with Rocco Angelo, March 2010.

3. Drucker, p. 399.

4. Ibid., pp. 400–401.

5. All of the quotes and references to Ritz-Carlton in this chapter were originally supplied to the authors by Patrick Mene, corporate director of quality for The Ritz-Carlton Hotel Corporation, Atlanta, Georgia, in the form of a series of articles, speeches, presentations, and other documents. The material was updated with the assistance of Marco Selva, General Manager, The Ritz-Carlton, Key Biscayne. The authors wish to acknowledge the generous assistance of Mr. Mene, Mr. Selva, and Ritz-Carlton for sharing this material.

6. Wess Roberts, *Leadership Secrets of Attila the Hun* (New York: Warner Books, 1990), pp. 74–75.

7. Janet Denefe, "Melman's Magic," *F&B Magazine,* July/August 1993, p. 24.

8. Zemke and Schaaf, p. 48.

9. *Competitive Benchmarking: The Path to a Leadership Position* (Xerox Corporation, 1992).

10. Joseph A. Michelli, *The Starbucks Experience: 5 Principles for Turning Ordinary into Extraordinary* (New York: McGraw-Hill, 2007), p. 8.

11. Drucker, p. 402.

12. Robert O'Brien, *Marriott: The J. Willard Marriott Story* (Salt Lake City: Deseret Book Company, 1987) p. 265.

13. Frederick W. Taylor, "A Piece Rate System," *Scientific Management,: A Collection of the More Significant Articles Describing the Taylor System of Management,* edited by Clarence Bertrand Thompson (Cambridge: Harvard University Press, 1914), p. 637.

14. "The Taylor System of Shop Management at the Watertown Arsenal," *Scientific Management,* p. 755.

15. Ibid., p. 743.

16. George Elton Mayo, *The Human Problems of an Industrial Civilization* (Boston: Macmillan, 1933), pp. 75–76.

17. This discussion of Maslow's theories is distilled from A. H. Maslow, *Motivation and Personality* (New York: Harper & Row, 1970).

18. Daniel A. Wren, *The Evolution of Management Thought* (New York: Wiley, 1979), p. 484.

19. The following discussion of Deming, Juran, and Crosby has been abstracted and paraphrased in part from "A Note on Quality: The Views of Deming, Juran, and Crosby," by Artemis March, associate for case development, under the supervision of Professor David A. Garvin of the Harvard Business School, 1986 (9–687–011), and from a teaching note by research associate Norman Klein and Professor David A. Garvin on the same subject, 1990 (5–691–022). Both documents are the property of the President and Fellows of Harvard College and are available from the Publishing Division of the Harvard Business School, Boston, Massachusetts 02163.

20. March, p. 2.

21. Ibid., p. 7.

22. Edwin McDowell, "Ritz-Carlton's Keys to Good Service," *New York Times,* 31 March 1993.

23. Ibid.

24. Tom Peters and Nancy Austin, *A Passion for Excellence* (New York: Random House, 1985), p. 4.

25. Ibid., p. 34.

26. The YP&B/Yankelovich Partners *National Leisure Travel MONITOR 2000.*

27. Marcus Buckingham and Curt Coffman, *First, Break All the Rules: What the World's Greatest Managers Do Differently* (New York: Simon & Schuster, 1989).

28. Ibid., pp. 129–132.

29. www.starwoodhotels.com/westin/careers/paths.

30. Darrell K. Rigby, *Management Tools 2009* (Boston, Mass.: Bain & Company, Inc., 2009).

31. www.businessweek.com, October 8, 2007.

32. www.balancedscorecard.org.

33. Ibid.

34. Warren Bennis and Burt Nanus, *LEADERS: The Strategies for Taking Charge* (New York: Harper & Row, Perennial Library Edition, 1986), p. 21.

35. Ibid., p. 22.

36. Ibid., p. 33.

37. Ibid., p. 56.

38. Ibid., p. 60.

39. Ibid., p. 64.

40. Ibid., p. 69.

Key Terms

behavioral school of management—Management theorists who sought to develop better ways to motivate workers than the rules, systems, and wages proposed by the classical management theorists.

classical school—A school of management thought in which workers are seen as rational people interested primarily in making money. This management approach addresses an employee's economic and physical needs, but not his or her social needs or need for job satisfaction.

competitive benchmarking—A phrase coined by the Xerox Corporation that refers to the continuous process of measuring products, services, and practices against those of a business's toughest competitors or other companies recognized as leaders.

contingency school—According to this school of thought, every management situation is different and every manager is different; therefore, there are few universal management principles. Also known as the situational management school.

customer focus school—The school of management thought that concentrates on designing and selling products and services that fit consumers' needs and lifestyles, rather than simply offering existing products and services.

empowerment—A management technique whereby front-line employees are authorized to solve customers' problems and make other decisions that were once made only at higher levels within the organization.

Hawthorne effect—The phenomenon that employees work harder and more efficiently when they know their managers are interested in them and their work.

Hawthorne studies—Studies of workers at the Western Electric Company's plant in Hawthorne, Illinois, involving Harvard Business School professor George Elton Mayo. The studies were originally designed to assess the effects of lighting conditions on worker productivity, but subsequently were broadened to include other working conditions, such as rest periods and type of supervision.

quality focus school—A school of management thought that emphasizes the importance of quality over all other aspects of management. Its founders were Deming, Juran, and Crosby.

quantitative school—A school of management that tries to integrate the management theories of the classical and behavioral management schools; it takes a mathematical approach to management problems.

situational management school—This school of thought believes that every management situation is different and every manager is different; therefore, there are few universal management principles. Also known as the contingency school.

systems school—A school of management thought that proposes that a company is a system of many interrelated parts. The company, in turn, is part of a larger external environment (system). Therefore, managers cannot act independently; what they can accomplish depends on factors inside and outside the company.

Theory X—A traditional set of assumptions some managers make about human nature that governs their management style. According to Theory X, the average employee (1) dislikes work and must be directed and threatened with punishment in order to put forth adequate effort, and (2) avoids responsibility and values security above anything else.

Theory Y—A set of assumptions some managers make about human nature that governs their management style. According to Theory Y, (1) the average employee does not inherently dislike work, (2) external control is not necessary if employees are committed to the organization's objectives, and (3) commitment to objectives is achieved by associating rewards with the attainment of those objectives.

three position plan of promotion—A plan developed by Frank and Lillian Gilbreth in which workers not only perform their jobs but also (1) learn the next higher job and (2) train a worker below them to take over their present job when they are promoted.

Review Questions

1. Managers must perform which five basic tasks?

2. Who are some of the primary figures within the classical school of management? the behavioral school of management? What were their contributions?

3. What were the Hawthorne studies?

4. What is the quantitative school of management?

5. How is the systems school different from the contingency school?

6. Who are some of the leaders within the quality focus school, and what did they contribute to this school of management thought?

7. What are the main ideas of the customer focus school?

8. How do the Six Sigma and Balanced Scorecard systems foster quality management?

9. What are four basic strategies of successful leaders?

10. What is employee empowerment?

Internet Sites

For more information, visit the following Internet sites. Remember that Internet addresses can change without notice. If the site is no longer there, you can use a search engine to look for additional sites.

Hotel Companies/Resorts

Fairmont Hotels
www.fairmont.com

Four Seasons Hotels and Resorts
www.fourseasons.com

Hampton Inn
www.hampton-inn.com

Hyatt Hotels Corporation
www.hyatt.com

Lettuce Entertain You Enterprises
www.lettuceentertainyou.com

Marriott International
www.marriott.com

Ritz-Carlton Hotels
www.ritzcarlton.com

Organizations, Resources

Business Process Reengineering
  and Innovation
www.brint.com/BPR.htm

The Malcolm Baldrige Award
www.quality.nist.gov

Publications

Inc. Online
www.inc.com

Strategy & Business
www.strategy-business.com

Restaurant Companies

McDonald's
www.mcdonalds.com

Taco Bell
www.tacobell.com

Chapter Appendix

Eight Managerial/Leadership Roles

Director Role

As a director, a manager must be a decisive initiator who defines problems, establishes objectives, generates rules and policies, and gives instructions. A manager directs by taking charge of a situation, focusing on results, and making things happen. As directors, managers must also set goals and define the action plans that will be needed to reach them. Finally, managers must know how to delegate effectively by recognizing that they cannot accomplish much by themselves. It is only through the work of others that things get done.

Producer Role

As producers, managers are expected to be task-oriented, work-focused, and highly interested in the task at hand. Managers must be able to motivate themselves to a high level of productivity, respond to challenges in a positive manner, and have the drive and ambition to continuously improve their performance.

Just as managers must motivate themselves, they must also motivate others by understanding that what they expect of their employees and how they treat them largely determines their employees' performances and career progress.

In the role of producer, a manager must also learn how to cope with and minimize the effects of negative stress that occurs regularly in many hospitality jobs, because often there are slow periods followed by peaks of frenzied activity.

Coordinator Role

As a coordinator, a manager makes sure that work flows smoothly and that activities are carried out according to their relative importance, with a minimum amount of conflict among individuals, departments, or groups of workers. This is accomplished by planning the use of financial and human resources to ensure the most effective delivery of services.

Managers must establish standards and priorities and schedule work by task and by employee. Managers must also establish lines of authority by clarifying who reports to whom and who is supposed to perform which jobs.

Finally, as coordinators, managers must learn to use controls as effective mechanisms that provide feedback on whether actual performance is consistent with planned performance and whether customers are actually receiving the level of service intended.

Monitor Role

As monitors, managers are expected to know what is going on and make sure people are complying with rules and producing as expected. Managers must be able to keep track of facts such as food costs or occupancy rates, analyze them, and decide what is important. To do this, managers must be good at handling paperwork, reading memos, and taking notes at meetings. Managers must also know how to make effective use of information by keeping an open mind and using good judgment. To solve problems, managers must be able to discover and weigh all possible factors and then decide which solution is likely to produce the desired result(s). This requires clear analytical thinking. Managers must also be able to present information to others by writing effective memos, proposals, and letters.

Mentor Role

As a mentor, a manager is expected to be helpful, considerate, sensitive, approachable, open, and fair. Managers do this by understanding themselves and others, by interpersonal communication—including developing active listening skills—and by developing employees through performance evaluation and training.

Facilitator Role

In the facilitator role, a manager fosters collective effort, builds cohesion and morale, and manages interpersonal conflict. This can be accomplished through team building. Effective managers are first of all team players. They believe that working together is better than working alone. They are able to get others to share that belief. Managers who are facilitators practice participative decision-making. When an important decision comes up, they involve the individuals whose work lives are affected by the decision. Furthermore, they are skillful in conflict management, which research shows may take between 20 and 50 percent of a manager's time. These managers know how to use collaborative approaches to resolve disputes.

Innovator Role

In today's rapidly changing environment, the ability of managers to initiate and implement change so that they can keep up with the times is an essential survival skill. Nowhere is change more evident than in the hospitality field, where new lifestyles and demographic profiles are constantly affecting how and where people travel as well as their diets and tastes. Managers must deal with changes that are unplanned and sometimes unwelcome. Doing this requires the creativity to generate new ideas and solutions. Innovative managers know how to plan for and manage change. They welcome new technology, new ideas, and are willing to take risks to find new and better ways of doing things.

Broker Role

In organizations, good ideas work only if people see a benefit in adopting them. Managers must be brokers who know how to build and maintain a power base, negotiate agreement and commitment, and present ideas effectively.

(continued)

Managers who are good brokers understand that power and authority are not the same thing. Real power doesn't come from a title or a position, but from the shape and impact a person's presentation of self has on others—the personal characteristics that people find attractive or influential or persuasive. Power can also be gained through the expertise a manager may possess in special areas like food preparation or computers. Managers who are effective brokers are good negotiators and know how to get agreement among groups or individuals with opposing ideas. They are also competent public speakers and know how to communicate not only on a one-to-one basis but to an audience.

13
Managing Human Resources

Outline

Competencies

1. Identify and discuss current labor trends and legislation affecting the hospitality industry. (pp. 388–393)

2. Describe elements of a good human resources program. (pp. 393–411)

Opposite page: The Fairmont Turnberry Isle Resort & Club; photo courtesy of Fairmont Hotels & Resorts.

I T HAS BEEN SAID that a manager can be compared to a conductor, whose job it is to instruct and direct all of the various musicians so that they perform well together. But before a conductor can direct a beautiful performance, all of the individual musicians must be able to play their instruments well. What kind of performance could you expect if the violinists did not know how to play their instruments or the flutists could not read music?

So it is in the hospitality industry. Before a manager can direct and shape employees' individual contributions into an efficient whole, he or she must first turn employees into competent workers who know how to do their jobs. Employees are the musicians of the orchestra that the members of the audience—the guests—have come to watch perform. If employees are not skilled at their jobs, then the performance they give will get bad reviews. Just as an orchestra can have a fine musical score from a great composer and still perform poorly because of incompetent musicians, so a hotel or restaurant can have the finest standard recipes, service procedures, and quality standards and still have dissatisfied guests because of poor employee performance.

That is why properly managing human resources within the hospitality industry is so important. No other industry provides so much contact between employees and customers and so many opportunities to either reinforce a positive experience or create a negative one. In this chapter we will talk about the shortage of qualified workers, high turnover rates, and labor-related legislation. We will then turn our attention to the chief strategies used by hotel and restaurant managers to combat this crisis: good human resources programs designed to help managers hire, train, motivate, and retain competent employees.

Labor Trends

By any measure, one of the most serious challenges the hospitality industry faces is the shortage of qualified workers. Many industry leaders feel that the shortage of qualified labor makes it difficult to expand their brands and provide excellent service. High turnover of staff also negatively impacts the industry's ability to provide consistent service and control labor costs. Demographic changes provide a clue to some of the causes of the industry's labor challenges.

Changing Demographics

Most observers agree that there are several key demographic trends that will have a significant impact on the American work force and consequently on all U.S. businesses in the next decade.

Population Growth. In the 1950s the U.S. population was growing at a rate of as high as 2 percent annually. Today's population growth rate is only slightly more than .9 percent, and the rate is projected to gradually decrease in the future. While the United States recently experienced an unexpected boom in births and a high increase in immigration, there was also a record number of deaths. As the U.S. birth rate continues to decrease and the number of deaths rise (due to an aging population base), immigration will play an ever more important role in shaping the American work force.

The Aging Work Force. Labor trends continue to show that the U.S. work force is aging. The median age of the U.S. labor force was 35.4 years in 1986, according to the U.S. Bureau

Opportunities to make a positive impression on guests abound in the hospitality industry.

of Labor Statistics; projections expect that by 2016, the median age will increase to 42.1 years. The number of older workers (55 years or older) is expected to continue to grow. This is due to a number of reasons, including:

- Individuals leading longer and healthier lives

- Today's higher-educated work force tends to stay longer in the workplace

- Defined contribution plans give incentives to older workers to continue to contribute to their retirement plans by remaining employed and delaying retirement

- The eligible age for collecting full retirement Social Security benefits began to increase as of 2000

- The rising costs of health insurance

The good news for hospitality managers is that an older labor force is usually more experienced and productive. However, the bad news is that there are fewer younger workers available in today's labor force, ready to start in entry-level positions and work their way up.[1]

Generation Y or Millennials. Those born between 1978 and 1995 and identified originally by advertisers and others as "Generation Y" or "Millennials" have entered the work force with attitudes about work different from those who preceded them. Millennials are technologically savvy, exhibit a high degree of independence, and seek flexibility in their work/life balance. They have high expectations of their employers and do not hesitate to challenge the status quo. Seeking to advance on their terms, they are ready to move to the next employment opportunity as soon as it arises. Their expectations differ greatly from their older counterparts in the work force, who tend to be more traditional, prefer the

The number of women employed in the hospitality industry continues to grow.

status quo, and remain loyal to their current employer. This may be especially challenging for managers in the hospitality industry, who are expected to lead an increasingly diverse work force with very different expectations.

The Increase in Women Workers. Because of the rising cost of living and the increase in the number of single-parent households, the number of women joining the U.S. work force has grown steadily since the middle of the twentieth century. In 1955 only 35 percent of women worked outside the home, but today more than half of all women are in the work force, and two-thirds of mothers in the United States are working outside the home. The growing number of working women is a boon for the restaurant business, since these women have less time for homemaking and they (and their families) eat out more. Employers who wish to recruit women must understand and possibly help to resolve the issue of dependent care, which was not necessary in the past when they dealt with a predominantly male work force.

The Shifting Population. There has been a large influx of immigrants from the Caribbean, Central and South America, and Asia who have settled in the southern and western United States. The ten fastest growing states are in the West and South. This means that there is a labor shortage in some areas of the country, but not in all.

The Growth in Education Levels. While the rate of college enrollments has been increasing, most American adults have still never been to college. Moreover, there is some evidence that literacy has been decreasing in some regions, due to the large number of non-English-speaking immigrants entering the country every year. However, as the demand for skilled workers increases, more adults are expected to seek degrees of some sort—either from a university, junior college, or technical school.

The Diversity of the Work Force. In 1960 only 10 percent of Americans belonged to a minority group. Today, 25 percent of all Americans are nonwhite. By the year 2050, blacks, Hispanics, Asians, and Native Americans will represent more than 50 percent of the U.S. population, and non-Hispanic whites will become the new minority. Clearly, as more and more managers and employees from diverse races and cultures are brought together in the workplace, there is an increasing need for diversity training and a better understanding on the part of managers of how to manage a diverse work force.

High Turnover

High turnover rates are another labor problem that hospitality managers must cope with. According to the American Hotel & Lodging Association, employee turnover in the hotel industry is between 60 percent to more than 300 percent annually. One hotel operator reports that most departing employees are room attendants, food servers, and bus help, and nearly half of them leave during the first two weeks of employment. One result of this high turnover rate is that many hotel and restaurant employees are not well-trained or experienced enough to provide the quality of service customers expect.

It is difficult to pin down all of the reasons for the industry's high turnover rates, but there are a few that may be universal:

- *Inefficient hiring systems.* Because it is so difficult to find employees, managers hire many individuals without screening them to see if they are the right people for the job, or fully explaining what their jobs involve. For example, a hotel is open and must be staffed 24 hours a day, seven days a week. New employees often don't understand what it is like to work all night, or on holidays or weekends, and that they are likely to be called on to fill some of those shifts. When they discover what a hospitality job can entail, they often get discouraged and look for other work.

- *Limited opportunities for advancement.* Most people want to better themselves. Few people are satisfied with minimum-wage employment at a hotel or restaurant if they can find a better job. Often they can. Another problem is that many hotels and restaurants have no training programs where entry-level workers can learn skills that will make them promotable within the company. A worker who wants to get ahead may have to quit and go somewhere else.

Diversity in the Workplace

When it comes to diversity in the workplace, most companies still operate using what David A. Thomas and Robin J. Ely of the Harvard Business School call the "discrimination-and-fairness" paradigm, which is based on the recognition that discrimination is wrong. Under it, progress is measured by how well a company achieves its recruitment and retention goals. The paradigm idealizes assimilation and color- and gender-blind conformism. But Thomas and Ely believe there is a better way. Instead, they advocate the "access-and-legitimacy" paradigm, which, instead of seeking conformism, *celebrates* differences. Under it, organizations seek access to a more diverse pool of workers, matching their demographics to the organizations' targeted consumers.

Here are the eight "pre-conditions" that Thomas and Ely believe need to be present in companies to make the transformation to the "access-and-legitimacy" paradigm successfully:

1. The leadership must understand that a diverse workforce will embody different perspectives and approaches to work, and must truly value variety of opinion and insight.

2. The leadership must recognize both the learning opportunities and the challenges that the expression of different perspectives presents for an organization.

3. The organizational culture must create an expectation of high standards of performance from everyone.

4. The organizational culture must stimulate personal development.

5. The organizational culture must encourage openness.

6. The organizational culture must make workers feel valued.

7. The organization must have a well-articulated and widely understood mission.

8. The organization must have a relatively egalitarian, nonbureaucratic structure.

One company that places diversity at the top of its list of priorities is Starbucks. The company has established six guiding principles that it says its managers will use in judging the appropriateness of all business decisions. The first two have to do with the work force:

1. Provide a great work environment and treat each other with respect and dignity.

2. Embrace diversity as an essential component in the way we do business.

Source: Adapted from David A. Thomas and Robin J. Ely, "Making Differences Matter: A New Paradigm for Managing Diversity," *Harvard Business Review on Managing Diversity* (Boston, Mass.: Harvard Business School Publishing Corporation, 2001), pp. 23, 52–53; and www.starbucks.com.

- *Lack of training and supervision.* People hired for entry-level positions should be trained to do their jobs. Many receive inadequate training, make mistakes, get discouraged, and quit. While on-the-job training may be the cheapest form of training, it is also the most traumatic for employees.

Legislation

It is important for hospitality managers to understand legislation that has an impact on the way they manage their businesses. In 1938 the U.S. Congress passed the Fair Labor

Standards Act (FLSA), which established laws concerning wages and overtime. Employees of service industries were exempt until 1967, and it was not until 1979 that all of the provisions were in force. The law addressed such issues as the employment of minors and equal pay for men and women who perform the same kind of work.

A number of other federal and local laws have influenced human resources practices. The Civil Rights Act of 1964 bans discrimination on the basis of race, sex, religion, or national origin. One result of this law was the formation of the Equal Employment Opportunity Commission (EEOC), which oversees the enforcement and administration of this law. In recent years the EEOC has expanded its horizons to cover sexual harassment cases.

The Occupational Safety and Health Act of 1970 spells out what constitutes safe working conditions. In addition, it requires employers to make sure that workers have necessary safety equipment while on the job, and that equipment such as meat slicers and ladders conforms to safety standards. OSHA—the Occupational Safety & Health Administration—was established to oversee worker safety.

The Americans with Disabilities Act of 1990 and the changes made by the ADA Amendments Act of 2008 are designed to protect the civil rights of persons who have physical or mental disabilities. Employers may not deny jobs to disabled persons who are capable of performing the jobs, and must provide reasonable access to the workplace for them (such as special parking spaces and ramps for wheelchairs).

The Family and Medical Leave Act of 1993 provides that employees must be given up to 12 weeks off a year without pay if they need it for the birth or adoption of a child, or because of an illness of the employee or a family member. Effective January 2009 the regulations were revised to add military family leave entitlements for eligible family members.

The Illegal Immigration Reform and Immigrant Responsibility Act of 1996 establishes penalties for employers who knowingly hire illegal aliens. It also prohibits employment discrimination on the basis of national origin or citizenship.

Human Resources Programs

A sound human resources program typically contains the following elements:

- It truly cares about employees
- It defines the job
- It establishes productivity standards
- It recruits the most suitable job candidates
- It selects the best applicants
- It implements continual training and career development programs
- It motivates employees so they want to stay with the company
- It offers competitive benefits
- It evaluates employees

We'll take a look at each of these elements in the following sections.

Caring About Employees

There is a growing recognition among managers in service industries that you can't expect employees to treat customers any better than they themselves are treated. The Ritz-Carlton Hotel Company refers to its employees in its mission statement as "internal customers," and believes that in order for its employees to offer quality service to guests, Ritz-Carlton must first offer it to employees. The company promotes a corporate culture that encourages employees to stop their day-to-day routine to help fellow employees. This helps eliminate internal competition and build stronger employee teams.

At McDonald's, teenage employees are told that "working part-time is an excellent way for you to learn about the real world. But it's more important for you to make education Priority #1. At McDonald's, our commitment is to help students explore the best of both worlds."[2] This communicates to employees McDonald's belief in the importance of education.

Both of these companies recognize that when they talk about being in the "people business," they mean the people who work for them as well as the people who buy from them. Companies with successful human resources programs recognize that people are the most valuable resource they have, and ensure that every step within their program takes into account the basic worth of individuals and their sensitivities and vulnerabilities. These companies say, in effect, "We are employers who care about the people who work for us."

Defining the Job

Before the right person can be hired to perform a particular job, managers must understand exactly what the job involves so that an applicant's skills and the requirements of the job can be matched accurately.

The task of analyzing a job is somewhat more complicated in the hospitality industry than elsewhere. The job of a spot welder, for example, is essentially the same whether the welding takes place on top of a skyscraper or in a machine shop. But a food server's job can vary tremendously, depending on the time of day, the operation's physical layout and design, whether he or she is working at a local diner or a fine-dining restaurant, the operation's equipment, and the guests' expectations. Even merchandising techniques can affect a food server's job: in most restaurants, guests order off a printed menu; in others, servers are expected to show a blackboard to diners or memorize the daily specials.

Since the same job can differ from property to property, independent hotels and restaurants must perform their own job analyses in order to understand how jobs are done at their particular properties. Hotels and restaurants that belong to chains do not typically perform their own job analyses; this task is done at corporate headquarters. For example, Days Inn's franchise division commissioned the School of Industrial and Systems Engineering at the Georgia Institute of Technology to prepare an analysis of Days Inn's room-cleaning procedures. The Georgia Tech analysts concluded that all major tasks in room cleaning fall into "natural groupings" or job blocks, and recommended that Days Inn adopt the room cleaning sequence shown in Exhibit 1.

Once a job has been analyzed, then a number of documents can be prepared to help employees understand and learn the job, among them job lists, job breakdowns, and job descriptions.

As the name implies, a **job list** is simply a list of the tasks that must be performed by the individual holding that particular job (see Exhibit 2). Job lists are useful as training tools and can serve as reminders for new employees.

Exhibit 1   Sample Guestroom Cleaning Sequence

Preliminary

The room attendant enters the room, turns on the light, and opens the curtains. He/she places the in-room cart at the side of the vanity. He/she then makes a forward sweep through the room, dumping ashtrays in the trash can bags, picking up these bags, and picking up room trash. He/she deposits the trash in the main cart outside the door and returns to the room, picking up ashtrays and washing them in the sink or leaving them there to soak if necessary.

Block 1

From the vanity, the room attendant makes a second sweep through the room, gathering all dirty terry, placing terry on the used bed, and wrapping the dirty linen around it. If two beds are used then he/she places the ball on the second bed, wrapping the dirty linen from that bed around it. Note that the procedure eliminates stuffing linen and terry into a pillow case. This is a time-consuming procedure. The room attendant takes the ball and places it in the main cart outside the door.

Block 2

From the main cart, he/she takes all necessary clean linen, re-enters the room, and makes the bed(s).

Block 3

From the beds he/she goes directly to the vanity and performs all necessary work, including terry re-stocking. He/she does not need to move away from the vanity due to the convenience of the in-room cart.

Block 4

He/she moves the in-room cart next to the bathroom. Here he/she performs all bathroom cleaning tasks.

Block 5

He/she makes a circuit of the room to dust. Returning to the in-room cart, he/she moves it next to the desk, cleans the desk mirror, replaces the trash can bag, re-stocks necessary stationery supplies, and replaces the desk ashtray. Then, moving the in-room cart toward the door, he/she replaces the air conditioner ashtray, and takes the in-room cart outside the room.

Block 6

Removing the vacuum (or other carpet cleaning tool) from the main cart, he/she vacuums the room.

This is only part of the job analysis of a typical room attendant position. The complete description might also cover the room attendant's responsibility for stocking the in-room cart with sheets, pillowcases, towels, glasses, soap, toilet paper, stationery, and other items, as well as more detail on how beds should be made, toilets cleaned, and so on.

Exhibit 2   Sample Job List

Date: xx/xx/xx

JOB LIST

Position: Housekeeping Room Attendant

Tasks: Employees must be able to:

1. PARK in designated area.
2. WEAR proper uniform.
3. PUNCH in.
4. PICK up clipboard and keys.
5. MEET with supervisor.
6. OBTAIN supplies.
7. PLAN your work.
8. ENTER the room.
9. PREPARE the room.
10. MAKE the beds.
11. GATHER cleaning supplies.
12. CLEAN the bathroom.
13. DUST the room.
14. CHECK/REPLACE paper supplies and amenities.
15. CLEAN windows.
16. INSPECT your work.
17. VACUUM the room.
18. LOCK the door and mark your report.
19. TAKE breaks at designated times.
20. RETURN and restock cart.
21. RETURN to housekeeping with clipboard and keys.
22. PUNCH out.

Job lists are the foundations for **job breakdowns**—specific, step-by-step procedures for accomplishing a task (see Exhibit 3). The first column in Exhibit 3 shows a task (7) from the job list shown in Exhibit 2. The second column breaks down the task by identifying the steps that an employee must take to accomplish the task. These steps are written as performance standards. The third column, "Additional Information," explains why each step of the task is performed and may also include such information as desired attitudes when performing the step, safety tips, or pointers on how to reach the performance standard. In column four, managers can record information for quarterly performance evaluations. As you can see, a job breakdown can be as useful in evaluating employees as in training them.

Once a job list and a job breakdown have been developed for a particular job, a **job description** can be written that outlines (1) the title that goes with the job, (2) the person to whom the employee reports, (3) the work to be performed (in general terms), (4) the education or skills the employee must have, and (5) the physical requirements of the job. A job description can be useful in a number of ways. It can be used as a recruiting tool to show prospective employees the nature of the work to be performed; it is an excellent

Exhibit 3   Sample Job Breakdown

POSITION: Housekeeping Room Attendant, morning shift

NAME:

SUPERVISOR:

JOB LIST	PERFORMANCE STANDARDS	ADDITIONAL INFORMATION	1st QTR Yes/No	2nd QTR Yes/No	3rd QTR Yes/No	4th QTR Yes/No
7. PLAN YOUR WORK.	A. STUDY your assignment sheet.	Early service requests, rush rooms, check-outs, VIPs and no-service requests will be noted on your chart.				
	B. CLEAN check-outs first, whenever possible.	Cleaning check-outs first gives the front desk rooms to sell.				
	C. CLEAN early service requests as noted on your report.					
	D. CLEAN VIP rooms before lunch, whenever possible.	A VIP is our most important guest.				
	E. LOCK your cart room door and proceed to your section.					
	F. HONOR "do not disturb" signs.	We must honor the privacy of guests. Many guests like to sleep in. Never knock on a door that has a "do not disturb" sign.				
	G. CHECK rooms marked c/o and then check the rooms which are circled on your report. These are rooms due to check out.	Rooms marked c/o have already checked out at the front desk. Check-out time is noon.				
	H. PLAN your work around early service requests.	If you have early service requests, be sure to clean these rooms at the proper time.				

training tool; supervisors can use it to monitor work in progress; and it can be used as the basis for employee evaluation. Job descriptions can also ease employee anxiety, because they specify in writing the person to whom the employee reports and the responsibilities of the employee.

Establishing Productivity Standards

A good human resources program has **productivity standards.** Productivity standards tell managers how long it should take employees to complete tasks using the best methods management has devised, and how much work can be performed in a given time period. Productivity standards are often based on a manager's personal experience, the business's historical records, and industry standards.

In order to know if productivity standards are being met, employee productivity must be measured. Productivity can be measured in dollars or units produced or served.

When productivity is expressed in dollars, it can be calculated by two different methods. The first consists of dividing sales by payroll costs:

$$\frac{\$10{,}000{,}000 \text{ (sales)}}{\$2{,}500{,}000 \text{ (payroll)}} = \$4$$

In this example, every $1 of payroll expended produced $4 of sales.

The second method of calculating productivity using dollars consists of dividing sales by the number of **full-time-equivalent (FTE) employees:**

$$\frac{\$10{,}000{,}000 \text{ (sales)}}{280 \text{ (FTE employees)}} = \$35{,}714 \text{ (rounded)}$$

In this example, $35,714 was generated for every FTE employee.

Units produced or served divided by the number of employees also yields a measure of productivity. For instance, suppose a restaurant with ten FTE employees serves 500 **covers,** or meals, on a particular evening:

$$\frac{500 \text{ covers (units produced or served)}}{10 \text{ (FTE employees)}} = \$50$$

In this example, 50 covers were served per FTE employee.

Fifty is the number of covers that were actually served that evening, but 50 covers might or might not meet the work productivity standard for the restaurant. The restaurant's standard might be that 65 covers should be served for every FTE employee, in which case the 10 FTE employees should have served 650 covers. Managers then have several options. They can investigate why employees served fewer covers that evening. It could be that guests at many tables stayed longer than average, so that the restaurant didn't seat enough guests to meet the productivity standard. Or it could be that several new food servers were scheduled that evening and they did not serve guests as quickly as the more experienced servers. Depending on the circumstances, managers might then decide to re-train the new servers or conclude that they just need a little more experience. Or managers might wait to see if an investigation is really necessary. Managers may decide not to investigate what happened that evening at all, but to keep a close eye on the covers-per-FTE-employee for the next week or two. Only if covers-per-FTE-employee stay below the standard for a significant period would they take the time to investigate the causes.

Productivity standards are not only essential for payroll control, they are also important in job analysis and as measures of expectation when recruiting, training, or evaluating an employee.

Managers should never assume that high productivity equals guest satisfaction and business success. While managers of service businesses must watch their productivity measures carefully in order to achieve their economic goals, they must also remember that success in business has qualitative as well as quantitative dimensions. In other words, successful businesses base their productivity standards in part on guest expectations, not on profitability or efficiency objectives alone. For example, the Bob Evans restaurant chain bases many of its productivity standards on its guests' expectations, and carefully measures how well it meets those expectations. Guests should not have to wait for a table for more than 15 minutes; after guests are seated, an employee should come by with water and a greeting within 60 seconds; food should arrive at the table no longer than 10 minutes after guests order it; and a vacated table must be readied for new guests within 5 minutes.

Recruiting Suitable Candidates

Once the various jobs have been defined and productivity standards established, recruiting workers becomes the top priority for managers. A major goal of recruiting is to find the best workers available who find the job attractive and are willing to work for the wages offered by the business. This task is complicated by the fact that, in the hospitality industry, work skills alone are not a sufficient measure of a person's suitability for a job. Personality must also be taken into consideration if the position involves interaction with guests.

To a large extent, whether an operation can recruit people who have the personality and skills to fit into a service-oriented business depends on the labor market in which it is functioning. Market areas differ as to levels of unemployment, diversity of the work force, and competitive industries. Hotels and restaurants might have trouble recruiting good employees in locales with a low level of unemployment and a number of large businesses with high wage scales. Even in some areas with high levels of unemployment, there may not be a wide selection of people with the basic skills and temperament to work in a hospitality organization. In some unfavorable market areas, employees must be transported daily from nearby towns to their place of work—a costly procedure. When McDonald's opened a new restaurant in Boca Raton, Florida—a town where the leading employer was IBM—it found it necessary to transport workers by bus from Miami, 50 miles away! The Hyatt Regency Hotel in Greenwich, Connecticut, assists workers who commute to the area by train from places like Mt. Vernon, New York, or Stamford, Connecticut. The hotel leased a van and hired two full-time drivers to pick up employees at the train station, ensuring that the workers get to work on time and saving them taxi fare.

Internal and External Sources of Employees. All sources of new employees fall into one of two categories: internal or external. Of these, internal sources are the least costly and often the most reliable. One internal source consists of recruits recommended by current employees. Since employees have a good understanding of the nature of the work involved, and since they tend to be careful about whom they recommend, employees often bring in recruits who do very well. In tight labor markets, employees may be paid a referral fee if the new recruit stays for a certain length of time (typically 90 days). Bulletin boards and company newsletters are ways of getting the news of job openings to employees.

Often employees will suggest friends and relatives for positions. Some businesses have rules prohibiting family members from working together. These rules are typically a result of previous negative experiences, or of fears that if one member of a family leaves the company, other members may leave as well. While these concerns are sometimes justified, there are many examples of family members working for the same employer, at the same time, quite successfully.

Another internal source of applicants for a vacant job is the current staff. Promoting from within establishes the operation as a good place to work—one in which opportunities are available for those who want them, are suitable for promotion, and work hard. In fact, a strong internal-promotion policy is in itself a valuable recruiting tool, and many companies spell out internal career ladders as part of their recruitment program. For example, many of the Domino's Pizza franchisees were once store managers—owning your own store is part of the career track that is offered as a recruitment incentive. More than 50 percent of Marriott's managers have been promoted from within. Nine out of ten salaried employees at tableservice restaurants started out as hourly workers. Loews Hotels has career development days for line-level employees.

In the hospitality industry, work skills alone are not a sufficient measure of a person's suitability for a job. Personality must also be taken into consideration, especially if the position involves interaction with guests. It's easier to teach job skills than to teach someone to have a pleasing personality and a warm smile; that's why some human resources managers "hire the smile" when recruiting for many positions. (Photo courtesy of Ernie Pick.)

There are also some potential problems associated with internal promotion. An employee-applicant who loses a position to another employee (or to an outside applicant) might turn his or her disappointment into negative actions, such as not performing up to standards or complaining on the job (which could affect the morale of others). In general, employers who use internal promotion effectively also have strong employee counseling programs.

External sources for employees can be informally tapped. Managers and supervisory staff often are able to locate new personnel through their social and professional contacts. In many cases this involves recruiting from competitive operations. Companies find that being heavily involved in local community affairs makes them more approachable, and that a larger number of people apply for job openings than would otherwise.

Classified advertising and direct mail are examples of formal external recruiting methods. Classified advertising can be placed in local daily newspapers, in industry journals, and even on radio stations. E-mail and direct mail to schools, colleges, and seniors' groups is also a good way to reach job candidates. An advantage of advertising and direct mail is that they generally produce a large number of applicants—everyone looking for a job is likely to apply for what sounds like an attractive position. A disadvantage of the direct mail recruiting method is that many applicants are not qualified and must be screened out by the human resources department. This can be time-consuming and expensive.

One of the most successful recruiting tools is the Internet. While sites like Monster.com post the largest number of job openings, there are some recruiting sites devoted just to the hospitality industry. The two most notable are hcareers.com and hospitalitycareernet. com. The latter also carries employment polls, compensation surveys, and career advice. Individual hospitality companies often have employment sections on their websites as well where a candidate can apply or submit his or her résumé online.

Other formal external sources that are often used to recruit employees are state government employment offices and private employment agencies. People who are out of work and wish to receive unemployment compensation are usually required to register with state employment offices, so these offices usually have sizable lists of candidates. Many of these individuals may not be qualified for hospitality jobs, however, and must be screened carefully. There are some private employment agencies that charge a fee for placing an individual with a company; the fee is paid by either the employee or the employer. These agencies are mostly used to find supervisory and management personnel.

The city school systems in New York City and Miami–Dade County have their own "Academies of Tourism." These academies help high school students gain an awareness and understanding of the hospitality and tourism industry. All of the students work in an internship in their senior year; some continue their education in culinary schools or hospitality programs in college, while others go directly into the work force. In many communities, students in hospitality, tourism, or culinary programs offered by junior colleges and four-year institutions are eager to gain work experience while in school.

The National Restaurant Association (NRA) has identified several sometimes overlooked population groups that can answer the needs of the restaurant industry and other hospitality organizations. These groups include minorities, disabled workers, senior citizens, and workers with limited skills. The NRA points out that some individuals within these groups might need help in improving their English-speaking skills. Special job trainers or equipment might be needed for workers with disabilities, and new career ladders might be needed for older workers.

A good deal of recruiting is done by companies at colleges that teach hospitality management. A hotel or restaurant chain may offer graduates an opportunity to enter a management training program that, upon completion, qualifies them for a supervisory position in one of its properties. Or graduates may receive direct placement offers. With these, graduates are put directly into supervisory or management positions and are given on-the-job training. Often, direct placement recruiting is done by independent hotels/ restaurants and private clubs that do not offer full-scale management training programs.

Some hotels and food service companies employ the services of executive recruiters or "headhunters." Companies usually engage these recruitment firms to find people for senior management positions. Executive recruiters receive substantial fees for their services.

Another recruitment technique is popularly called "networking." With networking, individuals either contact or are contacted by friends, classmates, and former associates about a job opening. Most observers agree that most management positions are filled via networking rather than through advertising.

Of course, many graduates from hospitality programs—and supervisors and managers already employed in the industry—find their own positions by directly contacting the companies they would like to work for.

Selecting the Best Applicants

Selecting the right employees has long been considered one of the keys to operating a successful hospitality business. As mentioned earlier, personality must be considered as well as skills. Almost 100 years ago, the great hotelier Ellsworth Statler told his hotel managers to "hire only good-natured people." That is still a good idea today.

Selecting an applicant to fill a position involves five steps:

1. Receiving and processing applications
2. Interviewing applicants
3. Evaluating applicants
4. Checking references
5. Hiring the selected person

These steps should not be taken lightly. Top-notch companies go about hiring people for even the lowest-paid positions carefully. Selectivity is the watchword. At the Walt Disney World Resort, no candidate for a salaried or managerial-level position is hired on the basis of one interview; at least two are required.

Receiving and Processing Applications. Most hotels and restaurants use exactly the same application form whether they are hiring unskilled or skilled personnel. The forms are typically found online at the company's website.

Applications generally cover an applicant's name, address, telephone number, work experience, references, and education, as well as some other miscellaneous items. Some applications also contain a clause in which the applicant agrees, upon accepting the job, to submit to a drug-screening test at any future time should the employer request it. After someone is employed, whether he or she can be tested is a matter for negotiation. Most employers believe it is better to secure permission up front so they can administer the tests on an as-needed basis.

Human resources managers are often more interested in a person's intellect and attitude than in his or her specific skills. With today's sophisticated training techniques, almost any entry-level job can be learned in a matter of weeks, so the key factors that managers look for are a person's talents, adaptability to a job, enthusiasm, and willingness to learn. That means a job application, at least in the hiring of entry-level employees, is a pre-screening tool more than anything else—it helps weed out people not suitable for

How Marriott Attracts and Retains Employees

In a speech before the Detroit Economic Club, J. W. Marriott, Jr., Chairman and CEO of Marriott International, told guests that "recruiting and retaining employees is the greatest challenge facing American business today." Marriott said that his company's "human capital strategy" focuses on five principles to generate even greater value for employees and the company. They include:

1. "Hire the right person for the right job. Good managers identify, hire, and wisely place top talent."

2. "Money is just one component of value, and managers must offer the whole package: competitive compensation and a great workplace. Our research shows that while pay is a top concern in decisions to stay or leave, other factors combine to outweigh money—such as work/life balance, leadership quality, career development opportunities, and work environment. The longer an employee is with us, the more important the non-monetary issues become."

3. "Pay may keep people on the job, but it won't motivate them to produce more value for the company or go the extra mile. In our industry, a genuinely warm, caring, empathetic workplace is a clear driver of the quality of our product."

4. "We give all associates the opportunity to advance as far as their abilities will take them. Not only does this help us build long-term leadership, it also enables us to perpetuate our culture, which provides our company with a sustainable competitive advantage. Employees specifically cite the opportunity for advancement as a key factor in their decisions to stay with Marriott."

5. "Consumer branding enables us to make a sale to customers who have unlimited choices. Employment branding enables us to attract potential employees, who also have a wide range of choices. Today more than ever, employees seek out brands with strong reputations and high standards."

a position, rather than identify the best candidates. Paul Breslin, an industry executive, puts it this way: "Hotels are no longer looking for people with five years' experience to be a front office clerk. They can learn the job with two weeks of training and two weeks of practical, hands-on experience. What hotels want are people who can adapt to a new environment and retain what they are taught."[3]

Interviewing Applicants. Once an application is filled out and submitted, the applicant is often called in and given a short screening interview by someone in the human resources office. In this interview, the interviewer reviews the facts on the application and notes the applicant's personal grooming and language skills. In small operations this interview can be extended to cover all aspects of the candidate's history, because the person doing the interviewing will also do the hiring. In large operations the human resources department only does the screening and first interviews; there is usually a second interview by the manager for whom the new employee will work.

Breslin has some advice about interviewing prospective employees: "Don't ask them any questions you don't need to know the answer to, such as 'Are you married?' or 'How many children do you have?'" As far as persons with disabilities are concerned, Breslin says, "Focus on what the person can do rather than what they cannot do."[4]

Some areas should be avoided altogether, since questions relating to them may be interpreted as violations of the applicant's rights. Topics to avoid during an interview include an applicant's birthplace, age, race or color, religion or creed, height, weight, marital status, sexual orientation, national origin, citizenship, membership in lodges and religious or ethnic clubs, and arrest record. The general rule of thumb is: Don't ask a question unless it has a direct bearing on whether the candidate can successfully perform the job in question. Since the standards for what constitutes discriminatory or otherwise unlawful questions vary from state to state and year to year, interviewers must keep abreast of current federal and state laws.

Evaluating Applicants. The goal when evaluating applicants is to find the right person for the job. Managers shouldn't put someone in a position where there's a lot of guest contact if the person is more suited to a back-of-the-house position. Housekeepers in hotels must bend over to make a bed or scrub the bathroom floor or tub; obviously, someone with a bad back would not be suitable for this kind of work.

Managers should pick the most interested candidate who enjoys the kind of work that must be done. Managers should also make sure that the candidate has the necessary language, writing, and physical skills, and (of course) good personal grooming habits. Beyond these traits, having an enthusiastic and optimistic attitude and the ability to function as part of a team are paramount.

Marcus Buckingham and Curt Coffman in their book, *First, Break All the Rules: What the World's Greatest Managers Do Differently*, report that the best managers hire for talent rather than experience. As the authors point out, "everyone has some unique talents. The point is to find the people with the special talent that you are looking for." In one study of hotel housekeepers, they found that great housekeepers are energized by their work, not dragged down by it. In their minds housekeeping gives them a chance to accomplish something tangible. The challenge gives them strength.[5]

When hiring housekeepers, managers should look for people who enjoy the challenge of keeping hotel rooms clean, not for people who simply want a job. The Marriott organization understands this very well. Bill Marriott likes to tell the story of Annie Krusheski. Annie cleans the ladies' room in one of their larger properties. Marriott says:

> We've received quite a few letters praising both the cleanliness of the ladies' room and Annie's happy disposition. Annie even brings in flowers she grows in her garden to brighten the countertops. Why did she go the extra mile? Because we hired the right person. Here's what Annie told us: "Being able to help people is what I like most about my job. I also like to clean, so this is the perfect job for me." As her story proves, if minds and attitudes are the materials and machines of today's economy, then hiring the right person is just as important as designing the right products. That may seem obvious, but in today's labor market, it also requires discipline. For a manager desperate to fill a shift, hiring the first person in the door is very tempting. But good managers identify, recruit, and place talent wisely—they decide what they need, and find it.[6]

Hospitality authors Casey Jones and Thomas A. Decotiis advocate "work sampling" as a method of predicting the performance of employees in guest-contact positions before they are hired. Work sampling tests employees by presenting them with situations simulating the actual job. Working with a major hotel company, Jones and Decotiis developed a video-based work-sample test that could be administered easily to large numbers of applicants and scored quickly.[7] Forty guest-service simulations based on actual guest/employee incidents were filmed. After each simulation is presented, a prospective employee is asked to choose among four possible responses to the guest's behavior. Here is a typical simulation:

The scene is the front desk, where a single front desk agent is on duty, checking out a guest. Several other guests are in line to check out. Suddenly, another guest rushes to the desk and says, "Hey, I'm going to miss my plane. I need to check out right now or I'm going to miss it." The frame freezes. The agent should: (A) ask the people in line if it's okay to check out the guest ahead of them, (B) say, "I'm sorry, sir, but I'll get to you as soon as I finish with Mr. Steinberg here," (C) say, "Yes sir, right away," or (D) look for a supervisor.

Action B is the best. It acknowledges the guest's special need by serving him next, but allows the agent to continue serving the guest who is at the head of the line (and may also have a time problem). Action A would shift the problem to the other guests, and if one of them objected, an embarrassing situation would arise. Action C would be viewed as extremely inconsiderate to guests in line and the guest being served. Action D is a last resort; supervisors should be called for help only in very difficult situations.[8]

According to the researchers, a work-sample test such as this one has proved valid as a predictor of job performance. It also has proven to be especially useful to applicants for whom English is a second language, because they can both see and hear the test problem.

Checking References. Before offering someone a position, managers should always check the person's references. Checking references is one of the most important steps in the hiring process. "Calling references can really give you greater insight into the applicant's previous overall job performance," says Breslin. "In addition, applicants usually know when you have called and that sends the message to them that they are important to you and that you are hiring them for the long term."[9] Of course, a former employer of the applicant may only confirm that the applicant worked for the organization from date X to date Y and decline to say anything more. Even that much information is useful, since it will help you check the accuracy of the candidate's application or résumé.

Some companies have a third party such as a private investigator do a further check on candidates for certain positions. If the candidate is interviewing for a position that involves being responsible for large amounts of money, managers may want to run a credit and criminal-background check. If the applicant is seeking a hotel position as a parking attendant or as a driver of a courtesy van, managers should run a check on the applicant's driver's license. Managers must be careful, however. Some checks are unlawful unless they clearly relate to the job the candidate is applying for.

Hiring the Selected Person. The key points for managers to keep in mind when hiring applicants is to make sure the applicants clearly understand the position they are being offered; what they will be required to do; what their hours will be; to whom they will report; their vacation and other benefits; the dress code or uniform requirements (if applicable); how much pay they will be getting to start; and when and under what circumstances they can expect a pay increase. If managers do not make these matters absolutely clear to applicants, misunderstandings can occur that could permanently spoil manager/employee relationships before they even get off the ground.

Implementing Continual Training and Career Development Programs

Training is one of the most crucial parts of a human resources program, but it is more often talked about than practiced. When an operation gets busy, training is often overlooked or temporarily suspended because of a lack of time or a lack of trainers.

Training is enormously demanding. It should be an ongoing process for all current employees; for new employees the training process or program has to be started all over again at square one. Training is also expensive, for employees who are learning are not fully productive. For these reasons, there is a great temptation to take shortcuts in training procedures. Managers often rationalize their negligence by telling themselves that current employees don't need to be trained, or on-the-job training is good enough for new hires. Yet without training at all levels within the organization, there can be no consistency of product and service. Training is the process that teaches trainees the knowledge and skills they need to operate within the standards set by management. Training also attempts to develop within employees a positive attitude toward guest service.

Poor training contributes to high turnover and substandard job performance. Employees should feel comfortable in their jobs and be able to do them well so that they do not become discouraged and quit. To train their employees well, many companies use techniques like the video-assisted testing described earlier for new job applicants. At Domino's, McDonald's, and Wendy's, front-line training is accomplished through CDs and DVDs sent to individual stores. These programs introduce new items and emphasize product consistency and control standards. McDonald's has updated its training to include the Internet and Web-based interactive e-learning technology, so its employees can study on their own home computers. The Cheesecake Factory has a comprehensive 14-week training course for new store managers and a 15-week curriculum for kitchen managers. At the end of the training the new-hires attend the Cheesecake Factory Institute. This is a five-day skills seminar that touches on everything from leadership and finance to customer relations. Trainees are told, "If you can't take care of a guest problem using any other means, get ready to grovel."[10]

According to Lewis C. Forrest, Jr., author of *Training for the Hospitality Industry*, the basic steps in the training process are:

1. Establish a training policy
2. Define training needs (needs assessment)
3. Plan the training
4. Prepare the employees
5. Conduct the training
6. Evaluate the training
7. Follow through with ongoing coaching[11]

Training should be continuous and ongoing. A company with an active training program expresses a commitment to its employees. A training program should define who will be trained (ideally, all categories and levels of employees), who will be responsible for training (corporate staff, on-site managers, supervisory personnel), and the training aids and techniques that will be used.

Regular, ongoing training on basic job tasks is necessary at all levels of an organization. Unless continuing positive reinforcement is provided, employees tend to forget some of what they learned. In addition to ongoing training in employees' regular duties, it is often necessary to hold extra training sessions on topics such as sanitation and fire safety.

While most training focuses on knowledge and skills, there are other issues that directly affect employees' job satisfaction and attitudes that are equally important. Many of these issues fall under the broad heading of diversity. **Diversity training** programs seek

Training helps give employees confidence.

to make all workers feel comfortable in the work atmosphere—no matter what their race, culture, sex, or age. Diversity programs are not the same as affirmative-action programs. Affirmative-action programs were created as a result of government mandates to eliminate discrimination based on gender and race. By their very nature, they have accelerated more diversity among workers, which has led to a greater need for diversity training.

Motivating and Retaining Employees

Finding ways to motivate and retain workers is perhaps a manager's most difficult challenge. The importance of having employees who are motivated is clear. The present shortage of workers demands that individual workers increase their productivity. How can managers increase productivity? According to a National Science Foundation report that reviewed 300 studies of productivity, pay, and job satisfaction,

> increased productivity depends on two propositions. First comes motivation: arousing and maintaining the will to work effectively—having workers who are productive not because they are coerced, but because they are committed. Second is reward. Of all the factors that help to create highly motivated and highly satisfied workers, the principal one ... appears to be that effective performance be recognized and rewarded in whatever terms are meaningful to the individual—financial, psychological, or both.[12]

The message is clear. Motivation is a matter of commitment. A manager can only motivate employees to do their best at what the manager wants them to do if it is something the employees want to do as well. Bill McLean, former CEO of a major bank, puts it this way: "You need not read further concerning motivation unless you genuinely understand that to get employees to perform minimum duties, one only needs to drive them. To gain their top performance, one must inspire them to drive themselves."[13]

Motivational Techniques. There are four techniques managers can use to create a self-motivational environment for employees.

Remove the fear of failure. Hospitality enterprises are busy and occasionally stressful places. For workers to function well, they must be well-trained and secure in the fact that they are valued and that they can count on keeping their jobs. Employees who are respected and aware of their importance to the company are not afraid of taking risks to do their best. Many hospitality companies don't even refer to their workers as employees: at McDonald's they are "crew members"; at the Walt Disney Corporation they are "cast members." These terms are intended to give workers a sense of importance.

Pay a fair wage. Employees who are worrying about how they're going to pay next month's rent or a big car-repair bill aren't usually in the mood to take care of other people's problems—they're too worried about their own. In a best-selling book on management called *Leadership Secrets of Attila the Hun,* the author attributed this management advice to Attila: "Grant your Huns the benefit of your interest in the welfare of their families and the condition of their stores; share your riches with those who are loyal and stand in need. They will be certain to willingly follow you into the mouth of Hell, should the occasion arise."[14] Many excellent companies view themselves as an extended family. Thomas J. Peters and Robert H. Waterman, Jr., the authors of *In Search of Excellence: Lessons from America's Best-Run Companies,* reported that "we found prevalent use of the specific terms 'family,' 'extended family,' or 'family feeling' at [such successful companies as] Disney, McDonald's, [and] Delta."[15]

In many cases, employees ask for promotions to other positions so that they can achieve an increase in their pay. This may not be good for the employee or the organization, since a great housekeeper or food server, for example, may make a very poor supervisor. In order to keep good employees satisfied without promoting them beyond their capabilities or inclinations, some companies employ a technique called "broadbanding." In broadbanding, pay for a particular job is defined in broad bands or ranges, with the top end of the pay range of the lower-level job overlapping the bottom end of the pay range of the job above. The Walt Disney company takes this approach. A great server in one of its fine-dining restaurants might earn more than $60,000 a year. If this server chooses to pursue Disney's career path for managers, his or her starting salary drops to $35,000 a year. This shows the amount of pay overlap between the two positions of server and manager trainee. Of course, once the server starts to excel as a manager and is promoted up and through various management levels, his or her total compensation package will grow far beyond $60,000. However, "broadbanding" allows great servers who are content to remain as servers to make a very good living. This also manifests itself in areas such as convention sales, where the sales executive might have a higher earning threshold than the manager of sales. "Broadbanding" allows the company to reward excellence in sales without forcing people into a role that may not suit them.

Offer incentives and rewards for performance. People like to be rewarded; it makes them feel good. The more rewards and awards a company gives, the more motivated its employees are likely to be. Incentives do not have to be monetary to be important. Peters and Waterman put it this way:

> We were struck by the wealth of non-monetary incentives used by excellent companies. Nothing is more powerful than positive reinforcement. Everybody uses it. But top performers, almost alone, use it extensively. The volume of contrived opportunities for showering pins, buttons, badges, and medals on people

It pays to have fun!

JOIN THE FAMILY.

APPLICATION ON INSIDE.
Always, An Equal Opportunity/Affirmative Action Employer.

This tabletop tent card asks job seekers to join the McDonald's "family."
(Courtesy of McDonald's Corporation.)

is staggering at McDonald's, Tupperware, IBM, and many other top performers. They actively seek out and pursue endless excuses to give out rewards.[16]

Operate with an open-door policy; keep everyone informed. Companies with highly motivated employees have few secrets. Communication is a two-way street in these companies. Everyone at the bottom knows what everyone at the top is thinking about important issues, and vice versa. When Ed Carlson was president of United Airlines, he said: "Nothing is worse for morale than a lack of information down in the ranks. I call it 'NETMA—Nobody Ever Tells Me Anything'—and I have tried to minimize that problem."[17] At Walt Disney World, employees receive monthly newsletters called *The EYES & EARS*. Weekly publications such as *Main Street Report* and *Resort Report* focus on specific business units. All of these publications focus on cast (employee) recognition and resort information. Walt Disney World managers also get *Five-Star Team*, a monthly newsletter that discusses current management issues and management development. Disney has designed a series of business-specific employee handbooks. Finally, there is an intranet portal that manages each cast member's entire human resource account, including work schedule and postings of jobs.

Besides using newsletters and handbooks, effective managers communicate with their employees via regular meetings, bulletins, and even paycheck stuffers. Operating results are posted where everyone can see them. A variety of techniques are used to make sure management at the top knows what workers on the front line think. Bill Marriott, Jr., still spends nearly half of his time in the field, first listening to and then talking to employees (the sequence is important). In addition to other forms of communication, the Marriott company conducts annual attitude surveys of all employees. One Marriott executive calls it "our early warning system."[18] Other progressive hotel companies, such as Loews Hotels, have implemented regularly held employee roundtables (quarterly is typical) where employees have the opportunity to speak directly with various members of senior management, including the managing director, and use this forum to ask questions or communicate concerns. At the same time, management is able to communicate what is new and happening at the hotel level and throughout the chain, encouraging two-way communication within the organization.

To keep the lines of communication open, top executives at Shoney's (frequently cited as one of the best limited-menu restaurant chains in the industry) regularly visit Shoney's restaurants. Operations managers are expected to spend as much as four days a week in the field. Jonathan Tisch, chairman and CEO for Loews, inspired a best-practice throughout his chain of hotels when he filmed *Who's the Boss Now*, a TLC television program that filmed executives taking on line staff responsibilities in their organizations. Today, many of the hotels in the Loews organization continue the tradition by having their executive teams take on positions such as housekeepers, stewards, and room service attendants throughout the year. As a result of this simple practice, changes to work practices and improvements in different areas have been implemented.

To ensure communication continues right to the end, excellent companies almost invariably hold exit interviews with departing employees, to collect information on why employees leave. Correctly used, these interviews can point to problems or new trends that cause turnover.

Employee Benefit Options

Including employee benefits as part of the compensation program has become even more important in the competitive environment in which hospitality organizations operate today. Benefits such as paid time off, vacation time, personal days, and paid holidays are critical in an industry that typically operates 24 hours a day, 365 days a year. "Work/ life balance" has become an important concept in an increasingly stressful society. Additionally, offering benefit options such as health insurance (medical, dental, vision), company-matched 401K retirement plans, and employee assistance programs contribute to a company's ability to attract and retain talented staff. Of course, there are expenses associated with these programs, but, in order to compete, most hospitality organizations find that these are necessary expenses.

Because of the increasing cost of health insurance, employers try to make plans more affordable by offering a variety of medical and dental plans with different options (high or low deductibles, varying office-visit co-pays, etc.) and by sharing the expense for these benefits with their employees (that is, asking employees to pay a portion of the cost). Due to the employer's purchasing power with the health insurance companies, the cost is less to employees than if they searched for insurance on their own.

Other employee benefits usually found in the hospitality industry include offering complimentary meals or meals offered at a minimal charge, free dry cleaning of uniforms, free parking, discounted or complimentary travel/room nights, and tuition reimbursement programs.

Evaluating Employees

Although we are discussing evaluation last, it should be clear by this time that evaluation occurs in almost every part of a human resources program, from selection and hiring to training and motivating. Companies that do a good job of developing, motivating, and retaining employees recognize that where there are problems, they are often the result of a flawed system rather than a flawed person. For example, if a server frequently has trouble delivering room service breakfast orders on time, you can't blame him or her for this problem if the only service elevator is always tied up by housekeepers eager to get their guestrooms cleaned.

Employee **performance reviews** are typically held every three, six, or twelve months. New employees are usually reviewed more frequently than experienced ones. The purpose of performance reviews is not to confront employees with their shortcomings. The performance review is a natural step that follows selection, training, and motivating. It lets employees know how well they have learned to do what the company expects of them, and it lets managers know how well they are doing in hiring the right people and training them. Performance reviews are also coaching tools that managers can use to improve employee performance.

Good performance reviews are specific and objective. Some managers fill out a review form before meeting with an employee, on which they can rate the employee's knowledge, skills, and personal attributes—often on some kind of numerical basis. During the review the manager shares these ratings with the employee and gives him or her a chance to comment on them. Some companies have the employee fill out the same form before the review meeting so that the manager and the employee can compare ratings. The manager can recommend follow-up training, coaching, and counseling if this seems called for. Some companies have the manager and the employee draw up a joint goal-setting agreement in which the two agree as to (1) what will be done on both sides to improve the employee's performance in his or her current job, and (2) what the manager and employee will do to prepare the employee for a more rewarding position.

Summary

It is critical that hospitality managers be prepared for the real challenges they will face in managing others. It is difficult to attract and retain the right talent within an industry where high turnover is almost a certainty. Managers must be prepared to lead others successfully in order to minimize the circumstances that cause turnover. With ever-increasing legislation that influences how a manager can deal with specific situations that arise in day-to-day operations, it is imperative that managers understand the implications of the various laws concerning workers and the workplace, including the Civil Rights Act, the Americans with Disabilities Act (ADA) and the ADA Amendments Act of 2008, and the Family Medical Leave Act, to name just a few.

As part of their strategy to deal successfully with employee issues, many hospitality companies have developed human resources programs. A human resources program typically involves a corporate philosophy that values employees. It also includes job analyses, productivity standards, and employee recruitment, selection, training, motivation, benefits, and evaluation programs.

Jobs should be analyzed to establish the best way to perform them. Once jobs are understood, job lists, job breakdowns, and job descriptions can be prepared. These are helpful in recruiting, training, and evaluating employees.

Productivity can be expressed in dollars or in units produced or served. But productivity standards cannot be based on numbers alone—they must take into account quality goals and guest expectations as well.

Effective recruiting demands an understanding of the local labor market. The goal of recruiting is to find the best workers available who find the vacant jobs attractive and are willing to work for the wages the business can pay. Recruiters can use internal sources (current employees, and people recommended by them) and external sources (those recruited through advertising, community involvement, and employment agencies). Sometimes-overlooked groups that can help answer the hospitality industry's labor needs include minorities, disabled workers, senior citizens, and workers with limited skills. There are many job programs in place to help hospitality businesses find and train potential employees in these groups.

Selecting a job applicant to fill a vacancy involves five steps: receiving and processing applications, interviewing applicants, evaluating applicants, checking references, and hiring the selected person.

Training is one of the most crucial parts of a human resources program. Unfortunately, training is often neglected. Basic steps in the training process are: establishing a training policy, defining training needs, planning the training, preparing the employees for training, conducting the training, and evaluating the training. Ongoing coaching by managers is a valuable follow-through on all types of training. Today many companies supplement traditional training methods with CDs, DVDs, and Web-based courses.

A manager who wants motivated workers must gain their commitment to the company and its goals. There are four techniques managers can use to accomplish this: (1) remove the fear of failure, (2) pay a fair wage, (3) offer incentives and rewards for performance, and (4) operate with an open-door policy—keep everyone informed. Offering a competitive benefit package is also important in an increasingly competitive environment for talented staff.

Evaluating employees is the final step in a human resources program. Employees need to know how they are doing; regularly scheduled performance reviews help accomplish this. Companies that do a good job of retaining, developing, and motivating employees recognize that where there are problems, they are often the result of a flawed system rather than a flawed person.

 Endnotes

1. Mitra Toossi, "Labor Force Projections to 2016: More Workers in Their Golden Years," *Monthly Labor Review,* November 2007, pp. 33–52.

2. From a letter by Edward H. Rensi, president, McDonald's U.S.A., printed as an introduction to *Ingredients for Success: Food for Thought on Finding Your First Job,* produced in conjunction with the American School Counselor Association.

3. From a personal interview with Paul Breslin, manager, Sheraton Atlanta Hotel.

4. Ibid.

5. Marcus Buckingham and Curt Coffman, *First, Break All the Rules: What the World's Greatest Managers Do Differently* (New York: Simon & Schuster, 1999), p. 67.

6. *Hotel* Online, October 2000. "How Marriott Attracts and Retains Employees" sidebar was also adapted from this source.

7. Casey Jones and Thomas A. Decotiis, "A Better Way to Select Service Employees: Video-Assisted Testing," *Cornell Quarterly*, August 1986.

8. Ibid.

9. Breslin interview.

10. Alan J. Liddle, "The Cheesecake Factory," *Nation's Restaurant News*, August 14, 2000.

11. Lewis C. Forrest, Jr., *Training for the Hospitality Industry*, 2d ed. (Lansing, Mich.: Educational Institute of AH&LA, 1990), p. 5.

12. Ron Zemke and Dick Schaaf, *The Service Edge: 101 Companies That Profit from Customer Care* (New York: New American Library, 1989), p. 72.

13. J. W. McLean, *So You Want to Be the Boss? A CEO's Lessons in Leadership* (Englewood Cliffs, N.J.: Prentice-Hall, 1990), p. 44.

14. Wess Roberts, *Leadership Secrets of Attila the Hun* (New York: Warner Books, 1990), p. 79.

15. Thomas J. Peters and Robert H. Waterman, Jr., *In Search of Excellence: Lessons from America's Best-Run Companies* (New York: Harper & Row, 1982), p. 261.

16. Peters and Waterman, p. 269.

17. Ibid., p. 267.

18. James L. Heskett, *Managing in the Service Economy* (Boston: Harvard Business School Press, 1986), p. 127.

⌐ Key Terms

covers—The actual number of meals served at a food function or during a meal period.

diversity training—Training that seeks to make all workers feel comfortable in their workplace, no matter what their race, culture, sex, or age.

full-time-equivalent employee (FTE)—A measure used for statistical purposes in which two or more part-time employees whose hours add up to 40 hours a week (the number of hours one full-time employee would work) equal one full-time-equivalent (FTE) employee. For example, four part-time employees who each work ten hours a week would, for statistical purposes, be recorded as one FTE employee.

job breakdown—The specific, step-by-step procedures for accomplishing each task of a particular job.

job description—A recruiting and training tool that outlines for a particular job (1) the title that goes with the job, (2) the person to whom the employee reports, (3) the work to be performed (in general terms), (4) the education or skills the employee must have, and (5) the physical requirements of the job.

job list—A list of the tasks that must be performed by the individual holding a particular job.

performance review—A meeting between a manager and an employee, to (1) let the employee know how well he or she has learned to meet company standards, and (2) let the manager know how well he or she is doing in hiring and training employees. Typically held every 3, 6, or 12 months, depending on the employee's performance and experience.

productivity standards—Measurements that tell managers how long it should take an employee to complete tasks using the best methods management has devised, and how many tasks an employee can perform in a given time period. This measurement differs according to the task the employee is performing.

Review Questions

1. What key demographic trends will have a significant impact on U.S. businesses within the next decade?

2. What are some common reasons for the hospitality industry's high turnover rates?

3. What are the differences between job lists, job breakdowns, and job descriptions?

4. What are some examples of productivity standards used within the hospitality industry?

5. What are some internal and external sources of employees?

6. What steps are involved in filling a vacant position?

7. Why is training important?

8. What are some techniques for motivating employees?

9. Why are performance reviews valuable to employees and managers?

Internet Sites

For more information, visit the following Internet sites. Remember that Internet addresses can change without notice. If the site is no longer there, you can use a search engine to look for additional sites.

Associations

American Hotel & Lodging Association
www.ahla.com

National Restaurant Association
www.restaurant.org

Hotels/Restaurants

Bob Evans
www.bobevans.com

Marriott International
www.marriott.com

The Cheesecake Factory
www.thecheesecakefactory.com

McDonald's
www.mcdonalds.com

Domino's Pizza
www.dominos.com

The Ritz-Carlton Hotel Company
www.ritzcarlton.com

Sheraton Hotels & Resorts
www.sheraton.com

Shoney's
www.shoneys.com

Organizations, Resources

Americans with Disabilities Act
www.usdoj.gov/crt/ada/adahom1.htm

ehotelier.com
www.ehotelier.org/browse/jobsearch.htm

hospitalitycareernet.com
www.hospitalitycareernet.com

hospitality careers online
www.hcareers.com

Hospitality Net
www.hospitalitynet.org

Hotel Jobs Network
www.hospitalityjobs.com

HRMagazine
www.shrm.org/hrmagazine

Walt Disney Corporation
www.disney.com

Wendy's
www.wendys.com

Human Resources Law Index
www.hrlawindex.com

Monster.com
www.monster.com

Occupational Safety & Health
  Administration (OSHA)
www.osha.gov

Society for Human Resource
  Management
www.shrm.org

U.S. Department of Labor
www.dol.gov

Workforce Online
www.workforceonline.com

14
Marketing Hospitality

Outline

The Marketing Concept
    The Four P's of Marketing
    Developing a Marketing Plan
Sales Management and Personal Selling
    How to Be a Successful Salesperson
Advertising
    Definition of Advertising
    What an Advertiser Needs
    Advertising Agencies
    Creating Effective Advertising
Public Relations
Publicity
Sales Promotion
Internet Marketing
    E-Mail Advertising and Promotion
    Social Media
Leveraging Your Marketing Dollars
Summary

Competencies

1. Distinguish marketing from selling, identify and explain the Four P's of Marketing, and describe how a marketing plan is developed. (pp. 418–429)

2. Describe how hotels organize their sales department and summarize the characteristics and qualities salespersons should possess. (pp. 429–431)

3. Define and describe advertising, including what an advertiser needs, advertising agencies, and how to create effective advertising. (pp. 431–440)

4. Explain the role and importance of public relations, publicity, sales promotion, and Internet marketing for hospitality businesses, and discuss how marketers can leverage their marketing dollars. (pp. 440–449)

Opposite page: The Savoy, London; photo courtesy of Fairmont Hotels & Resorts.

THIS CHAPTER DISCUSSES how hospitality companies market and sell their products and services. The Four P's of Marketing—product, place, price, and promotion—will be covered, along with how hotels and restaurants go about developing a marketing plan. Next we'll take a look at how important personal selling is to hotels and restaurants. A section on hospitality advertising follows, which ranges from how advertising is defined to how successful advertising is created. The chapter continues with a discussion of the marketing activities of public relations, publicity, sales promotion, and Internet marketing, then concludes with a section on how to leverage your marketing dollars.

The Marketing Concept

The purpose of a business is to get and keep customers, for without customers there is no business. Professor Theodore Levitt of the Harvard Business School points out that:

> customers are constantly presented with lots of options to help them solve their problems. They don't buy things, they buy solutions to problems.... No business can function effectively without a clear view of how to get customers, what its prospective customers want and need, what options its competitors give them, and without explicit strategies and programs focused on what goes on in the marketplace.[1]

That is what marketing is: the effort to determine and meet the needs and wants of current and potential customers.

There is an important distinction between selling and marketing that many students fail to recognize. This is due to confusing terminology that is commonly used in business. Often, people whose jobs are in sales are called "marketing representatives." The title suggests that the words "sales" and "marketing" are interchangeable; they are not. **Marketing** is a much broader term that includes sales and a great deal more. The difference between the two has often been stated this way: *selling is getting rid of what you have; marketing is having what people want.*

Some marketers look at it this way: marketing is the art of *buying from* customers, which is exactly the opposite of *selling to* customers. In other words, customers have money in their pockets that you, the salesperson, want to "buy." How can you buy the customer's money? By paying for it with a product or service. This marketing approach to selling can help you sell in two ways. First, your focus is on the customers rather than on your products. Instead of focusing on the attributes of your products, you focus on persuading customers to "sell" you their money—which usually leads you to study your customers and their needs and wants. Second, you have a different attitude toward customers—you value them more and approach them more carefully because you realize you are trying to convince them to give up something of value.

The Four P's of Marketing

The list of activities that can be included in the efforts to get and keep customers is quite extensive. For a restaurant, the things that influence whether customers eat there include the location, decor, menu, quality and presentation of food, type of service, and prices. All of these are marketing decisions first and foremost. To make these decisions, a restaurant's managers must determine (1) what their current and potential customers need or want, (2) how to provide it, and (3) how to persuade current and potential customers to patronize the restaurant. These activities break down into four basic responsibilities that are popularly called the **"Four P's of Marketing"**: product, place, price, and promotion.

How businesses allocate their resources among product, place, price, and promotional efforts varies widely, depending on the objectives of each business. In a sense, the Four P's are like the ingredients in a recipe for success, and the relative proportion of resources allocated to each effort and the way these four marketing efforts are combined is often referred to as the **marketing mix.**

Product: What Do You Sell? The term "product" as used in the hospitality field can have several meanings. Obviously, a product can be a guestroom or a meal that a hotel or restaurant provides to guests. A hospitality product can also be an intangible service, such as a food server serving a meal or a bellperson carrying a guest's luggage. Product can also refer to a hotel or restaurant's concept. For example, a Fairfield Inn is an economy product designed specifically to appeal to business travelers. In this case, "product" refers to all the things that make the experience of staying at a Fairfield Inn what it is—its philosophy, facilities, amenities, level of service, and the tangible products it sells to guests.

For many owners of small hospitality businesses, determining the concept for a hotel or restaurant was not considered a marketing decision. For example, many ethnic restaurants in the United States got their start because immigrant families from such countries as Italy, Greece, and France decided to open eating establishments offering the kind of

The term "product" as used in the hospitality industry can have several meanings. A hospitality product can be tangible—such as a bottle of fine wine—but it can also be an intangible service, such as a sommelier's suggestion for just the right wine for a special occasion. (Courtesy of Luxor Resort & Casino, Las Vegas, Nevada.)

food they knew how to prepare. Since these families generally opened their restaurants in neighborhoods where other people of the same ethnic background lived, their restaurants enjoyed a built-in market. It was not necessary for the owners to be marketing-oriented — they simply sold what they knew how to make, and as long as they did it well there were plenty of customers.

This approach no longer works, because those built-in markets have, for the most part, disappeared. While it is still true that people who have the same tastes and lifestyles are likely to live in the same neighborhood, consumers today have so many choices that simply opening a business in a location, no matter how good that location, cannot ensure success. This is especially true in the hospitality industry, where there are no revolutionary new developments that are likely to convince customers to give up their old buying habits and form new loyalties. People have been eating and sleeping the same way at hospitality businesses for thousands of years. While the surroundings have gotten nicer, the basic services offered by dining and lodging establishments have not changed. And yet, surprisingly enough, many hotels and restaurants still market themselves as if they were offering something truly unique in a marketplace without competitors. They first decide what they are going to sell and then wrestle with the problem of how to sell it.

A hotel or restaurant's concept — the type of establishment it is or will be — should be first and foremost a marketing decision that is based on providing a better solution to a customer's problem — which might be anything from finding a place for a quick bite to eat, to searching for a site to hold a wedding reception for 300 people. To come up with a successful concept for a hospitality business requires a clear understanding of what people are looking for and what competitors already offer them. Only a business that understands what problems consumers are hoping to solve — and can offer better solutions — has a hope of succeeding.

This reinforces what Professor Levitt says about people never buying a product, but rather the utility they expect to receive from it. In a speech for the American Association of Advertising Agencies at the Greenbrier in White Sulphur Springs, West Virginia, Levitt put it this way: "When you go into a hardware store you do not buy a quarter-inch drill, you buy the expectation of a quarter-inch hole."

It all comes down to what we pointed out earlier in this section — hospitality businesses do not simply sell rooms, meals, spas, airplane seats, or rental cars. What they sell is a service that uses these physical objects the same way a play in the theater uses a stage, sets, costumes, and props to put on a performance. Indeed, there are many similarities between service delivery and the theater, and it is useful to think about these similarities when looking at hospitality marketing from a customer's point of view.

First of all, there is the matter of the **front of the house** and the **back of the house**, terms used in the hotel business to describe the areas that guests see (the front desk, for example, is in the front of the house) and the areas that guests do not see (the kitchen and other behind-the-scenes areas). Theaters also have a front of the house (the seats for the audience and the stage on which the performance takes place) and a back of the house (dressing rooms, lighting booths, and so on). The front of the house in both hotels and theaters is designed to create an impression. Like actors in a play, hotel employees are given roles to play — front desk agent, dining room manager, housekeeper. The audience comes to a play to be entertained or distracted from their normal concerns in the same way that leisure travelers check into hotels or go to restaurants to get away from their familiar surroundings. There are many more comparisons that can be made, but for our purposes it is enough to remember that, as Hamlet pointed out in Shakespeare's tragedy of the same

"We're here to experience pleasure."

© Edward Koren/The New Yorker Collection/www.cartoonbank.com.

name, "The play's the thing." When people enter a hotel or restaurant, they expect to be transported to a place where everything looks beautiful and clean, and smiling people are friendly and want to help them and take care of them. They want a performance, and that is what hospitality managers and their staffs must be prepared to offer them.

Place: Where Do You Sell It? "Place" also has several meanings in hospitality marketing. To begin with, it clearly refers to the physical location of the business, which, as we have seen previously, can be crucial to its success.

Place can also have a profound effect on marketing methods. For instance, the fact that a large number of Holiday Inns are located all over the United States means that people are reminded of the Holiday Inn name wherever they go, so when they are in a strange town the Holiday Inn there is a familiar place. Moreover, because Holiday Inn is everywhere, its corporate management can advertise on national television or in national magazines, which would be too costly and inefficient for many of its competitors.

Place has another meaning as well, which is the location not of the hotel but of the site where the reservation for the hotel is made. This can be on the hotel's own website or the website of the chain to which the hotel belongs (in the case of chain properties), but it can also be via telephone at the hotel itself or at the hotel's central reservations office, at a travel agency (by phone or in person), or on the Internet with an online travel agency (OTA). The following are OTAs where it is possible to book hotel rooms, airline tickets, and more:

- Expedia.com, founded by Richard Barton in 1994 when he was working for Microsoft (currently it is owned by USA Interactive).

- Travelocity.com, which is owned by Sabre Holdings, a travel technology company.

- Orbitz.com, started by a partnership of major airlines but now a public company that owns cheaptickets.com.

- Priceline.com, an auction site where people can bid for low-priced airplane tickets, hotel rooms, vacation packages, and car rentals.

Price: What Do You Sell It For? Too often, hotels and restaurants set their prices on a cost-plus basis. It is assumed that food costs, for example, should be 30 percent of the menu item's total cost to a guest. But this model ignores how guests feel about what they are getting and what they are willing to pay for it. The basic flaw with **cost-plus pricing** is that guests don't care what your costs are. Moreover, it doesn't take into account a notion that almost all retailers understand: that some items are **loss-leaders** items that are not profitable in themselves but which attract customers to stores, where they may buy other items that are profitable. Typically, bars and lounges that offer a free or nominally priced buffet during happy hour are purposely sacrificing the low profit margin on their food in order to gain higher profits from beverage sales.

Cost-plus or product-driven pricing is used by many businesses to set prices, but ultimately consumers decide whether they will pay for what is being offered, and if they won't pay the price set by management, the price must be adjusted or the product or service must be dropped. Therefore, **consumer-based pricing** is a much more realistic method of setting prices. With consumer-based pricing, companies first determine what customers want, what they are willing to pay for it, and then figure out a way to deliver that product and service at the desirable price.

Hotels and restaurants that use consumer-based pricing try to give customers what they expect (or more than they expect) for the price being charged. Businesses that set prices with the customer in mind also recognize that consumers may perceive a larger difference between $9.95 and $10 than there actually is, and so try to keep their prices at the lower figure. There is another psychological factor at work in pricing—the assumption that quality costs money, and that you must pay more to get better quality. Many people are willing to pay more, and refuse to stay in the cheapest hotel. These customers believe that there are no free lunches and you always get what you pay for. Restaurants that have a real quality advantage over competitors in terms of product or service also have a definite pricing advantage. Even if it costs them less than it costs their competitors to produce a meal, they can charge more and their sales will actually increase, since many people believe that extra quality is worth more money.

There are many other methods of pricing besides cost-plus and consumer-based pricing. One is **competitive pricing**. With competitive pricing, hotels base room rates on what their competitors charge. This strategy can work only as long as consumers see all of the competing hotels as being equal. If there is a perceivable difference (such as one hotel being brand-new while the others are much older), then competitive pricing will favor the hotel that appears to offer the most, the newest, or the nicest facilities. Another problem with competitive pricing is that your competitors may be willing to lose money, or they might have lower costs, which would mean they can still make money by charging prices that would mean losses for you.

There is a phenomenon known as **elasticity of demand**—the response by customers to changes in price. Elasticity of demand is important to understand, because if demand for a product or service is elastic, then managers can raise or lower consumer demand through various strategies, including raising or lowering prices. If demand for a product or service is low at one price, then lowering that price may increase the demand. For example, in many cities, rates for hotel rooms are high during the week because business travelers will pay high prices for the rooms. Those same guestrooms may go unoccupied on weekends, however, when demand from business travelers drops off significantly. The rooms may be sold if the prices for them are lowered enough so that they appeal to a different guest group—families or singles wanting a weekend getaway package, for example.

If demand is inelastic, then demand will vary little if at all, no matter what type of price adjustments are made. This is the experience of resorts in areas such as Bermuda (in the winter when it is too cold) and Palm Springs, California (in the summer when it is too hot), where lowered room rates and special promotional advertising have not been entirely successful in raising room occupancies to an acceptable level during the off-season. Many people do not want to go to Bermuda or Palm Springs during the off-season, no matter how attractive the price.

Students interested in pricing should recognize that for the purposes of this introductory chapter we have simplified this subject considerably. For example, today many hotels use **revenue management** computer programs to set their prices. Revenue management programs seek to optimize the revenue a hotel receives in any given period by adjusting the rates that are offered to different market segments, based on the projected supply of rooms and the demand for them. Revenue management is a system originally developed by the airlines to allocate the number of seats on each flight that would be available for each of the different fares that airlines offer. These numbers change constantly as reservations come in and forecasts are adjusted accordingly.

In another example of a more complicated approach to pricing, Professor William Quain has developed a method for analyzing sales-mix profitability that looks at prices from the point of view of profit analysis by segment (PABS). Quain suggests that hotels that judge their performance simply by their ADR (the average daily rate they charge for guestrooms) are making "a mistake that occurs when hotels have a sales plan, not a marketing plan."[2] Quain's work suggests that the cost of making a sale should be a key component in setting guestroom prices. For example, it may be cheaper to sell a block of 100 rooms to one meeting planner than to process 100 individual reservations, so room prices can be set lower for the meeting planner. The amount of money a guest is likely to spend in the hotel should also be taken into consideration when setting guestroom rates. Guests attending meetings tend to have all of their meals on the property, so 100 meeting attendees may be more profitable than 100 individual guests, even if the meeting attendees are charged less for their guestrooms.

Christopher W. Nordling and Sharon K. Wheeler developed a market-segment accounting model for the Las Vegas Hilton that restructures the traditional approach of viewing each hotel department as a profit center and then using that information to account for revenues, costs, and profits, which in turn lead to pricing decisions. Nordling and Wheeler point out that "managers have always gone after what they believed to be the highest profit segment based on which type of guest pays the highest average room rate. But few operators have measured *all* of the attendant costs of servicing each segment and the non-room profit (or loss) produced by the segment."[3] They believe that only this kind of analysis, which shows the relative value of each market segment, can correctly help managers set prices that will produce optimal revenues for a property.

Promotion: How Do You Spread the Word? The fourth "P" in marketing stands for "promotion." It is placed last because promotional decisions ideally should be made after product, place, and price decisions have been made. Promotion consists of all the ways an enterprise tries to persuade people to buy its products and services, including use of online technologies through website advertising, e-mail promotions, and social networks. All promotional activities fall into one of six categories:

- Personal selling
- Advertising
- Public relations and sponsorship marketing
- Sales promotion
- Direct marketing communications
- Point-of-purchase communications

Traditionally, companies have looked at these functions separately. It is not uncommon for a hotel to use different people (either their own employees or outside agencies) to coordinate sales, public relations, direct marketing, and point-of-purchase merchandising. For example, a hotel's advertising and website might be designed and placed by the advertising agency that works with the general manager, while personal sales and public relations are handled by different people within the hotel. Direct response programs might be initiated by the marketing department, and point-of-purchase materials might be supplied to the food and beverage department by a local graphic designer or printer.

There is a school of thinking, however, that says that all of these tasks are various forms of *marketing communications* and that to be effectively managed they should be integrated. **Integrated marketing communications** has become the new model that many firms use in organizing their marketing activities. All activities, whether they involve personal sales calls, advertising programs, or tent cards for the dining room, are coordinated. This ensures that the organization sends out messages to its employees, customers, the press, and others that are consistent and directed at achieving the overall mission of the organization.

However, while these various forms of marketing communications should be integrated, each has unique strengths and weaknesses. Personal selling is used as the primary way to attract corporate and group business. Advertising both offline and online is often targeted at leisure travelers (who cannot be reached by direct sales), or designed to build an image for a brand name such as Hilton or Marriott. Public relations often has a much wider audience and attempts to influence individuals and groups not reached by traditional personal selling or advertising—employees, community opinion leaders, financial institutions, unions, and others. Sales promotion is used to quickly boost sales.

To succeed, a hotel or restaurant must know how to use promotional activities and how to organize and combine them so they work together to produce a synergistic effect—one where the whole is greater than the sum of its parts. The principal tool used to accomplish this is the hotel or restaurant's marketing plan.

Developing a Marketing Plan

All business activities should be planned. Although this seems obvious, it is often ignored. Managers sometimes feel that planning takes too much time. They argue that it is better to

Perhaps the most important marketing and sales promotion item in a restaurant is its menu. This menu cover is from Chili's. Inside, large four-color photographs and enticing menu descriptions encourage diners to spend. (Courtesy of Chili's Grill & Bar.)

go out and do something than to sit around and figure out how to do it. Nevertheless, in the case of marketing, where the expenses involved can be astronomical, planning may be regarded as essential to survival. Companies like McDonald's spend more than $2 billion a year on marketing and advertising activities. If those funds were not spent effectively and did not produce the desired results, those companies would suffer severe losses. Even a small restaurant owner with a marketing budget of $25,000 must make those dollars return themselves quickly in the form of increased revenue, or the dollars available for marketing will disappear in no time at all.

A marketing plan is a blueprint for organizing, in the most efficient way possible, a business's marketing strategies and activities. New marketing plans are usually created on a regular basis. Many businesses create one every year, others may create marketing plans every two, three, or five years. Good plans are always reviewed and often revised on a quarterly basis to take current conditions into account. A good marketing plan has several parts:

- Situation analysis
- Objectives
- Strategies
- Tactics
- Controls

Developing a marketing plan may sound like an intimidating procedure, but it is relatively uncomplicated and follows a series of logical steps.

Situation Analysis. The first step in developing a marketing plan is the situation analysis. A marketing department's situation analysis is in some ways similar to feasibility studies prepared for proposed restaurants or hotels, except that the marketing department's situation analysis is prepared for an already existing property and is even more marketing oriented.

A situation analysis prepared by a marketing department typically consists of a marketplace analysis, a competition analysis, a review of internal data, a target audience profile, and a problems and opportunities section. The situation analysis is often called a SWOT analysis; SWOT stands for strengths, weaknesses, opportunities, and threats.

Marketplace analysis. Before we can do anything about a situation, we must understand it. Therefore, the first thing a situation analysis contains is a description of the marketplace. If we were doing a situation analysis for a hotel, our first step would be to write down the important data that is likely to affect hotel occupancy in our area in the year ahead. Are businesses opening or closing? Is the economy growing? What is the outlook for tourism? Is the state or city planning any major new campaigns to attract tourists? Is the airport projecting more traffic or less?

Competition analysis. Marketplace information is very general. It concentrates on overall or big trends that are likely to affect your business in the years ahead. In addition to this kind of information, the situation analysis should include a competition analysis. The competition analysis seeks to pinpoint who your competitors are. They are not always easily spotted. For example, the Greenbrier Hotel in White Sulphur Springs, West Virginia, competes with the Arizona Biltmore in Phoenix for conventions. Quick-service establishments like Taco Bell and Subway compete not only with other quick-service restaurants, they also compete with convenience stores and supermarkets for market share.

Besides simply listing competitors, it is important to get down on paper a description of the competitors' establishments and how they compare with your facility, both in terms of the physical plant and the quality of service. The prices competitors charge should be compared with the prices you charge (or plan to charge). A competition analysis for a hotel also includes the number of hotel rooms or beds in the market, average occupancy rates, and the kinds of lodging properties found in the area—resorts, city hotels, motels, and so on. If the market is overbuilt, this fact should be noted. Finally, the analysis should include a careful look at who the competitors' guests are, where they come from, and whether you can reasonably expect to lure them away from your competitors. New business almost always comes from the customer-base of competitors, customers who either are unsatisfied or believe that you can offer them something superior.

Internal analysis. This section of the situation analysis compiles internal data that will be useful in formulating marketing strategies and tactics. This kind of data should include information on sales mix, such as the percentage and amount of revenue that comes from room sales, food, beverages, catering, and other activities. Finances should be taken into account as well—the capital and resources available, cash flow, and budgets. Human resources policies and operations data such as how well the reservation system and the website are functioning belong in this section.

Target audience profile. The most important part of the situation analysis is the target audience profile. You should begin with the demographics—that is, what you know about the ages, income, family size, and geographic location of your guests. You should also know as much as you can about your guests' lifestyles. How often do they travel or eat out? Where do they eat? Who makes the decision? This information will help you organize your sales efforts and select advertising media.

Ideally, a target audience profile should help you identify your current or potential heavy users. In the case of a restaurant, are they businesspeople grabbing a quick breakfast on the way to work, or mothers with young children meeting friends for lunch? A restaurant's heavy users sometimes represent only 25 percent of the guest base but as much as 75 percent of sales because they come in regularly several times a week. The same is true in hotels, where a small base of corporate guests can easily represent more than half of a hotel's total sales.

For many hotels (and some restaurants), the most important target audience is groups. These groups can range from motorcoach tour groups to meeting and convention groups. It is important to understand the specific needs of these groups. They may require large rooms for their main sessions and banquets, as well as smaller rooms for workshops. They may want several hospitality suites. They may also request special registration and check-out procedures.

Problems and opportunities. The "problems and opportunities" section is the one in which the strengths and weaknesses of the company are most often identified. Once you have completed the fact-finding phase of the situation analysis, the work really begins. Now you have to interpret what those facts mean. Does the fact that there are no Greek restaurants in your neighborhood mean that there is an opportunity to convert your restaurant to one, or does it simply mean that people in the area do not like Greek food? Does the fact that all of the hotels in your city are mid-price mean that there is a market for a luxury hotel? There may indeed be a market, but it may be so small that upgrading your property to go after it would not be a profitable venture. Many restaurateurs start a catering service, believing that their food service expertise is sufficient to attract customers and earn profits. This is often an illusion. There may already be several competent caterers in the area with established reputations and a loyal customer base. In such a situation it can be a long and costly process to start a new catering business, and it might never succeed unless there is a real point of difference between the established caterers and the new operation. Even then, success is not guaranteed. To paraphrase the old proverb, "The man who built a better mousetrap and then waited for the world to beat a path to his door starved to death."

The problems and opportunities section is the place to list, as objectively as you can, the problems that stand in the way of significantly increasing your sales or your market share. For example, if you operate a downtown dinner restaurant in a city where fewer and fewer people are coming downtown for dinner in the evening, put that down on paper. You have a genuine problem. You also may have an equally genuine opportunity to open a second restaurant in the suburbs, or open for lunch in your city location.

Objectives. Once facts about the current business situation have been gathered by a hotel or restaurant's marketers and outlined and analyzed in a situation analysis, managers can review the situation analysis and begin to create marketing objectives. Marketing objectives are clear and concise descriptions of exactly what managers want the marketing program to accomplish. These objectives are usually specific and measurable.

A business usually has several different types of marketing objectives. A financial objective is usually first. Most companies base their company-wide expense budget on expected income; expected income is stated in the marketing plan as monthly profit goals. Then there are usually growth objectives. Objectives to significantly increase your sales or expand into new markets are growth objectives. Sometimes financial objectives and growth objectives conflict with each other—building a new wing onto the hotel may diminish profits temporarily, for instance. Quality objectives are important in the marketing plans of service organizations. Quality objectives may encompass introducing new amenities or improving existing products or services. Finally, there are philosophical objectives that may address issues such as better working conditions for employees, more environmentally conscious operations, or support of local charities and cultural programs.

Strategies. After marketing objectives are established, marketing strategies can be devised. Strategies are simply descriptions of how the organization will go about trying to achieve its marketing objectives. For example, suppose one of your objectives is to increase the amount of leisure business at your hotel from 20 percent to 30 percent in six months. Your strategies to do this might include:

- Generating support from more travel agents
- Increasing consumer contact through e-mail, blogs, and other social networks
- Developing special honeymoon and other travel packages
- Promoting your website

To be sure that these strategies are realistic, projected cost figures should be attached to each of them. How much money is going to be spent on generating support from more travel agents, for example, or promoting the website? If a strategy costs too much, it can be modified, replaced with a less expensive strategy, or simply eliminated.

Tactics. Strategies are general in nature. Getting to specifics is where tactics come in. For example, how much of the marketing budget will be shifted from offline to online activities? Should we engage a manager for social networking? What promotions will be offered to our frequent customers via e-mail, Facebook, and Twitter?

The answers to these and other questions help managers develop tactics or action plans for achieving marketing objectives. Without tactics, a marketing plan is a useless document. It is not a plan at all. A real marketing plan contains tactics for every strategy, so that anyone with a copy knows what to do and how to do it.

Controls. Control is as important in marketing as it is in operations. If marketing's tactics are specific, you should be able to tell what is supposed to happen every month and how much it is expected to cost. Results can be anticipated too. Advertising a special honeymoon package ought to produce a number of reservations by honeymooners. If it doesn't, something is wrong. Marketing plans should not be inflexible—they should be reviewed on a regular basis and revised when necessary. That is the function of controls—to enable managers to monitor how well the plan is working and make adjustments when necessary.

Sales Management and Personal Selling

Some hotel and restaurant chains have millions of dollars to spend on advertising, public relations, and sales promotion, but most hotels and restaurants have limited marketing budgets. Therefore, personal selling by the owners, managers, or sales force is the business-building tool hotels and restaurants most frequently employ.

Most hotels have a marketing and sales or a sales department. Some of these departments are quite sophisticated. Salespersons generally report to a sales manager, who may in turn report to the director of marketing and sales (remember, sales is only one of the functions of marketing). In mid-size to small hotels, the director of marketing and sales and the sales manager are often the same person, although the functions of each job are different. Many hotel companies have adopted the cluster concept, whereby a staff in a central office performs the sales functions for a group of hotels in the region. Most private clubs, restaurants that have private meeting rooms, and caterers have at least one full-time salesperson on staff (unless the owner or manager takes on this function, which is usually not a good idea).

The sales manager is in charge of the sales office and is responsible for overseeing the sales staff. Some sales managers assign salespersons according to source of business. There may be a salesperson in charge of selling corporate programs targeted at individual business travelers, for example; another in charge of booking meetings and conventions business; and a third in charge of tour business. Other salespersons may be in charge of travel agency sales, military and government sales, and catering sales. Or, sales managers may use a regional approach—there may be an "East Region" salesperson, a "West Region" salesperson, and even an international salesperson, depending on the size and nature of the business. According to James Abbey, author of *Hospitality Sales and Advertising*, the general goals of a sales manager include:

- Increasing property revenue through personal sales calls, telephone calls, and correspondence

- Establishing guidelines for the number of personal sales calls, telephone calls, and sales letters required from each salesperson

- Assisting the general manager with obtaining the maximum sales effort from all employees

- Holding weekly and monthly sales meetings

- Maintaining sales reports and establishing a sales filing system to ensure that all files are processed and kept up-to-date[4]

In order to accomplish these tasks, a sales manager must first recruit and train salespersons. The ability to be an effective salesperson can be learned; it is not a skill that is inherited or based purely on natural talent. Nevertheless, some people are better at it than others.

There are individuals who do not like the idea of selling to someone else. They consider it to be manipulative or unethical behavior. To be sure, unethical salespersons are a part of American folklore. Some early American salespersons were peddlers whose wares included snake oil, charms, and fake antiquities, all of which required a certain amount of deception to sell. Even today, surveys show that used-car salespersons are some of the least-trusted of all businesspeople, and salespersons as a group are considered less trustworthy than most other professionals. Nevertheless, sales can be an honorable and rewarding career, and, as often as not, today's salesperson is regarded as an important partner, counselor, and helper. At IBM, for example, the mission of the sales team is to help companies solve problems, which is different from selling them computers. However, because IBM salespersons are good problem solvers, they also sell a great many computers.

How to Be a Successful Salesperson

There are certain characteristics that successful salespersons share, according to Professor Charles Garfield, a clinical professor of psychology at the University of California. Garfield, who has studied super-achievers in all areas, says that exceptional salespersons are similar in these ways:

- They are always innovating and taking risks to try and surpass previous levels of performance.

- They have a powerful sense of mission and set short-, intermediate-, and long-term goals to fulfill that mission. Their personal sales goals are higher than those set by their managers.

- Super-salespersons are more interested in solving problems than in placing blame or bluffing their way out of situations. Because they view themselves as professionals, they are always upgrading their skills.

- Super-salespersons see themselves as partners with their customers and as team players rather than adversaries. They believe their task is to communicate with people.

- Super-salespersons do not take rejection personally; rather, they treat it as information they can learn from.

- Super-salespersons use mental rehearsal. Before every sale, they review it in their mind's eye, from shaking the customer's hand when they walk in to discussing the customer's problems and asking for the sale.[5]

How does one become a good salesperson? One characteristic is essential in sales: intelligence. Derek Taylor, a successful hotel sales director in England for more than 30 years, puts it this way:

> Sales … is a cerebral occupation. It takes a great deal of thought, for in trying to convince a client to buy the product, you are trying to influence his mind. I

Successful salespeople know how to relate to other people and see themselves as partners and team players with their customers rather than adversaries.

have often been asked what book a prospective hotel salesperson should read to understand his job; my answer remains Freud's *Two Short Accounts of Psycho-analysis.* It is a nice simple book that tells you the rules of the game. The capacity to outthink the client who is not all that keen on buying your hotel is the vital difference between success and failure.[6]

Most professional salespersons would agree with Taylor that an understanding of how people think and how to relate to them is the most important characteristic of any salesperson. The idea that extroverted, sociable people make better salespersons than those who are quiet and introverted has little basis in fact. They make different types of sales-persons, but studies have shown that there is no difference in sales effectiveness between people who are outgoing and sociable and those who are quiet and reserved. The key is the ability to relate to other people, to be able to listen to them, and then to communicate with them in terms that they understand and in a manner that they can empathize with.

Advertising

The codfish lays a thousand eggs
The homely hen lays one
But the codfish never cackles
To show what she has done.
And so we praise the homely hen
The codfish we despise

Which clearly shows to you and me
It pays to advertise!

Anonymous

Advertising is a substitute for personal salesmanship. Through advertising, we attempt to talk to those prospects who, for one reason or another, will never get a personal sales call, as well as to prospects who never directly communicate with an advertiser. Advertising also has some unique advantages over personal selling. For instance, advertising can get into offices and homes where a salesperson can't. Many companies use advertising for exactly that reason—to get a "salesperson" past a closed door.

Another advantage of advertising is that it can be repetitive. Once we've seen a salesperson and heard his or her pitch, we are not likely to listen to the pitch again, but print and broadcast ads can reach us many times. This is an important feature, for many people need repeated exposures to sales messages before they understand and remember them.

Advertising can, and often does, increase the value of products and services in the customer's eyes. It does this in several ways; one way is by inspiring consumer confidence. Consumer confidence in a product or service can take a number of forms. A customer wants the security of knowing that he or she is not wasting money; a brand name—made familiar through advertising—can provide that security through the assurance of consistent quality. A plain two-story building doesn't stand for much until we put two words on it: Holiday Inn. Now, even though you don't know exactly what the inside looks like, you know that you'll get a clean room, reliable service, and well-thought-out amenities at a reasonable price. Other hotel brand names such as Four Seasons, Hyatt, Sheraton, Hilton, and Marriott all assure travelers that they are going to get whatever quality or value they have been promised. These companies understand that they risk everything if too many guests are disappointed, so they are careful to provide consistent products and services, and truthfully advertise them.

Another form of confidence is developed when a product is advertised in a way that boosts the consumer's self-esteem, telling a person that using the product will make him or her feel more successful, more important, or more self-confident. Travelers who stay at hotels like the Inn at Little Washington, Washington, Virginia; the Peninsula in Beverly Hills; and the Ritz-Carlton in Naples, Florida, know that they are paying for the best that money can buy. When businesspeople stay in a hotel that has achieved the reputation of being for top executives, it makes them feel successful and it signals their status to associates in that city. Advertising can let large groups of people know what status a hotel or restaurant has earned.

What advertising adds to the value of a product is known as **added-value.** The American Association of Advertising Agencies cites Dr. Thomas S. Wuster, vice president of the Boston Consulting Group:

> Chickens, water, and payment systems are all considered commodities. But Perdue has used advertising and quality controls to change chicken from a commodity into a product with distinct features; Perrier has used attractive packaging and advertising to make water into a drink of choice; American Express has continued to upgrade its brand value added through its gold- and platinum-card introductions. In each case a company has added something of value to consumers.[7]

Many hotel and restaurant managers say that, while stressing the value of what they offer is an interesting concept, they get better results by featuring low prices in their advertising. Wuster thinks otherwise:

Many believe that advantage based on lower costs is more real and lasting than advantage based on higher price realization and "elusive" concepts of superior consumer value. In fact, however, our experience and research suggest that the opposite is true: Value-based advantage is even more enduring than cost-based advertising.[8]

The bottom line, according to the Boston Consulting Group, is that "loyalty is a longer-lasting competitive barrier than low cost," and that companies that use advertising to make their name stand for quality will be able to hold on to their customers longer than those who compete by lowering their prices. Someone can always offer a lower price or a newer hotel, but a name that stands for superior value or service will outlast them.

To illustrate this, the Boston Consulting Group pointed out that in 19 of 22 consumer categories, the leading brand in 1925 was still the leader 75 years later. For instance, in 1925 Kellogg was the leading cereal brand, and it still is. Gillette razors, Hershey's chocolate, Wrigley chewing gum, Nabisco crackers, Ivory soap, Campbell's soup, Coca-Cola soft drinks, and Colgate toothpaste are other examples of leading brands that have held on to their position by competing on the basis of quality and value rather than price.

Although the Boston Consulting Group did not study hotels and restaurants, the same inferences for the most part can easily be drawn. The Broadmoor in Colorado Springs, Colorado, and the Greenbrier in White Sulphur Springs, West Virginia, are hotels that have never competed on the basis of price. Nor have such famous restaurants as Le Cirque in New York, Joe's Stone Crab in Miami, or the Tour D'Argent in Paris. These establishments have transformed themselves into institutions that cannot be displaced by newer or more trendy offerings.

The need for hospitality managers to understand the role of advertising is underscored by the significant amounts of money invested in advertising by hospitality enterprises. For example, McDonald's spends billions of dollars on advertising each year, making it one of the largest advertisers in the United States.[9]

No discussion of the role of advertising would be complete without mentioning the social concerns that are sometimes raised when advertising is discussed. Critics frequently charge that advertising makes people buy things they do not need and cannot afford. This is not true. Consumers' wants and needs are determined by society, not by advertising. Most advertisers have learned through experience that it is very difficult to change consumers' buying behavior. Usually, therefore, advertising is used to get consumers to choose between competing brands in a category in which they have already decided to buy something.

Critics also say that advertising is sometimes tasteless, it reinforces undesirable stereotypes, it exerts an unhealthy effect on social values, and it influences the character of the media. It would be naive to say that advertising is not guilty of these charges some of the time. However, most economists believe that advertising is, on the whole, a good thing for society because it supports a highly diverse media structure at a low cost to consumers. For example, usually only one–third of the cost of publishing a newspaper is paid for by its subscribers; the rest is covered by advertising. In the United States, commercial television programs are free to the public and paid for entirely by advertisers. In countries where advertising is restricted, television programs are subsidized by the government, which collects taxes from the public to pay for them and, in many cases, influences the content of programs, to the public's detriment.

Definition of Advertising

According to Professors Charles H. Patti of the University of Denver and Charles F. Frazer of the University of Colorado at Boulder, advertising has a number of characteristics that distinguish it from other forms of communication. Some of these are:

- *It is paid for by the sponsor rather than run at the discretion of the medium.* This distinguishes advertising from publicity (publicity is not paid for and is run at the discretion of the medium).

- *It is impersonal.* Advertising is disseminated to a mass audience. This distinguishes it from personal selling.

- *It identifies the sponsor of the message.* Advertising is distinguished from propaganda in that the source of the message is identified within the message itself.

- *It is persuasive.* Advertising is rarely designed to tell all sides of the story about a product or service; it is not designed to be objective. Advertising is a tool organizations use to persuade people to accept products, services, or ideas.[10]

In short, Patti and Frazer define advertising as "planned communication activity in which messages in mass media are used to persuade audiences to adopt goods, services, or ideas."[11]

What an Advertiser Needs

Advertising does not work equally well for all products and services under all conditions. To produce an effective advertising campaign, an advertiser needs a competitive advantage, unique positioning, and a segmented market.

Competitive Advantage. One of the key factors for advertising success is product differentiation—in other words, there must be a clear difference between what you offer and what your competitors offer. Produce wholesalers, for instance, do not need to advertise their lettuce or tomatoes to restaurants because most wholesalers sell similar grades and quality of produce. But if one wholesaler has a demonstrable difference, such as guaranteed fast delivery or lower prices, that is another matter. Advertising works best when a business has a demonstrable competitive advantage that it wants to communicate to consumers. This advantage might be superior service, lower prices, or higher quality.

The advantage must not only be demonstrable—that is, one that can be seen or experienced—it must be one that satisfies an important consumer need. For example, Hyatt Hotels, in promoting its weekend getaway packages in major cities, offered an 8 P.M. check-out on Sundays instead of the industry's usual noon check-out time. This was an important difference to guests, because the 8 P.M. check-out allowed them to spend Sunday afternoon at the beach or pool and even have dinner at the hotel before checking out. Another important competitive advantage in the hotel business can be location and price. The former Doral Inn in Manhattan, now a W hotel (W Hotels is a Starwood Hotels & Resorts Worldwide chain), ran an effective newspaper ad with the headline, "What Separates The Doral Inn From The Waldorf Astoria? Forty Feet And About $100."

Too often, advertisers ignore the principle of featuring an important difference and instead advertise features that consumers don't care about. One survey of the nation's most frequent travelers found that large numbers of travelers don't care much about in-room bars, computerized travel directions, or other new gimmicks. What they really want are simple pleasures—quiet hotel rooms, clean rental cars, comfortable airline seats. Delivering newspapers to guestrooms—which many hotels don't bother to do, or if they do, don't bother to advertise—appeals far more than a health club to most travelers.

Sometimes a business may have an important feature that competitors have as well, but if no one has advertised it, the first business that does so can gain an advantage. In an airfare war, all airlines may cut their prices to the same level, but the one that advertises the fare reduction first usually gets the lion's share of the business. Almost 80 percent of hotels offer a "kids-stay-free" plan, but many don't advertise it. The ones that do are more likely to get family business.

Unique Positioning. Another factor that contributes to effective advertising is **positioning**. This theory, first articulated by two advertising agency owners, Al Ries and Jack Trout, asserts that because of the number of products available in the marketplace today and the amount of "clutter" or marketing noise caused by the large number of advertising messages we are exposed to every day, most people do not remember (nor are they interested in remembering) what advertisers have to say. In short, advertising messages do not "get through" into the consumer's mind. Companies that aspire to offer everything in their advertising messages in reality don't offer anything of value or importance because people don't remember what they are saying. The secret, according to Ries and Trout, is to get inside the prospect's mind. "You concentrate on the perceptions of the prospect. Not on the reality of the product."[12]

According to Ries and Trout, an advertiser gets into our minds by linking its message to information we already know, not by getting us to remember new information. For example, in the classic case of Avis car rentals, Avis succeeded by telling consumers that "We Try Harder." At the time Avis ran this campaign, Hertz was the number-one car rental company and no one had even heard of Avis. By associating itself with this fact (without even mentioning the name of its competitor), Avis was able to quickly establish a "position" in its prospects' minds that was unique and compelling.

Of course, the name of your product can help position it. Few wanted to vacation at Hog Island in the Bahamas until Huntington Hartford bought it and changed its name to Paradise Island (now the home of the Atlantis mega-resort). That new position attracted a host of new resorts and visitors. Pictures can create a position as well. Bermuda's advertising has shown pink beaches, mopeds, horse-and-buggies, and British traffic bobbies in its advertising for the past 30 years. Hawaii is known for its tropical foliage, which it features in almost all of its ads.

Segmented Market. This brings us to the third factor that boosts advertising's effectiveness: a segmented market. **Market segmentation** refers to a company's ability to identify different segments of its market and separately promote its products and services to those segments. This is also called **target marketing**. Companies that practice target marketing make different products for each market segment and then create different advertising campaigns for each segment.

Marriott practices market segmentation very thoroughly. Marriott's Fairfield Inns aim for the economy segment of the market—that group of consumers who buy based on price. Courtyard by Marriott is aimed at business travelers willing to pay for mid–price rooms. Residence Inn, which offers mini–suites with cooking facilities, is targeted at business travelers who must spend an extended period of time in one location. Marriott Suites are full-service properties for travelers who want a larger-than-average guestroom. Then there are the upscale properties in Marriott's "Hotels, Resorts, & Suites" division, targeted at the upscale segment of the market. Marriott has different names and different advertising campaigns for each of these products. Instead of viewing its market as just "people who go to hotels," Marriott has segmented its market into smaller groups that it can identify, designed products with features that appeal to those groups, and then communicated those different features.

Almost all hotels practice some form of market segmentation. City hotels seek to appeal to traveling businesspeople on weekdays and tourists on weekends. Hotels in Bermuda advertise water sports to families in the summer months, but offer golf and tennis packages in the winter when it is too chilly to go swimming. Resorts may go after affluent consumers at the height of their season, then try to attract other groups by advertising lower prices in the off-season.

Price is only one way to segment customers. American Express segments its travel agency customers into different groups according to how they react to different travel products. With help from the Gallup organization, American Express identified five basic types of travelers:

- *Indulgers* are wealthy and confident people willing to pay for their comfort. They like to be pampered. These people prefer cruises and resorts that feature health spa programs.

- *Dreamers* read and talk a great deal about travel but lack confidence in their travel skills. They like to go to places recommended in guide books and tend to buy tried-and-true travel packages.

- *Economizers* see travel as an outlet for stress and a chance to relax. They scrimp on services and amenities even when they can afford them. Economizers are interested in price and value.

- *Adventurers* are young, confident, and independent. They prefer new experiences, cultures, and people. Many are interested in trips to the South Pacific and the Orient. Forty-four percent of Adventurers are between 18 and 34 years old.

- *Worriers* are afraid to fly and have little confidence in their decision-making while on the road. Half of them are over 50. Worriers need well-traveled, experienced agents to help them choose a destination and tell them how to get there.[13]

By dividing their markets into smaller market groups, American Express and other companies can tailor advertising campaigns to fit the wants and needs of each group and place ads in the media outlets that appeal to each group.

Advertising Agencies

The first decision hospitality business owners or managers encounter when putting together an advertising campaign is: Should they attempt to take care of their advertising themselves, or hire an advertising agency? Advertising agencies help clients create and place advertising. Agencies employ marketing strategists, artists, writers, production managers, and media selection experts. Agencies work on a negotiated fee basis or for a commission of 15 percent. If an agency is working on a 15-percent commission, that means that an advertiser who spends $1,000,000 on an ad campaign pays $150,000 for advertising agency services and $850,000 for space in the media where the advertising runs. Agencies bill their clients for the cost of media space or airtime and then—after receiving full payment from the client—are allowed by the media involved to deduct 15 percent from the client's payment before distributing the balance to the media.

Many advertisers opt to handle their advertising themselves by hiring freelance writers and artists to design their advertising, and then negotiating with the media directly for space and time. For a small advertiser this can mean considerable savings, since agency retainers plus fees for writing and designing ads can sometimes be substantial. On the other hand, many advertisers have found that there can be a big difference between customer response to a good ad versus a bad one, and argue that even small advertisers will get better results by using an agency instead of doing it themselves. While this may be true, there are some freelancers who can and do create outstanding ads (indeed, many freelancers are hired by ad agencies for certain projects), and therefore much depends on the nature of the advertising to be created, the freelancers available in an area, and the media to be used. Sometimes media prices are negotiable, and advertising agencies are in a better position to obtain the most favorable rates.

There is a wide variety of books and articles on how to choose an advertising agency, but one of the best ways is to simply take note of the advertising you like and then find out who did it by calling the advertiser or the media outlet in which the ad was placed. A note of caution, however: most agencies do not accept competing accounts unless they are located in different market areas.

Creating Effective Advertising

Movies and television shows have created an oversimplified and glamorous impression of how advertising is produced. Typically, writers and artists are shown as becoming suddenly inspired with an idea for an ad campaign—almost as if a bolt of lightning has come down from above. The truth is far more mundane. Good campaigns are based on marketing plans, which in turn are based on thorough market research. Effective advertising is almost always the product of a rational, methodical process. Most ads reflect a position that has been carefully worked out in advance, and are written to appeal to a specific target market. The people who create the ads are not geniuses who pull great ideas out of thin air. There is no doubt that talent is involved, but it is a special kind of talent that includes sorting out and synthesizing facts. Indeed, it is not uncommon to find advertising copywriters with strong backgrounds in research. Most professional advertising copywriters thrive on research reports, profiles of target audiences, demographics, and psychographics.

Think of the inventor Thomas Edison. He did not sit in his laboratory with his feet on his desk until the idea for a light bulb popped into his head. The idea grew out of years of collecting information about the properties of electricity and conductors. So it is with good advertising.

Using Print Media Effectively. Print advertisements consist of three basic elements: headline, body copy, and signature.

The **headline** is the heading or the title of the ad. It is similar to the headline of a newspaper story. The purpose of the headline is to draw readers' attention and get them to read the rest of the ad. Effective headlines often contain the main promise of the ad. Some advertisements contain a sub-headline that spells out the promise made in the headline.

The **body copy** is the main portion of an ad. This is text that usually contains an amplification of the promise or benefit offered in the headline.

Finally, ads usually contain **signatures** or logotypes. A "signature" is the name of the advertiser; a **logotype** or **"logo"** is "a unique trademark, name, symbol, signature, or device used to identify a company or other organization."[14] The golden arches of McDonald's are an example of a logo; so is the unique type that Coca-Cola uses to spell its name.

There are few rules as to what works and what doesn't in advertising. Since advertising is an art and a craft as much as a science, advertisers are always trying new techniques for getting and holding consumers' attention and persuading them to buy. However, over the years many advertising studies have been done by independent research companies, advertisers, and agencies that have led to some general guidelines that most advertisers follow.

Print advertising guidelines. Whether they appear in a newspaper, magazine, or some other print medium, all print ads should contain a promise. The promise can be stated or merely implied, but it is there, usually in the headline—the first thing most people read. Five times as many people read the ad's headline as read the body copy. That means that unless a headline sells, the advertiser has wasted most of its money.

Why does an ad need a promise? To attract readers. People won't remember an ad just because an advertiser wants them to, no matter how eloquently or clearly it is written. To be remembered, messages must include something that has personal meaning for readers. Consumers don't care about your hotel's features per se—they care about how those features can benefit them.

If you are advertising something that is only available to certain groups, it is a good idea to put something in the headline to flag them down. When Marriott advertises discounts available only to members of the American Association of Retired Persons (AARP), it usually puts a banner across the top of the ad that says "AARP Members Only."

There is conflicting evidence on how long a headline should be. While some studies show that headlines with less than ten words do better than longer ones, other studies show that people will read long headlines as well as long advertisements if they are interested in what the advertiser is saying. David Ogilvy, who founded Ogilvy & Mather Advertising and went on to be elected to the Advertising Hall of Fame, wrote one of the most famous automobile ads of all time for Rolls-Royce. The 17-word headline—"At 60 miles an hour the loudest sound you can hear is the ticking of the clock"—was followed by 607 words of factual copy.

Jim Johnston, chairman and co-founder of Jim Johnston Advertising, in an advertisement run by the *Wall Street Journal,* says this about headlines and advertising copy:

> Headlines *can* be visuals; words can stop readers. They can attract, intrigue, provoke—and pull the reader into the copy. But that's only the beginning. Copy is no task for tyros. It must work word for word, line for line. Effective copy is *simple* but not *simplistic*; intelligent but not obtuse; interesting but not frivolous. People *will* read long copy. They won't read dull, confusing copy, no matter how short.

In the body copy of the ad, advertisers should try to "make the sale"—that is, present the reasons why you should buy their product, stay at their hotel, or eat at their restaurant. The Regency Hotel in New York uses a headline to focus on its location: "As Preferred as Park Avenue." The body copy amplifies this promise: "Located in one of the world's most exclusive neighborhoods, it promises an enclave of quiet elegance. Here are superb accommodations, a restaurant, lounge, fitness center and select meeting facilities.... and of course, uncompromising service."

The final part of an ad should contain a call to action. In most cases ads don't make sales—salespersons make sales. The purpose of most ads is to interest the reader and put him or her in touch with a salesperson. "Go to Our Website," "Call This Number for Reservations," or "See Your Travel Agent" are typical calls to action. Salespeople who don't ask for the sale aren't successful; neither are ads that don't include a call to action.

An ad should always contain the signature or name of the advertiser and the advertiser's logo (if it has one). Sometimes advertisers are reticent about making their name too large—as if they are ashamed of who they are. But if the signature is not large and clear, people might miss it entirely. Often the only thing people see in an ad is the headline, picture (if any), and signature. This is why some advertisers always try to put their name in the headline. Readership studies show that many ads succeed in attracting attention and getting readership, but fail entirely in getting prospects to remember what company placed it. The Hong Kong Tourist Association puts its name in the headline as well as at the bottom of its ads, where it invites readers to take action.

Finally, there is the old proverb, "One swallow doesn't make a spring." One advertisement doesn't make a campaign, either. A campaign consists of a number of advertisements that bear a family resemblance in both style and content but are different enough to attract new attention from readers who may have already read a previous advertisement.

Using Broadcast Media Effectively. Unlike print media, in which a consumer chooses to read advertisements that are of interest, ads in broadcast media are intrusive. Listeners and viewers have tuned in to a program, and in the middle of that program they are interrupted by a commercial that they may not be interested in. Newspapers and magazines are primarily informational media, but radio and television are primarily entertainment media. Commercials interrupt that entertainment. Therefore, broadcast advertisers often seek to entertain in order to make their messages more palatable.

One way to entertain consumers is through humor. However, using humor requires great skill, because commercials are surrounded by professional entertainment and an amateurish commercial sticks out like a sore thumb. Moreover, a commercial needs "staying power" so audience members will enjoy hearing it or viewing it more than once, and unless it is well done they will tune out fast.

Some advertisers use a local broadcast personality in markets where the personality has a strong following. Local TV talk-show hosts or radio DJs often have a great deal of credibility with their listeners, especially when they endorse restaurants or other establishments that they personally patronize.

Music, too, can be effective in broadcast ads when it is correctly used. Music is not suitable for telling the whole message—commercials that are sung in their entirety are seldom remembered (with a few exceptions, such as the award-winning "I'd Like to Buy the World a Coke" TV commercial from the 1970s)—but music can enhance the ad's theme.

Broadcast advertising guidelines. *Fortune* magazine interviewed some of the top advertising executives on Madison Avenue and their clients to get an idea of what kind of broadcast advertising appealed to 21st-century consumers. They found three cutting-edge strategies that can reach out and grab today's consumer:

- *Make 'em laugh.* Cliff Freeman, president of Cliff Freeman and Partners, believes that humor and satire are the keys to many successful commercials. "The truth is, there is so little to say about a lot of products. So the marketing becomes about association, leaving people with a simple idea. And if you do humor well, people will love the brand."

- *Make 'em bond.* Many smart marketers now build campaigns around concepts that emphasize individual values. No advertisers, say top marketers, do this better than Coca-Cola, which links its soda to some vague, worldwide social movement, and Nike, which emphasizes achievement and rebellion. By transforming their brands into icons, both Coke and Nike have blown away their competitors and shown others how to break out of the "ours is better and cheaper" box. Companies should constantly redefine their image in the marketplace to keep up with shifting consumer attitudes.

- *Find out what they really like.* Consumers develop strong loyalties to certain media outlets and personalities—from the Discovery Channel to ESPN to Oprah Winfrey. By separating the media outlets and personalities that draw strongly loyal fans from those that attract mostly casual viewers, an advertiser with a relatively small ad budget can reach more desirable customers. Loyal viewers of a typical TV show are 30 percent more likely than casual viewers to buy the products of the show's advertisers, according to research by DDB Needham Advertising.[15]

Public Relations

A hospitality company does not function in a vacuum, but rather as part of a society that consists of the people who work for it, the people and companies who do business with it, the public at large, and the government that regulates and taxes it. These groups are known as a company's "publics." In order for a company to effectively deal with these publics, a relationship of trust must exist. Employees will not cooperate with or put forth their best efforts for a company that they do not trust or that they feel is taking advantage of them. The public will not buy services or products from a company that, in their estimation, is not responsible or trustworthy: if they can't trust the company or its owners, how can they trust the products or services it sells? And the government, as the protector of the society it governs, is especially vigilant in dealing with a company that it regards as not operating in the public interest. Given these circumstances, every hotel, restaurant, travel agency, tour company, and other hospitality business should give some thought to the relationships it has with all of the various publics it interacts with. The techniques that a company uses to improve these relationships are known as **public relations**, or **"PR."**

The goal of public relations is usually to improve the climate or atmosphere in which a company operates. Here are some results a company might expect from a successful public relations campaign:

- Its products and services are better known
- Its relationship with employees has improved
- Its public reputation has improved

A successful public relations campaign can get people to do something that will help a company, stop them from doing something that might hurt it, or at least allow the company to proceed with a course of action without criticism. "An organization with good public relations has a favorable image or reputation, perhaps as a result of public relations activities," says Richard Weiner, an award-winning public relations counselor and the author of *Webster's New World Dictionary of Media and Communications.*[16]

In developing and implementing public relations plans, companies often use a simple five-step process:

1. *Research or fact-finding.* The purpose of research or fact-finding is to identify the attitudes of the company's various publics, who the key opinion leaders are, and what must happen to change bad perceptions or reinforce good ones.

Exhibit 1   Public Relations at McDonald's

McDonald's uses booklets, posters, and other public relations materials to inform its customers of the many ways in which it tries to be socially responsible. (Courtesy of McDonald's Corporation.)

2. *Planning.* A public relations strategy is devised that will produce the desired outcome(s).

3. *Action.* Action steps are taken to implement the strategy.

4. *Communication.* The company's actions are communicated to the interested publics.

5. *Measurement or evaluation.* The results of the public relations campaign are studied to see if the desired outcomes have been achieved or if more action is needed.

McDonald's is a classic example of a hospitality company that practices good public relations (see Exhibit 1). It has always been important to McDonald's to be known as a company that values cleanliness. Indeed, founder Ray Kroc emphasized cleanliness along with quality, service, and value as being the four most important things in any McDonald's operation. For that reason Kroc instructed the first McDonald's franchisees to pick up all litter within a two-block radius of their stores, whether it was McDonald's litter or not.[17] However, by the mid-1970s McDonald's had grown so large that its discarded packages were found everywhere, from nearby city streets to campgrounds and beaches miles from the nearest restaurant. As public consciousness grew about the importance of not polluting, more and more critics pointed to McDonald's as a leading culprit, and the company realized it needed to take further action.

In 1976, McDonald's commissioned the Stanford Research Institute to do an environmental impact study comparing the paperboard packaging McDonald's was using at the time with polystyrene packages, an economical alternative that also offered some other product benefits. The study concluded that polystyrene was better from an environmental perspective when all aspects of the problem were taken into consideration. "Paper and paperboard used with food have to be coated, making them 'mixed materials' that are nearly unrecyclable. Polystyrene uses less energy than paper in its production, conserves natural resources, represents less weight and volume in landfills, and is recyclable."[18] McDonald's accepted the study's recommendations and switched to polystyrene wherever it could.

But in the 1980s new questions were raised. Environmentalists pointed out that the manufacturing process for polystyrene released halogenated chlorofluorocarbons into the earth's atmosphere, which harmed the ozone layer. By 1987 McDonald's had directed all of its packaging suppliers to eliminate these dangerous chemicals from the manufacturing process. At the same time it reduced by 29 percent the thickness of its containers, and by 20 percent the weight of plastic straws. It used a lighter paper for wrapping sandwiches and began using recycled paper for napkins and tray liners. At the same time the company launched a new investigation into recycling programs.

To make sure that everyone knew what it was doing, McDonald's made its concern for the environment the theme of its 1989 annual report and printed the report entirely on recycled paper utilizing paper waste from its offices and restaurants worldwide.[19] This was followed in 1990 by the announcement of McRecycle USA, a program in which McDonald's committed itself to buy $100 million in recycled materials in the next year for use in building and remodeling its restaurants, with a goal of spending $1 billion on recycled products by the year 2000. In 1999, McRecycle USA surpassed the $3 billion milestone—five years ahead of schedule.[20]

Despite all of these positive actions, many critics continued to question whether McDonald's was really an environmentally friendly company. As part of its response to these critics, in November 1990 the company made a decision to turn back the clock by phasing out polystyrene packaging and returning to paper while investigating other alternatives. Since 1990, McDonald's has reduced packaging by more than 20 million pounds through such actions as trimming the size of its napkins and straws, and reducing the paper content of Happy Meal bags and cartons by 20 percent. In 1993, McDonald's joined Environmental Defense (a national nonprofit organization concerned with environmental issues) on an innovative task force looking to increase the use of environmentally preferable paper products by businesses.[21]

It is important to understand the role public relations has played in all of these decisions. McDonald's has always been socially responsible and extremely concerned about its image. In 2002 McDonald's produced for the first time a special report on social responsibility, which it updated in 2004. But to McDonald's, public relations activities go much deeper than simply writing reports, sending out press releases, and having corporate officers serve on various charitable boards. The company understands that real public relations means taking significant actions first, then announcing them to the public. Without the first step, the second would be meaningless. Many companies do not understand this basic principle: if you want to make news, you must first do something newsworthy.

Publicity

Public relations and publicity are often confused with each other, but they are not the same thing. Richard Weiner defines **publicity** as "a public relations technique in which information from an outside source—usually a public relations practitioner—is used by the media. A message is developed and distributed, without specific payment to the media, through selected outlets (magazines, TV, and so on) to further particular interests of the clients."[22]

Publicity is sometimes called "free advertising," but this is a misnomer. Advertising is paid for and advertisers control the message in their ads. Publicity is not paid for by the advertiser, and the media—not the advertiser—control the message, because they are writing or broadcasting stories that they consider newsworthy, which also just happen to mention a company or be about a company. Because publicity is not paid for by an advertiser, it has more credibility with consumers than an ad. Unfortunately, from a company's standpoint, publicity can be unfavorable as well as favorable. A newspaper article about a restaurant's unlawful discrimination in hiring or a TV story about a cruise ship fire are examples of bad publicity.

New hotels and restaurants usually work hard to publicize their grand openings and often receive a good deal of attention and publicity. Press kits are the most common publicity materials prepared by a property. These kits generally consist of a series of fact sheets about the property; some news releases about the building, the architects, the general manager, and other key property personnel; and several glossy black-and-white photos that can be reproduced in newspapers.

However, grand openings occur only once and businesses need publicity throughout their lives. Newspapers receive thousands of press releases every week and generally discard most of them. Therefore it is often necessary to stage special events or create new products or services to focus the media's attention and give them something newsworthy to write about. One of Richard Weiner's most celebrated publicity stunts was the Texas Armadillo Race he created for Lone Star Beer. Weiner recruited "professional" armadillo racers and had them compete against one another. The cost was minuscule but the armadillo race (and Lone Star) appeared on several network TV shows.

Hotels and restaurants often try to stimulate publicity by inviting travel editors and writers to visit. Sometimes these invitations are arranged by publicists who organize all-expenses-paid press tours. However, while freelancers often accept invitations to go on these tours, many of the top newspapers and travel magazines will not publish anything that a journalist writes while enjoying a free trip, because they believe he or she is likely to be biased. Their editors and writers usually pay for everything when they visit a hotel or restaurant, and report on both the positives and the negatives they encounter.

Sales Promotion

Unlike advertising and public relations, which aim to achieve results over time, **sales promotion** consists of sales tools and techniques designed to encourage immediate

| Exhibit 2 | Sample Sales Promotion Materials |

HOTEL ADLON
BERLIN

Jahreswechsel
SILVESTER 2000/2001

HOTEL ADLON
BERLIN

Opera Soirees
Series

Pre-performance Lectures in English for
the Berlin Opera Premières 2000–2001

These brochures (only the covers are shown) from the Hotel Adlon in Berlin are designed to
encourage immediate action. The brochure on the left promotes a special New Year's package
developed by the hotel; the one on the right a special opera package. Inside, the packages are
described, prices are listed, and consumers are invited to call the hotel to make reservations.
(Courtesy of the Hotel Adlon, Berlin, Germany, and Kempinski Hotels & Resorts.)

action—not only by consumers (see Exhibit 2), but by others in the trade. Extra commissions
paid to travel agents, sales contests, and familiarization trips for agents are all examples
of hospitality industry sales promotions directed at the trade. For many years Carnival
Cruises has run a mystery-shopper program in which travel agents are handed $1,000
in cash on the spot for recommending a Carnival cruise to someone who asks about a
Caribbean vacation.

Probably the most widely used form of sales promotion directed toward consumers
is a loyalty marketing program, such as Marriott's Rewards, Hyatt's Gold Passport, or
American Airlines AAdvantage frequent-flyer program. All of these programs reward
people who travel frequently and do repeat business with these companies. Such programs
stimulate additional travel by offering incentives to fly and stay at hotels. Free travel is a
common form of sales promotion.

Sweepstakes are a popular form of sales promotion. Some years ago, faced with a
decrease in trans-Atlantic traffic due to travelers' fear of terrorism, British Airways created

an ambitious and successful "Go For It America" sweepstakes. Launched in June with entry blanks printed in newspapers, British Airways offered 5,200 readers free round-trip tickets for two to London with free first-night lodging. The July prize was 100,000 British pounds; in August the winner received a five-year London townhouse lease; and in September the prize was a new Rolls-Royce. The airline also included travel agents in this promotion—agents got an opportunity to win prizes every time they booked a passenger on British Airways.

Promotions are used extensively by restaurants to get publicity and stimulate business. For example, during the slow-business months of August and September, Miami restaurants have a promotion known as "Miami Spice." Participating restaurants offer a specially priced three-course menu. New York City restaurants have a similar program known as "Restaurant Week" that they offer in the slow winter months (January–February) and summer months (June–July).

Internet Marketing

Technology continues to transform the way we do business. In the past (in this case meaning the pre-Internet days), companies disseminated their marketing messages in several ways. As we have seen in this chapter, they used a sales staff, print and/or broadcast advertising, promotions, and perhaps a contracted public relations expert to help them get newspapers and magazines to take notice of the business. These traditional methods are still used, but there is also the new technology provided by the Internet. Today the Internet has become a major means of communicating with hotel, restaurant, airline, and other hospitality and travel customers.

More than eight in ten leisure travelers and approximately nine in ten business travelers access the Internet from their home or office computers, and the majority of travelers use that capability to plan their trips (fifty-six percent of leisure travelers and sixty-two percent of business travelers).[23] Internet bookings for the top thirty hotel brands, as opposed to reservations made via telephone or a global distribution system (GDS), have been climbing. In 2009 they increased by 6.6 percent over the previous year, while other sources of reservations declined.[24] The website has become a major tool in the marketing strategy of hotels and other hospitality companies. Accordingly, hotel websites must be attractive, easy to navigate (especially the reservations section), and display photographs of the hotel(s), rooms, and other facilities. It should give location information about the hotel(s) and feature special offers (if any), and provide a link for customers to ask questions. In other words, it must be functional, informative, and enticing.

Hotel websites are not limited to hotel reservations and information. For example, from the Marriott website one can connect to ShopMarriott, where lamps and bedding used in Marriott hotels can be purchased. Navigating to "Marriott in the Kitchen" allows Internet users to find recipes and information about foods served in the restaurants throughout the chain. Hilton's shopping channel is HiltonToHome.com. At TGIFridays.com, one can find store locations, join the frequent-diner program, and purchase retail food items and gift cards.

E-Mail Advertising and Promotion

One of the least costly methods of Internet marketing is via e-mail. In contrast to a print ad, an e-mail ad is more likely to be read, especially if it is addressed to an individual such as "Dear Ms. Jones" rather than "Dear Customer." Most segments of the hospitality and tourism industries have frequent-customer programs: Marriott Rewards, Hilton HHonors, AAdvantage, and World Club Member (Cunard) are just a few examples. Hence, they have a database of their loyal customers and their preferences. This information can be used to e-mail customers and address them by name, thank them for their loyalty, and offer them opportunities to participate in special programs or offers that might be of special interest to them. Links embedded in the e-mail make it easy for customers to respond. For good customer relations, e-mail ads should always include a way for recipients to opt out of future mailings if they do not want to receive additional marketing e-mails from the company.

Social Media

What is social media? One way to conceptualize how it works is to imagine sitting in a classroom listening to a lecture—the information is being given to you without an opportunity for you to participate—that's how a typical print advertisement works. Now think of a roundtable discussion, whereby everyone at the table is involved. That is social media marketing, a "one to many" conversation or a "many to many" conversation facilitated by the Internet. It is a sharing of opinions and information with friends or a community of those with like interests. Dan Zarella in his *Social Media Marketing Book* classifies **social media** as blogs, microblogs (Twitter), **social networks** (Facebook, LinkedIn, etc.,), and media-sharing sites (YouTube, for example).[25] As you can see, social networks can have audio and/or video capabilities as well as text.

A "blog" (a contraction from "web log") is a website created by an individual to present an opinion or commentary on a specific subject. Usually a blog allows for responses or additional commentary by others so that it becomes an online "conversation." On the other hand, Twitter is a microblog that limits commentary to 140 characters known as "tweets" that, in addition to being sent to the writer's "followers," is shown on the author's profile page.

Currently the most popular of the social media outlets is Facebook. Although it began as a social network for college students, it expanded to include anyone who cared to join, including businesspeople and businesses, making it possible for them to connect to communities (frequent users) and customers directly. YouTube, owned by Google, is a video-sharing website that is widely used by individuals and companies for uploading and sharing videos. Social networks are commonly associated with the term "Web.2.0," since these networks and other web applications that facilitate interactive information sharing and user-centered design are considered to be the second generation of web development. There are a number of other social networks, but those that have been noted are the most widely used by hospitality businesses thus far.

The hospitality industry has been quick to adopt social media. From the Marriott website one can find access to Bill Marriott's blog, where, in a friendly, informal style, he tells of different projects and accomplishments of the company and its employees. In a social network "war," Domino's Pizza used Twitter and YouTube to reach its customers in order to combat a negative video on YouTube. All hotel chains are on Facebook, using the social network to promote special packages and respond to guest questions and comments, both positive and negative. Social networks are also used as gathering places for members of frequent-guest programs, providing them a platform to share travel experiences, register complaints, or praise good experiences. Social media is being used to let guests sell to other potential guests. For example, at the San Juan Marriott Resort, guests have the opportunity to record a brief video at no cost that can be sent to family and friends. Arrangements are handled by a "YouTube Concierge." Combining traditional marketing with current technology can be a powerful combination. Denny's advertised during a Super Bowl its plan to give away in a contest one of its special breakfasts for a year. About 49 million people visited the Denny's website to download the coupon. Six hundred thousand entered the contest, of which 450,000 joined the company's Rewards program, providing Denny's with a huge database to promote its more than 1,500 restaurants.[26]

So, given the power of social media, is it time to abandon traditional marketing methods? Not yet, according to a study by Ypartnership and the U.S. Travel Association. Although there is widespread use of social media, only ten percent of Facebook users rely on the social network to reach destination or travel service suppliers, and even fewer have joined a community of like travelers.[27] However, as companies become more adept at using the technology and the oncoming generation of technologically savvy travelers comes into the mainstream, it is expected that the adoption of new marketing techniques to leverage the new social media outlets will grow. There are signs of that growth already. According to PKF Hospitality Research, e-commerce expenditures as part of full-service-hotel marketing expenses have been increasing, while expenditures in traditional marketing categories have been declining.

Leveraging Your Marketing Dollars

Up to now in this chapter, we have dealt with the good news. The good news is that there are a lot of consumers out there, they want to buy a lot of things, and many of them are interested in learning about new products and services through advertising and promotion. The bad news is that there is far too much advertising in the marketplace, and most consumers are turned off by much of it. Here's what the *New York Times* had to say about the current advertising glut:

> Add this to the endangered list: blank spaces. Advertisers seem determined to fill every last one of them. Supermarket eggs have been stamped with the names of CBS television shows. Subway turnstiles have messages from Geico auto insurance. Chinese food cartons promote Continental Airways. US Airways is selling ads on motion sickness bags, and the trays used in the airport security lines have been hawking Rolodexes.
>
> Marketers used to try their hardest to reach people at home, when they were watching TV or reading newspapers or magazines. But consumers' viewing and reading habits are so scattershot now that many advertisers say the best way to reach time-pressed consumers is to try to catch their eye literally at every turn.[28]

The market research firm Yankelovich estimates that a city dweller 30 years ago saw up to 2,000 ad messages a day, compared with up to 5,000 today. About half of the 4,110 people surveyed by Yankelovich said they thought marketing and advertising was out of control.[29]

Besides the consumer turn-off factor, marketers have to deal with an ever-changing consumer base. The key word here is multiculturalism. With their higher birth rates and increasing immigration, minorities will comprise one-third of the U.S. population by 2016. The U.S. Census Bureau predicts that by 2051 one in every four Americans will be of Latino ancestry. Hispanics represent both the fastest-growing and largest minority group in the

United States. By 2020, they will represent one half of the growth in the U.S. work force. African-Americans and Asians are becoming increasingly influential in American society and business. Marketers will need to understand these diverse consumer groups so that they can communicate with them on their own terms.

And then there is the aging population. Right now there are some 80 million baby boomers in the United States. On average, they are projected to live to be 77. In another 20 years, average life expectancy may surpass 80 years. Who knows what the average life expectancy will be in 50 years?[30]

How can marketers deal with these myriad demographic changes? Reaching U.S. consumers used to be relatively easy. There were only three major television networks, and if you advertised on all of them, you could reach perhaps 80 percent of television viewers. Most everyone got their news from the newspaper, so newspapers were seen as an effective advertising medium. And almost everyone listened to the radio, at least during drive time. But as the *Wall Street Journal* reported, "Today's consumers have a lot more than a handful of TV channels to watch, and are a lot less patient about sitting through ads, so advertisers are trying to win back their attention with a grab bag of new strategies."[31]

Chief among these strategies is the Internet. New ways to use this powerful communication tool are being discovered every day. Advertisers are targeting their Internet ads for diverse audience segments, and at the same time creating ads that don't look like traditional ads at all. Search-engine advertising is enjoying explosive growth. In 2005, search-engine advertising exceeded $5.1 billion in the United States and represented the largest category of Internet ads, according to the Interactive Advertising Bureau trade group and the consulting firm PriceWaterhouseCoopers. Search-engine advertisers bid in an online auction system to have their ads displayed every time a consumer uses the search engine to look for a specific key word or key word phrase. The advertisers pay only when consumers click on the site, forking over roughly $.50 per click on average, according to analyst estimates.[32]

Another new form of advertising is "viral advertising," so-called because the marketing message spreads from person to person like a virus. The technique is really very simple. You create an e-mail joke, or perhaps a game, or even a jingle of some sort, which you e-mail to a group of people, with the suggestion that they pass it along to their friends. In 2005, 1.3 million viewers watched a short online video for Budweiser that featured the brewer's famous ad characters Frankie and Louie, the lizards. When a consumer watches the video and passes it along, "it's like a personal endorsement," says Marlene Coulis, vice president for brand management at Anheuser-Busch, St. Louis.[33]

The traditional 30-second television commercial may well be on the way to extinction, simply because there are too many TV stations and too many commercials. Consequently, "the airwaves are filled these days with a dizzying array of commercial stunts—short ads, long ads, commercials thinly disguised as half hour pieces of entertainment, 'commercial-free' premieres sponsored by a single advertiser, and even several ads from one advertiser aired back-to-back during a single commercial break."[34] The conventional television ad was created during a very different time, when most people had a choice of just three big TV networks and a handful of independent TV stations. There was no cable TV, no Internet, and no video games to distract them. Back then, the ad world believed that, so long as viewers watched a couple of big-name TV shows each week, advertisers could be reasonably sure that the clever slogans and jingles they devised would be heard—and remembered.

Now, however, viewers have dozens, sometimes hundreds, of TV channels to choose from (not to mention websites, DVDs, video games, video-on-demand programs, and podcasts). At the same time, digital video recorders are making it easier for consumers to shun TV ads altogether; watching a program recorded on a DVR allows viewers to automatically skip the commercial breaks.[35] Advertisers are testing a lot of new ways to get around this problem. The traditional advertising campaign is simply too broadly targeted. Some advertisers are creating television ads specifically aimed at the audience of the TV program in which they are advertising. Others are creating television programs of their own. Another technique is to arrange to have products imbedded in the TV program itself—a more subtle form of advertising. Many marketers are using the same technique in feature films made in Hollywood. Here, advertisers pay the movie producer to have characters in the movie use their products onscreen, with the advertiser's name or logo clearly shown. For example, two characters sitting down for a cup of coffee might be specifically shown at a Starbucks.

Leveraging advertising dollars today means using all of these new techniques and more. It requires thinking outside the box and creating newfangled ways of delivering a message. Those advertisers who find those ways and utilize them effectively will win. Those who don't, won't!

Summary

There is a real difference between selling and marketing. Selling is getting rid of what you have; marketing is having what customers want. The marketing concept can be defined as the effort to determine and meet the needs and wants of current and potential customers.

The Four P's of Marketing are product, place, price, and promotion. The term "product" as used in the hospitality field can have several meanings. Obviously, a product can be a guestroom or a meal that a hotel or restaurant provides to guests. A hospitality product can also be an intangible service, such as a bellperson carrying a guest's luggage. Product can also refer to a hotel or restaurant's concept. For example, a Fairfield Inn is an economy product designed specifically to appeal to business travelers. In this case, "product" refers to all the things that make the experience of staying at a Fairfield Inn what it is—its philosophy, facilities, amenities, level of service, and the tangible products it sells to guests. The concept of a restaurant or hotel is first and foremost a marketing decision.

"Place" refers to the physical location of a property. It also refers to the place where a sale of a guestroom or a restaurant reservation is made, which can be over the Internet, via the telephone, or at a travel agency.

There are three methods of pricing commonly used in the hospitality industry: cost-plus pricing, consumer-based pricing, and competitive pricing. There are other, more complicated, approaches to pricing as well. Some hotels, for example, employ revenue management techniques to optimize the revenue they receive in any given period by adjusting the guestroom rates that are offered to different market segments, based on the projected supply of rooms and the demand for them.

Promotion decisions are made after the first three marketing P's are established. Promotion consists of all the ways a business tries to persuade consumers to buy its products and services. All promotional activities fall into one of six categories: personal selling, advertising, public relations and sponsorship marketing, sales promotion, direct marketing communications, and point-of-purchase communications.

To properly allocate marketing resources, a company should begin with a marketing plan. A good marketing plan consists of several parts: situation analysis, objectives, strategies, tactics (or action plans), and controls.

Personal selling by the owners, managers, or sales force is the business-building tool hotels and restaurants most frequently employ. Most hotels have a marketing and sales or a sales department. Hotel sales department personnel are often assigned to specific types of travelers or given specific regions. The sales manager is in charge of sales efforts. He or she is expected to increase property revenues through sales calls, establish guidelines for selling, assist the general manager with obtaining maximum sales efforts from all employees, hold weekly and monthly sales meetings, maintain sales reports, and establish a sales filing system. Successful salespeople have certain characteristics in common. The main ones are an ability to understand how people think and an ability to relate to them.

Advertising acts as a substitute for a personal salesperson. Advertising is valuable because it is repetitive and thus helps consumers understand and remember sales messages. It increases the value of products and services by adding value to the name and reputation of a company.

Some critics charge that advertising leads people to buy things they don't want or need, but in fact most advertising is used to influence the brand choice of something that consumers have already decided to purchase.

Advertising is paid for by the sponsor, is impersonal, identifies the sponsor, and is persuasive. It is a planned communication activity in which messages in mass media are used to persuade audiences to adopt goods, services, or ideas.

There are certain factors that favor the use of advertising. These include a demonstrable competitive advantage, unique positioning, and a segmented market. "Positioning" consists of getting inside a prospect's mind by linking the message the advertiser wishes to convey to something the prospect already knows. Market segmentation refers to a company's ability to identify different segments of its market and then create and promote products and services tailored for each segment.

Many hospitality advertisers employ advertising agencies. Advertising agencies consist of marketing strategists, artists, writers, production managers, and media selection experts. Agencies generally work for a negotiated fee or a 15-percent commission. Whether a company should use an agency depends on the nature of the company's advertising, the advertising agencies or freelancers available in an area, and the media to be used. Sometimes media prices are negotiable, and advertising agencies are in a better position to obtain the most favorable rates.

Effective advertising is not only inspired; it is almost always the product of a rational and methodical process. Print advertisements consist of several elements. Usually there is a headline; some advertisements also contain a sub-headline. The main portion of an ad is called the body copy. Finally, ads usually end with a signature and a logotype ("logo").

There are some general guidelines that most print advertisers follow: (1) put a promise in the headline, (2) "make the sale" in the body copy, and (3) close with a call to action, such as "Send for Our Free Brochure" or "Call This Number for Reservations." A successful print campaign consists of a series of advertisements that bear a family resemblance in both style and content but are different enough to attract new attention from readers.

Broadcast advertisers seek to entertain because commercials interrupt the entertainment provided by the broadcast medium. They often use humor.

Every hotel, restaurant, travel agency, tour company, and other hospitality enterprise should give some thought to its public relations—that is, the relations it has with all of the various "publics" (clients, employees, government agencies, and so on) it interacts with. The techniques that a company uses to improve these relationships are known as "PR" or public relations. In developing and implementing public relations plans, companies often use a simple five-step process: research or fact-finding, planning, action, communication, and measurement or evaluation.

Publicity is a public relations technique in which information from an outside source—usually a public relations practitioner—is used by the media. Hotels and restaurants often receive a lot of publicity at their grand openings. The need for publicity continues throughout the life of a business.

Sales promotion consists of sales tools and techniques designed to encourage immediate action by consumers or the trade. Probably the most widely used sales promotions directed toward consumers are loyalty marketing programs such as Starwood's Preferred Guest, Hyatt's Gold Passport, and American Airlines AAdvantage frequent–flyer program. Restaurants also use sales promotions to generate publicity and stimulate business; tie-ins with wine producers are common sales promotions among fine-dining restaurants, for example. Sweepstakes are widely used as a form of sales promotion among travel and hospitality companies.

There are a lot of consumers, they want to buy a lot of things, and many of them are interested in learning about new products and services through advertising and promotion—that's the good news. The bad news is that many consumers are turned off by the glut of advertising in the marketplace. Marketers used to try their hardest to reach people at home, when they were watching TV or reading newspapers or magazines. But consumers' viewing and reading habits are so scattershot now that many advertisers try to catch the attention of consumers literally at every turn. The result is that many people think advertising is out of control.

Reaching U.S. consumers used to be relatively easy. For example, years ago there were only three major television networks. But today, people have dozens, sometimes hundreds, of TV channels to watch (not to mention websites, DVDs, video games, video-on-demand programs, and podcasts), and they are a lot less patient about sitting through commercials. Consequently, advertisers are trying to reach them through new strategies and new media outlets, such as advertising on Internet search engines. On television, advertisers are trying many different ways to capture viewers' attention—short ads, long ads, commercials thinly disguised as half hour pieces of entertainment, "commercial-free" premieres sponsored by a single advertiser, and several ads from one advertiser aired back-to-back. Some advertisers are creating television commercials specifically aimed at the audience of the TV program on which they are advertising. Others are creating television programs of their own. Another technique is to imbed products in the TV program itself. (Many marketers are using this technique in movies as well.)

The Internet has become a major means of communicating with customers and has become an important tool in the marketing strategy of all hospitality enterprises. In some cases, websites, e-mail, and social networks have replaced traditional modes of advertising, sales, and promotion. Recent hotel studies have shown that expenditures for e-commerce as a percentage of total marketing expenses in full-service hotels are growing, in contrast to an overall decline in advertising and sales expenditures.

Leveraging advertising dollars today means using all of these new techniques and more. It requires thinking outside the box and creating new ways of delivering a message. Those advertisers who find those ways and utilize them effectively will win. Those who don't, won't!

Endnotes

1. Theodore Levitt, *The Marketing Imagination* (New York: Macmillan, 1983), pp. xii–xiii.

2. William J. Quain, "Analyzing Sales-Mix Profitability," *Cornell Quarterly,* April 1992, pp. 56–62.

3. Christopher W. Nordling and Sharon K. Wheeler, "Building a Market-Segment Accounting Model to Improve Profits," *Cornell Quarterly,* June 1992, pp. 29–36.

4. James R. Abbey, *Hospitality Sales and Advertising,* 3d ed. (Lansing, Mich.: American Hotel & Lodging Educational Institute, 1998), p. 91.

5. Philip Kotler and Gary Armstrong, *Marketing: An Introduction,* 2d ed. (Englewood Cliffs, N.J.: Prentice-Hall, 1990), p. 444.

6. Derek Taylor, *Sales Management for Hotels* (New York: Van Nostrand Reinhold, 1987), p. 23.

7. *The Value Side of Productivity* (New York: American Association of Advertising Agencies, 1989), pp. 17–18.

8. Ibid., p. 18.

9. McDonald's and Bear Sterns.

10. Charles H. Patti and Charles F. Frazer, *Advertising: A Decision–Making Approach* (New York: Dryden Press, 1988), p. 4.

11. Ibid., p. 5.

12. Al Ries and Jack Trout, *Positioning: The Battle for Your Mind* (New York: Warner Books, 1981), p. 8.

13. "Profiles in Travel," *Travel Agent Magazine,* 16 October 1989, p. 40.

14. Richard Weiner, *Webster's New World Dictionary of Media and Communications* (New York: Simon & Schuster, 1990), p. 272.

15. Edward A. Robinson, "Frogs, Bears, and Orgasms: Think zany if you want to reach today's consumers," *Fortune,* 9 June 1997, pp. 154–156.

16. Weiner, p. 381.

17. Scott Hume, "The Green Revolution," *Advertising Age,* 29 January 1991, p. 32.

18. Ibid.

19. Ibid.

20. "McDonald's USA Earth Effort—Frequently Asked Questions," www.mcdonalds.com, May 2001.

21. Ibid.

22. Weiner, p. 380.

23. The Ypartnership/Yankelovich, Inc., 2009 National Leisure Travel MONITOR and 2009 National Business Travel MONITOR.

24. Max Starkov, "2009: Another Year That Confirmed the Internet as the Only Channel in Hospitality," www.hospitalitynet.org/news, March 6, 2010.

25. Dan Zarella, *The Social Media Marketing Book* (Sebastopol, Calif.: O'Reilly Media, Inc., 2010).

26. Joseph De Avila, "Who Could Eat All This?" *Wall Street Journal,* March 17, 2010, p. D1.

27. Patrick Mayock, "Does Social Media Matter? Not Yet," www.hotelnewsnow.com, February 5, 2010.

28. Louise Story, "Anywhere the Eye Can See, It's Now Likely to See an Ad," *New York Times,* January 15, 2007, p. 1.

29. Ibid.

30. These demographic figures are from the public relations firm GolinHarris, cited in its pamphlet, "The Next 50 Years" (published in 2006). As of this writing, the publication could still be found by searching the GolinHarris website (www.golinharris.com).

31. Brian Steinberg, "The Marketing Maze," *Wall Street Journal,* July 10, 2006.

32. Kevin Delaney, "Wisdom for the Web," *Wall Street Journal,* July 10, 2006.

33. Suzanne Vranica, "Laughing All the Way to the Bank," *Wall Street Journal,* July 10, 2006.

34. Brianne Steinberger, "Testing Testing," *Wall Street Journal,* July 10, 2006.

35. Ibid.

Key Terms

added-value—What advertising adds to the value and reputation of the product, service, or company being advertised.

advertising—Planned communication activity in which messages in mass media are bought to persuade audiences to adopt goods, services, or ideas.

back of the house—The areas of a hotel or restaurant in which personnel have little or no direct guest contact, such as kitchen areas and the accounting department.

body copy—The main text of an ad.

competitive pricing—Basing prices on what competitors charge.

consumer-based pricing—Pricing based on what consumers are willing to pay.

cost-plus pricing—Determining a price by taking the total cost of providing a product or service and adding to it (1) a percentage to cover overhead or fixed expenses, and (2) a predetermined gross profit margin.

elasticity of demand—A measure of customer responsiveness to changes in price.

Four P's of Marketing—The four basic marketing responsibilities: product, place, price, and promotion.

front of the house—The areas of a hotel or restaurant in which employees have extensive guest contact, such as the front desk (in hotels) and the dining room (in restaurants).

headline—The most prominent part of a print advertisement, in which a promise or benefit is often expressed. It is used to get attention.

integrated marketing communications—A marketing model in which all marketing activities are coordinated, ensuring that all corporate marketing messages are consistent and directed at achieving the organization's overall mission.

logotype (logo)—A unique trademark, name, symbol, signature, or device used to identify a company or other organization.

loss-leaders—Items sold at or below cost in order to attract customers to a business, where they may buy other items that are profitable.

market segmentation—The process by which customers are classified into groups or segments, based on a variety of factors (depending on which factors prove most useful from a marketing point of view). Market segments can be based on demographic information (age, income), geographic information (where customers are located), psychographic information (lifestyles, social class), or a combination of these.

marketing—(1) A system of interrelated activities formulated to help managers plan, price, promote, and make available services or products to customers and potential customers in a particular target market. (2) The effort to determine and meet the needs and wants of present and potential customers. Marketing includes sales and a great deal more.

marketing mix—The variety of marketing activities a business engages in.

positioning—A marketing term used to describe how consumers perceive the products and services offered by a particular advertiser in relation to similar products and services offered by competitors. Positioning strategies attempt to establish in the minds of consumers a particular image of an advertiser's products and services.

public relations (PR)—A systematic effort by a business to communicate favorable information about itself to various internal and external publics in order to create a positive impression.

publicity—The editorial mention in the media of an organization's people, products, or services.

revenue management—A hotel pricing system, adapted from the airlines, that uses a hotel's computer reservation system to track advance bookings and then lower or raise prices accordingly—on a day-to-day basis—to yield the maximum revenue. Before selling a room in advance, the hotel forecasts the probability of being able to sell the room to other market segments that are willing to pay higher rates.

sales promotion—Sales tools and techniques such as contests, extra commissions, familiarization tours, and loyalty marketing programs that are designed to generate an immediate response.

signature—The name of the advertiser as it appears at the bottom of a print ad.

social media—A term for the tools and platforms people use to publish, converse, and share content online. These tools include blogs, podcasts, sites to share photos/videos, etc.

social networks—Places on the Internet where users can create a profile for themselves and then socialize with others using a range of social media tools, including blogs, videos, images, messaging, etc.

target marketing—Marketing that is designed to appeal to a specific consumer group.

Review Questions

1. What is the difference between marketing and selling?
2. What are the Four P's of Marketing?

3. Which methods of pricing are commonly used in the hospitality industry? How do they differ from one another?

4. Promotional activities fall into which six categories?

5. What are the differences between marketing objectives, strategies, and tactics?

6. What characteristics do exceptional salespeople share?

7. What characteristics distinguish advertising from other forms of communication?

8. Ideally, what three factors does an advertiser need in order to produce an effective advertising campaign?

9. What are some guidelines for creating print ads?

10. How can advertisers use broadcast media effectively?

11. What are the differences between public relations and publicity?

12. What is sales promotion?

 # Internet Sites

For more information, visit the following Internet sites. Remember that Internet addresses can change without notice. If the site is no longer there, you can use a search engine to look for additional sites.

Airlines

American Airlines
www.aa.com

British Airways
www.british-airways.com

Delta Air Lines
www.delta-air.com

Continental Airlines
www.continental.com

Qantas Airways
www.qantas.com

Hotels/Restaurants

Four Seasons Hotels
www.fourseasons.com

The Ritz-Carlton Hotel Company
www.ritzcarlton.com

Hilton Hotels
www.hilton.com

Sheraton
www.sheraton.com

Holiday Inn
www.holiday-inn.com

Starwood Hotels & Resorts Worldwide
www.starwoodlodging.com

Hyatt Hotels
www.hyatt.com

Taco Bell
www.tacobell.com

Marriott
www.marriott.com

Westin Hotels
www.westin.com

McDonald's
www.mcdonalds.com

Organizations, Resources

Advertising Age
www.adage.com

American Association of Advertising
  Agencies
www.aaaa.org

American Hotel & Lodging Association
www.ahla.com

Boston Consulting Group
www.bcg.com

Cheap Tickets, Inc.
www.cheaptickets.com

Environmental Defense
www.edf.org

Expedia.com
www.expedia.com

FORTUNE.com
www.pathfinder.com/fortune/

GetThere.com
www.getthere.com

Interactive Advertising Bureau
www.iab.net

National Restaurant Association
www.restaurant.org

TravelersNet.com
www.travelersnet.com

TravelNET Solutions
www.travelnetsolutions.com

Travelocity.com
www.travelocity.com

15

How Management Companies Manage Hotels

Outline

Why Management Companies Exist
The Evolution of Management Companies
Management Contracts
    Contract Provisions
    Advantages and Disadvantages
Summary

Competencies

1. Identify unique characteristics of the hotel business, explain why hotel management companies came into existence, and summarize the history of management companies. (pp. 460–463)

2. Describe a hotel management contract. (pp. 463–471)

Opposite page: The Atlanta Westin Peachtree Plaza; photo courtesy of Starwood Hotels & Resorts Worldwide, Inc.

THIS CHAPTER COVERS hotel management companies and their methods of operation. First it explains the beginnings of management companies and continues by describing their history and evolution. It then focuses on management contracts between hotel owners and management companies, identifying and explaining major contract provisions and the reasons for them. Finally, the chapter describes the opportunities and risks for hotel owners and management companies when they enter into a management contract.

Why Management Companies Exist

The growth and prosperity of hotel management companies, and the unique and changing nature of their relationships with hotel owners, underscore the fact that hotels are a special kind of real estate. They are very different from office buildings and shopping malls, for example.

To begin with, unlike most other businesses, hotels operate 24 hours a day. Moreover, unlike 24-hour operations such as all-night gas stations or drugstores, hotels must provide a multitude of readily available specialized services. At full-service properties, guests expect that food and beverage service will be provided—in some cases on a 24-hour basis. Rooms must be cleaned daily. Full-service hotels may also offer laundry and valet services, meeting and convention rooms and services, fitness clubs, tennis courts and golf courses, airport limousines, concierge services, business centers, Internet connections, and secretarial services. The number and range of facilities and services a lodging property offers depends on the property's biggest guest group, which may be business travelers, tourists, or conventioneers.

In fact, a hotel is a miniature self-sustaining society. Managers of large hotels often compare what they do to running a small city. Many large hotels have their own energy-generating facilities, security forces, and shopkeepers. Guests sleep, eat, work, play, and sometimes die in hotels. The hotel is the guests' headquarters—their office and home, the center of their daily business and social life. Because a hotel can be so many things, managing it can be complex and extremely demanding. Managers and their staffs must be prepared to cope with a variety of activities and emergencies while maintaining and controlling the hotel's physical plant.

Managing a hotel requires special expertise. Buying a franchise is one way inexperienced hotel owners can try to acquire that expertise. When they buy a franchise like Holiday Inn, they buy an established image, a tested and successful operating system, employee training programs, marketing and advertising programs, and reservation systems.

However, while a franchise may provide systems, programs, and training, it does not provide the cadre of experienced managers and employees necessary to run a hotel. For this reason, when hotel chains such as Hilton and Sheraton first expanded, they managed every new property themselves rather than sell franchises. They understood that they could not write down everything they knew in training manuals, and that mastery of the science of running a hotel could not be easily acquired in a short training course.

Rather than buy a hotel franchise, some inexperienced owners decided the best way to make sure their hotel was profitable was to hire professional hotel managers from established hotel chains or independent management companies. Thus the hotel management company was born.

The Evolution of Management Companies

For hundreds of years hotels were started and operated by hoteliers, just as restaurants were started by chefs. These hoteliers were professionals who knew how to manage a hotel.

But as the lodging industry grew in the last half of the twentieth century, a new breed of owners appeared. These new owners were entrepreneurs who regarded the buildings and land they occupied as attractive investments, or they were real estate developers who felt that a hotel would be the best use for a piece of property they owned. These new owners, who knew nothing about the hotel business and usually were not interested in it, had several options for running their hotels. Many hired professional hotel managers and operated their hotels as independent properties. In order to generate business and name recognition, they sometimes tied in with a referral service such as Best Western or a marketing group like Preferred Hotels.

Another option was to turn management of the property over to a hotel company. Hotel companies such as Hilton were receptive to the idea because it was a way to expand their earning base without the financial risk of developing a hotel from the ground up.

From the standpoint of these new owners—who were real estate investors, not hoteliers—the most logical way to employ a hotel company was a lease, an instrument that they were very familiar with. Under this arrangement, a hotel owner or developer—which might be an individual, a company, or even a government—would simply rent out a structure to a hotel company either as a fully developed and furnished turnkey operation or, more likely, as an unfurnished building that had to be outfitted by the hotel company. For instance, the government of Bermuda constructed the town of Saint George's first hotel, expecting the hotel would bring tourists to that part of the island. The building was then leased to the Holiday Inn Corporation. Subsequently the hotel has been leased to several other operators.

Under early lease arrangements, the hotel company was responsible for hiring and managing the entire staff of the hotel, collecting all the revenues from sales, and paying all operating costs. They also paid rent to the owners for the use of the facility. In return they received a share of the hotel's gross operating profit. Gross operating profit was determined by deducting operating costs from total revenue. Obviously, the hotel's fixed charges—such as depreciation, interest on borrowed capital, and real estate taxes—were paid by the owner of the building. For a few leased hotels, the rental agreement was based on a percentage of total sales. Sometimes the rent was based on a combination of a percentage of sales as well as a share of the gross operating profit.

Another typical arrangement was the two-thirds/one-third lease. Here, two-thirds of the gross operating profit went to the owner and one-third went to the hotel company. This kind of arrangement was the basis of the contract made in 1954 between Hilton Hotels and the Puerto Rican government, the lessee and lessor, respectively, of the Caribe Hilton Hotel in San Juan, Puerto Rico. Hilton used the same formula to expand to Turkey, Mexico, and Cuba. It was in Cuba, after Castro's takeover and the disruption of operations because of the revolution, that Hilton recognized the potential for losses due to circumstances beyond their control. According to Charles A. Bell, executive vice president of Hilton International in its formative years, "That is why Hilton converted their profit-sharing lease agreement into management contracts under which the owners took the risk of operating losses, as well as debt service, and had the ongoing responsibility of supplying working capital."[1]

While Hilton was growing by leasing new properties and creating new types of leases, the InterContinental Hotel Corporation (IHC) was pioneering the management contract.

This ad by Interstate Hotels emphasizes the experience it can offer to hotel owners who may be new to the industry. (Courtesy of Interstate Hotels & Resorts.)

In the early 1950s, IHC signed its first management contracts with the respective owners of the Techendama in Bogota, Colombia, and the Tamanaco in Caracas, Venezuela, while the hotels were still under construction. Instead of paying rent and keeping the hotels' profits, IHC did not pay rent and received from each owner a management fee (which originally was based on a fixed fee per room) and an "incentive fee." The incentive fee was a percentage of the hotel's gross operating profit, plus reimbursement of IHC's overhead—specific expenses incurred by IHC in managing the property.

Incentive fees are now a regular part of management contracts, but in the 1950s this concept was a real innovation. The term **"incentive fee"** describes that portion of the management fee that is based on a percentage of a negotiated level of profitability. For example, one basis is a percentage of operating cash flow after debt service (CFADS). It is called an incentive fee because it is designed to motivate the hotel company to produce maximum profit for the owners, so the hotel company can collect the maximum incentive fee. As it gained more experience with this concept, IHC switched from a fixed fee per room to a percentage of gross revenue plus a percentage of gross operating profit with no reimbursement of company overhead. At first, IHC made a small investment in each of the hotels it managed, to entitle it to a director on the boards of the companies that owned the hotels. Later, in Europe and the Far East, IHC invested as much as one-third of the project cost.

One of the pioneers of independent management companies in the United States was Robert M. James, CHA, former president (retired) of Regal-AIRCOA (now Richfield Hospitality, Inc.). When James started his company in 1971, few U.S. hotels were operating under management contracts. In 1970 there were fewer than 10 management companies operating 22 properties.

Since contracting with a hotel owner to manage the hotel for him or her was virtually a new field, there was little information or experience to guide the first U.S. management companies. To help remedy this situation, James started the International Council of Hotel and Motel Management Companies—a committee of the American Hotel & Lodging Association—which enabled management company representatives to meet with one another and learn more about management contracts.

As a result of the economic recession in the early 1970s, management companies' services were in great demand. They could provide professional management for U.S. hotels that had been taken back by the investors—many of them insurance companies. Exhibit 1 lists today's top management companies.

Management Contracts

A hotel **management contract,** as defined by Professors James Eyster and Jan de Roos of Cornell's School of Hotel Administration, is "a written agreement between the owner and the operator of a full-service or select-service hotel by which the owner employs the operator to assume full responsibility for operating and managing the property."[2] The operator (management company) can be a hotel chain with a familiar name and market image, such as Hyatt or Sheraton. It can also be an independent management company. Independent management companies operate franchise hotels as well as independent hotels. For example, Interstate Hotels & Resorts manages properties under various franchises such as Marriott, Hilton, and Sheraton, as well as independent hotels and resorts such as the Charles Hotel in Cambridge, Massachusetts, and the Roosevelt Hotel in New York City.

Exhibit 1	Top 20 Management Companies				
		Properties Owned & Managed		Properties Managed for Other Owners		Total Rooms Managed
Company Name	Rooms	Properties	Rooms	Properties	
1 Interstate Hotels & Resorts	2,500	7	44,500	219	46,550
2 Tharaldson Lodging	14,610	222	13,162	200	27,772
3 White Lodging Services	3,035	18	16,838	123	19,873
4 John Q. Hammons Hotels	19,021	78	0	0	19,021
5 The Procaccianti Group	15,025	57	0	0	15,025
6 Crestline Hotels & Resorts	1,340	6	13,239	64	14,579
7 Pyramid Hotel Group	0	0	12,792	38	12,792
8 Sage Hospitality Resources	10,614	50	1,905	12	12,519
9 Davidson Hotel Company	0	0	9,986	35	9,986
10 Outrigger Hotels & Resorts	3,129	6	5,554	28	8,683
11 Hei Hotels & Resorts	8,632	30	0	0	8,632
12 Kimpton Hotels	2,472	12	6,035	32	8,507
13 Crescent Hotels & Resorts	2,364	12	6,138	37	8,502
14 Winegardner & Hammons	6,426	26	1,585	8	8,011
15 Remington Hotel Corp.	199	1	7,769	43	7,968
16 GF Management	3,155	14	4,800	37	7,955
17 Hostmark Hospitality	0	0	7,420	36	7,420
18 Lodgian	7,363	40	0	0	7,363
19 Prism Hotels	0	0	7,079	35	7,079
20 Destination Hotels & Resorts	0	0	7,021	33	7,021

Source: *Lodging Hospitality,* December, 2009, p. 78.

Under the earliest management contracts, the operator was simply regarded as a company hired to perform a service, much as an architectural firm might be hired to draw the plans for a hotel. The management company got paid for performing those services, but took no financial risk and therefore was not entitled to any profits. However, as noted previously, that basic concept has evolved over time. Management companies now typically own a piece of the hotels they manage, thereby assuming a share of the financial risk. Other changes to the basic concept are as follows:

- Thirty years ago, most financing of lodging facilities in the United States was done by insurance companies and lending institutions. They invested for the long term, hoping to realize both profits and appreciation on the value of the property. Since the late 1980s the situation has become dramatically different. Current investors include "the major hotel brands and large well-capitalized management companies themselves, private equity funds, major Wall Street–sponsored funds, **real estate**

Thomas F. Hewitt, CEO of Interstate Hotels & Resorts, is a recognized leader within the hotel management company industry.

investment trusts (REITs), and high-net-worth individuals," according to Thomas F. Hewitt, Chairman and CEO of Interstate Hotels & Resorts, the nation's largest independent hotel management company.[3] (A real estate investment trust or REIT is like a mutual fund; it allows individuals to combine their resources to invest in income-producing properties or lend funds to developers or builders.) Hewitt states further that "brands, largely being public companies, favor joint ventures so they do not have to consolidate the entire investment on their books." Moreover, joint ventures, according to Hewitt, "also require less capital on the part of the brands to execute a transaction." Hence the hotel companies can use their financial resources to develop the brand rather than the real estate. In Europe and the Pacific Rim, financial institutions still play an important role in financing hotels, while in countries such as Mexico, Venezuela, and Argentina, governments often provide needed funds.

- The relationship between owners and operators has dramatically shifted. Writing in the *Cornell Quarterly,* Eyster says that there has been a significant change in management contracts due to increased competition among operators and the more active role of owners in managing their investments.[4] In their most recent study of hotel management contracts, Eyster and de Roos state that the relative bargaining strengths and negotiating abilities of the owner and the operator affect how the risks are shared.

- Environmental concerns have slowed hotel development in ecologically sensitive areas in the United States and abroad. Today it is recognized that hotels and resorts might damage ecologically sensitive areas, so it is harder to get approval to build. Often the cost of meeting environmental requirements can substantially increase the capital required to develop a new property.

- With the economic downturn at the end of the first decade of the twenty-first century, hotel development was stalled, resulting in few new management contracts available and shifting the bargaining power to the owners.

Because of these reasons, hotel owners have become even less willing than they were before to take all of the financial risk by themselves. The stakes have gotten too high. Moreover, some management companies have grown in size and power to the point where it makes economic sense for them to own all or part of the properties they manage. As part owners, they can take a share of the hotel's profits in addition to collecting their management fees. "I believe that more and more management contracts today require some form of investment on the part of the operator," says Hewitt. He adds, "Many management contracts involve some degree of ownership, lending, or something that involves risk for the management company. Owners today are keen to align the interests of the management company with their own interests and are much more comfortable with a management company that is willing to take a financial stake in a project."[5]

Contract Provisions

The provisions of a management contract are important not only to the owner and the operator, but also to the lenders who finance the project. Lenders want assurance that the hotel owner and the management company operating the hotel have a reasonable opportunity to make a profit. They also want to be sure that differences between the owner and the management company have been resolved in advance; otherwise, the viability of the project may be jeopardized.

Contract provisions detail the exact terms that the parties have agreed upon. Although the basic provisions of all management contracts are similar, there can be significant differences from contract to contract. These differences include the amounts invested by the owner and the management company; the nature and amount of control exercised by each party; fee structures, including the incentive arrangement; and contract termination provisions.

In the following sections, we discuss some of the major terms and provisions often addressed in hotel management contracts.[6]

Operating Term. The **operating term provision** defines the length of the initial term of the contract and its renewal options. The management company (hereafter referred to as the "operator") usually prefers a long initial period, while the owner usually prefers a shorter one. Eyster and de Roos explain that while a long-term contract offers stability for the operator, the owner, and the lender, it is a disadvantage to the owner if the owner wants to remove the operator before the contract comes up for renewal. Operators generally favor long-term contracts because such contracts give them more time to recover a return on their investment. The lenders' concern is that the term of the contract and the term of the loan coincide, making it probable that the hotel will be run by only one operator throughout the loan's payback period. Such a stable situation makes it more likely that there will be an uninterrupted flow of revenues and profits to cover debt payments.

The length of the contract is often a serious negotiating point. A Jones Lang LaSalle Hotels study reports that in the Americas the average initial term is 13 years, and the most common renewal options are one, two, and five years.[7] Their study reveals that "the length of management agreement terms has become more uniform as international operators spread their influence across the globe."[8]

Fee Structure. The **fee structure provision** outlines the fees the owner must pay to the operator for managing the property. This is one of the most important contract provisions because it affects both the owner's and operator's profits. The fee structure is negotiable, and will vary from contract to contract depending on the bargaining power of the parties. Eyster and de Roos categorize the payments owners make to operators into three areas.

Technical assistance fees cover the time and expertise of the operator as a consultant in the design of the facilities. Architectural and interior design are the services most commonly rendered, although help with restaurant layout, equipment selection, and security concerns such as lighting and locking systems are often involved as well.

Pre-opening management fees are similar to technical assistance fees in that they cover work done by the operator before the hotel opens. Pre-opening management activities include planning, staffing, training, marketing, budgeting, and other activities that the operator must perform before the property is ready to receive guests. These activities are very important—especially for hotel owners with no previous experience—since they may well influence the hotel's long-term success.

Post-opening management fees are almost always based on some kind of formula. It is typically a basic fee plus an incentive. **Basic fees,** also known simply as "management fees," are the fees paid to the operator for managing the property. In the case of a chain operator such as Hilton or Westin, the fee also covers the use of the established brand name. As has been noted, an independent management company does not bring a recognizable name to the negotiating table. If the owner wants a franchised name like Hampton Inn or Embassy Suites, or wants the property to be part of a referral reservation system like that of Best Western, he or she must deal directly with the franchisor or reservation system. That cost is distinct and separate from the management fee. This is the main justification for a chain operator's higher management fee; a chain operator gives the owner's hotel an already established name. The important thing in determining an equitable management fee is to relate the fee to the services received and to define the level of profit upon which the incentive fee is based. According to the Jones Lang LaSalle study, the average basic fee in the Americas is 2.8 percent of gross revenue. The incentive fee is a negotiated figure and there are a number of ways to calculate it. As mentioned earlier, one method utilizes a percentage of operating cash flow after debt service (CFADS). There are other methods that allow the owner to receive a designated percentage return on the total project cost or the owner's invested equity before the operator's incentive fee. While specific terms vary with each deal and are usually considered proprietary information, today's management contracts typically reflect base fees of 2 to 4 percent of total hotel revenue, coupled with an incentive fee of 5 to 10 percent of excess cash flow over and above a return to the equity investment. The incentive can also be tied to a small percentage, say 3 to 5 percent of EBITDA (Earnings Before Interest, Taxes, Depreciation, and Amortization) or NOI (Net Operating Income), according to Hewitt.[9]

Operator-reimbursable expenses are incurred when a management company's corporate office provides centralized reservation systems, bulk purchasing services, national advertising campaigns, and accounting services. Travel costs of corporate staff who supervise the hotel are also considered operator-reimbursable expenses. Each managed property reimburses the operator for its share of these costs.

Reporting Requirements. The **reporting requirements provision** defines the types of reports that will be provided by the operator to the owner, and outlines how frequently they will be provided. These reports include budgets, financial statements, variance reports between budget and actual performance, market plans, audited statements, and—in some cases—weekly and daily activity reports.

Approvals. Since the management contract is an agreement between the hotel's owner and operator, decisions about the hotel's development or operation generally require input from both parties, or at least an approval from one party of the other's decision. The agreement should have an **approval provision** that defines in what areas approvals are necessary. Most contracts require the owner's approval of the hotel's general manager, controller, and director of sales, says Hewitt. Today's lenders are no longer entirely passive; they may involve themselves in such areas as the hotel's asset positioning in the marketplace, capital programs, and fiscal budgets.[10] In many cases, owners are concerned about restaurant concepts and marketing and pricing strategies as well.

According to Hewitt, "In the '70s and '80s, a management company presented a marketing, capital, and business plan, then told the owners 'We'll see you next year.'" But things have changed dramatically, and the changes continue today, Hewitt says. "Owners, or their representatives—i.e., an **asset manager** retained by the owner entity—are involved in all aspects of the property on a regular basis." While some may disagree, Hewitt believes that owner participation through the management company, and through interaction with the general manager in some cases, is very beneficial. The danger, of course, is the potential for an owner to get directly involved with employees concerning day-to-day issues.[11]

Contract provisions relating to owner input have given owners and lenders, or their representatives (asset managers), more of a voice in operational decisions. According to James Eyster, involvement has increased considerably in operational decisions, the hotel's operating policies, the budgeting process, and personnel selection.

Although the operating companies continue to set standards, owners—through on-site representatives or representation on policy-making committees—take part in the decision-making process. In the past, the operator was responsible for developing and following the operating budget. Today, in most cases, owners provide input and have the right to approve the budget. Also, owner control over capital replacement or improvement budgets has increased significantly. Line staff members are sometimes employees of the owner under the relationship established by some management contracts, with the executive staff employed by the operator. Owners now have a greater say in the selection of the general manager and other key department heads.[12]

Even when communication between the owner and the operator is good, they may not always agree, so the contract should contain provisions for settling disputes. A number of management contracts contain an arbitration provision, specifying that the arbitration come from a qualified person or firm.[13]

Performance. Performance clauses that allow the owner to terminate the management company have become a more common addition to management contracts. According to Stephen Rushmore, performance clauses usually contain the following: "the criteria standard; an implementation period; ability for operator to cure; and exceptions to termination."[14] The criteria standard is generally a dual benchmark of revenue and a level of profitability. A common revenue test is revenue per available room (RevPAR) compared to that achieved by a competitive set of hotels. The level of profitability standard may vary according to the needs of the owner, but usually it is a level of net income that will provide a return on the owner's investment.

The implementation period is the time that the management company has to achieve the standards mentioned above. It could be anywhere from one to three years, depending on the market conditions. Also, it may vary between a new hotel, which requires a period of time to develop business, and an existing hotel, where the new management company must merely put in place its marketing and operating systems, rather than develop business from scratch.

If expected levels of profitability are not met, some contracts require that the management company give or lend the owner "sufficient funds to make up the difference between the stipulated level of net income defined in the standards and the actual level."[15]

Circumstances beyond the control of the management company, such as natural disasters or terrorist attacks, alter the market environment and are legitimate reasons for not achieving the negotiated performance standards. Hence the management agreement must be specific as to the exceptions that are acceptable.

Termination. All management contracts contain a provision that allows either party to terminate the management agreement under certain conditions:

- Non-performance of a contract provision by the other party (sometimes with a one-time right to "cure"—that is, make things right)
- One of the parties filing for bankruptcy
- One of the parties causing licenses to be suspended or revoked[16]

Some contracts include other reasons for termination. These relate to the damage or loss of the property or the sale of the property. Sometimes there is a "termination without cause" provision. If a contract is terminated without cause, the owner must pay a penalty fee to the operator to compensate for the loss of profits anticipated by the operator.

Operator Investment. Operators or management companies are primarily in the business of managing. On the other hand, owners prefer a good-faith investment on the part of the operator. Today, more operators are investing in the properties they manage, usually in the form of loans or equity. When an operator loans money to an owner, the management contract specifies the amount in the **operator investment provision;** how the loan will be used (as initial working capital, for example, or to cover negative cash flows); the term of the loan; and the interest rate. When the investment is an equity contribution, it may be in the form of cash, free technical services, waived pre-opening management fees, or even conversion of incentive fees.[17]

Operating Expenses. In addition to the normal costs of operating a hotel, an operator will incur expenses in its home office or on the premises of the property itself. Expenses such as centralized advertising, reservation systems, and computer and accounting services are typical of the costs that an operator sometimes charges to the hotel's owner. The operator should clearly state the operating expenses it will pass on to the owner in the **operating expenses provision**—this helps avoid challenges by the owner later on.

Other Provisions. Other provisions of most management contracts include those that:

- Restrict the operator from competing in the same market area by operating another property within the area (unless approved by the owner)
- Specify the methods of transferring ownership or management interests to others by either party through a sale or a lease
- Stipulate exclusive rights to work with each other on future hotels

- Define the rights of each party in case the property is damaged or condemned

- Provide indemnification for the adverse performance of the other party

- Lay out a plan for a cash reserve for the replacement of furniture, fixtures, and equipment

Advantages and Disadvantages

Management contracts have advantages and disadvantages for each of the parties involved.

One of the primary disadvantages for owners is that while a management contract relieves them of day-to-day operating responsibilities, they still have to carry all or most of the financial burden. Although operators have increasingly provided loans and equity investments in recent years, owners are still primarily responsible for funding their properties. They must make up for losses or insufficient revenues to cover operating costs. In addition, management fees reduce owner profits.

Owners do, however, benefit from management contracts. The primary advantage is that they buy the services of an established hotel operator with a proven track record and a good reputation. Although a management fee must be paid, the potential for profit is increased. An experienced operator can offer marketing expertise and systems of cost control that would otherwise not be available to the owner.

At first it may appear that operators have few serious disadvantages in a management contract arrangement. One of the greatest advantages, from an operator's point of view, is that it can control a large number of properties with a relatively limited investment. The operator's financial risk is much lower than the owners'.

Nevertheless, there are disadvantages to a management contract for operators as well. An operator's reputation is on the line every day at every hotel it manages. The operator must look to the owner for funding when there is a shortfall in revenues. If the owner refuses to supply it or doesn't have it, the resulting sub-standard services and facilities will reflect on the operator. In addition, today the operator's real opportunity for profit lies in the incentive fee. An operator dealing with a difficult or poorly financed owner will probably never realize the anticipated profits.

A further disadvantage is that, unless the operator has provided equity, the owner may make decisions regarding the property's development or sale without the operator's input. The owner can also dismiss the operator or not renew the contract at the end of its term, possibly damaging the operator's reputation and taking away its opportunity to realize profits from the work it has done. A hotel is rarely an overnight success; it usually takes years to realize an operating profit, and only those who are in it for the long haul are likely to reap the rewards.

On the whole, management contracts are carefully crafted so that all parties are well protected. But even with the best intentions, sometimes there are serious disagreements between owners and operators. An example of what can happen surfaced publicly when Broadreach Capital Partners, owners of the Four Seasons Aviara Resort in Carlsbad, California, attempted to oust the hotel company and replace Four Seasons with Dolce Hotels and Resorts. Broadreach had signed a 30-year contract with Four Seasons in 1995 that included three twenty-year options, so that the potential term of the contract had a 90-year span. However, a clash surfaced when the owners and the operator could not agree on the 2009 operating budget. Although the contract contained a provision for settling disputes, both parties brought the disagreement to court. The owners claimed that Four Seasons was not operating in a cost-effective manner and they wanted the hotel company out immediately. In fact, representatives of the owners arrived at the property late at night to change the locks of management offices, according to a Four Season's assertion. On the other hand, Four Seasons argued that Broadreach burdened the hotel with onerous debt and requested that the court stop the owners from seizing the hotel and require them to abide by the dispute-settlement provision in the management contract—namely, arbitration. The court agreed and ordered the parties to arbitrate. They did so, and the arbitration panel ruled that Broadreach had to pay Four Seasons in order to sever the contract.

According to Eyster and de Roos, dispute-settlement provisions are relatively new to management contracts and they appear now rather frequently. According to their research, "Most owners and operators interviewed recommend that the arbitration clause state clearly whether all contract provisions should be subject to arbitration or whether arbitration should be limited to specific disputes."[18] In the case of the Broadreach and Four Seasons dispute, the management agreement had a broad arbitration clause. If an "owner wants to reserve its right to litigate certain aspects of the relationship with the manager in court, then it should customize the provision appropriately" by either explicitly excluding or stating potential areas of dispute.[19]

While this kind of incident is highly unusual, serious disagreements do happen occasionally, and it illustrates the necessity of both parties understanding what they get and what they give up in a management contract.

Summary

Hotels are a special kind of real estate. They are small, self-sufficient communities, and they need people with hotel expertise to operate them. In the last half of the twentieth century, inexperienced hotel owners such as investors and real estate developers began to acquire hotel properties. These owners realized that the best way to gain hotel management expertise was to bring in experienced hotel operators by (1) leasing the hotel to them, or (2) signing a management contract with them that allowed them to run the hotel.

With the first leasing agreements, the operator paid rent for the building but kept whatever profits were made. With the first management contracts, operators did not pay rent and did not keep all of the hotel's profits—they received a basic fee to cover their overhead costs plus a share of the profits or an incentive fee.

A management contract is a written agreement between an owner of a hotel and a hotel management company (operator) in which the owner employs the operator as an agent to assume full responsibility for managing the property. The operator can be a hotel chain with an established brand name or an independent management company.

Management contracts are still evolving, for several reasons. Most new hotel owners are only interested in short-term involvement. Hotel development has slowed because the tax structure and business climate have changed and environmental concerns have become more important. In addition, owners are no longer willing to take all of the financial risks by themselves; operators are now sharing some of the risks.

The most important provisions in a management contract are those dealing with the operating term, the fee structure, reporting requirements, approvals, performance, termination of the contract, operator investment, and operating expenses.

From an owner's point of view, the advantage of hiring a management company is that it relieves him or her of the burden of running the hotel and provides the hotel with experienced management personnel and operating systems. The disadvantages are that the owner is still responsible for paying the bills even though the management company operates the hotel, and management fees reduce the owner's profits.

Hotel management companies benefit from management contracts because the companies can grow without putting up large amounts of capital, keeping their financial risk low. However, difficult or under-financed owners can damage an operator's reputation and deprive it of profits it has earned. The owner can also dismiss the operator who built the business, even if the hotel is showing a profit.

Endnotes

1. Charles A. Bell, "Agreements with Chain-Hotel Companies," *Cornell Quarterly,* February 1993, p. 28.

2. James J. Eyster and Jan A. de Roos, *The Negotiation and Administration of Hotel Management Contracts,* 4th rev. ed. (Pearson Custom Publishing, 2009), p. 5.

3. Thomas F. Hewitt, personal interview, November 2009.

4. James J. Eyster, "Hotel Management Contracts in the U.S.," *Cornell Quarterly,* June 1997, p. 14.

5. Hewitt interview.

6. These provisions and some of the comments about them are adapted from Stephen Rushmore, "Make Sure Management Contracts Contain These Terms," *Lodging Hospitality,* April 1988. The authors also wish to acknowledge their debt to Professor James J. Eyster. Many of the observations and comments relating to these provisions are based on Eyster's *The Negotiation and Administration of Hotel and Restaurant Management Contracts.*

7. "Global Hotel Management Agreement Trends," Jones Lang LaSalle Hotels, in conjunction with CMS Cameron McKenna LLP and Baker & McKenzie, June 2005.

8. Ibid.

9. Hewitt interview.

10. Ibid.

11. Ibid.

12. Eyster, "Hotel Management Contracts in the U.S.," p. 15.

13. Ibid., p. 33.

14. Stephen Rushmore, "Performance Clauses Essential in Contract," *HOTELS,* November 2002, p. 36.

15. Ibid.

16. Eyster, *Negotiation and Administration.*

17. Eyster, "Hotel Management Contracts in the U.S.," p. 22.

18. Eyster and de Roos.

19. Cecelia L. Fanelli and Jonathan D. Twombly, "Four Seasons Aviara Case: Using An Arbitration Clause," *Hotels,* June 3, 2009.

Key Terms

approval provision—The provision of a hotel management contract specifying which operator decisions require management approval. The mechanism for settling owner/operator disputes is sometimes included in this provision.

asset manager—The owner's representative monitoring the operation of the hotel.

basic fees—Fees paid by a hotel owner to a management company for managing the property. In the case of a chain management company, the fees also cover the use of the established brand name. Also called "management fees."

fee structure provision—A provision in a contract between a hotel owner and a hotel management company that outlines the fees the owner must pay to the management company for managing the property.

incentive fee—That portion of the management fee (paid by hotel owners to hotel management companies) that is based on a percentage of income before fixed charges (also known as gross operating profit), or on a percentage of cash flow after debt service.

management contract—A written agreement between an owner and an operator of a hotel or motor inn by which the owner employs the operator as an agent (employee) to assume full responsibility for operating and managing the property.

operating expenses provision—The provision in a hotel management contract that outlines the expenses the management company will pass on to the hotel's owner.

operating term provision—The provision of a hotel management contract that defines the length of the initial contract and its renewal options.

operator investment provision—The provision of a hotel management contract outlining the details of the operator's investment in the property.

operator-reimbursable expenses—Expenses a hotel management company's corporate office incurs in providing services (bulk purchasing services and national advertising campaigns, for example) to its managed properties. Each managed property reimburses the management company for its share of these costs.

pre-opening management fees—Fees paid by a hotel owner to a management company for work done before the opening of the hotel, including planning, staffing, training, marketing, budgeting, and other activities that the management company must perform before the property is ready to receive guests.

real estate investment trust (REIT)—An investment instrument, somewhat like a mutual fund, that allows individuals to combine their resources to invest in income-producing properties or lend funds to developers or builders.

reporting requirements provision—The provision of a hotel management contract that stipulates the types of reports the management company must provide to the owner and how often they must be submitted.

technical assistance fees—Fees paid by a hotel owner to a management company covering the time and expertise of the company as a consultant in the design and plan of the facilities.

Review Questions

1. How can a hotel owner who is not a hotelier ensure that the property is managed effectively?

2. What is an incentive fee?

3. What three provisions are common to almost every management contract?

4. What are the differences between a lease and a management contract?

5. What are some of the industry-wide changes responsible for the evolution of management contracts?

6. In negotiating a management contract, which party prefers a long-term contract and which party prefers a short-term contract? Why?

7. What are four types of fees owners pay to operators?

8. What do the "approval" and "termination" provisions of a management contract cover?

9. What are the advantages and disadvantages of management contracts, from both the owner's and operator's points of view?

 Internet Sites

For more information, visit the following Internet sites. Remember that Internet addresses can change without notice. If the site is no longer there, you can use a search engine to look for additional sites.

Hotel Companies/Resorts

Best Western
www.bestwestern.com

Doubletree Hotel Corporation
www.doubletreehotels.com

Hilton Hotels
www.hilton.com

Host Marriott Corporation
www.hostmarriott.com

Interstate Hotels & Resorts
www.ihrco.com

Preferred Hotels & Resorts
www.preferredhotels.com

Richfield Hospitality Services
www.richfield.com

Ritz-Carlton Hotels
www.ritzcarlton.com

Sheraton Hotels
www.sheraton.com

Starwood Hotels & Resorts Worldwide
www.starwood.com

Organizations, Resources

Bison.com
www.bison1.com

16

Franchising Is
Big Business

Competencies

1. Explain what a franchise is, describe types of franchises, summarize the history of franchising, and explain how franchising works. (pp. 478–485)

2. State common reasons individuals give for wanting to buy a franchise, outline the advantages and disadvantages of owning a franchise, list advantages and disadvantages for franchisors, and summarize other franchising issues. (pp. 485–492)

Opposite page: Photo courtesy of the Renaissance Nashville Hotel.

T HIS CHAPTER DEALS WITH FRANCHISING in the hospitality industry. It covers
the history of franchising, the reasons for its popularity, the advantages and
disadvantages of owning a franchise, and how franchising works.

What Is a Franchise?

In its simplest form, the word *franchise* refers to the authorization given by a company to
another company or an individual to sell its unique products and services. Franchising is
a marketing or distribution system: the franchisor grants an individual or company the
right to conduct business according to the franchisor's guidelines, for a specified time and
in a specified place, for a fee.

A franchisee may be a single-unit owner or have a multi-unit franchise. As the term
suggests, a single-unit owner has the right to open and operate one franchise unit. It does
not exclude that individual from buying additional single units. If that occurs, the franchisee is a multiple, single-unit owner. A multi-unit franchisee is given the right to open
and operate more than one unit in a defined area.

Let's review the following terms, which will be used throughout the chapter:

- **Franchise**—In addition to the meaning mentioned earlier, "franchise" can also refer
  to the name of the business format or product that is being franchised. The Marriott
  Corporation grants Residence Inn franchises as well as Courtyard by Marriott franchises and others.

- **Franchisor**—The franchise company that owns the trademark, products, and/or
  business format that is being franchised.

- **Franchisee**—The individual or company granted the right to do business under the
  franchisor's name. A person who buys a Dairy Queen franchise is a franchisee.

- **Franchising**—The major trade association in franchising, the International Franchise Association, defines franchising as "a continuing relationship in which the
  franchisor provides a licensed privilege to do business, plus assistance in organizing, training, merchandising, and management in return for a consideration from
  the franchisee."

Franchise rights vary. Most franchisors grant franchisees the right to use the franchise
name and its distinctive trademark, logo, architecture, and interior design. Some franchisors also sell their method of operation, or designate territories in which the franchisee
may operate. In some cases, the franchisor may grant the franchisee the right to sell the
franchisor's product(s); for example, franchisees of Baskin-Robbins ice cream stores have
the right to sell Baskin-Robbins ice cream.

Types of Franchises

There are two types of franchises: the product or trade-name franchise and the business
format franchise.

The **product** or **trade-name franchise** is a supplier-dealer arrangement whereby the
dealer (franchisee) sells a product line provided by the supplier (franchisor) and, to some
degree, takes on the identity of the supplier. This is the type of franchise that exists in

Marriott is one of the most recognized names in hotel franchising.
(Courtesy of Marriott.)

the automobile, gasoline service station, and soft drink industries. The majority of total franchise sales in the United States are from product or trade-name franchising.

Business format franchises, which include quick-service restaurants and lodging chains, are characterized by an ongoing business relationship between franchisor and franchisee that includes not only the product, service, and trademark but the entire business concept itself.

The majority of the growth in franchising has been in the business format franchise category. Besides food service operations and hotels, this category includes non-food retailers, personal and business services, real estate services, and other service businesses. Restaurants make up the majority of business format franchises.

The History of Franchising

Franchising is not a new concept. A precursor of modern franchising occurred in Roman times, when private citizens bid for the right to operate tax-collecting "franchises" for the government. These "franchisees," called "publicans," kept a percentage of the taxes they collected for themselves. It was a lucrative business—especially for the unscrupulous—and publicans were generally detested, as the Biblical phrase "publicans and sinners" reminds us.[1] This form of franchising existed in the Middle Ages as well, when royalty and church officials rewarded important citizens with the right to collect revenues in return for "various services or considerations."[2]

Product or Trade-Name Franchising

All of the early franchises were product or trade-name franchises that allowed individuals or companies willing to put up their own capital to sell and, in some cases, make the franchisor's product. The only restrictions on franchisees were on what they sold and the territory where they sold it.

In 1851, I. M. Singer & Company used franchising to develop a network of sewing-machine dealers throughout the United States. Under the Singer concept, a dealer was allowed to open a Singer Sewing Machine store in return for an agreement to sell only Singer machines and supplies. Since people did not know how to use these new sewing machines, the dealers also provided service in the form of sewing lessons. This was the beginning of modern franchising systems.

Because the Singer company had a unique product that was in demand, and one that dealers could not obtain unless they agreed to open a Singer Sewing Machine store, the company did very well. However, franchising did not catch on in a big way until the early 1900s, with the production of automobiles and soft drinks.

Just as in the case of Singer sewing machines, automobiles were new and complicated mechanical devices requiring service and repair. No one was willing to buy a horseless carriage unless there was someone nearby who could fix it if it broke down. Automobile manufacturers, most notably General Motors at first, came up with a solution similar to the Singer company's: they established dealerships to sell and service their cars. Because dealers were located in the communities where the cars were sold, they were trusted neighbors who could be relied on to back up the promises made by the automobile manufacturers. Not surprisingly, the petroleum companies that grew along with the automobile dealers adopted the same form of distribution. Even today gas stations are, for the most part, individually owned small businesses that have the right to use a company's trade name and sell its products.

The first Coca-Cola franchise was granted in 1899. Franchising was necessary because Coca-Cola was packaged in a unique glass bottle that consumers paid a deposit for and returned to the company. Handling the bottles required local bottling companies that could pick them up, wash them, and re-use them. Moreover, it was expensive to ship bottled drinks all over the country from the company's headquarters in Atlanta, Georgia. In order to expand, Coca-Cola gave franchisees the right to build Coca-Cola bottling plants in return for purchasing Coca-Cola's bottles and syrup. Coca-Cola also agreed to train its bottlers in production techniques and marketing. Soon Coca-Cola bottling plants were established all over the United States.

Each Singer or General Motors franchise involved a relationship between the manufacturer (franchisor) and the retailer (franchisee) who sold the manufactured product(s) directly to the public. Note that in both cases the retailer performed a service (product servicing and repair) for the franchisor in addition to selling the product. This was one reason why franchising was the most efficient form of distribution for these products. In the case of

Coca-Cola, the relationship was between the manufacturer (franchisor) and a wholesaler (franchisee). Coca-Cola's wholesalers did not sell directly to the public, but delivered Coca-Cola to retail soda fountains and grocery stores. Again, however, the franchisee (wholesaler) performed a service for the franchisor: in this case, bottling the product. These new products—sewing machines, cars, and soft drinks—required the seller to provide services as well as the product itself, making franchising necessary and practical.

Business Format Franchising

The first person to pioneer the idea of the business format franchise in the hospitality industry was Howard Dearing Johnson, founder of the Howard Johnson Company. Johnson started his chain in 1925 with a drug store that he successfully converted into an ice cream parlor. By 1928 he had two thriving ice cream parlors and decided to open a third that would serve food as well. This was his first restaurant. A friend offered Johnson some land so Johnson could build a second restaurant. Johnson had no more capital to invest, however, and convinced his friend to build the restaurant. Johnson would provide him with a franchise to sell Howard Johnson ice cream as well as assist in the design and supervision of the restaurant.

The friend's restaurant was an instant success, and Johnson realized that he had found a way to expand his business without investing any money of his own. Johnson decided

LOOKING FOR SOMETHING TO ADD TO YOUR MENU?
HOW ABOUT A NEW RESTAURANT.

- Looking for experienced multi-unit restaurant owners.
- Multi-Unit territories *still* available.
- Dual branding opportunities with T.J. Cinnamons® Classic Bakeries.
- Training, marketing and operations support.
- 3200 restaurants and growing.
- 14 straight quarters of same store sales increases

Arby's and other quick-service restaurant franchises are examples of business format franchises. This ad targets those who might be interested in owning an Arby's franchise. (Courtesy of Arby's.)

to continue with the strategy of encouraging others to build Howard Johnson restaurants, which would sell Howard Johnson ice cream and other products that he would supply. He continued to assist in the design and management of these new restaurants so that he could help make them a success. Johnson did not ask for a royalty on sales for these extra services; his sole profit came from the sale of Howard Johnson products. By the end of 1936 there were 61 Howard Johnson's restaurants, most of which were franchises; by 1939 there were 107 restaurants operating in a half dozen states.[3] In 1954 Johnson entered the lodging business by franchising his first motor lodge in Savannah, Georgia. By 1969 there were 391 lodges, 90 percent of which were franchises. (After 11 more years of continued growth, Howard B. Johnson, son of the founder, sold Howard Johnson's to Imperial Group Ltd., a British corporation. Imperial sold the company to Marriott in 1985. Marriott kept a few of the bigger hotels and quickly sold the rest of the lodging properties to Prime Motor Inns; Marriott then sold the free-standing Howard Johnson's restaurants to various buyers over the next few years. The "Howard Johnson" hotel name is now owned by Wyndham Hotel Group.)

In spite of Johnson's success, franchising did not catch on with the rest of the hospitality industry until the early 1950s. Lodging's most notable early franchising success was Holiday Inn. Kemmons Wilson and a partner owned three successful Holiday Inn motor hotels in the early 1950s and wanted to expand nationwide. They decided to finance their expansion by selling Holiday Inn franchises to franchisees who would build their Holiday Inns according to a set format and contribute some money from each guestroom for advertising.

The beginning of the franchise giant McDonald's was a drive-in self-service restaurant in San Bernardino, California, built in 1948 by two brothers, Maurice and Richard McDonald. In 1954, Ray Kroc, a milkshake-machine salesman, called on the McDonald brothers to deliver eight of his Multimixer machines. What he found was an efficient octagonal assembly-line operation turning out beverages, french fries, and 15-cent hamburgers. As Kroc tells it, "When I saw it working that day in 1954, I felt like some latter-day Newton, who'd just had an Idaho potato caromed off his skull."[4] Kroc understood what made the restaurant a success. In his book, *Grinding It Out: The Making of McDonald's*, he explained what went through his mind:

> I've often been asked why I didn't simply copy the McDonald brothers' plan. They showed me the whole thing and it would have been an easy matter, seemingly, to pattern a restaurant after theirs. Truthfully the idea never crossed my mind. I saw it through the eyes of a salesman. Here was a complete package. I could get out and talk up a storm about it.... Besides, the brothers did have some equipment that couldn't be readily copied. They had a specially fabricated aluminum griddle for one thing, and the set up of all the rest of the equipment was in a very precise step-saving pattern. Then there was the name. I had a strong intuitive sense that the name McDonald's was exactly right. I couldn't have taken the name. But for the rest of it, I guess the real answer is that I was so naive or honest that it never occurred to me that I could take their idea and copy it and not pay them a red cent.[5]

The McDonald brothers, who drove Cadillacs and lived together in a luxurious home, were not interested in expanding. They were happy with what they had achieved and did not want to work any harder. In exchange for $2 million, they granted Kroc an exclusive ten-year franchise. He agreed to put up buildings exactly like the one their architect had drawn up, complete with the golden arches. The McDonald brothers inserted contractual clauses that obligated Kroc to follow their plans down to the last detail—even to signs

McDonald's in Guangzhou, China. (Courtesy of McDonald's Corporation.)

and menus. And there was a clause that prohibited Kroc from doing anything differently without a registered letter of permission from the two brothers. It was agreed that Kroc could charge franchisees 1.9 percent of their gross sales and that he would give .5 percent of that to the McDonalds. Kroc was also allowed to charge a franchise fee of $950 to cover the expenses he incurred in finding a suitable location for each franchise and a contractor who would build to the McDonalds' specifications.

Kroc brought in Harry Sonneborn to assist him, and the two planned the future of their new enterprise. They realized that for their franchise to succeed they had to do more than simply sell prospective franchisees a name and a menu. Besides, a hamburger—ready-made according to the franchisor's specifications—could not be sold to a franchisee like Howard Johnson's ice cream; franchisees would have to cook their own hamburgers. Kroc wrote:

> We agreed that we wanted McDonald's to be more than just a name used by many different people. We wanted to build a restaurant system that would be known for food of consistently high quality and uniform methods of preparation. Our aim, of course, was to ensure repeat business based on the system's reputation rather than on the quality of a single store or operator. This would require a continuing program of educating and assisting operators and a constant review of their performance. It would also require a full-time program of research and development. I knew in my bones that the key to uniformity would be in our ability to provide techniques of preparation that operators would accept because they were superior to methods they could dream up for themselves.[6]

Here Kroc expresses the heart of the concept of modern franchising: a franchise company's reputation depends on the quality and consistency of all of its franchises, and quality and consistency are maintained by ongoing training and development. In 1961 Kroc bought out the McDonald brothers for an additional $2.7 million. Today there are more than 32,000 McDonald's units in 117 countries.

How Franchising Works

In order to obtain a license from a franchisor, a franchisee must pay a fee for the privilege of using the franchisor's name, identity, business systems, operating procedures, marketing techniques, and (in the case of hotels) reservations system. The typical franchise fee arrangement has two parts: (1) an initial franchise fee, payable upon signing the franchise agreement, and (2) ongoing fees.

Initial franchise fees vary. They are calculated by assigning a monetary value to the following:

- The franchisor's goodwill

- The value of the new franchise unit's trading area or territory

- The average cost of recruiting a franchisee

- The cost of training a franchisee

- The cost of signs, ads, plans, and other aids

The goodwill of a business—the reputation or prestige it enjoys among customers—is an intangible asset that is easier to estimate for an established franchisor such as McDonald's than for a new franchisor. Although intangible, goodwill can be calculated by relating it to the franchisor's profits, profits being one measure of the amount of goodwill a franchisor enjoys. For example, if a franchisor's franchises average $150,000 in profits per year, the value of the goodwill for a new franchise might be 2½ times that, or $375,000. A percentage of the goodwill charge—anywhere from 4 percent to 12 percent—could be part of the initial franchise fee. Franchisors differ in how they calculate goodwill and how they charge it to their franchisees.

Some territories are more valuable than others, due to their demographic makeup and the propensity of their residents to eat out. Therefore, a new franchise's location would be considered in setting the initial franchise fee.

The value of recruiting, training, and aids such as signs and advertising is easier for the franchisor to calculate, since it can refer to actual costs.

Restaurant franchisors generally charge a flat franchise fee for one unit; some franchisors charge a reduced rate for additional units. On the other hand, hotel franchisors base their initial franchise fees on the number of guestrooms the franchisee builds, with a minimum fee plus an amount per room over a defined minimum number of rooms. For example, a minimum fee for a hotel with 100 rooms would be $50,000, but a hotel with 150 rooms would be $50,000 plus $300 per room over 100 rooms, or $65,000 ($50,000 + $15,000). Some hotel companies quote an amount per room with a total minimum. Here are some examples of initial franchise fees:

Franchisor	Initial Franchise Fee
Subway	$15,000
Little Caesars	$15,000–$20,000
McDonald's	$45,000
Hilton	$85,000 minimum for 275 rooms, $300 each additional room
Holiday Inn Hotels & Resorts	$500 per room with a $50,000 minimum

Ongoing franchise fees vary. All franchisors charge a royalty fee, usually calculated on a percentage of the franchisee's sales. As with initial franchise fees, royalties are related to the value of the franchise. Examples of typical royalty fees are as follows:

Franchisor	Percent of Gross Revenues
Subway	8.0%
Beef 'O' Brady	4.0%
Hilton	5.0%
McDonald's	12.5%

Some hotel franchisors operate a central reservations system and charge franchisees a fee to cover the cost of operating the system. The calculation of this fee varies. It is usually a percentage of rooms revenue, an amount per available room per month, or an amount per reservation.

Initial Investment

Although most restaurant franchises are still considered small businesses, the initial investment required to establish a successful franchise can be substantial, due (among other factors) to the cost of real estate, construction, and property taxes. For example, the total investment to open a McDonald's ranges from $1 to $1.8 million! The land is owned by McDonald's and the rent is included in the continuing royalty fee of 12.5 percent. (McDonald's also has a leasing plan for new franchisees who cannot afford the total investment required to purchase a unit.) Some hotel franchises cost even more. For example, a Hilton Garden Inn can cost from $10 to $16 million. Because of the high cost of franchises, franchisors want to be sure that their franchisees will have enough capital to operate their units until they start making a profit. For this reason, some franchisors require their franchisees to have a minimum personal net worth. This amount varies from franchisor to franchisor.

Franchise Regulations

Franchising is regulated in the United States by the Federal Trade Commission and a number of states. In those states with special regulations, a franchisor must register with the proper state authority before offering a franchise for sale within the state. State and local restrictions take precedence if they are more demanding than federal requirements.

All franchisors must comply with Federal Trade Commission Rule 436.1, which requires that a prospective franchisee be given a prospectus—the **Uniform Franchise Offering Circular** or **UFOC**. This prospectus is a disclosure document that informs the franchisee about certain vital aspects of the franchisor and the franchise agreement before the agreement is signed. This disclosure statement must be in the hands of the prospective franchisee ten business days prior to signing the franchise agreement, so that the franchisee will have ample time to study it and understand the risks involved. The UFOC covers everything from the franchisor's history and financial condition to the detailed terms of the sales agreement. Franchisees should study the UFOC carefully before buying a franchise. (See the chapter appendix for more information on what a UFOC must contain.)

Owning a Franchise

Franchising has not only been a boon to companies seeking to expand quickly; it is one of the ways individuals can realize the dream of having their own business. Ray Kroc

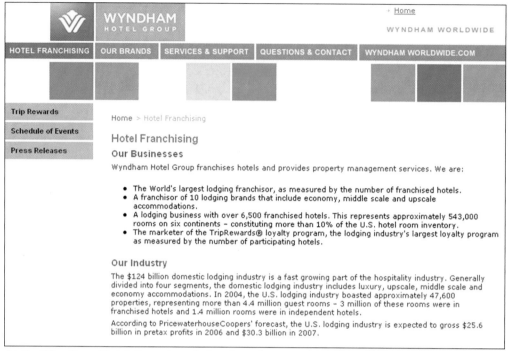

At the Wyndham Hotel Group's website, those interested in owning a property in one of the company's hotel brands (from Baymont Inn & Suites to Wyndham Hotels and Resorts) can learn about franchising opportunities. (Courtesy of Wyndham Hotel Group.)

considered it the quickest way to capture the American dream and was proud of the fact that people credited him with making many of his associates millionaires.

Success doesn't happen for every franchisor, however. A study conducted by a professor of economics at Wayne State University found that within four to five years of opening, 38.1 percent of new franchised businesses failed.[7] Starting a business is risky, and success depends heavily on the franchisor. Obviously, the franchise company also plays a role. Experienced franchise companies with successful track records are more likely to provide the kind of advice and support that translates into profitability.

Franchising gives an individual entrepreneur a chance to compete in the marketplace against giant companies. It provides some insurance for success, for when franchisees buy a franchise, they buy (1) a format and formula, and (2) the experience of the franchisor, who is expected to teach them what they need to know to succeed.

The Development Group, a consulting firm that sells franchises for its clients, asked prospective franchisees why they wanted a franchise. Their answers were revealing:

- Self management was the most important reason given: 73 percent of applicants saw owning a franchise as a way to be their own boss.

- Financial independence was a close second: 69 percent of applicants thought owning a franchise was a better way to ensure financial security than depending on a paycheck from someone else.

- Career advancement ranked third (53 percent of applicants). If you own your own franchise you don't have to wait for someone else to promote you. You can move as fast as you are able.

- New skills/training was cited by 49 percent as their main reason for buying a franchise. Many people, for example, would like to own their own hotel or restaurant but simply don't know how. Good franchise companies provide training and assistance.

- A franchise was seen by 32 percent as a long-term investment that would appreciate in value.

Advantages

There are many advantages to owning a franchise in addition to those just cited, including:

- Site-selection assistance
- Credit
- Construction expertise
- Fixtures and equipment assistance
- Training
- Opening support
- Promotional assistance
- Economies of scale
- Ongoing support

Site-Selection Assistance. The first advantage for franchisees is that their franchisor will help them select a good site for their business. Almost all successful franchisors know exactly what kinds of sites work best for their franchises. In many cases the franchisor selects the site, buys or leases the land, puts up the building, and then leases it to the franchisee. In other instances, the franchisees do all of this for themselves, but even then, franchisors almost always approve sites based on their experience of the amount and kind of population needed in an area, traffic patterns, and other considerations.

Choice Hotels International, which franchises Comfort Inn, Quality, Clarion, and Econo Lodge, among others, offers prospective franchisees help with not only site selection but also site acquisition and site and market assessment. Restaurant franchisors do the same. In its franchise-offering circular, filed with the Federal Trade Commission in Washington, D.C., the Subway sandwich chain states:

> The location of the store must be approved by the franchisor and the franchisee. The franchisor, or a corporation it designates, will then endeavor to lease the approved site and sublet the premises to the franchisee at cost. The responsibility for finding a site rests solely with the franchisee, and the franchisor will not unreasonably withhold approval of a location found by a franchisee. In rendering its assistance, the franchisor considers the population in the area of the site.

While Subway requires franchisees to find their own locations, McDonald's picks locations for its franchisees, based on sophisticated airplane and helicopter surveys and demographic studies.

Credit. Some franchisors may help provide financing to qualified applicants. This help can be in the form of offering loans or guarantees, locating potential lenders, or preparing a loan package or business plan that can be shown to a bank or other potential lender. Some franchisors have been known to accompany franchisees in their visit to the lender. Many people have been able to get into the franchise business by using all kinds of creative financing plans and more than one source of capital. These include lines of credit, Small Business Administration loans, Employee Stock Options (ESOPs), credit unions, insurance policies, venture capital, and trade credit (from suppliers). Some franchisors even have lease programs that allow prospective franchisees to lease units with an option to buy them.

Construction Expertise. Most franchisors supply franchisees with architectural and floor plans for the franchise building. Choice International has plans available for three different styles of two-story, 100-unit Sleep Inns, and furnishes all interior and exterior designs and site plans, including landscaping. McDonald's and Burger King have a large variety of interior designs to choose from, depending on the market and the amount the franchisee is able to invest.

Some franchisors also help the franchisee employ the builder and supervise the construction. Since most franchisees do not have experience in this area, the assistance of a construction professional can mean considerable savings. Choice International provides preliminary and code-modified working drawings, elevations, and floor plans, as well as all structural, mechanical, plumbing, and electrical drawings necessary to complete the hotel. When the hotel is finished, a Choice International representative conducts a final site inspection to make sure that everything was done properly.

Fixtures and Equipment Assistance. Franchisors help franchisees select, purchase, and install fixtures and equipment. The Subway chain has an equipment-leasing program for franchisees who do not have sufficient capital to purchase necessary fixtures. Sheraton issues a product catalog as well as a guestroom design catalog with different interior design schemes that fit the Sheraton image.

Training. Classroom and on-the-job training is a major part of most franchise programs. As noted earlier, 49 percent of all franchisees list training as their main reason for buying a franchise. Many franchisors have extensive training programs because it is in their best interest to see that franchisees meet franchise standards.

Subway offers an intensive two-week training program that includes basic business operations, management techniques, and hiring skills. The program is conducted in a classroom and at one of the Subway restaurants. There are also follow-up programs for management. The KFC training program is four days of eight to ten hours per day. The franchisee or the manager and one other key person must attend the training. McDonald's has a two-week training program at Hamburger University in Oak Brook, Illinois, that follows on-the-job training at an operating store; every seven years franchisees are invited back for an additional one-week course. McDonald's has twenty-two regional training teams throughout the world as well as six other Hamburger Universities in Hong Kong, London, Munich, Sao Paulo, Tokyo, and Sidney. Most of the hotel franchisors have training at their headquarters or conducted at individual hotels by field representatives.

Opening Support. Just about all franchisors help their franchisees prepare and open their franchise units for business. McDonald's opens its restaurants with a series of champagne receptions for local politicians and families of the crew. In 1990, when McDonald's opened its first Russian franchise on Pushkin Square in Moscow, 700 people attended a champagne and caviar reception!

Promotional Assistance. Promotional assistance—that is, help with advertising, sales, and public relations—is one of the main strengths a franchisor can offer a franchisee. Most franchisors charge franchisees a marketing or advertising fee that is used to purchase television time, radio spots, newspaper ads, and produce other promotions such as coupons, sweepstakes, or contests. Burger King charges each franchisee an advertising royalty of 4 percent of monthly sales. This money is used for newspaper and magazine advertisements, mailers, promotional displays, and television and radio commercials. The company also helps franchisees with cooperative advertising plans, offers ongoing sales incentives, and sponsors periodic awards for superior sales and quality. Wendy's charges 2 percent of gross sales for national advertising, and another 2 percent for local advertising efforts.

Advertising and sales efforts in the lodging industry can be complicated. For Hilton Hotel's Garden Inns, a monthly program fee of 4.3 percent of gross rooms revenue is charged. The program fee covers advertising, promotion, publicity, public relations, market research, hotel directories, and developing and maintaining the reservation system. Additional charges are levied for marketing programs not covered under the program fee, including Hilton HHonors Worldwide, Hilton's guest frequency and reward program.

Economies of Scale. Because they are part of a franchise chain, franchisees receive the advantages of economies of scale in purchasing supplies, equipment, and advertising.

Ongoing Support. The franchisor remains available to the franchisee on an ongoing basis after the franchise unit becomes operational. Franchisors have regional representatives and

A franchisor's regional representatives give franchisees ongoing support. (Courtesy of McDonald's Corporation.)

district managers who regularly meet with franchisees. Franchisors help franchisees with merchandising and day-to-day problems. As members of a franchise organization, franchisees have access to many types of specialists that they would otherwise have to hire.

Disadvantages

Despite all of the advantages of franchising, there are problems that have caused some franchisees to regret their decision to purchase a franchise. Disadvantages include:

- Restrictions
- Unwanted products or procedures
- Unwanted advertising
- Unprotected territories
- Cancellation
- Inadequate training

Restrictions. A major disadvantage of franchising is that most franchise contracts restrict franchisees a great deal. A franchisor's success depends on having consistent quality throughout the system. When people check into a Holiday Inn anywhere in the United States, they expect to find the same kind of room, similarly priced and furnished, with the same kind of amenities. A Big Mac or a Whopper is expected to taste exactly the same, whether it is purchased in Los Angeles, California, or London, England. This means that franchisors must strictly enforce their standards. Operators of Holiday Inns *must* furnish and maintain guestrooms in a certain way; Holiday Inn kitchens *must* adhere to certain standards, and staffing *must* be at required levels. A McDonald's franchisee *must* throw away unsold hamburgers after ten minutes no matter how much it costs, and a Dunkin' Donuts franchisee *must* make new donuts every four hours. All of these franchisors run regular and unannounced inspections, and franchisees who fail to adhere to standards run the risk of having their franchise canceled. This is not an idle threat. Every year some franchisees have their contracts canceled for failure to follow company guidelines.

These restrictions mean that some franchisees cannot be as creative as they'd like to be. They can't come up with their own advertising campaigns or introduce new menu items on their own. Restaurant chains are especially strict about their menus. Franchisees cannot add or subtract anything from menus or change recipes in any way without permission, and permission is seldom granted, though on very rare occasions a franchisee will get an idea approved. McDonald's likes to point out that several of its menu items evolved from the ideas of its operators. Ray Kroc credited franchisee Lou Groen with inventing Filet-O-Fish to help him in his battle against the Big Boy chain in the Catholic parishes of Cincinnati; Jim Delligatti in Pittsburgh came up with the idea for the Big Mac; Herb Peterson in Santa Barbara created the Egg McMuffin; and Harold Rosen in Enfield, Connecticut, came up with the Shamrock Shake, a special green milkshake served around St. Patrick's Day.[8]

Unwanted Products or Procedures. When new products or procedures are introduced, franchisees must embrace them whether they want to or not. Originally, many McDonald's operators did not want to open for breakfast—it meant dramatically increased labor costs and a whole new shift. They doubted that they would sell enough breakfasts to make it pay. But when the company decided to advertise the new breakfast hours on television, every franchisee was forced to open at 6:00 A.M., even in areas where there was no business.

Many franchising companies operate worldwide. Sometimes the franchisor must make adjustments to menus, architechture, or other franchise elements in order to accommodate unique circumstances within a given country or locale. This McDonald's is in Romania.

Unwanted Advertising. A franchisor's advertising program can be another cause of franchisee dissatisfaction. When Burger King decided to launch a television campaign featuring "Herb the Nerd," many franchisees did not like it. They felt it actually drove away customers. Nevertheless, they were forced to accept it and pay for it until the company itself decided the campaign was not effective and canceled it. In some cases, franchisees feel the franchisor's national campaign does not help them, although it may benefit franchisees elsewhere.

Unprotected Territories. Another area of dispute between franchisors and franchisees involves territories. Many franchisors do not grant specific territories. This means they allow a new franchisee to establish a new unit as close as a mile or two away from an existing unit if business in the area warrants it. This is called **encroachment.**

There have been a number of lawsuits brought against franchisors by franchise operators over this issue. In Iowa, the legislature responded to franchisee anger by passing a law banning any new quick-service outlet within three miles of an existing franchise from the same system or within a population radius of 30,000.[9]

According to a report in the *New York Times:*

> McDonald's negotiates compensation agreements for some owners faced with encroachment from a new store, or minimizes the potential for conflict by offering them a new franchise. In general, though, it argues that extending the chain also stimulates people to eat more often at existing restaurants, offsetting encroachment concerns.[10]

Legislation to protect franchisees' rights, and the formation of a number of franchise owners groups, are restricting the power of franchisors to control their operators' destinies. In many cases, these groups now have a voice in determining company policies on encroachment into their territories, as well as input on new product introductions and advertising campaigns.

Cancellation. Franchisees are not always guaranteed that they will be able to renew their franchise after the initial 20-year period (the usual length of a franchise contract). If a franchisee has not been adhering to the standards set by the company, for example, the franchisor may decide not to renew the franchise. The franchisor may also decide not to renew for reasons outside the franchisee's control. Theoretically, a franchisee might spend a lifetime building a business and then be unable to pass it on to his or her children because the franchise contract expired and was not renewed.

Inadequate Training. Not all franchisors provide high-quality training programs to their franchisees. Sometimes a franchisor's salespersons misrepresent the training franchisees will receive.

Advantages and Disadvantages for Franchisors

Franchising has advantages and disadvantages for the franchisor as well. On the advantages side, little to no capital is required for expansion, because the franchisees provide the funding. Franchisors can expand their companies quickly, while transferring the investment risk to the franchisees. Because a franchise unit is owned by a local individual or company, the franchisor gains an involved and motivated on-site manager who is a member of the community. This means the franchisee is likely to be accepted by the local community, and the franchise is in the hands of someone who knows local authorities and ordinances.

The downside is that the franchisor gives up the profits generated by its franchise units, settling for royalties instead. Also, the franchisor surrenders a certain amount of control to the franchisees. In company-owned units it is easier to make changes in operating procedures and marketing approaches and get feedback from unit managers.

Franchising Issues

Franchising will continue to be a major force in the expansion of the hospitality industry. There are problems, however, that strain franchisor/franchisee relations. The most common areas of disagreement include encroachment, financial violations such as unpaid royalty charges, and contract violations.

Some segments of the hotel and restaurant business have reached a mature stage of growth. New concepts are more difficult to come by, and franchise chains and individual franchisees are competing for market share with each other. Franchisors, however, have not been taking these signs of a mature market lying down. Instead, they have reached out to penetrate new markets. The strategy of a number of restaurant chains is to establish outlets in nontraditional locations such as supermarkets, convenience stores, airports, schools and colleges, ballparks, and hospitals. Pizza Hut offers room service in a number of Choice Hotels nationwide. Several California high schools offer fare from Pizza Hut and Taco Bell. Taco Bell has even installed carts along the Moscow subway to sell to the roughly nine million Russians who ride the subway each day.

In the lodging industry, too, franchising is in transition. Hotel chains have introduced new brands under their trade name or a new name. As a result of this branding strategy, some franchisees have accused hotel franchisors of encroachment. Franchisors have countered with impact studies and defined geographic areas for each franchisee to allay their fears.

Summary

Franchising is a marketing or distribution system. In its simplest form, the term "franchise" refers to the authorization given by one company to another to sell its unique products and services.

There are two types of franchises: the product or trade-name franchise and the business format franchise. The product or trade-name franchise is a supplier-dealer arrangement whereby the dealer (franchisee) sells a product line provided by the supplier (franchisor) and to some degree takes on the identity of the supplier. Business format franchises are ongoing business relationships between franchisors and franchisees in which franchisors sell their product(s), service(s), trademark, and the business concept itself to franchisees in return for royalties and other franchise fees.

Franchising is not a new concept. In 1851, I. M. Singer & Company used franchising to develop networks of sewing-machine dealers all over the United States. The first person within the hospitality industry to pioneer the idea of the business format franchise was Howard Johnson, founder of the Howard Johnson Company.

The evolution of franchising was driven by the desire of some companies to expand their business, coupled with the desire of entrepreneurs like McDonald's founder Ray Kroc to take a successful idea and build on it, rather than risk starting from scratch. Franchising also provided companies with an alternative method of financing growth other than through company-owned units.

The typical franchise fee arrangement has two parts: (1) an initial franchise fee, payable upon signing the agreement, and (2) ongoing fees, which consist of royalties (based on monthly gross sales) and advertising and marketing fees. In addition to these fees, there is an initial investment required to purchase or lease the physical facility, equipment, and supplies necessary to operate the franchise.

Before selling a franchise, franchisors are required by the Federal Trade Commission to submit a Uniform Franchise Offering Circular (UFOC) to the prospective franchisee. The UFOC must contain the sections shown in the chapter appendix.

Franchising is one way for individuals to run their own businesses. When people buy a franchise, they buy (1) a format and formula, and (2) the experience of the franchisor, who will teach them what they need to know to succeed. One study showed that prospective franchisees had the following reasons for wanting their own franchise: self management, financial independence, career advancement, new skills/training, and long-term investment.

There are many other advantages to owning a franchise. Franchisors help franchisees with site selection, credit, construction, fixtures and equipment, training, pre-opening and opening activities, promotional assistance, economies of scale, and ongoing support.

Franchising is not for everyone. Many franchisees do not like the restrictions imposed on them by their franchise agreement. Franchisors have tough standards and usually do not hesitate to cancel the franchises of operators who will not adhere to those standards. Franchisees must also go along with—and help pay for—the franchisor's advertising and marketing program, whether they agree with it or not. Sometimes there are disputes over territories.

Franchising has disadvantages for the franchisor as well. While little or no capital is required to expand (because funding is provided by the franchisee), the franchisor gives up the profits generated by the franchise units, settling for royalties instead. Also, the franchisor surrenders a certain amount of control to the franchisees.

There is no doubt that franchising will continue to be a major force in the expansion of the hospitality industry. But there are many upheavals taking place, due to the expansion strategies of franchisors.

 Endnotes

1. N. G. L. Hammond and H. H. Scullard, eds., *The Oxford Classical Dictionary* (Oxford England: Clarendon Press, 1979), pp. 613, 898–899.

2. Charles L. Vaughn, *Franchising* (Lexington, Mass.: Lexington Books, D. C. Heath and Company, 1974), p. 11.

3. Ibid., pp. 15–17.

4. Ray Kroc and Robert Anderson, *Grinding It Out: The Making of McDonald's* (New York: Berkeley Books, 1978), p. 71.

5. Ibid., pp. 72–73.

6. Ibid., p. 86.

7. Eric Schlosser, *Fast Food Nation* (New York: Houghton Mifflin Company, 2001), p. 98.

8. Kroc, pp. 173–174.

9. "Indigestion at Taco Bell," *Business Week,* 14 December 1992, p. 67.

10. Barnaby J. Feder, "McDonald's Finds There's Still Plenty of Room to Grow," *New York Times,* 9 January 1994, p. F-5.

Key Terms

business format franchise—An ongoing business relationship between a franchisor and a franchisee in which the franchisor sells its products, services, trademark, and business concept to the franchisee in return for royalties and other franchise fees.

encroachment—Placing a branded hotel or restaurant in the vicinity of other hotels or restaurants with the same or a related brand.

franchise—Refers to (1) the authorization given by a company to an individual or another company to sell its unique products and services, or (2) the name of the business format or product that is being franchised.

franchisee—The individual or company granted a franchise.

franchising—A continuing relationship in which the franchisor provides a licensed privilege to do business, plus assistance in organizing, training, merchandising, and managing, in return for a financial consideration from the franchisee.

franchisor—The franchise company that owns the trademark, products, and/or business format that is being franchised.

product or trade-name franchise—A supplier/dealer arrangement whereby the dealer (franchisee) sells a product line provided by the supplier (franchisor) and to some degree takes on the identity of the supplier.

Uniform Franchise Offering Circular (UFOC)—A prospectus that outlines certain vital aspects of a franchisor and its franchise agreement. By law, the UFOC must be given to a potential franchisee before the franchisee signs the franchise agreement.

Review Questions

1. What is the difference between a franchisor and a franchisee?

2. What are two types of franchises?

3. How did I. M. Singer, General Motors, and Coca-Cola contribute to franchising?

4. How are initial franchise fees calculated by the franchisor?

5. What is the Uniform Franchise Offering Circular?

6. According to a poll by the Development Group, why do franchisees purchase a franchise?

7. From a franchisee's point of view, what are the advantages and disadvantages of franchising?

8. Why do franchisors hold franchisees to such strict standards?

9. From a franchisor's point of view, what are the advantages and disadvantages of franchising?

Internet Sites

For more information, visit the following Internet sites. Remember that Internet addresses can change without notice. If the site is no longer there, you can use a search engine to look for additional sites.

Food Service Operations

Arby's
www.arbys.com

Baskin-Robbins
www.baskinrobbins.com

Burger King
www.burgerking.com

Dairy Queen
www.dairyqueen.com

Domino's Pizza
www.dominos.com

Dunkin' Donuts
www.dunkindonuts.com

KFC
www.kfc.com

McDonald's
www.mcdonalds.com

Pizza Hut
www.pizzahut.com

Taco Bell
www.tacobell.com

Wendy's
www.wendys.com

Hotel Companies/Resorts

Accor
www.accor.com

Best Western
www.bestwestern.com

Carlson Companies, Inc.
www.carlson.com

Choice Hotels International
www.choicehotels.com

Hawthorn Suites
www.hawthorn.com

Hilton Hotels
www.hilton.com

Holiday Inn
www.holiday-inn.com

Marriott International
www.marriott.com

Sheraton
www.sheraton.com

Organizations, Resources

American Association of Franchisees &
  Dealers
www.aafd.org

Franchise Handbook: Online
www.franchise1.com

FranInfo
www.franinfo.com

International Franchise Association (IFA)
www.franchise.org

Chapter Appendix

Uniform Franchise Offering Circulars

All franchisors must comply with Federal Trade Commission Rule 436.1, which requires that a prospective franchisee be given a prospectus—the Uniform Franchise Offering Circular (UFOC). The purpose of a UFOC is to inform the franchisee about certain vital aspects of the franchisor and the franchise agreement *before* the franchisee signs the agreement. A UFOC must contain the following:

1. **Background.** The franchisor's background, including the franchisor's personal and business background and financial history, must be disclosed. Franchisors must state if they have any previous experience operating the kind of business they propose franchising. However, they are not required to disclose background that is not connected with their current enterprise.

2. **Key associates and managers.** The franchisor must identify and give the backgrounds of directors, trustees, partners, principals, and other managers of the franchising company.

3. **Litigation.** The franchisor must disclose any criminal or civil action involving unfair business practices, fraud, or violations of the franchise law. In those states where laws forbid revealing criminal records, only civil actions are revealed.

4. **Bankruptcy.** The statement must reveal whether the franchisor, partners, officers, or predecessors in the business have declared bankruptcy in the last 15 years.

5. **Initial Fee.** This section describes the initial franchise fee and how it must be paid. The refund policy must also be stated.

6. **Other fees and ongoing royalties.** Here the franchisor states the amount of monthly royalty plus advertising, marketing, reservation, and other fees the franchisee must pay. If the franchisor charges for training or for the time and expenses of its field representatives, such charges must be disclosed.

7. **Initial investment broken down into components.** In this section the amount of investment needed to open the franchise is stated. This includes the cost of the real estate, equipment, and supplies. If the amount is likely to vary due to local conditions, a range must be stated. In some cases, these figures do not include a figure for working capital, but anyone considering a franchise should add this to cover the period until the business starts making a profit.

8. **Designated suppliers.** The franchisor must state whether the franchisee is required to purchase or lease products, services, and equipment from a

(continued)

specified source. Generally this practice is frowned upon—and in some cases, is unlawful—except in certain instances. For example, the franchisee may be required to lease the building and land from the franchisor and buy certain signs from the franchisor.

9. **Obligation to purchase supplies according to franchisor specifications.** Franchisors cannot force a franchisee to buy from them or suppliers they designate (except as noted above), but in most cases it is reasonable to expect that the supplies a franchisee buys must meet franchise specifications. In the case of fast-food franchises, the specifications for all products to be used are often contained in the operating manuals. In lodging franchises, typical specifications include such items as size and quality of furnishings and construction materials.

10. **Financing.** In cases where financing assistance by the franchisor or others is offered, details of the parties involved and conditions should be set forth.

11. **Obligations of the franchisor.** Here the franchisor must describe all of the services promised to a franchisee after the agreement is signed. These include services provided before and after opening, such as site selection and training. If a franchisee is expected to pay for personal travel and living expenses while being trained at the franchisor's headquarters, this must be disclosed.

12. **Exclusive territory.** In many cases, the territory of the franchise is limited to the actual location. In others, protection may extend to a certain geographical area or be described in terms of population density. In any case, the franchisor must disclose what protection, if any, is offered to the franchisee. Even when the franchisor forbids another franchise unit from being built within the franchisee's territory, the franchisor cannot protect the franchisee from other franchisees who may wish to solicit business within the franchisee's territory. For instance, several franchised travel agencies with different owners located in different parts of a city may compete with each other by advertising the same tours in the same newspaper.

13. **Trademarks, logotypes, and commercial symbols.** Since a franchisee often is buying the use of a recognized name, the franchisor is obligated to state whether that name is fully protected, and, if not, what steps are being taken to register and protect it. It should be noted that names of particular products served as well as that of the establishment can be protected. For example, McDonald's has registered not only its name and its golden arches but also names like "Big Mac."

14. **Patents and copyrights.** Some franchisors have unique, patented equipment or designs as part of their franchise. If this is part of the franchise, it must be disclosed.

15. **Obligation of the franchisee to participate in the conduct of the business.** If the franchisor requires the franchisee to personally operate the business, such a requirement must be stated. Some franchisors allow absentee ownership; others forbid it.

16. **Restrictions on goods and services.** Almost all restaurant franchisors restrict the variety of menu items that franchisees can sell. Lodging franchises usually limit the sales of goods and services on the premises to those that are normally incident to the operation of the facility.

17. **Renewal, termination, repurchase, and assignment.** This section covers the rights of both of the parties to renew, terminate, or assign the franchise. It is often the clause that is most litigated, because franchises can be terminated for non-performance and because franchisees sometimes wish to sell or otherwise terminate their franchise.

18. **Arrangements with public figures.** Some franchises are named after real people or use the names of celebrities in their promotions. If there is a formal arrangement with one or more public figures to use their name or reputation, the details and compensation must be disclosed.

19. **Projected earnings.** If franchisors project earnings, they must disclose the formula used in the calculation process. Names and addresses of units that have achieved these earnings are sometimes given. However, most franchisors do not project any sales or profits, since these figures can easily be misleading or misinterpreted and lawsuits can be filed for misrepresentation.

20. **Information regarding the franchises of the franchisor.** Franchisors are required to list the number of franchises they have sold as well as the franchises' addresses and the names of their owners. Prospective franchisees are well-advised to contact current owners for information before purchasing their own franchises.

21. **Financial statement.** An audited financial statement of the franchisor that is no more than six months old must be a part of the UFOC.

22. **Contracts.** The franchise agreement and any other agreements—such as a lease that the franchisee will be required to sign—must be attached to the UFOC.

23. **Acknowledgment form.** A form that requires the franchisee to acknowledge receipt of the offering circular must be part of the UFOC.

17
Ethics in Hospitality Management

Outline

Competencies

1. Define ethics, distinguish social responsibility from business ethics, describe six kinds of moral reasoning, and compare the ethical standards of business and poker. (pp. 502–507)

2. Explore whether honesty is always the best policy, give examples of different viewpoints concerning morality, contrast deontology with utilitarianism, and explain the concept of ethical relativism. (pp. 507–511)

3. Describe ethical issues in the hospitality industry, explain the need for a code of ethics for hospitality businesses, define the term "stakeholder," and identify three questions individuals should ask themselves when making a decision. (pp. 511–522)

Opposite page: Emirates Palace, Abu Dhabi, United Arab Emirates; photo courtesy of Emirates Palace and WATG.

I N THIS CHAPTER we define and discuss ethics in the hospitality industry. The chapter distinguishes ethics from social responsibility and explores how values are arrived at. Concepts such as whether it is ever right to lie are examined. Ethical issues in hospitality such as discrimination, AIDS, advertising claims, and truth-in-menu laws are discussed. Finally, an ethical litmus test is offered.

What Is Ethics?

There is a children's story about a group of blind men from "Indostan" who, by touching an elephant, attempt to describe to each other what it is like. The first man, falling against the elephant's side, says the elephant is like a wall. The second, feeling the elephant's tusk, tells the others that the elephant is like a spear. The third, with the animal's trunk in hand, says the elephant is like a rope. The fourth is certain an elephant is like a tree, having touched a leg, while the fifth blind man feels the elephant's ear and concludes elephants are like fans. The sixth, seizing its tail, pronounces that an elephant is like a snake:

> So these men of Indostan
> Disputed loud and long
> Each in his own opinion
> Exceedingly stiff and strong;
> Though each was partly in the right
> And all were in the wrong![1]

Trying to describe ethics is similar to the blind men describing the elephant. Depending on how we approach the question and our own system of values, we can come up with very different answers.

Ethics is a set of moral principles and values that we use to answer questions of right and wrong. Ethics can also be defined as the study of the general nature of morals and of the moral choices made by individuals in their relationships with others.

There is evidence that many people have forgotten the true meaning of ethics. Today we tend to think of ethics in pragmatic terms—our choices are based on what seems reasonable or logical to us according to our own personal value system. This is called "ethical relativism," because it casts ethics in the role of being relative to what the situation is or how we feel about it.

In truth, ethics is something different. The very concept of ethics suggests that there is a real distinction between good and bad, right and wrong, and that it is our obligation to do our best to distinguish between these and then always try to do what is right. Although we all have different personal values and morals, we should recognize that there are some universal principles that virtually all religions, cultures, and societies agree upon. These principles form the basis of ethical behavior. The foundation of all of these principles is the belief that other people's rights are as important as our own, and that it is our duty not to harm others if we can avoid it. In fact, it is our duty to help them whenever possible. This idea is at the heart of the value system of most societies, tribes, and organizations. Without it, we would not find it possible to live and work together.

Social Responsibility and Business Ethics

It is important to distinguish between social responsibility and business ethics. The concept of social responsibility suggests that "at any one time in any society there is a set of generally accepted relationships, obligations, and duties between the major institutions and the people. Philosophers and political theorists have called this set of common understandings 'the social contract.'"[2] This contract differs among societies and may change over time. For example, today we expect that businesses will take care (1) not to pollute the air we breathe or the water we drink, (2) not to damage the ozone layer, (3) to offer fair wages and employee benefits, (4) to provide a satisfactory product or service at a reasonable price, and (5) to in some way participate in making the community in which they operate a better place. These are not ethical considerations—they are part of a "deal" that says that we as consumers expect companies to act in this manner because they are a part of the society we all share (see Exhibit 1).

Many companies recognize this and have stated publicly their belief that it is good business to be a good citizen. They support local arts, build parks, protect the environment, raise funds for charities, and try to put back some of their profits into the communities that have made their success possible. For example, Domino's Pizza has raised $4.7 million over a period of four years for St. Jude's Children's Research Hospital. In McDonald's nine largest markets, 82 percent of the consumer packaging is made from renewable materials. Recently the Environmental Protection Agency named McDonald's an ENERGY STAR Partner of the year for the company's efforts in energy conservation.[3] *Time* magazine singled out McDonald's as being an outstanding example of a company that understands the meaning of social responsibility in an article entitled, "'America's Hamburger Helper': McDonald's gives new meaning to 'we do it all for you' by investing in people and their neighborhoods."[4] Marriott International is another company with an outstanding social conscience. In selecting Marriott as one of the "100 Best Companies to Work For," *Fortune* magazine noted that 60 percent of the company's associates are from minority groups.

Ethical behavior is a whole different matter. In the past few years the United States has seen unethical behavior by corporate executives far in excess of anything ever witnessed before. For example, in 2009 Bernard Madoff, an investment advisor and stock broker, was sentenced to 150 years in prison for masterminding and operating a Ponzi scheme[5] that defrauded thousands of his clients of a reported $21 billion—the largest financial investor fraud in history committed by a single person. A few years earlier, Enron's executives were charged with hiding billions of dollars of debt through unethical accounting practices. In another spectacular failure of business ethics, Dennis Kozlowski, the former CEO of Tyco, and two other executives were charged with looting their company of $600 million and using the money to fund lavish lifestyles that included expensive Manhattan condos, vacation homes, ski chalets, and fine art collections. Investigators charged that Kozlowski once spent $1 million in company funds on a birthday party thrown on the island of Sardinia for his second wife, a party that featured gladiators, chariots, horses, lions, and an ice sculpture of Michelangelo's David with vodka gushing out of it for partygoers.

How We Arrive at Our Values

Author Hunter Lewis says that there are six ways in which we arrive at our values—our personal beliefs about what is "good" and "just." The six kinds of moral reasoning are:

Exhibit 1   Environmental Fact Sheet from Starbucks

From Bean to Cup:
Starbucks Environmental Efforts Along Its Supply Chain

1

Bean: Conservation
Starbucks has partnered with Conservation International (CI) to encourage the use of ecologically sound growing practices that help protect biodiversity and provide economic opportunities for small-scale farmers.

2

Harvest: Coffee Sourcing Guidelines
Starbucks Coffee Sourcing Guidelines reward farmers who meet strict environmental, social, economic and quality standards with preferred supplier status.

3

Storage:
Burlap Bag Recycling
Starbucks recycles all grass and jute bags used for the delivery of unroasted coffee. More than 1.37 million pounds of these bags were recycled in 2003.

4

Roasting:
Environmental Management
State-of-the-art emissions control technology is used to control the smoke and odors from coffee roasting. As new plants are designed, the best available control technology is employed. Other efforts to minimize environmental impacts at the roasting plants include reprocessing light bulbs to prevent mercury-halide from reaching landfills and recycling coffee chaff, stretch wrap, and corrugated cardboard.

5

Starbucks Support Center:
Packaging and Paper Purchases
Starbucks considers recyclability, reusability and recycled content in its purchasing decisions. Efforts are aimed at reducing packaging, and Starbucks has set a target of 30 percent post-consumer content in all paper purchases.

6

Retail: Reusing and Recycling
Starbucks offers a $0.10 discount to customers who bring in their own commuter mug. In 2003, customers used their own mugs 13.5 million times, which prevented more than 586,000 pounds of paper waste from reaching landfills. Starbucks seeks to recycle cardboard boxes, milk jugs and other waste products where commercial recycling facilities exist.

7

Cup: Grounds for Your Garden
While coffee grounds are the heaviest part of Starbucks waste stream, they can serve as a nutritious additive to gardens and compost piles. Through *Grounds for Your Garden,* Starbucks encourages reuse of coffee grounds by giving them to customers who garden.

This diagram is just part of the material that appears on Starbucks' website, describing the efforts of Starbucks to be a socially and environmentally responsible company. (Courtesy of Starbucks Coffee Company.)

1. *Authority.* Beliefs can be derived from an authority. Here we take someone else's word, such as that of the Bible or the church.

2. *Deductive logic.* Deductive logic is another basis for our beliefs. Here is a simple example of deductive logic: If all chocolate is fattening, and if this dessert is chocolate, then this dessert must be fattening.

3. *Sense experience.* Often, beliefs are arrived at through sense experience. In these cases we gain direct knowledge through our five senses. We decide that something is true because we heard it; can see it with our own eyes; or can touch it, taste it, or smell it.

4. *Emotion.* Emotion can dictate our beliefs. We may "feel" that something is true. Sometimes our emotions concerning others influence our ideas about them. For example, if we love someone, we tend to idealize him or her. Violent criminals might have parents who say, "He's a nice boy" or "But she's really a good girl."

5. *Intuition.* Intuition is another way to arrive at knowledge. Here we use our unconscious or intuitive mind to process information and discover the solution to a problem. Sometimes we refer to our intuition as our "gut feeling."

6. *Science.* Science is the basis of some beliefs. When we use the scientific method, we use our senses to collect facts, our intuition to develop a hypothesis, our logic to experiment, and our senses again to complete the test. Physicians use this process to arrive at their beliefs about the causes of disease and what cures to prescribe.[6]

Although we may use all six techniques of moral reasoning at one time or another, Lewis believes that each of us has a dominant or primary technique. To discover your dominant technique, Lewis suggests you ask yourself whom you would confide in if you had a serious personal issue on your mind and wanted advice.

If your answer is a priest, a minister, a rabbi, or another religious leader, your primary mode may be to use authority as the basis for your beliefs. If you would ask a professor of philosophy to help you, you would be looking for someone who could think through your problem in a highly structured or logical way. If your confidant were a professor of history and literature who is also a good friend, you might be relying on his or her own personal sense experience plus the experience of Western culture as contained in its history and literature. Suppose you turn to a family member or close friend. Here your dominant reasoning style could be characterized as emotional. Clearly you are looking for empathy from a member of your peer group. Some people would seek an answer from a Buddhist or guru of immense calm and unspoken wisdom. They would be hoping to use meditation and other tools to unlock their powers of intuition. If you don't recognize yourself in any of these groups, perhaps you would consult a psychiatrist who could offer an appraisal based on social science methods and principles.[7]

The point is that we are all likely to have a different set of values or ethics, depending on which moral reasoning technique is our dominant one. To many of us, some actions are wrong because the Bible or the Torah or the Koran says so. To others, actions are wrong only if our friends and family would condemn them. Some believe that anything is okay "so long as it isn't against the law" or even "so long as you don't get caught." Nearly everyone agrees that it is a good idea to tell the truth, and that stealing from others is wrong.

Is Business Like Poker?

There is a school of thought that recognizes that honesty is the best policy and it is never right to lie or steal, but holds that the rules of business are different and that behavior that

Some companies, such as McDonald's, choose to have a direct and positive influence in local communities. (Courtesy of McDonald's Corporation.)

is unacceptable elsewhere is legitimate in the business world.

Business writer Alfred Carr attracted a good deal of attention by comparing business to a poker game:

> No one expects poker to be played on the ethical principles preached in churches. In poker it is right and proper to bluff a friend out of the rewards of being dealt a good hand. Poker's own brand of ethics is different from the ethical ideals of civilized human relationships. The game calls for distrust of the other fellow. It ignores the claim of friendship. Cunning, deception and concealment of one's strength and intentions, not kindness and open-heartedness, are vital in poker. No one thinks any worse of poker on that account. And no one should think any the worse of the game of business because its standards of right and wrong differ from the prevailing traditions of morality in our society.[8]

While Carr's argument might seem to make sense at first glance, Robert Solomon and Kristine Hanson—authors of *It's Good Business,* a book about business ethics—point out that it shows a misunderstanding of both poker and business:

> Bluffing isn't lying, which is as forbidden in playing poker as it is in business. Most business is conducted in conversation where truth and mutual trust are essential....A poker game involves only its players; business is essential to the well-being of the entire society. The rules of poker protect the game and its players; the rules of business protect everyone else, too. Carr's suggestion ignores that core of ethics that does not vary from community to community—which we call 'morality.' Morality consists of those basic rules which are not merely a matter of a single game or practice, but provide the preconditions of every game, every practice. Carr may be trivially correct when he says the rules of poker are different from the rules of other games and practices, but he is quite wrong when he suggests that this constitutes a divergence from morality.[9]

Solomon and Hanson point out that the ultimate goals of business are to promote a good life for every individual and wealth for the nation as a whole. The goal of poker is to redistribute the wealth among a small group of players. Because the goals are different, and because in the business world much more is at stake, the rules of poker and business should and must be different.

Is Honesty Always the Best Policy?

According to some moral philosophers, honesty is the only acceptable policy. They argue that all lying, whether "little white lies" or vicious falsehoods, injures both the liar and the person lied to, and may injure society as well. When someone lies to Congress about the extent of the United States' military involvement in an area, or the cost of a weapon or social welfare program, the result is that our elected officials do not have the information they need to protect our interests, which is what we elected them to do.

The principle involved here is described by Sissela Bok, author of *Lying: Moral Choice in Public and Private Life,* who writes, "All our choices depend on our estimates of what is the case; these estimates must in turn often rely on information from others. Lies distort this information and therefore our situation as we perceive it, as well as our choices."[10] When we lie to others, Bok argues, we take away their right to make their own choices and instead manipulate them by giving them false information on which to base their decisions. In a real sense we are taking away their freedom. Unless we have a very strong reason for doing so, lies cannot and should not be tolerated.

Liars like to believe that their reasons for lying are sound. Most liars do not believe anyone ought to lie to them, but justify their own behavior on the grounds that they are protecting someone else's feelings or confidences, or that their lie is necessary to protect their business or their employees. But according to Bok, when we lie—for any reason—we run risks that we may be found out and our credibility will be damaged. Even worse, few lies are solitary ones. The first lie "must be thatched with another or it will rain through."[11] Eventually

> psychological barriers wear down; lies seem more necessary, less reprehensible; the ability to make moral distinctions can coarsen; the liar's perception of his chances of being caught may warp.... For all these reasons, I believe that we must at the very least accept as an initial premise Aristotle's view that lying is "mean and culpable" and that truthful statements are preferable to lies in the absence of special considerations.... Only where a lie is a last resort can one even begin to consider whether or not it is morally justified.[12]

Solomon and Hanson take a slightly more liberal view of lying. "Lying may always be wrong, but some lies are more wrong than others."[13] While they too believe that it is never right to lie, they suggest that sometimes it may be prudent or preferable to telling the truth. A sales representative, for instance, might understandably sound more enthusiastic about a product than he or she really is, and most people understand that salespeople present the favorable side of a product or service, not all sides. On the whole, however, they take the position that in business as in personal life, "telling a lie always requires extra thought and some very good reasons to show that this cardinal violation of the truth should be tolerated."[14]

Each person must decide for him- or herself what such a good reason would be. Clearly, if a robber walks into your business and asks for all your money and you say all you have is in the cash register, when in fact there is a considerable amount stored in the back room, this is a matter of self-preservation and one can justify lying. What about telling an employee whom you are letting go that you haven't got enough work, when in fact your real reason is that the person is incompetent? In this case it might be easier to lie, but one can argue that such a lie is easily seen through and it might be kinder in the long run to be honest with the employee, so that he or she can look for more suitable work. Each situation must be looked at individually, with our bias always on the side of telling the truth.

The Search for a Common Moral Ground

Despite the fact that everyone may use a different set of values to determine what is ethical, many philosophers and educators who have spent their lives thinking about ethics have concluded that there are some universal moral imperatives or obligations that form the basis of civilized behavior and are necessary for any society to function. Michael Josephson is an attorney and founder of the Joseph and Edna Josephson Institute for the Advancement of Ethics, a non-profit institute that has been at the forefront of defining ethical behavior for businesses. In an interview with Bill Moyers on the Public Broadcasting System (PBS), Josephson said:

> History, theology, philosophy will show that every enlightened civilization has had a sense of right and wrong and a need to try to distinguish them. Now we may disagree over time as to what is right and what is wrong—but there has never been a disagreement in any philosophy about the importance of knowing the difference. The things that are right are the things that help people and society. They are things like compassion, honesty, fairness, accountability. They are absolute universal ethical values.[15]

Josephson points out that the Golden Rule, which says "Do unto others as you would have them do unto you," occurred in Greek culture and Chinese culture thousands of years before Christ articulated his version.[16]

Josephson believes that most people have a built-in sense of what is right and wrong. The proof, he says, is that we feel guilt and shame when we do the wrong thing. Despite that knowledge, we often ignore our ideals about what constitutes proper behavior. There are a number of reasons for this. We have become a rights-oriented society. Sometimes we feel we have a right to certain things, but we have forgotten that with those rights come certain responsibilities. Too often, says Josephson, we measure our lives by what we get, what we acquire, and who we know. "It's the need to win, to be clever, and to be successful in other people's eyes that sometimes causes people to sacrifice the fundamental ideals," he says.

Ambassador Max Kampelman puts it this way: "There is a hole in our moral ozone layer. There is a vast difference between the right to do something, which is important, and doing something right, which is equally important."[17]

Sometimes businesspeople feel that the only way to be competitive and win is to be completely selfish—put their own interests above those of everyone else. Josephson tells the story of a lawyer who goes on a camping trip with a friend. They both are hiking with backpacks when suddenly they see a cougar about 20 yards away. The lawyer takes off his backpack, and the friend says, "What are you going to do?" The lawyer says, "I'm going to run for it." The friend says, "But you can't outrun a cougar." And the lawyer says, "I don't have to outrun the cougar. I just have to outrun you."[18]

Some justify the philosophy of putting our own interests ahead of everyone else's by saying that life is like having your hand in a bucket of water—when you remove it, the water settles down within moments and no one knew you ever lived; therefore you should try to get everything you can for yourself, because it will make no difference to anyone else in the long run. There is another way of looking at the world and your place in it that holds that you can make a permanent and positive impact on society by doing what you can to make positive differences in the lives of the people you come in contact with. You can bring some of them happiness and joy, and help alleviate the pain and suffering of others.

Sometimes people argue that when you are dealing with unethical people, you have to be unethical, too, or you will be stepped on. Josephson says, "There is usually a choice of ethical and unethical behaviors. We tell people, unless you have three alternatives to every major problem, you haven't thought hard enough. As soon as you have three, you can find one that's ethical."[19]

Eventually most of us come to believe in the philosophy of helping people rather than taking advantage of them or using them for our own benefit, but the sad thing is that for many of us this occurs late in life, when we have learned that accomplishing a particular task or career goal did not bring us the satisfaction we had hoped for. As Josephson observes, "We know that nobody on a deathbed says, 'I wish I had spent more time at the office.' People's values begin to change when they reflect upon how futile most of the flurry of activity was. And the fact is that a good conscience is the best pillow. Living a good life is the most important thing for us."[20]

Deontology versus Utilitarianism. There are two major traditions that dominate current thinking in moral philosophy: deontology and utilitarianism.[21]

Deontology holds that there are basic or universal ideals that should direct our thinking. Deontology is based on the beliefs of Immanuel Kant, an eighteenth-century German philosopher. Kant thought that the human mind could not possibly comprehend or arrive at the truth about God or the universe through pure logic or thought. He said that the only judgments we were capable of making were those based on evidence that we could see or prove the existence of. Kant believed in the existence of God, but said we have to take this on faith, since we can't prove it by pure logic. Once one admits there is a God, then it is possible to make logical and reasonable assumptions about what is expected of us and how we are required to act. In short, there is a scientifically arrived-at ideal that is necessary for humans to adhere to and for which adequate evidence exists, once one admits there is a God. Deontology proposes that ethical behavior is simply a matter of doing God's will. Since most of us believe that God is good, then goodwill or loving other human beings as God loves us is the universal principle on which all moral behavior must be based.

Along with the concept of goodwill goes a concept of duty to keep one's promises, which is known as Kant's **categorical imperative**—an absolute and universally binding

Immanuel Kant (1724–1804) was a German philosopher who advanced the theory of deontological ethics or deontology—"the theory of duty or moral obligation."

moral law. Kant believed in always telling the truth because if we cannot believe what others tell us, then agreements and even conversations between people are not possible. Would you loan money to someone if you knew that he or she had no intention of repaying it, even though he or she promised to? Deontology, in effect, says that the only way to measure whether an action is ethical is to ask whether we would be willing to live in a world where *everyone* routinely did the same thing. If our actions would be acceptable to us as a universal law, then they are correct and ethical.

Conversely, **utilitarianism** does not seek universal principles that can be applied to all situations, but instead says that ethical behavior consists of acting in such a way as to achieve the greatest good for the greatest number. One determines this by "performing a social cost/benefit analysis and acting on it."[22] Authors Donald Robin and Eric Reidenbach show that this philosophy is grounded in the ideas of Adam Smith, who said that "capitalistic systems, by providing the greatest material good for the greatest number, are considered ethical from a perspective of economic philosophy."[23] They point out, however, that there are some major criticisms of utilitarianism that should be considered. One is that an action might do a small amount of good for a large number of people while at the same time severely injuring a small group. For example, is it always ethical to build a mega-resort on a pristine beach in an underdeveloped country? Such a complex benefits tourism, but is often a disaster for the local community. A mega-resort introduces pollution, large numbers of visitors and noise to the area, and may lead to the destruction of the local culture. Moreover, utilitarianism suggests that each action should be judged on its own merits. When we do this there is a lack of consistency that opens the door to generalizations and excuses. One cannot say that anything is either moral or immoral, ethical or unethical, if "it all depends." For example, can an accountant embezzling company funds be excused because he or she believes the company is "ripping people off, so why shouldn't I?" Generally, we reject that kind of rationalization because it is entirely subjective.

"This might not be ethical. Is that a problem for anybody?"

© Dean Vietor/The New Yorker Collection/www.cartoonbank.com.

Ethical Relativism. Ethical relativism suggests that there are no universal ethical principles at all; each issue must be considered in its situational or cultural context. For example, it might be unethical to bribe a government official in the United States to obtain a building permit or zoning variance, but quite acceptable in some other countries where bribes are a routine part of doing business. (Students should note that while one can debate whether bribing government officials is ethical or not, it is most definitely against U.S. law for any American corporation or citizen to do so.) This kind of reasoning is also known as "situational ethics." It is a convenient ethical code for those who are not sure what their ethical values are or how they are arrived at, but, like utilitarianism, it provides little guidance for those who believe in a clear and consistent code of ethics.

Ethical Issues in Hospitality

Each day hospitality managers are faced with a variety of business decisions with ethical overtones. Too often, managers ignore ethical considerations when making business decisions.

Here are a few examples of decisions that a hotel general manager or someone in a similar position at a club or restaurant might make in the ordinary course of business:

New Menu
You have just approved a new menu that retains many of your favorite high-calorie, high-cholesterol, high-sodium foods. There are no nutritious alternatives on the menu. You reason that hotel guests liked what was on the old menu and they will keep coming back.

Bumped Reservation
You have just been approached by an influential guest regarding a birthday party he would like to hold at the hotel two months from now. Unfortunately, just

yesterday the hotel's meeting room was booked for that date. The guest asks you to bump the person who reserved the room. He suggests you tell that person the sales manager made a mistake in booking the room when it had previously been reserved. You agree to do so.

Cashier's Integrity
You decide to test a cashier's integrity. The cashier has been with the company ten years and has a flawless record. You slip a $50 bill in the register receipts. At the end of the day, the cashier shows a $5 overage. Upon questioning, the cashier admits to pocketing the $45 difference.

Free Wine
You recently purchased 20 cases of wine for the hotel from a new beverage supplier. Without your advance knowledge, the supplier delivered one free case of wine to your residence. You decide to keep the free case for your personal use, since it did not influence the purchase of the 20 cases for the hotel.[24]

In a *Lodging* magazine poll, 400 lodging managers were asked if they agreed with the ethics of the manager's decision in each of these hypothetical scenarios. The results of that poll are shown in Exhibit 2.

The "new menu" scenario considers how much responsibility each of us must take for the welfare of others. We may not consider ourselves our brother's keeper, but it can be argued that as hospitality professionals it is our duty to include low-calorie, nutritious meals on the menu, so we can meet the needs of guests who must, for health reasons, be careful about what they eat.

We were told by one knowledgeable hotelier that meeting room reservations get "bumped" all the time. That may be so, but if we are going to respect the rights of others, the fair thing is to allow the person who made the reservation first to keep it. Moreover, it is wrong to lie and say the other reservation was made earlier when it was not. On the other hand, if we are ethical relativists we might argue that, if we do not go along with this influential guest, we may lose a substantial amount of business, which could mean laying off employees and facing other consequences that might hurt others.

The case of the cashier's integrity also bears on the rights of others. Is it fair to put a loyal employee to a test of this nature without warning him or her in advance, especially when there is no evidence that anything is wrong? Would we like to be treated this way?

The free wine scenario poses the question of what constitutes honesty. The wine may have been delivered after the hotel's wine was ordered, but it still represents an unauthorized payment to the manager for "services rendered." The manager could return the free case and ask the supplier to show his or her appreciation for the order by giving the hotel an appropriate discount on its next wine purchase. Or the manager might give the extra case of wine to the hotel so that the hotel could profit from its sale. One test of whether it is ethical to keep this wine for personal use would be for the manager to ask how he or she would feel if other managers at the hotel found out about it. Along with many other hospitality companies, Hilton Hotels Corporation has a strict policy that prohibits its managers and other company personnel from accepting gifts from people with whom they do business; there is even a sample "gift response" letter in the company's *Code of Conduct* booklet for managers.

Linda K. Enghagen surveyed 113 four-year colleges and universities on ethical issues in hospitality and tourism. While a total of 35 different issues were raised, the ten that received the most mentions were:

Exhibit 2   Ethics Poll of Lodging Managers

The New Menu, Bumped Reservation, Cashier's Integrity, and Free Wine scenarios (described in the text) were presented to lodging managers by *Lodging* magazine. When rating the manager's decision in each of the scenarios, the polled managers were asked whether they (a) strongly agreed, (b) moderately agreed, (c) were unsure, (d) moderately disagreed, or (e) strongly disagreed with the actions of the managers in the scenarios. Here are the results.

New Menu

(a)	Strongly agree	6.1%
(b)	Moderately agree	15.5%
(c)	Unsure	8.9%
(d)	Moderately disagree	24.9%
(e)	Strongly disagree	44.6%

Comment: The responses suggest a fairly high level of health consciousness among hotel managers.

Bumped Reservation

(a)	Strongly agree	1.3%
(b)	Moderately agree	5.1%
(c)	Unsure	4.6%
(d)	Moderately disagree	13.7%
(e)	Strongly disagree	75.3%

Comment: Clearly, managers believe that guest favoritism leads to guest dissatisfaction.

Cashier's Integrity

(a)	Strongly agree	36.5%
(b)	Moderately agree	25.6%
(c)	Unsure	9.4%
(d)	Moderately disagree	11.7%
(e)	Strongly disagree	16.8%

Comment: A minority of managers evidently believed that the test put too much pressure on the employee; however, 62.1% agreed with the manager's test.

Free Wine

(a)	Strongly agree	7.4%
(b)	Moderately agree	16.5%
(c)	Unsure	10.6%
(d)	Moderately disagree	17.5%
(e)	Strongly disagree	48.0%

Comment: 65.5% of respondents apparently felt that acceptance of the wine could influence future beverage purchases by the hotel.

Adapted from Raymond S. Schmidgall, "Hotel Scruples," *Lodging,* January 1991, pp. 38–40.

- Managing an ethical environment
- Relations with customers and employees
- Honesty

- Employee privacy rights
- Alcohol/drug testing
- Environmental issues
- Relations with foreign governments
- Codes of ethics and self-governance
- Employee abuse of alcohol/drugs
- Conflicts of interest[25]

These issues reflect the academic perspective. Industry leaders have cited many other ethical problems that concern them. These include:

- Travel agent commissions
- Overbooking
- AIDS
- Employment discrimination by age, sex, or race
- Kickbacks
- Concealing income from the Internal Revenue Service
- Revenue management
- Advertising claims
- Raiding of competition's staff
- Truth-in-menu laws
- Meeting the needs of disabled customers and employees
- Adequate safety and security measures

Let's take a closer look at some of these industry issues.

Environmental Issues

Preserving and protecting the resources of tourist destinations has become a topic of major importance. Every time a hotel or an attraction is added to an area already crowded with visitors, there is a legitimate concern about its long-term impact on the environment. At an international symposium on ecology and tourism in Mazatlan, Mexico, James Speth, administrator of the U.N. Development Program, warned that "tourism and environmental protection are on a collision course." Speth urged that "rapid and forceful changes be made in the tourism industry to incorporate environmental protection policies."[26] At the same meeting, officials from the Mexican government said that Mexico was undertaking a major review of development plans at resorts like Huatulco and Los Cabos to stop the deterioration of coastal ecology.[27] Mexico's neighbor, Belize, is also taking steps to limit and control growth by keeping 80 percent of its land in tropical forest and turning down several proposals for resort development.[28]

Many destinations have already taken major steps to preserve their natural resources. In Bermuda, the number of hotel rooms has been restricted to 10,000 for a number of years, and cruise ship visits are restricted. In Egypt, officials have reduced the visiting hours at the Pyramids at Giza and limited the number of tourists who can visit at one time.

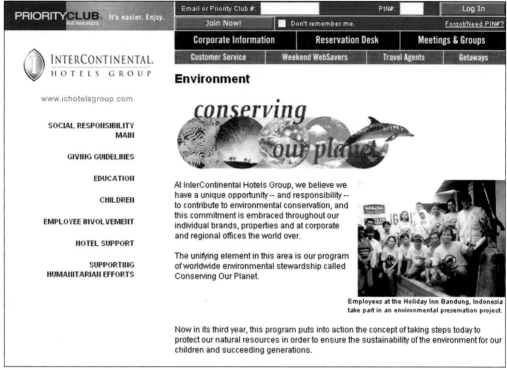

Recognizing the value of environmental responsibility, many hospitality companies make a point of publicizing their progress. (Courtesy of InterContinental Hotels Group.)

Much of the concern revolves around hotel and restaurant development, which is inevitable at popular tourist destinations, because if visitors are allowed to visit a site, they need to be accommodated while they are there. This dilemma is faced not only by developing nations, but also by highly developed industrialized countries where overbuilding has already caused major damage.

One hotel company that takes its environmental responsibilities seriously is Inter-Continental Hotels Group, which has created an online sustainability system for use in all of its almost 4,500 properties. The system, known as "Green Engage," advises the company's hotels on "what they can do to be a green hotel and gives them the means to conserve resources and save money." Furthermore, the hotels are given guidelines to manage, assess, and report on energy and water usage, waste consumption, and the hotels' effect on their communities.[29]

Walt Disney Resorts has implemented a substantial number of procedures to reduce waste. Of the total waste generated by Disney parks and resorts in 2006, 298,000 tons, or 43 percent, was diverted from landfills and was either recycled, reused, donated, or sent for composting. But that meant that 57 percent of solid waste was still entering landfills. It is Disney's goal to decrease this to 50 percent by the year 2013.[30]

Many hotels urge guests to save water (the water used by the hotels' laundries) by reusing towels rather than asking for fresh ones every morning. Modern cruise ships burn waste in onboard incinerators or compact and store it until it can be properly disposed of on land.

Fairmont Hotels & Resorts has a chain-wide Fairmont Green Partnership program. At each Fairmont hotel, a "green team" (made up of staff volunteers) oversees existing environmental initiatives and looks for new areas where environmentally friendly practices and policies can be introduced. Fairmont's director of environmental affairs believes that environmental responsibility is also good business. For example, recently Fairmont's five properties in British Columbia saved enough energy through environmentally friendly practices to power one hotel for an entire year.[31] In 2008, Fairmont Hotels was selected as one of Canada's "Top 100 Employers" for its "earth-friendly" programs, based on the company's success at integrating environmental values as part of the company culture.

In addition to the hotel companies just mentioned, most of the other major hotel organizations have green programs. Marriott International, Wyndham Worldwide, Hyatt Hotels Corp., Hilton Worldwide, and Starwood Hotels & Resorts have corporate environmental officers and property green teams that train and measure green program effectiveness.[32]

You don't have to be big to be environmentally sensitive. In Ohio, Izzy's, a small deli-restaurant chain, encourages customers to bring in their own take-out packaging by charging customers extra for take-out orders packed by the restaurant. One small restaurant in Chicago has a successful recycling program despite the fact that it does not have room to store recyclable materials on-site. Its employees drop off bags of recyclables at recycling centers on their way home from work.[33]

Discrimination

Even though it is unlawful, and companies may have their own policies forbidding it, discrimination of one sort or another can still occur in the workplace, simply because some managers may have value systems that lead them to discriminate in certain instances, perhaps unconsciously. Because there are so many subtle forms of discrimination—based on age, race, religion, gender, sexual preference, nationality, or physical attributes—discrimination may be one of the most common violations of ethics found in the hospitality industry, and one of the most difficult to recognize. In many cases it is neither malicious nor intentional. That does not excuse it, however, and managers must know where they are likely to find it and how to eliminate it.

Almost all discrimination involves fear of one sort or another. We live in uncertain times; huge political and social upheavals have taken place. These changes are bound to make us uneasy. Many of us are afraid of losing our jobs. Others are afraid of losing power or prestige, or simply not "belonging" anymore. One way these fears manifest themselves is through discrimination. Discrimination allows us to express those fears and rationalize them by giving them faces and names. Unfortunately, many opportunists have made a career out of exploiting our concerns and thus have muddied the waters even more. Their ideas fuel our fears, and sometimes these fears express themselves in the workplace.

One of the most serious and blatant forms of discrimination still practiced in many parts of the world is racial. Many people believe that affirmative action programs are necessary to give minority groups and others the opportunities that have been denied them in the past. The hospitality industry faces the same challenges as the rest of society.

Discrimination also occurs in policies sometimes found in clubs and hotels that try to restrict the use of their facilities by certain racial and ethnic groups. Hotels have been known to discourage group business from certain groups of people because "our regular guests might feel uncomfortable." While some managers may think in these terms when making a business decision, ethical managers must ask if they can in good conscience be a party to a policy that clearly conflicts with ethical standards.

Many hospitality companies recognize the problem of racial discrimination and are doing something about it:

> Marriott points with pride to its selection as one of the 25 best employers for blacks in a readership poll conducted by *Black Enterprise* magazine. One of the reasons for that designation: The chain has had roughly a 50 percent increase in the number of minority hotel general managers in the last year, according to David Sampson, Marriott's vice president for human resources. In addition, Marriott has recently added a black woman, Floretta McKensie, a former District of Columbia schools superintendent, to its board of directors.
>
> Sheraton sponsors scholarships for hospitality students at historically black colleges, including Grambling State University and Tuskegee Institute, and runs an internship program for minority students.[34]

Sex discrimination is another form of discrimination that must be addressed. For years, most male chefs believed that women had no place in professional kitchens, and even today that belief is widely held. Sometimes this is based on fallacies such as "it's a man's world" or "those large pots are too heavy for a woman to lift." But discrimination is not confined to the kitchen. Female general managers of hotels are still relatively scarce when one considers that more than half of most hotels' employees are women. There are also questions of salaries and promotions. Male managers often assume that, since a married woman has a husband to help support her, she is in less need of a raise. Sometimes a female manager is not offered a promotion that involves a transfer to another city because it is wrongly assumed that her husband's job dictates where the family will live. Women have been denied sales positions because it was felt that men were better suited for traveling and going out drinking with clients. In other words, a female manager is just not "one of the boys." Discrimination on this basis is clearly unethical, as well as being unlawful in the United States.

Finally, no discussion of discrimination would be complete without mentioning age discrimination, a global problem. Companies under economic pressure to cut costs often look first to older workers, who often enjoy high earnings (due in part to their years of service) and may in the long run cost the company more if they stay employed until retirement and become entitled to a pension. Many companies favor younger applicants when reviewing job applications.

While age discrimination is illegal in the United States, European employers legally can—and do—refuse to consider job applications from older people, reports the Wyatt Company (a consulting firm). Wyatt reports that many Europeans who lose their jobs after age 45 can only find short-term contract or temporary work. Employers in most European countries can also force employees to retire when they reach the normal age of eligibility for pensions—between 55 and 67, depending on the country.[35]

Sexual Harassment

Another ethical problem in the workplace is sexual harassment. Men as well as women can be victims of sexual harassment by superiors. Sexual harassment by employers includes asking their employees for dates, making sexual jokes or comments, touching employees inappropriately, or suggesting that sex will result in a promotion. The pressure to not complain when one's job and economic well-being are on the line is sometimes overwhelming. Companies cannot and should not allow anyone to believe for a moment that such behavior will go unnoticed or be excused.

The U.S. Equal Employment Opportunity Commission (EEOC) has developed guidelines designed to prevent discrimination on the basis of sex. The guidelines detail the following three examples of misconduct that constitute sexual harassment:

- When submission to such conduct is made a term or condition of an individual's employment, either explicitly or implicitly;

- When submission to or rejection of such conduct by an individual is used as a basis of employment decisions; and

- When such conduct has the purpose or effect of unreasonably interfering with an individual's work performance or creating an intimidating, hostile, or offensive work environment.[36]

The third guideline, which cites a "hostile" work environment, should be of particular interest to managers, since it is a more subtle violation of the law and may not manifest itself in such obvious circumstances as employment or promotions. In 1986 the United States Supreme Court handed down a landmark decision, *Meritor Savings Bank* v. *Vinson,* that acknowledged the existence of a "hostile work environment" as a basis for a claim of sexual harassment.[37] The courts have, in a series of subsequent decisions, clarified the types of conduct that might support a claim of a hostile work environment. These include "treating women with less respect than men or being abusive to women but not men, and published images or remarks or spoken comments portraying women or men in a sexually demeaning manner."[38]

What this comes down to is that sexual harassment is largely subjective. If people feel that they are being sexually harassed, then they have a right to be protected from such behavior. Managers need to be extremely sensitive to the feelings as well as the behavior of employees.

AIDS in the Workplace

AIDS is a good example of how prejudice and hysteria have affected some managers' ability to make fair and impartial decisions. Some people believe that AIDS carriers ought to be identified through testing, so that they can be informed and prevented from spreading the disease. But as columnist William Schneider points out, "What about their right not to be forced to learn whether they are under a probable sentence of death?"[39] There are other rights involved as well. Should employees who have tested HIV positive, but have not yet come down with AIDS (and may never come down with it), be promoted? One could argue that they should not be, because they may not be able to stay in their new position long enough to benefit the employer, but no one knows how long a person in this situation will remain healthy, and to deny him or her a well-deserved promotion seems unfair by any standard. The issue is most often not one of promotion but simply of keeping one's job. It is illegal in the United States to discriminate against AIDS-infected workers, since (1) they are considered to be "disabled," and (2) their condition cannot be transmitted via food or casual contact, according to the latest scientific studies.

Many hotel and restaurant operators have no written or expressed policy on the subject, though a few operators are quite explicit about their attitudes. Fuddruckers, a hamburger chain based in Wakefield, Massachusetts, clearly states that "the company's policy is not to discriminate in any way against someone infected with AIDS, and if asked, to provide a list of AIDS-related social services."

Advertising Claims

The purpose of advertising is to sell products and services. Most people understand this and therefore are skeptical about advertising claims. They are used to puffery and know that some restaurants that claim to serve "gourmet" meals may offer quite ordinary fare, and that resorts that offer "a luxury vacation" may in reality offer a mediocre one. Most people rely on recommendations from friends, relatives, and travel agents when making dining or travel plans, and take the claims made in brochures and advertising with a grain of salt.

Exaggeration in brochures and other travel advertising is "motivated by the fact that so much of the industry is so price-driven that the line between telling people a reasonable truth and beefing it up to be competitive is crossed all the time," says Sven-Olof Lindblad, president of Special Expeditions, a specialty cruise line. Travel advertising shouldn't give people "an impression that something is going to be something that it absolutely is not," such as "a picture of a beach in Honolulu with not a footprint on it, and two people walking alone into the sunset. Give me a break. That's out of the question."[40]

There is a difference between puffery and outright deception. Resorts that advertise that they are "on the beach" should be on the beach and not across the street from it. Some resorts advertise that they offer golf, but neglect to mention that the course they use is 20 miles away and starting times are difficult to come by. If a rate is advertised, it should be one that is readily available.

In an unusual dispute that garnered a good deal of negative publicity for all concerned, Killington Ski Resorts of Vermont hired an engineering firm to measure its ski terrain and the terrain of nine other New England resorts. It then launched an advertising campaign charging its competitors with exaggerating their number of trails, the depth of their snow, snow conditions, and acreage of skiable terrain. The resort placed large advertisements in national newspapers that said, "You can't ski on hype. This time of year, the hype on the trails is usually thicker than the snow." The ad then illustrated how much terrain Killington had that could be skied, and compared it with other resorts in the area.[41] In a related case, Sunday River Ski Resort in Maine filed a complaint charging Sugarloaf/USA with misleading advertising. In its advertising, Sugarloaf claimed that it was only 35 miles farther from Portland, Maine, than Sunday River. Sunday River said Sugarloaf was at least 42.6 miles farther. Sugarloaf changed its ads to say it was 39 miles farther.[42]

Unlike a television set or a sweater, which can be returned if it is not satisfactory, a vacation is not returnable and represents an investment in time that cannot be replaced. Hoteliers have a moral duty to disclose all of the relevant details of their properties so that consumers can make a fair judgment as to whether their expectations are going to be met.

Truth-in-Menu Laws

Many states have enacted truth-in-menu laws. In some states, fines can be as high as $500 for misrepresenting a menu item. But beyond legal obligations, there is a moral one to present what is being sold fairly and honestly. People have a right to know what they are eating, as well as to have enough information to make a fair evaluation about whether they are getting their money's worth. If a menu offers a 12-ounce sirloin steak, it ought to be 12 ounces every time it is served. Honest restaurateurs are proud of the fact that their gulf shrimp really comes from the Gulf of Mexico and their prime beef really is prime and not a lower grade. These may seem like minor points, but consumers have indicated that they are important to them.

Advances in the genetic engineering of food products have raised an interesting ethical question concerning truth-in-menu issues. After the Food and Drug Administration announced that it was not necessary to test or label genetically engineered (GE) fruits or vegetables that had been altered to extend their freshness or increase their size, a group of chefs protested. Rick Moonen, chef at the Water Club in New York City, put it this way:

> As a professional chef, I'm responsible for every plate of food that's served to every one of my patrons. And I must know what's on it. People come to your restaurant because of their confidence in you, because they feel you'll take care of them and their needs. If I'm serving GE foods, unlabeled and untested, I'm not fulfilling my obligation.[43]

Even if many patrons don't care if they are eating genetically engineered foods, it can be argued that they ought to know about it, especially since these products have not been sufficiently tested in the eyes of some critics.

Must There Be a Code of Ethics?

Hospitality businesses that do not already have a code of ethics should develop one employees can live by and make decisions with while at work. Without such a code, how can a manager know what the company considers ethical or unethical? If every manager makes decisions based on his or her own ethical code, then a corporation may have no ethics at all or a lot of different ethical codes, depending on who is calling the shots. "Thirty years ago all [business] values and ethics were primarily informal," says Michael G. Daigneault, president of the Ethics Resource Center. "It was assumed you were a good person and would do the right thing.... Today organizations are realizing they are the transmitters of values. Many institutions have created codes of ethics, put ethics officers in place, and are offering ethics training. The pendulum has now swung over to formal ethics."[44]

A company's ethics should reflect the company's mission and must be communicated to those who are responsible for carrying out that mission. Hospitality is a "people business"; ethics deals with our relationships with other people. For this reason, a code of ethics is almost mandatory for hospitality businesses whose managers want to achieve a unified direction and a satisfactory level of control over the conduct of business.

There is ample evidence to suggest that, without a code of ethics, some managers will make unethical decisions. According to a survey done by *Personnel Journal* magazine, middle managers—especially those 40 to 45 years old—are the most likely executives to do something unethical.[45] Some of these managers have a desire to "make it before it's too late," and strive to advance by shortcuts. In addition, they may have developed the attitude that "the company owes me" and therefore may be prone to cheating on expense accounts or making purchasing deals that benefit them.[46]

Other managers don't cheat or lie on purpose; they just make decisions without thinking out all of the ethical implications or potential pitfalls. Archie B. Carroll, an ethics professor at the University of Georgia, divides businesspeople into three categories—moral, immoral, and amoral—and says the vast majority fall into the third category. It's not that they aggressively cheat; it's just that they don't think about ethics, and they stumble into unethical territory without realizing it. That's why a written ethics policy is so important. Ask most businesspeople about their basic responsibilities and they'll list two: making money and obeying the law, says Carroll. In fact, there's a third: "They have a responsibility to be ethical. Which essentially means to be fair and just and to avoid harm in the marketing and sales of their product." Responsibility to ethics, he says, is no less fundamental than profitability and legality.[47]

One hotel company that has a strict and explicit code of ethics is Sheraton Hotels & Resorts. Sheraton's managers are expected to strictly comply with all of the company's business ethics policies. The policies are quite lengthy and include the following:

Conflicts of Interest

Employees are to exercise sound judgment, guided by the highest ethical standards of honesty and integrity, in all matters. No employee may abuse a corporate position for personal advantage or promote any actions contrary to stated ethical standards....

Employees and their immediate families shall not accept any gifts of cash or items of more than token value from third parties in connection with Sheraton business. All employees shall report immediately to their supervisors any offer or gift of more than token value.

Quality

Our success as a corporation in fulfilling its obligation to shareholders is ultimately measured in terms of customer satisfaction. It is our policy to provide products and services that satisfy the needs and expectations of our customers; conform to appropriate specifications and contractual agreements, including reliability requirements; are safe for intended use and foreseeable misuse; and meet all applicable statutory requirements of local, regional, and national agencies.

Stephen S. J. Hall, a quality assurance consultant and the founder of the International Institute for Quality and Ethics in Service and Tourism (IIQEST), has proposed the ethics code for hotels shown in Exhibit 3.

Some Ethical Litmus Tests

Even with laws and company policies and rules, ethical behavior is an intensely personal matter that every manager and employee must wrestle with. There are no easy guidelines that apply equally well in all circumstances. Ethical philosophers often talk about the moral duty of taking into account the interests of all stakeholders in arriving at a decision. A **stakeholder** is anyone who is affected by the outcome of a given decision. These could be your employees or your boss, the owners of the company you work for, the families of your employees, or the community in which the business operates. Sometimes managers or employees who are forced to implement unethical policies become whistleblowers and let other stakeholders know what is happening rather than be a silent part of an unethical action or plan.

In their book *The Power of Ethical Management*, Ken Blanchard and Norman Vincent Peale list three simple questions that they believe managers should ask themselves when making a decision:

1. *Is it legal?* Will I be violating either civil law or company policy?

Exhibit 3	Sample Code of Ethics for Hotels

1. We acknowledge ethics and morality as inseparable elements of doing business, and will test every decision against the highest standards of honesty, legality, fairness, impunity, and conscience.

2. We will conduct ourselves personally and collectively at all times such as to bring credit to the service and tourism industry at large.

3. We will concentrate our time, energy, and resources on the improvement of our own products and services, and will not denigrate our competition in the pursuit of our own success.

4. We will treat all guests equally regardless of race, religion, nationality, creed, or sex.

5. We will deliver all standards of service and product with total consistency to every guest.

6. We will provide a totally safe and sanitary environment at all times for every guest and employee.

7. We will strive constantly, in words, actions, and deeds, to develop and maintain the highest level of trust and understanding among guests, clients, employees, employers, and the public at large.

8. We will provide every employee at every level all of the knowledge, training, equipment, and motivation required to perform his or her own tasks according to our published standards.

9. We will guarantee that every employee at every level will have the same opportunity to perform and advance, and will be evaluated against the same standard as all employees engaged in similar tasks.

10. We will actively and consciously work to protect and preserve our natural environment and natural resources in all that we do.

11. We will seek a fair and honest profit, no more, no less.

Source: IIQEST Ltd.

2. *Is it balanced?* Is it fair to all concerned in the short term as well as the long term? Does it promote win-win relationships?

3. *How will it make me feel about myself?* Will it make me proud? Would I feel good if my decision were published in the newspaper? Would I feel good if my family knew about it?[48]

Summary

Ethics is a set of moral principles and values that we use to answer questions of right and wrong. It focuses on moral choices and relationships with others. Although we all have different personal values and morals, there are some universal principles which virtually all religions, cultures, and societies agree upon. The basis of all of these principles is that other people's rights are as important as our own, and that it is our duty not to do anything to harm others.

Social responsibility is not the same as ethics, although the concepts are related. Companies have an unwritten social contract with society covering their rights and obligations. Ethics consists of "doing the right thing" in areas that may be entirely unrelated to that social contract, such as dealing with employees and customers.

There are six ways in which we arrive at our values about what is "good" and "just": authority, deductive logic, sense experience, emotion, intuition, and science. One of these ways is usually dominant within an individual and tends to influence the way he or she arrives at personal values. Although everyone is likely to have different values, on the whole most agree that it is a good idea to tell the truth whenever possible, and that stealing from others is wrong.

While some have argued that business is like poker and thus principles of ethical behavior do not apply in business, a careful examination shows that because businesses have different goals and there is much more at stake, the rules of business and poker must and should be different.

Honesty is always the best policy. When we lie we manipulate other people and impair their ability to make choices based on true information. People should think carefully before telling a lie, and have some very good reasons for violating this cardinal rule of ethics.

The most basic ethical rule is the Golden Rule: Do unto others as you would have them do unto you.

There are two major traditions that dominate current thinking in moral philosophy: deontology and utilitarianism. Deontology holds that there are basic or universal ideals that should direct our thinking. These include keeping one's promises and always telling the truth. Utilitarianism says there are no basic or universal ideals; ethical behavior consists of doing the greatest good for the greatest number. This philosophy is based on the ideas behind capitalism.

Many people who cannot choose between these two traditions prefer ethical relativism, also known as situational ethics. However, by definition situational ethics is ambiguous and thus cannot be incorporated into any management system.

Hospitality managers are faced with a variety of ethical decisions daily. What should be done to preserve and protect the environment has become an ethical question of major importance in the hospitality industry. Many destinations have already taken major steps to preserve their natural resources, and hotel and restaurant companies are implementing recycling programs.

One of the most serious ethical issues facing the industry is discrimination, not only in hiring and promotion, but in treatment of guests. Discrimination can be based on race, ethnicity, gender, or other characteristics.

Another ethical problem that must be addressed in the workplace is sexual harassment. Companies cannot and should not allow anyone to believe that sexual harassment will go unnoticed or will be excused.

AIDS is an issue that forces managers to make ethical decisions in regard to such things as testing and promotion policies. Advertising claims should not misrepresent the truth or create unrealistic expectations. Menus should honestly describe what is being sold.

Companies should adapt an ethical code such as the one suggested by IIQEST. A good litmus test of an ethical decision is: (1) Is it legal? (2) Is it balanced? and (3) How will it make me feel about myself?

Endnotes

1. John Godfrey Saxe, *The Blind Men and the Elephant* (New York: McGraw-Hill, 1963).

2. George A. Steiner, "Social Policies for Business," *California Management Review,* Winter 1972, pp. 17–24, cited by Donald P. Robin and Eric Reidenbach in "Social Responsibility, Ethics, and Marketing Strategy: Closing the Gap Between Concept and Application," *Journal of Marketing,* January 1987, p. 45.

3. Information taken from Domino's and McDonald's Social Responsiblity Reports found on their websites.

4. Edwin M. Reingold, "America's Hamburger Helper," *Time,* 29 June 1992, p. 66.

5. A Ponzi scheme is an investment scam in which individuals are enticed by a fraudster or fraudsters to make "investments" in a financial venture that promises an unusually consistent and/or unreasonably high rate of return. Money from later investors is used to pay earlier investors, giving the illusion of profitability and encouraging both current and new "investors" to contribute more money to the scheme. The scheme does little or no legitimate business, it just recycles money from its investors and depends on a constant stream of new investors to fund the payouts to earlier investors and line the pockets of the fraudster(s). Ultimately, a Ponzi scheme will collapse when there are no more new investors to supply new money for the older investors, or when an economic downturn leads a large number of investors to demand their money back. The fraudster(s) will face multiple criminal charges when caught. This method of financial fraud is named after U.S. swindler Charles Ponzi, who ran an investment scheme in 1919–20, but the method predates him.

6. Adapted from Hunter Lewis, *A Question of Values* (New York: Harper & Row, 1990), pp. 10–11.

7. Ibid., pp. 16–17.

8. Alfred Carr, "Is Business Bluffing Ethical?" *Harvard Business Review,* January/February 1968, cited by Robert C. Solomon and Kristine R. Hanson in *It's Good Business* (New York: Atheneum, 1985), p. 91.

9. Solomon and Hanson, pp. 90–93.

10. Sissela Bok, *Lying: Moral Choice in Public and Private Life* (New York: Random House, 1979), p. 20.

11. Ibid., p. 26.

12. Ibid., pp. 26–27, 32–33.

13. Solomon and Hanson, pp. 93–94.

14. Ibid., p. 96.

15. Bill Moyers, "Ethical Dilemmas," *New Age Journal,* July/August 1989, p. 45.

16. Ibid. The phrase Josephson is referring to appears in the New Testament: "Therefore all things whatsoever ye would that men should do to you, do ye even so to them: for this is the law and the prophets" (Matthew 7:12, King James Version).

17. Ambassador Max Kampelman, speaking at Florida International University's graduation ceremony, May 3, 1993, Miami, Florida.

18. Moyers, p. 97.

19. Ibid.

20. Ibid.

21. Robin and Reidenbach, p. 46.

22. Ibid.

23. Ibid., p. 47.

24. Adapted from Raymond S. Schmidgall, "Hotel Scruples," *Lodging*, January 1991, pp. 38–40.

25. Linda K. Enghagen, "Ethics in Hospitality/Tourism Education: A Survey," supplied by the author. Professor Enghagen has been most helpful in the formulation of some of the ideas presented here.

26. "Hot Line," TravelAge East, 20 September 1993, p. 4.

27. Ibid.

28. Eugene Sloan, "Belize Tries to Avoid the Eco-Tourism Trap," *USA Today*, 17 December 1992, p. 8-D.

29. David Jerome, Senior Vice President, Corporate Responsibility, IHG.com, 2010.

30. The Walt Disney Company, 2008 Corporate Responsibility Report, www.disney.go.com/crreport.

31. Jeff Hale, "We'll Leave the Lights On for You? Not Any More," *The Globe (Toronto) and Mail*, 20 April 2007, p. B8.

32. Nancy Loman Scanlon, "Sustainability," *Hotel Business*, February 7–20, 2010.

33. Susan M. Bard, "Conference Takes Look at Hotel Recycling," *Hotel & Motel Management*, 16 December 1991, p. 18.

34. David Ghitelman, "Racism: Let's Face It," *Meetings & Conventions*, November 1992, p. 58.

35. "Labor Letter," *Wall Street Journal*, 27 July 1993, p. A-1.

36. Arthur J. Hamilton and Peter A. Veglahn, "Sexual Harassment: The Hostile Work Environment," *Cornell Quarterly*, April 1992, p. 88.

37. Ibid.

38. Ibid., p. 90.

39. William Schneider, "Homosexuals: Is AIDS Changing Attitudes?" *Public Opinion*, July/August 1987, p. 59.

40. Gary Langer, "Business Ethics," *travel COUNSELOR*, June 1996, p. 19.

41. Marj Charlier, "Resort Ads Caught Snowing the Ski Set," *Wall Street Journal*, 22 December 1992, p. B-1.

42. Ibid.

43. Julie Mautner, "Culinary Crusaders," *Food Arts*, December 1992, p. 29.

44. Cheryl-Anne Sturken, "What's Your Ethics IQ?" *Meetings & Conventions*, August 1997, p. 50.

45. Study by *Personnel Journal*, November 1987, cited in "Survey: Middle Managers Most Likely to Be Unethical," *Marketing News*, 6 November 1987, p. 6.

46. Ibid.

47. Langer, p. 19.

48. Ken Blanchard and Norman Vincent Peale, *The Power of Ethical Management* (New York: Morrow, 1988), p. 27.

🔑 Key Terms

categorical imperative—A moral obligation or command that is unconditionally and universally binding.

deontology—A system of ethics that assumes God exists and holds that there are basic or universal ideals.

ethical relativism—A philosophy that holds that ethical choices should be based on what seems reasonable or logical according to one's own value system. Also known as situational ethics.

ethics—(1) A set of moral principles and values that individuals use to answer questions of right and wrong; (2) the study of the general nature of morals and of the specific moral choices to be made by individuals in their relationships with others.

stakeholder—Anyone who is affected by the outcome of a given decision.

utilitarianism—A system of ethics based on the greatest good for the greatest number of people.

❓ Review Questions

1. What is ethics?
2. What is the difference between social responsibility and business ethics?
3. What are the six techniques of moral reasoning?
4. Is business like poker?
5. Is honesty always the best policy?
6. What is the difference between deontology and utilitarianism?
7. What is ethical relativism or situational ethics?
8. What are some typical ethical dilemmas hospitality managers face?
9. Why should businesses have a code of ethics?
10. What three questions should managers ask themselves to test whether they are making an ethical decision?

💻 Internet Sites

For more information, visit the following Internet sites. Remember that Internet addresses can change without notice. If the site is no longer there, you can use a search engine to look for additional sites.

Hotel Companies/Resorts

InterContinental Hotels
www.intercontinental.com

Sheraton Hotels
www.sheraton.com

Walt Disney Resorts
www.disney.com

Organizations, Consultants, Resources

The Better Business Bureau
www.bbb.org

Institute for Business and
Professional Ethics
www.depaul.edu/ethics

Restaurant Companies

Domino's Pizza
www.dominos.com

McDonald's
www.mcdonalds.com

Institute for Global Ethics
www.globalethics.org

International Business Ethics
Institute
www.business-ethics.org

Starbucks
www.starbucks.com

Appendix
Hospitality Associations and Periodicals

The following is a list of some of the associations and periodicals that may be of interest to hospitality students, managers, and employees. Phone numbers are not included because they change somewhat frequently.

ASSOCIATIONS

Associations are organizations of persons having a common interest or purpose. They can be a valuable resource for individuals seeking job opportunities, information about their profession, news of current trends, or just the camaraderie of individuals in similar fields with similar interests. What follows are representative associations related to the travel and tourism industry.*

American Bed and Breakfast
    Association (ABBA)
1407 Huguenot Road
Midlothian, VA 23113-2644

American Franchise Association (AFA)
10850 Wilshire, No. 700
Los Angeles, CA 90025

American Hotel & Lodging Association
    (AH&LA)
1201 New York Avenue, NW,
    Suite 600
Washington, DC 20005

American School Food Service
    Association (ASFSA)
1600 Duke Street, 7th Floor
Alexandria, VA 22314

---

*All association names and addresses have been quoted from Deborah M. Burek, ed., *Encyclopedia of Associations* (Detroit, Mich.: Gale Research Company). This encyclopedia is updated each year.

American Society of Bakery Engineers
    (ASBE)
2 North Riverside Plaza, Room 1733
Chicago, IL 60606

American Society of Heating,
Refrigerating and Air-Conditioning
    Engineers (ASHRAE)
1791 Tullie Circle NE
Atlanta, GA 30329

American Society for Hospital Food
Service Administrators (ASHFSA)
c/o American Hospital Association
840 N. Lake Shore Drive
Chicago, IL 60611

American Society of Sanitary
    Engineering (ASSE)
P.O. Box 40362
Bay Village, OH 44140

American Society of Travel Agents
    (ASTA)
1101 King Street
Alexandria, VA 22314

American Travel Inns (ATI)
349 South 200 East, Suite 170
Salt Lake City, UT 84111

Association of Corporate Travel
    Executives (ACTE)
P.O. Box 5394
Parsippany, NJ 07054

Association of Group Travel
    Executives (AGTE)
c/o Arnold H. Light
The Light Group, Inc.
424 Madison Ave., Suite 705
New York, NY 10017

Association of Retail Travel Agents
    (ARTA)
1745 Jefferson Davis Hwy., Suite 300
Arlington, VA 22202-3402

Bed and Breakfast League/Sweet
Dreams and Toast (BBL)
P.O. Box 9490
Washington, DC 20016

Center for Hospitality Research and
Service (CHRS)
c/o Department of Hotel, Restaurant
and Institutional Mgt.
Virginia Polytechnic Institute and State
University
Blacksburg, VA 24061

Chinese American Restaurant
Association (CARA)
173 Canal Street
New York, NY 10013

Club Managers Association of
America (CMAA)
1733 King Street
Alexandria, VA 22314

Council on Hotel, Restaurant, and
Institutional Education (CHRIE)
1200 17th Street, NW
Washington, DC 20036-3097

Cruise Lines International Association
(CLIA)
500 5th Avenue, Suite 1407
New York, NY 10110

Food Industries Suppliers Association
(FISA)
P.O. Box 2084
Fairfield Glade, TN 38557

Food Processing Machinery and
Supplies Association (FPMSA)
200 Dangerfield Road
Alexandria, VA 22314

Food Service Marketing Institute
(FSMI)
P.O. Box 1265
Lake Placid, NY 12946

Foodservice and Packaging Institute
(FPI)
1025 Connecticut Ave. NW
Washington, DC 20036

Franchise Consultants International
Association (FCIA)
5147 S. Angela Road
Memphis, TN 38117

Hospitality Lodging and Travel
Research Foundation (HLTRF)
c/o Raymond C. Ellis, Jr.
American Hotel & Lodging Association
1201 New York Avenue, NW,
Suite 600
Washington, DC 20005

Hotel-Motel Greeters International
(HMGI)
P.O. Box 20017
El Cajon, CA 92021

Hospitality Sales and Marketing
Association International (HSMAI)
1300 L Street NW, Suite 800
Washington, DC 20005

Institute of Certified Travel Agents
(ICTA)
148 Linden Street
P.O. Box 56
Wellesley, MA 02181-0503

International Association of Holiday
Inns (IAHI)
3 Ravinia Drive, Suite 2000
Atlanta, GA 30346

International Association of Hospitality
Accountants (IAHA)
Box 27649
Austin, TX 78755-2649

International Food Service Executive's
Association (IFSEA)
1100 S. State Road, Suite 103
Margate, FL 33068

International Franchise Association
(IFA)
1350 New York Ave. NW,
Suite 900
Washington, DC 20005

International Society of Hotel Association
   Executives (ISHAE)
P.O. Box 1529
Tallahassee, FL 32302

Meeting Planners International (MPI)
1950 Stemmons Freeway
Infomart Building, Suite 5018
Dallas, TX 75207-3109

Mexican Food and Beverage Board
   (MFBB)
314 E. 41st Street
New York, NY 10017

Mobile Industrial Caterer's Association
   (MICA)
7300 Artesia Blvd.
Buena Park, CA 90621

National Association of Black Hospitality
   Professionals (NABHP)
P.O. Box 5443
Plainfield, NJ 07060-5443

National Association of Catering
   Executives (NACE)
304 W. Liberty Street, Suite 201
Louisville, KY 40202

National Association of Concessionaires
   (NAC)
35 E. Wacker Drive, Suite 1545
Chicago, IL 60601

National Association of Institutional
   Linen Management (NAILM)
2130 Lexington Road, Suite H
Richmond, KY 40475

National Association of Pizza Operators
   (NAPO)
P.O. Box 1347
New Albany, IN 47150

National Association of Restaurant
   Managers (NARM)
5322 N. 78th Way
Scottsdale, AZ 85250

National Bed-and-Breakfast Association
   (NB&BA)
P.O. Box 332
Norwalk, CT 06852

National Black McDonald's Operators
   Association (NBMOA)
c/o Mrs. Fran Jones
6363 W. Sunset Blvd., Suite 809
Los Angeles, CA 90028-7330

National Business Travel Association
   (NBTA)
1650 King Street, No. 301
Alexandria, VA 22314-2747

National Food Service Association
   (NFSA)
P.O. Box 1932
Columbus, OH 43216

National Restaurant Association
   (NRA)
1200 17th Street, NW
Washington, DC 20036

National Soft Serve and Fast Food
   Association (NSSFFA)
7321 Anthony Hwy.
Waynesboro, PA 17268-9736

Preferred Hotels Association (PHA)
1901 S. Meyers Road, Suite 220
Oakbrook Terrace, IL 60181

Roundtable for Women Food-
   Beverage-Hospitality (RWFBH)
145 W. 1st Street, Suite A
Tustin, CA 92680

Shakey's Franchised Dealers Association
   (SFDA)
5820 Wilshire Blvd., No. 500
Los Angeles, CA 90036

Small Luxury Hotels of the World
   (SLHW)
337 S. Robertson Blvd., Suite 202
Beverly Hills, CA 90211

Society for the Advancement of Food
   Service Research (SAFSR)
University of Nevada, Las Vegas
William F. Harrah College of Hotel
   Administration
Food and Beverage Department
4505 S. Maryland Parkway
Las Vegas, NV 89154-6022

Society of Corporate Meeting
Professionals (SCMP)
2600 Garden Road, #208
Monterey, CA 93940

Society for Foodservice Management
(SFM)
304 W. Liberty Street, Suite 201
Louisville, KY 40202

Tourist House Association of America
(THAA)
RD 2, Box 355A
Greentown, PA 18426

Travel Industry Association of America
(TIAA)
2 Lafayette Center
1133 21st Street, NW
Washington, DC 20036

Travel Industry and Disabled Exchange
(TIDE)
5435 Donna Avenue
Tarzanna, CA 91356

Travel and Tourism Research Association
(TTRA)
P.O. Box 58066
Salt Lake City, UT 84158

U.S. Travel Data Center (USTDC)
2 Lafayette Center
1133 21st Street, NW
Washington, DC 20036

PERIODICALS

If you are interested in a periodical, the
business section of your local library may
carry it. If not, call information to obtain
the phone number of the periodical's
business office, call the office, and ask the
representative to describe the publication
or send you a sample copy. Subscriptions
to these periodicals vary from a few
dollars to a few hundred dollars. (Students: Many periodicals offer student
rates—be sure and ask.) It is a good idea to
make sure the periodical meets your needs
before subscribing.

Airline Companies
American Business Directories, Inc.
5711 S. 86th Circle, Box 27347
Omaha, NE 68127-4146

Airline Financial News
Phillips Business Information, Inc.
1201 Seven Locks Road
Potomac, MD 20845-3394

*Airline, Ship & Catering Onboard
Services*
International Publishing Co. of
America Inc.
665 La Villa Drive
Miami Springs, FL 33166-6095

Airliners Monthly News
World Transport Press Inc.
Box 52-1238
Miami, FL 33152

Airport Highlights
Airport Council International-North
America
1220 19th Street, NW, #200
Washington, DC 20036-2497

Airports
McGraw-Hill Aviation Group
1200 G Street, NW, Suite 200
Washington, DC 20005

Annals of Tourism Research
Pergamon Press, Inc.
660 White Plains Road
Tarrytown, NY 10591-5153

Asia Pacific Foodservice Product News
Young/Conway Publications, Inc.
1101 Richmond Ave., Suite 201
Point Pleasant Beach, NJ 08742-3094

AsiaPacific Travel Magazine
AsiaPacific Travel Co.
1540 Gilbrett
Burlingame, CA 94010-1605

Asian Pacific Travel Facts
6414 Kelly-Elliott Road
Arlington, TX 76017

ASTA Notes
American Assn. of Travel Agents
1101 King Street
Alexandria, VA 22314-2944

ASTA Travel Agency Management
1301 Carolina Street
Greensboro, NC 27401

Bermuda Shorts
Bermuda Department of Tourism
310 Madison Avenue, Suite 201
New York, NY 10017-6083

Britainews
British Tourist Authority
40 W. 57th Street, 3rd Floor
New York, NY 10019-4001

Bus Tours Magazine
National Bus Trader, Inc.
9698 W. Judson
Polo, IL 61064

Business Travel Management
Coastal Communications Corporation
488 Madison Avenue
New York, NY 10022-5772

Business Travel News
CMP Publications, Inc.
600 Community Drive
Manhasset, NY 11030

Business Traveler International
Business Traveler
51 E. 42nd Street, #1806
New York, NY 10017-5404

CKC Report, The Hotel Technology
   Newsletter
Chervenak, Keane & Co.
307 E. 44th Street
New York, NY 10017-4400

Cameron's Foodservice Marketing
   Reporter
Cameron's Publications
5325 Sheridan Drive, Box 1160
Williamsville, NY 14231-1160

Canadian Hotel & Restaurant
Maclean Hunter Ltd.
Maclean Hunter Building
777 Bay Street
Toronto, ON M5W 1A7
Canada

Canadian Intitutes of Travel Counsellors,
   Update
3300 Bloor Street West, #2880
Etobicoke, ON M8X 2X3
Canada

Canadian Travel Press Weekly
Canadian Travel Press
Baxter Publishing Co.
310 Dupont Street
Toronto, ON M5R 1V9
Canada

Caribbean Travel and Life
8403 Colesville Road, #830
Silver Spring, MD 20910-3368

Casino Magazine
115 South State Street
Waseca, MN 56093
Casino World
Gramercy Information Services Inc.
Madison Square Station, Box 2003
New York, NY 10010-9998

Casinos: The International Casino Guide
B.D.I.T. Inc.
P.O. Box 1405
Port Washington, NY 11050

Caterers
American Business Directories, Inc.
5711 S. 86th Circle, Box 27347
Omaha, NE 68127-4146

Cheers
Jobson Publishing Corp.
100 Avenue of the Americas
New York, NY 10013-1678

Chef Institutional
Talcott
222 Merchandise Mart Plaza,
   Suite 1529
Chicago, IL 60654-1301

Club Management
Finan Publishing Co., Inc.
8730 Big Bend Blvd.
St. Louis, MO 63119-3730

College/University Foodservice
Who's Who
Information Central, Box 3900
Prescott, AZ 86302-3900

The Concessionaire
National Association of Concessionaires
35 E. Wacker Drive, Suite 1849
Chicago, IL 60601-2202

Condé Nast Traveler
Condé Nast
350 Madison Avenue
New York, NY 10017-3136

Convene
Professional Convention Management
Assn.
100 Vestavia Office Park, #220
Birmingham, AL 35216-3781

Cooking for Profit
CP Publishing Inc.
Box 267
Fond du Lac, WI 54936-0267

Cook's Illustrated
Natural Health Limited Partners
17 Station Street, Box 1200
Brookline, MA 02147

Cook's Index
John Gordon Burke Publisher, Inc.
Box 1492
Evanston, IL 60204-1492

Cornell Hotel & Restaurant Administration
Quarterly
Elsevier Science Publishing Co.
Subscription Customer Service
655 Avenue of the Americas
New York, NY 10010

Corporate & Incentive Travel
Coastal Communications Corporation
488 Madison Avenue
New York, NY 10022-5772

Corporate Travel
Miller Freeman, Inc.
1515 Broadway
New York, NY 10036

Correctional Foodservice
International Publishing Co. of
America Inc.
665 La Villa Drive
Miami Springs, FL 33166-6095

Cruise & Vacation Views
Orban Communications
60 E. 42nd Street, Suite 905
New York, NY 10165

Cruise Industry News
Nissen-Lie Communications
441 Lexington Ave., #1209A
New York, NY 10017-3959

Cruise Trade
Travel Trade Publications
15 West 44th Street
New York, NY 10036-6611

Current Food Additives Legislation
Columbia University Press
562 W. 113th
New York, NY 10025-8099

Desserts!
House of White Birches
306 E. Parr Road
Beme, IN 46711-9509

Destinations
American Bus Association
1015 15th Street NW, #250
Washington, DC 20005-2681

Dietary Manager
Dietary Managers Association
One Pierce Place
Itasca, IL 60143

Directory of College and University
Foodservice
Chain Store Guide Services
3922 Coconut Palm Drive
Tampa, FL 33516-8321

*Directory of High Volume Independent
    Restaurants*
Chain Store Guide Services
3922 Coconut Palm Drive
Tampa, FL 33516-8321

*Directory of Restaurant and Fast Food
    Chains in Canada*
Maclean Hunter Ltd.
Maclean Hunter Building
777 Bay Street
Toronto, ON M5W 1A7
Canada

FIU Hospitality Review
School of Hospitality Management
Florida International University
North Miami Campus
3000 N.E. 145 Street
North Miami, FL 33181-3600

F&B Magazine
Hospitality Communications
1251 West Webster Street, Suite 2
Chicago, IL 60614

F&B News
Hospitality Communications
1251 West Webster Street, Suite 2
Chicago, IL 60614

Food and Beverage Marketing
Charleson Publishing
505 Eighth Avenue
New York, NY 10018-6505

Food and Beverage Newsletter
National Safety Council
1121 Spring Lake Drive, #558
Itasca, IL 60143-0558

Food & Drink Daily
King Communications Group
627 National Press Building
Washington, DC 20045

Food Arts Magazine
M. Shanken Communications, Inc.
387 Park Avenue South, 8th Floor
New York, NY 10016

Food Broker Quarterly (FBQ)
National Food Brokers Association
1010 Massachusetts Ave., NW
Washington, DC 20001-5499

Food Business
Putman Publishing Co.
301 E. Erie Street
Chicago, IL 60611-3059

Food Business Letter
Make It Tasty Spice Co.
Box 416
Denver, CO 80201

Food in Canada
Maclean Hunter Ltd.
Maclean Hunter Building
777 Bay Street
Toronto, ON M5W 1A7
Canada

Food Chemical News
CRC Press Inc.
1101 Pennsylvania Avenue
Washington, DC 20003

Food Engineering
Chilton Publishing
One Chilton Way
Radnor, PA 19089

Food Engineering International
Chilton Publishing
One Chilton Way
Radnor, PA 19089

Food Facts
National Research Bureau
Box 1
Burlington, IA 52601-0001

*Food Industry Futures—A Strategy
    Service*
C.R.S. Inc.
Box 430
Fayetteville, NY 13066-0430

Food Industry Newsletter
Newsletters Inc.
Box 2730
Bethesda, MD 20827-2730

Food Industry Report
Food & Nutrition Press Inc.
2 Corporate Drive, Box 374
Trumbull, CT 06611-1338

Food Irradiation Update
Technomic Publishing Co. Inc.
851 New Holland Ave., Box 3535
Lancaster, PA 17604-3535

Food Management
Penton Publishing
100 Superior Avenue
Cleveland, OH 44114-2518

Food and Nutrition News
National Livestock and Meat Board
444 N. Michigan Ave.
Chicago, IL 60611-3978

Food Professional's Guide
American Showcase
915 Broadway, 14th Floor
New York, NY 10010-7108

Food Protection Report
Charles Felix Associates
Box 1581
Leesburg, VA 22075-1581

Food Safety Notebook
LYDA Associates
Box 700
Palisades, NY 10964-0700

Food Trade News
119 Sibley Avenue
Ardmore, PA 19003

Food World
Best-Met Publishing Co., Inc.
5537 Twin Knolls Road, Suite 438
Columbia, MD 21045

Foods—Carry Out
American Business Directories, Inc.
5711 South 86th Circle, Box 27347
Omaha, NE 68127-4146

Foodservice Director
Bill Communications, Inc.
355 Park Avenue South, 3rd Floor
New York, NY 10010-1706

*Foodservice Equipment & Supplies
  Specialist*
Cahners Publishing
1350 East Touhy Ave.
Des Plaines, IL 60018-3358

Foodservice & Hospitality Magazine
Kostuch Communications Ltd.
980 Yonge Street, Suite 400
Toronto, ON M4W 2J8
Canada

Foodservice Information Abstracts
National Restaurant Association
1200 17th Street, NW
Washington, DC 20046-3097

Foodservice Product News
Young/Conway Publications, Inc.
1101 Richmond Ave., Suite 201
Point Pleasant Beach, NJ 08742-3094

Gaming International Magazine
Boardwalker Magazine Inc.
Box 7418
Atlantic City, NJ 08404-7418

Gourmet News
United Publications, Inc.
38 Lafayette Street
Box 1056
Yarmouth, ME 04096-1600

Guide to Cooking Schools
ShawGuides, Inc.
625 Biltmore Way, #1406
Coral Gables, FL 33134-7539

*Guide to Food & Beverage Industry
  Publications*
Food Processing Machinery &
  Supplies Association
200 Dangerfield Road
Alexandria, VA 22314-2884

Guide to Hospitality Education
CHRIE
1200 17th Street, NW
Washington, DC 20036-3006

HSMAI Hotel Facilities Digest
Hotel Sales and Marketing Association
    International
1300 L Street NW, #800
Washington, DC 20005-4133

Healthcare Foodservice Magazine
International Publishing Company of
    America, Inc.
665 La Villa Drive
Miami Springs, FL 33166-6095

Healthcare Foodservice Who's Who
Information Central
Box 3900
Prescott, AZ 86302-3900

Hospitality and Automation
2180 Pleasant Hill Road, Suite 5370
Duluth, GA 30136

Hospitality Design
Bill Communications, Inc.
355 Third Avenue South, 3rd Floor
New York, NY 10010-1706

Hospitality Education and Research
    Journal
CHRIE
311 First Street NW
Washington, DC 20001

Hospitality Law
Magna Publications
2718 Dryden Drive
Madison, WI 53704-3005

Hospitality and Tourism Educator
CHRIE
311 First Street NW
Washington, DC 20001

Hospitality World
International Food, Wine & Travel
    Writers Association
Box 1532
Palm Springs, CA 92263-1532

HOSTEUR
CHRIE
1200 17th Street, NW
Washington, DC 20036-3006

Hotel Business
ICD Publications
1393 Veterans Highway, #214N
Hauppauge, NY 11788

Hotel & Motel Management
Advanstar Communications
7500 Old Oak Blvd.
Cleveland, OH 44130

Hotel & Resort Industry
Coastal Communications Corporation
488 Madison Avenue
New York, NY 10022-5772

Hotel and Travel Index
Reed Travel Group
Subscription Department
P.O. Box 5820
Cherry Hill, NJ 08034

Hotel/Motel Security and Safety
    Management
Rusting Publications
402 Main Street
Port Washington, NY 11050

Hotels
Cahners Publishing
1350 East Touhy Ave.
Des Plaines, IL 60018-3358

ICTA Update
Institute of Certified Travel Agents
148 Linden Street, Box 812059
Wellesley, MA 02181-0012

ID (Institutional Distribution)
Bill Communications, Inc.
355 Third Avenue South, 3rd Floor
New York, NY 10010-1706

Inn Business Magazine
Zanny Publishing
11966 Woodbine Ave.
Gormley, ON L0H 1G0
Canada

Inn Touch
Wisconsin Innkeepers Association
509 W. Wisconsin Ave., #622
Milwaukee, WI 53203-2006

Innkeeping
P.A.I.I.
Box 90710
Santa Barbara, CA 93190-0710

Innkeeping World
Box 84108
Seattle, WA 98124-5408

International Hotel Trends
Pannell Kerr Forster
420 Lexington Avenue, Suite 2400
New York, NY 10170

International Journal of Hospitality Management
Pergamon Press, Inc.
660 White Plains Road
Tarrytown, NY 10591-5153

International Gaming & Wagering Business
BMT Publications, Inc.
7 Penn Plaza
New York, NY 10001-3900

International Travel News
Martin Publications, Inc.
2120 28th Street
Sacramento, CA 95818-1910

Journal of College & University Foodservice
Haworth Press
10 Alice Street
Binghamton, NY 13904-1580

Journal of Ecotourism Development
International Ecotourism Education Foundation
Box 676
Falls Church, VA 22040

Journal of Foodservice Systems
Food and Nutrition Press, Inc.
Corporate Drive, Box 374
Trumbull, CT 06611-1338

Journal of Restaurant & Foodservice Marketing
Haworth Press
10 Alice Street
Binghamton, NY 13904-1580

Journal of Travel & Tourism Marketing
Haworth Press
10 Alice Street
Binghamton, NY 13904-1580

Journal of Travel Research
Business Research Division
University of Colorado
Campus Box 420
Boulder, CO 80309-0420

Just Go!
1459 18th Street, #175
San Francisco, CA 94107-2801

Lodging Hospitality
Penton Publishing
1100 Superior Ave.
Cleveland, OH 44114-2518

Lodging
American Hotel & Lodging Association
1201 New York Avenue, NW
Washington, DC 20005

Lodging and Restaurant Index
Restaurant, Hotel & Institutional Management Institute
Purdue University
3572 Young Graduate House, Room 101
West Lafayette, IN 47906-3572

Lodging Outlook
Smith Travel Research
P.O. Box 659
Gallatin, TN 37066

Mature Group Traveler
Meetings Info-Resources, Inc.
1000 Prospect Street, 1st Floor
Stamford, CT 06901-1640

Meat Price Report
National Provisioner, Inc.
15 W. Huron
Chicago, IL 60610-3812

Meeting Manager Magazine
Meeting Planners International
1950 Stemmons Freeway, #5018
Dallas, TX 75207-3109

Meeting News
Miller Freeman, Inc.
1515 Broadway
New York, NY 10036

Meeting Planners Alert
Darrells Graphic & Print
8554 Lorretto Ave.
Cotati, CA 94931-4471

Meeting Planners Guide
Worth International Communications
5979 NW 151st Street, Suite 120
Miami Lakes, FL 33014

Meetings & Conventions
Reed Travel Group
500 Plaza Drive
Secaucus, NJ 07096

Meetings Monthly
Publicom Inc.
CP 365 Place D'Armes
Montreal, PQ H2Y 3H1
Canada

Mexico Update
Travel Mexico Magazine Group
Box 188037
Carlsbad, CA 92009

Military Club & Hospitality
825 Old Country Road
Westbury, NY 11590

Military Clubs and Recreation
Club Executive, Inc.
Box 7088
Alexandria, VA 22307-0088

Military Market
Army Times Publishing Co.
6883 Commercial Drive
Springfield, VA 22159-0001

Mobile and Industrial Catering
Mobile Industrial Caterer's Association International
7300 Artesia Blvd.
Buena Park, CA 90621-1804

Nation's Restaurant News
Lebhar-Friedman, Inc.
425 Park Ave.
New York, NY 10022-3506

Nevada Casino Journal
3100 West Sahara Avenue, Suite 205
Las Vegas, NV 89102
Organic Food Business News

Hotline Publishing
Box 161132
Altamonte Springs, FL 32716

Pasta Journal
National Pasta Association
2101 Wilson Blvd., #920
Arlington, VA 22201-3055

Pizza Today
ProTech Publishing & Communications
Box 1347
New Albany, IN 47151-1347

Recommend Magazine
Worth International Communications
5979 NW 151st Street, Suite 120
Miami Lakes, FL 33014

Report on Institutional Foodservice
Information Central
Box 3900
Prescott, AZ 86302-3900

Ron Paul's Future Foods Report
Technomic Inc.
300 S. Riverside Plaza, #1940
Chicago, IL 60606-6613

Resort Management
Western Specialty Publications, Inc.
2431 Morena Blvd.
San Diego, CA 92110

Resort Management Report
Rouge Et Noir Inc.
Box 1146
Midlothian, VA 23113

Restaurant Business
Bill Communications, Inc.
355 Park Avenue South, 3rd Floor
New York, NY 10010-1706

Restaurant Hospitality
Penton Publishing
1100 Superior Ave.
Cleveland, OH 44114-2518

Restaurant Merchandising News
Mortimer Publishing
53 Sterling Road
Trumbull, CT 06611

Restaurants & Institutions
Cahners Publishing
1350 East Touhy Ave.
Des Plaines, IL 60018-3358

Restaurants USA
National Restaurant Association
1200 Seventeenth Street, NW
Washington, DC 20036-3097

Russia & East Travel Newsletter
Printing Consultants
Federal Square, Box 636
Newark, NJ 07101

Sales & Marketing Management
Bill Communications, Inc.
355 Park Avenue South, 3rd Floor
New York, NY 10010-1706

School Food Service Journal
American School Food Service
   Association
1600 Duke Street, 7th Floor
Alexandria, VA 22314

School Foodservice Who's Who
Information Central
Box 3900
Prescott, AZ 86302-3900

Seafood Trend Newsletter
Seafood Trend Association
8227 Ashworth Avenue, North
Seattle, WA 98103-4434

Student Travels
Student Travel Catalog
Council on International Educational
   Exchange
205 E. 42nd Street
New York, NY 10017-5776

Successful Meetings
Bill Communications, Inc.
355 Park Avenue South, 3rd Floor
New York, NY 10010-1706

Survey of State Travel Offices
U.S. Travel Data Center
1133 21st Street, NW
Washington, DC 20036

Toll-Free Travel & Vacation Information
   Directory
Pilot Books
103 Cooper Street
Babylon, NY 11702-2349

Total Quality In Hospitality
2718 Dryden Drive
Madison, WI 53791-9618

Tour and Travel News
CMP Publications, Inc.
600 Community Drive
Manhasset, NY 11030

TravelAge East
Official Airline Guide Travel
   Magazines
1775 Broadway, 19th Floor
New York, NY 10019

TravelAge West
Official Airline Guides
49 Stevenson, Suite 460
San Francisco, CA 94105-2909

Travel Agent Magazine
801 Second Avenue
New York, NY 10003-4404

Travel & Leisure
American Express Publishing Corp.
1120 Avenue of the Americas
New York, NY 10036-6770

Travel Counselor Magazine
Miller Freeman Inc.
600 Harrison Street
San Francisco, CA 94107

Travel Industry Personnel Directory
Fairchild Publications
7 West 34th Street
New York, NY 10001

*Travel Industry World Yearbook—The Big
  Picture*
Child and Waters, Inc.
Box 610
Rye, NY 10580-0811

Travel Market Report
U.S. Travel Data Center
1133 21st Street, NW
Washington, DC 20036

Travel Trade
15 West 44th Street
New York, NY 10036-6611

Travel to the USSR
Victor Kamkin, Inc.
4956 Boiling Brook Parkway
Rockville, MD 20852

Travelin' Talk Directory
Travelin' Talk Network
Box 3534
Clarksville, TN 37043-3534

Traveller Accommodation Statistics
Statistics Canada, Marketing Division
120 Parkdale Avenue, Room 1710
Ottawa, ON K1A 0T6
Canada

Travel Weekly
P.O. Box 7661
Riverton, NJ 08077

Trends in the Hotel Industry, USA
PKF Consulting
425 California Street, Suite 1650
San Francisco, CA 94104-2201

Who's Who in the Lodging Industry
American Hotel & Motel Association
1201 New York Avenue, NW
Washington, DC 20005

World Cruise Industry Review
Sterling Publications
86-88 Edgware Road
London W2 2YW
England

Index